Special Events

The Wiley Event Management Series

Series Editor: Dr. Joe Goldblatt, CSEP

Special Events: The Roots and Wings of Celebration, Fifth Edition
by Dr. Joe Goldblatt, CSEP

Dictionary of Event Management, Second Edition
by Dr. Joe Goldblatt, CSEP and Kathleen S. Nelson, CSEP

Corporate Event Project Management
by William O'Toole and Phyllis Mikolaitis

Event Marketing: How to Successfully Promote Events, Festivals, Conventions, and Expositions
by Leonard H. Hoyle, CAE, CMP

Event Risk Management and Safety
by Peter E. Tarlow, Ph.D.

Event Sponsorship
by Bruce E. Skinner and Vladimir Rukavina

Professional Event Coordination
by Julia Rutherford Silvers, CSEP

The Complete Guide to Event Entertainment and Production
by Mark Sonder, MM, CSEP

The Guide to Successful Destination Management
by Pat Schaumann, CMP, CSEP

The Sports Event Management and Marketing Playbook
by Frank Supovitz

Art of the Event: Complete Guide to Designing and Decorating Special Events
by James C. Monroe, CMP, CSEP

Global Meetings and Exhibitions
by Carol Krugman, CMP, CMM, and Rudy R. Wright, CMP

Special Events

The Roots and Wings of Celebration

Fifth Edition

Dr. Joe Goldblatt, CSEP

WILEY

John Wiley & Sons, Inc.

Copyright © 2008 by John Wiley & Sons, Inc. All rights reserved
Published by John Wiley & Sons, Inc., Hoboken, New Jersey
Published simultaneously in Canada

For general information on our other products and services or for technical support, please contact our Customer Care Department within the United States at (800) 762–2974, outside the United States at (317) 572–3993 or fax (317) 572–4002.

Wiley also publishes its books in a variety of electronic formats. Some content that appears in print may not be available in electronic books. For more information about Wiley products, visit our web site at www.wiley.com.

Library of Congress Cataloging-in-Publication Data

Goldblatt, Joe Jeff, 1952–
  Special events : the roots and wings of celebration / Joe Goldblatt.—5th ed.
    p. cm. — (The Wiley event management series)
  Previous editions have different subtitles.
  Includes index.
  ISBN: 978–0–471–73831–2 (cloth : alk. paper)
1. Special events—Management.   I. Title.   II. Title: Roots and wings of celebration.
GT3405.G65 2008
394.26'068—dc22

                                                                2006100241

Printed in the United States of America

10 9 8 7 6 5

DEDICATION

The **Fifth Edition** of **Special Events** is dedicated to both life and memory. One of the greatest exemplars of these intertwined concepts is the group of people who live in the United States Gulf Coast region. This group includes my first cousins who have remained and are rebuilding their homes and lives. Following the tragedy of Hurricane Katrina, my cousins and the other people of this region embraced life and sallied forth to stage the annual Mardi Gras celebration only a few months following these catastrophic events. They understand, perhaps better than most, how important it is to celebrate life every day.

The second exemplar is found not in a group but within an individual human being. Linda F. Higgison (1947–2007) dedicated her professional and personal life to creating and advancing knowledge in the field of special events. She introduced the term "eventology" to the North American lexicon. As a result of her selfless pioneering efforts and her inspiration of hundreds of students worldwide, the global events industry will perpetually celebrate her blessed memory.

Dr. Joe Goldblatt, CSEP

"Call it a clan, call it a network, call it a tribe, call it a family. Whatever you call it, whoever you are, you need one."

Jane Howard (1998) (1935–1996) *Families,*
Transaction Publishers/Great Britain

CONTENTS

Foreword   ix
Preface   xi
Acknowledgments   xxvii

PART ONE
Theory of Event Leadership

CHAPTER 1 Welcome to Event Leadership   3

CHAPTER 2 Models of Global Event
Leadership   37

PART TWO
Event Administration

CHAPTER 3 Developing and Implementing
the Event Plan   71

CHAPTER 4 Event Leadership through Human
Resource and Time Management   117

CHAPTER 5 Financial Administration   143

PART THREE
Event Coordination

CHAPTER 6 Managing Vendor Contracts   171

CHAPTER 7 On-Site Event Production   207

PART FOUR
Event Marketing

CHAPTER 8 Advertising, Pubic Relations,
Promotions, and Sponsorship   261

CHAPTER 9 Online and Computer-Generated
Media   295

PART FIVE
Legal, Ethical, and Risk Management

CHAPTER 10 Risk Management: Legal
and Financial Safeguards   307

CHAPTER 11 Inclusivity, Morality, Law, and
Ethics in Event Leadership   333

PART SIX
Technology for Professional Development

CHAPTER 12 Technology for Modern Event
Leadership   355

CHAPTER 13 Career Development,
Advancement, and Sustainable
Success   367

CHAPTER 14 Best Practices in Event
Leadership 393

CHAPTER 15 Case Studies in Twenty-First-
Century Event Leadership 401

APPENDICES

APPENDIX 1 References 417

APPENDIX 2 Organizations and Resources 430

APPENDIX 3 Internet Sites 441

APPENDIX 4 Periodicals 451

APPENDIX 5 APEX Resources 454

APPENDIX 6 Directories 456

APPENDIX 7 Audio and Video Resources 460

APPENDIX 8 Software 462

APPENDIX 9 Sample Client Agreement 464

APPENDIX 10 Sample Vendor Agreement 467

APPENDIX 11 Sample Insurance Certificate 470

APPENDIX 12 Sample Catering Menu 472

APPENDIX 13 Sample Incident Report 474

APPENDIX 14 Sample Purchase Order 477

APPENDIX 15 Sample Event Evaluations 479

APPENDIX 16 Sample Event Survey 484

APPENDIX 17 International Special Events
Society Principles of Professional
Conduct and Ethics 487

Index 489

FOREWORD

By Robert Z. Shapiro

Hollywood film and television producer whose illustrious career includes serving as the senior executive consultant for twelve Academy Awards telecasts.

You are running an event, and everyone involved has expectations, and they have demands, and they have an investment, and they deserve satisfaction. They don't care about problems; they only want to have all of the expectations that they have for the event fulfilled easily and flawlessly, with only pleasant surprises.

When I work on the Academy Awards show (I have worked on 12) I am always awed by how many people work on the show. From the armies of professional people; directors, camera, editors, art department, wardrobe, makeup, and lighting technicians, to florists, caterers, and security people, to the seat fillers, presenters, and Academy Award nominees, there are more than 1,000 people who work on the show. I am always amazed at this great number of people who must perform their jobs in a highly professional manner in order for the show to be flawless and a success. The show consists of a lot of working links, and if one link breaks there could be dire results.

What to do? Get prepared. How to get prepared? Reading this book, **Special Events, Fifth Edition,** by Joe Goldblatt is the ultimate tool for future and present event planners to learn exactly what to do to get the perfect party started.

Picture this; you are barefoot and you are on a bed of hot coals. Now look above you. There are many people above who are throwing little pieces of meat towards you at the same time. It is raining meat confetti. Your job is not to let any of the little pieces of meat reach the hot coals and burn. You must not only catch the little meat pieces, but you must juggle them at the same time. Oh yes, and smile in a calm and reassuring fashion. That's what a good event planner does, catches all the hundreds of details and requests that come their way and turns them into entertainment. While looking good to the client at the same time. In order to pull off this seemingly impossible task, you must be fast on your feet, you must be well organized, and you must be well prepared.

For every event there are thousands of things that can go wrong, either one at a time, like a waiter who spills a glass of red wine on the next speaker's white shirt, or one first of many, which cause a ripple effect that in turn can cause hundreds of things to go wrong like demon dominoes, like when there's a storm that causes all surrounding airports to close and half the people who were supposed to come to your event, including the entertainment, can't. To learn how to recover from calamities and be prepared for the worst, an event professional needs knowledge in many areas of expertise.

It will be your job as an Event Leader to make sure that what can go wrong doesn't. It is your responsibility to make sure that the execution of your event is flawless, and it appears that the event runs itself.

Whether you are involved in the planning of an event for a celebration, a reunion, or an educational or marketing event, as an event management person you are responsible for researching, designing, planning, coordinating, and evaluating events. Yes, Event Leadership represents a unique body of knowledge. This book provides a great foundation and road map for event management professionals and students alike.

PREFACE

May you be cursed to live in interesting times.
—*Ancient Chinese saying*

My father once told me, "Children need both roots and wings." He further explained, "Every human being should know where they have come from, so they may build upon this history to achieve their full potential." My father was indeed a wise man who provided my sister and me with deep roots and strong wings.

Once more, it is time, through the pages of the *Fifth Edition* of *Special Events,* to gather together and explore and strengthen the roots and wings of celebration for the future. Through this exploration, we will be able to better serve others by understanding and appreciating our past while advancing our profession into the twenty-first century.

The contents of this *Fifth Edition* are drawn from the many great continents of the earth. In my travels around the globe, I have searched for our collective celebratory roots with the hope that I would also discover new tools to strengthen our wings and enable our profession to soar even higher in the future.

I have traveled throughout five continents: Africa, Asia, Australia, Europe, and North and South America in search of the rituals, ceremonies, customs, and traditions from whence our contemporary celebrations have developed. Although I have not yet traveled to Antarctica, perhaps one day soon I will visit the South Polar Ice Cap and discover even more powerful examples of celebration among the explorers who have worked and lived there.

One decade ago I hosted a conference entitled, "The Future of Event Management" at the Biosphere2 research facility in Oracle, Arizona. One of the many discoveries we made during that conference was that the scientists who lived inside the facility for extended periods managed to survive by looking forward to their communal celebrations such as birthdays, anniversaries and other special events.

We also know that there is anecdotal evidence that some people achieve certain celebratory milestones before they die. In my own family, my father celebrated his sixtieth wedding anniversary and then died the next day from a heart attack. He had suffered from heart disease for many years but seemed determined to achieve this important milestone. And he did!

In the heart of Africa, in the country of Uganda, I observed a Buganda tribe marriage introduction ceremony and also participated in the Batwa Pygmies ritual dances and their ancient ceremonies. In Australia, while studying and interviewing aboriginal elders, leaders of one of the world's oldest and most complex cultural groups, I learned about men's and women's rituals that are thousands of years old. Throughout Asia, Europe, North America, and South America, I observed and learned why and how people celebrate their triumphs, their joys, and even their sorrows (Victor Turner, 1977). These lessons will serve as further instruction for you, the next generation of tribal leaders, who will produce new rituals, ceremonies, and celebrations.

In the Swahili language, the term *embizo* means "a gathering." As we approach the twentieth anniversary of the **First Edition** of **Special Events,** I am reminded that each new edition of this book represents a unique gathering of new associates as well as a reunion of those who have joined us once again. Indeed, each new edition represents our roots in history as well as the wings of our aspirations.

As I begin the journey of revising the **Fifth Edition** of **Special Events,** I am in Almaty, Kazakhstan in Central Asia. Almaty is perhaps best known as a point where Marco Polo journeyed along the Great Silk Road from Italy to China. Polo was not only a great trader; he was one of the first tourists in recorded history. As I explore this ancient land, I, too, feel as though I now have the rare opportunity of further advancing Marco Polo's research by discovering ancient and new rituals along the Great Silk Road.

I have been appointed by the relatively new independent government of the Republic of Kazakhstan as a consultant to help them develop their meetings, incentives, conventions, and exhibition industry. At the same time, I will provide recommendations regarding the potential for developing the first convention/congress center in this region. I believe Marco Polo would smile if he knew that almost 1,000 years later the Great Silk Road would still be traveled by future traders. In fact, if the congress center is built, it will be the first facility of its kind in Central Asia.

Kazakhstan is a land of people with deep roots and strong wings. Throughout their troubled history, rituals and ceremonies have provided them with a source of continuity and stability. Ray B. Browne (1980) defines rituals and ceremonies as "codifications and statements of attitudes." He states, "Ideas create rituals, and rituals spawn ideas. They are codes of and methods for behavior."

Nearly everywhere in the world, human beings take part in rituals and ceremonies to recall their collective history and express their individual aspirations.

Wilson and Goldfarb (1994) further define ceremony and ritual:

A ceremony is a formal religious or social occasion, usually led by a designated authority figure, such as a priest or chief; examples would include a graduation or inauguration and a marriage ceremony. A ritual is the acting out of an established, prescribed procedure; rituals can range from a family event, such as Thanksgiving or Christmas dinner, to elaborate religious events, such as the Roman Catholic mass and the Jewish Yom Kippur service during the High Holy Days.

In the postmodern world, the designated authority figure is often the Event Leader. This is the trained professional who researches, designs, plans, coordinates, and evaluates the ritual or ceremony. Increasingly, thanks in large part to readers like you, who are committed to continuing professional education, the event management profession is now for the first time firmly established and recognized throughout the world.

For example, my letter of invitation from the Government of Kazakhstan stated: "We have identified two major sources of future economic impact for our country. The first is petroleum, and the second is *event management*." This type of recognition for our profession would have been inconceivable 20 years ago.

As I travel throughout the world, I have noted that, for the first time, federal governments are taking a sincere interest in our profession and are seeking methods to study, evaluate, and determine how best to benefit from the assets Event Leaders bring to their nations.

Whether it is the World Cup in South Africa or the Miss Universe Pageant in Thailand, governments throughout the world actively compete through million-dollar annual investments to attract special events to their destination. Government leaders realize that events such as meetings, conventions, exhibitions, incentives, festivals, fairs, weddings, and others represent not only big business, but they also produce new jobs and establish or promote the overall image of a destination, which is a central part of the global tourism industry. In fact, when well planned and coordinated, events contribute significantly to the quality of place, something that citizens and businesses desire and political leaders must provide.

Events not only help establish a quality of place, they often transform communities. In Providence, Rhode Island, the *Waterfire*™ event (www.waterfire.org) has helped transform a decaying urban center into a thriving entertainment district. *Waterfire* is an event conceived by the artist Barnaby Evans and uses the basic elements of water, fire, and music to create a dramatic and inspiring tourism experience. One hundred bonfires are placed in metal cauldrons in the middle of a river in the center of Providence. Using highly fragrant wood, new age and classical music, and hundreds of volunteers as bonfire builders and lamplighters, this event has literally helped rekindle the tourism economy of Providence.

This is but one example of the hundreds of thousands of small and large events being produced throughout the world where ceremonies and rituals draw on ancient symbols to create new outcomes. This *Fifth Edition* of *Special Events* reminds us how modern events such as *Waterfire* use rituals and ceremonies to explore how planned events promote both continuity and stability within human societies. In this edition, you will discover, as Victor Turner stated, the "fons et origo" (fountainhead and origin) of social structure. Perhaps through this discovery you will find the resources, ideas, and inspiration to raise this ancient tradition and modern profession to a higher level of excellence and meaning.

New to This Edition

The *Fifth Edition* of *Special Events* differs from all others in these ways:

✦ New interviews in the "Profiles in Events Leadership" section with the leaders and luminaries of the global events industry. Now you will learn what makes the great ones and their events truly spectacular. Perhaps more important, you will also learn about their personal celebrations and how these events influence the ones they produce.

✦ Streamlined discussion of event leadership and human resources management.

✦ Broader coverage of production schedules and event résumés.

✦ Revised discussion of law and ethics in special events.

✦ Over 100 new web resources in the text and appendices to help you save money, save time, and improve the overall quality of your events.

✦ A comprehensive model to enable you to measure and analyze the economic as well as social, environmental, and other impacts on your events.

✦ Dozens of new photographs (all photographs are by the author unless identified otherwise) to better help you see and understand the wide scope of resources and opportunities within this growing global industry.

An *Instructor's Manual* (ISBN 978–0–470–13506–8) accompanies this book. It can be obtained by contacting your Wiley sales representative. If you do not know who your representative is, please visit *www.wiley.com/college* and click on Who's My Rep? An electronic version of the *Instructor's Manual* is available to qualified instructors, and Power-Point slides are available to students and instructors on the companion Web site, at *www.wiley.com/college/goldblatt*.

From Event Manager to Event Leader

Throughout this book, you will see numerous examples of how the profession of Event Leadership has evolved both naturally and strategically to focus more and more on the leadership skills that are needed for long-term career success.

In the first edition of this textbook, the primary focus was on developing creative resources and then applying logistics to turn these dreams into plans that could be executed to achieve successful events.

The Event Leaders agreed that, although creativity is important, it is not the primary duty or task needed for long-term success in this field. In fact, out of eight duties and tasks of associated Event Leaders, only one duty, creating the event, addresses the creative aspect of the profession. While one could argue that creativity is a continuous thread throughout all of the duties associated with the Event Manager, the Event Leaders believe the priority of responsibilities, and the knowledge associated with those priorities, have indeed expanded, as outlined in Figure P.1.

Event Manager*	Event Leader†
Administration	Provide strategic planning
Coordination	Cultivate business development
Marketing	Control financial operations
Legal, Ethical, Risk	Standardize operations systems
Management	and procedures
	Facilitate human resources
	Create the event
	Orchestrate the event
	Pursue professional development

*Body of knowledge for Certified Special Event Professional (CSEP) (1996)
†Duties of Event Leader identified during Developing a Curriculum (DACUM) process conducted by Johnson & Wales University (2002)

Figure P.1 Comparative Analysis of Event Manager versus Event Leader

The emerging research within the special events profession continues to validate and confirm the findings of the Event Leaders. There appears to be a newfound body of knowledge linking the modern process of Event Management with the more established field of project management. Project management requires a clear identification of the goals and objectives of the event and a thorough review and evaluation of each milestone that is established. Event Leaders are increasingly being held accountable for understanding and embracing similar competencies. Throughout this book and the others in **The Wiley Event Management Series,** you will be able to develop and expand your competency as an Event Leader and, therefore, increase your marketability and expand your career options.

New Data Creates the Knowledge You Need to Lead

Event Solutions™ magazine (*www.event-solutions.com*) conducts an annual survey of the event industry. In 2004, 1,300 persons answered approximately 250 questions on behalf of themselves and the organizations where they are employed. *Event Solutions* has been collecting this data for five years.

Between 1993 and 2000, I conducted a similar survey with members of the International Special Events Society. Interestingly, the results of both data sets are very similar.

The conclusions that are drawn from this research should not be considered absolute or final. Rather, this information, along with other surveys conducted by industry organizations such as the Center for Exhibition Industry Research (*www.ceir.org*), the Convention Industry Council (*www.conventionindustry.org*), the International Congress and Convention Association (*www.icca.nl*), the International Festivals and Events Association (*www.ifea.com*), and others provide a series of snapshots representing trends within the global events industry. By monitoring these trends, you, as an Event Leader, may be able to make better informed decisions in the future.

Employment

One barometer of a healthy economic environment is employment. According to the *Event Solutions* 2004 survey, only 8.5 percent said they decreased the number of employees. The rest reported that either they increased the number of employees or their workforce levels remained the same as 2003.

Web Site Growth

According to *Event Solutions,* there has been an 11 percent increase in the number of event companies that have their own Web site between 2000 and 2005. Similarly, in my studies with ISES members, the number of Internet users grew from 56 to nearly 100 percent during the same period.

Certification

A significant percentage of planners, especially association planners, have earned a certification designation, such as Certified Meeting Professional (CMP) or Certified Special Events Professional (CSEP). According to the *Event Solutions* survey, over 6 percent of all event professionals hold the CSEP certification designation.

Gross Revenues

Event Solutions reported that in all categories, event professionals gross revenues were under $250,000 per year. This corresponds with the surveys I have conducted with ISES members. Therefore, most event organizations are small businesses. However, according to *Event Solutions,* in 2004 gross revenues increased 15 percent in all categories from 2003.

Number of Corporate Events

Event Solutions reported nearly a 100 percent increase in the number of events held by corporations with attendance of 100 or more persons per event. Generally, the data collected and analyzed by *Event Solutions* portrays a rosier outlook for the corporate events industry than reported in previous years.

Corporate and Association Event Planner Salaries

Event Solutions discovered that there was a 15 percent decrease in corporate event planner salaries. This is a trend that actually began to appear in 2003. Perhaps this trend is due, as *Event Solutions* postulates, to the hiring of many new entry-level employees at typically lower salaries. Or, could this signal the maturation of this industry in terms of employment? This could be an early indicator that event professionals, especially in the corporate sector, must work harder to justify fair and equitable compensation for the complex and high-level tasks they perform.

However, the salaries are still healthy in this sector, with a senior event producer earning on average over $55,000 per year. By comparison, the association planners reported an average salary for a senior event producer or meeting manager of $47,000. Their salaries also decreased from those reported in 2003. Generally salaries may be seen as flat or slightly increased when all categories and factors are considered. Therefore, event professionals must continue to demonstrate the added value for their services to help promote well deserved increases in the future.

■ Festival Executives and Special Event Director/Operations Compensation and Benefits

In 2003, the International Festivals and Events Association (IFEA) conducted a compensation and benefits survey to identify trends in this important budget area. The largest single percentage of the 300 respondents managed events with budgets of $1.5 million, and nearly 45 percent of the respondents managed events with budgets under $500,000.

Most festival organizations have small staffs of fewer than six persons; however, they average per-festival involvement of 533 volunteers. These organizations are highly dependent on volunteer labor including interns.

Seventy-seven individuals responded to the question regarding compensation for executive director or chief executive officer (CEO) and stated that the average salary was $66,752. Fifty percent of these respondents received bonuses ranging from $500 to a maximum of $15,000. Seventy-nine percent of the respondents reported receiving raises in 2002.

By contrast, those individuals reporting their title as Special Events Director/Operations earned on average $46,051.

■ Exhibition Industry Growth

According to the 2004 Center for Exhibition Industry Research Industry Index report, the exhibition industry generally has returned to the levels of activity it experienced before 2000. The index measures net exhibit space, the number of exhibiting companies, professional attendance, and revenue. Net square footage showed the greatest improvement, rising from an index value of 102 to 109 in one year.

■ Convention Industry Impact

The Convention Industry Council reported in their Economic Impact report that the meetings industry is the twenty-ninth largest contributor to the U.S. gross national product. In 2004, total direct spending amounted to $122.31 billion.

The meetings industry supports nearly 1.7 million jobs and provides employment for over one-third of the hotel industry.

■ Global Event Growth

The International Congress and Convention Association (ICCA) is the leading global association for members of the meetings, incentives, conventions, and exhibitions (MICE) industry. In their International Meetings Market Report of 2005, the ICCA stated that their members reported over 5,000 events took place in 2005, an increase of nearly 500 events over 2004. They further reported that the United States, Germany, and Spain hosted the most international meetings in 2005. Vienna, Austria, was the city that hosted the most international events, closely followed by Singapore and Barcelona, Spain. Interestingly, Seoul, Korea, is a newcomer to the ICCA data annual list of top-10 cities that host international meetings. This may further confirm the future potential of Asia as a region for growth in the events sector.

■ Conclusions

All industries experience different economic periods over time. The events industry, closely related to the tourism industry, is similarly experiencing a period of slow but steady growth. Generally, economic downturns in the tourism industry are not long lasting due to the continued need of human beings to experience periods of leisure. However, exogenous shocks, such as terrorism attacks or the rising cost of energy (automobile and airplane fuel especially), could slow the growth of the events industry in the future.

However, the global events industry also has the benefit of providing goods and services that are always in demand as individuals mark and therefore celebrate the many milestones (births, deaths, and everything in between) in their lives. The worldwide phenomenon of aging populations is rapidly influencing the modern events industry; more events are celebrated as people are living longer.

Furthermore, the demand for professional event planners may grow due to the increasing work requirements of most adults that leave little time to plan even the simplest of celebrations. Finally, the harder one works often correlates with the level of stress in one's daily life.

Therefore, the forces of aging, increased work leading to greater stress, and reduced time for planning events may help fuel the sustained growth of the global events industry. And this industry will need Event Leaders like you to plan and produce these events. And to succeed, you will need to continue to learn, grow, and demonstrate through credentials such as professional certification and successful events the added value of your efforts.

According to one study conducted by the Professional Convention Management Association (PCMA), the chief executive officers who hire, supervise, and promote event professionals expect them to be effective leaders.

The Event Leader

The Johnson & Wales University Event Leader DACUM process not only revealed the principal duties for Event Leaders but also identified the tasks assigned to each duty area. In addition, the experts who participated in this forum further identified the general knowledge, skills, worker behaviors, future trends and concerns, tools, equipment, supplies, and materials.

Figures P.2 through P.6 summarize these findings.

Duties	Tasks
A. Provide Strategic Planning	A-1 Establish/support organizational mission, vision, and values; A-2 Develop stakeholder commitment; A-3 Conduct a SWOT (strengths, weaknesses, opportunities, threats) analysis; A-4 Develop a multiyear plan; A-5 Evaluate strategic plan effectiveness; A-6 Update strategic plan; A-7 Conduct forecasting activities
B. Cultivate Business Development	B-1 Determine market niche; B-2 Determine target audience(s); B-3 Develop innovative concepts; B-4 Implement a strategic marketing plan; B-5 Implement an advertising and promotions plan; B-6 Implement a sales plan; B-7 Establish strategic alliances and partnerships; B-8 Pursue industry/market recognition
C. Control Financial Operations	C-1 Establish accounting practices; C-2 Develop financial relationships; C-3 Establish pricing structure; C-4 Establish compensation structure; C-5 Establish profitability target; C-6 Conduct budgeting procedures; C-7 Manage cash flow; C-8 Oversee asset management; C-9 Evaluate profitability
D. Standardize Operations Systems and Procedures	D-1 Establish policies, practices, systems, and procedures; D-2 Adhere to legal/fiduciary compliance; D-3 Establish equipment requirements; D-4 Establish technology requirements; D-5 Create internal documents; D-6 Coordinate database management; D-7 Review/update policies, practices, systems, and procedures
E. Facilitate Human Resources	E-1 Establish ethical expectations; E-2 Establish job descriptions; E-3 Promote a diverse workforce; E-4 Manage recruiting program; E-5 Conduct orientation program; E-6 Provide training; E-7 Manage compensation program; E-8 Manage benefits program; E-9 Conduct review process; E-10 Implement feedback procedures; E-11 Execute recognition program; E-12 Implement retention strategies
F. Create the Event	F-1 Identify stakeholders; F-2 Establish goals and objectives; F-3 Define quality standards; F-4 Research industry "best practices"; F-5 Design the event; F-6 Establish the budget; F-7 Create the marketing plan; F-8 Create the proposal; F-9 Secure proposal approval

Figure P.2 Event Leader Duties and Tasks (listed in order of engagement) *(Continued)*

Duties	Tasks
G. Orchestrate the Event(s)	G-1 Implement project-management system; G-2 Coordinate human resources (e.g., volunteers, participants, staff, vendors); G-3 Negotiate vendor contracts; G-4 Facilitate regulatory compliance; G-5 Execute the marketing plan; G-6 Coordinate logistics integration (e.g., venue, vendor/supplier, audience/participant, media, environment); G-7 Monitor quality standards; G-8 Manage the budget; G-9 Service the stakeholders; G-10 Monitor risk management activities (e.g., safety and security insurance); G-11 Coordinate follow-up activities; G-12 Analyze outcomes
H. Pursue Professional Development	H-1 Develop a professional network; H-2 Participate in industry conferences; H-3 Document career achievements; H-4 Assess publications; H-5 Evaluate research and trends; H-6 Participate in industry organization; H-7 Pursue professional credentials; H-8 Pursue academic credentials; H-9 Pursue speaking, writing, and consulting opportunities; H-10 Engage in mentoring opportunities; H-11 Develop internship, externship, and in-service opportunities; H-12 Maintain life/work balance; H-13 Support community activities; H-14 Conduct benchmarking activities; H-15 Develop alliances with education providers; H-16 Participate in industry competitions

Figure P.2 *(Continued)*

After carefully reviewing these figures, it may seem that the Event Leader must first step into a nearby telephone booth, don a cape, and emerge as some sort of super hero or heroine. However, the opposite is actually true. Event Leaders are ordinary human beings tasked with performing a series of complex duties and, some may argue, extraordinary tasks. These duties and tasks are not necessarily always performed in the sequential order presented in the DACUM analysis, nor are all of the duties and tasks relevant for every event. As the old saying goes, "There are many roads to Boston," and the experienced Event Leader will adjust his or her navigational system to find the most direct, efficient, and effective route to achieve success.

One of the significant outcomes of the DACUM process is that the portrait or profile of the Event Leader is beginning to emerge for the first time in the history of this profession.

Former U.S. Secretary of Labor Robert Reich described this type of worker in his book *The Work of Nations* (Alfred A. Knopf, 1992). Reich identifies a new worker he defines as the *symbolic analyst* who assembles abstract raw materials (ideas) in a logical pattern to create something of value for the consumer. He also suggests that these types of workers

- Communication skills*
  - Oral
  - Listening
- Writing
- Accounting
- Computer
- Negotiation
- Marketing
- Sales
- Psychology
- Interpersonal*
- Organizational*
- Stress management*
- Cultural sensitivity
- Detail oriented*
- Leadership*
- Androgogy (helping adults learn versus pedagogy, teaching adults)
- Managerial*
- Conflict resolution*
- Industry knowledge
  - Catering
  - Facilities
- Multiple languages†
- Adaptability*
- Union knowledge
- Industry customs/standards*
- Teaching
- Networking
- Sociology

- Artistic
- Anthropology
- Board leadership
- Multitasking*
- CPR/First aid
- Heimlich maneuver
- Sales
- Personality types
- Team building*
- Coaching
- Presentation
- Project management
- Public speaking
- Storytelling
- Financial management
- Crisis management
- "Jack or Jill of all trades"
- Entrepreneurial
- Analytical
- Messianic
- Evangelical†
- Good judge of quality/character
- Change management
- Consensus-building skills
- Ability to improvise*
- Committee leadership
- Knowledge of state and federal laws
- Time management*
- Visionary

*100 percent of the participants agreed that these are important/essential general knowledge and skill traits for Event Leaders.
†More than 90 percent of the participants did not agree that these general knowledge and skill traits are important for Event Leaders.

Figure P.3   Event Leader General Knowledge and Skills

- ✦ Resourceful*
- ✦ Self-motivated*
- ✦ Team player
- ✦ Detail oriented
- ✦ Creative
- ✦ Competent*
- ✦ Cordial
- ✦ Dedicated
- ✦ Committed*
- ✦ Diplomatic
- ✦ Confident
- ✦ Kind
- ✦ Inspirational*
- ✦ Open-minded*
- ✦ Ethical
- ✦ Even-tempered
- ✦ Mature
- ✦ Opinionated
- ✦ Articulate
- ✦ Consistent*
- ✦ Well read
- ✦ Loyal
- ✦ Lifelong learners
- ✦ Conversational
- ✦ Extroverted
- ✦ Compassionate
- ✦ Reliable*

- ✦ Passionate
- ✦ Honest
- ✦ Integrity*
- ✦ Risk taker
- ✦ Positive*
- ✦ Tireless
- ✦ Hardworking*
- ✦ Decisiveness*
- ✦ Punctual*
- ✦ Competitive
- ✦ Poised
- ✦ Visionary
- ✦ Professional
- ✦ Common sense
- ✦ Make people feel special*
- ✦ Provide transformational events
- ✦ Promote value of education
- ✦ Sense of humor*
- ✦ Change agent
- ✦ Responsible*
- ✦ "Do whatever it takes" attitude
- ✦ Global thinker
- ✦ Educator
- ✦ Focused*
- ✦ Disciplined
- ✦ Empowering
- ✦ Learn from your mistakes/failures*

*100 percent of the participants agreed that these are critical Event Leader worker behaviors.

Figure P.4 Worker Behaviors for Event Leaders

will be the most valued in the new economy. I heartily endorse Reich's theorem and further argue that the outputs from the DACUM support his suppositions.

The DACUM for Event Leader depicts the complex worker identified in Figure P.7.

The summary in this figure establishes a portrait of a very different Event Leader from that of only a decade ago. Success, indeed, does come by degrees, and to sustain that success throughout a demanding career, the Event Leader must aspire to achieve the eight degrees depicted in Figure P.7. According to the Event Leaders surveyed across the globe, these are the leadership qualities that will provide a sustainable

- ✦ Increased risk management*
- ✦ Increased focus on celebration of life
- ✦ New market: "Remembrance Days for 9/11/01"
- ✦ Nutritional requirements
- ✦ Social drinking declines
- ✦ Entertainment + education = "Edutainment"
- ✦ Combining business/theatre
- ✦ More focused on each event
- ✦ Small events, deliver more value
- ✦ Unstable economy*
- ✦ Changing workforce*
- ✦ Multiculturalism*
- ✦ Changes in the travel industry
- ✦ Changes in worker values
- ✦ Regulations/laws
- ✦ Compacting of our industry
- ✦ Specialization
- ✦ Impact of the Internet

- ✦ Need for continuing education
- ✦ Consolidation
- ✦ Increased competition*
- ✦ More volunteers
- ✦ Fewer volunteer hours
- ✦ Expectation of instant gratification
- ✦ Increased cost of advertising
- ✦ E-commerce
- ✦ "Cocooning" (term coined by author/futurist Faith Popcorn of The Brain Reserve, Inc., to describe growing trend of increased psychocentric behavior as evidenced by more and more individual participation through the Internet, television watching, etc., rather than group activities outside the home or office)
- ✦ Changing lifestyles
- ✦ Demographic changes*

*96 percent or more of the participants agreed that these trends and concerns would be significant in the immediate short-term future.

Figure P.5 Future Trends and Concerns for Event Leaders

career in the new world—a new world that will continue to value and greatly need experienced and professional individuals who will create and orchestrate meaningful rituals and ceremonies.

My mother, another wise being, once told me, "You stand upon the shoulders of giants." She meant that each of us is the sum and substance of the great ones who have

- ✦ Communications equipment
- ✦ General office equipment
- ✦ Resource library
- ✦ Professional membership
- ✦ Information-management system
- ✦ Financial resources
- ✦ Operations equipment

Figure P.6 Tools, Equipment, Supplies, and Materials for Event Leaders

Critical Responsibilities and Behaviors	General Knowledge	Essential Tools to Support Responsibilities, Behaviors, and Knowledge	Future Trends and Concerns	Key Requirements
1. Strategic Thinker	Visionary, global thinker, consensus builder, focused, learns from mistakes	Communications equipment, resource library	Increased risk management	Strong facilitation skills essential
2. Business Developer	Marketing, sales	Professional membership, information-management system	Increased competition, E-commerce demographic changes	Strong sensitivity to changing market trends through forecasting
3. Financial Operations Control	Financial management, accounting, honest, integrity, ethical	Financial resources, office equipment	Unstable economy, regulations/ laws	Strong ability to collect and analyze financial data to forecast future supply and demand factors
4. Operations Systems and Procedures Standardization	Detail oriented, computer, industry knowledge, project management, time management, multitasking	Operations equipment	Increased risk management, regulations/ laws	Strong background in project management and ability to multitask
5. Facilitate Human Resources	Psychology, sociology, interpersonal, organizational, cultural sensitivity, androgogy, conflict resolution, multiple languages, board leadership, personality types, coaching, team building, good judge of quality, character, union knowledge	Communications equipment, information-management system	Changing workforce, multiculturalism, more volunteers and fewer volunteer hours, expectation of instant gratification	Strong ability to connect with, persuade, and motivate human resources to achieve consistent optimum performance

Figure P.7   Portrait of an Event Leader

Critical Responsibilities and Behaviors	General Knowledge	Essential Tools to Support Responsibilities, Behaviors, and Knowledge	Future Trends and Concerns	Key Requirements
6. Create the Event	Artistic, storytelling, entrepreneurial, visionary	Resource library, professional membership, information-management system, communications equipment		Strong ability to design complex events to consistently satisfy rapidly changing demographics
7. Orchestrate the Event	Communication skills, negotiation, organizational, detail oriented, leadership, managerial, conflict resolution, adaptability, multitasking, team building, coaching, crisis management, change management, ability to improvise, industry customs/ standards, time management	Communications equipment, office equipment, information-management system, operations equipment	Increased risk management, specialization, smaller events, deliver more value	Strong communications, prioritization, and delegation skills
8. Professional Development Pursuits	Industry knowledge, knowledge of state and federal laws, well-read education	Resource library	Need for continuous education	Strong commitment to and evidence of perpetual professional development

Figure P.7   *(Continued)*

come before us. In the pages to come, you will meet many of the giants of the global celebrations industry upon whose strong shoulders we now stand. May you discover even deeper roots, develop stronger shoulders, and create even greater opportunities for those to come. Perhaps you will soon spread your wings and fly to unprecedented heights to others, who, just like you and I, are in search of the roots and wings of celebration.

DR. JOE GOLDBLATT, CSEP
Senior Lecturer, Executive Director for Professional Development and Strategic Partnerships, Temple University School of Tourism and Hospitality Management, Philadelphia, Pennsylvania.

ACKNOWLEDGMENTS

A book that has continued through five editions is very much like a mighty tree. Its root system is very complex indeed. I wish to acknowledge the following Event Leaders whose intellectual and creative contributions have helped form the extensive root system for this book.

Fifth Edition Profiles in Event Leadership:

Dr. Dessislava Boshnakova, Bulgaria
Gene Colombus, USA
Jay Downie, USA
Zeren Earls, USA
Sheila Graham, Captain, USN
    (Ret.) USA
April Harris, USA
Mary Jordan, USA (deceased)
Windsor Jordan, USA
Peter Kagwa, Uganda
Jin Kawamura, Japan
Josh McCall, USA
Jean McFaddin, USA
Lucky Morimoto, Japan
Patrick Muyonjo, Uganda
David Rich, USA
Frank Supovitz, USA
Connie Zambelli, USA
Danabeth Zambelli, USA
George "Boom Boom" Zambelli, USA
    (deceased)
Marcy Zambelli, USA

Additional contributors:
Richard Aaron, CSEP, CMP
Dr. Debra Kaye Blair
Gail Bower
Maricar Donato
Jerry Edwards, CPCE
Robert Estrin
Dana Giovinetti, CMP, CMM
Katy Handley
Linda F. Higgison
Janet Landey, CSEP
Dion Magee
Bill Morton
Jack Morton (deceased)
Michelle D. Pearl
Ira Rosen, CFEE
Steven Wood Schmader, CFEE
Robert Sivek, CSEP, CERP
Fred Stein
John Tempest
Mark H. L. Wells
David Wolper

The following individuals participated in the DACUM process to identify the duties and tasks of Event Leaders:

Tina Carlson
Burt Ferrini
Stedman Graham
Robyn Hadden, CSEP
Linda Higgison
Kathy Lobdell
Kathy Nelson, Ph.D., CSEP, CMP

Mark Putnam
Mary Ann Rose
Stephen Wood Schmader, CFE
Robert Sivek, CSEP, CERP
Mary Kay Weber, CSEP
Dana Zita, CSEP, CMP

Throughout the previous editions of **_Special Events,_** these individuals and organizations have provided invaluable insights and contributions:

Dr. Betsy Barber
Eva Barkoff
Jaclyn Bernstein
Angelo Bonita
Sara and Frank Cohen
Alice Conway, CSEP
John J. Daly, CSEP
Sally Estrod
Linda Faulkner
Dr. Daniel Fesenmaier
The George Washington University
Max Darwin Goldblatt
Max Goldblatt (deceased)
Rosa Goldblatt (deceased)
Sam deBlanc Goldblatt
Dr. Joseph Arthur Greenberg
Earl Hargrove, Jr.
Jack Hartzman
Dr. Donald E. Hawkins
Linda Higgison
Robert Hultsmeyer
Sir Thomas and Lady Emma Ingilby
Klaus Inkamp
Bertha Jacob (deceased)
Sam Jacob (deceased)

Johnson & Wales University
Glenn Kasofsky
Alexey Khripunov
Tim Lundy
Louise Lynch
Nancy R. Lynner
Robert J. Miller
Jeffrey Montague
Doris Morales
Leah Pointer (deceased)
Dr. Catherine H. Price
The Professional Convention
    Management Association
Jason Quinn
Julia Schiptsova
Dr. Oleg Schiptsov
Dr. Ira Shapiro
Patti Shock
Carolina Sicilia
Mary Ellen Smith
Dr. Wright Smith
Mary Ellen Smith
Stephen Joel Trachtenberg
Temple University
Dr. Brunetta Wolfman

Those who reviewed this book in its various stages of development:

Emma Good of Florida State University
Bo Hu of Oklahoma State University
Kathleen Nelson of University of Nevada,
    Las Vegas

Kimberly Tranter of Johnson &
    Wales University

I wish to acknowledge and express great appreciation for the continuous support and encouragement of our John Wiley & Sons publishing team, Melissa Oliver and JoAnna Turtletaub. These talented professionals are longtime dear friends and excellent colleagues whose many talents have helped ***Special Events*** find new wings in the ***Fifth Edition.***

Furthermore, I was most fortunate in benefiting from the editorial expertise and judgment of Tzviya Siegman in the final preparation of this manuscript. Ms. Siegman's good taste, attention to detail, and devotion to this work greatly improved the ***Fifth Edition*** of this book. Kerstin Nasdeo, Production Manager at Wiley, is responsible for the final editing, design, and production of this volume. I am very grateful for her excellent judgment and for encouraging me to enter the digital age of copy editing.

In 2005 I organized a tour for my Temple University students of the Kodak Theater in Los Angeles, California. The tour was requested by the students as they unanimously declared the production of the Academy Awards as their favorite live event. During that behind the scenes visit, we met with Mr. Robert Z. Shapiro, who is the senior executive consultant for the Academy Awards telecast. Mr. Shapiro is one of Hollywood's most successful television and film producers. He was kind enough to write the foreword for this ***Fifth Edition*** of ***Special Events*** for which I am most grateful. Mr. Shapiro has helped produce more Academy Awards telecasts than any other producer. I am most grateful to Mr. Shapiro for helping to inspire my students, the readers of this book, and millions of television viewers worldwide through the magic of live television spectaculars such as the Academy Awards.

Finally, this work would not have been possible without the loyal and expert assistance provided by Elizabeth Denniston. Liz has provided immeasurable contributions to this edition of ***Special Events*** and at the same time has been a joy to work with. Her meticulous attention to detail, curious mind, and keen intellectual analysis have both improved and expanded this volume. The ***Fifth Edition*** of this book has greatly benefited from her expert talents.

PART ONE

Theory of Event Leadership

Zeren Earls (left), founder of First Night, is joined by colleagues as she leads the grand procession at the First Night International annual convention.

CHAPTER 1

Welcome to Event Leadership: The Roots and Wings of Celebration

In This Chapter You Will Learn How To:

+ Understand and appreciate the historic roots of celebration
+ Recognize and understand the demographic changes affecting the global events industry
+ Utilize the psychographic changes affecting event length, purpose, and outcomes to improve performance
+ Identify new and emerging career opportunities
+ Understand why education has become the most important factor in Event Leadership growth
+ Identify industry certification programs
+ Advance your career throughout the twenty-first century
+ Develop new ways to sustain your career

The professional Event Leadership host knows that the word *Welcome!* is an essential part of the guest experience at any event. Therefore, I warmly welcome you to the fifth edition of *Special Events*. However, in the global spirit of the fifth edition, allow me to add:

- ✦ Beruchim Habaim! (Hebrew)
- ✦ Benvenuto! (Italian)
- ✦ Bien venue! (French)
- ✦ Bienvenidos! (Spanish)
- ✦ Dobre doshli! (Bulgarian)
- ✦ Dobro pozhalovat! (Russian)
- ✦ Fun ying! (Cantonese Chinese)
- ✦ G'day! (Australian English)
- ✦ Hos geldin! (Turkish)
- ✦ Huan ying! (Mandarin Chinese)

- ✦ Kali meta! (Greek)
- ✦ Kwaribu! (Swahili)
- ✦ Laipni ludzam! (Latvian)
- ✦ Sabah al kher! (Arabic)
- ✦ Tusanyuse Kulamba! (Bugandan)
- ✦ Urakasa neza! (Kinyarwandan)
- ✦ Urseo oh se yo! (Korean)
- ✦ Velkomst! (Danish)
- ✦ Willkommen! (German)
- ✦ Yokoso! (Japanese)

With the rapid development of the Internet, the world as we once knew it has rapidly changed. For example, to learn how to say "welcome" in over 325 different languages, visit *www.elite.net/~runner/jennifers/welcome.htm*. The local or regional nature of the Event Leadership business was replaced with lightning speed by global connections throughout the world. I discovered this while seated at my home computer receiving e-mail messages from distant lands. "Thanks for your excellent book—it changed my perspective about the profession," wrote one industry member from the Far East. These types of messages were quickly followed by requests for information and, ultimately, offers to fly me to lands that I had only read about. Indeed, the Internet has had the same (or perhaps a greater) influence as that of Gutenberg's printing press. The World Wide Web has woven the Event Leadership profession together into a new global community. As a result of this new "web," each of us now has far greater opportunities for career and business development than we previously imagined or aspired to.

During the past two decades (since the first edition of *Special Events*), the field of Event Leadership has seen numerous changes, and Figure 1.1 summarizes these paradigm shifts.

Event Aspect	From:	To:
Event organization	Amateur	Professional
Event guests	Younger	Older
Event technology	Incidental	Integral
Event markets	Local	Global
Event education	Nonessential	Essential
Event evaluation	Narrow	Comprehensive

Figure 1.1 A Decade of Change

These six aspects of the profession reflect how the Event Leadership field has experienced sweeping changes in the past decade. The letters above the massive doors to the National Archives in Washington, DC, announce "Where past is prologue." And so it is with our profession of Event Leadership. To go forward, we must first reflect on the historical roots of a field of study.

From Roots to Wings

The term *special events* may have first been used at what is often described as the "happiest place on earth." In 1955, when Walt Disney opened Disneyland in Anaheim, California, he turned to one of his imagineers, Robert Jani, and asked him to help solve a big problem. Each day at 5:00 P.M., thousands of people, in fact almost 90 percent of the guests, would leave the park. The problem with this mass exodus was that Walt's happiest place on earth remained open until 10:00 P.M. This meant that he had to support a payroll of thousands of workers, utilities, and other expenses for five hours each day with no income.

To correct this problem, Robert Jani, then director of public relations for Disneyland and later the owner of one of the most successful Event Leadership production companies in the world, Robert F. Jani Productions, proposed the creation of a nightly parade that he dubbed the "Main Street Electric Parade." Dozens of floats with thousands of miniature lights would nightly glide down Main Street, delighting thousands of guests who remained to enjoy the spectacle. This technique is used today in all Disney parks, with perhaps the best example at Epcot, where a major spectacular is staged every night. According to the producers, this spectacle results in millions of dollars of increased spending annually.

One of the members of the media turned to Robert Jani during the early days of the Main Street Electric Parade and asked, "What do you call that program?" Jani replied, "A special event." "A special event—what's that?" the reporter asked. Jani thoughtfully answered with what may be the simplest and best definition: A special event is that which is different from a normal day of living. According to Jani, nowhere on earth does a parade appear on the main street every night of the year. Only at Disneyland, where special events are researched, designed, planned, managed, coordinated, and evaluated, does this seemingly spontaneous program take place every night. Jani, who would later produce National Football League Super Bowl half-time spectaculars as well as the legendary Radio City Music Hall Christmas Show, among many other unique events, was a man whose motto was "Dream big dreams and aim high."

Anthropological Beginnings

Some 35 years later, in the first edition of this book, I defined *special event* as a unique moment in time celebrated with ceremony and ritual to satisfy specific needs. My definition emerged from that of anthropologist Victor Turner, who wrote: "Every human society celebrates with ceremony and ritual its joys, sorrows, and triumphs." According to Turner and other researchers whom I had studied in my exploration of anthropology, ceremony and ritual were important factors in the design, planning, management, and coordination of special events.

The term *event* is derived from the Latin term *e-venire,* which means "outcome." Therefore, every event is in fact an outcome produced by a team that is led by the Event Leader. After interviewing thousands of experts in special event leadership for the past five editions of *Special Events,* I have discovered that, while special events may represent many professions, one person is always at the helm of this large vessel. That person is the *Event Leader.*

Growth Opportunities

Only six decades ago, when an orchestra was needed to provide music for a wedding or social event, one consulted an orchestra leader. Very often, the orchestra leader would provide references for additional talent to enhance the event. Mike Lanin, of Howard Lanin Productions of New York City, tells the story of a meeting his father, Howard Lanin, the renowned society maestro, had with a client in Philadelphia during the late 1920s. Having already asked Lanin to provide music for her daughter's coming-out party being held at the Bellevue-Stratford Hotel (now the Park Hyatt at the Bellevue), the client asked that he provide décor as well. When Lanin asked how much the client would like to spend, the client replied, "Just make it lovely, Howard—just make it lovely." Lanin immediately realized that making this huge ballroom "lovely" might require an investment of five figures. With inflation, the cost of such an undertaking today would well exceed six figures. But Lanin was fortunate to have earned his client's total trust. Without further discussion, the orchestra leader and decorator went to work. Few clients of any era would offer such an unlimited budget. But more and more often, special events professionals such as the Lanins are being asked to provide more diversified services. And although orchestra leaders may have been comfortable recommending decorations and other services and products for social events three decades ago, they and others with specific areas of expertise found that, when it came to events designed for advertising and public relations opportunities, they required specialized assistance.

Public relations is a proud ancestor of the celebrations industry. Less than 50 years ago, the modern profession of public relations and advertising became an accepted tool in American commerce. When a corporation wished to introduce a new product, increase sales, or motivate its employees, its corporate leaders turned to public relations and advertising professionals to design a plan. Today, the celebrations industry includes tens of thousands of hardworking professionals, who, for the first time in the industry's history, are truly working together to offer their clients the excellent services and products they deserve. As an example of the growth of Event Leadership in the public relations field, consider this comment from the first person in the United States to receive a master's degree in public relations, Carol Hills, now a professor at Boston University: "My students are extremely interested in events. They recognize that public relations and events are inseparable. Event leadership is certainly a growth area in public relations practice."

According to the International Council of Shopping Centers (ICSC) in New York, marketing directors who produce events for local and regional shopping centers can earn in the high five figures. Marketing professionals have recognized the need for specialized training and the benefits of certification within their industry. Events help attract and influence consumers to purchase specific products and services from small retail stores up to major regional shopping centers with hundreds of shops. In this age of entrepreneurship, the creation of new business is far greater than the growth of established firms. With each new business created, there is a new opportunity to celebrate through a grand opening or other special event. There are over 1 million new businesses created annually in the United States that may require an event leader to produce an opening celebration.

The 2005 convention of the International Amusement Parks and Attractions revealed even more changes occurring in the leisure field. According to recent studies, the newest lifestyle trends bear watching. Fifty percent of the new so-called baby boomer or limbo generation have discretionary income. Due to longevity and what is defined as vacation starvation, they are spending this income on leisure products.

Many of these individuals are described as "wanderlust singletons" because most are indeed single adults. They are socially aware and environmentally sensitive, support fair trade, and desire nature-based tourism experiences.

They have a strong need to escape a working environment that is increasingly stressful and therefore seek experiences in the great outdoors, where there is a greater opportunity for controlled risk through activities such as whitewater rafting with an experienced guide.

One final psychographic change identified at this meeting was the development of "tribing" and mass customization. Affinity or special interest groups, where individuals can bond with people of similar interests and experience levels, and the need to customize experiences are both growing in importance. Therefore, the ability to satisfy both needs, tribal as well as individual activities, will determine in the future which Event Leaders will succeed and which may fail.

Demographers believe that India and China will soon emerge as the major exporters of tourists due to the population density and the rising average income. However, in developed countries such as the United States, a new group nicknamed "SKIN" is developing. SKIN means "spending kids' inheritance now." As adults find new ways to extend their lives as well as the quality of their lives, leisure, through special events, will become even more popular.

An *Event Leader* historically was a person responsible for *researching, designing, planning, coordinating,* and *evaluating* events. You will learn about each of these phases in the pages to come. However, the logical question one may ask is: What is the Event Leadership profession?

The Event Leadership Profession

Event Leadership is a profession that requires public assembly for the purpose of *celebration, education, marketing,* and *reunion.* Each of these overarching activities is encompassed by the profession of Event Leadership. Although it can be argued that, like tourism, Event Leadership is actually comprised of many industries, increasingly, as data are gathered and scientific tests conducted, it becomes more apparent that Event Leadership represents a unique body of knowledge.

According to experts in the field of professional certification, all professions are represented by three unique characteristics: (1) the profession must have a unique body of knowledge, (2) the profession typically has voluntary standards that often result in certification, and (3) the profession has an accepted code of conduct or ethics. The profession of Event Leadership meets each of these qualifications.

Let us explore further the definition of Event Leadership. The term *public assembly* means events managed by professionals who typically bring people together for a purpose. Although one person can certainly hold an event by him- or herself, arguably it will not have the complexities of an event with 10 or 10,000 people. Therefore, the size and type of group will determine the level of skills required by a professional Event Leader.

The next key word is *purpose.* In daily lives, events take place spontaneously and, as a result, are sometimes not orderly, effective, or on schedule. However, professional Event Leaders begin with a specific purpose in mind and direct all activities toward achieving this purpose. Event Leaders are purposeful about their work.

The third and final key component consists of the four activities that represent these purposes: *celebration, education, marketing,* and *reunion.*

Celebration

Celebration is characterized by festivities ranging from fairs and festivals to social life-cycle events. Although the term *celebration* can also be applied to education, marketing, and reunion events, it serves to encompass all aspects of human life where events are held for the purpose of celebration.

When one hears the word *celebration,* typically one has an image of fireworks or other festivities. In fact, the word *celebration* is derived from the Latin word *celebro,* meaning "to honor." Another commonly accepted definition is "to perform," as in a ritual. Therefore, celebrations usually refer to official or festive functions such as parades, civic events, festivals, religious observances, political events, bar and bas mitzvahs, weddings, anniversaries, and other events tied to a person's or organization's life cycle or of historical importance.

Education

From the first event in preschool or kindergarten to meetings and conferences where many adults receive continuing education throughout their entire adult lives, educational events mark, deliver, test, and support growth for all human beings. This growth may be social, such as the high school prom, or it may be professional, such as a certification program. Regardless of the purpose, a school public assembly may be primarily or secondarily educationally related.

The term *educate* is also derived from Latin and means "to lead out." Through education events, Event Leaders lead out new ideas, emotions, and actions that improve society. Examples of education events include convocations, commencements, alumni events, training at a corporation, meetings and conferences with specific educational content, and a fairly new activity known as *edutainment*. Edutainment results from the use of entertainment devices (e.g., singers and dancers) to present educational concepts. Through entertainment, guests may learn, comprehend, apply (through audience participation), analyze, and even evaluate specific subject matter. Entertainment may be used to lead out new ideas to improve productivity.

Marketing

Event marketing, according to *Advertising Age,* is now an intrinsic part of any marketing plan. Along with advertising, public relations, and promotions, events serve to create awareness and persuade prospects to purchase goods and services. These events may be private, such as the launch of a new automobile to dealers or the public. Retailers have historically used events to drive sales, and now other types of businesses are realizing that face-to-face events are an effective way to satisfy sales goals. The appearance of soap opera stars at a shopping center is an example of many types of promotions used to attract customers to promote sales.

Reunion

When human beings reunite for the purposes of remembrance, rekindling friendships, or simply rebonding as a group, they are conducting a reunion activity. Reunion activities are present in all the Event Leadership subfields because once the initial event is successful, there may be a desire to reunite. The reunion activity is so symbolic in the American system that President Bill Clinton used this theme for his inaugural activities.

Event Leadership Subfields

The desire and need to celebrate are unique characteristics that make us human. The humorist Will Rogers is reported to have said: "Man is the only animal that blushes . . . or needs to!" Human beings are the only animals that celebrate, and this not only separates us from the lower forms but perhaps raises us to a transcendent or even spiritual level. The growth of Event Leadership subfields certainly reflects this extraordinary capability of celebration to transform humans and entire industries.

As noted earlier, anthropology historically has recognized a four-field approach to Event Leadership. However, the profession of Event Leadership encompasses many specialized fields: advertising, attractions, broadcasting, civic, corporate, exposition, fairs, festivals, government, hospitality, meetings, museums, retail, and tourism. Event Leaders may specialize in any of these fields; however, rarely is an Event Leader an expert in more than a few of these areas. For example, a director of Event Leadership for a zoological society may plan events for the zoo, and some of those events may involve retail promotions. Therefore, a knowledge of education and marketing as well as administration and risk management is important.

These subfields are not scientifically categorized—there are many linkages between and among them. However, this list provides an overview into the possibilities for Event Leaders as they seek to chart their future course of study:

- ✦ Civic events
- ✦ Expositions/exhibitions
- ✦ Fairs and festivals
- ✦ Hallmark events
- ✦ Hospitality
- ✦ Meetings and conferences
- ✦ Retail events
- ✦ Social life-cycle events
- ✦ Sports events
- ✦ Tourism

Once trained in the fundamentals of Event Leadership, Event Leaders must specialize or concentrate their studies in one or two event subfields. By concentrating in more than one area, Event Leaders are further protected from a downturn in a specific market segment. For example, if association meeting planners suddenly were no longer in demand, due to outsourcing, cross-training in corporate Event Leadership may allow them to make a smooth transition to this new field. Use the descriptions of subfields that follow as a guide to focus your market or future employment options. The appendixes list contact details for many of the industry organizations.

Civic Events

Beginning with the U.S. bicentennial celebration in 1976 and continuing with individual centennials, sesquicentennials, and bicentennials of hundreds of towns and cities, Americans in the twentieth century created more events than at any other time in the history of the republic. In both Europe and Asia, celebration is rooted in long-standing religious, cultural, and ritual traditions. The United States has not only blended the traditions of other cultures but has created its own unique events, such as the annual Doo-Dah Parade in Pasadena, California. Anyone and everyone can participate in this event, and they do. There is a riding-lawn-mower brigade, a precision briefcase squad, and other equally unusual entries. As the United States matures, its celebrations will continue to develop into authentic made in the U.S.A. events.

Expositions/Exhibitions

Closely related to fairs and festivals is the exposition. Although divided into two categories—public and private—the exposition has historically been a place where retailers meet wholesalers or suppliers to introduce their goods and services to buyers. Some marketing analysts have suggested that it is the most cost-effective way to achieve sales, as people who enter the exposition booth are more qualified to buy than is a typical sales suspect. Furthermore, the exposition booth allows, as do all events, a multisensory experience that influences customers to make a positive buying decision. A major shift in this field has been to turn the trade show or exposition into a live multisensory event with educational and entertainment programs being offered in the various booths. Like many other fields, this field is growing. Although some smaller trade shows have consolidated with larger ones, just as many or perhaps more shows are being created each year. This spells opportunity for savvy event marketers who wish to benefit from this lucrative field.

Fairs and Festivals

Just as in ancient times, when people assembled in the marketplace to conduct business, commercial as well as religious influences have factored into the development of today's festivals, fairs, and public events. Whether a religious festival in India or a music festival in the United States, each is a public community event symbolized by a kaleidoscope of experiences that finds meaning through the lives of the participants. This kaleidoscope is comprised of performances, arts and crafts demonstrations, and other media that bring meaning to the lives of participants and spectators.

These festivals and fairs have shown tremendous growth as small and large towns seek tourism dollars through such short-term events. Some communities use these events to boost tourism during the slow or off-season, and others focus primarily on weekends to appeal to leisure travelers. Regardless of the reason, fairs (often not-for-profit but with commercial opportunities) and festivals (primarily not-for-profit events) provide unlimited opportunities for organizations to celebrate their culture while providing deep meaning for those who participate and attend.

Hallmark Events

The growth of the Olympic Games is but one example of how hallmark events have grown in both size and volume during the past decade. A hallmark event, also known as a mega event, is best defined as a one-time or recurring event of major proportions, such as the Summer or Winter Olympic Games, the National Football League Super Bowl, or other event projects of similar size, scale, scope, and budget. According to Colin Michael Hall (*GeoJournal* 1989), a hallmark event may also be defined "as major fairs, expositions, cultural and sporting events of international status which are held on either a regular or a one-off basis. A primary function of the hallmark event is to provide the host community with an opportunity to secure high prominence in the tourism market place. However, international or regional prominence may be gained with significant social and environmental costs." From the Olympic Games to the global millennium celebrations, the 1980s and 1990s were a period of sustained growth for such mega-events. Although television certainly helped propel this growth, the positive impact of tourism dollars has largely driven the development of these events. Ironically, the world's fair movement appears to have ebbed, perhaps due to the fact that the inventions showcased in previous world's fairs (space travel, computers, teleconferencing) have become commonplace and because supposedly future happenings actually occurred before the fairs opened. This provides an opportunity to reinvent, revive, and perhaps sustain this hallmark event.

Hospitality

In the hospitality industry, hotels throughout the world are expanding their business interests from merely renting rooms and selling food and beverages to actually planning events. Nashville's Opryland Hotel may have been the first to create a department for special events as a profit center for the corporation. It was followed by Hyatt Hotels Regency Productions, and now other major hotel chains, such as Marriott, are exploring ways to move from fulfilling to actually planning and profiting from events. According to Maricar Donato, president of WashingTours, cultural sensitivity in hospitality will grow rapidly as events increasingly become multicultural experiences.

Meetings and Conferences

According to the Convention Industry Council, an organization that represents dozens of organizations in the meeting, conference, and exposition industries, these industries contribute over $122.31 billion annually to the U.S. economy. Since widespread use of the jet airplane in the 1950s, meetings and conferences have multiplied by the thousands as attendees jet in and out for three- and four-day events. These events are primarily educational seminars that provide networking opportunities for association members and corporate employees. Despite the recent challenge of terrorism, the globalization of the economy has produced significant growth in international meetings, and as a result, Event Leaders are now traveling constantly both domestically and internationally.

Retail Events

From the earliest days of ancient markets, sellers have used promotions and events to attract buyers and drive sales. The paradigm has shifted in this subindustry from the early 1960s and 1970s, when retailers depended on single-day events to attract thousands of consumers to their stores. Soap opera stars, sports celebrities, and even live cartoon characters during a Saturday appearance could increase traffic and, in some cases, sales as well. Today, retailers are much more savvy and rely on marketing research to design long-range promotional events that use an integrated approach, combining a live event with advertising, publicity, and promotions. They are discovering that cause marketing, such as aligning a product with a worthy charity or important social issue (e.g., education), is a better way to build a loyal customer base and improve sales. This shift from short-term quick events to long-term integrated event marketing is a major change in the retail events subindustry.

Social Life-Cycle Events

Bar and bas mitzvahs, weddings, golden wedding anniversaries, and other events that mark the passage of time with a milestone celebration are growing for two important reasons. As the age of Americans rises due to improvements in health care, there will be many more opportunities to celebrate. Only a few years ago, a fiftieth wedding anniversary was a rare event. Today, most retail greeting-card stores sell golden-anniversary greeting cards as but just one symbol of the growth of these events.

In the wedding industry, it is not uncommon to host an event that lasts three or more days, including the actual ceremony. This is due to the great distances that families must travel to get together for these celebrations. It may also be due to the fast-paced world in which we live, which often prevents families and friends from coming together for these milestones. Whatever the reason, social life-cycle events are growing in both length of days and size of budgets.

Funeral directors report that business is literally booming. Coupled with the increase in number of older U.S. citizens is the fact that many people are not affiliated with churches or synagogues. Therefore, at the time of death, a neutral location is required for the final event. Most funeral chapels in the United States were constructed in the 1950s and now must be expanded to accommodate the shift in population. New funeral homes are being constructed and older ones are being expanded.

In the first edition of this book, I predicted that in the not-too-distant future, funerals might be held in hotels to provide guests with overnight accommodations and a location for social events. Now I predict that in some large metropolitan areas, due to aging demographics, funeral home construction will be coupled with zoning decisions regarding hotel and motel accommodations to provide a total package for out-of-town guests. With the collapse of the traditional family of the 1950s and Americans' proclivity for relocation, it is not unreasonable to assume that weddings, funerals, and reunions are central to our lives for reconnecting with family and friends. Perhaps one growth opportunity for future Event Leaders will be to design a total life-cycle event environment providing services, including accommodations, for these important events in a resort or leisure setting.

Social life-cycle events have always been important. While conducting focus group research at a local nursing home, a 97-year-old woman told me: "When you get to be my age, you forget almost everything. What you do remember are the important things: your daughter's wedding, your fiftieth wedding anniversary, and other milestones that make life so meaningful." Increasingly, due to limited time availability, people are turning to Event Leaders to organize these important milestone events.

Sports Events

One example of the growth in popularity in professional sports is the rapid development of sports hall of fame and museum complexes throughout the United States. The 1994 World Cup soccer craze generated excitement, visibility, and, in some cases, significant revenue for numerous destinations throughout the United States. Before, during, or following the big game, events are used to attract, capture, and motivate spectators, regardless of the game's outcome, to keep supporting their favorite team. In fact, the line has been blurred between sport and entertainment, due largely to the proliferation of events such as pregame giveaways, postgame fireworks and musical shows, and even promotions such as trivia contests during the game.

Tourism

Since the U.S. bicentennial in 1976, when literally thousands of communities throughout the United States created celebrations, event tourism has become an important phenomenon. According to a study I conducted in 1994, those communities that do not have the facilities to attract the largest conventions are turning increasingly to event tourism as a means of putting heads in beds during the off-season and weekends. Whether it is in the form of arts and crafts shows, historical reenactments, music festivals, or other events that last anywhere from 1 to 10 days, Americans are celebrating more than ever before and profiting from event tourism. From taxpayers to political leaders to business leaders, more and more stakeholders are becoming invested in event tourism. According to studies by the Travel Industry Association of America, an increasing number of adults visit a special event (fair, festival, other) while on vacation. In the period immediately after September 11, 2006, when transportation changed from fly to drive, many events benefited from local and regional visitors who took advantage of the opportunity to experience a local festival, often for the first time.

Stakeholders

Stakeholders are people or organizations who have invested in an event. For example, the stakeholders of a festival may include the board of directors, the political officials, the municipal staff, the participants (craftspeople), the utility companies, and others. The Event Leader must scan the event environment to identify internal as well as external stakeholders. An internal stakeholder may be a member of the board, the professional staff of the organization, a guest, or other closely related person. External stakeholders may include media, municipal officials, city agencies, or others. A stakeholder does not have to invest money in an event to be considered for this role. Emotional, political, or personal interest in a cause is evidence of investment in an event.

The Event Leadership Professional Model

The analysis herein, from defining the profession, to identifying the principal activities conducted within this profession, to listing some of the subfields where Event Leaders work, is not intended to be comprehensive. Rather, it is a framework within which you can begin to see a pattern emerge. This pattern is reflected in Figure 1.2, a model that depicts the linkages among the definition, activities, subfields, and stakeholders. It will be useful to you as you begin or continue your studies in Event Leadership, as it provides a theoretical framework supporting the organization of this profession. The term *eventology* was first introduced in North America in 2003 by Linda Higgison (1947–2007) Higgison was a prolific writer, speaker, and successful business entrepreneur. However, the concept was first explored twenty years earlier by the Institute for Eventology in Japan. This scientific field of study incorporates previous studies in sociology, anthropology, psychology, business, communications, technology, theology, and other more established scientific fields. Eventology is a synthesis of studies conducted in previous fields and advances these fields of study to systematically explore the outcomes resulting from human events.

THE PROFESSION

EVENT LEADERSHIP

The function that requires human assembly for the purpose
of celebration, education, marketing, and reunion

⇓

THE PROFESSIONAL TITLE

EVENT LEADER

The person responsible for researching, designing, planning,
coordinating, and evaluating an event

⇓

SUBFIELD SPECIALIZATION

Examples of subfields: civic events, conventions, expositions, fairs and festivals,
hallmark events, hospitality, incentive travel, meetings and conferences, retail
events, reunions, social life-cycle events, sport events, and tourism

⇓

STAKEHOLDERS

Individuals or organizations financially, politically,
emotionally, or personally invested in an event

Figure 1.2   Goldblatt Model for the Event Leadership Profession

Change: The Only Constant in Event Leadership

A six-year study entitled *The Profile of Event Management* (International Special Events Society, 1999) has identified many significant changes in the Event Leadership profession. Many of these shifts were identified in Figure 1.1; now let's explore these changes further and see how they may affect your career.

Demographic Change

Within the next decade, nearly 70 million Americans will turn 50 years of age. As a result of the graying of America, not only will millions of Americans celebrate a major milestone (middle age) but Event Leaders will be forced to rethink the types of events they design. For example, as Americans age, it is likely that they will experience more health problems, such as loss of hearing and vision and restriction of movement. Therefore, Event Leaders must respond to these changes with improved resources, such as large-type printed programs, infrared assisted-listening devices, and event ramps and handrails to accommodate persons with physical challenges. The good news is that, as people age, so do their institutions, creating a multiplier effect for the number of celebrations that will be held. The other news is that Event Leaders must anticipate the requirements the aging population will have and be prepared to adapt their event design to satisfy these emerging physical and psychological needs.

Psychographic Change

Tourism researchers have identified the adventurist or allocentric tourist as the fastest-growing market in leisure travel. This projection is further evidenced by the rapid growth in ecotourism programs throughout the world. In both developed and developing countries, Event Leaders must rethink the approach to events to preserve the high-touch experience for guests. This need for high levels of stimulation may be a direct response to the decade-long fascination with the Internet, which is essentially a solitary endeavor. The Internet may have directly or indirectly created an even greater demand for high-touch, in-person, face-to-face events. By understanding the psychographic needs of event guests and providing high-touch experiences, Event Leaders may, in fact, have greater opportunities for maximizing the outcomes that guests desire.

Career Opportunities

Figure 1.3 lists 15 established and emerging Event Leadership careers. No one can determine accurately how many more careers may be added to this list in the near-, mid-, or long-term future. However, using the demographic and psychographic cues identified in this chapter, the Event Leader may begin to imagine what is most likely to develop in terms of future careers.

Event Management Position	Background and Experience Typically Required
Attraction Event Leader	Organization, marketing, logistical, human relations, financial, negotiation
Catering Director	Food and beverage coordination, organization, financial, supervisory, sales, negotiation
Civic Event Leader	Organization, legal and regulatory research ability, human relations, financial, marketing, logistical, negotiation
Convention Service Leader	Organization, supervisory, financial, logistical, human relations, negotiation
Family Reunion Leader	Human relations, marketing, financial, organization, supervisory, negotiation
Festival Event Leader	Organization, financial, marketing, volunteer coordination, supervisory, entertainment, cultural arts, negotiation
Fundraising Event Leader	Research, fundraising, proposal writing, marketing, human relations, volunteer coordination, financial
Political Event Leader	Affiliation with a cause or political party, volunteer coordination, financial, marketing, human relations, fundraising
Public Relations Event Leader	Writing, organization, research, financial, marketing, human relations, public relations, logistical, negotiation
Retail Event Leader	Marketing, advertising, organization, financial, human relations, logistical, negotiation
School Reunion Event Leader	Research, organization, financial, marketing, negotiation, volunteer coordination
Social Life-cycle Event Leader	Human relations, counseling, organization, financial, negotiation
Sport Event Leader	General knowledge of sport, organization, financial, marketing, negotiation, volunteer coordination, supervisory
Tourism Event Leader	Organization, political savvy, financial, marketing, research
University/College Event Leader	Organization, financial, supervisory, marketing, logistical, human relations, negotiation

Figure 1.3   Fifteen Event Leadership Positions and Background and Experience Typically Required

The aging population in North America will certainly require a strong health care system to provide a comfortable lifestyle. This growth in the field of health care will inevitably create new positions for Event Leaders in tourism, recreation, leisure, and education related directly to serving older people with programs tailored to their physical abilities and personal interests.

The rapid technological development we have experienced in the past decade will probably continue and even accelerate. Therefore, professional Event Leaders must meet the technological challenges of the twenty-first century through a commitment to continuing education. As these new technology platforms emerge, Event Leaders must improve their skills continually to meet these fierce challenges or risk being left behind as technology advances.

Will we see the emergence of an *eventologist,* one who combines high touch and high tech to provide a virtual and live event enabling guests to achieve high levels of customization, speed, and service through appropriate technology and greater emphasis on satisfying each person's unique needs? Although we cannot predict with total accuracy what will occur one year from today, much less five years from this moment, we must be prepared by accepting responsibility for harnessing the new technologies to best serve event guests.

Gender Opportunities

Although studies of gender in Event Leadership consistently indicate that females outnumber males in this profession, recent studies (*Profile of Event Management,* 1999) also indicate that more men are beginning to enter the profession. For a variety of reasons, it is essential that the profession attract both men and women.

Males will continue to enter the profession, due to the rich array of career opportunities that await them and the lucrative salaries that are being offered. However, to achieve long-term success, the profession must provide upward mobility for all workers. Upward mobility is tied only partially to compensation. Greater upward mobility specifically requires that, as an Event Leadership employer, you must provide advancement, lifestyle, and training opportunities for event workers, to enable them to achieve professional growth within specific event organizations. Without these internal opportunities, Event Leaders will continue to seek new employment and take with them the institutional memory and experience they have gained while working for your firm.

Educational Opportunities

When the second edition of *Special Events* was written in 1996, I identified 30 to 40 colleges and universities that offered courses, degrees, and certificates in event-related studies. In a study commissioned in 1999 by the Council for Hospitality, Restaurant, and Institutional Education, I identified over 140 institutions of higher education that offer educational opportunities related to meetings, conferences, and special events. Now, as of 2006, there are hundreds of institutions that offer courses in the fields related to eventology. A listing of these schools may be seen at www.wiley.com/goldblatt.

Finally, the technological advancement we have experienced is directly responsible for the contraction and consolidation of global markets. To ensure future success and career advancement, an Event Leader must embrace the global market as an opportunity rather than a challenge. Through research, focus, and sensitivity to cultural differences, the professional Event Leader will be able to reap infinite benefits from the new global economy. In this book, we provide a strategic plan for learning how to identify and conquer these markets to ensure further long-term personal and professional growth. Perhaps the fastest growth has been in the development and delivery of distance learning programs. At The George Washington University, hundreds of annual registrations are received annually for the distance learning certificate program.

Certification

Historically, modern professions have used voluntary professional certification as a means to continually improve their practice and to slow or discourage regulatory bodies (e.g., local and state governments) from creating licensing requirements. When a profession can demonstrate the ability to regulate itself effectively, government is less likely to interfere. The Event Leadership profession first addressed the issue of certification in 1988, when the International Special Events Society announced formation of the Certified Special Events Professional (CSEP) task force. This organization studied a wide variety of certification programs to determine which one would serve as a valid model for the event profession. Ultimately, the Canadian model emerged as the best template from which to construct the CSEP program.

The Canadian government, through the Alberta Tourism Education Council (ATEC), conducted an in-depth study that produced two vocational standards: Event Manager and event coordinator. The International Special Events Society (ISES) merged these two standards into a single comprehensive position entitled *Event Manager* and utilized the ATEC research to develop a body of knowledge for this new vocation. The four knowledge domains identified by ATEC and ratified by ISES are administration, coordination, marketing, and risk management.

This book is based on a comprehensive review of six event-related certification programs and provides an excellent study manual for the CSEP certification program as well as others in the events industry.

Developing Your Career

Now that Event Leadership has emerged as a professional career, it is essential that you manage your growth carefully to sustain your development for many years to come. There are numerous challenges in developing any professional career, whether in medicine, law, or Event Leadership. Identifying these challenges and developing a strategic plan to address them is the most effective way to build long-term success. The four primary challenges that professional Event Leaders encounter are time, finance, technology, and human resources. They are the four pillars upon which you will reconstruct or construct a successful career (see Figure 1.4). This chapter will help you transform these challenges into opportunities for professional growth and better understand the emerging resources available in this new profession.

Mastering Yourself

The first person to be managed is you. Your ability to organize, prioritize, supervise, and delegate to others is secondary to being able to manage your time and professional resources efficiently and effectively. Once you are sufficiently well managed, you will find that managing others is much easier. Managing yourself essentially involves setting per-

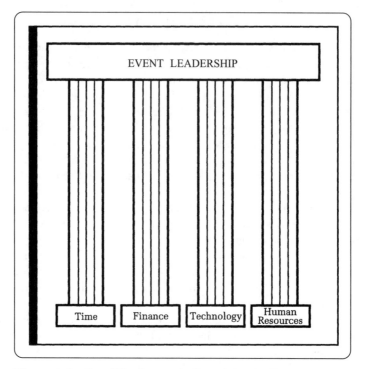

Figure 1.4 Four-Pillar Approach: Foundation for Success

sonal and professional goals and then devising a strategic plan to achieve them. Doing this involves making choices. For example, you may want to spend more time with your family, and that will determine in what field of Event Leadership you elect to specialize. Certain fields will rob you of time with your family and friends, especially as you are building your career; others will allow you to work a semiregular schedule. Association or corporate meeting planning may require that you work 9:00 A.M. to 5:00 P.M. for 40 weeks of the year and 7:00 A.M. to 10:00 P.M. or later during convention preparation and production. Hospitality Event Leadership positions, by contrast, may require long hours every day for weeks on end. After all, the primary resource of the Event Leader is time. It is the one commodity that, once invested, is gone forever. Setting personal and professional goals has a direct correlation with the type of work you will perform as an Event Leader. It is hoped that the fruits of your labors will represent an excellent return on your investment.

Mastering Time Management

One key element in effective time management is the ability to use your time effectively by distinguishing between what is urgent and what is important. Urgency is often the result of poor research and planning. Importance, however, results from a knowledge of priorities of time, resources, and the overarching goals of the event. I recognized this principle when I sold my business, when for the first time in my adult life I was able to distinguish between my personal and my professional time. Too often, the Event Leader—one who usually loves what he or she is doing for a living (thereby distinguishing this person from most of the working population of the world)—combines personal and professional time to his or her detriment. In my own experience, I carefully analyzed the capacity for personal and professional time each week and learned that only 168 hours are available. Of these hours, 56 are invested in sleeping and 21 in eating, leaving 91 hours for work and personal commitments. For nearly 15 years I had used between 70 and 80 of these valuable hours for work-related activities, leaving only 10 or so per week for my family and myself. After I had completed this analysis, I set about matching my time to my new goals.

One of the reasons I sold my business was to spend more time with my family and improve myself both mentally and physically. I realized that, by working smarter instead of longer, I could accomplish in 50 hours the tasks that it had formerly taken me 25 percent more time to do. This new plan would allow me to spend additional time with my family and work toward achieving other personal goals that I had set.

Effective time management must begin with setting personal and professional priorities, especially as this profession is one with a high degree of burnout. Finding a healthy balance among the worlds of work, family, leisure, recreation, and spiritual pursuits is essential to your long-term success as an Event Leader. This book will not only help you find this balance but also show you how to integrate time management principles into every aspect of your Event Leadership professional career. This integration of time management principles will ultimately allow you more hours for recreation, leisure, and self-improvement, while providing increased earnings with fewer working hours. The 10 suggestions for event time management will help you develop an effective system suitable for your personal and professional style:

1. Budget your time and relate this budget directly to your financial and personal priorities. For example, if you value your family life, budget a prescribed period of time to be with your family each week.
2. Determine, by an analysis of your overhead, what your time is worth hourly. Remind yourself of the value of your time by placing a small sign with this amount on or near your telephone. Condense extraneous phone calls and other activities that are not profit producing.
3. Make a list of tasks to complete the next day before you leave the office or go to bed. Include in this list all telephone calls to be made, and carry it with you for ready reference. In the age of cellular communications, you can return calls from anywhere. As each task is completed, cross it off triumphantly. Move uncompleted tasks to the next day's list.
4. Determine whether meetings are essential and the best way to communicate information. Many meetings can be conducted via telephone conference call rather than in person. Other meetings can be canceled and the information communicated through memoranda, newsletters, or even video or audio recordings.

5. When receiving telephone calls, determine if you are the most appropriate person to respond to the caller. If you are not the most appropriate person, direct the caller to the best source. For example, when people contact you for information about the Event Leadership industry, refer them immediately to the ISES Website www.ises.com. Tell them that if they have additional questions, you will be pleased to answer them after they contact ISES.

6. Upon opening mail or reading faxes, handle each item only once. Respond to casual correspondence by writing a note on the document and returning it with your business card. Not only is this efficient, but it is also good for the environment. Respond to business documents upon receipt by setting aside a prescribed time of day to handle this important task.

7. When traveling for more than three business days, have your mail sent to you through an overnight service. Doing this allows you to respond in a timely manner.

8. Prepare a written agenda for every meeting, no matter how brief. Distribute the agenda in advance and see that each item includes a time for discussion. When appropriate, ask meeting participants to prepare a written summary of their contributions and deliver them to you prior to the start of the meeting. This summary will assist you in better preparing for the contributions of the meeting participants.

9. Establish a comprehensive calendar that includes the contact name, address, and telephone number of people with whom you are meeting. Use computer software contact-information programs to take this information on the road with you.

10. Delegate nonessential tasks to capable assistants. The only true way to multiply your creativity is to clone yourself. A well-trained, well-rewarded administrative assistant will enhance your productivity and even allow you occasionally to take some well-deserved time off.

Mastering Finance

Becoming a wise and disciplined money manager is another pillar upon which you can construct a long-term career in Event Leadership. During your Event Leadership career, you will be required to read and interpret spreadsheets filled with financial data. You cannot entrust this to others. Instead, you must be able to understand their interpretations of these data and then make judgments based on your final analysis. Many Event Leaders are uncomfortable with accounting. When interviewing students for admission to the Event Leadership program at The George Washington University, I noted that over 90 percent said that they were not comfortable with their financial or accounting skills.

Sharon Siegel, executive vice president of Deco Productions of Miami, Florida, has owned her company for several years and understands well the importance of prudent financial management. "Watching your overhead is extremely important," she says, "especially if you are constructing and storing props." Siegel, former owner of Celebrations, merged her company with an entertainment firm and provides full-service destination management services, including design and fabrication of decorations. To help control overhead, her firm is located in the building that houses her husband's large party rental operation. Not only does this protect the bottom line, but it improves gross income through referral business generated through the party rental operation.

Sound financial practices allow savvy Event Leaders to better control future events by collecting and analyzing the right information through which to make wise decisions. In this book, we look at many ways in which you may become more comfortable with accounting. As a result of your new confidence, you will greatly improve your profitability, to ensure a long, prosperous future in this profession. These five techniques for Event Leadership financial success will assist you with establishing your own framework for long-term profitability:

1. Set realistic short-, mid-, and long-term financial goals.
2. Seek professional counsel.
3. Identify and use efficient financial technology.
4. Review your financial health frequently and systematically.
5. Control overhead and build wealth.

Mastering Technology

New advances ranging from personal digital assistants (PDAs) as well as Radio Frequency Identification (RFID) to the broadband capability of the Internet itself are rapidly transforming the way in which Event Leaders conduct business. As an example, most résumés that I review describe computer skills and software literacy. Although this is a basic requirement for most administrative jobs, it is surprising that some Event Leaders are still somewhat intimidated by the computer age.

Overcoming this intimidation through the selection of proper tools to solve daily challenges is an essential priority for modern Event Leaders. These basic tools may include software programs for word processing, financial management, and database management.

Word processing skills allow the Event Leader to produce well-written proposals, agreements, production schedules, and other important documents for daily business easily and efficiently. Many successful Event Leaders incorporate desktop publishing software with word processing tools to produce well-illustrated proposals and other promotional materials.

Earlier we discussed the importance of prudent financial management. Financial spreadsheet software allows modern Event Leaders to process quickly, efficiently, and accurately hundreds of monthly journal entries and determine instantly profit or loss information from individual events. These same software systems also allow you to produce detailed financial reports to satisfy tax authorities as well as to provide you with a well-documented history of income and expense. Most important, the use of electronic financial management tools will enable you to determine instantly your cash flow to further ensure that at the end of the month, you have enough income to cover bills and produce retained earnings for your organization.

Learning to use these systems is relatively simple, and most Event Leaders report that they are impressed with the ease and efficiency of this technology compared to the days of pencil or pen entries in financial journals. There are numerous brand names available for purchase, and I encourage you to determine at the outset your financial management needs and then select software that will meet those needs cost-effectively now and for the immediate future.

A database system will allow you to compile huge amounts of information, ranging from vendor to prospective client to guest lists, and organize this information for easy retrieval. Event Managers coordinate hundreds of resources per year, and the ability to store, organize, and retrieve this information quickly, cost-efficiently, and securely is extremely important for business operations and improved earnings.

There are numerous software systems available; many can be customized to fit the individual needs of your organization. However, Event Leaders may fail to recognize the time required to enter the data initially and the discipline required to continue to add to the original database in a systematic manner.

Whether for human, financial, or organizational purposes, information technology is the critical link between an average organization soon in decline or a great Event Leadership firm with expansive growth potential. Use the next five steps to acquire and maintain the right technology to match your needs:

1. Identify the technology needs within your organization.
2. Review and select appropriate technology.
3. Establish a schedule for implementation.
4. Provide adequate training for all personnel.
5. Review needs systematically and adapt to new technology.

Mastering Human Resource Skills

Empowering people is one of the most important human resource skills the Event Leader must master. Thousands of decisions must be made to produce successful events, and the Event Leader cannot make all of them. Instead, he or she must hire the right people and empower them to make a range of important decisions.

Although the empowerment of event staff and volunteers is important, the primary reason why most Event Leadership concerns fail is not creativity but financial administration. Perhaps this is why in many companies the chief financial officer (CFO) is one of the best compensated at the executive level.

As Event Leaders become more educated in finance, human resource management, and other business skills, they are actually demonstrating entrepreneurial skills to their current employers. Many employers reward entrepreneurs (or, as they are commonly referred to, *intrapreneurs*) as they exhibit the skills needed to manage a complex competitive environment autonomously.

Navigating the Internet for Event Leadership Success

Millions of people are currently using the Internet to satisfy their information, marketing, and other personal and professional needs. It is predicted that this number will soon rise to billions. Will the Internet reduce or eliminate the need for human beings getting together in person? On the contrary, futurists such as Alvin Toffler and William Hallal predict that this unprecedented information technology will increase the desire for public assembly, as hundreds of millions of people assemble virtually and find common interests that require public assembly to fully satiate their needs.

The Internet is a complex network of millions of computers that sends and receives information globally. Initially conceived by the Department of Defense Advanced Research Projects Agency, the Internet was installed as a highly stable network with no single point of origin. Initially, only the government, university scientists, and technical people used the Internet to share information, due to its inherently technical interface. With the invention of the *browser,* a software program that allows the users to view parts of the Internet graphically (known as the World Wide Web), the Internet is now the fastest-growing communications device in the world. Not since the invention of the printing press has communications been so rapidly transformed.

To use the Internet, you will need to identify a local access server, such as one of the major online subscription services or one of hundreds of local access firms. Once you are admitted to cyber- (meaning "to steer") space, you may easily navigate between thousands of sites (or *home pages*) using search engines that allow you to search for information that has been indexed.

In the Event Leadership profession, there are hundreds of home pages on the Internet system (see Appendixes 1 and 2 for some examples). Viewing sites with a browser on the World Wide Web using the point-and-click method is easy and fun. Many of the pages contain *hyperlinks,* which are a way to access more information. After you click your mouse on a highlighted key word (*hypertext*) on a home page, a related home page appears.

One of the easiest and fastest ways to conduct research is through the Internet system. For example, the Event Leader who desires to identify sources for entertainment may either review a variety of home pages related to this subject or visit a *chat room*—a live link across the Internet—to query other people who are interested in the same subject.

If you can wait a day or two to retrieve the information you require, the bulletin board may be a feasible option. However, if you need the information now, you will want to go directly to the chat room or home page.

Regardless of what service you use, the Internet system is the Event Leader's most dynamic tool in transforming tomorrow's events through unlimited education and research. Get connected, log on, navigate, and surf the Event Leadership superhighway to find greater success.

Therefore, one of the benefits of mastering skills in Event Leadership is the ability to learn how to run your own business effectively to improve your performance as an employee. In addition, you may be improving your opportunity to one day own and operate your own successful Event Leadership consulting practice. As the Chief Event Officer (CEO), you must empower others to lead as well.

There Is No Substitute for Performance

When meeting with his team and listening to their assurances of improving profits, Harold Gineen, the former chairman of ITT, would invoke the most sacred of all Event Leadership business principles: "There is no substitute for performance." Four pillars of long-term success in event leadership—time, financial, technology, and human resource management—must be applied to achieve consistent success. Setting benchmarks to measure your achievements will help you use these pillars to build a rock-solid foundation for your Event Leadership career. According to Sharon Siegel of Deco Productions of Florida and many of her colleagues, all Event Leaders are ultimately measured only by their last performances. Steadily applying these best practices will help ensure many stellar event performances to come.

Challenges and Opportunities

Three important challenges await you in developing a long, prosperous professional career in Event Leadership. Each of these challenges is related to the other. The environment in which business is developed, the rapid changes in available resources, and the requirement for continuous education form a dynamic triangle that will either support your climb or entrap you while limiting your success. You will find that your ability to master each of these challenges dramatically affects your success ratio throughout your career.

Business Development

Every organization faces increased competition as the world economy becomes smaller and you find that you no longer compete in a local market. Performing a competitive analysis in your market area is an important step in determining your present and future competitors and how you will differentiate yourself to promote profitability. One way to do this is to thoughtfully consider your organization's unique qualities. After you have identified these qualities, compare them to the perception your current and future customers have of other organizations. Are you really all that different from your competitors? If you have not identified your unique differentiating qualities, you may need to adjust the services or products you provide to achieve this important step. The five steps that follow are a guide to best practices in competitive advantage analysis.

1. Audit your organization's unique competitive advantage: quality, product offering, price, location, trained and experienced employees, reputation, safety, and so on.
2. Survey your current and prospective customers to determine their perception of your unique attributes compared to competing organizations.

3. Anonymously call and visit your competitors, and take notes on how they compare to your unique competitive advantage.
4. Share this information with your staff, and adjust your mission and vision to promote greater business development.
5. Review your position systematically every business quarter to determine how you are doing and adjust your plan when necessary.

Whether you are the owner, manager, or employee, maintaining a competitive advantage in Event Leadership is the secret to success in long-term business development. To maintain your most competitive position, combine this technique with constantly reviewing the trade and general business literature as well as information about general emerging trends.

Relationship marketing is increasingly important since the development of affinity programs by retailers in the 1950s. Modern organizations are just now learning what buyers and sellers in markets knew thousands of years ago: All sales are based on relationships. Implied in that relationship is the reality that the buyer and seller like, respect, and trust one another. The higher the price, the more important this process becomes. Therefore, Event Leaders must use events to further this important process.

According to *Advertising Age* and other major chroniclers of global marketing relationships, relationship marketing is the fastest-growing segment in the entire marketing profession. The Event Leader must invest the same time that larger organizations do to understand how to use events to build solid relationships that promote loyalty, word-of-mouth endorsement, and other important attributes of a strong customer and client relationship.

Resource Development

As more and more organizations create their own home pages on the World Wide Web, consumers will be exposed increasingly to infinite resources for Event Leadership. Your challenge is to select those resources that fit your market demand and cultivate them to ensure the highest consistent quality. One of the reasons that brand names have grown in importance is due to consumers' desire for dependability and reliability. Positioning yourself and your organization as a high-quality, dependable, and reliable service through your careful selection of product offerings will further ensure your long-term success. Whether you are selecting vendors or determining the quality of paper on which to print your new brochure, every decision will reflect your taste and, more important, that of your customers. Determine early on, through research, whom you are serving and then select those resources to match their needs, wants, desires, and expectations. This may be accomplished in five ways:

1. Identify through research the market(s) you are serving.
2. Establish a database to collect information about the needs, wants, desires, and expectations of your customers.

3. Regularly review new products (some Event Leaders set aside a specific day each month to see new vendors), and determine if they meet the standards set by your customers.

4. Match the needs, wants, desires, and expectations to every business development decision. For example, do your customers prefer to do business with you in the evening? If so, stay open late one night per week.

5. Regularly audit your internal procedures to make certain that you are developing new business by positioning your products and services as quality, dependable, and reliable resources for your customers.

Lifelong Learning: A User's Guide

If the twentieth century represented the age of innocence in Event Leadership, the twenty-first century may be described as "the renaissance." You are part of an era of unprecedented learning and expansion of knowledge in the field of Event Leadership. This book will serve as your primer to direct you to additional resources to ensure that you stay ahead of rather than behind the learning curve in this rapidly changing and expanding profession. One way to do this is to establish learning benchmarks for yourself throughout your career. Attending one or two annual industry conferences, participating in local chapter activities, or setting aside time each day to read relevant literature (see Appendixes 1 and 4) about the profession will certainly help you stay current. Perhaps the best proven way to learn anything is to teach someone else what you have learned. Collecting information that can later be shared with your professional colleagues is an excellent way to develop the habit of lifelong learning. Consider these five techniques for lifelong learning:

1. Budget time and finances to support continuing education on an annual basis.

2. Require or encourage your employees to engage in continuous Event Leadership education by subsidizing their training. Ask them to contribute by purchasing books that are related to the course work.

3. Establish a study group to prepare for the certification examination.

4. Set aside a specific time each week for professional reading. Collect relevant information and then highlight, clip, circulate, or file this information at this time.

5. Attend industry conferences and expositions to expose yourself to new ideas on an annual basis. Remember that, upon returning to your organization, you will be required to teach what you have learned to others. Therefore, become a scholar of your profession.

When you audit the business environment, select resources that demonstrate your quality, dependability, and reliability, and engage in a program of lifelong learning, you will be far ahead of your current and future competitors. This book will help you understand the profession of Event Leadership as both an art and a science, requiring not only your creativity but also your exacting reasoning ability. However, any book is only a catalyst for future exploration of a field of study. As a result of using this book to promote your future growth, you will have established the rigor required to become a scholar of Event Leadership and an authority in your organization. To maintain your position, you will need not only to return to this book as a central reference but to begin a comprehensive file of additional educational resources. This book provides several appendix resources from which you may assemble this base of knowledge. Upon completing this book, use Appendix 1 to expand your comprehension of the profession by contacting the organizations listed to request educational materials to improve and sustain your practice. Doctors, lawyers, and accountants, as well as numerous other established professionals, require continuous education to meet licensing or certification standards. Our profession must aspire to this same level of competence. Your use of this book and commitment to future educational opportunities will enhance your competence.

Getting Focused

Although ISES has identified nearly two dozen professions within the events industry, you must soon decide how you will focus your studies. After reading the preface and this chapter, you should be able to comprehend the macroprofession of Event Leadership through brief descriptions of the many subfields. Now is the time to begin to focus your studies on one or two specific subfields, such as tourism, meetings, conventions, festivals, reunions, and social life-cycle Event Leadership. Use the list of Event Leadership positions described in Figure 1.3 as a tool to get focused, and select the one or two areas where you wish to concentrate your studies.

Did you note the similarities in background and experience in each position? The key to your success in this business (or any other for that matter) is a thorough grounding in organization, negotiation, finance, and marketing. Human relations experience is also essential, as is the related volunteer coordination skill. Increasing in importance is your ability to design, conduct, and analyze research. Throughout the book each skill is discussed in detail. However, you must now begin to focus on how you will apply these skills to your particular career pursuits.

Event Leadership is a profession that provides skills for use in a variety of related disciplines. The field is grounded in the science of management, but you will also learn skills in psychology, sociology, and even anthropology as you develop your career. As you move from one subfield to another, these foundational skills will serve you well. They are the portable elements of this curriculum that you may take with you and apply to a variety of different types of events.

How to Use This Book

Self-Education: The Reading Log

Each chapter of this book represents the sum of many years of professional reading by this author. Therefore, as you approach a new chapter, look for related writings in industry trade and professional journals as well as general media, such as the daily newspaper. As you identify these readings, save them for your study time. When you complete your two 20-minute study periods, give yourself a bonus by reading the related material and then noting in your reading log the title, author, date, and a short description. Developing this habit during your study period will begin a lifelong process that will reward you richly throughout your career. Make certain that you develop a filing system for these readings for future reference, and use the reading log as a classification system for easy reference.

Benchmark Checklists

Self-improvement is the goal of every successful person. It is a continuous process. Ensuring continuous self-improvement and business improvement requires utilizing an old tradition in a new context. The term *benchmarking* was first used by Xerox Corporation to describe the way its corporate leaders reinvented its organization to compete more effectively. This process was so successful that Xerox won the most coveted award in corporate America, the Malcolm Baldridge National Quality Award. The principles of benchmarking are simple; however, the application requires commitment and discipline.

Benchmarking is a management process in which you study similar organizations to determine what systems they are using that can become quality benchmarks for your own organization. Once you have identified these benchmarks, your organization's goal is to meet or exceed these standards within a specified period of time.

The checklists throughout this book are your benchmarks. They are the result of 25 years of study of successful individuals and organizations in the profession of Event Leadership. Your goals should be to develop the rigor to meet or exceed these standards during your Event Leadership career.

Critical Connections for Career Advancement

In addition to the numerous tables, charts, and models in this book, each chapter includes four critical connections to help you rapidly advance. The very nature of special events is to connect people through a shared activity; therefore, each chapter includes specific instructions for global, technological, resource, and learning connections. Make certain that you carefully review these sections at the end of each chapter to expand, reinforce, and strengthen your connections in the twenty-first-century global Event Leadership profession.

Profiles in Event Leadership

This edition provides a series of new profiles of distinguished Event Leaders throughout the world. Each of the profiles demonstrates through practice the core competencies of the chapter in which it is presented. The Event Leaders who were selected for this edition will inspire you with their devotion to the field of special events leadership. These Event Leaders have also agreed to provide professional mentoring for you. To facilitate that opportunity, their e-mail addresses are included within their profiles.

Appendixes

The 17 appendixes are designed to provide you with extensive resources in one location to use throughout your professional life. Review these listings and determine what gaps you currently have in your operations, marketing, or other areas, and use these resources to add to your knowledge. As Event Leadership is an emerging discipline and rapidly expanding profession, you may notice gaps in the appendixes that you can fill. Send me your resources at joe.goldblatt@jwv.edu, and you will be acknowledged in the next edition.

Role and Scope

This book's role is to expand the knowledge base in the emerging discipline of Event Leadership. The scope of its task is to provide concrete techniques to immediately improve your practice as an Event Leader. Your career needs will determine how you use this book to improve your business. However, if you are sincerely interested in expanding the knowledge base in Event Leadership, your practice will improve in equal proportion to your level of commitment. This is so important that it bears repeating. If you are interested in expanding the body of knowledge in Event Leadership, your skills will improve in equal proportion to your level of commitment.

Therefore, as in most professions, the harder you work, the more you will learn. And as is also true in all professions, the more you learn, the more you will earn. I encourage you to become a scholar of this fascinating profession and, as suggested earlier, read this book as if someday, somewhere, you will be requested to teach others. I challenge you to achieve mastery through these pages so that those you will influence will leave this profession even better prepared for those who will follow.

I, like you, am a student of this profession. There are new learning opportunities every day. Over two decades ago, I stood outside a hospital nursery window gazing lovingly on our newborn son, Sam. Only a few hours earlier, I had telephoned my cousin Carola in New Orleans to announce his birth and, choking back tears, to tell her and the family that he would be named for my uncle, her father, who had recently died. Celebrating this new

Profile in Event Leadership:
Peter Kagwa and Patrick Muyonjo

REINVENTING EVENTS IN THE LAND OF THEIR BIRTH

Uganda is located in a region that was once described by the British prime minister and world traveler Sir Winston Churchill as "the pearl of Africa." In this special land, the savannahs of East Africa meet the jungles of West Africa, and for thousands of years human beings have commemorated their joys and triumphs through various celebrations.

The Buganda tribe, representing 18 percent of the total population, comprises what is the largest traditional kingdom in Uganda. For thousands of years, this tribe has created and sustained colorful and dramatic rituals, many of which are still practiced today.

From 1939 to 1966, this tribe was led by King Edward Mutesa II. In 1963, Mutesa II became figurehead president of Uganda. In 1966, Apollo Milton Obote suspended the Ugandan constitution, declaring himself president and thus forcing Mutesa II into exile in Great Britain.

In 1993, the current leader of Uganda, President Yoweri Kaguta Museveni, reinstated

Peter Kagwa

Patrick Muyonjo

traditional and cultural leadership and hence the return of Mutesa II's son, Ronald Muwenda Mutebi II as the king of the Buganda people.

The history of Uganda includes numerous revolutions and dictators. However, over the last two decades, under the leadership of President Museveni, the country has experienced an era of political stability that has ushered in steady growth of the tourism and education sectors and economic development in general. The modern events industry is definitely contributing to this recent period of tourism growth and economic development.

Peter Kagwa, managing director of Events Warehouse Uganda, a leading events management and experiential marketing company, is currently the only member of the International Special Events Society in this country of 27 million people. Kagwa believes that the future of Uganda lies in strengthening and developing the tourism and hospitality sectors of the economy.

"By taking our events to the next level of professionalism, we will contribute toward restoring pride in Uganda as a leading business and travel destination in the region," says Peter. This is exactly what Peter and his partner, Patrick Muyonjo, are doing. Annually, they plan, manage, and execute dozens of corporate and public events, such as music festivals featuring prominent local and international artists.

In their bid to develop Uganda's potential as a major travel destination in sub-Saharan Africa, Peter and Patrick are careful about overpromising and underdelivering their event services and products. According to Patrick, who is the firm's technical production expert, "When a major international music star comes to Uganda, we carefully review his contract rider and then communicate to his production crew what is available in the country, what we can confidently acquire from other nearby countries, and finally, advise the team on what they should carry along."

Peter Kagwa sees a bright future for the Ugandan event community because "tourism is the sunshine our country greatly needs." With the influx of larger local and international conferences and events into the country—for instance, the upcoming 2007 Commonwealth Heads of Government Meeting—and with VIPs such as Her Majesty Queen Elizabeth and other high-level dignitaries, tourism is beginning to shed the first streams of sunshine seen by the country in many years.

According to Peter, first-class hospitality facilities and reliable services are the keys to developing a vibrant and lucrative event tourism industry. With the development of new facilities, such as Speke Resort Munyonyo (*www.spekeresort.com*) located on the shores of beautiful Lake Victoria, Peter Kagwa and other event professionals are on their way.

Although Peter and Patrick have made significant contributions to the development of the emerging events industry in Uganda, Peter acknowledges that "if I have created a goal and it has been achieved, I must then aim higher the next time." He believes that he achieves these goals by practicing core values, such as integrity and consistency of quality in delivering his event services.

"Some of our traditional and cultural values, such as warm reception, hospitality, courtesy, integrity, and respect, have shaped my identity. It is important for me to transmit those values to the next generation of event professionals in Uganda and, indeed, throughout the world." Peter adds, "To know where you are going, it is important to know where you have come from. These values blended with my international exposure, give me an edge in finding my wings in the modern event world."

As Uganda and the continent of Africa continue to develop, pioneering professional events organizers from developing countries, such as Peter Kagwa and Patrick Muyonjo of Events Warehouse Uganda, will forever be remembered. As early event leaders, they have cultivated quality and professionalism while spreading the hopes and dreams of a better events industry.

We are indeed fortunate that they have retained their cultural values and, at the same time, brought these traditional values into the new event world for the greater benefit of all of us.

Peter Kagwa and Patrick Muyonjo: peter.kagwa@eventswarehouse.biz, patrick@eventswarehouse.biz life together, we laughed out loud about the "curse" that might come with my son's name. Would he be as funny, charming, irascible, and generous as my uncle Sam? His potential was limitless. Confucius declared several thousand years ago that "we are cursed to live in interesting times indeed." Like Sam, regardless of what road you take in the infinitely fascinating Event Leadership profession, you can be assured of finding many opportunities in these very interesting and challenging times. In the closing lines of his best-seller *Megatrends* (Warner Books, 1982), John Naisbitt exalted the world he had spent years analyzing: "My God, what a fantastic time in which to be alive." The future that you and your colleagues will create will carry the curse of Confucius, the joy of Naisbitt, and the final assurance of the French poet Paul Valéry, who wrote: "The trouble with the future is it no longer is what it used to be." Your future is secure in knowing that there are millions of new births annually in the world and, therefore, just as many future events (and many more) to lead.

Career-Advancement Connections

🌐 Global Connection

Connect globally with Event Leaders throughout the world through an Internet Listserv, such as "World of Events," which is managed by Leeds Metropolitan University in Great Britain. World of Events provides a global forum for discussion of Event Leadership topics by researchers, academics, students, and practitioners throughout the world (*www.worldofevents.net*).

💻 Technology Connection

Develop an interactive Web-based data management system to enable you to collect and access your Event Leadership data from throughout the world. The best system for achieving this is to create a password-protected Internet-based database that can be accessed by an authorized Event Leader from any remote point on earth. It is critical to protect your valuable data. The protection can be enforced by setting different levels of access: to review data only, to add data, or to delete and modify data.

📚 Resource Connection

Use the appendixes of the book to connect with associations for future study. Hundreds of colleges and universities throughout the world offer courses, curricula, degrees, certificates, and other resources. Temple University's School of Tourism and Hospitality Management offers a comprehensive certificate in Event Leadership. For more information, visit *www.temple.edu/STHM/EL*.

Learning Connection

Construct a 1-, 3-, 5-, and 10-year plan or blueprint to identify your career goals and path. Assess your current skill and experience level and list the educational, practical, and theoretical resources that you will need to achieve your goals and objectives. Read *Dollars and Events: How to Succeed in the Special Events Business* (Wiley, 1999) by Dr. Joe Goldblatt, CSEP, and Frank Supovitz, as well as *What Color Is Your Parachute? 2006* (Ten Speed Press, 2006) by Richard Nelson Bolles.

Chinese dragon boat races such as this one have been re-created in cities and towns throughout the world, demonstrating the globalization of the events industry.

CHAPTER 2

Models of Global Event Leadership

In This Chapter You Will Learn How To:

+ Recognize and use the five phases of the modern Event Leadership process

+ Identify the strengths, weaknesses, opportunities, and threats of your event

+ Create an accurate blueprint for your event

+ Conduct a comprehensive needs assessment

+ Complete a gap analysis for your event

+ Communicate effectively with event stakeholders

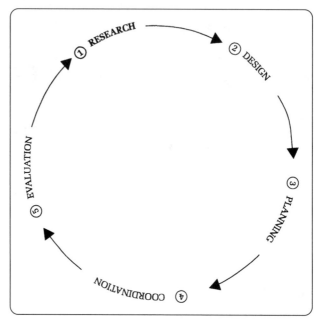

Figure 2.1 Event Leadership Process

All successful events have five critical stages in common to ensure their consistent effectiveness. These five phases or steps of successful Event Leadership are *research, design, planning, coordination,* and *evaluation* (see Figure 2.1). In this chapter, we explore each phase to enable you to produce successful events every time.

Research

Excellent event research reduces risk. The better research you conduct prior to the event, the more likely you are to produce an event that matches the planned outcomes of the organizers or stakeholders. For many years, public relations professionals and other marketing experts have realized the value of using research to pinpoint the needs, wants, desires, and expectations of prospective customers. Government leaders regularly conduct feasibility studies prior to authorizing capital investments. These feasibility studies include exhaustive research. An event is a product that is placed before members of the public with the reasonable expectation that they will attend. Therefore, it is imperative that you conduct careful and accurate consumer research to reduce the risk of nonattendance.

I have interviewed hundreds of leading Event Leadership professionals, and they have stated their belief that more time must be devoted to research and evaluation of events. According to these experts, if more time were devoted to these phases of the Event Leadership production process, ultimately less time and expense would be needed to complete the following steps.

The three types of research that are used for pre-event research are quantitative, qualitative, or a combination or hybrid of both. Matching the research type to the event is important and is determined by the goals of the research, the time allowed for conducting the research, and the funds available.

Market Research Techniques

Before bringing a new product or service to market, the inventor or manufacturer will conduct market research to determine the needs, wants, desires, and expectations of the target market. Whether your event is a new or a preexisting product, market research is required to determine how to obtain the very best position in a sometimes crowded marketplace. Typically, qualitative and, in most cases, focus group research is used for this purpose.

Market research will help you determine the target or primary market as well as the secondary and tertiary markets for your event. Market research will also enable you to study the service levels expected by guests as well as the perceptions by internal stakeholders of the services currently being delivered. By studying the market in depth, you are able to spot emerging trends, develop new service delivery systems, and solve minor problems before they become major catastrophes.

One example of this is the Event Leader who discovered through research that attendees could not register for the upcoming convention during normal business hours due to workplace regulations. Therefore, she invested in an answering service for six months prior to the meeting to accept registrations between the hours of 5:00 P.M. and 8:00 A.M. This new service was a major success, and registrations for the conference increased markedly.

Quantitative versus Qualitative Research

■ Quantitative Pre-Event Research

Event Leaders primarily use quantitative research to determine demographic information such as gender, age, income, and other pertinent facts about the future market for an event. This research is relatively inexpensive to conduct and easy to tabulate and analyze with computers. Figure 2.2 provides a model of a typical quantitative pre-event research survey.

Whether you use a written survey, an in-person interview, or a telephone interview method of construction, the research survey is of prime importance. To achieve the greatest possible response, offer a reward, such as "enclose your business card and we will share the research findings with you," or offer an immediate incentive, such as enclosing a $1 bill.

Questions may be developed in two different styles. As noted in Figure 2.2, Question 4 uses a *Likert scale* to allow a respondent to select the response that states his or

This survey will enable the organizers of XYZ event to determine the feasibility of producing the following event. Your participation is important in this effort. Answer all questions by checking the appropriate box. Return this survey by January 1, 2008.

1. Gender? ☐ Male ☐ Female

2. Age? ☐ Under 25 ☐ 26–34 ☐ 35–44 ☐ 45–60 ☐ 61 and over

3. Income? ☐ Under $24,999 ☐ $25,000–44,999 ☐ Over $45,000

4. If the event were held during the summer I would: *(Likert scale)*
   ☐ Not attend ☐ Maybe attend ☐ No opinion ☐ Probably attend ☐ Positively attend

5. If the event were held during the fall I would: *(semantic differential scale)*
   Not Attend ☐ 1 ☐ 2 ☐ 3 ☐ 4 ☐ 5 Positively attend

6. If you checked number 1 above, please describe your reasons for nonattendance in the space below: *(open-ended question)*

   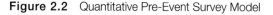
   _____

   _____

   _____

Return this survey by January 1, 2008 to:
Dr. Joe Goldblatt, CSEP
Temple University
1700 North Broad Street, Suite 412D
Philadelphia, PA 19122
or fax to 215-204-9015

To receive a *free copy* of the survey results, please include your business card or e-mail.

Figure 2.2 Quantitative Pre-Event Survey Model

her opinion precisely. Question 5 uses a *semantic differential scale* to allow a respondent to select a continuum between two opposing adjectives. The number that the respondent chooses indicates the likelihood of attending or not attending an event.

■ Qualitative Pre-Event Research

Market research consultants rely on qualitative research to probe for hidden meanings in quantitative studies. Qualitative research tells the research organization what is beneath the numbers in quantitative research and, therefore, is an important step in the research process. This type of research may take the form of a focus group, participant/observer research, or a case study. Selecting the proper methodology depends on your goals, the time available, and the funding.

The *focus group* is typically comprised of 8 to 12 people of similar background and experience who assemble for the purpose of discussion. A trained facilitator leads the group through specific questions that will provide clues to the goals or outcomes desired from the research. A focus group may be one hour in length, although, in most cases, they last between 90 minutes and two hours. In some instances, a room with a one-way mirror is used to allow the other stakeholders to observe participants for subtle changes in body language, facial reactions, and other gestures that may reveal information in addition to their verbal opinion. The focus group is audiotaped, and the tapes are later transcribed and analyzed to identify areas of agreement or discord.

The *participant/observer* style of qualitative research involves placing the researcher in a host community to participate in and observe the culture of those being studied. For example, if you desire to determine whether a certain destination is appropriate for relocation of an event, you may wish to visit, participate, and observe for an extended period of time before making a decision. Interviews with key informants are essential to this research.

The third type of qualitative research is the *case study.* In this style, a preexisting event is singled out as a specific case to be studied in depth. The event may be studied from a historical context, or the stakeholders may be interviewed to determine how personality, skill, and other factors drive the success of the event. The case study enables the event researcher to draw conclusions based on the research gleaned from a comparable event.

■ Cost

Qualitative research is generally more expensive than quantitative research due to the time that is involved in probing for deeper, more meaningful answers than only digits. The cost of training interviewers, the interviewers' time, the time for analyzing the data, and other costs contribute to this investment. Although the cost is greater, many Event Leaders require both qualitative and quantitative studies to validate their assumptions or research their markets.

■ Combined Research

In most cases, Event Leaders use a combination of quantitative and qualitative research to make decisions about future events. Event Leaders obtain large volumes of information in a cost-efficient manner using the quantitative method and then probe for hidden meanings and subtle feelings using the qualitative approach.

Effective quantitative research includes elements of qualitative research to increase the validity of the questions. Event Leaders should use a small focus group or team of experts to review the questions before conducting a survey. These experts can confirm that a question is understandable and valid for the research being conducted. Figure 2.3 provides a simple way for Event Leaders to determine what research methodology is most effective for their purpose.

The goals and required outcomes of the research, combined with the time frame and funding available, will ultimately determine the best method for your pre-event research.

Goal	Method
Collect gender, age, and income data	Written survey
Collect attitudes and opinions	Focus group
Examine culture of community	Participant/observer
Identify comparable characteristics	Case study
Collect demographic and psychographic data	Combined methods

Figure 2.3   Selecting the Appropriate Pre-Event Research Method

Regardless of the type of research you conduct, it is important that you take care to produce valid and reliable information.

Validity and Reliability: Producing Credible Pre-Event Research

All research must be defended. Your stakeholders will ask you bluntly, "How do you know that you know?" If your research has high validity and reliability, you can provide greater assurance that your work is truthful. Validity primarily confirms that your research measures what it purports to measure. For example, if you are trying to determine if senior citizens will attend an event, you must include senior citizens in your sample of respondents to ensure validity. Furthermore, the questions you pose to these seniors must be understandable to them to ensure that their responses are truthful and accurate.

Reliability helps prove that your research will remain truthful and accurate over time. For example, if you were to conduct the same study with another group of senior citizens, would the answers be significantly different? If the answer is yes, your data may not be reliable. Designing a collection instrument that has high validity and reliability is a challenging and time-consuming task. You may wish to contact a university or college marketing, psychology, or sociology department for assistance by an experienced researcher in developing your instrument. Often a senior-level undergraduate student or a graduate student may be assigned to help you develop the instrument and collect and analyze the data for college credit. The participation of the university or college will add credibility to your findings. Use software applications such as Microsoft Excel for analyzing data. For more complex analysis, use statistical applications such as SAS, Minitab, and SPSS.

Interpreting and Communicating Research Findings

Designing and collecting pre-event research is only the beginning of this important phase. Once you have analyzed the data carefully and identified the implications of your research, as well as provided some recommendations based on your study, you must present the information to your stakeholders. The way that you do this will determine the level of influence you wield with stakeholders.

If the stakeholders are academics or others who have a research background, using tables or a written narrative may suffice. However, if, as is most often the case, stakeholders are unsophisticated with regard to research, you may instead wish to use graphs, charts, and other visual tools to illustrate your findings. To paraphrase Confucius, "One picture is certainly worth a thousand numerals." Use these five steps to present your pre-event research findings effectively:

1. Determine your audience and customize your presentation to their personal communication learning style.
2. Describe the purpose and importance of the research.
3. Explain how the research was collected and describe any limitations.
4. Reveal your findings and emphasize the key points.
5. Invite questions.

Distributing a well-produced written narrative with copies of the information you are presenting (e.g., graphs from slides) will be helpful to the stakeholders, as they will need more time for independent study before posing intelligent questions. In the written narrative, include a section describing the steps you have taken to produce research that demonstrates high validity and reliability; also list any independent organizations (e.g., a university or college) that reviewed your study prior to completion.

Communicating your research findings is an essential phase in the research process. Prepare, rehearse, and then reveal your data thoughtfully and confidently. Summarize your presentation by demonstrating how the findings support the goals and objectives of your research plan.

The Five W's: How to Produce Consistently Effective Events

Too often students will ask me *what* event they should produce for a class project instead of *why* they should produce the event in the first place. After the economically rocky early 1990s, corporations, associations, governments, and other organizations began to analyze carefully why a meeting or event should occur. This solid reasoning should be applied to every event decision.

The first step is to ask: "*Why* must we hold this event?" Not one but a series of compelling reasons must confirm the importance and viability of holding the event.

The second step is to ask: "*Who* will the stakeholders be for this event?" Stakeholders are both internal and external parties. Internal stakeholders may be the board of directors, committee members, staff, elected leaders, guests, or others. External stakeholders may be the media, politicians, bureaucrats, or others who will be investing in the event. Conducting solid research will help you determine the level of commitment of each of these parties and help you define whom this event is being produced for.

The third step is to ask "*When* will the event be held?" You must ask yourself if the research-through-evaluation time frame is appropriate for the size of the event. If this time period is not appropriate, you may need to rethink your plans and either shift the dates or streamline your operations. *When* may also determine where the event may be held.

The fourth step involved is to ask: "*Where* will the event will be held?" As you will discover in this chapter, once you have selected a site, your work becomes either easier or more challenging. Therefore, this decision must be made as early as possible, as it affects many other decisions.

The fifth and final *W* is to determine, from the information gleaned thus far: "*What* is the event product that you are developing and presenting?" Matching the event product to the needs, wants, desires, and expectations of your guests while satisfying the internal requirements of your organization is no simple task. You must analyze the *what* carefully and critically to make certain that the *why, who, when,* and *where* are synergized in this answer.

Once these five questions have been answered thoroughly, it is necessary to turn your deliberations to *how* the organization will allocate scarce resources to produce maximum benefit for the stakeholders. SWOT (strengths, weaknesses, opportunities, threats) analysis provides a comprehensive tool for ensuring that you review each step systematically.

SWOT Analysis: Finding the Strengths, Weaknesses, Opportunities, and Threats

Before you begin planning an event, you usually must implement SWOT analysis to underpin your decision making. SWOT analysis assists you in identifying the internal and external variables that may prevent the event from achieving maximum success.

■ Strengths and Weaknesses

The strengths and weaknesses of an event are primarily considerations that can be spotted before the event actually takes place. Typical strengths and weaknesses of many events are shown in Figure 2.4. The strengths and weaknesses may be uncovered through a focus group or through individual interviews with the major stakeholders. If the weaknesses outnumber the strengths and there is no reasonable way to eliminate the weak-

Strengths	Weaknesses
Strong funding	Weak funding
Good potential for sponsors	No potential for sponsors
Well-trained staff	Poorly trained staff
Many volunteers	Few volunteers
Good media relations	Poor media relations
Excellent site	Weak site

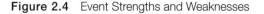

Figure 2.4   Event Strengths and Weaknesses

nesses and increase the strengths within the event planning period, you may wish to postpone or cancel the event.

■ Opportunities and Threats

Opportunities and threats are two key factors that generally present themselves either during an event or after it has occurred. However, during the research process, these factors should be considered seriously, as they may spell potential disaster for the event. *Opportunities* are activities that may be of benefit to an event without significant investment by your organization. One example is that of selecting a year in which to hold an event that coincides with your community's or industry's hundredth anniversary. Your event may benefit from additional funding, publicity, and other important resources simply by aligning yourself with this hallmark event. Other possible beneficial outcomes, sometimes indirect, such as the potential of contributing to the political image of the event's host, are considered opportunities.

Threats are activities that prevent you from maximizing the potential of an event. The most obvious threat is weather; however, political threats may be just as devastating. Local political leaders must buy in to your civic event to ensure cooperation with all agencies. Political infighting may quickly destroy your planning. A modern threat is that of terrorism. The threat of violence erupting at an event may keep people from attending. A celebrity canceling or not attending can also create a significant threat to the success of an event. Typical opportunities and threats for an event are listed in Figure 2.5.

You will note that, although strengths and weaknesses are often related, opportunities and threats need not be. Once again, in making a decision to proceed with event planning, your goal is to identify more opportunities than threats. All threats should be considered carefully, and experts should be consulted to determine ways in which threats may be contained, reduced, or eliminated.

SWOT analysis (see Figure 2.6) is a major strategic planning tool during the research phase. By using SWOT analysis, an Event Leader can not only scan the internal and external event environment but also can proceed to the next step, which involves analyses of the weaknesses and threats, and provide solutions to improve the event planning process.

Opportunities	Threats
Civic anniversary	Hurricanes and tornadoes
Chamber of Commerce promotion	Political infighting
Celebrity appearance	Violence from terrorism
Align with environmental cause	Alcoholic consumption
Tie-in with media	Site in bad neighborhood
Winning elections	Celebrity canceling or not attending
Developing more loyal employees	

Figure 2.5 Event Opportunities and Threats

S = strengths		
1. Strong funding	Internal	
2. Well-trained staff	Internal	
3. Event well respected by media	External	
W = weaknesses		Existing conditions
1. Weak funding	Internal	
2. Few human resources	Internal	
3. Poor public-relations history	External	
O = opportunities		
1. Simultaneous celebration of a congruent event	External	
2. Timing of event congruent with future budget allocation	Internal	
T = threats		Future/predictive conditions
1. Weather	External	
2. New board of directors leading this event	Internal	

Figure 2.6   SWOT Analysis

The research phase of the event administration process is perhaps most critical. During this period you will determine through empirical research whether you have both the internal and external resources essential to make a decision to produce an effective event. Your ability to select the appropriate research methodology, design the instrument, and collect, analyze, interpret, and present the data will ultimately determine whether an event has sufficient strength for future success. The first pillar of the Event Leadership process—research—rests squarely in the center of the other four supporting columns. Although each is equal in importance, the future success of an event depends on how well you conduct the research phase.

Design: Blueprint for Success

Having researched your event thoroughly and determined that it is feasible, time may now be allotted to use the right side of the brain—the creative capacity—to create a general blueprint for your ideas. There are numerous ways to begin this process, but it is important to remember that the very best event designers are constantly visiting the library, attending movies and plays, visiting art galleries, and reviewing periodicals to maintain their inspiration. This continuous research for new ideas will further strengthen the activities you propose for an event.

Brainstorming and Mind Mapping

Too often in volunteer-driven organizations, the very best ideas are never allowed to surface. This occurs because well-meaning volunteers (and some not so well-meaning volunteers) tell their colleagues "This will never work" or "This is impossible at this time." Although their opinions are certainly valid, the process of shooting down ideas before they are allowed to be fully developed is an unfortunate occurrence in many organizations. Event Leaders must encourage and support creativity because, ultimately, the product you will offer is a creative art. Creativity is an essential ingredient in every event management process.

Therefore, when beginning the design phase of this Event Leadership process, conduct a meeting where creative people are encouraged to brainstorm the various elements of the event. The Event Leader is the facilitator of this meeting, and, in addition to various creative stakeholders, you may choose to invite other creative people from the worlds of theater, dance, music, art, literature, and other fields. At the outset of the meeting, use a flip chart to lay out the ground rules for the discussion. In large bold letters write "Rule 1: There are no bad ideas. Rule 2: Go back and reread Rule 1."

You may wish to begin the session with an activity that will stimulate creativity. One activity I've used is to place an object in the center of the table and invite participants to describe what it might become. For example, a shoebox might become a tomb, a rocket, or a small dwelling. As each person offers his or her ideas, the others should be encouraged to be supportive.

Once you have completed these warm-up activities, members should be given simple suggestions regarding the *why* of the event. From these suggestions, they should be encouraged to provide creative ideas for *who, when, where, what,* and *how.* If one member (or more than one member) tends to dominate the discussion, ask him or her to summarize and then say "Thank you" as you quickly move on to others to solicit their ideas. Use the flip chart to list all the initial ideas, and do not try to establish categories or provide any other organizational structure.

Mind mapping allows an Event Leader to begin to pull together the random ideas and establish linkages that will later lead to logical decision making. Using the flip chart, ask each member of the group to revisit his or her earlier ideas and begin to link them to the four *W*'s and ultimately help you see how the event should be developed. Write *Why? Who? When? Where? What?* and *How?* in the center of a circle on a separate page of the chart. From this circle, draw spokes that terminate in another circle. Leave the circles at the end of each spoke empty. The ideas of your team members will fill these circles, and they will begin to establish linkages between the goal (Why? Who? When? Where? What? and How?) and the creative method. Figure 2.7 is an example of a successful event mind-mapping activity.

Mind mapping is an effective way to synthesize the various ideas suggested by group members and begin to construct an *event philosophy.* The event philosophy will determine

Why?	+	Who?	+	When?	+	Where?	+	What?
What is the compelling reason for this event? Why must this event be held?		Who will benefit from this event? Who will they want to have attend?		When will the event be held? Are the date and time flexible or subject to change?		What are the best destination, location, and venue?		What elements and resources are required to satisfy the needs identified above?
				= How?				
		Given answers to the five *W*'s, how do you effectively research, design, plan, coordinate, and evaluate this event?						

Figure 2.7   Event Leadership Needs Assessment

the financial, cultural, social, and other important aspects of the event. For example, if the sponsoring organization is a not-for-profit group, the financial philosophy will not support charging high fees to produce a disproportionate amount of funds, or the tax status may be challenged. Mind mapping allows you to sift through the ideas carefully and show how they support the goals of the event. As you do this, an event philosophy begins to emerge. Those ideas that do not have a strong linkage or support the philosophy should be placed on a separate sheet of flip chart paper for future use. Remember Rule 1?

The Creative Process in Event Leadership

Special events require people with the ability to move easily between the left and right quadrants of the cerebellum. The right side of the brain is responsible for creative, spontaneous thinking, while the left side of the brain handles the more logical aspects of our lives. To function effectively, Event Leaders must be both right- and left-brained. Therefore, if you have determined that one side of your brain is less strong than the other, you must take steps to correct this to achieve maximum success in Event Leadership.

Most of this book is concerned with logical, reasoning activities. Therefore, assuming that one of the aspects of Event Leadership that you find attractive is the creative opportunities afforded in this profession, I will provide some insight into ways to develop your creativity to the highest possible level. Remember that developing creativity is a continuous process. The reason that some corporations put their advertising accounts out for review to other agencies periodically is to be sure that the current agency is working at its highest possible creative level. As an Event Leader, you too must strive for constant review of your creative powers to make certain that you are in high gear. Following are some tips for continuously developing your creativity:

✦ Visit one art gallery each month.
✦ Attend a live performance of opera, theater, or dance each month.

◆ Read great works of literature, on a continuing basis.
◆ Enroll in a music, dance, literature, visual arts, or acting class or discussion group.
◆ Apply what you are discovering in each of these fields to Event Leadership.

Perhaps the best way to stretch your creativity continually is to surround yourself with highly creative people (see Figure 2.8). Whether you are in a position to hire creativity or must seek creative types through groups outside the office, you must find the innovators in order to practice innovation.

Richard Carbotti's company, Perfect Surroundings, Inc., of Newport, Rhode Island, provides consulting, design, fabrication, and on-site management to events throughout the world. Carbotti, a graduate of the prestigious Parsons School of Design and the 2001 *Event Solutions* Magazine Event Designer of the Year, says that event design began to change before September 11, 2001. According to Carbotti, "We still have clients who want the design to reflect simplicity, as well as those who wish to focus upon indulgence. Although they still want the 'oh wow!' look, they do not want to pay for it. Clients are more specific about each line item in the décor budget." Carbotti notes that labor costs for décor are about 25 percent of the total client investment, the remaining 75 percent being administration, product materials, transportation, storage, and other operational costs.

Sometimes Carbotti bills as a consultant for his services; typical fees range up to $1,000 per day. He notes that successful designers pay close attention to the personality of the venue where the event is being held and incorporate that personality in the design

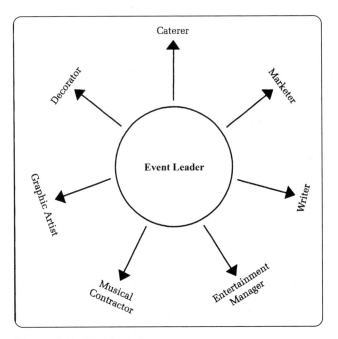

Figure 2.8   Creative Influences

approach. In addition, the three-time Gala Award–winning designer says, "Effective Event Leaders pay close attention to the attitude of the culture of the organization sponsoring the event and the politics that are driving that culture."

After nearly 20 years as one of the leading event designers, Richard Carbotti says that he is now focusing on a select list of clients in the corporate and social markets. He notes that there is much crossover between the corporate and social market; the father or mother of the bride or the bride herself can often become his next corporate client. "As an Event Leader, my job is to make certain my managers have the resources they need to lead while I go one step further, looking at the long-term strategic goals of my organization," says Carbotti. Whether it is a vision of the event design or a vision of his company, Richard Carbotti focuses on quality and innovation to continually expand the possibilities within the new world of event design.

Making the Perfect Match through Needs Assessment and Analysis

Once you have completed the brainstorming and mind-mapping activities satisfactorily, it is time to make certain that your creative ideas perfectly match the goals and objectives of your event. This is accomplished through *needs assessment and analysis.*

Needs assessment and analysis enables you to create an event that closely satisfies the needs of your stakeholders. You actually began this process by asking "Why?" and "Who?" Now it is time to take it one giant step forward and survey the stakeholders to determine if your creative solutions will satisfy their needs. To accomplish this part of the design phase, develop your ideas into a series of questions, query the key constituents for the event, and determine if the various elements you have created—from advertising to décor, from catering to entertainment, and everything in between—meet their expectations. Once you are confident that you have assessed the needs of the stakeholders adequately and confirmed that you have, through analysis, determined how to meet these needs, you are well prepared to confirm the final feasibility of your event design.

■ Is It Feasible?

Feasibility simply means that you have looked at the event design objectively to determine if what you propose is practical given the resources available. This is the final checkpoint before actual planning begins and, therefore, must be given adequate time for review. Municipalities often engage professional engineers or other consultants to conduct lengthy feasibility studies before approving new construction or other capital expenditures. Although you may not need a battery of consultants, it is important for you to review all previous steps thoroughly when determining the feasibility of an event plan.

The three basic resources that will be required are financial, human, and political. Each of these resources may have varying degrees of importance, depending on the nature of the event. For example, a for-profit or large hallmark event will require significant financial investment to succeed. A not-for-profit event will rely on an army of volunteers, and, therefore, the human element is more important. A civic event will require greater political resources to accomplish. Therefore, when assessing and analyzing feasibility, first determine in what proportions resources will be required for the event. You may wish to weigh each resource to help prepare your analysis.

Financial Considerations

You will want to know if sufficient financial resources are available to sustain development and implementation of the event. Furthermore, you must consider what will happen if the event loses money. How will creditors be paid? You will also want to know what resources you can count on for an immediate infusion of cash, should the event require this to continue development. Finally, you must carefully analyze the cash-flow projections for the event to determine how much time is to be allowed between payables and receivables.

The Human Dimension

In assessing the feasibility of an event, you must not only know where your human resources will come from but how they will be rewarded (financially or through intangibles, such as awards and recognition). Most important, you must know how they will work together as an efficient event team.

Politics as Usual

The increasingly important role of government leaders in event oversight must be viewed with a practiced eye. Politicians see events as both good (opportunities for publicity, constituent communications, and economic impact) and bad (drain on municipal services and potential for disaster). When designing civic events, it is particularly important that you understand and enlist the support of politicians and their bureaucratic ministers to ensure smooth cooperation for your event. Furthermore, for all events, it is essential that you carefully research the permit process to determine if the event you have designed is feasible according to the code within the jurisdiction where the event will be held.

■ The Approval Process

The research and design phases add to the event history once an event is approved. The approval process may be as simple as an acceptance by the client or as complex as requiring dozens of signatures from various city agencies that will interact with the event. Regardless of the simplicity or complexity of this step, you should view it as an important milestone that, once crossed, assures you that the plan has been reviewed and deemed reasonable and feasible, and has a high likelihood of success. All roads lead to official approval, whether in the form of a contract or as individual permits from each agency. Without official approval, an event remains a dream. The process for turning dreams into workable plans requires careful research, thoughtful design, and critical analysis. This could be called the planning to plan phase, because it involves so many complex steps related to the next phase. However, once the approval is granted, you are on your way to the next important phase: the actual planning period.

Project Management Systems for Event Leaders

According to William O'Toole and Phyllis Mikolaitis, CSEP, the authors of *Corporate Event Project Management* (Wiley, 2002), there are several reasons why project management offers you unique resources for improving your practice. Using a project management system will help you establish a systematic approach to all events. Like the five phases of Event Leadership, the project management system provides you with a superstructure to enable you to systematically approach every event using the same framework.

Many events—especially those in the social market—are driven by emotional decisions rather than systematic or logical approaches. The project management system will depersonalize the event as it provides you with an objective process for reviewing the event development.

Communication is critical throughout the Event Leadership process, and the project management system will help you facilitate clear communications with stakeholders from many different fields. Through meetings and documents, project management provides a transparent system to promote better communications.

Many corporate and government organizations already utilize project management systems; therefore, using this system will help you conform to those that are already in place in your clients' organizations.

Accountability is increasingly one of the more important outcomes of any event project. The project management system helps ensure accountability through the continuous outputs that are required to update the progress of the event.

O'Toole and Mikolaitis believe that, through the adoption of project management systems, you will be able to increase the visibility for the profession of Event Leadership. If your work is often invisible until the actual start of the event, the project management system will provide a continuous flow of information charting the progress of the event as it develops and will provide your client and others with an overview of the complexity of your job.

Training is critical for your staff and volunteers. By providing them with a project management system to follow, you simplify and expedite this training. The project management system will put your staff and volunteers to work more quickly and will motivate them to consistently perform better over the life span of the event.

In addition to facilitating training, project management competency helps develop transferable skills that will help you attract the best people. As a result of working within your project management system, your staff and volunteers will learn a system that can be transferred and applied to a seemingly infinite number of jobs and careers.

Finally, as an event project manager, you will establish a diverse body of knowledge that may be transmitted to other organizations. In addition, you will be able to accumulate and refine the knowledge you receive from specific events and related projects from around the world. Whether it is a moon landing mission by NASA or the development and deployment of the new Transportation Security Administration, you can benefit from the successful project management experiences of other organizations.

In traditional project management, a technique called the project breakdown structure (PBS) is often used to establish the organizational structure. Similar to the traditional organizational chart, the PBS provides a thorough overview of all of the event requirements.

After the event has been thoroughly defined, the work that will be required must be carefully analyzed. During this decomposition period, the work that will be conducted for the event is broken down into smaller units of work called *tasks*. This process is described in project management as the work breakdown structure (WBS). Tasks or activities are generally singular, independent entities that may be individually managed. They also have specific start and finish times. Finally, they require clearly assigned resources (labor, finance, time). When several tasks are bundled together, they form a *work package*. A *milestone* is the accomplishment or completion of an important task.

Scheduling is perhaps one of the most valuable advantages of using a project management system for your event. Tasks are usually divided into two types of scheduling systems. *Parallel scheduling* refers to tasks that may be performed at the same time. *Serial scheduling* refers to tasks that must be performed in a sequence, such as when the lighting company must first hang the lights before the rental company places the tables and chairs for a banquet. Timelines for your events may benefit from a pictorial tool, such as the GANTT chart or bar chart, which demonstrates the major tasks that need to be accomplished. Creating and documenting the critical tasks and critical path are major responsibilities for the event project manager. The ability of the event project manager to list, prioritize, and sequence the tasks will ultimately determine the overall success of the event from an operational and financial standpoint.

Influence diagrams and sensitivity analyses are used to mitigate future challenges. The *influence diagram* is a chart that demonstrates through boxes and arrows what tasks are interdependent on others. Most importantly, it clearly demonstrates that events are part of larger systems and that one change in the system can affect hundreds of other components in the event. The *sensitivity analysis* is the identification of the degree of influence any part of the event has on the entire event as a whole. This analysis also aids in the risk-management controls for the event because it demonstrates how a small change in one area can affect other areas of the entire event. As a result of this careful documentation, a series of outputs are created, including charts and reports. Later you can use these outputs to form a handbook or manual to educate or train others as well as provide important documentation and historical detail of the event.

Event Leaders will greatly benefit from project management training. The use of this system, as outlined by O'Toole and Mikolaitis, provides Event Leaders with a system that bridges the most accepted practices of their clients. For this reason and many more, it is important that Event Leaders become familiar with how to apply project management techniques to their Event Leadership system.

Planning Consistently Effective Events

The planning period is typically the longest period of time in the Event Leadership process. Historically, this has been due to disorganization. *Disorganization* is best characterized by frequent changes resulting from substitutions, additions, or even deletions due to poor research and design. Ideally, the better the research and design, the simpler and briefer the planning period will be. Since events are planned by human beings for other human beings, this theory is fraught with exceptions. However, your goal should be to develop a smooth planning process based on careful research and design procedures. The planning phase involves using the *time/space/tempo laws* (see Figure 2.9) to determine how best to use your immediate resources. These three basic laws will affect every decision you make; how well you make use of them will govern the final outcome of an event.

Timing

The *law of timing* refers to how much time you have in which to act or react. The first question that many Event Leaders ask the client is: When would you like to schedule the event? The answer to that question tells you how much time you have to prepare. Often that timetable may seem incredibly short.

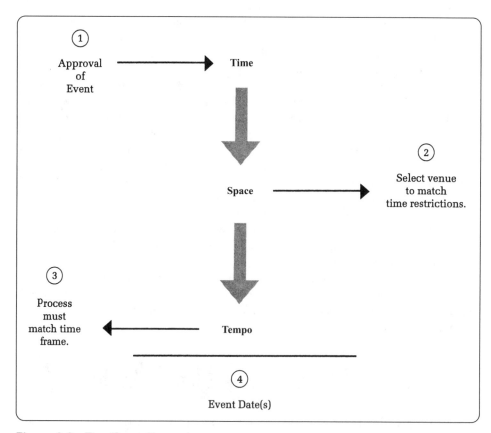

Figure 2.9 Time/Space/Tempo Laws

The length of time available for planning and for actual production will dramatically affect the cost and sometimes the success of the event. Equally important, as you discovered earlier, is how you use your time. According to the Greek philosopher Theophrastus, "Time is the most valuable thing a human can spend."

Mona Meretsky, president of COMCOR, a Fort Lauderdale corporate events firm, notes that, when budgeting her time to prepare a final cost estimate for a client, she realizes that the time she invests will exceed the number of billable client hours because she is a perfectionist. She will "take as much time as is required for each event to make certain that the details are attended to. It pays off in the long run. I've never had a corporate client not come back." As Meretsky's words indicate, budgeting your time is not an exact science but rather a dynamic experience that must be governed by the importance of each event.

When budgeting time for a proposed event, some independent Event Leaders estimate the amount of time necessary for pre-event client meetings, site inspections, meetings with vendors, ongoing communications and contract preparations, actual event time from time of arrival through departure, and post-event billable time. You may wish to allocate your billable time to follow the five phases of the event process: research, design, planning, coordination, and evaluation.

Because you can only estimate the time involved in these tasks, you must add a contingency time factor to each phase. Meretsky believes that using a 10 percent contingency factor will help you cover extra time required but not originally projected.

Like Meretsky, Audrey Gordon, sole proprietor of Audrey Gordon Parties of Chicago, admits that her actual time often exceeds her projected time. "A bar mitzvah could, if necessary, be planned in one eight-hour day. The worst-case scenario is days of planning, as people usually change their minds often."

By paying careful attention to the research and design phase, you will be able to budget your time more precisely. This is particularly true for the event itself. This part of planning involves when to arrive for a particular event, when to cue the appropriate musician or performer, when to take breaks, and, of course, when to stop. Planning the time of an event is as important as managing your planning time.

Meretsky says, "I request that my personnel be set up for our events one hour in advance. In Florida, guests often arrive early, and we must be ready when they are."

Gordon, owner of a one-person firm, must rely on legions of vendors to produce her social life-cycle events. Her planning must be careful and precise, even to the point of listing what song is to be played at a specific time. The net result of her exhaustive preparation is that guests are able to relax and enjoy the event, as every element happens logically, sequentially, and on time.

The moment the client approves the date of an event, the Event Leader must begin assessing how the planning period will affect other business operations. Therefore, the law of timing sometimes requires that, when an unreasonable time frame is allotted to produce an event professionally, the Event Leader must decline to accept the opportunity. Ultimately, timing is the factor that will govern every decision when you ask yourself: "Given this amount of time, can I produce an event that displays the quality and professionalism I am known for without losing equal or possibly larger opportunities?" Your answer will determine whether the light turns green, fades to yellow, or becomes red.

Space

The *law of space* refers to both the physical space where an event will be held and the time between critical decisions pertaining to the event. The relationship of timing to space is one that is constant throughout the entire event process.

For the 1988 Super Bowl half-time show in Jack Murphy Stadium, Radio City Music Hall Productions designed an elaborate show featuring 88 grand pianos. Suddenly, without warning, the day before the actual production, the producer was instructed that his setup time for the production was reduced to only a few minutes. Further complicating matters, the groundskeepers at the stadium raised serious concerns that the movement of the pianos onto the field would affect the turf on the field. In this example and numerous others, the actual physical space governs the time required for various elements of the event.

When selecting a *venue* for an event, the location and physical resources present will significantly affect the additional time that must be invested. If you select a historic mansion with elaborate permanent décor, less time will be required to decorate the site. By comparison, if you select a four-walled venue, such as a hotel or convention center (where you are literally renting the four walls), significant time and expense must be invested to create a proper atmosphere for the event.

Burt Ferrini, director of University Events at Northeastern Illinois University in Chicago, recognizes the importance of space. As the manager of commencement exercises, Ferrini must coordinate thousands of people in a space most are not familiar with. Furthermore, he must ensure that the event runs precisely on time. "I prepare individual schedules for each group of participants and then, after rehearsing them individually, I blend them together in a master schedule. Breaking the large event down into component parts and then reassembling it on the day of the event helps ensure a smooth ceremony."

When considering the space for an event, some Event Leaders prepare an elaborate checklist to review each element carefully. The checklist should reflect the goals and objectives of the event and not merely replicate a form you have copied for convenience. One of the primary considerations when selecting space is the age and type of guest who will be attending. Older guests may not be able to tolerate extreme temperatures, and this may preclude you from selecting an outdoor venue. For events with young children, you may or may not wish to select a site in a busy urban setting. Go back to the research and needs assessment phase, and review why this event is important and who the stakeholders are. Then select a venue specifically to match their needs, wants, and expectations.

The terms *ingress* and *egress* are important concepts when reviewing a potential venue. *Ingress* defines the entrances or access to the venue, and *egress* refers to the exits or evacuation routes. When considering ingress and egress, you must consider not only people, including those with disabilities, but also vehicles, props, possibly animals, and indeed any element that must enter or exit the site. You must also keep in mind the time available for ingress or egress, as this will determine the number of *portals* (doors) that may need to be available for this purpose.

Parking, public transportation, and other forms of transportation, including taxis, limousines, and tour buses, must also be considered when analyzing a site. These considerations should include the number of parking spaces, including those for the disabled, the availability and security/safety of public transportation, and the time required to dispatch a taxi.

Tempo

The final law of event planning is concerned with the rate or *tempo* at which events take place during both production planning and the event itself. From the moment the client approves an agreement or authorizes you to proceed with planning to the final meeting, you must be aware of the projected rate at which events will happen. Improved technology, such as faxes and online services, has dramatically accelerated the process and the demands of clients to "do it now." However, "now" is often not as efficient as later. When an Event Leader is pressured to deliver a product before it is fully developed, the results may be less than exemplary. Therefore, as you manage the rate at which tasks will be completed and events will occur, it is important to consider if each action is being performed at the best time. "Maybe" is not an acceptable response. To determine if this is the best moment for this task to be handled, ask yourself if you have sufficient information and resources to implement it. If not, try to delay the action until you are better prepared.

Establishing the proper tempo is not an exact science. Rather, like a conductor of an orchestra, you must allow your personal taste, energy, and experience to guide you as you speed up or slow down the tempo as required. By analyzing the event site and estimating the time required for a project, the Event Leader is better able to set the tempo or schedule for the setup, production, and removal of the equipment. Without this advance analysis, the Event Leader becomes an orchestra conductor without benefit of a score, a musician without benefit of a maestro.

Understanding the needs of guests also helps establish and adjust the tempo during an event. If guests are concerned primarily with networking, a leisurely time frame should be followed to allow for plenty of interaction. For example, while the transition from cocktails to dinner may be brisk when the program is more important than networking, the transition may be slowed when the emphasis is on the connections the audience members make among themselves.

Jerry Edwards, CPCE, past president of the National Association of Catering Executives (NACE), and owner of Chef's Expressions, Inc., in Timonium, Maryland, is convinced that the best Event Leaders are those who are focused on quality outcomes for their guests. "I was very fortunate to own a business in the era of high demand, and I was able to continually upgrade my staff. Now, thanks to The Food Channel and other food-related programming, customers are more sophisticated and demanding," says Edwards.

When Edwards began his catering business, there was little information regarding high-end catering or ethnic menus. Today, due to changing tastes, everyone is concerned with the food components and the final presentation. In terms of changing tastes, Edwards reports that the use of full-liquor bars is up by 21 percent in his events. "Perhaps the nostalgia exhibited by the baby boomers has brought back the name brand or call liquor consumption. They will actually pay for liquor but may not pay as much for food. Nine out of ten will ask for liquor by brand name. The drink reflects personal taste, sophistication, and success," says Edwards. The three-term president of NACE said that he learned the catering business through the NACE meetings he attended. His involvement in NACE helped take his business from $500,000 to over $2 million per year in revenues.

Edwards envisions that, through organizations such as NACE, Event Leaders in the near future will earn credentials from either certifications or college degrees and that specific career paths will be identified for young people to help them break the glass ceiling that continues to exist in the hospitality industry. Finally, he believes that human nature plays a significant role in developing Event Leaders and that schools and associations must work closer together to promote leadership development. "We need to begin developing the next level of Event Leaders in the catering industry, and we can do this best by working together to help insure the future for our profession," suggests the man who bought a small lunch counter for $2,000 and then developed a multimillion-dollar off-premise catering enterprise while serving as a leader for one of the industry's major associations.

These three basic laws, as old as human creation itself, govern the planning of all events. To become an expert Event Leader, you must master your ability to manage time in the most minute segments. You must develop the vision to perceive the strengths, weaknesses, opportunities, and threats of every space. Finally, you must be able to analyze the needs of your guests to set tempos that will ensure a memorable event.

Gap Analysis

Too often, Event Leaders proceed by rote memory to produce an event in a style with which they are most familiar. In doing this, they often overlook critical gaps in the logical progression of event elements. Identifying these gaps and providing recommendations for closure is the primary purpose of *gap analysis.*

This planning tool involves taking a long, hard look at event elements and identifying significant gaps in the planning that could weaken the overall progression of the plan. An example is an Event Leader who has scheduled an outdoor event in September in Miami Beach, Florida. September is the prime month of the hurricane season. The Event Leader has created a wide gap in his or her plan that must be closed to strengthen the overall event. Therefore, finding a secure indoor location in case of a weather emergency would be a good beginning toward closing this gap.

Use a critical friend—a person whose expertise about the particular event is known to you—to review your plan and search for gaps in your logical thinking. Once you have identified the gaps, look for opportunities to close them. By implementing the findings from SWOT and gap analysis, you are able to begin executing your plan. This execution phase is known as *coordination.*

Coordination: Executing the Plan

As the light turns green, the tempo accelerates, and now you are faced with coordinating the minute-by-minute activities of the event itself. I was once asked, "What does it take to be a competent Event Leader?" "The ability to make good decisions," I swiftly answered. I realize now that it requires much more than good decision-making ability; however, it is also true that during the course of coordinating an event you will be required to make not dozens but hundreds of decisions. Your ability to use your professional training and experience to make the correct decision will affect the outcome of the entire event. While it is true that Event Leaders should maintain a positive attitude and see problems as challenges in search of the right solution, it is also important that you apply critical analysis to every challenge that comes your way. These five steps are a simple but effective way to make these decisions:

1. Collect all the information. Most problems have many sides to review.
2. Consider the pros and cons of your decision in terms of who will be affected.
3. Consider the financial implications of your decision.
4. Consider the moral and ethical implications of your decision.
5. Make a decision and do not look back.

Evaluation: The Link to the Next Event

The Event Leadership process, as shown in Figure 2.10, is a dynamic spiral that is literally without end. The first phase—research—is connected with the last—evaluation. In this last phase, you will ask: "What is it we wish to evaluate, and how will we best accomplish this?" You can evaluate events by each part of the Event Leadership process or through a general comprehensive review of all phases. It is up to you and your stakeholders to decide what information you require to improve your planning and then implement effective strategies to accomplish this phase.

Perhaps the most common form of event evaluation is the written survey. Usually the survey is conducted immediately following the event, to identify the satisfaction level of the participants and spectators. As with any evaluation method, there are pros and cons to immediate feedback. One bias is the immediate nature of the feedback, which prohibits respondents from digesting the total event experience before providing feedback.

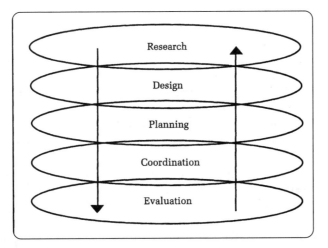

Figure 2.10 Event Leadership Process

Another form of evaluation is the use of monitors. A *monitor* is a trained person who will observe an element of the event and provide both written and verbal feedback to the Event Leader. The event monitor usually has a checklist or survey to complete and will then offer additional comments as required. The benefit of this type of evaluation is that it permits a trained, experienced event staff member or volunteer to observe the event objectively while it is taking place and provide instructive comments.

The third form of event evaluation is the telephone or mail survey conducted after the event. In this evaluation, the Event Leader surveys the spectators and participants after the event through either a mail or a telephone survey. By waiting a few days after the event to collect these data, the Event Leader is able to glean from the respondents how their attitudes have changed and developed after some time has passed since participating in the event.

A new form of evaluation that is growing in popularity is the pre- and post-event survey. This evaluation allows an Event Leader to determine the respondents' knowledge, opinions, and other important information both before and after their attendance at an event. This is especially helpful when trying to match expectations to reality. For example, an event guest may state upon entering an event that he or she expects, based on the advertising and public relations, to enjoy nonstop entertainment. However, upon completing the exit interview, the guest registers disappointment because of the gaps in the programming. This type of evaluation helps event organizers close gaps between overpromising and underdelivering certain aspects of an event. Registration mail-in rebates and other incentives may be offered for filling out both surveys.

Regardless of the form of evaluation you use, it is critical that you not wait until the end of the event to find out how you are doing. If you were to attend any banquet where I am responsible for the event, you might be surprised to see me wandering from table to table and asking guests how they are enjoying dinner. In doing this, I am able to uncover gaps in execution of the plan. One guest might say: "I ordered vegetarian and was served meat." I am able to correct this error immediately. If I had waited until the person had filled out an evaluation form, it would have been too late. Take the temperature of your guests hourly to make certain that you are on target in meeting your goals and objectives. By doing this, you are able to reset your course immediately and ensure that, together, you will arrive at the same destination: a successful event.

Professor Helmut Schwagermann lectures at the University of Applied Science of Osnabrueck in Germany. A longtime veteran of the global meeting industry, Schwagermann has developed an original theory to control the outcome of events.

He recommends that the control of events take place in three phases.

1. Control the event concept in a pre-event test.
2. Control the event during the process itself during what he describes as the in-between test.
3. Control the results of the event through a post-test. During this post-test, ask questions such as: Did the event satisfy the economic results and strategic communication goals?

Schwagermann cautions that so-called hard economic facts such as profits are not always justified. Long-term effects, such as changes in opinions and behavior as well as the effect on remembering and emotional excitement, can be measured with instruments of comprehensive event marketing research.

On the other side of the world, Leo Jago, deputy chief executive officer and director of research of the Australian federal government's Sustainable Tourism Cooperative Research Center, has similarly conceived and tested a new Triple Bottom Line theory for event evaluation. According to Jago, events cannot be measured or evaluated in strictly economic terms. Rather, he recommends a triple evaluation process that includes comprehensive analysis of the economic, sociocultural, and ecological outcomes of the event.

The event evaluations standards being established in Australia may be the direct results of the successful Summer Olympic Games of 2000 that were held in Sydney. In preparation for the games, the Sydney Organizing Committee for the Olympic Games developed, in cooperation with the International Olympic Committee (IOC) and Monash University, an information-sharing and knowledge transfer program. The IOC requires every official organizing committee to provide a final comprehensive report. However, the Sydney Olympic Games were the first time this process was coordinated in a systematic process that was originally called "Athena" in honor of the Greek goddess of knowledge and wisdom. As a result of the Sydney initiatives, the IOC has formalized the knowledge transfer process as part of their Olympic Games operations plan.

The future of event evaluation and knowledge transfer will most certainly include more comprehensive processes as recommended and demonstrated by Schwagermann, Jago, and the IOC. Regardless of how you establish the metrics for final evaluation of your event, you must insure that you have provided the appropriate resources to evaluate the outcome of your efforts thoroughly and systematically. Evaluation is the fifth phase in the event management process; however, it propels the first phase of research by collecting and analyzing the history that is needed to continually improve your event process in the future.

This Event Leadership process is the conceptual framework for every effective event. The process is dynamic and selective, in that the Event Leader must determine where to begin and how to proceed to best accomplish the objectives. One event may be past the research stage, and the Event Leader may be retained merely to coordinate the elements. Still another may be midway through the planning phase. The effective Event Leader will immediately recognize that the event process cannot be complete or totally effective unless each phase is considered carefully. It does not matter where you begin the process. What is essential is that every phase be considered, visited, and understood.

Communications: The Tie That Binds

Event Leadership is a profession whose success or failure ratio often depends on people's ability to communicate effectively with one another. It does not matter whether this communication is oral, written, electronic, or all three. What is important is that Event Leaders become practiced communicators in order to maintain clear communications with all stakeholders. Regardless of the communication channel that you are using, you want to make sure that you make your point clearly and establish the right priorities in your message.

Often both visual and auditory noise provides a barrier to open communication. Visual noise includes those visual distractions that take place when you are trying to communicate with others. Auditory noise may be music, traffic, or other distractions that interfere with others' ability to hear and concentrate on what you are saying. Remove all noise before trying to communicate with others. Find a quiet place to meet, remove visual distractions, and verify and confirm that those you are communicating with comprehend what you are sharing.

Written communications are essential not only for record keeping but also for purposes of mass distribution. It is impossible to transmit verbally to 1,000 people an event update without distortion. (Remember the children's game "telephone"?) Use memorandums, briefing statements, bulletins, and other documents to communicate effectively to one or many others. Memoranda should include an "Action Required" statement to inform the reader how best to respond and in what time frame.

Bulletins must be sporadic, or you run the risk of becoming the person who cried "wolf" once too often and now is ignored by everyone. Newsletters are a particularly effective tool for communications; however, use caution, as they are extremely labor intensive to continually write, edit, produce, and distribute on a regular basis.

Perhaps one of the best ways to communicate is through a meeting. When scheduling a meeting, make certain that you prepare an agenda in advance that lists the items for discussion. Distribute this document prior to the meeting to those who will attend and ask them to comment. This will help them prepare for the meeting. Use the agenda to guide the meeting, and, as the leader, serve as a facilitator for discussion. Using a flip chart will help you capture ideas while sticking to the agenda. One extremely effective device is to assign participants work prior to the meeting so that they come to the meeting prepared and ready to make specific contributions. Make sure that your meeting does not take much longer than initially planned; otherwise, you will give the impression of being a disorganized person who does not value your own time and the time that others invest in the meeting.

Alternative communication techniques include producing audiotapes and videotapes as well as using teleconferencing through compressed video (telephone lines). The average person commutes to the office 20 or more minutes twice daily and can use this time to listen to your audiotape. Put your meeting or information on audiotape, add a little music, and share your ideas. The major drawback to this alternative is that the communication is one-way. Videotapes also allow you to express your thoughts creatively with photos, interviews, and music. By showing the tape before a large group of people, you can create group excitement. Two-way video using existing telephone lines and a compressed system is an effective way to present data, visuals, and some person-to-person interaction. It is also relatively inexpensive compared to traditional satellite uplink/downlink technology.

The use of computer online chat rooms has grown in popularity due to the rapid expansion of the Internet technologies. When using chat rooms, avoid personal issues and conduct postings in a businesslike manner. Personal issues may be addressed through other mediums, such as telephone calls. Chat rooms are excellent information-exchange opportunities, and you will find that your colleagues will provide you with new resources for producing better events.

Event Management Body of Knowledge Project

In 2004 the first Event Management Body of Knowledge (EMBOK) Embizo was held at the Edeni Private Game Reserve near Kruger National Park in South Africa. The term *embizo* comes from the Sulu language and means "a gathering." The purpose of this historic meeting was to identify and develop a global model for producing professional live events. Many years earlier, the Project Management Institute (PMI) (*www.pmi.org/info/pp_pmbok2000welcome.asp*) had used a similar process to standardize the project management process. Therefore, the EMBOK participants used the PMI model as a way to standardize the body of knowledge in the global event industry.

The convener for this meeting was Janet Landey, CSEP, the managing director of the South African Institute for Event Management. The event educators included Glenn Bowdin of Leeds Metropolitan University; this author; Matthew Gonzalez of Events Education; Dr. Kathy Nelson of the University of Nevada at Las Vegas; William O'Toole of the University of Sydney, Australia; Julia Rutherford Silvers, CSEP of Speaking of Events; and Dr. Jane Spowart of the University of Johannesburg.

Following several days of intensive meetings and friendly but lively debate, a preliminary model was developed. A second Embizo was held in the summer of 2005, also in South Africa, and further work was completed regarding the development of the model and in establishing communications channels to share this valuable information with others. Figure 2.11 demonstrates one example of this model. EMBOK is still very much a work in progress. However, it has tremendous potential in creating a set of unifying standards around which Event Leaders may work together to continuously improve the profession. For more information about EMBOK, visit the Web site at *www.embok.org.*

Synergy: Linking Administration, Coordination, Marketing, and Risk Management

At one time, the Walt Disney Company was the only organization of its size with an executive board position titled vice president for synergy. Due to the diversity in the Disney product line (theme parks, retail stores, movies, recordings, sport, television), the leaders of this successful organization believe that one person must be responsible for ensuring that there is synergy among all aspects of the business operation.

Up to one year in advance, before Disney rolls out a new movie, the retail stores are developing new products, the theme parks are planning new live shows, and the other aspects of the corporation are preparing for joint promotion and distribution of the new product. This kind of synergy allocates Disney's scarce resources in the most efficient manner.

Your event also has scarce resources. These resources include your ability to administrate, coordinate, market, and manage the risk for the event. You must link these four

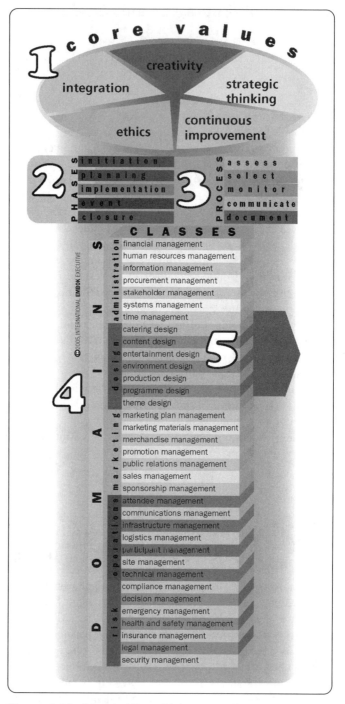

Figure 2.11 Model of Event Management Body of Knowledge (EMBOK) Project. Courtesy of Janet Landey, CSEP.

competencies together carefully and thoroughly throughout the event process in order to produce the very best and most profitable event product.

The administration process of an event serves as the foundation for the resources you will select and manage during the coordination process. Poor administration will later undermine your ability to coordinate the event. Strong coordination will result in better marketing results. Unless your operations people are aware that today's tickets are discounted, for example, all the advertising in the world will be wasted. The link between coordination and marketing, and for that matter administration, is vital. Finally, legal, ethical, and risk-management issues form a strong river current that runs through every decision you make in Event Leadership. If your marketing team leader overpromotes or promotes an event inaccurately, he or she will place those who must coordinate event operations at a great disadvantage. In subsequent chapters, we introduce each of these competencies in detail, but at this stage it is important for you to recognize the connection between them. Together, and with the potential adoption of EMBOK, they weave a strong tapestry that will help shield you from future problems and provide you with a rich understanding of how all team members must work together productively.

Career-Advancement Connections

Global Connection

Internet online discussions help to establish communication among Event Leadership organizations and various other event stakeholders. This will also help to reduce operations costs, especially for international events. Since international events usually require more time for logistical preparations, it is important to use the fastest methods of communication to facilitate the planning stage.

Technology Connection

With the development of the Internet, many Event Leader organizations started using Internet-based applications that allow secured sharing of information among multiple parties. Using password-secured Web sites, you can post files and exchange information from anywhere in the world. Large event organizations such as Jack Morton Worldwide (*www.jackmorton.com*) and The George P. Johnson Company (*www.gpjco.com*) effectively use this communications medium with their clients and staff.

Resource Connection

Contact Event Leadership industry associations to stay abreast of quickly developing industry trends. The International Special Events Society (ISES, *www.ises.com*) is committed to continuous education in the Event Leadership community.

Profile in Event Leadership:
Jean McFaddin

THE LEGENDARY PRODUCER OF MACY'S THANKSGIVING DAY PARADE

Jean McFaddin

From the time she produced her fifth birthday party, Jean McFaddin was directing people. Years later, her high school drama teacher, Tom Jack Lucas, recognized her talent for design and organization and taught her how to capitalize on her talents. Lucas and others taught Jean to "define the structure and break the barriers," something she has been doing exceptionally well throughout her long and successful career.

From her hometown of Lufkin, Texas, she traveled to Columbia, Missouri, to attend the renowned Stephen's College, where she first worked with professional actors from New York City. During the summers, she was a production intern at Houston's acclaimed Alley Theatre for the well-respected regional theater director Nina Vance, who inspired Jean to produce her own theater for children the following summer. After completing her Associate of Arts degree at Stephen's, she transferred to the University of Texas (UT) Drama Department, where she earned her undergraduate and graduate degrees in Theatre Production/ Design and Direction. During her graduate work, Jean discovered how to express her vision in terms of imagery and action. At UT, she learned "how to think, how to look at, and how to visualize the show."

Alongside her natural design ability, she was able to apply many of the techniques she mastered at UT to the Macy's Thanksgiving Day Parade. "To me, the success of Macy's parade was in achieving a larger-than-life scale. Remember, the parade is marching through the canyons of New York City, competing with giant skyscrapers for attention. I learned how to magnify and expand my staging and design choices in tone, spirit, dimension, and color to create the dynamic size and overwhelmingly spectacular that is the modern parade."

One of the many innovations Jean brought to the parade was the use of multiple layers of imagery to fill every level of the sky. Thanks to Jean McFaddin, today's Macy's Thanksgiving Day Parade is a kaleidoscope of giant balloons, floats, thousands of costumed marchers, and even hundreds of pounds of confetti.

According to Jean McFaddin, "Learning how to properly cast, motivate, and direct people is a critical skill for an event producer." Furthermore, her theatrical training as a director taught her the importance of delegation as well as trust in the production team she empowered to express her ideas.

The key, says McFaddin, is to "get people supporting you, the Event Leader, in your event." Early in her theatrical career, she was sent to Oklahoma to design costumers at the famous Mummers Theater. While struggling on her tenth all-night session with both designing and building costumes, the theater's

75 year-old seamstress walked in and said, "Look, you design them, and I will build them." From this mentor, Jean learned the importance of delegation and trust, plus a great appreciation for the expertise that comes with years of experience.

After quickly advancing from costume designer to theatrical director at the Mummers Theater, Jean set her sights on New York City theater, when she found the right show for her debut, an innovative production entitled *The James Joyce Memorial Liquid Theatre*. Originally developed by a performance group in L.A., the show was a series of trust exercises involving the audience, and took place in a highly visual, sensory environment to stimulate the audience's awareness. Jean and her creative partners brought the show to the Guggenheim Museum in New York. According to Jean, preview night was a disaster, and the producers threatened to close the show. Addressing the show's problem, Jean determined that the New York audience, unlike the relaxed California public, needed to experience and be prepared through the same physical exercises and games that the cast had undergone in rehearsals, in order for audience to "trust" the experience and be brought "into the party" with the cast. Overnight, Jean re-created and restructured the entire event, and then incorporated these changes into the show with the actors as they performed. As a result of Jean's enhancements and insight into the audience, critics described the show as a theatrical milestone, bringing a new emotional energy and a unique experience to participants. The New York show became so successful it was produced in both Paris and London, where, Jean notes, the production was adjusted for each city to address cultural differences in the audience.

Her sojourn to Europe introduced her to various festivals, and she continued to develop as a mega-event producer. From 1974 to 1975, she produced promotional projects for the Philadelphia Bicentennial celebration. Her Americana performance project was so successful that the U.S. National Endowment for the Arts asked her to produce similar events in Washington, DC, to celebrate the different national monuments.

In 1976 Jean was consultant to New York City's Bicentennial Events when she met her predecessor at Macy's, who was leaving the job and identified Jean as her replacement. According to Jean, "I was in the right place at the right time with the right creative talents and leadership experience for the Macy's job." At that time, Macy's and NBC, the parade's main sponsors, were not pleased with the parade, and its future was uncertain. Jean says, "I walked into an enormous challenge, which demanded that I re-create Macy's Parade into a state of the art, multifaceted event in entertainment, design, and sponsor values, making it a dynamic branding tool for Macy's. In addition to building many spinoff events around the parade, I had the opportunity to build an annual calendar of seasonal holiday spectaculars and to develop a wonderful production organization that still thrives today."

McFaddin later worked with George Zambelli, Sr. (see Chapter 7), whom she describes as her early partner in designing fireworks displays. She remembers proposing to George that they join the techniques of theatrical lighting design with pyrotechnics. Together with George and later with the Souza Family of Pyro Spectaculars of Rialto, California, she developed the first ever computer-programmed, musically choreographed pyrotechnic displays for the Macy's Fourth of July celebrations, setting new benchmarks in the pyrotechnic industry. With NBC, she established a national

(continues)

(continued)

telecast of the annual Macy's fireworks spectacular.

When asked about weather contingency plans for outdoor events, Jean cautions, "Be completely prepared. Keep safety foremost in your event. Have a contingency plan in place, and communicate it well to others. If you carry an umbrella, it probably won't rain."

As a director of an event, Jean believes that the most important challenge is to create a dynamic, entertainment event for your audience, but as a producer, it is equally essential to ensure a firm business plan for your organization with great partners and a shared vision to grow the event if it is to go forward. She adds that the fun of both jobs, director or producer, is to create the magic and mystery for all to enjoy: "When you see your audiences say "WOW, that's your big payback!"

Since retiring from Macy's in 2001, Jean continues to spread this theatrical energy and creative expertise to corporations and to the festivals and events industry nationwide, as a consultant and speaker. Whether directing children's theater, creating experimental theatrical events, delighting millions of New Yorkers with the annual Macy's Fourth of July Fireworks Spectacular, or leading the world's most popular televised parade, Jean McFaddin's creative designs and careful structure both "define and break the barriers" for the modern special events industry. Thanks in large part to her enormous and pioneering contributions, our modern celebrations have become theatrical events or, as Jean first imagined, spirited spectaculars that fill the heart.

Jean McFaddin: jeanmcfaddin@aol.com

Contact the National Laboratory for Tourism and *e*Commerce at Temple University for technical support in designing and conducting valid and reliable event evaluations (*www.temple.edu/sthm*).

Learning Connection

In this chapter, you have explored the five stages of each event. To enhance your understanding of the chapter, complete this activity:

You are managing a new European car launch in the United States. Over 5,000 attendees are expected to be at the event over a three-day period. The event will include various elements, such as a car show, indoor test-driving, and a gala reception. The contract requires that you develop the complete event program and implement it. This event requires a lot of creativity and excellent organizational skills. You need to produce the event and execute it flawlessly. What tasks will you perform in each of the five stages?

PART TWO

Event Administration

An inflatable costumed character at Tokyo Big Sight toy show demonstrates how expositions often involve a series of special events within the larger special event.

CHAPTER 3

Developing and Implementing the Event Plan

In This Chapter You Will Learn How To:

+ Conduct comprehensive research for your event

+ Identify key sources of information for planning

+ Design a program creatively

+ Develop an appropriate theme

+ Establish and manage an effective strategic plan

+ Develop and manage the timeline for an event

The administration of a professional event is the first competency that must be mastered in the Certified Special Events Professional body of knowledge. Comprehensive administration is the foundation for all successful events. The administration of an event provides you and the stakeholders with data with which to design the dream that will produce the deliverables you desire.

During the administration process, the Event Leader must make certain that data identified during research are used to drive the design and ultimately to produce the measurable outcomes required by event stakeholders:

research (data) + design = planned successful outcomes

Research without the important phase of design will result in a dry, one-dimensional, and perhaps boring event. To produce a multidimensional and multisensory event experience that transforms guests, you must research as well as design the event outcome. The research and design phases ultimately produce the tools with which you can construct a blueprint of the event plan. The final event plan is, in fact, a direct reflection of the research and design phases.

Stretching the Limits of the Event

Whereas research is either inductive or deductive in form and often proceeds in a linear fashion, the design phase is weblike and often kaleidoscopic. Just as the Internet provides you with literally millions of resources for event design, your own mental process must mirror this technology. During the design process, the professional Event Leader considers every possibility and challenges every assumption determined during the research phase. This pushing of the research envelope is essential if you are to produce innovative, highly creative, unique special events that will exceed the expectations of guests.

As B. Joseph Pine and James H. Gilmore state in *The Experience Economy* (Harvard Business School Press, 2000), "You are what you charge for." If you are to steadily increase the value of your work as an event researcher, designer, planner, coordinator, and evaluator, you must strive continually to collect the best information and resources to produce a solid plan that satisfies the needs, wants, desires, and, ultimately, expectations of event guests.

Designing the Event Environment

Like a playwright who molds his or her play to create a setting that a theater's limited confines can accommodate, Event Leaders face a similar challenge each time they are called on to create an environment. Whether the site is a palatial mansion or a suburban park, the challenges remain the same. How can the site be adapted to meet the needs of guests?

Ballrooms with their four bare walls, department stores filled with products, and even main streets upon which parades are staged offer the same problems and opportunities as those confronting playwrights and set designers.

When creating an environment, the special events professional must again return to the basic needs of the guests. To be successful, the final design must satisfy these needs. Lighting, space, movement, decor, acoustics, and even such seemingly mundane concerns as restrooms all affect the comfort of the guests and so play vital roles in creating a successful environment.

Five-Card Draw: Playing the Five Senses

When attempting to satisfy the needs of guests, remember that the five senses are very powerful tools. Like five winning cards in the Event Leader's hand, combining the five senses—tactile, smell, taste, visual, and auditory—to satiate the needs of guests is the primary consideration when designing the event environment. The olfactory system creates instant emotional and creative reactions within your guests. How many times have you walked into a room, noticed a familiar smell, and suddenly experienced déjà vu? Event Leadership pioneer Jack Morton says that smell is the most powerful sense because of the memories it produces. In fact, smell may generally be the strongest sense in terms of generating emotional response; however, this will vary among individual guests. Therefore, as the Event Leader you must actively seek to employ in your environmental design elements that will affect all the senses.

When designing a *Gone With the Wind* banquet, you may erect a backdrop that immediately conjures memories of Tara, play music from the famous movie's theme, and even have Rhett and Scarlett look-alikes at the door to greet and touch your guests. However, that magnolia centerpiece on the table is sadly missing one element. When you add a light scent of Jungle Gardenia perfume, the event suddenly becomes a total sensory experience.

Just as some guests are sensitive to certain stimuli, such as smell or hearing, other guests have a primary sense that they rely on. Due to the influence of television, many baby boomers may rely primarily on their visual sense. When designing the environment, this fact is important to recognize when you are trying to communicate your message quickly. Use the senses as instruments to tune the imagination of guests. Be careful to avoid playing sharp or flat notes by overdoing it. Find the perfect sensory melody and guests will become involved in your event creatively and emotionally.

Five procedures will enable you to survey guests to determine their level of sensitivity as well as their primary sensual stimuli in order to create an effective event sensory environment:

1. Use a focus group to determine the primary sensory stimuli of your guests.
2. Identify any oversensitivity or even allergies guests may have that could be irritated by certain sensory elements.

3. Use the draft diagram of the event environment to identify and isolate the location of certain sensory experiences.
4. Share this design tool with typical guests and solicit their attitudes and opinions.
5. Audit the venue to determine the preexisting sensory environment and what modifications you will be required to implement.

Soundscaping

To communicate with the guests at an event, you must design a sound system and effects that are unique and powerful enough to capture their attention. Do not confuse powerful with loud, however. Poignant background music at a small social event has as much power as a booming rock beat at a retail promotion. As with other components of event production, successful use of sound requires gauging and meeting the needs of the audience.

Sound by itself is a most powerful sensation. When asked which of her senses she would like to have returned to her, the late Helen Keller, blind and deaf since birth, explained that the ability to hear is more important than the ability to see. The eyes can deceive, but the way in which others speak and the thoughts they share reveal much about personality and intentions. Sound unlocks our imagination and allows us to visualize images buried in our subconscious. When planning the sound design for your event, many questions need to be considered. What is to be the dominant sensory element for the event? Sound may be the dominant sensory element for your event; for example, if live music or extensive speeches are the major component of your event, your investment in high-quality sound production may be paramount.

How will sound help support, reinforce, or expand the guests' perceptions of the event? Consider the theme of your event and devise ways in which sound can be used to convey that theme to the guests. For example, if you are planning a Polynesian theme event, the use of recorded island-type music at the entrance will help communicate that theme.

Are the architectural conditions in the venue optimal for sound reproduction? This question is most important considering the number of new sites being created every day. The majority of these sites were not designed for optimum sound reproduction, and the event planner or sound designer must, therefore, consider how to improve the sound conditions in the venue. In the five special events markets, sound design, like lighting, is growing tremendously. In the social market, not only are live bands used more than ever, but with the addition of new electronic instruments, the repertoire of a small live band can be increased manyfold. Moreover, the rise of the disc jockey format and the more frequent use of videotape require that the sound quality must be better than ever before. As the sophistication of the audio components available to the average consumer has increased, the sound systems for retail events have had to improve in quality as well to match the sound many guests can experience in their living rooms. Whether it is a fashion show or a visit with Santa, excellent sound is required to give the event credibility and value in the eyes (or ears) of the guest. Millions of dollars' worth of merchandise may be on display, but if the sound system is poor, the guest perceives less value and is less inclined to buy.

Meetings and convention events also place more importance on sound reproduction for their programs. Gone are the days when a meeting planner was content to use the hotel house speakers for live music. Today, many musical groups carry their own speakers, mixing boards, and operators.

Visual Cues

Baby boomers and subsequent generations, raised in front of television sets, may require strong visual elements to assist them with experiencing your event. This includes using proper signs to orient the guest and provide clear direction. Additional visual elements that must be considered are the proper and repetitive use of key design elements such as the *logo*. A logo is the graphic symbol of the organization sponsoring the event. Not only must this symbol be represented accurately, but it also must always appear in the same manner to benefit from repetitive viewing and establish consistency to promote retention.

Touch

Whether you are considering the cloth that will dress the banquet table, the napkins, or the printed program, touch will immediately convey the quality of the event environment. To establish this sense, use several different textures and, while wearing a blindfold, touch the various elements to determine what feelings are promoted. When handling the cloth, do you feel as if you are attending a royal gala or a country picnic? When holding the program, are you a guest of the king or the court jester? Use this blindfold test to help you narrow your choices and effectively select the right fabric, paper, or other product to properly communicate the precise sense of touch you desire.

Smell

Earlier we discussed the use of a perfume such as Jungle Gardenia to stimulate the sense of memory through smell. Remember that throughout the event environment a series of smells may be present that will either create the correct environment or confuse and irritate the guest. When conducting the site inspection, note if the public areas are overdeodorized. This smell is often a clue that chemicals are being used to mask a foul smell. Instead, you may wish to look for venues whose aromas are natural and the result of history, people, and, of course, natural products such as plants and flowers.

Some people are extremely sensitive to strong odors. Therefore, when using the sense of smell, do not overdo it. Instead, establish neutral areas where the smell of a scented candle, flowers, or food odors is not present, to provide the nose with a respite from this stimulation. However, establishing individual areas that have a strong aroma of pizza baking or chocolate melting is also important to both attract and convey the proper atmosphere. You may, for example, wish to incorporate the smell of barbecue into your western-themed event or pine trees into your Christmas wonderland. Again, when establishing these areas of smell, try to isolate them so that the guests can return to a neutral zone and not feel overwhelmed by this sense.

Taste

The sense of taste will be discussed later; however, the Event Leader must realize that the catering team members play a critical role in establishing a strong sensory feeling for the event. Consult in advance with the catering team and establish the goals and objectives of the food presentation. Then determine how best to proceed in combining the other four senses with the sense of taste to create a total olfactory experience for the guests. Keep in mind the age, culture, and lifestyle of the guests. Older guests may not be as sensitive to taste, whereas other guests may require spicier food combinations to engage their sense of taste. The taste sense historically has been linked with a strong sensual experience. Play the taste card for all it is worth, and you will transform guests from spectators to fully engaged participants who will long remember the succulent event you have designed.

Blending, Mixing, and Matching for Full Effect

Make certain that you carefully select those event-design sensory elements that will support the goals and objectives of the event. Do not confuse or irritate guests by layering too many different senses in an effort to be creative. Rather, design the sensory experience as you would select paint for a canvas. Determine in advance what you hope to achieve or communicate, and then use the five senses as powerful tools to help you accomplish your goals.

Bells and Whistles: Amenities That Make the Difference

Once you have established the atmosphere for your event environment and satisfied the basic needs of all guests, you have the opportunity to embellish or enhance their experience by adding a few well-chosen amenities. An *amenity* is best defined as a feature that increases attractiveness or value. In today's added value–driven business environment, amenities are more important than ever before. These amenities may include advertising specialty items given as gifts at the beginning or the end of the event, interactive elements such as virtual environments, and even child care.

A popular way to stretch the budget is to transform the guests into décor elements. This is accomplished by distributing glow-in-the-dark novelty items, such as necklaces, pins, or even swizzle sticks. As guests enter the darkened event environment, their glowing presence suddenly creates exciting visual stimuli. Firms such as Liquid Light in Los Angeles specialize in customizing these items with the slogans, logo, or name of the sponsoring organization.

Another effective amenity that is growing in popularity is the virtual event environment. Using virtual-reality software, guests are able to experience many different environments at the same time. When they wear specially constructed goggles, guests are propelled visually to the top of a skyscraper, where they do battle with evil demons or may stroll casually through a virtual trade show environment, pausing to visually inspect a variety of different booths. These systems have become integral to the success of high-tech industries and are gaining in importance in helping guests to maximize their time while at an event by providing the opportunity to visit several different environments in a short time period.

Whether dealing with glow-in-the-dark jewelry or virtual-reality software, you must evaluate consistently the needs, wants, and desires of guests to determine if the communications media you are using are effective and efficient. Using feedback from specific populations will help you achieve this purpose rapidly.

Identifying the Needs of Your Guests

Once you have gathered all the quantitative data from the site inspection, it is time to analyze your findings and determine what implications emerge for your event environment design. Important considerations include the legal, regulatory, and risk management issues that are uncovered during site inspection.

Provision for Guests Having Disabilities

If the venue is not in full compliance with the Americans with Disabilities Act, you may need to make certain modifications in your design. See Chapter 11 for a complete discussion of compliance with this act.

Implications of Size, Weight, and Volume

Let us assume that your design requires massive scenery and that the ingress to your venue is a door of standard width and height. How do you squeeze the elephant through the keyhole? The answer is, of course, "Very carefully." Seriously, make certain that your design elements can be broken down into small units. Using component parts for the construction process will enable you to design individual elements that will fit easily through most doorways.

Weight is an important consideration, as many venues were not built with this factor in mind. Before bringing in elements that have extraordinary weight, check with the facility engineer to review the construction standards used in the venue and then determine if the stress factor is sufficient to accommodate your design. Shifting weight also can cause serious problems for certain venues. Therefore, if you are using a stage platform and simply placing a heavy prop, you may not experience any problems. However, if on this same platform you are showcasing 50 dancers performing high-energy routines, the platforms may not be sufficiently reinforced to handle this shifting weight. In addition to reviewing with the engineer or other expert the stress weight that the area can accommodate, conduct independent tests yourself by actually walking across the stage or examining the undergirdings to ensure that what goes up will not come down.

The final consideration is volume. The fire marshal determines the number of persons who can be safely accommodated in the venue. You, however, greatly influence this number by the seating configuration, the amount of décor, and other technical elements that you include in the final event environment. Less equals more. Typically, the fewer design elements you incorporate, the more people you can accommodate. Therefore, when creating your total event design, first determine the number of people you must accommodate, then subtract the number of square feet required for the guests. The remainder will determine the volume of elements that contribute to the event environment.

Julia Rutherford Silvers, CSEP, in *Professional Event Coordination* (Wiley, 2003), notes:

> *A unique venue should be carefully examined to determine its capabilities and challenges. You should be looking at accessibility for the vendors providing the goods and services for the event, as well as accessibility for the guests, workable space for preparations and event activities, power and parking capabilities, safety and sanitation issues, and, of course, protection for the property rights of the venue as well as its neighbors—for example, in regard to noise, light, and other forms of disturbance or pollution.*

One example of protecting the property rights of neighbors is evident at the famous Hollywood Bowl amphitheater, which is located in a residential neighborhood in Hollywood, California. Prior to the start of the performance and immediately afterward, the audience is reminded through an audio announcement to please exit the venue quietly and not honk auto horns, play loud car radio music, or make other noise that will inconvenience the neighbors. As a result of the Station nightclub fire in Providence, Rhode Island, the National Fire Protection Association has revised its standards and now requires an announcement be made prior to the start of each performance notifying the audience members of the location of the nearest fire exits and how to exit the venue in an orderly manner.

■ Example: Calculating and Sizing the Event Environment

1. Identify the total number of persons and multiply the square feet (or meters) required for each person. For example:

$$\begin{array}{r} 50 \text{ couples} \\ \times\, 10 \text{ square feet per couple} \\ \hline = 500 \text{ square feet} \end{array}$$

2. Subtract the total number of square feet required for the couples from the total space available. For example:

$$\begin{array}{r} 1{,}000 \text{ square feet available for dance floor} \\ -\, 500 \text{ square feet required by couples} \\ \hline = 500 \text{ square feet available for props,} \\ \text{tables, chairs, and other equipment} \end{array}$$

Do not do this in reverse. Some event leaders create a lavish design first, only to find later that the number of guests will not allow them to install this design.

Securing the Environment

Just as the fire marshal is responsible for determining occupancy, the police and local security officials will determine how to secure an environment to reduce the possibility of theft or personal injury. When considering the theme and other important design elements, remember that people will be walking under, over, and within this environment, and their safety must be paramount in your planning. Providing adequate lighting for traversing the event environment, securing cables and other technical components with tape or ramps, and posting notices of "Use Caution" or "Watch Your Step" are important considerations when designing beautiful, as well as safe, event environments.

Theft, sadly, is a major concern in designing an event environment. Do not make it easy to remove items from the event environment. Secure perimeter doors with guards or provide bag-check stations at the entrance to discourage unscrupulous persons from removing valuable event elements. This is especially important when designing expositions where millions of dollars of merchandise may be on display for long periods of time. Furthermore, do not allow event participants to store merchandise or personal goods, such as purses, in public areas. Instead, provide a secure area for these elements, to ensure a watchful eye.

In today's post–September 11 world, securing the environment also involves additional considerations. For example, Event Leaders must ask questions concerning biochemical risks, terrorism threats, communicable disease threats (pandemics and epidemics), and effective crowd-control procedures.

As a direct result of the Station nightclub fire mentioned earlier, several new laws have been adopted and the Rhode Island state legislature has outlawed the grandfathering of buildings. Adopting the National Fire Protection Association (NFPA) 101, the *Life Safety Code,* and the NFPA 1, the *Uniform Fire Code™,* as their guides, Rhode Island has virtually banned indoor pyrotechnics except in major theater auditoriums and arenas. In addition, the state is requiring venues to provide one trained crowd manager for all events with 300 or more persons and one additional trained crowd manager per each additional 300 persons. Within a few years, the majority of nightclubs, restaurants, and other event facilities will have fire-suppression equipment (sprinklers) as a direct result of the tragic loss of 100 lives in the Station nightclub fire. It is the responsibility of every Event Leader to anticipate potential risks and proactively create an environment that is as risk-free as possible.

Transportation and Parking Factors

Event safety and security expert Dr. Peter Tarlow, in his book *Event Risk Management and Safety* (Wiley, 2002), states that the area that unites security and safety is the parking lot. Tarlow reminds us that parking lots can be dangerous for six reasons.

1. People tend to drive in parking lots as if there are no rules or laws. Having parking attendants or traffic directors can help alleviate this problem.
2. Pedestrians often assume that parking lots are safe and that drivers will follow the rules and see them. The use of parking attendants will help separate unaware pedestrians from clueless drivers.
3. Event attendees often lose their cars and may inadvertently set off the alarm of another car that looks like theirs. This type of behavior could cause a panic, so it is best if signs are posted reminding drivers to note the location of their vehicle.
4. Catastrophic weather conditions can create dangers for people who have parked in outdoor locations. Providing enclosed shuttle buses or trams can help alleviate these problems.
5. Poor lighting has been proven to promote criminal activity in parking lots. When possible, make certain the parking areas have sufficient lighting and/or adequate patrols.
6. Children can run off while parents are loading or unloading cars and can easily be injured. Having a drop-off area for children where they can be safely secured before parents park their cars is an excellent way to mitigate this problem.

As you develop and implement the event plan, remember that often transportation and parking is the first and last impression. Therefore, it makes good sense to follow Dr. Tarlow's wise counsel. For example, a clean parking area and a spotless restroom create and sustain a lasting impression of professionalism and quality.

The venue may or may not provide easy vehicle ingress. Therefore, well in advance, you must locate the proper door for load-in of your equipment, the times the dock is available for your deliveries, and other critical factors that will govern your ability to transport equipment and park your vehicles. Another consideration for transportation relates to approved routes for trucks and other vehicles. In some jurisdictions, such as Washington, DC, truck and large vehicular traffic is strictly regulated. Once again, confer well in advance with transportation and venue officials to determine the most efficient route.

Whether you are parking your vehicles in a marshaling facility or on the street, security must be considered as well as easy access. Some venues may not be located in the safest of neighborhoods, and, therefore, securing your vehicles and providing safe and fast access to them are important. Well-lit, fenced-in areas are best for parking; however, the proximity of the vehicles to the loading area of the venue is the prime concern.

You may think that transportation and parking have little to do with creating a proper event environment, but these two considerations should be given significant attention. Many events have started late or suffered in quality due to late or lost vehicles and inefficient load-in operations. Remember, you may design the most incredible event environment, but until it is shipped, loaded in, and installed properly, it is only your idea. Proper transportation and installation will turn your idea into a dynamic event environment.

Effectively Manage the Event Environment and They Will Come Back

Understanding the basic needs of the guest is of paramount importance, especially when you are working with a smaller budget than you would like. In circumstances where the budget is severely restricted, there are ways, using your imagination, to stretch limited funds. Use your budget to enhance the beginning and the end, as these are what the guest will most remember. Following are some considerations for managing the design of an event environment.

Entrances and Reception Areas

The Event Leader must immediately establish the theme of the event with environmental design. The use of proper signs, bearing the group's name or logo, and appropriate décor will reassure guests that they are in the right place. Consider the arrival process from the guests' point of view. They received the invitation some time ago and probably did not bring it with them to the event. Therefore, they are relying on memory to guide them to the right building and the right room. Once they have located parking, they ask the attendant to direct them to XYZ event. The attendant is rushed, having to park several hundred cars for perhaps as many as six different functions, and cannot recall the exact location of the affair. Should the guests stumble upon your site and not recognize it because the logo is absent or the entrance does not communicate the theme of the party, they will become confused and lost. Providing your own personnel in costume or professional wardrobe will help guests locate your event, as will proper signage. Upon arrival, guests should have an "Aha!" experience, knowing that they have arrived at the right place at the right time. You can offer guests this experience and create a positive impression by proper design of the reception area at which they are greeted. When guests must wait in long lines, they often begin to resent the event or its hosts. You must plan for these delays and offer solutions.

Figures 3.1 to 3.4 demonstrate how to place greeters, or "damage control" hosts, to handle problems in the reception area. In Figure 3.1, the guests have begun to form a second row at the reception table. When this occurs, greeters should immediately invite the second-row guests to step forward to the additional tables set behind the primary tables. Having extra tables available will be perceived by guests as an added courtesy and will help ease heavy arrival times. Note that the guests at the primary tables enter between them so as not to conflict with the guests at the additional tables.

Figure 3.2 shows a solution to the problem of guests arriving without an invitation and without their names appearing on the list of invitees. To avoid embarrassment and delay, the guest is invited to step forward to the courtesy table, conveniently isolated from the general crowd flow. There the problem can be resolved quietly and courteously, or the guest may be ushered out a back door without disrupting the event.

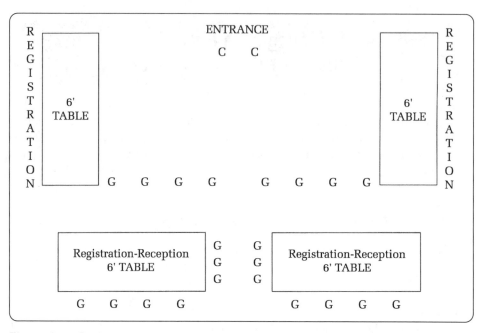

Figure 3.1 Registration-Reception Setup with Secondary Tables Supporting a Primary Table (G, guest; C, control)

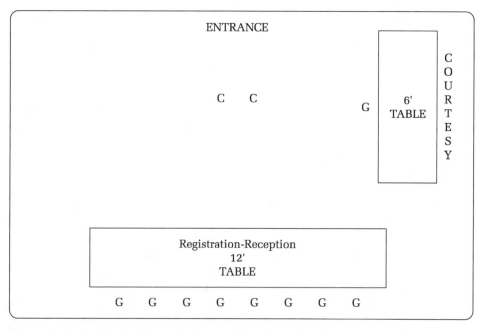

Figure 3.2 Registration-Reception Setup with a Secondary Courtesy Table (G, guest; C, control)

The scenario depicted in Figure 3.3 is one that every experienced event planner has known. During heavy arrival time, such as the second half-hour of a one-hour cocktail party preceding the main event, long lines of guests are forming while those staffing the reception tables are trying to greet arrivals quickly and efficiently and keep the line moving. Professional greeters can make the guests' wait less annoying. Their job is simply to greet the guests in line, quietly thank them for coming, and answer any questions they may have while waiting. Often professional performers, such as strolling mimes, clowns, jugglers, or magicians, may be used in this area to entertain, thereby distracting guests while they wait in line.

When you expect long lines over a brief period, the best arrangement is a variation of Figure 3.1. By using two additional courtesy tables, positioned at an angle, as shown in Figure 3.4, you can alleviate crowding. The reception setup integrating the profes-

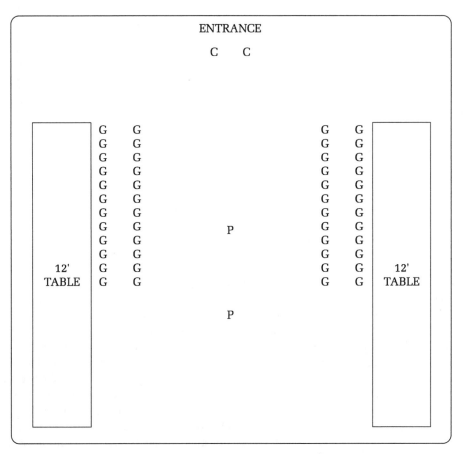

Figure 3.3 Reception Setup Integrating the Professional Greeter into the Flow of Guest Traffic (G, guest; C, control, P, professional greeter)

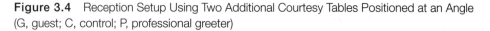

Figure 3.4 Reception Setup Using Two Additional Courtesy Tables Positioned at an Angle (G, guest; C, control; P, professional greeter)

sional greeter into the flow of guest traffic further ensures the ease and comfort of guests.

In Figure 3.4, you can keep guests moving forward and handle disputes at the same time. The hosts and hostesses at these courtesy tables should be trained to resolve disputes quickly and know when to refer a guest to a supervisor for further assistance. Most disputes can be remedied simply, requiring no more than preparation of a name badge, a payment, or other minor business. If handled at the primary table, such tasks become cumbersome. Experienced planners know that the floor plan for the reception area should facilitate guests' arrivals and is critical to the success of the event. The way in which a guest is first received at an event determines all future perceptions that he or she will have about the event program you have designed. Take time to plan this area carefully to ensure an efficient and gracious reception.

Function Areas

The reception area may create the first impression, but the main function area will determine the effectiveness of the overall design. This is the area in which guests will spend the most time, and this is the area where your principal message must be communicated to guests in a memorable manner. Traditional space designs are currently being rethought by meeting planners as well as psychologists to develop a more productive environment. Dr. Paul Radde is a psychologist who has pioneered the development of physical-space planning for conferences that provides a better environment in which to learn. Radde has, often to the chagrin of various hotel setup crews, determined that speakers prefer and often deliver a better talk when there is no center aisle. In the traditional theater- or classroom-style setup shown in Figure 3.5, all of the speaker's energy escapes through the center aisle. When this lane is filled with live bodies, the speaker's interaction is increased, as is the human connection among audience members themselves.

Figure 3.6 demonstrates the optimum setup, complete with wide aisles on each side to allow for proper egress. With this setting, each row should be at least 6 inches farther

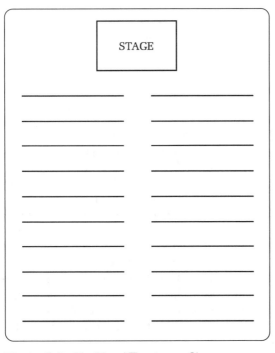

Figure 3.5 Traditional Theater- or Classroom-Style Setup

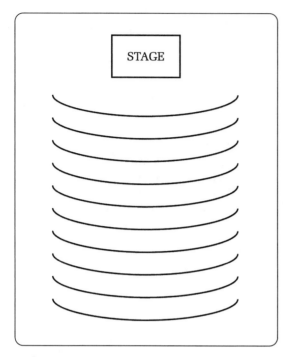

Figure 3.6 Optimum Theater- or Classroom-Style Setup

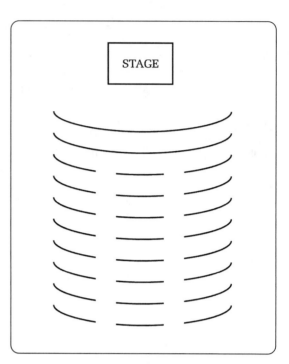

Figure 3.7 Modified Theater- or Classroom-Style Setup

apart than in Figure 3.5, to allow for more efficient egress. Some fire marshals prohibit the arrangement in Figure 3.6 because some audience members will be seated too far from an aisle. An excellent alternative is shown in Figure 3.7, in which the front two rows are solid, with side aisles beginning behind the second row.

Perhaps the best adaptation is shown in Figure 3.8. In this arrangement, all rows except the first five are sealed, and the center aisle is easily reached by latecomers in the rear of the auditorium. Planning an effective seating arrangement is only the beginning. Masking tape or rope on stanchions can be used to seal the back rows, as shown in Figure 3.8, encouraging guests to fill in the front rows first.

Once the rows are filled with guests, the tape is removed. After 30 years of watching audiences head for the back rows, I experimented a few years ago with this method to determine if I could control seating habits without inconveniencing the audience unduly. Much to my delight, several audience members have thanked me for this subtle suggestion to move up front. Without this direction, audience members become confused and revert to old habits.

Interestingly, once a guest claims a seat, he or she will return to it throughout the event. However, unless I have predetermined that they will sit up front by making the

```
                    ┌─────────────┐
                    │    STAGE    │
                    └─────────────┘

                                        R
                                        O
          M                             P
          A                             E
          S
          K                             &
          I
          N                             S
          G                             T
                                        A
          T                             N
          A                             C
          P                             H
          E                             I
                                        O
                                        N
```

Figure 3.8 Modified Theater- or Classroom-Style
Setup with Roped-off Rear Section

back rows unavailable, all of the coaxing and bribing (I once placed dollar bills under front-row seats) will not move audience members from the back-row comfort zone.

Innovative Sites

The purpose of creatively designing your environment is to provide a dynamic atmosphere within which your guest may experience the event. Decorator Terry Brady knows all too well how important such an atmosphere can be, as he once staged a banquet in a tractor-trailer. The guests were escorted up the steps and dined inside an actual tractor-trailer decorated by the Brady Company's team of artists. The goal of this creative design was to surprise and intrigue guests, who were picked up in limousines and brought to this isolated and inelegant site. Inside the tractor-trailer, they found luxurious décor, complete with chandeliers, tapestries, and fine linens. Brady recalls that the total tab for the 40 guests, including catering, service, and décor, was roughly $16,000. Not every client will allocate over $400 per person for an event. Nonetheless, the Event Leader is increasingly faced with the challenge of finding innovative, creative environments in which to stage events. Curators of museums and public buildings in record numbers throughout the United States have begun setting fees and offering their buildings to groups that wish to host a reception or meeting in a novel atmosphere. With these new opportunities for use of public space come increased challenges for decorators, who must now cope with the increased demand for atmospheric props in place of flats, banners, murals, and other more traditional scenic devices. Figure 3.9 includes a sampling of ideas for unusual sites in which to hold special events. Use this list to brainstorm with your event stakeholders to determine the best venue for your next event. The possibilities for exciting, innovative, and offbeat event sites are infinite. It is important, however, that your selection be logical and practical in terms of location, parking, setup, budget, and use of space.

One important book, entitled *New York's 100 Best Party Places: Weddings, Special Occasions, Corporate Events,* by S. Stuman and H. Sheets (City & Co., 2000), lists 100 event sites in New York City. The publication may be obtained by telephoning (212) 737–7536. In a Northern California–based publication entitled *Perfect Places,* by Lynn Broadwell and Jan Brenner (Hopscotch Press, 2001), venues ranging from historic homes to modern museums are described, with careful attention to both aesthetic and logistical detail. This publication may be obtained by calling (510) 525–3379. A companion book by Broadwell is entitled *Here Comes the Guide* (Hopscotch Press, 2001) and focuses on sites for weddings. According to Broadwell, writing in *ISES Gold* (ISES, 1994): "Twenty years ago event sites were a rare commodity. What's changed? Everything."

Wherever you turn, you will find new products and new services available to help you transform an environment for a creative special event. Many unusual products can be found at gift shows (trade shows featuring new and unusual gift items), antique stores and shows, flea markets, used and classic clothing stores, hotel closeout sales, and other businesses selling off stock. The ISES worldwide resource directory lists additional groups and organizations that can help create an environment for your next special event.

Amenities and Furnishings

The possibilities for linens, silverware, glassware, centerpieces, and even costumes for servers are greater in the profession today than ever before. Sites, sources, and suppliers for these items can be found in journals such as *Event Solutions* and *Special Events Magazines,* and various industry newsletters. See Appendixes 4, 5, and 6 for dozens of additional resources.

■ Edible Centerpieces and Displays

The centuries-old European custom of including elaborately designed food displays as part of the décor is finally becoming popular—indeed, in some regions, de rigueur—in the United States. This important area of setting design can range from fancy carved crudités for the hors d'oeuvres to elaborate centerpieces carved from thick dark chocolate. Today's special events professionals are as concerned with the aesthetic appeal of food selections as they are with taste. In fact, food presentation has become an art form in the United States, one in which annual competitions are held in areas ranging from ice sculpture and

In Transit

Aircraft carrier	Moving railroad train	Stationary caboose
Blimp	Orient Express	Subway platform
Cruise ship	Paddle-wheel steamboat	Tractor-trailer
Double-decker bus	Roller coaster	Trolley
Hot-air balloon	Space shuttle	Yacht
Monorail		

Design by Mother Nature

Apple orchard	Christmas-tree farm	National forest
Arboretum	Dude ranch	Pasture
Botanical center	Formal garden	Rose garden
Caverns	Greenhouse	Summer camp
Central Park	Meadow	Underneath a waterfall

Music, Music, Music

Rave nightclub	Grand Ole Opry stage	Symphony hall
Estate of deceased music star	Opera house	Television décor of
Gazebo or bandshell in a park	Recording studio	The Grammy Awards™

On Stage

Circus center ring	Famous actor's dressing room	Theater green room
Circus museum	Professional theater—lobby	Theatrical museum
Comedy nightclub	backstage, on stage	
Community theater		

At the Movies

Any movie theater	Former movie or television location	Former movie set (such as
Drive-in movie	(such as the bridge in Madison	Universal Studios' back lot
Estate of a deceased film star	County or Southfork Ranch in	or Granada Studios tour)
	Dallas)	Historic movie theater
		Radio City Music Hall

Food, Glorious Food

Apple orchard	Cornfield	Kitchen of a bakery
Bottling plant	Distillery	Vineyard
Cannery		

Infamous

Alcatraz	Microbrewery	Saloon in a ghost town
Former speakeasy	Nightclub	
Homes of famous outlaws (now often museums)		

Figure 3.9 Event Sites

(Continued)

Stately

Castle	Convent	Monastery
Cathedral	Mansion	

The Child in You

Amusement park	Clown alley at a circus	Laser-tag center
Arcade	Fairgrounds	Puppet theater
Children's museum	Family entertainment center	Virtual-reality center
Children's theater		

Wild Places

Animal shelter	Pet kennel	Wild-animal park
Aviary	Stable	Zoo
Local animal farm or ranch		

In Scholarly Pursuits

University/college dining hall	University/college private dining	University/college theater,
University/college library	facility (president's dining room)	meeting room, chapel

In Glass Cases

Aquarium	Medical museum	Science museum
Art museum	Natural-history museum	Sculpture museum
Aviation museum	Planetarium	Textile museum
Historical society museum	Potter's studio	

Behind the Scenes

Aircraft hangar	Empty swimming pool	Movie sound stage
Baseball dugout	Football locker room	Presidential library
Current embassy	Former embassy	Television studio
Diplomatic reception rooms at the U.S. Department of State		

The Winner Is You

Basketball court	Hockey rink	Racetrack
Fifty-yard line of a football field	Home plate on a baseball diamond	Roller rink
Swimming pool	Miniature golf course	Former Olympic Games venue

Ghoulish and Ghastly

Abandoned hospital morgue	Cemetery	Mausoleum
Abandoned hospital operating room	Funeral home	Tombstone manufacturer

Highly Scientific

Astrological observatory	Computer laboratory	General science laboratory

Figure 3.9 *(Continued)*

sugar works to chocolate and pastry design. When incorporating food into an overall design, remember that, ultimately, most food is intended to be eaten. The display must be accessible to guests and still look appealing after they are served. If possible, a server should offer the first guests who visit the display a serving of the decorated or carved item. This will help encourage other guests to help themselves. You may wish to prepare two versions of an item: one for show on an elevated, lighted platform and one for serving, placed within reach of guests. This will allow every guest to appreciate the work of your culinary artists throughout the event.

■ Decorating the Environment

The decorating profession has undergone a rapid transformation since the days when Howard Lanin's client told him: "Just make it lovely." Today, making it lovely involves a specialized professional in touch with the latest styles and products with which to create specific environments that will satisfy guests' individual needs. Today's designers are creating more profound, if only temporary, works of art to frame special events. Sixty years ago special events were most often held in private rooms, private clubs, churches, public sites, or hotels. Modern decorators are faced with the challenge of turning almost any conceivable space into a suitable environment for a special event. From football fields to tractor-trailers, today's decorators must display more imagination, creativity, and skill than ever before to keep pace with changing styles and trends. The designer/decorator's craft is one of transformation. Turning a polo field into a castle, a ballroom into the land of Oz, or a black tent into an extraterrestrial fantasy, decorators transport guests from the ordinary to the extraordinary by creating a world of fantasy.

Regional customs and geographic location may determine, to some extent, what types of products are used for some events. Very often, for example, a client in Florida will request a mariachi theme, and a client from the Southwest will desire a Polynesian holiday. But expanded delivery services, which allow suppliers to send almost anything overnight, have enabled designers and decorators to obtain almost any product for a special event, regardless of location.

One challenge that decorators face is designing an environment that will satisfy both primary and secondary audiences. Creating designs and products that will translate to television, film, and still photography is becoming increasingly important. Consequently, when formulating design ideas, consider both the primary and secondary audiences: Who will view this event and in what format? Perhaps the design will be detailed in such a way that it will show well in close-up photography. Many stock décor items available in today's events marketplace did not exist 60 years ago. Synthetic fibers and plastics have become increasingly sophisticated, enabling the fabrication of countless imaginative pieces. Even as these lines are written, products continue to be developed, providing greater selection at lower cost. Trying to describe all the products and techniques available to the event practitioner is impossible. The discussions that follow will introduce you to some of the more popular products and the imaginative ways that some innovative special events planners use them. Their continual exploration of new ways to satisfy clients' needs is the ultimate key to creative design.

■ Interactive Décor

Today's guests want to be more than just spectators at a special event—after all, movies and television provide plenty of opportunities to watch fantastic special effects and see gorgeous set designs and wonderful performances. To provide more than just a passive viewing experience, the event designer must create an environment that allows the guests to participate—to be actors in the decorator's dream world.

In Atlanta, Georgia, I experimented with this idea of interactive décor with an audience of prestigious and somewhat jaded professional catering executives. The challenge was to show these hospitality professionals something new, working, as always, within a specific budget. The theme of the banquet was "Starship NACE" (National Association of Catering Executives). As the guests entered the foyer, they passed between two 25-inch color television monitors that featured a close-up view of an extraterrestrial's face. As each guest passed, the alien greeted him or her by name and offered a warm welcome to the event. I stood in the shadows, out of sight, and watched the guests' reactions—they suddenly stopped and laughed, clearly baffled by how an image on a screen could recognize and greet them. In actuality, an actor was hidden in a side room. As each guest stepped into the reception area, a technician using a two-way radio revealed the name to the actor, who in turn announced the name on television. Fog machines were set a few feet beyond the television monitors; just as the guests were recovering from one experience, they would receive a small blast of dry chemical fog to surprise them again. Throughout the cocktail reception, a prerecorded endless-loop cassette tape featuring space sounds and a professional narrator making preboarding announcements was played. When the time came to open the ballroom doors for dinner, four astronauts dressed in white jumpsuits, with NACE embroidered on their breast pockets, and blue and white space helmets, also featuring the NACE emblem, appeared in front of each door. As the doors were slowly opened, more fog seeped from the ballroom into the cocktail area. The guests entered the ballroom via a tunnel constructed of black pipe and drape and hundreds of miniature white lights. They tiptoed over a moonscape atmosphere, created by thousands of Styrofoam peanuts covered by ground cloth. Walking through that tunnel, the guests were entering another world. Once inside the ballroom, a robot welcomed the guests from the dance floor and instructed them to "be seated quickly, as the starship will be departing soon." "Also Sprach Zarathustra," the music used in the movie *2001: A Space Odyssey*, played in the background, and the sound effects of sonic blasts were added, projected through four speakers to create a true sense of surround sound. One-dimensional scenic pieces of planets were hung from the walls, and miniature strobe lights created the effect of starlight.

Later chapters explore how the use of video and live action helped to provide constant interaction for the guests attending this event. At this point, it is sufficient to understand the importance of creating a design that will meet the needs of the guests. Today, any site can be transformed through décor, using a variety of products and techniques. Regardless of the site and the decoration details, however, the designer's objective remains the same: satisfying the guests. To accomplish this goal, the designer must involve the guests in the event as much as possible through their senses, their activities, and their emotions. Site design can facilitate such involvement, as the "Starship NACE" event demonstrates.

In another example of interactive décor, my firm was involved in designing a theme event entitled "A Dickens of a Christmas," in which the streets of Victorian London were re-created to bring the feeling of Charles Dickens's England to a hotel exhibit room. Since one of Dickens's best-known tales is *A Christmas Carol,* we decided to employ a winter setting and scattered artificial snow throughout the hall. I was delighted to see the usually staid guests kicking the snow throughout the room as they traveled down each lane, participating actively in the setting. We also included a group of street urchins (actually, professional boys and girls with extensive Broadway credits), who were instructed to attempt to steal food from the lavish buffets throughout the room. Each time they snatched a scone, the waiters would grab them and say, "All right, if you want to eat, you must sing for your supper!" The children then proceeded to sing a 10-minute medley of holiday carols. The guests reacted first with surprise when the waiter reprimanded the children and then, within seconds, became emotionally involved as the adorable and talented children sang for their supper. A life-sized puppet of Ebenezer Scrooge was also used. As guests wandered by his house (a display piece), he popped his head out and shouted, "You're standing on my kumquats! Get out of my garden now! Bah, humbug!" The guests, of course, loved this Christmas nemesis. Those who were recognized by the puppeteer were called by name, much to their delight and the delight of their friends. Mr. Scrooge created gales of laughter, once again emotionally stimulating the guests.

The potential for effective design is truly greater than ever. To succeed, the guest must be involved sensuously, physically, and emotionally. The Bible tells us that "There is nothing new under the sun." The late Cavett Robert, chairman emeritus of the National Speakers Association, has said, "Much that is described as 'new' is actually old wine in new bottles." These maxims apply to the décor industry because, with every advancement of new technology, the basic principles of satisfying the guest's sensual, physical, and emotional needs remain unchanged.

Inside the World of Event Design

Hargrove, Inc., of Lanham, Maryland, was founded in the late 1930s by Earl Hargrove Sr., who specialized in what was then called *window trimming,* decorating store windows of retail establishments in the Washington, DC, area to promote sales. With the advent of television, Hargrove's clients began to funnel their advertising dollars into the new medium, and his business soared. When Hargrove's son, Earl Jr., returned home from a stint in the Marine Corps in the late 1940s, he joined his father's company. Earl Jr. wanted to pursue the new and lucrative field of convention and trade-show display and exposition decorating, but his father wanted to remain solely in the specialty decorating market. Although they separated for a time, Earl Jr. pursuing the convention market and Earl Sr. struggling in the specialty decorating market, they eventually rejoined forces.

Their longevity in the Washington, DC, events arena is best symbolized by their association with the national Christmas tree located beside the White House. In 1949, Earl Hargrove Jr. placed the star high atop the tree; in that same year, he and his father renewed their business partnership, and a new brilliance in special events décor began. Today that partnership includes many more members of the Hargrove family, a talented team of employees, and a large warehouse-studio filled with thousands of props, scenic items, and parade floats. When Earl Hargrove Jr. began in partnership with his father, he discovered the lucrative market for Washington social events. He recalls receiving an order in the early 1950s to decorate a country club for which the total bill was $350. Times certainly have changed, both in terms of budget and available products with which to decorate. Today a third-generation Hargrove, Carla Hargrove McGill, helps lead a sales team that provides décor for major casinos, corporations, and associations as well as private individuals who seek decorations for their bar and bas mitzvahs, weddings, and other celebrations. McGill believes that her mission in the social-event field is to bring the client's theme to life through décor. Doing so today, however, is trickier than in past years, in part because of more stringent fire regulations. According to McGill, "Many states have particularly tough fire laws governing interior décor, and others are following. Every product we use must be flame-proofed, which in the balloon industry, for example, is very difficult to accomplish, largely due to high manufacturers' costs." When Earl Jr. began with his father, the available materials were paper, cloth, and wood. Today the Hargroves enjoy many more options, including foam, fiberglass, a wide selection of flame-proofed fabrics, and a full range of plastics, to mention only a few. Forty years ago, guests were content merely to view the decoration. Today Hargrove, Inc., is challenged to give guests a feeling of participation and interaction with the décor.

Hargrove, Inc. designs sets for themed events using devices such as time tunnels, which the guests walk through to enter the main event, or three-dimensional props that the guests may touch. The Hargroves agree that a successful decorator must offer a full range of services and products to be successful. Hargrove, Inc., will rent out a single prop or create an entirely new themed event. This diversity has proven successful for over 40 years. The Hargroves, along with other professional decorators, suggest that, although there are millions of new decorating ideas for special events, not all of them are practical. Therefore, it is always important to consider these points when choosing decorations:

+ What will the venue (site, building) allow in terms of interior/exterior décor?
+ What are the policies regarding installation? What are the policies or laws of the local municipality regarding decorating materials?
+ What is the purpose of the décor?
+ Are you conveying a specific theme?
+ Is there a specific message?
+ What period or style are you attempting to represent?
+ What are the demographics and psychographics of your attendees?
+ Are they spectators or participants?
+ What are the budgetary guidelines for the décor?
+ How long will it be in use?
+ Which existing scenic pieces can be modified to fit your theme or convey your message?

■ Parades and Float Design

Starting with the original Cherry Blossom parade in Washington, DC, the Hargrove artists have been recognized as leaders in the U.S. float design and construction industry. Many nationally known parades, including the annual Miss America parade in Atlantic City and the 1987 We the People parade in Philadelphia, celebrating the bicentennial of the U.S. Constitution, have featured Hargrove floats. Designing, building, transporting, and operating floats can be a costly enterprise. But the rewards for the sponsor, in terms of publicity, can be priceless, provided that the right steps are taken. These questions should be addressed before contracting to design a float:

+ What does the parade committee or organization allow in terms of size, materials, and thematic design?
+ Under what meteorological conditions and in what climate will the float be used? (Some float builders specialize in designs suitable for particular climates.)
+ Will the float appear on television?
+ What investment will the sponsor make?
+ What constraints are imposed by the parade itself regarding construction, size, weight, materials, and themes? (For example, spatial constraints may limit a float's dimensions.)
+ What message does the sponsor wish to convey?
+ Where will the floats be stored prior to the parade?
+ What is the physical environment of the parade route?

When asked why he continues to pursue this extremely labor-intensive sector of the decorating profession, Earl explains with a story: "A few years ago, I was in Atlantic City with the Miss America Parade, and a man in the convention pipe-and-drape industry saw me watching my floats go down the boardwalk. He said, 'Earl, why don't you get out of the float business and just concentrate on the convention draping part? That's where the profits are.' Well, I didn't answer him, but I knew at that moment how different our company is from all the others. This guy was the unhappiest guy in the world. He didn't really love what he did. On the other hand, we do what we love to do, and I hope it shows in our work."

Parade floats are a perfect example of the need to consider the ultimate viewership of your design. Corporations sponsor floats in an effort to develop positive publicity and influence consumers to buy their products and services. Since only a few parades are televised nationally, most floats need only ensure that the sponsor's theme is conveyed to the live audience viewing the event. Many floats include people—pageant queens, actors, actresses, costumed characters, and celebrities—in their design. When planning the float design, it is essential to consider their place in the display. The wardrobe color of the person riding on the float, for example, will affect the total look of the float and, therefore, is an important design concern. Additionally, the lighting at the time of the parade will determine, to some extent, which colors and materials will best convey your message.

As I noted earlier, it is essential to review the parade organization's requirements for parade floats before making any design choices. In most cases, it will be appropriate to feature the float sponsor's name prominently in the design. The manner in which you incorporate the sponsor's name or logo into the float design will affect the integrity of the display itself. Be careful to make the sponsor's name and/or logo a cohesive part of the design whenever possible instead of merely tacking a loose sign on the side as if it were an afterthought. Your ability to incorporate the sponsor's message into your final design in a seamless manner will determine the effectiveness of the float in the eyes of both the viewer and the sponsor. Whether it's themed décor for social events or major parade floats for the Philadelphia Thanksgiving Day parade, the Hargrove family, starting with the founder, Earl Sr. and continuing today with Earl Jr. and his children, bring innovations to the art and science of décor. They are serious businesspeople concerned with profit and growth, but they are guided ultimately by the feeling that they bring a special magic to special events. The Hargrove family still ensures the placement of the star high atop the national Christmas tree; perhaps this is a symbol of the bright, shining influence their art has shone upon the special events universe.

Say It with Flowers

Flowers are usually more costly than stock rental decorations (props) because of their perishable nature. According to some designers, the markup for floral is often four times the cost. If the cost of the floral centerpiece is $20, the designer will sell it to the client for $80 or more to recover his or her labor, materials, and overhead costs, plus retain a margin of profit.

John Daly, CSEP, president of John Daly, Inc., of Santa Barbara, California, began his successful design firm with floral products. He suggests that, when designing vertical centerpieces, these guidelines should be observed: "The centerpiece height should not exceed 14 inches unless it is loose and airy, therefore see-through, over the 14-inch mark. This, of course, does not apply to the epergne arrangement. An epergne is a flower holder, such as a candelabra or mirrored stand, that raises the flowers from the table. When using the epergne, the base of the floral arrangement should begin at least 24 inches above table height."

Daly believes that event design has truly matured into both a fine art and a science because of the new materials available and the speed at which they can be obtained. Today, a wider range of floral products is available because of the advances in transportation and shipping. With the advent of overnight delivery systems, Daly can have virtually any product he wishes for any event in any location. As designer for events in Seoul, Korea, and in the Virgin Islands, this advantage has increased his ability to use fresh and exciting ideas in many far-off event sites.

Balloon Art

Balloon décor can range from a simple balloon arch to more elaborate designs, such as three-dimensional shapes or swags of balloons, intertwined with miniature lights, hung from the ceiling. Balloons can create special effects, such as drops, releases, and explosions. Balloon drops involve dropping balloons over the audience from nets or bags suspended from the ceiling. Releases including setting helium-filled balloons free outdoors from nets, bags, or boxes, all commercially available. Explosions might include popping clear balloons filled with confetti or popping balloons mounted on a wall display to reveal a message underneath.

From centerpieces to massive walls of balloons, such as the U.S. flag displays that Treb Heining (Balloonart by Treb) created for the city of Philadelphia, balloon art has become an established part of the special events industry. Organizations such as the National Association of Balloon Artists (NABA) and Pioneers Balloon Company's Balloon Network are working to educate both balloon professionals and their clients to the uses of this art form as well as to ensure greater responsibility in employing it.

Balloon art has become an integral part of event décor largely because of the innovations in the 1980s and 1990s by Treb Heining of California. From creating an enormous birthday cake for a tenth-anniversary celebration at a shopping mall to supervising the balloon effects for the opening and closing ceremonies of the Los Angeles Olympic Games, Heining has been at the forefront of his profession for many years. He began by selling balloons at Disneyland in Anaheim, California, and later used the same products for decoration at both social and corporate events. He designed the massive balloon drops for the Republican National Conventions, incorporating the balloon-holding nets in the décor prior to the actual drop. Heining also designed the gigantic confetti displays for the New York City Times Square New Year celebrations.

In recent years, there has been much discussion regarding the effect of balloon releases on the environment. Marine biologists have determined that wind currents cause balloons to drift out over bodies of water, where they lose velocity and eventually fall into the waters below. They are concerned that sea animals may ingest these products and become ill or die. Although there is currently no conclusive evidence that balloon releases have harmed marine animals, what goes up must eventually come down, and both the balloon professional and his client must act responsibly. Electric power companies in some jurisdictions throughout the United States have reported incidences where foil balloons have become entangled in power lines following a release, causing power failures due to the conductivity of the metallic balloon. All balloon professionals disapprove of foil balloon releases as well as releases where hard objects are included in or on the balloon itself. Although it is impossible to regulate a balloon's final destination after a release, it is possible to design and stage releases that will not adversely affect the environment. A tethered release—where the balloons are released on long tethers and not allowed to float freely—may be one alternative. In some jurisdictions, the Federal Aviation Administration requests notice of balloon releases in order to advise pilots in the area.

Tents: Beyond Shelter Is Décor

One example of a new adaptation of a classic environment is in the tenting industry. Developments in materials and workmanship in this industry have multiplied the design possibilities of tents. Half a century ago, the standard tent available for a special event was a drab olive U.S. Army tarpaulin. Flooring was rarely considered, and lighting was most elementary. Today, however, thanks to significant pioneers such as Bob Graves, former owner of the Van Tent company, Harry Oppenheimer, the founder of HDO Productions, and major innovators such as Edwin Knight, CERP of EventQuip, the tenting industry has truly come of age. Oppenheimer sees his service as "essentially solving a space problem. For that special occasion, such as a fiftieth anniversary, you don't have to build a family room to accommodate your guests. You can rent a tent with all of the same comforts of a family room." Oppenheimer believes the successful tenting professional prepares for the unforeseen, imagining the structure in snow, wind, rain, and perhaps hail. Most professionals in the tenting industry will not only carefully inspect the ground surface but will also bore beneath the surface to check for underground cables and pipes that might be disturbed by the tent installation. When Oppenheimer receives an inquiry for tenting from a prospective client, he first dispatches an account executive from his firm to meet with the client in person and view the site. Once the site has been inspected, the account executive is better prepared to make specific recommendations to the client. HDO Productions uses a computer network to track the client's order. The computer will first tell HDO if equipment and labor are available to install the tent on the date requested. The computer then lists the number of employees needed for the installation and prints the load sheet for the event.

Today's tent fabrics are more likely to be synthetic than muslin. Synthetics provide a stronger structure that is easier to maintain and aesthetically more pleasing. Oppenheimer particularly likes such innovations as the Parawing tent structure, which can be used indoors as well as outdoors in venues that need aesthetic enhancement to mask unfinished portions or obnoxious views. The addition of lighting to these sail-like images will make the event even more aesthetically pleasing. Heating, air conditioning, and flooring are also now available for tented environments. Each of these important elements can help ensure the success of your tented event. A competent tenting contractor will survey your installation area and determine if flooring is advisable, or perhaps essential, because of uneven topography. Listen carefully to his or her recommendations. I had the misfortune of watching 3,000 women remove their fancy dress shoes as they sank ankle deep in mud under a tent. The client refused to invest in flooring, although the additional cost was quite minimal. A pouring rain arrived just before the guests stepped under the canopy and flooded the public areas of the tent. It is a wonder the client did not have to replace 3,000 pairs of ruined shoes. From wooden floors to Astroturf, your tent contractor can recommend the most cost-efficient ground surface for your event. In some instances, the location for the tent may require grading or other excavation to prepare the land for effective installation. Many tent contractors provide a preliminary evaluation and recommendation at no charge in order to prepare a proper bid for an event.

Heating or air conditioning can increase the comfort of your guests, thus helping increase attendance at your tented event. Once again, your tent contractor will assist you in determining whether to add these elements and what the cost will be. If you elect to air-condition or heat your tent, make certain that the engineer in charge of the temperature controls remains on-site during the entire event. The temperature will rise as the tent fills with guests, so the heating or air conditioning must be adjusted throughout the event to ensure comfort. When you use a tent, you not only take responsibility for ensuring the comfort and safety of the guests, but in some jurisdictions you are actually erecting a temporary structure that requires a special permit. Check with local authorities.

A tent provides a special aesthetic appeal; like balloons bobbing in the air, white tent tops crowned with colorful flags seemingly touching the clouds signal an event to your arriving guests. Few forms of décor make as immediate and dramatic an impression as a tent does. With a competent tent contractor, the problems you might anticipate are easily manageable, and the possibilities for an innovative event, year-round, are limitless.

■ Décor Costs

When hiring a design professional for an event, expect to cover not only the cost of labor, delivery, and the actual product, but also the designer's consultation fee. In some cases, this consultation fee may be included in the final bid for the job. If you are soliciting many different proposals, it is best to outline your budget range for the project to the prospective designers up front. This openness may dictate the selection of products for your event. Labor is a major component of design charges because the designer-decorator's craft is so time-consuming.

The complexity of the design will affect costs, as will the amount of time available for installation. The longer the time allowed for installation, the fewer persons required. I have seen décor budgets double when less than one hour was allotted for installation of a major set. Allow enough time for the designers to do their work from the very beginning, alleviating the need for extra last-minute labor to complete the job. While many variables are involved in pricing décor, a typical margin of profit above the direct cost of materials and labor is 40 percent. This does not include the general overhead associated with running a business, including insurance, rent, promotion, vehicles, and the like. Therefore, today's designers must be very careful when quoting prices, to ensure that costs are recovered adequately and allow for a profit. When purchasing design services, remember that each designer possesses a unique talent that may be priceless to your particular event. This perception of value may, in your estimation, overrule the pricing formulas described above.

Themed Events

The theme party or theme event originated from the masquerade, where guests dressed in elaborate costumes to hide their identity. From these masquerade events a variety of themes were born. Today, it is typical to attend western-, Asian, European, or South and Central American–themed events, as themes are often derived from destinations or regions of the country or world. Robin Kring, author of *Party Creations: A Book of Theme Design* (Clear Creek Publishing, 1993), says that "theme development and implementation are really very easy. Themes can be built on just about any item you can think of."

Themes usually are derived from one of three sources. First, the destination will strongly influence the theme. When guests travel to San Francisco, they want to enjoy a taste of the city by the bay rather than a Texas hoedown. The second source is popular culture, including books, movies, and television. Whether the theme is a classic (*Gone With the Wind*) or topical (*Lord of the Rings*), the idea is usually derived from popular culture. The third and final source is historical and current events. Themes reflecting the Civil

War, World War II, or the landing of a human on the moon, as well as the collapse of the Berlin Wall, have strong historical or current significance and may be used to develop themes. See the examples of themed events in Figure 3.10.

An important consideration when planning theme parties is to understand the history of the group. Themes can be overused, and it is important that you rotate themes to maintain the element of surprise. When planning theme parties, ask your client these questions:

◆ What is the history of your theme parties? What did you do last year?
◆ What is the purpose or reason for this event?
◆ Is there a specific theme you wish to communicate?
◆ To convey the theme, is food and beverage, décor, or entertainment most important for your group's tasks?
◆ Remembering that first and last impressions are most important, what do you want the guests to most remember from this event?

The answers to these questions will provide you with ample instructions to begin your planning of a terrific themed event. The list of themes in Figure 3.10 is by no means exhaustive. However, it does reflect a sample of the top themes currently in use in American events. When selecting a theme, make sure you are certain that the theme can be communicated easily and effectively through décor, entertainment, food and beverage, and of course, invitation and program design.

John P. Tempest is a funeral director in Leeds, England, who notes that, while fashions come and go when planning "the ultimate final tribute," tradition governs the format of most funeral rites. For example, Tempest notes that, in Great Britain, many families engage a funeral director to arrange for the burial of their deceased family member. The services Tempest provides include providing essential staff, preparing all official documentation and liaison with the proper authorities, making and receiving all necessary telephone calls, arranging for the attendance of the minister for the funeral service, placing obituary notices in newspapers, and making the necessary disbursement payments on behalf of the family. In addition, his firm will supply a traditional coffin with fittings for cremation (more frequently selected as a burial option in Great Britain than in the United States), vehicles, and professional fees for the director.

When planning this important final event, Tempest suggests that most families select a traditional service rather than deviate from the norm. After the funerals of public figures, such as Princess Diana, Tempest noted that, for a short time, certain new customs are adopted, such as the use of white flowers, in an effort to emulate the funeral rites of the departed celebrity. However, these are the exceptions to the rule, in a country where hundreds of years of tradition and precedent govern most decisions.

Tempest states that the total cost for these services is approximately $3,000. Deviation from tradition resulting in further customization will increase the costs. Event Leaders may elect to use the formula of basic pricing for standard services that is customary in the funeral industry to create standard packages and improve efficiency when providing price quotations. Although every event represents the unique tastes and sensitivities of the

Theme	Audience	Elements
The Wild Wild West	All ages; very popular with men	*Décor:* hay bales, western-style bar, western jail set for photos, saloon with swinging doors *Entertainment:* gunslingers, lariat act, whip act, knife-throwing act, medicine-man magic show, western band, western dancers, fiddle ensemble, harmonica act, strolling guitarist, cowboy singer on live horse, steer, trainer *Food and beverages:* barbecue, hamburgers, biscuits, baked beans, rattlesnake, fowl, fresh pies
South of the Border	All ages; international guests; events held in states or areas bordering Mexico	*Décor:* small bridge over the Rio Grande; Customs officials and signs at the entrance; bright yellow lighting inside entrance; carts with vendors in Mexican attire selling novelties; cacti; colorful blankets in southwestern designs; umbrella tables with tequila logo on top *Entertainment:* mariachi musician, flamenco and folk dancers, folk artists weaving baskets and other handicrafts *Food and beverages:* tacos, fajitas, refried beans, rice, chili, tamales, guacamole, margaritas
The New Millennium	Younger guests; men and women; businesspeople; scientists; engineers; scholars	*Décor:* large video projection screens projecting star pattern at entryway, followed by a darkened tunnel with thousands of miniature lights and spacelike sound effects; dance floor covered in light fog with pulsing lights; Internet stations on personal computers set throughout the room *Entertainment:* robots, actors in astronaut costumes, actors in alien costumes, high-tech band performing space-associated music *Food and beverages:* space food preset at each setting with freeze-dried ice cream and jellybeans representing various vitamins
Mardi Gras	Younger guests; especially appropriate for New Orleans events	*Décor:* two large papier-mâché heads or floats framing the entrance; one doubloon given to each guest to exchange for a drink; purple, green, and gold balloons; exterior facades of Bourbon Street landmarks

Figure 3.10   Themes from Popular Culture, History, and Current Events   *(Continued)*

Theme	Audience	Elements
		Entertainment: quick-sketch artists; jazz band, including second-line parade; Mardi Gras revelers throwing beads
		Food and beverages: muffaleta sandwiches; seafood, including crawfish and oysters; gumbos; red beans and rice; shrimp Creole, biscuits; po'boy sandwiches; snowball; king cakes; hurricane-style drinks
Riverboat	All ages, especially older audiences	*Décor:* small gangplank bridge leading to doorway; life preserver over doorway with name of event displayed; inside main function room is casino, theater, long bar, colorful pennants, and flags
		Entertainment: Dixieland jazz band, banjo players, close-up magicians masquerading as gamblers
		Food and beverages: Southern cuisine, including ribs, pork, fried chicken, grits, mint juleps, bourbon served in souvenir shot glasses
Paris Nights	All ages, especially younger audiences	*Décor:* entryway marquee with chaser lights representing a Paris nightclub; in the center of the room, a three-dimensional replica of the Eiffel Tower outlined in miniature lights; ficus trees on the perimeter with miniature lights; backdrops or sets of typical Parisian facades, including the Louvre, the Folies Bergère, and the Comédie Française
		Entertainment: quick-sketch artists, cancan dancers, café orchestra, chanteuse
		Food and beverages: crepes, cheeses, pastries, wines, champagne
Hooray for Hollywood	All ages	*Décor:* sign announcing "The Hollywood Palladium"; red carpet with rope and stanchion on either side; follow spotlights sweeping the carpet; inside the function room, film props such as directors' chairs, cameras, lights, backdrops, a wind machine
		Entertainment: a team of young male and female fans screaming as the guests arrive; a recording studio for instant sing-alongs; improvisational movie-set area with instant replay; photo area with guests wearing wardrobe items from famous movies
		Food and beverages: menu items from Hollywood

Figure 3.10 *(Continued)*

Theme	Audience	Elements
Broadway Bash	All ages	*Décor:* large entrance sign proclaiming "Opening Night Starring [the name of the guests]"; fake ticket booth distributing programs; guests enter through stage door and actually walk onto the stage *Entertainment:* actors portraying ticket sellers, ticket takers, stage doormen, actors; Broadway orchestra in pit performing selections from top Broadway shows; musical-comedy performers performing popular Broadway songs; photos taken with Broadway look-alikes *Food and beverages:* New York cuisine, including Coney Island frankfurters, New York strip steak, Manhattan clam chowder
Rock Around the Clock	Younger audiences; baby boomers	*Décor:* giant jukebox facade serves as entranceway; interior transformed into gymnasium complete with basketball hoops at each end of dance floor and school name and logo on dance floor; bright ribbon in the school colors swagged from the ceiling; mirror ball for lighting effect *Entertainment:* 1950s, 1960s, 1970s rock 'n' roll; hula-hoop contest; servers on roller blades; a phone booth–stuffing contest; a '57 Chevy for photos *Food and beverages:* beer, pizza, hot dogs, hamburgers, malts, French fries, cherry Cokes
Dickens of a Christmas	All ages	*Décor:* entryway with Covent Garden design; fake snow scattered throughout; cemetery area with the tombstones of Marley and famous British writers; facades of London landmarks, including the Tower of London, Big Ben, and Parliament *Entertainment:* a team of strolling urchins sings for their supper; a Salvation Army worker plays harp; Father Christmas poses for photos; a woman strolls by selling live geese in cages *Food and beverages:* cider, ale, beer, wassail, holiday punch
Rave Party	Generation X; teenagers	*Décor:* fencing, salvage, industrial equipment *Entertainment:* punk-rock band; DJ with lighting effects *Food and beverages:* fast food

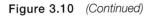

Figure 3.10 *(Continued)*

host/purchaser, many standard steps can be priced well in advance to ensure consistent profit when providing individual quotations.

Big Theme Success with Small Budgets

Even the slightest budget can enjoy big results through a carefully planned theme event. First, you must decide what elements are most important, because it is not likely that you will be able to fund equally everything you desire. If your guests are gourmets, the largest percentage of the budget will be dedicated to food and beverage. However, if they are creative, fun-loving people who are only slightly interested in the menu, you will want to shift your expenditure to décor and entertainment. Make certain that the first impression (entrance area) is well decorated, as this not only sets the tone for an event but is often the most photographed area. Next, include a series of surprises, such as a dessert parade or the arrival of a guest celebrity as your auctioneer, to keep guests on the edges of their seats.

Finally, share your resources with others. Check with the director of catering at the hotel and find out if other groups are meeting in the hotel before, during, or following your stay. Ask for permission to contact their Event Leader and determine if you can produce the same event and split the costs for décor and entertainment. You will find that you can afford 50 percent more by allocating your scarce resources in this manner.

Trends in Theme Events

Interactive events are transforming couch potatoes into fully participatory guests. David Peters of Absolute Amusements in Florida annually produces hundreds of interactive events, ranging from the Team Excellence Olympics for Xerox Corporation to school picnics. Peters features unusual interactive equipment such as sumo wrestling (where participants wear giant foam rubber suits), the Velcro wall (where the participants wear Velcro-covered jumpsuits and jump and land in various positions on a large wall covered with Velcro), and virtual surfing (where surfers stand on boards attached to electronic terminals and see themselves on a large video monitor as they roll, slide, and sometimes tumble into the virtual ocean). When designing interactive events, keep in mind the safety of the participants. Alcohol will, of course, increase the margin of risk for a guest. Some Event Leaders require guests to sign hold-harmless waivers to acknowledge the risk involved with the activity.

Your event environment is the opportunity to explore dozens of opportunities in décor, entertainment, and other elements to make every moment unique and memorable. Every Event Leader has essentially this same opportunity. By understanding how the various pieces fit together to solve the puzzle that is the event environment, you provide a finished picture that will be remembered by your guests for years to come. Your ability to design, balance, and mold this collage will be rewarded by the guests' total immersion in the environment, leaving an indelible impression for many years. Especially in the new world of Event Leadership, you must be sensitive to the cultural, political, and other unique factors represented by your event guests. Remember, this is one reason why you are so valuable. You are the artist and scientist; use your experience, sensitivity, good taste, and talent to create and plan this unique moment in time.

Sustainable Event Leadership: Conserving the Environment

When I addressed the Nature Conservancy, a major U.S. environmental research and educational organization that focuses on environmental issues, I was impressed with how these leaders use events to communicate the important message of conservation. You can use every event as an opportunity to stress environmental sensitivity. Whether implementing a recycling plan or selecting products that do not harm the ecosystem, the Event Leader has an implied responsibility to produce events that are environmentally sensitive.

Environmental Ecological Sensitivity

Environmental and ecological sensitivity are important for two major reasons. First, they are the right thing to do. When allocating scarce resources for an event, remember that no resource is as scarce as the environment in which we live, work, and play. Second, clients are increasingly requesting that every event meet or exceed certain environmental standards. Major corporations have been criticized by their customers for not demonstrating enough sensitivity to the environment. Therefore, when these corporations retain you to manage an event, they want you to reflect their renewed commitment to environmental concerns.

The best way to accomplish this is to clearly define the organization's environmental policy and then incorporate these policies into your event environment design and operations. Event sponsors who practice recycling in all likelihood will want recycling bins at an event they sponsor. Event sponsors who do not use foam products for disposable serving utensils will not want you to specify these items in your catering orders. Meet with the key environmental policy person for the organization sponsoring your event and determine, with his or her help, how to incorporate such policies within the event environment.

Why not create your own policies? To ensure that events enjoy sustainable growth, it is important for you to establish your own environmental policies that will demonstrate to prospective event sponsors your knowledge and sensitivity regarding these issues. These policies need not be repressive. However, they must be consistent. Do not alter your policies merely to satisfy the budget considerations for the event. Instead, seek creative solutions, such as finding a sponsor for the recycling station, to make certain that your environmental ideals are well protected at every event.

Recycle Your Success

In the exposition event field, a growing trend is the recycling to local schools of leftover materials such as paper, pens, pencils, and other reusable supplies. Usually these items end up in the dumpster when, only a few blocks from the venue, there may be a school with children who cannot afford these basic supplies. You may wish to incorporate this program in your agreements to inform your sponsor of your policy of recycling your success to help others.

Many event sponsors recycle leftover food products to local homeless shelters or food distribution agencies. Doing this assures your guests that you are committed to sharing the success of your banquet with those less fortunate. Some venues require the recipients to sign a hold-harmless form; however, regardless of the legal technicality, this opportunity to feed others should be seized for every event.

Still another way to recycle your success is to build into your event a project to benefit a local organization. Some event organizers schedule a day before or after the event for attendees to use their skills to clean up a local playground, paint a school, or perform some other community service. To arrange this activity, contact the volunteer center in the local community. The office of the mayor is a good place to start to locate the local volunteer coordinating organization. Tell the office what resources you are bringing to their destination and then apply your success to help others.

Inspiration and Perspiration

A famous novelist once stated that writing is 10 percent inspiration and 90 percent perspiration. Although the design phase provides inspiration, it also expands and tests the limits of research. At the conclusion of the design phase, the Event Leader should have a clear idea of the needs and desires of event stakeholders. The goals and objectives that were identified in the research phase represent the skeletal structure in the anatomy of an event, and the flexible elements identified in the design phase represent the musculature needed to move event research forward. Now it is time to add the cardiovascular system to give and sustain life for the event. This is the beginning of the event's life, and the primary organ that will sustain this life is the *event strategic plan*.

Event Strategic Planning

The event strategic plan (ESP) provides the definition for event stakeholders of the steps, people, time frame, and other critical elements needed to ensure that an event reaches a successful outcome. Your ESP can be compared to the tracks driving a locomotive. Without tracks, the train cannot reach its destination. Without a workable plan, an event cannot achieve the optimum outcome and arrive at the destination that you and the stakeholders desire.

The planning phase is a direct result of the data collected during research and the color, luster, and texture mixed into the process during design. The plan must be reasonable (as confirmed during the research phase) and match the expectations of the stakeholders (as identified during the design phase). The planning phase involves the key informants or leading stakeholders who will manage the event. During the planning meeting, it is important to involve those people who not only have the responsibility but also the authority to make decisions. The plan will reflect those decisions, and these important stakeholders must be included to ensure that they take ownership in the creation of the plan. These key informants should be involved in the planning process:

+ Admissions coordinator
+ Advertising coordinator
+ Assistant Event Leader
+ Audiovisual coordinator
+ Caterer
+ Decorator
+ Entertainment coordinator
+ Event coordinators
+ Event Leader
+ Exposition coordinator
+ Facility manager
+ Fire department
+ Food and beverage coordinator
+ Insurance coordinator
+ Legal advisor
+ Lighting, sound, and technical production coordinator
+ Logistics coordinator
+ Marketing coordinator
+ Medical coordinator
+ Municipal, state, and federal officials
+ Police/public safety
+ Public relations coordinator
+ Registration coordinator
+ Risk management coordinator
+ Safety coordinator
+ Security coordinator
+ Sponsorship coordinator
+ Transportation coordinator
+ Ushering coordinator/house manager
+ Volunteer coordinators
+ Weather and meteorological experts and officials

Planning to Plan

Tom Kaiser, author of *Mining Group Gold* (Irwin Professional Publishing, 1995), suggests that, prior to any meeting the participants should be assigned prework to prepare them to participate actively in the meeting. The scope and level of the prework is determined by the Event Leader based on the skills and responsibilities of the planning team members. The planning team members should, however, be prepared to contribute empirical information in addition to their opinions as a result of their preparation.

The planning process begins with the announcement of the planning meeting. This announcement should include a time and date for the meeting that is convenient for the planning team members. One of the most common mistakes is to schedule this meeting without consulting with the participants in advance. An effective planning meeting requires that the planning team members be fully committed to the process. This commitment requires advance approval of the date, time, location, and format. Another common mistake is not allowing sufficient time for the first meeting. Prior to scheduling the first meeting, you should assemble a small group of senior members of the team to actually plan the planning process. This planning to plan (or *preplanning*) is a critical part of the ESP process.

Most Event Leaders require several planning meetings to establish the final timeline and thorough event plan. During the preplanning meeting, you should reach consensus on how many planning meetings will be needed and when and where they should be scheduled. The location and length of the planning meeting will have a direct impact on the efficiency you achieve. It is important to locate a site for the meeting that is convenient for the participants yet free of distraction. It is also important to remind stakeholders that they will need to leave beepers, cell phones, and other personal distractions outside the meeting.

The length of the meeting will ultimately influence the productivity. The maxim "less is more" is appropriate for planning meetings. Limit meetings to 90 minutes maximum. If the meeting must last longer than 90 minutes, schedule frequent breaks. The agenda for the ESP meeting will guide the team toward their eventual goal: the production of a workable and sustainable plan. Therefore, the agenda should be developed during the preplanning process and distributed to the full team in advance of the first planning meeting. A typical agenda for the ESP meeting follows.

    I. Welcome and introduction of team members
   II. Review of goals and objectives of event
 III. Review of critical dates for event
 IV. Reports from team members from prework
   V. Discussion of event preproduction schedule
 VI. Consensus regarding event preproduction schedule
VII. Discussion of production schedule
VIII. Consensus regarding production schedule
 IX. Final review of plan to check for any illogical elements, gaps, oversights, or other
   X. Adjournment

Confirming Validity, Reliability, and Security

After the planning meeting or meetings are concluded, the Event Leader must make certain that the event plan is valid, reliable, and easily communicated to a wider group of stakeholders. Prior to distribution of the plan, make certain that your event plan passes the "grandmother test." Show the plan to those stakeholders who were not directly involved in the planning process. Ask these stakeholders pointed questions, such as: "Is this logical? What is missing? Does the plan support the goals and objectives of the event?"

Once the plan is validated and prior to distribution to a wider group of stakeholders, make certain that there are no security implications of this release. For example, if a very important person (VIP), such as a high-ranking elected official or celebrity, is included in the plan, you may wish to assign the individual a pseudonym or limit the distribution of the plan to preserve the security of your event.

Timeline

The tracks that your event train will travel to reach its successful destination are reflected in the instrument known as the *event timeline*. The event timeline literally reduces to writing the major decisions that will be included in the event from the beginning of research through the final tasks involved in evaluation. Often I am asked, "When does the event timeline begin?" After many years of experience and literally thousands of event experiences, I can state that it must begin with the first inquiry about the potential or prospective event. For example, the first telephone call from a prospective client researching your availability to manage an event or from an Event Leader who is researching information about your catering services may quickly lead to design, planning, coordination, and, finally, evaluation.

Therefore, I suggest that you begin the construction of the timeline when you first hear that unmistakable sound that telegraphs curiosity and enthusiasm or that twinkle in the eye that immediately and firmly announces that a potential spectacular is hiding just around the corner (from research and design). In fact, the only distance between you and the ultimate realization of the event may be a few hours, days, weeks, or months. To best control this period, it is essential that you construct a realistic time frame.

One reason that many events fail is due to an insufficient time frame to effectively research, design, plan, coordinate, and evaluate them. When time is not sufficient to research an event properly, you may end up paying more later, due to insufficient or incorrect information. When time is not sufficient to design an event, you may overlook some of the more creative elements that will provide you with the resources to make the event magical and, therefore, memorable.

Each Event Leader should construct a timeline that begins with the research phase and concludes with the evaluation phase. The timeline should cover each aspect and component of the event. It should include the start and ending times for each activity or task. It must be comprehensive and incorporate the individual timelines established by auxiliary organizations, such as vendors and government regulations. The Event Leader should carefully collect individual timelines from all vendors and other service providers. The timeline should detail the elements or components that appear in other people's timelines. This process of purging and merging the various timelines into one master production instrument is essential for communication between all parties.

Prior to distribution of the final copy, the Event Leader should seek consensus among all stakeholders before codifying the final results. The timeline must be acceptable to all stakeholders. One way to ensure the careful review and approval of each critical stakeholder is to require that they initial their acceptance on the final document. The final timeline should be distributed to all stakeholders as well as appropriate external officials (i.e., police, fire, media) to ensure timely service and provide effective damage control. By providing media and other external stakeholders with accurate information in a timely manner, you may avoid problems with innuendo and hearsay that cause erroneous reporting of your event planning process.

The way you depict your timeline ultimately will determine its effectiveness in communication to the broadest possible number of event stakeholders. Figure 3.11 shows a typical event timeline in summary form. Although the information in the figure is pre-

Phase	Task(s)	Participants in Event and Responsible Persons	Start Date and Time	End Date and Time
Research	Collect and analyze three years of event history or review comparable events	Key stakeholders and informants: Event Manager, financial manager, marketing manager, and volunteer coordinator	June 1, 9 A.M.	June 14, 5 P.M.
Design	Collect ideas from similar events; brainstorm with key informants and vendors	Event Manager, key informants, vendors, creative staff	June 15, 12 noon (luncheon)	June 16, 5 P.M.
Planning	Preplan planning meetings, announce/ schedule planning meeting, assign prework, facilitate planning meeting, develop timeline	Event Manager, key informants, critical stakeholders, key advisors	June 18, 9 A.M.	June 29, 5 P.M.
Coordination	Identify prospective vendors, contract vendors, develop final production schedule, implement production schedule	Event Manager, event coordinators, vendors, key external stakeholders	July 1, 9 A.M.	August 1, 5 P.M.
Evaluation	Prepare and distribute surveys, collect data, tabulate data, analyze data, prepare report of findings and recommendations, submit final report	Event Manager, evaluation team, client representative	Sept. 1, 9 A.M.	Sept. 30, 5 P.M.

Figure 3.11   Event Timeline Summary

sented in summary form, it demonstrates that the timeline must be a comprehensive instrument that provides a separate column for each task, list of participants, and start and end dates and time. For example, in the *evaluation* phase, only the quantitative survey evaluation is listed as the task to be performed. In fact, as you will discover later in the book, evaluation is a comprehensive process, and in this phase you will also evaluate factors ranging from finance to timing. Each of these factors will be listed on a separate task line with specific participants assigned to supervise this process.

The timeline provides the Event Leader and event stakeholders with a precise tool for managing the event. It is the comprehensive map that results from the event planning process. Just as with any map, there may be shortcuts; however, you must depict the entire map to ensure accuracy to provide the traveler with the best choices for gaining efficiency during the journey. The same may be said of the timeline. Once you have created this master planning document, in subsequent meetings you may adjust the timeline to gain speed and save time and money, ensuring that you will also ultimately reach your destination in order to achieve your goals and objectives.

The process of planning—from preplanning through the essential corrective planning during the coordination phase—forces the Event Leader and his or her team to logically assemble the best ideas to produce added value for the client. In addition, the planning process must result in a document or instrument that will guide and memorialize the journey of the stakeholders. From a legal standpoint, the timeline, organizational chart, and production schedule can be used to show illogical planning or, even worse, gaps in the planning process. As an expert witness in numerous trials involving negligence by event professionals, I often see attorneys use these three documents to prove that the Event Leader and his or her organization did not meet or adhere to the standard of care generally accepted in the modern profession of Event Leadership.

As the modern profession of Event Leadership transforms into the twenty-first-century global marketplace, Event Leaders must not only meet and exceed the standard of care that is generally accepted in developed countries but also use these instruments to begin to communicate a global standard for the worldwide event industry. Through standardized planning instruments and processes, Event Leadership will join other well-developed professions, such as medicine and engineering, in establishing protocols that will lead to better communication, increased safety, and higher-quality performance wherever Event Leaders research, design, plan, coordinate, and evaluate professional events.

Profile in Event Leadership:
Jay Downie, CFEE

FIRST IN FESTIVAL INNOVATION AND IMAGINATION

"Celebrations are not just food, drink and entertainment. There must be a sense of the greater experience level. It must result in planned serendipity," says event producer Jay Downie.

During his quarter of a century of transforming communities through events, Downie developed what he calls a celebration matrix. His passion for entertainment is the fuel behind his innovative events, such as the 2004 Grand Excursion, the top-rated MAIN ST. Arts Festival of Fort Worth, Texas, Tall Stacks and Sundance Square Parade of Lights.

As one of five children, Jay had to finance his college education through scholarships and odd jobs, such as performing as a tuba player at King's Dominion amusement park and as a euphonium player at Busch Gardens in Williamsburg. In time, however, the amusement park industry recognized Jay's leadership and management skills.

Taft Broadcasting, now Paramount Parks, which once owned King's Island amusement park, appointed Jay to a management position in the entertainment department, where Jay "was responsible for the care and feeding of 400 to 500 entertainers. I handled training,

Jay Downie, CFEE

quality control, performer relations and much more," says Jay.

Kings Productions, the creative arm of Paramount Parks, who has produced numerous live entertainment shows, later appointed Jay director of productions. In 1981, for an annual salary of $15,000 per year, Jay was responsible for conducting worldwide auditions for the company. He triumphed in this position because he believes that it "is important to do what you love and then get paid." At Kings Productions, he could do both.

Downie also believes that you must constantly explore to find the better path. He says, "In basketball you miss 100 percent of the shots you do not take." Therefore, he was constantly trying new approaches. "From private dates for AT&T to public performances," Jay worked hard at opening up new markets for Kings Productions.

In 1986, with only $2,800 in the bank as start-up capital, Downie began his own business. Through the many positive relationships he developed in the theme park industry, he began producing major events for prestigious clients, such as Avon and Procter & Gamble. In 1988 he produced the events for the Bicentennial of Cincinnati, Ohio.

To launch his new business, Jay "did lots of networking, going out door to door and visiting prospective clients. We joined the convention and visitors bureau and then had access to their list of conventions that were coming to our city." His access to advanced communication systems allowed him to contact event planners, who were bringing their conventions to his city. One of these clients was the American Legion Festival, an event that included 60,000 attendees.

Jay says that his on-the-job training during his years in the theme park industry enabled him to develop the imaginative and innovative environments for his events. He attributes his success to "taking the values of the theme park industry's fantasy environment. A festival becomes the celebration of a milestone. The event becomes the environment."

Downie's pioneering perseverance is exemplified in his work with rooftop pyrotechnic shows. He once designed a citywide pyrotechnic celebration for 2 million people in Cincinnati but was initially denied permission by local fire officials. To overcome their objections, he brought in the leading pyrotechnic safety officials to demonstrate he could safely manage this event. Ultimately, the local fire department granted their permission.

Another one of Jay's major achievements was the design and production of the Centennial Celebration of Fiesta San Antonio in San Antonio, Texas, an event in which over 1 million people participated. Once again, he turned to the Hemisphere Tower of San Antonio to safely create a spectacular pyrotechnic display.

Jay's most recent achievement was 2004's $8 million event called "Grand Excursion." The original Grand Excursion occurred in 1854, when the owners of the nation's major railroads wanted to celebrate their unprecedented expansion with a major event. However, with 20 full-time staff members, 1,500 volunteers, and over 1 million participants, the chief purpose of the 2004 Grand Excursion, according to Jay, was "community building." "For me," he says, "the hub of any event is its relevance. The event should cultivate and transmit a sense of pride and celebration. This is my core mantra. I do not want to do the *big* thing. I want to do the *relevant* thing."

Overall, Jay's family has perhaps made the most impact on his career. "Our personal celebrations always included selecting the Christmas tree, all of us decorating it the night before, Mom and Dad waking me up Christmas morning, and of course lots of photos being taken as we opened our gifts." In recent years, he has enjoyed reunions in Pennsylvania with over 300 family members in attendance. "I have always loved the accessibility of family, the warmth, the feeling of inclusiveness that occurs at these reunions. They make us feel as though we are part of the whole as we experience the things that connect us to our history and motivate our future actions."

Jay Downie's family celebrations have undoubtedly taught him the sense of unity among people and influenced the events he has produced for millions in both large and small communities throughout America. His innovations in entertainment development, event environmental design, and technological advancement, among many others, have helped dramatically transform traditional rituals and ceremonies into unforgettable modern celebrations.

Jay Downie: jaydownie@s1mc.com

CAREER-ADVANCEMENT CONNECTIONS

Global Connection

When planning events in countries outside North America, these considerations must be incorporated to ensure a smooth planning process:

+ Some countries and cultures have a more rigid planning framework. Ask experienced event organizers in the country where you are working to offer their insights as to the best way to organize and lead your planning team.
+ In many countries, Event Leaders hold the title of professional congress organizer (PCO). This person is usually responsible for multiple functions, including financing the event as well as marketing the overall program. When working with a PCO, determine in advance the range of his or her responsibilities regarding the planning phase. Some PCOs adhere to the requirements identified by the International Association of Professional Congress Organizers (IAPCO). For more information about IAPCO, visit its Web site at *www.iapco.org*.

Technology Connection

Although planning software is increasingly global in configuration, nuances in languages can lead to critical oversights and even errors. Therefore, it is important for you to appoint a local technology consultant to assist you with technology planning in the country where your event will be held. These suggestions will further expedite your technology connections in the global event marketplace:

+ Use the World Wide Web to research, confirm, and communicate inexpensively prior to your first site inspection. For more information about useful Web sites, see the Web directory lists in Appendix 3.
+ Make certain that your planning process includes a thorough review of the technological capability of the venue and destination where the event will be held. Not all phone systems are created equal. In many developing countries, you may have difficulty with sending and receiving large files due to bandwidth limitations. Consult with local technology experts to plan in advance to overcome these challenges.
+ The technological infrastructure of many event venues in countries outside North America is superior to systems in place in the United States and Canada. When planning the meeting site, keep in mind the critical importance of technology and select the site based on the technological capabilities to support your event.

◆ Plan to use technology to create a 24-hour, seven-day time band for your event. Your event can easily begin with online marketing and registration; this can lead to chat rooms prior to the event, and be followed after the event with new online chat rooms. Furthermore, you can create a password-protected site for people to log into your event when they cannot be there in person. You can also develop this site as an electronic commerce area and sell products, services, and access to information to create new revenue streams for your event budget.

 ## Resource Connection

To identify resources for the planning phase, remember these key points:

◆ Review the hundreds of comparable events described in the Wiley Event Management series of books to identify models that may assist you in your development.

◆ If you need models of comparable events, such as the complete planning guide for the National Football League Super Bowl or the Goodwill Games Opening Ceremony, visit The George Washington University Gelman Library Event Management and Marketing Archives (*www.gwu.edu/gelman*).

◆ If you use software to create a planning matrix like a PERT chart (*www.critical-tools.com*) or a GANTT chart, make certain that you select the model that will be easiest to communicate to each of your stakeholders.

◆ The Convention Industry Council (*www.conventionindustry.org*) through its Accepted Practices Exchange (APEX) provides 200 planning templates for meeting, convention, exhibition, and event-planning purposes in a software package called *APEX Meeting and Event Toolbox by Office Ready.*

 ## Learning Connection

Answer these questions and complete the activities.

1. Who are some of the key informants for your event, and why should they be included in the planning meeting?
2. What information should you send to the key informants prior to the first planning meeting?
3. How can you make certain that the planning meeting includes the input and consensus of all participants?
4. Write a memorandum to announce the first ESP meeting and assign prework to the participants.
5. Create a schedule for the planning process and show the linkages between the planning steps and the goals and objectives of the event.

The Mummers Parade in Philadelphia requires careful coordination of human resources and excellent time management.

CHAPTER 4

Event Leadership through Human Resource and Time Management

In This Chapter You Will Learn How To:

+ Identify leadership characteristics in an Event Leader and in yourself

+ Make critical decisions and act decisively

+ Solve problems

+ Overcome communication challenges

+ Improve human resource management

+ Recruit excellent staff and volunteers

+ Orient, train, inform, educate, motivate and inspire staff and volunteers

+ Create effective organizational charts

+ Develop policies, procedures, and practices

+ Improve time management

+ Benefit from diversifying your staff

Professional event management is truly a leadership process. Linda Higgison (1947–2007), former chair and chief executive officer (CEO) of the TCI Companies and curriculum designer for the Temple University Event Leadership Executive Certificate Program, describes the leadership process this way: "The global Event Leader must be a leader and he or she must wear many hats in various leadership roles. One role is the creator, another is the communicator, another is the visionary, and still another is the problem solver. The successful Event Leader must not only wear these hats and many more but must also become adept at continually changing hats (roles) to achieve the goals and objectives of the event." Higgison is correct in her assumption that the Event Leader must, indeed, play many roles. However, historically, management has been a command-and-control approach rather than a collaborative process. How much command and control should the Event Leader relinquish if he or she is to become an effective Event Leader?

Julia Rutherford Silvers, author of *Professional Event Coordination* (Wiley 2003), states: "Leadership requires trust, and trust depends on integrity, competence, and confidence. *Managers* analyze information, make inferences, and make decisions. They allocate resources to solve problems, assign tasks, and make schedules. Leaders influence and inspire others to achieve a goal. Leaders motivate. Leaders evaluate decisions, imagine consequences, and build contingencies."

Leadership Styles

When teaching, I often use a leadership exercise to dramatically convey the three different leadership styles found among Event Leaders. I divide the class into three groups and give each team a set of Popsicle sticks. I then instruct each group to construct an event site using the sticks. One group will do this using a democratic approach, the other with autocratic principles, and the third from a laissez-faire approach.

The *democratic group* arranges the Popsicle sticks easily and efficiently in a pleasing formation, and their conversations, discussions, and decision making flows smoothly. The arrangement of the sticks is a dramatic representation of the effectiveness of their process.

The *autocratic group* can barely decide how to place their Popsicle sticks, due to dissension and arguments regarding turf. This group is too busy battling among themselves to accomplish the goals required by the event.

The *laissez-faire group* constantly arranges and rearranges their Popsicle sticks, as without clear direction or facilitation they have trouble achieving consensus; their Popsicle sticks demonstrate this confusion.

Each of these Event Leadership styles has an important role to play in the Event Leadership process. Your ability to navigate among these styles and use the one that is appropriate at the right time is essential to achieving success.

Democratic Style

Typically, the democratic leadership style, which involves considering the thoughts of all members of a group and coming to a collaborative decision about how to proceed, is used during the early stages of the event process. It is an excellent approach for facilitating discussions, conducting focus groups, and building consensus as you assemble your stakeholders. It is also effective as you move from the design phase into the coordination phase. Before you can coordinate your team members' efforts, you must demonstrate that you are willing to listen and that you are able to function as a good facilitator. These two skills—listening and facilitation—are hallmarks of democratic Event Leadership.

Autocratic Style

When the fire marshal tells you to evacuate an event site, you should not use the democratic approach. The democratic Event Leadership style has one major drawback: It takes time to reach consensus. When an emergency evacuation is required, there is no time or any reason to try and reach consensus. Instead, you must use the autocratic approach and give the order to evacuate. Then you must supervise carefully to make certain that your instructions are being followed. The autocratic approach should be used sparingly. It is impossible, for example, to force volunteers and increasing staff members to do things they do not wish to do. Therefore, the autocratic approach should be used only when time is of the essence.

Laissez-faire Style

The laissez-faire approach of individuals working toward a common goal as opposed to a team working together toward a common goal is least used in event management because it requires a team whose members have skills that are equal in level; therefore, the Event Leader does not have to facilitate to ensure that goals are being achieved. It is rare that an event organization has a team with skills at a similar level. Most event organizations are comprised of many people with a variety of different skills and even commitment levels. Therefore, it is impossible for the Event Leader to sit back and let the group decide for itself how to proceed. Beware the laissez-faire Event Leader. He or she may be unskilled and trying to transfer his or her incompetence to the entire event team.

When you are faced with this scenario, move quickly to empower others on the team to assist this person with decision making to ensure that the event goals and objectives are being met. The most common way to reduce large amounts of complex information about an event to a manageable communications process is through published policies and procedures. All events of substance have such a document, and it helps drive the event's decision making.

Leadership Characteristics

Throughout ancient and modern human history, a number of people have been identified by historians as effective leaders. Some of these people became leaders due to a defining moment or event in their lives, while others sought leadership opportunities to cause positive change. In Figure 4.1, the general traits associated with effective leaders are

Traditional Leaders	Event Leaders
1. Communication skills	1. Integrity
2. Confidence	2. Confidence and persistence
3. Courage	3. Collaboration
4. Decision making	4. Problem solving
5. Enthusiasm	5. Communication skills
6. Integrity	6. Vision
7. Persistence	
8. Planning	
9. Problem solving	
10. Vision	

Figure 4.1   Leadership Characteristics

compared to those specialized characteristics that Higgison and Rutherford Silvers have identified within successful Event Leaders. Although some will argue with this list and ranking, I am firmly convinced, based on my observation of literally thousands of Event Leaders throughout the world, that the six characteristics listed in the right column of the figure generally define the qualities of the top Event Leadership leaders. These qualities or characteristics are ranked in this order for a specific purpose. It is important for Event Leaders to understand that not all leadership characteristics are equal; however, integrity is paramount. Integrity is the value that determines the external perception by others.

Integrity

The Event Leader must set the standard for integrity. If he or she does not exemplify integrity in performance and decision making, event stakeholders will soon lose faith and trust not only in the Event Leader but also in the event organization. For example, if an Event Leader reminds his or her staff that it is inappropriate to accept gifts from vendors and then is seen by subordinates receiving a substantial gift from a vendor, the credibility of the person as well as that of the organization may be shattered. The Event Leader who exhibits high integrity will not only refuse the gift but will effectively communicate to his or her colleagues that the gift has been refused and why it would be inappropriate to accept this gift. Figure 4.2 demonstrates perceptions of high and low integrity by event stakeholders.

Confidence and Persistence

When your back is against the wall, will you have the confidence and persistence to forge ahead? Typically, most events have a reality check where funds are low, morale is even lower, and impending disaster seems just around the corner. During these times of trial

Perception of High Integrity	Evidence	Perception of Low Integrity	Evidence
Consistency	Punctuality	Tardiness	Communications
Inclusiveness	Participation	Absenteeism	Intolerance
Participation	Consistency	Inconsistency	Participation
Tolerance	Inclusiveness	Exclusiveness/favoritism	Exclusiveness
Punctuality	Tolerance	Intolerance	Inconsistency

Figure 4.2 Integrity Quotient

and tribulation, all eyes will be on the Event Leader. Your ability to stay the course, maintain the original vision, and triumph is what is expected by your event stakeholders.

Let us suppose that you are responsible for acquiring sponsors for your event. Only a few weeks before the event, your biggest sponsor backs out. There is no time to replace the sponsor. In addition, the neighbors whose houses are near your event venue are starting to make rumblings in the media about noise, traffic, and other disruptions that they believe will result from your event. A traditional manager would collect all the necessary information and perhaps assign each problem to an appropriate subordinate after making a decision as to the best course of action. An Event Leader, however, will use these challenges as opportunities for the event organization to learn and grow. The Event Leader may ask members of the board as well as staff for recommendations on how to replace or at least mitigate the damage that could be caused by the missing sponsor. Furthermore, the Event Leader will meet with the neighbors or their association and work collaboratively with his or her staff to offer the assurances they need to provide new and long-term support for the event. Event Leaders use their confidence and persistence as teaching tools to influence other event stakeholders.

Event Leaders must work effectively with cross-functional teams. One definition of effective leadership is to occasionally look behind you and see if anyone is actually following you. A great leader must be supported by an even greater team. In 2006, when the Temple University Event Leadership Executive Certificate Program was selected by the International Festival and Events Association to receive the Haas & Wilkerson Gold Pinnacle Award for Best Certificate Program in Events Education, I immediately notified and acknowledged the team that achieved this success. However, despite camaraderie that may result from effective teams, challenges do occur and must be anticipated and addressed by the Event Leader.

Collaborative Decision Making

Since Frederick Winslow Taylor (1856–1915) Taylor created the management methods used to propel industrialized America, most management theory has focused on achieving efficiency to maximize profits. As workers began to organize into labor unions, they challenged this approach and sought an equal share in the decision-making process regarding not only the type of work they do but how they do it. Event organizations are not linear organizations like factories. Instead, they are pulsating organizations that may start with a small staff, swell to a large part-time and volunteer organization as an event grows near, and then rapidly deflate to the original small staff as the event winds down. This type of organization requires close collaboration between the Event Leaders and those who will actually deliver the services that provide the final perception of the event by the guests.

Collaborative organizations or quality teams have been used for the past three decades by numerous for-profit and not-for-profit organizations to achieve high quality and, consequently, better financial results. Event Leaders should always perceive their associates (permanent and part-time staff), volunteers, and others as collaborators who share a mutual goal of producing a successful event. Therefore, all decisions should be preceded by close collaboration among the stakeholders. However, there are also times when the Event Leader must lead by making timely decisions without consulting all affected stakeholders. For example, when the Event Leader is notified of an unsafe, illegal, or unethical activity taking place, he or she must intercede swiftly. Following the decision to act, the Event Leader must make certain that he or she has used this action as a teachable moment to explain why it is important. The Event Leader must notify the affected stakeholders that he or she has taken an action, then seek their input in case a similar decision has to be made in the future.

Problem Solving

A colleague of mine once said that she counted thousands of potential problems during the development of an event and, therefore, concluded that events consist of a series of problems whose solutions determine the level of success achieved by event stakeholders. I prefer to see a problem as a challenge that temporarily tests the skills of the Event Leader and his or her stakeholders. Few Event Leaders continue in the field unless they are comfortable with their ability to solve problems. Therefore, it is understood that Event Leaders who are experienced and trained possess the skills not only to analyze problems but also to provide a solution or solutions that will improve the outcome of the event. This five-step list provides a framework for Event Leaders to understand, analyze, and solve event problems:

1. Make certain that you thoroughly understand the size, scope, and time sensitivity of the problem.
2. Identify the key informants and stakeholders affected by the problem.
3. Determine if there is a model or comparable problem whose solution could be used for this problem.
4. Test the potential solution by seeking the collaborative input of those affected by the problem. If the problem is urgent and requires an immediate response, use a precedent or other model to frame your response.
5. Once a decision has been made, monitor the impact to determine if anything further must be done to mitigate future problems resulting from your decision.

Here is an example of how this model would work during an actual event. A prominent Texas university had a tradition of allowing students to construct a giant bonfire before the major football game of the year. This tradition stretched back several decades and had become a hallowed ritual/rite for students and alumni. Unfortunately, one year the bonfire materials collapsed, killing several students and critically injuring many others. University officials then had to decide whether to allow the bonfire to be rebuilt the following year. The framework just given may be applied to this problem to produce an outcome that can be accepted by a majority of stakeholders.

First, the president of the university and other administrators had to hold a thorough investigation to make certain that they had all the facts concerning the scope, size, and time sensitivity of the problem. Next, they had to make certain that their empirical information represented input from key stakeholders (those most seriously affected by the problem). Then they had to conduct further research to determine if there had been a similar problem and solution that may be used as a model for this incident. By researching academic journals, conducting interviews with administrators at other schools, and seeking anecdotal information from other institutions, the administrators can identify responses that may guide them to an appropriate solution.

The institution must first test the potential solutions with key informants and other critical stakeholders to make certain that their response is accurate, thorough, and appropriate. The input that will be received from other stakeholders will further refine not only the strategic solution but also the implementation tactics. Due to the gravity of this problem, university administrators decided immediately to cancel further bonfire structures for the next 12 months, pending an official investigation and analysis of the problem. This decision was made to prevent other groups, including off-campus organizations, from continuing the tradition.

Finally, the solution to the problem (canceling the bonfire for a period of years) must be monitored to determine if other challenges occur as a result of the solution. Indeed, as soon as the cancellation was announced, an off-campus alumni organization announced that it wanted to build a bonfire to continue the tradition. University administrators strongly discouraged this activity and promoted their concern to media to go on record opposing this activity.

Most event problems are not of the magnitude of the university bonfire tragedy. However, unless problems are solved efficiently and appropriately, they can easily escalate to a level that may threaten the reputation of the event. Once the reputation is injured or ruined, it may be difficult to sustain the future of the event. That is why it is critical that the Event Leader design and promote a carefully crafted internal communications strategy.

Communication Skills

Although communication is a critical component of the entire event process, it is also the single largest culprit when it comes to problems that may arise. How many times has a lack of communication or, more often, miscommunication resulted in a missed opportunity, an error, an oversight, or even a dangerous situation? Although an Event Leader need not be particularly articulate or even eloquent, he or she must be an excellent communicator. Communication is a continuous process that involves both sending (transmitting) and receiving information. This information may be verbal, written, or even abstract symbols, such as body language. The Event Leader must be able to receive and transmit complex information to multiple stakeholders throughout the event process. The glue that literally binds the various disparate components of the event plan together is the communications process. Therefore, the Event Leader must lead through excellent communications from research through evaluation. Following are the most common communications problems that may affect the planning process in Event Leadership and how to correct them:

✦ *Communication is not received by stakeholders:* Confirm receipt.
✦ *Communication is misunderstood by stakeholders:* Ask questions.
✦ *Communication is blocked among stakeholders:* Promote open communications.

Without open and continuous communication, event stakeholders cannot form the collaborative team needed to achieve common objectives. To promote open communications, the Event Leader must listen, analyze, and act. To listen effectively, an event manager must be intuitive, set specific criteria for the analysis of facts, and, when necessary, act quickly and decisively to unblock communications among stakeholders.

Julia Rutherford Silvers recognizes that coordinating events requires a complex set of skills, including effective communication. She states in *Professional Event Coordination* (Wiley, 2003), "Creating and producing events is an exhilarating and sometimes exhausting occupation, but it is always rewarding emotionally, spiritually, and often economically. The professional event coordinator must be flexible, energetic, well organized, detail-oriented, and a quick thinker. As a professional event coordinator you must understand the integrated processes, plans, and possibilities specific to each event you coordinate so that you will be a better planner, producer, purchaser, and partner in delivering the special event experience that exceeds expectations." One important communications strategy is the Event Leader's presentation of the vision of the event to his or her team.

Vision

The professional Event Leader must clearly demonstrate that he or she has a vision of the event's outcome. During early meetings with the stakeholders, the Event Leader must describe in a visual manner the outcome that will result from the event. For example, the Event Leader may state: "On the opening day thousands of guests will line up to buy tickets and, once inside, they will smile, participate, and have a good time, all due to your efforts." Furthermore, the Event Leader must "lead" the stakeholders toward that vision of the event by asking leading questions, such as "Can you see this happening? Are you prepared to help me make it happen? What will you do to help us achieve this goal?"

Achieving the goals and objectives of the event is the ultimate challenge for every event leader and his or her team. Six unique factors promote the rapid and complete achievement of your event goals.

Event Leadership Factors

These six leadership factors ultimately result in an Event Leader who has the skills, experience, and intuition to form the best judgment and act appropriately to advance the goals of the event organization. This is no small task. It requires continuous monitoring by stakeholders to ensure that the Event Leader is doing his or her best to lead the team. Event Leadership requires constant vigilance and continuing education to ensure that the power that is entrusted to the Event Leader is used wisely, judiciously, and thoughtfully.

Finally, it is important to note that Event Leadership is neither charisma nor control, the ability to command nor the talent to inspire. Rather, it is that rare commodity, like good taste, that one recognizes when one sees it. Every Event Leader should aspire to become the kind that others will not only recognize but will follow to see where he or she leads them. Ultimately, the best Event Leaders become ones whom other event stakeholders not only admire but also emulate as they seek to develop their own leadership potential. Through this admiration and emulation, these event stakeholders will soon become leaders themselves, producing even greater events in the twenty-first century.

Challenges of Teamwork

If you have ever served on a committee, marched in a band, sung in a choir, or played on a team, you know the challenges of developing successful teams. The most frequent challenges that Event Leaders face when developing teams are (1) communications, (2) self-interest, (3) dependability, (4) trust, and (5) collaboration.

Communications

Excellent event coordination is the result of continuous, consistent, high- quality communications between the event stakeholders. The Event Leader is responsible for developing and sustaining the event communications to ensure that all stakeholders are informed, in touch, and involved in each of the phases of managing the event. Several methods that you may use to establish and/or improve a high-quality communications network for your event follow.

- ✦ Conduct a communications audit and find out how your event stakeholders best send and receive information.
- ✦ Avoid communications that are blocked by noise, visual distraction, or other interference.
- ✦ Include an "Action Required" statement on all written communications to confirm that communications have been received and understood.
- ✦ Use nontraditional communications such as audio- and videotapes to increase impact, retention, and action.
- ✦ Use written change orders to record changes during your event. Make certain the client or other responsible person signs the change order to authorize the addition, deletion, or substitution of services or products.

Self-Interest

Many committees are comprised of people who essentially bring their personal views, biases, and agendas to the event planning process. It is the responsibility of the Event Leader to persuade each person to forgo personal interest for the sake of group interest. Only through a strong group effort can an event achieve a successful outcome. You may wish to invite an expert in team building or conduct team-building exercises yourself to develop trust, congeniality, and a common purpose among the team members. One way to begin this process is through an informal series of events such as social functions where the event stakeholders get to know, like, and trust one another before they sit down to deliberate (plan) an event. During this social period the Event Leader may observe the participants to begin to identify those who naturally work best in teams and those who will need more coaching or persuasion to feel comfortable working on a group project.

Dependability

One of the biggest management problems in working with volunteers is time and attendance. Because volunteers are not compensated for their efforts, many do not feel the obligation to arrive on time or even to show up at all. To compensate for the serious problem of attrition at events, many Event Leaders actually schedule between 25 and 50 percent more volunteers than will be needed.

The Sydney Organizing Committee for the Olympic Games (SOCOG) developed a unique passport system for the 60,000 volunteers who helped coordinate the 2000 Summer Olympic Games. Each volunteer was issued a personal passport and asked to have it stamped each day by his or her supervisor. When the passport was completely stamped, the volunteer would be entered in a drawing to win a wide range of valuable prizes.

Jason Quinn, a professional stage manager, states that most vendors do not want to be late when purveying an event. Therefore, for the first infraction he waits for a calm moment and asks, "What happened?" Later he may state: "Let me know if there is anything I can do to help you with your scheduling, because we are depending on you being on time to ensure a successful event."

Of course, the easiest way to ensure dependability is to recruit dependable people. Keep accurate records of time and attendance, and use the records to determine who to engage for future events. During the interviewing or recruiting process, check references carefully to make sure that your stakeholders have a pattern of punctuality that can be shared with your event.

In the Event Leadership profession, the correct definition of punctuality is "arrive early." Because of the numerous variables that can occur before, during, and after an event, it is essential that all event stakeholders arrive at an event site early enough to be able to spot potential challenges and overcome them before the guests or other vendors arrive. When interviewing potential event coordination staff, I often ask: "If the event setup time is at 8 A.M., what time do you believe is the best time for you to arrive at the venue?" Those who answer between 7 and 7:30 A.M. are most likely to receive final consideration for employment. This is because I have often arrived at an event venue to coordinate the setup only to find that it takes up to one hour to open the locked parking lot, contact security to gain entrance to the building, and locate engineering to turn on the lights in order to be ready for the vendors' arrival.

Trust

Trust must be earned by the Event Leader. Trust is the result of the Event Leader's sustained effort to develop an atmosphere and environment wherein the event stakeholders invest their trust in his or her behavior and judgments. Trust, in fact, is the net result of a pattern of positive behaviors exhibited by the Event Leader. When the Event Leader's behaviors are erratic or quixotic, the trust factor begins to diminish. To develop, establish, and sustain trust, the Event Leader must earn it and ask for it from his or her stakeholders.

Event stakeholders cannot blindly trust every Event Leader. Rather, they must use their best judgment to determine when and how to invest their trust. Trust should not be invested without question or careful analysis by the stakeholders. However, an event organization that is not firmly rooted in trust between the Event Leader and his or her stakeholders is one that is precarious and cannot achieve the level of success required to meet the expectations of all the stakeholders.

Collaboration

The final quality of effective event coordinators is the ability to develop close collaboration between all the stakeholders. This is extremely difficult, due to the disparity between the personalities, skills, and experiences of each stakeholder. Imagine a pre-event conference with all the stakeholders. You may have at the same table persons with a wide variety of formal education, an even wider range of skill and experience level, diverse ethnic backgrounds, and completely different technical abilities. How does the Event Leader inspire and encourage close collaboration between such a varied group of stakeholders? The key to collaboration is purpose. The Event Leader must clearly articulate the purpose of the event and convince each stakeholder that he or she must work with others to achieve or exceed the expectations of the guests. The distinguished anthropologist Margaret Mead once wrote: "Never doubt that a small group of thoughtful, committed citizens can change the world; indeed, it's the only thing that ever has." Your world or universe is the event you are responsible for managing. Therefore, you must firmly remind the stakeholders that self-interest must be left out of the event environment. The purpose of the event team is to cooperate and collaborate to achieve the goals and objectives of the event, and the Event Leader is the leader of this effort.

Human Resource Management

The Event Leadership industry is primarily a service industry. Therefore, its vital function often consists of intangible things such as customer service. You cannot touch it or smell it, but it exists, and moreover, it can make your events a disaster or a complete success. You are being paid for creating memorable positive experiences, and you and your staff are the critical resource that makes a guest's experience memorable. Issues such as your human resource organization, training, and employee retention are vital if you are to remain competitive. For example, most Event Leadership organizations offer similar services, but it is their people that makes the difference. Members of your association are not very likely to attend next year's convention if they had a bad experience this year, and without trained and experienced people, the event cannot succeed. That is why you should always remember that you and your colleagues are the most important asset of any Event Leadership organization. You are the locomotive that makes the Event Leadership train move forward. The human resources for your event represent the fuel that will drive the successful outcomes for your program. This fuel represents scarce resources that must be conserved and carefully deployed to achieve maximum benefit for your events organization. Southwest Airlines refers to their human resources department simply as the "people" department. And in fact, the event industry's most important resource is people.

The global human resource sector endured major changes during the past several years. With the rapid growth of the global economy, the employee turnover in many fields, including the Event Leadership field, increased tremendously. An average of five-year employee retention decreased to less than a year and a half per employee. This high turnover became a constant challenge to human resource and department managers. Under these circumstances, it is more important than ever to motivate your employees and offer various soft benefits in addition to monetary rewards. Benefits such as travel, employee meals, subsidized parking in big cities, employee-appreciation events, employee-performance awards, training, and company-paid memberships in industry associations are no longer a rarity. In many cases, you can encourage your employees greatly by creating growth and learning opportunities, supporting promotions, and creating valuable titles.

Celebrate Your Success

The effective Event Leader looks for opportunities to celebrate the individual and the success experienced by your organization. Is registration way ahead of last year? Break out the champagne! Mary confirmed that $10,000 sponsorship? Blow up the balloons and cut the cake that reads "Way to go, Mary!" Your team has won an award for your recent event? Celebrate with dinner and dancing for the entire team. Your team will readily recognize that every good deed can be rewarded if you take the time to notice and mark the occasion.

You may wish to appoint one person from your organization as the internal event specialist in charge of these celebrations so that you can readily delegate these tasks and be assured that each one is handled by a capable person. Too often, event employees are like the shoemakers' children in that their managers plan wonderful events for others but scrimp on their own behalf. Your internal events should be models for all external events, and your team should feel proud not only to be part of your celebration but to have made a positive contribution to the event. This is especially true of volunteers who work long hours for no financial remuneration.

Diversify Your Staff

It is extremely important to diversify staff to better represent your guests as well as to provide new, creative viewpoints to develop your events. This will help the Event Leadership profession to grow and develop successfully. Currently, female representation in the profession is much higher than male. However, this may change in the future to better represent parity between men and women. More minorities in the United States will also join the exciting field of Event Leadership and bring their magnificent ethnic ceremonial traditions from African, Asian, Hispanic, and other cultures. The fusion of diverse cultures can weave a beautiful and strong tapestry to best display the potential of global Event Leadership.

One excellent suggestion for promoting diversity within organizations was offered by Judith McHale, president of Discovery Communications. In cases where managers are slow to recognize the importance of promoting women and others who are underrepresented in management, McHale recommends that *diversity goals* be made part of their bonus package. "That, at the end of the day, has a pretty positive impact," suggests McHale (*Washington Post,* March 18, 2001).

Volunteer Coordination

Volunteers are the lifeblood of many events. Without volunteers, these events would cease to exist. In fact, the vast majority of events are entirely volunteer driven. The profile of the volunteer has changed dramatically during the past three decades, and it is important that the Event Leader recognize this change.

The emergence of the two-income family has resulted in the fact that half of the volunteer force in the United States (women) is no longer available to work as full-time volunteers. Furthermore, since many people have more than one job and must carefully balance school, children's activities, and other commitments with their volunteer responsibilities, it is increasingly difficult to attract volunteers to assist with events.

According to the Institute for Volunteer Research (*www.ivr.org.uk*), although there are more volunteers than ever before, there is a net deficit in the number of volunteer hours due to the time pressures that all workers are facing today. Therefore, Event Leaders must be highly creative and persistent when recruiting, training, and rewarding their future volunteer resources.

Effectively recruiting, training, coordinating, and rewarding volunteers is a vital part of many Event Leadership operations. Although challenging, the recommendations that follow will help you streamline this critical function.

Julia Rutherford Silvers, CSEP, in *Professional Event Coordination* (Wiley, 2003), describes how using "reverse scheduling" assists Event Leaders with realistic scheduling of human resources. According to Rutherford Silvers, "When estimating the time required for each task defined, you must consider all constraints, assumptions, capabilities, historical information, and mandatory dependencies (the tasks that must be completed before another task can begin)."

■ Recruitment

Many Event Leaders are now turning to corporate America to recruit legions of volunteers for their events. First, the corporation is asked to serve as an event sponsor, and as part of its sponsorship, the corporation may provide key executives to give advice and counsel or a team of 100 or more volunteers to manage the beverage booths, games, or other aspects of the event. A good source for volunteer leadership through corporations is the office of public affairs, public relations, or human resources. Toni McMahon, former executive director of the Arts Council of Fairfax County and producer of the International Children's Festival, goes right to the top. "I start with the chief executive officer. If I can get this person to buy into the event, others will surely follow," McMahon says. Her track record speaks for itself, with literally dozens of major corporations providing hundreds of volunteers for this annual event.

Other sources for volunteers are civic and fraternal organizations. Part of the mission of these organizations is community service, so they will be receptive to your needs. A related organization is that of schools, both public and private. In many school districts across the United States, high school students are required to complete a minimum number of community service hours in order to graduate. And do not overlook colleges and universities. Many institutions of higher learning have dozens of student organizations that also have a service mission and may be willing to participate in your event.

The key to attracting these groups is the WIFM ("What's in it for me?") principle. When you contact these organizations, learn a little bit about their needs and then use the objectives of your event to help them fulfill their needs. The service aspect is a natural. Ron Thomas, CEO of the Tennessee Walking Horse National Celebration, coordinates dozens of community organizations, such as the Kiwanis, who provide concessions for his events. Their activity is the major fund-raising aspect of the organization each year. They know exactly what's in it for them: cash. This cash enables them to do good work all year long. Determine what's in it for them and you will quickly find volunteers standing in line to help your event succeed.

■ Training

All volunteers must be trained. This training need not be time-consuming, but it must be comprehensive. One way to reduce the amount of time required is to publish a handbook for volunteers that summarizes event policies and procedures. Training may take the form of a social gathering, such as an orientation, or it can be formalized instruction in the field at the actual event site. It does not matter how you deliver this training, as every group of volunteers will require a different method in order to help them learn. However, what is important is that you test for mastery to make certain that they are learning and applying the skills you are imparting. Testing for mastery can be done through a written exam, observation, or a combination of both.

■ Coordination

The on-site management of volunteers entails coordinating their job performance to ensure that you are accomplishing the goals of the events. Depending on the skill level of the volunteers, you must assign team leaders or supervisors in sufficient number to oversee their performance. Remember that the coordination of volunteers involves coaching and mentoring. Make certain that your team leaders or supervisors are skilled in these areas.

■ Rewarding Excellent, High-Quality Performance

Don't wait until the end of the event to say "thank you." Some organizations publish volunteer newsletters; others host holiday parties to thank the volunteers for their help during the annual summer festival. Giving volunteers early, frequent, and constant recognition is a critical component in developing a strong and loyal volunteer team. You may wish to create an annual contest for Volunteer of the Year or some such recognition to encourage good-natured competition among your team members. Make certain that you carefully research with your volunteers how to effectively recognize and reward their service to the event.

Contract Temporary Employees

You may incorporate cost-efficient human resource management with cost control by contracting temporary employees for peak seasons. This will allow you to keep in place only those employees whom you need all year long. This will also help you to retain your permanent staff longer, since you will be in a better position to extend your resources to a smaller number of permanent staff. The biggest downside of this strategy is the challenge of attracting qualified personnel for short-term assignments. You can minimize the risk of having to deal with unprofessional behavior by hiring hospitality and event students from your local colleges and universities or by establishing long-term trusting relationships with a specialized staffing agency. Your collaboration with local schools can be based on offering shorter- and longer-term professional internships. Such programs can also be helpful for screening your potential future employees.

One of the scarcest resources within any event organization is time. In fact, some event leaders describe their time as their only real resource. Therefore, it is important that every event leader become a master of time management.

Time Management

Your return on your event investment is in direct proportion to your ability to manage your time efficiently and meet various deadlines. This is so important that it bears further explanation. If you have only 8 hours to produce an event that normally requires 12 or more hours, you can either lose money or make money by how you plan and use the available time. For example, you may ask yourself what resources can be consolidated, what meetings combined, and what tasks delegated to allow you to remain focused on your 8-hour deadline. You can hire extra labor, purchase additional resources, schedule more meetings, and try to handle all the details yourself. The choice is yours.

These principles of time management are first applied in your daily life. How you spend your time performing everyday activities directly influences how you achieve your goals during your Event Leadership career. The ability to manage your time does not decrease as the number of assignments and tasks that you are involved in increases. The opposite is true. The busier you get and the more things you have planned, the more efficient you are in your time management and the more projects you manage to complete. It simply proves the famous Parkinson rule, which states that "a task can be accomplished within the amount of time assigned for its accomplishment"; getting a time extension on a project would normally push back the time of its accomplishment. Although in many situations this rule is true, you should, however, be careful and not overestimate your capacity. Always remember that it is better to underpromise event expectations and overdeliver final event perceptions.

Organizational Chart

Although not all Event Leadership organizations have their organizational charts in document form, all organizations have an internal structure that determines important things such as promotion and growth, and simply regulates everyday operations. Even if you have never seen an organizational chart, you know to whom you report, who reports to you, and at what level of responsibility and authority you are at a certain point in time. However, it is important to be able to evaluate organizational charts from the employer and employee standpoints. Figure 4.3 represents a typical "flat" organizational structure with little opportunity for growth and significant power in two managers' hands. Although these structures exist, it is important to realize that employee retention under this structure is likely to be low, since most people would like to see a potential for growth and promotion within their organization. If they do not find it, they will soon start looking for other opportunities elsewhere. The few managers in such organizations share high power and probably will keep their positions for a lengthy time period. However, if for some reason the organization structure cannot be changed, you can develop loyalty in your employees by creating incentive programs, improving the work environment, and increasing compensation. Figure 4.4 represents a more dynamic and complex organizational structure that offers its employees better growth potential, higher titles, and more focused work assignments. In this kind of organization, you can offer your employees cross-training opportunities that will add to their professional growth. You can clearly see identifiable departments, which will make it easier to form teams.

Less frequently, you can find other types of organization structures (see Figures 4.5 and 4.6). For example, some organizations have one subordinate reporting to three supervisors. This kind of situation rarely works out successfully and often leads to frustration

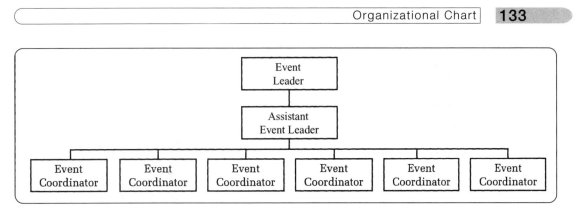

Figure 4.3 Flat Traditional Organizational Structure

for both employee and manager. Many small event organizations run into difficulties when they hire very few people to complete a vast variety of tasks due to limited financial resources. If the relationship is built on trust and mutual cooperation, such alliances can be beneficial for either party for a limited period of time. However, when the company gains more business, the situation needs to be changed. If an employee is overscheduled with work and is not physically able to complete it due to the lack of help, this employee will probably quit and look for another job. You have to remember that valuing your employees, investing in their development, and building their loyalty will be more finan-

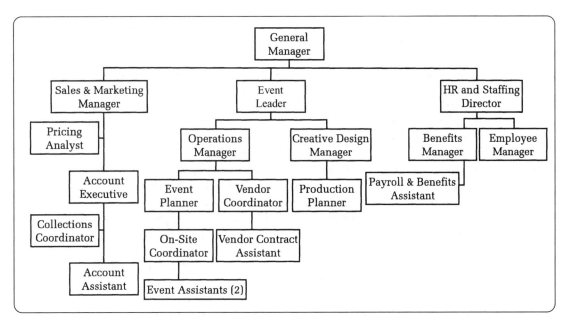

Figure 4.4 Dynamic Organizational Structure

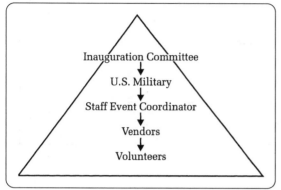

Figure 4.5 Top-Down Organization

Figure 4.6 Bottom-Up Organization

cially rewarding to you in the long run than saving money on employee incentives and generating extra costs for recruiting and training.

Developing Policies, Procedures, and Practices

The best organizational chart will not completely communicate to your stakeholders the precise actions they should take in specific situations before, during, and following the event. This is why it is important that you carefully develop policies, procedures, and practices that reflect the culture of your event organization.

Everyone benefits from well-written policies and procedures. First, the internal stakeholders benefit from having a clear process through which to make decisions. Second, the external stakeholders benefit from using a tool to help them understand the organization and the decision-making process of the event team. Finally, the guests themselves benefit. Although they may never see a copy of the policies and procedures, in the event of a life-threatening emergency, thanks to this document, lives may be saved.

This document is used in a variety of ways. It may be given to all full-time staff and volunteers as a reference tool. It may be distributed to members of the board of directors to guide the development of future policies. Most important, it may be used by the Event Leader to implement the board's policies through carefully developed procedures.

Policies are conceived and approved by the sponsoring organization's trustees. Typically, the trustees are the owners of the event, such as a private businessperson, a corporate board of directors, or the trustees of a not-for-profit group. The policies that are developed and approved reflect the vision and mission of the organization as well as comply with local, state, provincial, and federal laws.

Procedures are the implementation tactics for policy. Policy may be broad, overarching rules of conduct, whereas procedures are the regulations that administrators or Event Leaders use to implement policy. Both policies and procedures are essential to produce and sustain successful events.

Many events have well-crafted policies and procedures that can serve as a model for an organization. Contact another event organization of similar size and scope, and ask it to share a copy of its policies and procedures. In addition, ask the company how it most effectively communicates these policies and procedures to its stakeholders.

Carefully review your vision and mission statement, and use your event strategic plan as a litmus test for every policy and procedure you create. Appoint experts in a variety of event fields, including volunteer coordination, risk management, sponsorship, and others to help you review and create the final draft of your policies and procedures.

Convene a focus group comprised of typical event stakeholders to make certain that what you have written can be implemented easily and effectively. Next, survey a wider group to sample their opinions. This group should include external stakeholders, such as government, police, fire, and other officials.

Make certain that your policies and procedures are fully in compliance with local, state, provincial, and federal laws. Retain an attorney to review your document to ensure compliance. Your document may be beautifully written, but unless it is in full compliance with all laws, it will be of no value.

Finally, regularly evaluate and revise your policies and procedures. Laws change, events mature, and other changes require that your policies, procedures, and practices document be revisited annually to look for gaps and provide updates to close these gaps. One example of this is the massive revisions that were required after the implementation of the Americans with Disabilities Act. A typical event policy and procedure can be outlined as follows:

I. Media conferences. Media conferences will be held prior to the annual event and at other times as required. (Policy)
   A. The Event Manager will schedule the media conference with staff. (Procedure)
      1. The public relations coordinator will implement the media conference. (Practice)
   B. Participants will include but not be limited to credentialed members of the media, members of the board of trustees, and invited guests.
      1. The public relations coordinator will issue these credentials.
   C. The chair of the board of trustees will serve as the official spokesperson for the event organization at all media conferences. In the absence of the chair, the Event Leader will serve in this position.
      1. The official spokesperson will prepare in advance a copy of his or her written remarks and distribute it for comment to the board.
      2. An audio recording will be made of each media conference.
      3. The public relations coordinator will be responsible for recording the media conference and providing a written transcription.

Event leaders are only as effective as the teams that support them. By creating a culture of professionalism, quality, and yes, fun, you will not only educate and inform but even occasionally inspire your event team to exceed the expectations of their guests. Two examples of successful Event Leaders who have led their teams to continually exceed expectations and positively transform their organizations at the same time follow.

Profile in Event Leadership: Josh McCall

HOW HELPING OTHERS ADVANCED AN INDUSTRY

In the early 1960s, when the McCall family moved to Greenwich, Connecticut, to find the best school for Josh's older brother, Chris, a career path began to form. The primary components of this path were the values that Josh's parents and later mentors instilled in him through their actions.

Chris has Down syndrome and now successfully lives in a group home in Idaho. When he was a child, Josh knew that Chris had special needs, which provided a unique opportunity for his family to help him continue to grow and develop as a human being.

Josh McCall, Chairman
Jack Morton Worldwide

While attending the University of Pennsylvania and majoring in sociology and anthropology, Josh had a strong interest in advertising. He would spend many of his free hours in the library thumbing through copies of *Advertising Age* to research the latest advertising trends.

When Josh graduated from Penn in the spring of 1982, he, like many college students, was ready to embrace the world, but due to a challenging economic downturn, he received no job offers. Fortunately, a good friend who was a senior executive at the advertising agency Ogilvy and Mather told him about a firm called Cablevision Systems Corporation. This firm offered direct selling experience, and Josh was hired as a door-to-door salesman.

He spent many months going door to door to thousands of homes in the Metropolitan New York suburbs of Connecticut's Fairfield County. After leaving a leaflet at prospects' front door, Josh would then follow up to convert them to become cable subscribers. "This is where I first recognized the importance of my sociology degree from Penn." According to Josh, the demographics of his potential customers often predicted their buying habits.

He also quickly realized that "If I didn't sell, I didn't eat." Josh traces the ambition required to sustain his enthusiasm, while visiting thousands of strangers to sell what at the time was a new and unknown service, back to his great-grandfather, Joseph B. McCall. Mr. McCall was the son of immigrants from Scotland, and he became the chief executive officer (CEO) of the Philadelphia Electric Company.

Josh's path to the CEO position at Jack Morton Worldwide took a dramatic turn one evening when he was selling cable television in Greenwich, Connecticut. One of his prospects was Bill Morton, who was then the president of Jack Morton Productions. Morton, the son of founder Jack Morton, told Josh that he was interested in bringing young, motivated people to work with him, and on January 2, 1984, Josh began his now-long career at Jack Morton.

In the early days, Morton and McCall commuted to work together for many months. Josh says that this time "provided us a rare opportunity to get to know one another, talk about opportunities and challenges, role play scenarios, talk about proposals in progress, and develop a true friendship."

During his 20 years with the firm, Josh prepared himself for future leadership by gaining extensive broad experience in business development, client services, recruiting staff, and analysis of compensation and acquisition programs. One of his final preparations for leading the firm occurred in 2001, when his business experienced the "perfect storm." "We needed to recalibrate our business after the shocks of September 11, 2001, and the general downturn in the global economy. These were tough decisions that had to be made in order for the business not only to survive but also to move forward and grow."

When he was appointed CEO, he became only the third individual, and first nonfamily member, to hold this position in the 67-year-history of this venerable firm. As he looks to the future, Josh states: "The ongoing challenge will be the recruitment, training, and mentoring of staff to ensure that we maintain a position of leadership as an organization. We also need to maintain our relevancy and deliver on our brand promise to meet or exceed our clients' expectations."

Most industry insiders know Jack Morton Worldwide as producers of the spectacular opening and closing ceremonies of the 2004 Summer Olympic Games. One columnist who wrote about the televised ceremonies seen by over 1 billion people around the world said, "They were the most memorable ceremonies in human history." In addition to the Olympic Games, the firm has produced the Commonwealth Games in Manchester, Great Britain, and Melbourne, Australia. Its corporate projects include companies on the Fortune 100 list as well as international television broadcasters. Jack Morton Worldwide designs and fabricates the television scenery seen by millions for productions such as NBC's *Today Show* and the 2004 NBC television election set at Democracy (Rockefeller) Plaza in New York City.

One of the most important future challenges for the firm will be its ability to measure the effectiveness of experiential marketing. "I sincerely believe we can prove that we can measure this marketing service more effectively than the way we traditionally measure advertising's effectiveness. The interaction of face-to-face communication provides marketers with highly meaningful data," Josh explains.

According to Josh, "In the old days, we measured advertising and marketing in terms of awareness and recall of brand image and messages. Now, in the age of experiential marketing, the foundation of our success is consumer engagement with the product or service."

Josh McCall's improbable career path was, in fact, highly possible. By learning about and listening to elders, learning from the values of mentors, helping others, and gaining intense direct selling experience, he has forged a career unlike any other in the modern events industry.

McCall remembers that whenever the founder of his firm, Jack Morton (1910–2004), received a compliment, he would often respond by saying "I had lots of help." Morton always generously gave the credit to others who had helped him succeed. Josh's career demonstrates that, similar to his company's founder, the late Jack Morton, asking for help and then helping others is an important career advancement strategy.

As the CEO of the world's largest and most successful experiential marketing firm, Josh McCall emulates these values in his day-to-day interactions with associates and customers. Of course, he had a good foundation as he traveled up this amazing career path. It began with a great-grandfather, father, and a brother who faced every challenge with hard work, dignity, and grace. And it continues today with Josh, as he incorporates, builds on, and transmits these important values to others. Through his leadership, he is helping to positively transform and advance the global event and experiential marketing industry.

Josh McCall: josh_mccall@jackmorton.com

Profile in Event Leadership:
Sheila Graham, CSEP

HELPING PEOPLE BY MARKING A MAJOR MILESTONE

In 2006 the American Red Cross commemorated 125 years of service since being founded by Clara Barton in 1881. Today, in communities throughout the United States, the American Red Cross relies on nearly 1 million volunteers, 35,000 employees, and more than 800 chapters to respond to over 70,000 disasters each year. This humanitarian organization mobilizes people to provide aid and comfort to millions across the nation each year. The long and proud history of this respected organization certainly merits a major celebration, and the person who was in charge of the Anniversary Gala commemorating 125 years was veteran event producer, Sheila Graham, CSEP.

Sheila Graham, CSEP
(Captain, U.S. Navy, retired)
American Red Cross

A graduate of the U.S. Navy's Officer Candidate School, Sheila served as a public affairs specialist for six Navy admirals and was responsible for media relations, employee communications, and community events and programs. She coordinated countless Navy events that included color guards, bands, aircraft fly-overs, and ship open houses.

Her expertise in ceremonial precedent and protocol was developed during her Navy career and has been put to good use in all her positions. In 1998 she retired from the Navy as a captain and transitioned to the public sector, becoming the communications director and public spokesperson for the City of Falls Church, Virginia. During this period, she enrolled and graduated with honors from the George Washington University Event Management Certificate Program. She also became active in the International Special Events Society, serving as a committee member, director, and vice president of the Washington, DC, chapter. Through this broader exposure to the events industry, she resolved, "In my next career, what I really want to do is produce corporate and nonprofit events."

She had just that opportunity when she joined Hayes & Associates, a prominent special events and public relations firm in the DC area that produces corporate, nonprofit, and government events and meetings. As the senior account executive, she managed National Race for the Cure events, the Girl Scouts' ninetieth anniversary gala, a presidential inaugural ball, and other events with more than 1,000 attendees. Shortly after joining Hayes & Associates, she earned her Certified Special Events Professional (CSEP) designation from the International Special Events Society.

Her success in managing large events led to her 2002 promotion to vice president of events and creative resources for the national headquarters of the American Red Cross, where she was in charge of events and meetings, national conventions, a museum, and creative resources.

In this position, she was able to blend her personal and professional experiences together to successfully achieve the complex requirements of these events and meetings.

As she prepared to help the American Red Cross celebrate 125 years of their history, she realized this as a rare opportunity to communicate to supporters and the public the important role and mission the Red Cross plays in responding to disasters. Prior to the gala, Sheila organized several cultivation events for benefit, leadership, and honorary committee members to encourage their involvement in accomplishing this commemoration. "The gala, with a focus on 'Then, Now, & Always,' will include historical videos that reflect our history, celebrity performers and donors that support us now, and volunteers and employees who make it possible for us to carry out our humanitarian mission today and always," said Sheila as she enthusiastically described the gala.

"We want to honor all these 'stakeholders' who support us daily—from our volunteers and employees to our Celebrity Cabinet, corporations, and community and government partners who help us serve those in need. The ceremonial part of the gala honored all those who serve—from Clara Barton to the thousands of people and organizations across the U.S. who have responded to devastating hurricanes. In addition, the gala honored corporate partners and included a Humanitarian of the Year award."

This gala was staged in the round from a stage shaped like a Red Cross as a way to be more inclusive and to place as many stakeholders as possible closer to the excitement of celebrating the traditions and history of the American Red Cross as they mark the milestone of their 125th anniversary.

Sheila Graham's passion for celebration extends seamlessly into her personal life. Her family's floral business gave her an early introduction to the celebrations industry. In addition, Sheila was born on her grandmother's birthday, so this day was annually a dual celebration. Her long career with the U.S. Navy influenced her strong devotion to protocol and precedent, the value of rituals, and the importance of quality events achieved through attention to detail.

Sheila and her husband, Steve Epstein, love to celebrate rituals with family and friends, including birthdays, anniversaries, Halloween, and an annual white elephant party gift exchange. They annually lead their neighborhood in organizing a festive celebration commemorating America's Independence Day.

Her career has been positively influenced by many outstanding mentors. "There have been so many people who helped me and I believe in giving back. I always urge people interested in entering the special events profession to find a mentor as a way to gain connections and to volunteer with organizations, such as ISES, to gain valuable experience," she says.

From the proud traditions of the U.S. Navy to the remarkable achievements as now-executive producer in the external events office of the American Red Cross, Captain Sheila Graham (U.S. Navy, Retired) has effectively utilized her experience, training, and skills to advance in every organization where she has been a member. The key to her successful career is her commitment to continuous professional development as an event professional. "You must continue to learn and improve throughout your career," she explains. "The ultimate reward I've had, and I hope others have, is the rare opportunity to stand at center stage with dedicated and important individuals, saluting an organization whose unique mission it is to provide relief to disaster victims and to prepare for and respond to emergencies."

Sheila Graham: grahams@usa.redcross.org

Career-Advancement Connections

Global Connection

Appoint people from different cultural and ethnic backgrounds who will contribute to the success of your event. You can learn more about other national traditions and how to incorporate them into your theme by researching the Center for Popular Culture at Bowling Green State University (*www.bgsu.edu/departments/popc/center .html*). However, diversity also presents potential challenges, and you should encourage training, orientation, and other employee assistance to support mutual respect and understanding.

Technology Connection

+ As technology becomes more affordable, one of the growing trends is to use tele- and videoconferencing for group projects and team-building activities. In many cases, this helps to save money on travel expenses and improve productivity. One excellent (and free) online resource for this form of communications is Skype (*www.skype.com*).
+ Use the Internet to improve communications among all stakeholders through real-time online conversations.
+ Maintain the vision of your event by designing a Web site for your event staff and volunteers that is password-protected.
+ Provide your staff and volunteers with a downloadable screen saver of your event logo to remind them constantly of the mission, vision, goals, and objectives that you share as an event organization.

Resource Connection

+ Use the Microsoft Organization Chart to practice constructing a top-down or bottom-up event organization chart.
+ Visit the American Society for Training and Development (ASTD) Web site (*www.astd.org*) for additional resources.

Learning Connection

+ Draft an organizational chart of your event organization or another event organization with which you are familiar. Evaluate this chart from a long-term perspective, and answer these four questions:
  1. Based on this chart, what are the educational, promotional, and growth opportunities for employees?
  2. How can this chart be modified to increase employee retention?

3. What kind of cross-training programs can be incorporated in the organization to make employees more valuable and at the same time create additional learning opportunities for them?

4. Based on the chart, what teams can be formed within the organization?

✦ Improve your personal leadership skills by training and actual practice offered through organizations such as the International Special Events Society (*www.ises.com*), Meeting Professionals International (*www.mpiweb.org*), and Professional Convention Management Association (*www.pcma.org*).

✦ Complete these activities to advance your growth in the area of Event Leadership:

1. What are the five most important qualities of twenty-first-century Event Leadership leaders?

2. How do these qualities differ from those in other fields, such as politics, education, and others?

3. What are the best methods for improving communications among event stakeholders?

4. Use Microsoft Word organizational chart to construct an organizational chart for your event. What is the "best fit" for the Event Leader within the organizational chart?

5. Analyze and discuss this case study by incorporating the principles included in this chapter. A small event organization has an annual music festival, and each year for the past five years the number of volunteers has decreased. This decrease can be attributed to a perception by potential volunteers that the organization is too exclusive and does not really value new ideas and opinions. How will you increase the number of volunteers for the next festival without seriously jeopardizing the relationship that you have with other volunteers who have been with the organization for many years?

6. Write a one-page description of the type of leader you believe your staff and volunteers perceive you to be, and then describe the type of leader you can become with proper training and practice (experience).

The Mardi Gras in New Orleans produces millions of dollars of economic impact and raises the spirits of the local citizens and tourists in the post–Hurricane Katrina city.

CHAPTER 5

Financial Administration

In This Chapter You Will Learn How To:

✦ Understand basic Event Leadership financial and accounting terminology

✦ Maintain event financial records

✦ Understand and interpret the event balance sheet and income statement

✦ Calculate the break-even point and profit margin for your event

✦ Forecast projected revenues and expenses for your event

✦ Estimate reliable budget goals for your event

✦ Plan and allocate your event budget

The most common deficiency I have identified in all Event Leaders relates to the area of financial management. Event Leaders by nature rely on the right side of the brain and often ignore the important logical thinking abilities that help ensure long-term success. Whether you use the services of a professional bookkeeper and/or accountant or not, knowledge of financial management is essential to the practice of modern Event Leadership. This knowledge is not difficult to master. With modern software systems, it is actually simple and, many say, fun to practice. Whether you enjoy financial management is not the issue. Few people enjoy studying for and taking their driver's license exams. However, can you imagine what the streets would be like without this baseline of knowledge? Accidents, death, and destruction everywhere might result from this lack of rigor. Financial ignorance can just as easily wreck a creative, successful Event Leadership business and destroy one's reputation as well as have serious legal ramifications. This chapter is essential if you are planning not only to make money but to keep it as well. Additionally, as your business ages along with you, this chapter will help you learn how to work a little less and earn a little more.

Budgeting

The budget represents an action plan that each successful Event Leader must carefully develop. Budget preparation is probably the most challenging part of financial management since the entire preparation is usually based on limited information or assumptions. To complete the budget preparation, you should come up with estimates based on assumptions.

The event budget is the most important tool you will use to manage the financial decisions within your Event Leadership business. Each event represents a separate budget. All individual budgets are combined into an annual budget. Your daily business operations also require an annual budget to reflect your earnings and expenses. Event Leaders should use the expression "staying within the budget" every day and for every project.

Each budget represents the financial philosophy of the event. Since different events are designed for different purposes, they may fall into one of three categories:

1. *Profit-oriented events.* In this type of event, revenue exceeds expenses. Typical examples are events produced by corporations for the purpose of generating new sales.
2. *Break-even events.* In this type of event, revenue is equal to expense. A good example is an association conference. In this case, event professionals should budget the event, keeping the break-even assumption in mind. Admission fees should be calculated at the rate that will cover all expenses and break even.
3. *Loss leaders or hosted events.* These events are designed from the very beginning to lose money. Good examples of such events are university graduations or governmental celebrations. These events usually are organized for the purpose of promoting a cause or agenda and not designed to break even or generate a profit.

If your event is a charitable endeavor, your financial philosophy will be markedly different from that of a commercial venture. First, determine what is the financial philosophy of your event before you begin the budget process. A budget represents the income and expenses of your organization or the individual event. An event budget is based on five factors:

1. Marketing projections and estimates
2. The general history of previous identical or similar events
3. The general economy and your forecast for the future
4. The net profit or excess you reasonably believe you can expect with the resources available (return on investment)
5. The type of financing that you choose to use to finance your event (borrowed funds, prepayments, existing funds)

Financial History

The best financial history is that which occurs over a three-year period. In some cases, it is not possible to construct a precise history, and the Event Leader must rely on estimates or on what is known at the time the budget is prepared. In still other cases, the Event Leader will have to rely on events of similar size and scope to develop the budget because his or her event is a first-time venture and no history exists. Not only is it important to base your budget on history, it is equally important that you develop controls to begin collecting financial data on the event budget you are currently preparing. These data will become the next event's historic information and help you construct a better budget.

The longer you are in the Event Leadership industry, the more accurate your estimates will be. A good technique used for developing income projections is *high–low*. The logic is that an Event Leader compares two scenarios: the best and the worst. Next, the Event Leader decides whether the losses that may occur under the worst-case scenario are bearable and, if so, accepts the projects. If not, the project is refused. This method is especially beneficial to small and mid-size Event Leadership businesses that operate under financial constraints and do not have much margin for error.

General Economy

The economy is chaotic, unpredictable, and, some economists would add, a disaster waiting to happen. You, however, must not be a victim of these predictions; instead, you must use general economic data to assist you with the development of your budget. Reams of secondary data are available about the local, state, and national economy from offices of economic development as well as the U.S. Department of Commerce. No event takes place in a vacuum. Whether you are managing the International Special Olympics in New Haven, Connecticut, or the local food and wine festival, your event's success will be affected by the general economy. Indicators of strong economic health usually include low unemployment, a steady rate of inflation, and healthy retail sales. Other indicators include new home building activity, new industry, and capital investments by local, state, or federal government. Before locking in your final budget, consult with an economist from a local college or university, a representative from the local office of economic development, or the editor of the business section of your local newspaper and ask for his or her opinion on the health of the economy.

Reasonable Projected Income

The Greek word *logos* (or logic) means to "act reasonably." A budget based on certain logical assumptions of projections of income is one that is within reason. To logically project revenue based on the resources available, you must consider market research as well as a general knowledge of the economy. For example, if your city festival is being held this year on the local payday from the area's largest industry, does that mean you can reasonably expect that spending will be increased for your event? The only way to test this theory is with research. You may wish to contact other events of similar size and scope and evaluate their experience with similar circumstances. Furthermore, you may wish to survey some of the workers to determine if they are more likely to attend the event this year and, if so, if they will be inclined to increase their spending due to the coincidence of their payday and the event date. Making reasonable assumptions about projected revenue is one of the most important decisions that you must handle as you begin the budgeting process. Gather all the facts, seek objective opinions and counsel, and then conservatively project the revenue you hope to achieve.

Typical Income Categories

Due to the wide range of events represented by the subfields within the Event Leadership profession, it is difficult to list categorically every type of income. However, there are some general items that most budgets include:

- ✦ Advertising revenues
- ✦ Concession sales
- ✦ Donations
- ✦ Exhibit or exposition booth rental fees
- ✦ Gifts in kind (actual fair market financial value)
- ✦ Grants and contracts
- ✦ Interest income from investments
- ✦ Merchandise sales
- ✦ Registration fees
- ✦ Special events ticket sales
- ✦ Sponsorship fees
- ✦ Vendor commissions (hotels)

Expenses

When preparing your budget, the first thing you will note under the expense category is how many more items are listed as compared to income. My late father-in-law, a successful businessman, once told me, "The income comes in through one or two doors, but the expenses can leak out of many doors." In the strange economic times of the mid-1990s, organizations placed greater emphasis on monitoring expenses because it was easier to control costs than to project revenue. My father-in-law also reminded me that Benjamin Franklin observed some 200 years ago, "A penny saved is a penny earned." Developing solid, predictable expense categories is critical to sound financial management. These expense items often come from historical data or comparing your event to others of similar size and scope. The actual amount budgeted for each expense line item is what you and your advisors believe to be reasonable based on the information known at the time the budget is prepared. Therefore, the more you know, the more precisely you can budget for expenses. This is another reason why record keeping is so vital to the success of your financial management operations. The general expense categories for most events are:

- Accounting
- Advertising
- Advertising specialties
- Audiovisual equipment rental
- Audiovisual labor
- Automobile mileage reimbursements
- Automobile rental
- Awards and recognition
- Brochure and other collateral design
- Brochure and other collateral mailing
- Brochure and other collateral mechanical preparation
- Brochure and other collateral printing
- Complimentary registrations or admission
- Consultants
- Décor
- Entertainment
- Evaluations
- Food and beverage
- Gratuities
- Guest transportation
- Insurance
- Legal counsel
- Licenses
- Lighting equipment rental
- Lighting labor
- Local, state, provincial, and federal taxes
- Materials shipping/freight fees
- Miscellaneous or other
- Percentage of administrative overhead
- Permits
- Photocopying
- Photography
- Postage
- Proceedings editing, design, and printing
- Public relations
- Registration contract labor
- Registration materials
- Report preparation and publishing

- Research
- Risk management corrections
- Signs
- Site office furniture rental
- Site office supplies
- Site rental
- Site telephone expense
- Sound equipment rental
- Sound labor
- Speakers' fees and/or honoraria
- Speakers' travel
- Staff travel
- Videography
- Volunteer appreciation activities and gifts

Structuring Account Codes

Each income or expense item must have a corresponding account code. Accounts are those general budget categories where items of similar type and impact on the overall budget are grouped together for more efficient analysis. For example, in the administration category, these items would appear:

- Décor
- Insurance
- Site telephone expenses

Under the account category "staff/volunteers," these items would be grouped together:

- Staff accommodations
- Volunteer accommodations
- Volunteer appreciation activities and gifts

Each account code has a numerical listing to make it easy to find individual entries. The general categories start with the 100 series. For example, administration would be 100, marketing would be 500, and so on. Each item would have a separate sequential numerical listing:

100 Administrative
500 Marketing
501 Advertising
502 Advertising specialties
503 Brochure and other collateral design
504 Brochure and other collateral mechanical preparation
505 Brochure and other collateral mailing
506 Brochure and other collateral printing
507 Public relations

Finding and Supervising an Accountant

Contact your local chamber of commerce to obtain a referral for an accountant who may be familiar with event budgets or service businesses. Once you have prepared a draft budget, seek the counsel of the accountant to review your budget and help you with establishing the various line items and account codes. Your accountant will be able to interpret the tax codes for you to make certain that your accounts match the terms and requirements for the local, state, provincial, and federal tax authorities.

Make certain that you discuss billing and fees with your accountant. You may retain the accountant to handle specific operations or to coordinate all of your financial procedures. Obviously, the cost will fluctuate greatly based on the number of tasks you ask the accountant to perform. Using accounting software may help you reduce your costs and provide you with better, faster information.

Accounting Software

Since the invention of the spreadsheet program for computers, accounting has never been the same. Commercial software packages such as Quicken have allowed small-business owners to record their journal entries quickly, accurately, and cost-effectively. What once required many hours with a pencil and eraser has, thanks to modern computer science, been reduced to a fraction of the time. Microsoft Excel is also very useful in budgeting and creating financial projections. I encourage you to spend some time familiarizing yourself at least with basic functions of this software.

Although using commercial software is time-efficient, it does require certain additional safeguards. First, make certain you always back up your data on a disc and store this information in a safe, fireproof location. Next, regularly send a copy of your data to your accountant so that he or she can prepare your monthly, quarterly, and annual financial reports. The first step should be to consult with your certified professional accountant to determine the best type of software to invest in because, to a large extent, you will be partners, and you should be using software that will allow you to communicate effectively on a regular basis.

Producing Profit

The financial purpose of every for-profit business is to produce a fair net profit. The term *profit* means the earnings over and above all expenses.

$$\text{profit} = \text{revenue} - \text{expenses}$$

Not-for-profit organizations do not, for obvious reasons, use the term *profit*. Instead, they refer to this excess of income over expenses as *retained earnings*. In fact, the earnings are not retained for long, as the organizations are required by the tax code to reinvest the earnings in their business operations rather than distribute them to shareholders as some for-profit businesses do.

Producing a fair net profit is both challenging and possible for Event Leadership businesses. The challenge is that Event Leaders must work with a wide range of clients, and it is difficult to budget for each event carefully to ensure a net profit. There are too many variables to ensure that this happens every time. However, if the business is to remain healthy at year-end, the business activities must result in a net profit.

Although there is no average for net profit, let us consider, for the purposes of discussion, that your financial goal is to achieve an annual net profit of 15 percent. To do this, you must guard all fixed overhead expenses carefully. All expenses can be divided into two major categories: (1) fixed overhead expenses and (2) variable expenses. Although both of these categories are expenses, the methods you use to manage and control them are different. To understand how you can minimize your expenses, you should be able to make a distinction between these two categories.

Fixed Overhead Expenses

Fixed overhead expenses of an organization are those predictable items such as rent, salaries, insurance, telephone, and other standard operating expenses required to support the Event Leadership business. The better you are able to achieve a lower cost of sale, the greater net profit you will achieve. To lower your cost of operations, it is imperative that you try to reduce your fixed overhead expenses. Many Event Leadership firms have suffered great losses or have even gone out of business entirely because they tried to expand too rapidly. Expansion brings increased cost of sales, and increased cost of sales means that you must produce much greater income. As we discussed earlier, due to the volatility of the world economy, this is not always possible. Once you have cut your fixed overhead expenses to a level that allows you to maintain quality but at the same time produce a fair net profit, you must return your attention to *variable,* or *direct, expenses.*

Fixed expenses of an individual event do not depend on the number of participants. For example, rent is a fixed expense. Rent expense usually does not vary when the number of participants increases or decreases slightly. The expense of live music is similar. If an Event Leader contracts a local band to entertain guests, the cost of this entertainment is fixed. Variable costs are the costs that depend on the attendance (e.g., food and beverages). Food and beverage expenses for 100 people will be approximately twice as large as if only 50 people attend the event.

This example will help you to understand the difference. The Event Leader of a mid-size corporation has to budget expenses for a reception. He or she is not sure about the exact number of guests; however, the minimum and the maximum number of guests are known. The minimum number is 200 guests and the maximum is 400. The catering company has provided the Event Leader with its price quote of $25 per person for food and $15 per person for beverages. The Event Leader creates the expense calculation shown in Figure 5.1.

Variable Expenses

Variable expenses are more difficult to predict because often they relate to items that are purchased at the last minute from vendors, and the prices may fluctuate. Variable, or

Number of people	200	400	
Food $25 per person	$5,000	$10,000	} Variable
Beverages $15 per person	3,000	6,000	} expenses
Rent expense	2,000	2,000	} Fixed
Entertainment expense	1,000	1,000	} expenses
Total expenses	$11,000	$19,000	

Figure 5.1   Fixed and Variable Expenses

direct, expenses include audiovisual rentals and labor, registration materials, proceedings design and printing, and other items with a total cost that relies on the final number ordered and your ability to negotiate a fair price. Due to last-minute registrations and an increase in walk-up guests for a variety of events, it is extremely difficult to wait until the last minute to order certain items. Printing, as well as advance notice for audiovisual equipment rental and labor, requires a sufficient window of time to deliver a quality product. This means that your ability to use historical data to project the volume of items you will need or to order less with an option to obtain additional supplies rapidly will greatly help you reduce your variable or direct expenses. In addition, your ability to negotiate the best deal for your event organization will have tremendous impact on these items.

Net Profit versus Gross Profit

Event Leaders endeavor to produce a fair net profit. The difference between net profit and gross profit is the percentage of fixed overhead expenses that was dedicated to producing a specific event. Fixed overhead expenses dedicated to the individual event include a percentage of staff salaries and benefits, a percentage of the office expense, and other shared expenses. This percentage will fluctuate, but by using time sheets you can easily calculate the staff time directed to the event. The other expenses, such as rent, insurance, and telephone, may be given a percentage based on the time recorded from the time sheets.

Break-even Point

To understand the break-even calculation, you have to understand one more term: *contributional margin,* the difference between the revenue received from a single person and the variable costs incurred for one person. For example, if an Event Leadership company receives revenue of $50 per person but the total variable cost for one person is $40 ($25 food and $15 beverages), the contributional margin is $10 per person:

contributional margin = revenue per person—variable costs per person

The final step to calculate the break-even point is to divide the total fixed costs by the contributional margin:

	Loss	Break-even	Profit
Number of people	290	300	310
Revenue:			
$50 per person	$14,500	$15,000	$15,500
Expenses:			
Variable expenses:			
Food $25 per person	7,250	7,500	7,750
Beverages $15 per person	4,350	4,500	4,650
Fixed expenses:			
Rent expense	2,000	2,000	2,000
Entertainment expense	1,000	1,000	1,000
Total expenses:	$14,600	$15,000	$15,400
Profit (revenue − expenses)	$(100)	$—	$100

Figure 5.2 Break-even Analysis

$$\text{break-even point} = \frac{\text{total fixed costs}}{\text{contributional margin}}$$

For example, if the total fixed costs are $3,000 and the contributional margin is $10, the break-even point is 300 people:

$$300 = \frac{\$3,000}{\$10}$$

or

$$300 \times \$50 = \$15,000$$

If fewer than 300 people attend the event, it loses money. It turns profitable once the attendance exceeds 300 people. Therefore, the break-even point is achieved when you collect $15,000 in revenue. Figure 5.2 demonstrates the break-even analysis.

Cutting Costs

As an Event Leader, your ability to cut costs rapidly to ensure consistent profits is one that will serve you well throughout your career. To decide which costs may be cut without sacrificing the integrity of the entire event, you must begin with the budgeting process by prioritizing expenses. Seek counsel from your stakeholders and honestly determine what, in the worst-case scenario, if certain items must be cut from the budget, they would like to preserve and which should go to ensure a profit. Although this is a difficult decision process, it is wise to make such decisions free from internal and external pressures during the final phases of the Event Leadership process. Typically, these costs are associated with variable or direct expenses. Therefore, the expenditure is not made until later in the Event Leadership process. Cutting your event's costs is one way to help improve your cash flow.

Ensuring Positive Event Cash Flow

It is not enough to just have profitable operations. Many Event Leadership companies were unsuccessful because they were always out of cash. These companies showed profit on their books but had an empty checking account. This situation is called *insolvency*. The best way to avoid insolvency is to execute sound cash-flow management.

Cash flow is the liquidity that allows you to pay your bills, including salaries, in a timely manner. When this liquidity is gone, your reputation may not be far behind. To ensure a positive event cash flow, two measures are necessary. First, you must prearrange with your vendors payment terms and conditions that will allow you to collect revenues adequate to honor these obligations. Second, you must diligently collect those funds that are due and payable to you in a timely manner in order to meet your obligations to your vendors.

Payables are those financial accounts that you have established with vendors. These are funds that are due according to the agreements you have arranged with individual vendors. *Receivables* are those funds due to your event organization by a certain date. *Aging receivables* are simply those funds that were not collected at the time they were due. Five simple techniques for collecting Event Leadership receivables follow.

1. Log on your calendar the day the receivable is due.
2. Telephone early in the morning to ask when your payment will be processed.
3. If possible, arrange to pick it up.
4. If it is not possible to pick it up, offer to provide an overnight mail service.
5. Courteously but firmly request payment until it is received.

One of the challenges with the value of Event Leadership services is that there is often rapid depreciation as soon as the curtain rises. Consider this scenario. Your client has invested $50,000 with your firm to produce a gala awards dinner. Midway through the dinner, the client's spouse notices a cigarette burn in the tablecloth. Later, he or she comments on "skimpy" floral arrangements. Finally, he or she complains loudly about the inferior music and food. Before long, the client locates you and wants to discuss the bill. Ironically, only three hours earlier, the client walked through the ballroom and told you effusively how beautiful everything looked. Buyers of Event Leadership services and products are not usually experts in your profession. That is why they have retained you. Because the purchase of Event Leadership services and products is sometimes an emotional decision, the buyer may easily be influenced by others. *The only leverage you have as the professional provider of these services is to collect your full fee as soon as possible, because otherwise the value of your performance will deflate rapidly.* As in medicine and other established professions, the old maxim "people only value what they pay for" is absolutely true in this profession.

Effective management of accounts receivable is only half of the equation needed for solid cash flow. The second half requires that you become knowledgeable about typical accounts-payable agreements and learn to negotiate for the best possible payment terms. The best policy is to collect cash as fast as possible but pay off your bills on the last day allowed by the contract.

Accounts Payable: Finding the Best Terms

When establishing relationships with vendors, it is important that you learn as much as possible about the size, scope, and nature of their business. You will want to know if they own or lease their equipment. You will also want to know when they may have periods of slow business. Their off-season can produce favorable terms and perhaps discounts for your event. You will also want to know if a vendor could benefit from exposure through your event. Some Event Leaders have a stringent rule about not letting vendors promote themselves directly to their clients. However, it is my belief that these hard-and-fast rules may prevent you from providing your client with the products and services your vendor may be able to offer. In one example, a video production company telephoned me after a major corporate event and asked permission to contact the corporate headquarters to provide services directly. Not only did I encourage the company to do so, I wrote letters to my client and others on the company's behalf. As a result of this courtesy and flexibility, this firm will work with me on price in the future for other clients whom I may serve. Therefore, beware the dangerous word *always,* as it may cause you to provide less service than possible.

The key to negotiating excellent terms with vendors is first to establish professional friendships and conduct business in an atmosphere of mutual respect. The more you know about your professional partners (vendors) and the more they know about you, the easier it is to do business. There are typical accounts-payable customs and traditions in the Event Leadership profession; however, your ability to make friends and provide assistance to your vendors will alter these customs to your benefit.

Typical Accounts-Payable Customs

One accounts-payable custom is for the vendor to require a deposit of 50 percent of the final contracted cost as a deposit and receive the full balance plus any additional agreed-upon charges immediately following the event. Entertainment vendors, especially those representing major celebrities, are even more stringent. They may require full payment in the form of a certified check prior to the first performance as a guarantee.

Another accounts-payable custom is for the vendor to require a small deposit (as low as 10 percent) and then invoice you for the balance due net 10 or 30 days after the event.

Still another custom allows you to pay your balance on account. In this custom, typically you are a regular good customer of the vendor, and the company allows you to pay off the balance monthly or within a reasonable amount of time without interest, late charges, or other penalties. Sometimes vendors even provide small discounts if you pay off your balance faster than required. There is a special terminology for this situation. For example, if a vendor offers you a 3 percent discount if you pay off your balance within the first 10 days, you may hear this formula: "3/10, net 30." This means that if you pay off the balance within 10 days, you receive 3 percent off your total bill; otherwise, you have to pay the entire balance within the next 30 days.

The final custom is for the vendor to extend credit to your organization, allowing you to authorize purchases and be invoiced by the vendor at a later date. This is the best scenario, as you are able to negotiate credit terms well in advance. Although most accounts are due within 30 days of the date of the invoice, I have heard of some arrangements where the vendor will extend credit for 60 or even 90 days to maintain the account. It is up to you to negotiate the best possible terms.

Negotiating Accounts Payable

Always negotiate from a position of strength. Strength in the area of accounts payable means that you have collected as much information as possible about the vendor with whom you need to negotiate. The answers to six questions will enable you to negotiate favorable terms for your accounts payable:

1. How important is your business to this vendor?
2. During what time period is your business most needed?
3. Are your clients the types of organizations your vendor would like to do business with? How well funded/capitalized is your vendor?
4. How does your vendor market his or her services and products? How sophisticated are your vendor's business operations?
5. What are your vendor's standard and customary accounts-payable terms?
6. Most important, can you speak with other clients of this vendor to determine what types of terms they are receiving?

Once you have the answers to these questions, it is time to ask your vendor for more favorable terms. To do this, you will need to provide your vendor with documentation about your own business health. Testimonials from recent clients, a list of accounts receivable, and other financial data will also help you create a favorable impression. Once you have established your credibility with the vendor, ask for the most favorable terms. You might ask for credit and 90 days. The vendor may counter with 30 days, and you then agree on 60 days. Do not play hardball. Remember, this vendor will be servicing your clients, and maintaining their goodwill is of supreme importance. However, you have a responsibility to your event organization to negotiate the most favorable terms and must remain firm in your pursuit of what you believe to be a fair agreement.

Your vendor may ask for a trial period, after which he or she may extend better terms once you have demonstrated your ability to meet your obligations consistently and provide the benefits your vendor expects. I cannot emphasize enough how important your relationships with your vendors are in the full spectrum of your event operations.

Controlling Purchases

The most common device for approving purchases is the *purchase order* (PO). No purchase should be authorized without an approved purchase order. This form specifies the product or service approved for purchase, the number of units, the price per unit, and the total amount due, including taxes and deliveries. The type of shipping and date and time of arrival should also be clearly specified. The PO should also state the payment terms. Instruct all your vendors by letter that you will be responsible only for purchases preceded by a valid purchase order. Include this statement on each purchase order: *"Vendor may not substitute or alter this order without the written permission of the purchaser."* This statement helps you avoid the creative vendor who is out of red tablecloths and believes that you will accept blue instead at the same price.

Finally, the purchase order must have a signature line that grants approval and the date of the approval. The PO is the most important tool you have to control your purchases and, therefore, monitor those numerous doors where expenses leak and potentially drain your event economic engine. Since your PO is a very important financial document that can hold you or your company liable, it is important to ensure a safe procedure for issuing and approving all purchase orders. All your vendors should be informed as to who in your company is authorized to sign purchase orders. A PO signed by the authorized person should be mailed to a vendor at the beginning of the transaction. This PO procedure is very important, and it can help save you money when you compose the final invoice.

Common Event Financial Challenges and Solutions

The Event Leadership profession is a business. As in other businesses, there are common problems and solutions. When Event Leadership business owners assemble for annual meetings and conferences, they can be heard discussing many of the same challenges year after year. As one wag said, "The problems don't change, the solutions only become more difficult." Perhaps by reviewing the examples that follow you will be able to anticipate some of these challenges and thereby take measures to avoid them entirely.

+ **Challenge:** Negotiating employees' salaries and benefits.
  Solution: Collect information from the Event Solutions Black Book (*www.event-solutions.com*), Salaries.com (*www.salaries.com*), or from firms in similar market areas. Use this information to determine a market basket figure from which you can negotiate up or down based on the potential value of the employee to your firm.
+ **Challenge:** Proper compensation for Event Leadership salespeople.
  Solution: Three methods are customary. First and most prevalent is the *draw against commission*. This approach requires that you provide the salesperson with a

small stipend until his or her commissions have equaled this amount. After he or she has equaled the amount of the draw, the stipend stops and the salesperson receives only sales commissions. The second approach is *straight commission.* In this case, usually the salesperson has existing accounts and is earning commissions immediately. Typical commissions range from 3 to 7 percent of the gross sale. Therefore, a salesperson who produces $500,000 in gross revenue will earn $35,000. The final custom is to offer the salesperson a *salary plus bonuses* based on sales productivity. This bonus is typically awarded after the salesperson reaches a certain threshold in sales, such as $1 million. A typical bonus is 1 or 2 percent of sales. A salesperson earning a salary of $50,000 could earn an additional $20,000 based on a 2 percent bonus on $1 million in sales.

Straight salary as compensation is the least desirable because it provides no financial incentive, and salespeople typically are driven by financial incentives. Whatever arrangement you agree on, do not change it for one year. You will need one year of financial data on which to base your review and future course of action.

✦ **Challenge:** Client is slow to pay balance of account.

   Solution: Inquire how you can help expedite payment. Can you pick up the check? Is there a problem, and could the client pay the largest portion now and the rest later? Are other vendors being paid? Does the client have a history of slow payment? What leverage do you have? Can you suspend services until the balance is paid or payment on account is made? Can you speak with one of the owners or principals and solve this problem? Can you find a creative solution, such as the one that Andy Stefanovich of Opus Event Marketing, Richmond, Virginia, found? Andy had his dog send a collection notice, complete with begging for food and a paw print.

✦ **Challenge:** Out of cash.

   Solution: With prudent management of accounts payable and receivable, this problem should not occur. Assuming that a business emergency has caused this unfortunate situation, you must contact vendors immediately and notify them of your intent to pay. Then notify all past-due accounts receivable and accelerate collection. Reduce or stop spending with regard to fixed overhead. Next, contact your lenders to access a line of credit based on your receivables until you have sufficient cash to meet your expenses.

✦ **Challenge:** Vendor promotes himself or herself to your client directly.

   Solution: Do you have written policies and procedures outlining what is and what is not permissible by your vendors? Realistically, how will their promotion injure your business? Can you negotiate with your vendor to receive a commission from any future sales to this client since you were the first contact?

✦ **Challenge:** Employee is terminated, starts own business, and takes your clients.

   Solution: Does the employment agreement forbid this practice? Assuming that it does, you can have your attorney send a cease-and-desist letter. This rarely helps because clients have no constraints on whom they do business with. Either way you lose. Instead, suggest to the former employee that he or she may wish to provide you with a commission on the first sale he or she makes with your former client, as a courtesy for providing the first introduction. This way you can release the client and also receive some compensation for your effort in first identifying the account. If former employees refuse to provide you with a commission, chances are that their bad business ethics will eventually alienate them from enough industry colleagues that it will limit the amount of sales that they are able to achieve and reduce significantly the level of services they receive from vendors suspicious of their behavior.

These common challenges and typical solutions should serve as a guide or framework to guide your decision making. Although most of the solutions in modern business still rely on common sense, I have noticed that there is nothing as uncommon in today's business environment as common sense. You will want to test each of these solutions with your business advisors (attorney, accountant, mentor) before implementing it to make certain that it addresses your particular problem and provides the most logical solution. There is no such thing as a general solution for a specific problem. All business problems are specific in nature, and you must seek a solution that addresses your precise problem.

Foreign Exchange Rates

It is important in this global world that you understand exchange rates, their fluctuations, and the differences that international exposure brings to your financial operations. Remember that although large international Event Leadership companies depend greatly on global changes that occur regularly in various countries, mid-size and small Event Leadership companies are also affected by these changes. Event Leadership today is a global economic enterprise. Food and beverages that you purchase in the United States or elsewhere are often produced outside of the country in which they are sold. Payments that your organization makes or receives from overseas can be conducted in either local or foreign currency.

The *foreign exchange rate* is the price of one currency expressed in another currency. For example, DKK 6.79/1 USD means that for 1 U.S. dollar (USD), the market requires 6.79 DKK (Danish krona); USD 0.1472/DKK means that for 1 Danish krona, the market requires 14.72 U.S. cents. The currency exchange rates change every day, sometimes even several times per day. Changes are usually not significant for small and mid-size businesses and affect mainly large banks and investment companies. Exchange rates generally are affected by market conditions and government policy and also by national disasters (especially for small countries).

Market Conditions

The general rule is that currencies of countries with strong economies are in greater demand than currency of countries with weak economies. If the economy of country A is getting stronger and stronger but the economy of country B is getting weaker and weaker, the exchange rate between the currencies of these countries will favor the currency of country A.

Government Policy

The currency of countries with strong governments that have predictable policies is always preferred over the currencies of countries whose governments have unpredictable policies. Even during the close 2000 U.S. presidential election between George W. Bush and Al Gore, the U.S. dollar exchange rate was not greatly affected because the United States is known for its predictable domestic and foreign policy. Major financial newspapers, such as the *Financial Times* and *Wall Street Journal,* contain daily information about currency exchange rates and projections. You should monitor journals to forecast the economic conditions in countries where you will be doing business.

Changes in exchange rates affect all companies. Large businesses are affected directly; small businesses are affected indirectly. In one example, a large Event Leadership company based in the United States signs a contract with a U.K.-based corporation to produce a large event in London. The U.S. Event Leadership company is paid in pounds sterling. The total cost of the contract is £400,000. The contract is signed on June 1 and the event is to be held on December 21. The contract says that the U.K. company must make a 50 percent advance payment in June with the balance payable on the day of the event. On June 1, the exchange rate between the U.S. dollar and the British pound is USD 1.658£. If the exchange rate between the pound and the dollar stays unchanged until December 21, the income statement of the event would appear as shown in Figure 5.3. Note that since the Event Leadership company is U.S.-based, all expenses that it incurs are in U.S. dollars and total $500,000.

The gross profit is calculated to be $163,000. This represents a 25 percent profit margin ($163,000/$663,200). Obviously, the project looks very attractive. The question is how attractive the project would be if the exchange rate were to change by December 20. Suppose that, due to the strong economy in the United States, you predict that the U.S. dollar will appreciate (its value will increase). Now suppose that the exchange rate in December will be $1.5£. Figure 5.4 shows how this change could dramatically reduce your margin of profit. Due to the exchange rate change in December, £200,000 will be worth only $300,000 but total expenses are still $500,000 (since they occurred in U.S. dollars). Therefore, the gross profit dropped to $131,000 and the profit margin dropped to 20 percent.

The more expensive the U.S. dollar becomes, the less profit the U.S. organization makes from its overseas events that are paid in foreign currency. This means that the U.S.

	U.K. Pound	U.S. Dollar
Revenue		
50% advance on June 10	£200,000.00	$331,600.00
50% payment on December 20	200,000.00	331,600.00
Total	400,000.00	663,200.00
Total expenses	n/a	(500,000.00)
Gross profit	n/a	$163,200.00

Figure 5.3 Income Statement: No Exchange Rate Fluctuation

	U.K. Pound	U.S. Dollar
Revenue		
50% advance on June 10	£200,000.00	$331,600.00
50% payment on December 20	200,000.00	300,000.00
Total	400,000.00	631,600.00
Total expenses	n/a	(500,000.00)
Gross profit	n/a	$131,600.00

Figure 5.4   Income Statement: With Exchange Rate Fluctuation

organization can purchase fewer dollars for the amount of foreign currency earned. To attain the same level of profitability, the organization should start charging more for its service event; however, if it does so, it becomes less competitive. Alternatively, when the U.S. dollar depreciates, services provided by U.S. Event Leadership organizations overseas become less expensive, hence more competitive.

Typical Event Budgets

Your budget is a general guide to the income and expense projected for your event. It may be adjusted as necessary, provided that you can justify these changes and receive approval from the stakeholders. For example, if your revenue projections are way ahead of schedule, your variable costs will also increase proportionately. Use the budget as a valuable tool that may be sharpened as needed to improve your percentage of retained earnings.

The sample budgets shown in Figure 5.5 will serve as a guide as you develop your financial plans for various events. Each budget has the same structure; however, you will note that in the case of not-for-profit organizations, the term *retained earnings* has been substituted for the term *profit*. Use these budgets as a model as you endeavor to create consistently effective financial management systems for your organization.

Although most Event Leaders find that financial matters are the least interesting aspect of their role and scope of their jobs, you now understand that to sustain long-term success, it is critical that you firmly control this important management area. The better you become at watching the bottom line, the more resources will become available to you for other more creative activities.

Julia Rutherford Silvers, CSEP, believes that financial goals, objectives, and tactics must be considered when evaluating the event elements being deployed. In *Professional Event Coordination* (Wiley, 2003), Rutherford Silvers puts this concept into perspective by offering this example. "Suppose you are coordinating a conference for your professional association. The costs to a delegate may include a registration fee of $600, an airline ticket at $500, a hotel room at $600 (four nights at $150 per night), and meals, business center services, and other incidentals that may add up to $400. Add to that $900 for a week away from work (a factor too many organizers ignore), and the cost to the delegate is $3,000. To

AWARDS BANQUET

Income
100	Registrations	
101	Preregistrations	$ 25,000
102	Regular registrations	50,000
103	Door sales	5,000
	Subtotal	$ 80,000
200	Marketing	
201	Sponsorships	$ 15,000
202	Advertising	10,000
203	Merchandise	5,000
	Subtotal	$ 30,000
300	Investments	
301	Interest income	1,000
	Subtotal	$ 1,000
400	Donations	
401	Grants	$ 5,000
402	Individual gifts	10,000
403	Corporate gifts	25,000
	Subtotal	$ 40,000
	Total income	$151,000

Expenses
500	Administration (fixed expense)	
501	Site office furniture rental	$ 1,000
502	Site office supplies	1,000
503	Site rental	3,000
504	Site telephone expense	1,000
	Subtotal	$ 6,000
600	Printing (fixed expense)	
601	Design	$ 3,000
602	Printing	5,000
603	Binding	1,000
	Subtotal	$ 9,000
700	Entertainment (fixed expense)	
701	Talent fees	$ 10,000
702	Travel and accommodations	1,000

Figure 5.5 Sample Budgets   (Continued)

703	Sound	2,000
704	Lights	2,000
	Subtotal	$ 15,000
800	Food and beverages (variable expense)	
801	300 dinners @ $50	$ 15,000*
802	Open bar for one hour	3,000*
803	Ice sculpture	500
	Subtotal	$ 18,500
	*Include taxes and gratuities.	
900	Transportation (variable expense)	
901	Staff travel	$ 1,000
902	Valet parking	750
	Subtotal	$ 1,750
1000	Insurance (fixed expense)	
1001	Cancellation	$ 1,000
1002	Host liability	500
	Subtotal	$ 1,500
	Total expenses	$ 51,750
	Total variable expense	$ 29,250
	Total projected income	$151,000
	Total projected expense	51,750
	Gross retained earnings	$ 99,250
	Percentage of fixed overhead	25,000
	Net retained earnings (reinvestment)	$ 74,250

MUSIC FESTIVAL

Income

100	Ticket sales	
101	Regular advance	$ 50,000
102	Student advance	25,000
103	Regular door sales	100,000
104	Student door sales	50,000
103	Group sales	25,000
	Subtotal	$250,000
200	Marketing	
201	Sponsorships	$ 50,000

Figure 5.5   *(Continued)*

202	Advertising	25,000
203	Merchandise	30,000
	Subtotal	$105,000
300	Investments	
301	Interest income	3,000
	Subtotal	$ 3,000
400	Donations	
401	Grants	$ 10,000
402	Individual gifts	0
403	Corporate gifts	25,000
	Subtotal	$ 35,000
	Total income	$393,000

Expenses

500	Administration (fixed expense)	
501	Site office furniture rental	$ 500
502	Site office supplies	500
503	Site rental	10,000
504	Site telephone expense	1,500
	Subtotal	$ 12,500
600	Printing (fixed expense)	
601	Design	$ 1,000
602	Printing	5,000
	Subtotal	$ 6,000
700	Entertainment (fixed expense)	
701	Talent fees	$ 50,000
702	Travel and accommodations	5,000
703	Sound	5,000
704	Lights	5,000
	Subtotal	$ 65,000
800	Transportation and parking (variable expense)	
801	Staff travel	$ 500
802	Parking lot rental	3,000
	Subtotal	$ 3,500
900	Insurance (fixed expense)	
901	Cancellation	$ 1,000
902	Host liability	500

Figure 5.5 *(Continued)*

903	Comprehensive general liability	2,000
904	Pyrotechnics rider	1,000
	Subtotal	$ 4,500
	Total expenses	$ 51,750
	Total variable expense	$ 29,250
	Total projected income	$393,000
	Total projected expense	91,500
	Gross retained earnings	$301,500
	Percentage of fixed overhead	150,000
	Net retained earnings (reinvestment)	$151,500

CONFERENCE AND EXPOSITION

Income

100	Registration	
101	Early-bird discount	$100,000
102	Regular	50,000
103	On site	25,000
104	Spouse/partner	10,000
105	Special events	15,000
	Subtotal	$200,000
200	Marketing	
201	Sponsorships	10,000
202	Advertising	15,000
203	Merchandise	10,000
	Subtotal	$ 35,000
300	Investments	
301	Interest income	$ 1,000
	Subtotal	$ 1,000
400	Donations	
401	Grants	$ 5,000
	Subtotal	$ 5,000
500	Exposition	
501	200 booths @ $1,500	$300,000
502	50 tabletops @ $500	25,000
	Subtotal	$325,000
	Total income	$566,000

Figure 5.5   *(Continued)*

Expenses
600	Administration (fixed expense)		
601	Site office furniture rental	$	1,500
602	Site office supplies		500
603	Site rental		30,000
604	Site telephone expense		1,500
	Subtotal	$	33,500
700	Printing (fixed expense)		
701	Design	$	2,000
702	Printing		10,000
	Subtotal	$	12,000
800	Postage (fixed expense)		
801	Hold this date	$	1,000
802	Brochure		5,000
803	Miscellaneous		500
	Subtotal	$	6,500
900	Entertainment (fixed expense)		
901	Talent fees	$	5,000
902	Travel and accommodations		500
903	Sound		0
904	Lights		0
	Subtotal	$	5,500
1000	Transportation and accommodations		
1001	Staff travel	$	1,500
1002	Staff accommodations		1,500
	Subtotal	$	3,000
1100	Insurance (fixed expense)		
1101	Cancellation	$	3,000
1103	Comprehensive general liability		2,000
	Subtotal	$	5,000
1200	Speakers (variable expense)		
1201	Honoraria	$	10,000
1202	Travel		3,000
1203	Accommodations		1,000
1204	Complimentary registrations		3,000
1205	Per diem		1,000
	Subtotal	$	18,000

Figure 5.5   *(Continued)*

1300	Audiovisual (variable expense)	
1301	Rentals (general sessions)	$ 25,000
1302	Labor (general sessions)	10,000
1303	Rentals (breakouts)	2,000
1304	Labor (breakouts)	1,000
1305	Prerecorded modules	5,000
	Subtotal	$ 43,000
1400	Exposition (variable expense)	
1401	Pipe and drape	$ 10,000
1402	Aisle carpet	20,000
1403	Signs	5,000
	Subtotal	$ 35,000
	Total projected income	$566,000
	Total projected expense	161,500
	Gross retained earnings	$404,500
	Percentage of fixed overhead	199,000
	Net retained earnings (reinvestment)	$205,500

Figure 5.5 *(Continued)*

achieve a positive return on his or her investment, the delegate will have to come away from the conference with a $3,000 idea."

Jerry Edwards, CPCE, is the owner of Chef's Expressions and the immediate past president of the National Association of Catering Executives (NACE). Edwards has observed significant changes in spending since the September 11, 2001, attacks. "Although September 11 marked the beginning of significant cutbacks in two major lines of catering business (conventions and corporate events), social business has become all the more important. Clients desire a very classic look that reflects high quality instead of ostentatiousness. Therefore, our catering budgets must reflect these changing tastes."

Career-Advancement Connections

Global Connection

The role that international finance plays in the Event Leadership industry was highlighted by the changes that occurred within the industry from the moment the North American Free Trade Agreement (NAFTA) was implemented. The entire economy of the United States, including the Event Leadership industry, has undergone major changes. Major labor-intensive industries were moved to Mexico because of cost savings in the labor force. At the same time, more knowledge-intensive industries were concentrated in the United States and Canada. Today the term *outsource* no longer means hiring domestic freelancers; rather, it refers to employing workers in countries where wages and, therefore, costs are lower.

Technology Connection

To learn more about financial management and financial markets, I encourage you to visit these Web sites:

◆ *www.ft.com Financial Times*
◆ *www.wsj.com Wall Street Journal*
◆ *www.sec.gov* Securities and Exchange Commission
◆ *www.freeedgar.com* EDGAR (Electronic Data Gathering, Analysis, and Retrieval) database, which contains information about financial performance of all companies, including Event Leadership, whose stocks are traded publicly
◆ *www.rubicon.com/passport/currency/currency.html* for easy, fast currency exchange-rate data

Resource Connection

The best strategy for understanding event financial management is practice. Excellent textbooks to assist you further include: *Analysis for Financial Management,* Sixth Edition, by Robert C. Higgins (McGraw-Hill, 2000); *Financial Management: Theory and Practice,* by Eugene F. Brigham and Louis C. Gapenski (South-Western Educational Publishing, 1998); and *Financial Analysis with Microsoft Excel,* by Timothy Mayes (South-Western Educational Publishing, 1996).

Learning Connection

Your Event Leadership organization is seeking a contract with a large corporation. It is a promotional event that will be organized to promote a new service. In order to make a final decision on whether you want to accept the project, you have to conduct financial calculations and a break-even analysis. Your Event Leadership organization is willing to accept the project if the total gross profit for the event is more than $5,000. Your client estimates that there will be somewhere between 100 and 300 guests. The company pays $100 per person with a minimum of $10,000. You know that your variable costs (food and beverage) total $30 per person. The total fixed costs are $4,000. Now calculate the maximum and the minimum gross profit that you can achieve for this event.

Profile in Event Leadership: Frank Supovitz

CONTROLLED CREATIVITY LEADS TO FINANCIALLY SUCCESSFUL EVENTS

In 2003 Frank Supovitz became one of the first individuals in the events industry to receive an honorary doctorate in business administration. After earning this prestigious honor, Dr. Supovitz achieved yet another milestone in a long and distinguished career when he was promoted to senior vice president for special events for the National Football League (NFL). Upon completing his undergraduate degree in biology, he rose from ushering audience members to their seats to helping produce the special events at the famed Radio City Music Hall. Following his tenure at Radio City Music Hall, he served as a senior executive with Eventures, a mega–event production firm that produced acclaimed spectaculars for the NFL Super Bowl Halftime Show Spectacular, the U.S. Olympic Festival, and other important clients. Prior to joining the NFL, he led the event and entertainment operations for one of the world's premier sports organizations, the National Hockey League (NHL).

Frank Supovitz
Senior Vice President of Events
National Football League

Reflecting on his own career progression, Supovitz states, "As any industry matures, there is a natural progression from competent manager to strategic leader. You need a competent manager to establish sufficient revenues, and you need leaders who are capable of responding to economic pressures." Using his own experience as an example, he observed, "There are only two major revenue streams in the sport event industry: ticket sales and sponsorship. In our case, the Event Leaders at the NFL must deliver interesting products to sponsors. As sponsors' financial pictures become more uncertain, it is more and more important that we find more effective ways to help them invest their marketing dollars." For nearly a quarter of a century, Frank Supovitz has effectively used his leadership skills to produce creative and memorable events for millions of people.

Frank Supovitz: frank.supovitz@nfl.com

PART THREE

Event Coordination

Vendor contracts may include various interactive experiences, such as this Oxygen Bar, where guests such as Katy Handley of Jack Morton Worldwide may find refreshment and enjoyment. *Photo courtesy of Dr. Joe Goldblatt, CESP*

CHAPTER 6

Managing Vendor Contracts

In This Chapter You Will Learn How To:

- ✦ Develop and implement the design for your event
- ✦ Develop appropriate resources
- ✦ Coordinate catering operations
- ✦ Use trends in event catering
- ✦ Coordinate technical resources, including lighting, sound, and special effects
- ✦ Conduct and analyze the site inspection
- ✦ Develop and construct the production schedule
- ✦ Anticipate and resolve operational conflicts

The International Special Events Society (ISES) annually awards several Esprit prizes for excellence in the spirit (esprit) of teamwork. This is the only awards program that I am aware of in the hospitality, meeting planning, and related industries that salutes achievement through high-quality teamwork. No single person is honored; rather, the awards are bestowed to teams that are responsible for innovative, excellent event production. ISES members understand that great events are the result of great people working together to achieve a common goal.

Developing and Implementing the Design for Your Event

Once the design has been developed and the plan finalized, the two must be merged to begin the implementation process. During the coordination phase, we arrive at the intersection of research, design, and planning and through the convergence of these three places begin to operationalize the event itself. The coordination phase provides us with the opportunity to see the results of our early labors in research, design, and planning. It is also the opportunity to ensure that we preserve the integrity of our early efforts. Too often, changes are made during the coordination phase that negatively affect the outcome of the event because they do not preserve the integrity of the design and planning process. One technique for ensuring that you continually preserve the integrity of your event design is to appoint one person to monitor the coordination and make certain that there is an obvious relationship between the design, the plan, and the final version of the event. Another method is to develop a series of written or graphic cues, such as design renderings or goals and objectives to make certain the stakeholders hold fast to the early vision of the event.

Developing Appropriate Resources

Event resources generally include people, time, finances, technology, and physical assets. Although each is important, each is also extremely scarce. Occasionally someone will tell me that he has unlimited resources for his event. I am skeptical about this because of the economic theory, which states that you must learn to allocate scarce resources to achieve maximum benefit. No matter how many resources you have, the fact is that they are always limited. The way you stretch your resources is through careful and creative allocation.

The Event Leader must first identify appropriate resources for his or her event during the proposal stage. It is not unlikely that you will receive a telephone call one morning at 9 and be told that you need to deliver a proposal by 12 noon to be eligible to earn the right to produce the event. Given this short time frame, the Event Leader must be able to identify appropriate resources quickly and accurately. Figure 6.1 provides a general guide to where to find these important resources.

Category	Examples	Sources
Money	Starting capital, emergency funds	Investors, credit, vendors, sponsors
People	Volunteers, staff, vendors	Convention and visitors' bureaus, destination management companies, schools, colleges, organizations, public relations, event alumni, advertising
Physical assets	Transportation, venue, catering	Destination management companies, school districts, caterers, convention and visitors' bureaus
Technology	Software, hardware	Internet, industry organizations
Time	Scheduling, organization, management, expanded time bands	Scheduling software, delegation strategies and tactics, cloning yourself

Figure 6.1   Event Resources and Where to Find Them

The Event Leader must be able to identify quickly the most appropriate resources for the event. Furthermore, the Event Leader has to attest that these resources are reliable. This is not always possible, due to time constraints. Therefore, after every effort is made to verify the quality of an event resource such as entertainment or catering or venue, the Event Leader may wish to include this statement in the proposal to reduce his or her liability: *"The information contained herein is deemed to be reliable but not guaranteed."* It is impossible to verify and confirm every resource within the brief time constraints imposed by most events. Therefore, the Event Leader should do what is reasonable and inform the client of the status of the level of reliability of the information that he or she is providing. The most common method for identifying appropriate resources consists of 10 steps:

1. Conduct a needs assessment.
2. Determine the budget.
3. Develop the request for proposal document and evaluation criteria.
4. Identify appropriate firms or individuals to submit proposals.
5. Distribute a request for proposal.
6. Review the proposals.
7. Select the suppliers.
8. Negotiate with the suppliers.
9. Develop and execute contracts with the suppliers.
10. Monitor contract performance.

Steps 1 and 2 are critical in order to proceed to develop an effective request for proposal (RFP). They may be conducted during the research phase and will include using historical as well as comparable data. The RFP must include the history of the event and/or the goals and objectives as well as the budget parameters. You may wish to establish a broad list of qualified organizations or individuals to receive the RFP. These lists can come from the resources shown in Figure 6.1 or through historical or comparable information. Regardless of how you acquire these lists, it is wise to qualify them further by calling each potential proposer to ask if he or she would like to receive the RFP. The initial list of proposers may be lengthy; however, the final list should not include more than five organizations or individuals. Typically, no more than three proposers receive the RFP.

The average Event Leader responsible for a large event such as the one described in Figure 6.2 may have as many as 50 or 60 proposals to receive and review. Therefore, it is important that you develop a methodology or system for receiving, reviewing, and responding to these proposals. Figure 6.3 provides an example of how to manage this process. Coordinating the flow of documents is the first step in this phase in managing a successful event. The system shown in this figure will help you track these important documents and evaluate the qualifications and value of each proposer. This system will also help you develop a historical profile for each vendor so you can plan more efficiently in the future.

The Convention Industry Council through its APEX initiative is currently developing a standard request for proposal form for the meetings and events industry. For more information about this project, visit *www.conventionindustry.org/apex/in_progress.htm*.

William O'Toole and Phyllis Mikolaitis report in *Corporate Event Project Management* (Wiley, 2002) that the ideal situation for contracting goods and services is with the use of the black box view system. The black box view dictates that the way in which the vendor accomplishes the deliverable is usually of no interest to the Event Leader. According to O'Toole and Mikolaitis, "Only the results matter." Using the black box approach, the inputs include the event charter, the design specifications, the performance specifications, and the contract additions. These requirements are given to the vendors who process these components into outputs or deliverables, which are the event goods and services. In order for this process to be successful, you must first clearly and accurately communicate to your vendors the requirements for your event.

Working with Suppliers and Vendors

Your ability to work with your vendors to satisfy the needs of your guests will ultimately help determine the level of success you achieve as an Event Leader. There are innumerable vendors; for example:

- ✦ Advertising agencies
- ✦ Advertising specialty providers
- ✦ Amusement-games providers
- ✦ Animal providers
- ✦ Audiovisual providers
- ✦ Balloons
- ✦ Caterers
- ✦ Clowns
- ✦ Décor specialists

Event title:	Med-Eth Conference and Exposition
Sponsoring organization:	International Medical Ethics Society
Description of organization:	Med-Eth is the world's largest professional society in the field of medical ethics
Tax status:	Med-Eth is a 501.c3 U.S. tax-exempt membership organization
Description of attendees:	Medical doctors, medical administrators, suppliers to the medical ethics profession
Event date(s):	June 6–11, 2002
Event location:	Washington, DC, Convention Center
Service(s)/product(s) to be proposed:	Audiovisual equipment and labor
Total budget not to exceed:	$5,000

Technical specifications:

1. Equipment and labor for video magnification and sound for two general sessions with 1000 persons using rear projection.
2. Equipment and labor for seven breakout sessions with an assortment of equipment, including slide projectors, video projectors, personal computers with PowerPoint, front projection screens, microphones, flipcharts (pads and markers), and laser pointers. Average audience size is 55 persons. Audience size will range from 30 to 75 persons.

Submission requirements:	All proposers must follow these guidelines to be considered for this assignment

1. Company/organization profile and history, including names of owners or principals as well as persons assigned to coordinate the event.
2. Itemized list of equipment and labor that will be provided, including redundant (backup) equipment.
3. Complete listing of all costs, including taxes if applicable.
4. Evidence of insurance company and evidence of commercial general liability with minimum limits of $2 million per occurrence.

Deadline for submission:	5 P.M. EST May 30, 2001
Submission instructions:	Proposals may be submitted electronically to Ms. Jane Doe via e-mail to: jdoe@med-eth.com or by mail to:

Attn: Jane Doe
Med-Eth
6000 Massachusetts Avenue, N.W.
Washington, DC 20039

Figure 6.2   Typical Request for Proposal

Event name: Med-Eth Conference and Exposition
Service(s)/product(s) required: audiovisual products and labor
Proposal due date: May 30, 2001

Ranking	Proposer	Date and Time Received	Qualifications	Value	Total Score
3	Sound and Pictures, Inc.	May 15, 2001, 4 P.M.	4	2	6
1	Techno Services	May 17, 2001, 10 A.M.	5	4	9
2	Light and Sound, Inc.	May 25, 2001, 2 P.M.	5	2	7
4	Microphones, etc.	May 27, 2001, 5 P.M.	3	2	5
5	Video, Inc.	May 29, 2001, 4 P.M.	2	2	4

[a]Scoring matrix: 1, poor; 2, fair; 3, acceptable; 4, good; 5, excellent

Figure 6.3 Proposal Tracking System[a]

+ Destination management companies
+ Entertainment providers
+ Envelope addressers
+ First-aid providers
+ Flag providers
+ Florists
+ Government agencies
+ Hotels
+ Insurance brokers and underwriters
+ Invitation designers
+ Legal counsel
+ Lighting providers
+ Magicians
+ Printers
+ Public relations counselors
+ Puppeteers
+ Pyrotechnic designers
+ Security providers
+ Simultaneous interpreters
+ Special effects providers
+ Translation providers
+ Valet parking providers
+ Venue lessors

In this chapter, we explore two of the more frequently used resources: caterers and technical production specialists.

Catering Management

Historically, events have been associated with food and beverages. Here we examine how to ensure that the catering elements of an event are well coordinated.

Event caterers are usually one of three business types, and each is defined by location. First is the *institutional caterer,* commonly described as an in-house or on-premises caterer, who may or may not have permanent kitchens and offices at the event venue. This caterer may limit the choices for the Event Leader but can provide greater security by being familiar with the idiosyncrasies of the venue.

The second business type is the traditional *off-premises caterer,* whose clients engage him or her to cater meals at a temporary location. The location or venue may or may not have permanent kitchen facilities. However, the off-premises caterer is responsible for providing the necessary equipment and services to create an atmosphere of permanence in this temporary locale.

The third and final type of event caterer is the *concessionaire.* This person may use a mobile kitchen or concession trailer to dispense his or her product or may work in a fixed venue from a permanent or temporary concession area. In some venues, the in-house catering operation operates all concession activities simultaneously as well.

Obviously, there is significant variation in these event-catering business operations. Generally, however, when contracting caterers, the three types will be on-premises, off-premises, and concessions. A growing trend in an effort to boost revenues is for on-premises caterers to begin catering off-premises in private homes and even other venues.

Although the on-premises caterer provides the lion's share of major event-catering operations, the off-premises caterer may actually feed the broadest possible constituency. The off-premises caterer must have the ability to establish a temporary kitchen in a tent, in an aircraft hangar, or even in a jewelry store. This type of caterer works closely with party rental specialists to ensure that he or she can provide the appropriate equipment on a moment's notice. Furthermore, the off-premises caterer must establish adequate resources for utilities, deliveries, waste disposal, and other critical elements of any catering operation. Finally, the off-premises caterer must stay abreast of local health and sanitation regulations to ensure that he or she is in compliance regardless of an event's location.

In actuality, although many off-premises caterers may boast of their ability to provide their services uniformly in any location in most major metropolitan areas, relatively few are able to do so. When you add multiple events on the same date, this number shrinks dramatically.

As the on-premises caterer continues to expand off-premises, he or she is learning that the rigor of the temporary location is much greater than the fixed or permanent venue. Some on-premises caterers have ceased off-premises operations for this very reason. They quickly discover that on- and off-premises are two very different catering skills and that, when trying to conquer both worlds, one inevitably suffers.

Location, Location, Location

Of the five W's in Event Leadership, "where" is perhaps one of the most critical to the on- and off-premises caterer for a variety of reasons. First, the caterer must comply with specific health department codes and regulations that will govern where he or she may operate. Second, food and beverage preparation is time-dependent, and the distance between the food preparation area and the serving location can determine an entire range of quality and service issues. What happens if hot food becomes cool or even cold during transit? How will the guests feel about slow food delivery? Finally, what utilities, equipment, and other resources are available to the caterer to prepare, serve, remove, and clean up successfully?

The location of the event is, therefore, a critical consideration for the off-premises caterer. However, the on-premises caterer must also be sensitive to these issues, as even the most routine event can suffer from logistical problems. As one example, what happens in the convention center when the caterer must serve 1,000 guests on the ground floor, the kitchen is located on the second floor, and the elevator stops working? Or perhaps the Event Leader has asked the caterer to serve the meal in an unusual location, such as in a tent in the parking lot. Does the caterer have the necessary equipment and additional labor to accomplish this task successfully? These questions and many more must be considered well in advance of establishing the location for the catered meal.

Equipment

Obviously, tables, chairs, china, silver, and other standard equipment will be required to serve a high-quality meal. However, the Event Leader must ensure that the caterer has access to the appropriate style and quantity to match the needs of the event. Some caterers own a sufficient inventory of rental equipment, while others have close relationships with party and general rental dealers to provide these items. The Event Leader must inspect the equipment to ensure that the caterer not only has sufficient quantity but that the quality is appropriate for the event.

When considering quantity, remember that the caterer may have multiple events on the same date. Make certain that additional inventory is available in case your guest list increases at the last moment. Furthermore, make certain that if the quantity of items is increased, the inventory will remain high quality.

Beyond china and silver, some caterers also maintain a healthy inventory of tables, chairs, linens, and other serving utensils, such as chafing dishes, props, and other elements that will provide you with a cohesive look. Some caterers stock unusual items from a specific historic period or feature items that reflect their style of catering. A caterer who primarily services the social life-cycle market may provide latticework props and gingham linens, while the caterer who works in the corporate event market may provide white linens and more traditional china and silver. The Event Leader must select a caterer who has equipment and experience that matches the goals and objectives of the specific event.

Utilities

As the caterer plugs in the coffee urn, the music from the band suddenly comes to a screeching halt. The guests on the dance floor look confused, but both the Event Leader and catering director know what has happened: an overloaded circuit caused by the coffee urn. The Event Leader must audit the caterer's utility needs as well as those of the other vendors to determine if the venue can support these requirements.

In addition to electricity, the caterer will require water. The proximity of the water will also be an important factor, as costs may increase if water must be transported from a great distance. The third and final requirement for all catering operations is waste management. The caterer must have a system for disposing of waste materials. The Event Leader must ensure that the caterer has the necessary resources to perform professionally.

Time Constraints

Time is of the essence in most catering operations, for a variety of reasons. First, the caterer must prepare and deliver his or her product within a reasonable amount of time to ensure freshness and quality. Second, the caterer must carefully orchestrate the delivery of his or her product within a complex setting in which multiple activities are being staged. For example, a dinner dance may require that the caterer serve various courses between dance sets. At some events the caterer must provide the entire service within a short time frame to ensure that all servers are out of the function room in time for speeches or other aspects of the program.

Service Styles

The term *service* refers to the method used for serving a catered meal. In the United States, the three most popular forms of service are the seated banquet, the standing or seated buffet, and the standing reception, where food items are passed by servers to guests. Each of these service types helps satisfy specific goals and objectives. Figure 6.4 provides a simple guide on when to employ a specific type of service.

In addition to these service styles, the exposition is an important venue for effective catering. Exposition managers know that food and beverages serve as a strong attraction and increase traffic greatly in an exposition hall. One of the more popular methods is to provide guests with an apron (usually donated by a sponsor and imprinted with their logo) and then distribute pocket sandwiches. With this technique the guests can walk, talk, shop, and eat. It is a very efficient way to provide food service for guests at an exposition and resembles a giant walking picnic.

Picnic style is also a popular technique for corporate and reunion events. Although this style is difficult in terms of service, it is extremely popular among guests who want to sit together as one large group. This style is also popular with Oktoberfest events, as it resembles a German beer hall.

Event	Service Style
Brief networking breakfast	Standing buffet
Breakfast with speaker	Seated buffet
Breakfast with speaker, program	Seated banquet
Brief networking luncheon	Standing buffet
Luncheon with speaker	Seated buffet
Luncheon with speaker, program	Seated banquet
Brief cocktail reception	Passed items
Extended cocktail reception	Standing buffet or individual stations
Brief dinner	Standing buffet or individual stations
Dinner with speaker, program	Seated banquet
Formal dinner	French service

Figure 6.4 Event Catering Service Styles and When to Use Them

English and Russian services, although not very popular in the United States, are two styles that may be implemented for the right occasion. English style involves serving each table from a moving cart. In Russian service, the server uses silver platters from which he or she places each course onto a guest's plate. Both styles of service may be requested, but the caterer must be equipped and schooled properly to produce an effective result.

Logistical Considerations

Proper and efficient guest flow as well as effective methods for ensuring timely delivery of food and beverages are essential considerations for a catered event. The event caterer may have substantial experience working in a permanent venue, but when asked to provide services off-premises, he or she may not be aware of the additional rigor required to survive in the jungle. To survive and thrive, one must know these basic laws of the event jungle:

✦ Determine in advance the goals and objectives of the catered event and match the logistical requirements to these objectives. For example, a brief networking event should use fewer chairs and tables, to allow guests time to mix and mingle.

✦ Determine the ages and types of guests and match the requirements to their needs. For example, for older guests, more chairs may be needed to provide additional comfort during an extended reception.

✦ Identify the food preparation and other staging areas and ensure that there is a clear passageway to the consumption area. Check the floors to make sure that they are free of debris and allow the service staff to move quickly.

✦ Whenever possible, use a double-buffet style for this type of service. The double buffet not only serves twice as many guests but also allows guests to interact with one another as they receive their food.

✦ Do not place food stations in areas that are difficult to replenish. Large crowds of guests may prevent service personnel from replenishing food stations efficiently.

✦ When passing food items, place a few servers at the entryway so that guests notice that food is available. This technique ensures that most guests will see and consume at least one of the food items being offered.

✦ Use lighting to highlight buffets, carving, and other stations. Soft, well-focused lighting directs guests' eyes to the food and makes it easier to find as well as more appetizing.

✦ Use servers at the entryway to pass drinks rapidly to guests as they enter, or open the bars farthest from the entrance first. For smaller events with ample time, passing drinks may be preferable; however, for larger events where the guests must be served quickly, staggering bar opening may be beneficial. Once the distant bars begin to experience lines of 10 or more persons, succeeding bars are opened, working back toward the entryway.

✦ Instruct the bar captain to close all bars promptly at the appointed time. Use servers to line up at the entryway to assist in directing guests into the main function room.

✦ Provide return tables to accept glassware as guests go to the next event. Staff these areas to avoid too many glasses accumulating.

✦ Request that servers distribute welcome gifts or programs during the setup period and be staged in each dining station to assist with seating. Servers should be requested to offer chairs to guests without hesitation, to expedite seating.

✦ Use an invocation, moment of silence, or a simple "bon appetit" to signal the beginning of the meal.

✦ These service times typically should be used for catered events:
  ✦ *Cocktail reception:* 30 minutes to 1 hour
  ✦ *Seated banquet:* 1 to 2 hours
  ✦ *Preset salad consumption and clearing:* 15 to 20 minutes
  ✦ *Entrée delivery, consumption, and clearing:* 20 to 40 minutes
  ✦ *Dessert delivery, consumption, and* clearing: 15 to 20 minutes
  ✦ *Coffee and tea service:* 10 to 15 minutes

✦ Make certain that all service personnel have exited the function room prior to the program or speeches. If this is not possible, make certain that front tables have been served and that servers continue service as quietly as possible in back of the function area.

✦ Request that servers stand at exit doors and bid guests good-bye and distribute any parting gifts from the host or hostess.

Your catering event professional will suggest other ideas to help you accomplish your goals and objectives. However, remember that you must prioritize the event's goals and objectives, and catering may or may not be high on the list. Therefore, it is important to maintain balance as you decide where to focus during specific periods of the event.

Once you have identified the event's goals and objectives, you choose the service style to make certain that your guests' needs are satisfied. After basic needs are satisfied, it is time to add some magic to turn an ordinary catered affair into an extraordinary special event.

Coordinating Catering Operations

As caterers assume increased responsibilities in the Event Leadership profession, other members of the professional team will need to adjust their marketing and operations strategies to cope with this new phenomenon. "Can and will caterers charge for Event Leadership services beyond the cost of food and service?" and "Will all future catered events place significant emphasis on food and beverage at the risk of ignoring other elements and producing a more balanced event?" are but two of numerous questions that will be raised.

Earlier I stated that, historically, caterers have provided Event Leadership services. Now the question becomes: Will caterers develop these services further to reflect full depth and breadth of resources available within the Event Leadership industry? If they choose to broaden their education, their impact can have substantial implications within the industry. The future of Event Leadership may include both good food and beverages as well as equally excellent services managed by the caterer. This consolidation will be welcomed by some clients who desire one-stop shopping and rejected by others who may, for a variety of reasons, prefer to entrust their event to another Event Leader. Regardless, the future force in catering will include offering many diversified services carefully combined into a nutritious, filling, and satisfying buffet. At the center of the bountiful buffet of these diversified services may be Event Leadership.

Global Event Leaders must also recognize that trends are typically regional and then national in scope. For example, recently I have noticed a trend that involves the elaborate design and construction of full-scale ice martini bars. These bars are constructed entirely of ice; fiber-optic lights illuminate them internally. The bartenders dispense hundreds of martinis, which are well received by baby boomers who want to relive the classic moments from the 1930s and 1940s enjoyed by their parents. The same is true of cigars, which are very popular in many parts of the United States. In other countries, cigars and martinis are usual and customary; in North America, they are often reserved for special occasions.

To best utilize the trends in event catering, I recommend that you first review all event literature to be sure that you are incorporating a trend that is on an upward trajectory. Next, make certain that you test the trend idea with a focus panel of your event guests and others to make certain that it is appropriate and can be implemented with high quality. Finally, remember the difference between fads and trends. Fads are often short-lived. You may purchase 1 million Pet Rocks only to discover that they were in vogue for only six months. Cautiously incorporate trends into your event design to enhance your plan.

Catering Ideas

■ Living Buffet

Effect
As guests browse along a seemingly normal buffet table, they are startled as the head of lettuce suddenly starts talking to the cauliflower and the cauliflower turns to the guest for advice on how to handle the unruly lettuce.

Method

Using a standard buffet table, cut two 24-inch holes in the top. The holes should be located approximately 12 to 18 inches apart and away from the front edge of the table. Place two actors, in headpieces that resemble lettuce and cauliflower, under the table with their heads penetrating the hole. It is best if the headpiece covers the eyes or they keep their heads slightly bowed until time to speak. Elaborately garnish all the area around the fake lettuce and cauliflower. Use theatrical lighting to soften the light on this area of the buffet.

Reaction

Guests will shriek with delight, and the talking lettuce and cauliflower will become one of the best memories of your catered event.

Bonus

Write a brief script between the lettuce and cauliflower in which they engage in a heated discussion about health and nutrition. Have the actors turn to the guests to ask their opinions.

■ Human Buffet Table

Effect

A person supports an entire buffet on his or her garment.

Method

Place a male or female actor in the center of two buffet tables. The buffet should be slightly elevated on platforms so that the edge of the table is at eye level. Construct a costume that appears to support the entire buffet. A woman may wear a long dress and the skirt may be supported with matching fabric used to skirt swag the front edge of the buffet table (see Figure 6.5), or a male may wear a colorful tailcoat with the tails extended with matching fabric to drape the tables. Place bright light on the actors in colors to complement their costumes and slightly softer light on the buffet tables. Match the lighting for the actor's wardrobe with softer lighting in matching colors on the buffet skirting.

Reaction

Guests will *ooh* and *ah* as your elegant actors wave and invite them to dine.

Bonus

Direct the actors to freeze and come to life periodically. This will create an ongoing activity for the guests to observe and enjoy.

Resource

Roberts Event Group (*www.robertseventgroup.com*) offers this attraction and many other innovative entertainment ideas.

Figure 6.5 Roberts Events Group of Jenkintown, Pennsylvania, rewards their many satisfied clients with a living martini bar at the Benjamin Franklin Institute in Philadelphia, Pennsylvania.

■ Old Black Magic

Effect
Thirty servers enter once the guests are seated. Each server is carrying a silver tray with two top hats. Suddenly the entire room begins to glow in the dark.

Method
Purchase 60 black-plastic top hats. Fill each top hat with 20 glow-in-the-dark bracelets and sticks. Line the waiters up outside the room service entrance of the function. Dim all the lights and instruct the servers to enter as you play music such as "Old Black Magic" or "Magic to Do." As the servers arrive at the tables and place their hats in the center, quickly turn off the lights. Instruct the servers to place their trays under their arms, clap their hands, and distribute the glow-in-the-dark pieces from inside the hats to the guests.

Reaction

Your guests may first wonder why there are no centerpieces for this elaborate catered event. However, once the glow-in-the-dark gifts are distributed, the guests will applaud as they become the room décor and you produce magic at a fraction of the cost of traditional décor.

Bonus

Purchase white gloves for the servers and color them with glow-in-the-dark dye. As the lights go dim, have the servers wave their hands above their heads and then clap them before producing the glow-in-the-dark gifts.

Resource

The Oriental Trading Company, Inc. catalog (*www.orientaltrading.com*) offers hundreds of inexpensive party supplies.

■ Dessert Parade

Effect

Your guests receive a unique dessert that has been created for them as your team of servers parades the dessert to their tables.

Method

Use glow-in-the-dark swizzle sticks or other items to decorate the dessert trays. Play a lively march or theme music that reflects the style of the catered event as the servers march forward. Stage the servers so that they enter at the rear of the room and march through the tables holding the trays high above their heads. Lower the lights and use follow spotlights to sweep the room to create additional excitement. Prior to their entrance, announce: "The chef has prepared a once-in-a-lifetime dessert creation to celebrate this momentous occasion. Please welcome your servers!" The servers march (or dance) to each table and serve dessert.

Reaction

Your guests will respond with spontaneous applause followed by clapping rhythmically to the music as your servers deliver dessert.

Bonus

At the conclusion of the dessert parade line, have the servers line up in front of the stage and gesture to the left or right as the pastry chef appears for a brief bow. Make certain that the pastry chef is dressed in all white with a traditional chef's hat so that he or she is easily recognized. This will cause an additional ovation, perhaps a standing one.

Resource

The Culinary Institute of America (*www.ciachef.edu*) or Johnson & Wales University College of Culinary Arts (*www.jwu.edu*) can refer you to their graduates throughout the world who are among the leading pastry chefs working in the modern food and beverage industry.

■ Incredible Edible Centerpiece

Effect
Your guests will notice that their centerpiece is both beautiful and edible. They will see and smell as well as taste this delicious work of art.

Method
Engage a chocolatier to carve a centerpiece out of chocolate for your guests to enjoy. The carving may represent the symbol of the event or the logo of the organization sponsoring the program. Use a pin light to illuminate each sculpture independently. Make certain the sculpture is on a raised platform, such as a gold or silver epergne. Include fresh fruit in your display to add color to your final design. One excellent subject is a large chocolate cornucopia filled with fresh red strawberries.

Reaction
Your guests will soon notice the work of art gracing their table and engage in lively conversation about its origin. Some guests will take photos, and others may try to nibble.

Resource
Belvedere Chocolates (*www.belvederechocolates.com*) has standard chocolate sculptures, such as a signature Bonsai Tree or magician's top hat, or it can create original designs for your event.

■ Ice-Cold Logo

Effect
As your guests arrive for the cocktail reception, they observe an ice carver putting the finishing touches on an elaborate sculpture.

Method
Your caterer can refer a professional ice carver who will pre-carve from a large block of ice your organization's logo, image, name, or other important and valued symbol of your group. Place the carver on a raised platform, and use rope and stanchion to provide ample working room and keep your guests from being hit by flying chips of ice. Make certain that the ice carver completes his or her work of art at the very moment your main function is to begin. Upon completion, stage several photos of your key leaders with the new work of art and then announce that the main function will begin.

Reaction
Your guests will crowd around the carver and begin intense discussions with one another about the creation. At the conclusion of the carving, they will erupt into applause and begin taking numerous photos.

Bonus

Ask the ice carver to use an electric chain saw, as this creates noise and excitement. In addition, the use of flame (fire and ice) is another dramatic touch that your ice carver may wish to incorporate into the final design (e.g., a dragon breathing fire).

Resource

An excellent and creative resource for this type of production is called Fear No Ice (*www.fearnoice.com*). A multimedia, performance art team of professional ice carvers create masterpieces in ice, including corporate logos, while performing to high-energy music.

Selecting the Best Caterer

The best caterer is the organization best equipped with experience, knowledge, creativity, personnel, and resources (human and actual equipment) to achieve your goals and objectives. In each community, there may be several full-service off-premises caterers with excellent reputations. However, you can narrow the list to one, two, or perhaps three by using these 20 criteria:

1. Find out how many years the company has been in business and the size of events it has catered.
2. Ensure that caterer has health and occupancy permits (and all other necessary permits).
3. If serving alcohol, make sure that caterer has on- and off-premises alcoholic beverage permits.
4. If permits are in order, make sure that caterer has liquor liability insurance.
5. Ask to see references and/or client letters.
6. Ask to see pictures of past events—look for professionalism and setup of kitchen/staging area.
7. Identify past and present events that caterer has handled and find out maximum and minimum sizes.
8. Check to see if site meets Americans with Disabilities Act requirements and complies with laws.
9. Find out policies on client tastings.
10. Review printed materials—menu descriptions will tell about level of professionalism.
11. Ask to see design equipment and/or in-house rentals—look for innovation and cleanliness.
12. Leave messages with company receptionist—see how long it takes to return calls.
13. If on-premises, make sure that any electronic or live music complies with Broadcast Music, Inc. (BMI) or American Society of Composers, Authors, and Publishers (ASCAP) regulations.
14. Check for membership in professional organizations (i.e., National Association of Catering Executives [NACE] and ISES).
15. Find out where executive chef received training.

16. Find out how waitstaff is attired for different levels of services.
17. Find out if servers are proficient in French service, modified French service, or plated service.
18. Find out deposit requirements and terms.
19. Review and analyze contracts and cancellation agreements.
20. Call the local party-equipment rental company and find out about its working relationship with the caterer.

▪ Catering Coordination

The Event Leader must closely coordinate all event activities with the director of catering or other catering team leader. Within the catering team, each member has particular responsibilities:

+ *Director of catering:* Senior catering official who coordinates sales and operations
+ *Catering manager:* Coordinates individual catered events, including sales and operations
+ *Banquet manager:* Manages specific catered functions; servers report to banquet manager
+ *Server:* Person responsible for serving the guests
+ *Bartender:* Person responsible for mixing, pouring, and serving alcoholic and non-alcoholic beverages

To ensure that you are coordinating each element effectively with your catering team, make certain that you hold a series of telephone or in-person meetings to review the various elements that will be included in your event. The first meeting should be used to review the proposal and answer any questions you may have about the food, beverage, equipment, or service and terms of payment. The next meeting will be held prior to signing the contract to negotiate any final terms, such as the inclusion of a complimentary food tasting. Some caterers prefer that you attend a comparable event and taste similar items that will be served at your event. However, if your event is introducing new cuisine, it is essential that you insist on a separate food tasting to ensure the quality of each item prior to serving your guests. In some instances, there will be a charge for this service; you should confirm this prior to signing the contract. The final meeting should include a thorough review of all elements, including the schedule, equipment, and service levels, and answer any final questions the caterer may have regarding delivery, utilities, or other important issues.

▪ Reviewing Proposals

Most caterers will provide a complete proposal, including the type of cuisine, number of servers, schedule, equipment rentals, payment terms, and other pertinent information. Using the next checklist will ensure that all important information is included in the catering proposal:

+ History of the catering organization, including other clients of similar size and scope they have served.

✦ Letters of reference from other clients of similar size and scope

✦ Complete description of cuisine.

✦ Complete description of style of service, including the number of servers/bartenders that will be provided.

✦ Complete description of equipment that will be provided by the caterer. Equipment may include tables, chairs, and serving utensils as well as other items. Make certain that each is described and that quantity is included.

✦ List of additional services to be provided by the caterer, such as floral, entertainment, or other special requirements.

✦ Complete description of payment terms, including date of guarantee, taxes, gratuities, deposits, balance payments, and percentage of overage provided by the caterer.

✦ All schedule information concerning deliveries, setup, service, and removal of equipment through load-out.

✦ Insurance, bonding, and other information pertinent to managing the risk of your event.

✦ Any additional requirements, including utilities such as water, electric power, and so on.

Negotiating with the caterer is an important step in the process of selecting the best caterer. In smaller Event Leadership markets, where competition is not as great as in larger markets, negotiation may be more difficult. Still, regardless of size, five areas often can be negotiated:

1. Ask to pay the lowest deposit in advance or to pay a series of smaller deposits spread evenly over a period of months. Even better, if your organization has a good credit record, ask to pay net 30 days after your event.

2. Ask for a discount for prepayment. You may receive up to a 5 percent discount if you pay your entire bill in advance.

3. Ask for a discount if you are a not-for-profit organization. Although all not-for-profit organizations ask for this concession, you may be successful if you can convince the caterer that your guests may bring him or her additional new business. Offer to actively promote the presence of the caterer at the event to ensure high visibility.

4. Ask for a complimentary service. Some caterers will provide services ranging from a complimentary ice sculpture to a pre- or post-event reception.

5. Ask for a complimentary food tasting for yourself and your key decision makers. This should not take the form of an additional event; rather, it is a business activity for the purpose of inspecting the food presentation, taste, and other important elements of the event.

■ Final Step

The final meeting should be held in person. Often it is held in conjunction with the food tasting or final walk-through. This important meeting is your final opportunity to review the critical details regarding the caterer's contribution to your event. Five major points must be covered during this meeting:

1. Confirm the day, date, time, location, parking, and other critical information with the caterer.
2. Carefully coordinate all catering deliveries and access to the loading entrance with other vendors.
3. Review the times for the service, and instruct the caterer regarding the other elements of the program and how he or she will interface with these aspects.
4. Review the caterer's alcohol management program. Ask the caterer if his or her staff has received training and how they will handle guests who are obviously inebriated.
5. Review all payment terms and any elements you are required to provide as part of your agreement.

■ Cost-Saving Measures

Increasingly, both clients and their Event Leaders are concerned with cost. In some corporate circles, it is not the actual cost but the perception of a high-priced event that is of greater concern. Use this list to avoid these concerns and lower your overall catering costs:

+ Carefully analyze the meals that must be provided. Some meals may be taken by guests on their own, such as at networking dinners, where all guests pay their individual bills. You may also wish to substitute concessions for some meal functions. An individually priced buffet line may be a good alternative for some meal functions.
+ Use buffets and boxed lunches instead of seated banquet service. Reducing labor cost may reduce expense.
+ Price food items by the lowest possible unit (cup, piece, or dozen) rather than by the tray or gallon. Order only the amount of food you will require based on the history of your event.
+ Secure sponsors for meal functions. In a recent study, we learned that sponsors are very much interested in providing funding for meals that are related to educational programs.
+ Secure in-kind sponsorships from bottlers and others in the food and beverage industry.
+ Reduce or eliminate alcohol from your event. Many events are becoming beer-and-wine functions in place of full-open-bar affairs. This change is happening due to concerns about health but also because of the perceived association between heavy drinking and drunk driving.
+ Serve a signature drink to everyone. A signature drink is an original drink that your bar manager creates for consumption by the entire group. At a catered function, the first need of most guests is to occupy their hands with a drink. Offer your sig-

nature drink at the entrance to your event and solve this need while reducing your budget by controlling consumption.

✦ Allow guests to serve themselves. This is especially popular with children's events. Make Your Own Sundae bars and the making of a five-foot-long submarine sandwich are not only entertaining but may also result in cost savings.

Catering Trends

A *trend* is a pattern of behavior that is likely to be sustained over time. Although the event catering profession is susceptible to shifting tastes and is certainly affected by the state of the economy, several trends are emerging. These trends are well worth noting, as they will certainly influence many of the decisions you will make.

Use of nutritious food and beverages is a trend that will affect both perception and reality in the catering field. As the world's population ages (especially in the United States), guests will be more and more concerned with good health and will turn to nutritious foods as a primary means of promoting this lifestyle. Not only must the food perception be that of healthy presentation, but the ingredients must also be carefully considered. Increasingly, more and more people and their hosts will want to know the ingredients in their food and beverages to make wise decisions regarding menu items. Therefore, caterers will want to make available the ingredients and may even wish to list these items in a menu on signs posted near the food items. Furthermore, caterers will continue the practice of promoting heart-healthy menu items, as offering these items will provide a popular alternative but also differentiate the caterer from competitors because of this attention to low cholesterol.

A second trend is the shift away from beer and wine in the 1990s to the increased popularity in the twenty-first-century of martinis that are now being featured at many event bars. In fact, some bars *only* feature martinis. The martini was probably derived from the sweeter drink called the Martinez and invented in California in the 1870s. Whether the popularity of the James Bond films or the nostalgia craze being experienced and promoted by the baby boomers, more and more events are featuring this classic drink. Figure 6.6 depicts a modern martini bar constructed entirely of ice.

The third trend relates to the second trend in that, increasingly, caterers are seeking additional revenue streams and some are even moving from strictly food and beverage operations into full Event Leadership services. This change comes with great challenge as well as potentially great opportunity. Historically, caterers have been involved in all aspects of Event Leadership. Caterers, especially in the social life-cycle event market, have been responsible for providing or recommending the services of florists, musicians, decorators, invitation designers, and other allied professionals. Today's trend merely quantifies this historic business opportunity and repositions the caterer as an Event Leader who specializes in catering services. However, to take full advantage of this trend, the catering professional must be willing to round out his or her education with a rigorous course of study in Event Leadership. In every profession, eventually, superior quality combined with good value can conquer fierce competition. Event Leadership is no different from other professions in this regard. If catering professionals are to expand their services to include those of Event Leadership, they must be willing to acquire the new skills that

Figure 6.6 The 2005 *Event Solutions* off-premise party entitled Southern Exposure produced at the magnificent Flint Hill mansion (*www.flinthill.com*) by Kendall Collier, CSEP, and Teresa Day of MMinc Catering & Special Events and Tim Lundy, CSEP, of Rosewood Market/Distinctive Design Events (*www.distinctiveevents.com*) featured a martini bar made entirely of ice that served as a cool refuge.

will complement their existing talents to improve their quality and provide them with the tools to compete effectively in the event marketplace.

Therefore, these three trends—nutritious and healthy menus, a wider range in alcohol service, and the expansion of the caterer's services to include those of an Event Leader—may be viewed as economic opportunities provided that education and commitment to quality is implemented consistently.

Coordinating Technical Resources

The Event Leadership profession has seen perhaps the greatest paradigm shift in the live production sector of this industry. Live production is also what differentiates events from other entertainment or creative products. Although one may argue that television specials are billed as "special events," in most instances these events are filmed or taped before a live audience. Productions ranging from the National Football League Super Bowl halftime show to the Three Tenors concert combine live production with various audiovisual, lighting, sound, special effects, and video resources to produce a well-crafted event that ultimately is viewed by millions via television. The modern Event Leader cannot ignore this major shift and must understand as well as implement these resources when appropriate.

Why = What

Earlier I described that, prior to selecting the most effective resources for your event, you must establish clear goals and objectives by asking why this event is necessary. Due to the myriad new technologies now offered, this question is more important than ever before. The inexperienced Event Leader may decide to mix and match a wide array of new technology to impress his or her guests during the event. In fact, this mixture becomes a collage of inappropriate resources that results in confusion to the guests. An award-winning designer reportedly cautioned his young apprentices that "less is indeed more." The Event Leader must also use caution when selecting appropriate resources to support or enhance the event to make certain that each device is well integrated rather than extraneous. The list that follows can be used as a primary coordination tool for selecting and engaging these resources:

✦ Identify the purpose of event technology for your program. Will the event technology be used to attract attention or to improve communications?

✦ Determine the size of the live audience. The technology you select for the audience will be determined by the number of guests.

✦ Identify the age, culture, and learning style of your guests. Some guests are visual learners, while others are more attuned to audio influences. Still other audiences, due to their age, may prefer a louder or more quiet sound level.

✦ Inspect the venue and inventory preexisting light (natural and artificial), in-house audiovisual equipment, utilities, the experience of local technical labor, and any other elements that will interact with your event.

✦ Sit in a guest's chair or stand in the guest's place and try to envision the event through his or her eyes and ears. Check for obstructed views and other distractions. Identify potential solutions to develop optimum enjoyment through the entire event.

Purposes of Event Technology

Whether the purpose of your event is to educate or entertain or, perhaps, both, the technology that you select will help you best achieve your goals and objectives. In the conference event field, you may select slide projectors, overhead projectors, a TelePrompTer, or perhaps one microphone to improve communications between the presenter and the participant. The entertainment field may require theatrical lighting and special effects, such

Style	Purpose	Technology
Civic	Attract attention	Special effect: pyrotechnics
Conference	Communicate	Audiovisual: video magnification
	Focus	Lighting: key lighting of lectern
Education	Build retention	Audiovisual: interactive CD
Entertainment	Attract	Sound and lights: announce and chase
Exposition	Educate	Video: product description
Festival	Communicate	Sound: public address
Reunion	Excite	Audiovisual: slide show of guests

Figure 6.7 Matching Technology to Style and Purpose

as fog, laser, or strobe lights. Other fields will require different technologies; however, ultimately the purpose of the event will determine the final selection and coordination of the event technology. Figure 6.7 provides a guide for general use in selecting equipment for the event style and purpose.

Audiovisual Effects

The term *audiovisual* was probably first coined in the 1950s, when schools and, later, businesses and then associations used slide and overhead projectors and sound recordings for instructional purposes. During the 1970s, this technology expanded rapidly with more sophisticated audio tools as well as video enhancement due to the invention of video-projection systems. Indeed, today dozens of audiovisual tools are available for use by Event Leaders. However, I concentrate on those 10 tools used most often in the production of civic, entertainment, exposition, festival, and conference events. These tools are readily available in most event markets or may be obtained from nearby larger markets.

Audiovisual projection is divided primarily into two projection fields: visual and audio. The tool and its power depend on the factors described in the checklist in Figure 6.8. Audience size, distance, and the age and type of attendee are critical considerations when selecting a tool. The right tool will make your task easier and the event more enjoyable for your guests; the improper tool will cause you frustration and irritate your guests. Therefore, when selecting audiovisual tools for an event, refer to the checklist to check and balance your decision.

Digital images have replaced traditional photography in the Event Leadership production industry. Yesterday's slide projector has been replaced by the notebook computer loaded or the Universal Serial Bus (USB) storage device with hundreds of slides and entire educational programs, including music and video. Monitor industry publications such as *Sound and Video Contractor* (*www.svc.online.com*) and *Digital Content Producer.com* (*www.digitalcontentproducer.com*) to stay current with the latest technological advancements in the audiovisual field.

Conducting and Analyzing the Site Inspection

Site inspection occurs during both the planning and coordination phase. During the planning phase, potential sites are inspected to identify those that should receive requests for proposals. Increasingly, this task is conducted using the Internet. However, I caution you whenever possible to visit the site yourself or send a representative to inspect the physical assets. Even using three-dimensional technology on the Internet will not allow you to view every nook and cranny of the venue. Therefore, a physical inspection is essential to confirm and verify the quality of the physical space.

It is particularly important that you schedule a site inspection during the coordination phase to reconfirm that there have been no changes to the site since the planning period. I recommend that you visit the site no less than 30 days prior to the event to reinspect and make certain that you will be able to conduct the event effectively within the venue. If there have been dramatic changes, this type of lead time will give you sufficient time to rework your event design or even, if necessary, change venues. Figure 6.8 is a good beginning for you to be able to develop a customized site inspection checklist.

Site Inspection

Perhaps the most important activity involving space is the site inspection. Using a comprehensive, customized checklist will make this task efficient and thorough. It will also allow you to delegate this task to others if you are not able to travel to the site yourself. Always carry a retractable or digital tape measure, digital or video camera, notepad, and pencil on such an inspection.

Upon arrival, note the ingress to the parking facilities for up to one mile away. What will be the estimated travel time in heavy to moderate traffic, and are there alternative routes if the main artery is blocked by an accident or construction? Determine where the parking area will be for your official and VIP vehicles. Find out if special identification is required for those vehicles to park in these preapproved areas. Measure the height of the loading dock (if available) from the driveway to make certain that your vehicles can deliver directly onto the dock. This knowledge alone may save you thousands of dollars in additional labor charges.

Ask the venue officials to show you the entrance door for your personnel and the walking route to the pre-event waiting area (dressing rooms, green rooms, and briefing rooms). Write down these instructions and read them back to the official. Note who supplied these instructions, as they will later be given to your personnel, and should there be a problem, you must be able to refer back to your original source for clarification.

Measure the square footage of the waiting area and determine how many persons can be accommodated when official furnishings are included. Locate the restrooms and note if they are adequate or require upgrading (e.g., bringing in nicer amenities, such as specialty soaps, toiletries, perfumes, full-length mirrors, and fresh flowers).

Ask the venue official to lead you from the waiting area to the location of the actual event. Thoroughly examine the event site from the perspective of the spectator or partic-

Amenities:
1. Ability to display banner in prominent location
2. Limousines for very important persons (VIPs)
3. Upgrades to suites available
4. Concierge on VIP floors
5. Room deliveries for entire group upon request
6. In-room television service for special announcements
7. Personal letter from venue manager delivered to room
8. Complimentary parking for staff or VIPs
9. Complimentary coffee in lobby
10. Complimentary office services, such as photocopying for staff

Americans with Disabilities Act
1. Venue has been modified and is in compliance
2. New venue built in compliance with act
3. Modifications are publicized and well communicated

Capacity
1. Fire marshal approved capacity of venue for seating
2. Capacity of venue for parking
3. Capacity for exposition booths
4. Capacity for storage
5. Capacity for truck and vehicle marshaling
6. Capacity for pre-event functions such as receptions
7. Capacity for other functions
8. Capacity for public areas of venue such as lobbies
9. Size and number of men's and women's restrooms

Catering
1. Full-service, venue-specific catering operation
2. Twenty-four-hour room service
3. Variety of food outlets
4. Concession capability
5. Creative, tasteful food presentation

Equipment
1. Amount of rope (running feet) and stanchions available
2. Height, width, and colors available for inventory of pipe and drape
3. Height, width, and skirting colors available for platforms for staging
4. Regulations for use and lift availability for aerial work
5. Adequate number of tables, chairs, stairs, and other equipment

Financial considerations
1. Complimentary room ratio
2. Guarantee policy
3. Daily review of folio

Figure 6.8 Event Site-Inspection Checklist Criteria

4. Complimentary reception or other services to increase value
5. Function-room complimentary rental policy

Location/proximity
1. Location of venue from nearest airport
2. Distance to nearest trauma facility
3. Distance to nearest fire/rescue facility
4. Distance to shopping
5. Distance to recreational activities

Medical assistance/first aid
1. Number of staff trained in CPR, Heimlich maneuver, and other first aid
2. Designated first-aid area
3. Ambulance service

Portals
1. Size and number of exterior portals
2. Size and number of interior portals, including elevators
3. Ingress and egress to portals

Registration
1. Sufficient well-trained personnel for check-in
2. Ability to provide express check-in for VIPs
3. Ability to distribute event materials at check-in
4. Ability to display group event name on badges or buttons to promote recognition
5. Effective directory or other signs for easy recognition

Regulations
1. Designation of a civil defense venue to be used in emergencies
2. Preexisting prohibitive substance regulations
3. Other regulations that impede your ability to do business
4. Fire-code requirements with regard to material composition for scenery and other decoration
5. Local fire officials' requirements for permission to use open flame or pyrotechnic devices
6. Requirement regarding the use of live gasoline-powered motors
7. Policy regarding live trained animals

Safety and security
1. Well-lit exterior and interior walkways
2. Venue has full-time security team
3. Communications system in elevators in working order
4. Positive relationship between venue and law-enforcement agencies
5. Positive relationship between venue and private security agencies
6. Fire sprinklers controlled per zone or building-wide; individual zone can be shut off, with a fire marshall in attendance, for a brief effect such as pyrotechnics

Figure 6.8 *(Continued)*

7. Alarm system initially silent or announces a fire emergency immediately
8. Condition of all floors (including the dance floors)

Sleeping rooms
1. Sufficient number of singles, doubles, suites, and other required inventory
2. Rooms in safe, clean, working order
3. Amenities such as coffeemakers and hair dryers available upon request
4. Well-publicized fire emergency plan
5. Balcony or exterior doors secured properly

Utilities
1. Electrical power capacity
2. Power distribution
3. Working on-site reserve generator (and a backup) for use in the event of a power failure
4. Responsible person for operation of electrical apparatus
5. Sources for water
6. Alternative water source in case of disruption of service
7. Separate billing for electricity or water

Weight
1. Pounds per square foot (meter) for which venue is rated
2. Elevator weight capacity
3. Stress weight for items that are suspended, such as lighting, scenic, projection, and audio devices

Figure 6.8   *(Continued)*

ipant. Most important, can the spectator see and hear comfortably? Sit in the seat of the spectator farthest from the staging area. Determine how the person with the most obstructed view can best see and hear.

When possible, ask the venue official to supply you with a floor plan or diagram of the site. Use this site diagram as a general blueprint and then confirm and verify by using your measuring device to measure random locations. Note any variances for later adjustment on the final diagram.

Finally, before you leave the venue, sit for a minimum of 15 minutes in one of the chairs your spectator will occupy. Determine if it is comfortable for your guests. If not, ask if alternate seating is available and at what cost.

Developing the Diagram

At one time transferring the results of the site inspection to a final, carefully produced diagram was a major labor-consuming operation. Using computer tools such as Computer Assisted Design and Drawing (CADD) systems, this task has been simplified and automated. For those Event Leaders who are uncomfortable with computers, a manual system has been developed involving scale cutouts of magnets that correspond to the typical inventory of most venues (chairs, tables, platforms, pianos, etc.). Once assembled, the final product can be photocopied for distribution. A resource called Room Viewer™, using a CADD system, may be found at *www.timesaversoftware.com/roomviewer/aspx.*

Before beginning the process of developing the diagram, audit all internal and external stakeholders and create a list of every element that must be depicted on the diagram. These elements may range from décor to catering tents and from first-aid centers to parking locations. You will later use this checklist to cross-check the diagram and make certain that every element has been included.

After the first draft diagram has been developed, it must be distributed to stakeholders for a first review. Ask the stakeholders to review the diagram for accuracy and return it within a fixed amount of time with any additions, deletions, or changes.

After you have received comprehensive input from the stakeholders, prepare a final copy for review by officials who must grant final approval for the event. These officials may include the fire marshal, transportation authorities, or others responsible for enforcing laws and regulations.

Once you have constructed a final, approved diagram, you have made the giant step forward from dream to idea to final plan. Event Leadership planning requires that you consistently implement your plan effectively.

Determining the Production Schedule

The production schedule is the primary instrument (other than the event diagram) that is used during the coordination phase. During this phase, the Event Leader must implement a minute-by-minute plan and monitor the tasks that lead to the ultimate conclusion of the event itself. The production schedule ensures that you will be able to achieve this goal efficiently. Figure 6.9 is an example of a typical production schedule. Note how it is different from the timeline shown in Figure 3.11.

As Figure 6.9 suggests, the production schedule begins with load-in and concludes with load-out. The first line in the production schedule generally is "inspect venue" and the last line is "reinspect venue" to review and return the venue to the best condition. You will note that the production schedule is much more precise than the timeline and includes minute-by-minute precision. Typically, the Event Leader will include the production schedule in the timeline in the coordination phase and then provide a full version on-site at the event for the event coordination staff to manage the minute-by-minute operations.

The Convention Industry Council has adopted the term *Event Specification Guide* as the official standardized term for the previously used résumé or production schedule. The function schedule in this document is similar to the production schedule. To view a template of the *Event Specification Guide,* visit *www.conventionindustry.org,* click APEX, and then click Accepted Practices.

Task	Start Time	Stop Time	Details	Person(s) Responsible	Notes
Inspect venue	7 A.M.	7:45 A.M.	Check for preexisting damages, problems	Event Leader	
Lighting and sound company loads in	8 A.M.	9 A.M.	Arrivals and load-in	Event coordinator	
Lighting and sound company installs	9 A.M.	12 noon	Set up, hang, focus, test	Event coordinator	
Lunch break	12 noon	1 P.M.	Lunch for 10 stage hands	Caterer	
Florist loads in and installs	1 P.M.	3 P.M.	Decorate stage and prepare centerpieces	Florist	
Rental company loads in and sets tables, chairs, and cloths	1 P.M.	3 P.M.	Place tables and chairs and clothe the tables	Rental company	
Place centerpieces on table	3 P.M.	4 P.M.	Position centerpieces	Volunteers	
Caterer loads in and sets up preparation area	3 P.M.	4 P.M.	Set up staging area for food preparation	Caterer	
Caterer sets tables	4 P.M.	5 P.M.	Final setting of tables	Caterer	
Inspection of tables, décor, lighting, sound by Event Leader	5 P.M.	5:30 P.M.	Final review	Event Leader	
Sound check and rehearsal with band	5:30 P.M.	6:30 P.M.	Final sound check	Event Leader and talent and technicians	
Waiters in position to open doors	6:45 P.M.	7 P.M.	Workers ready to open doors for guests	Event coordinator	
Open doors	7 P.M.	7:15 P.M.	Guests enter and are seated by waiters	Event coordinator	Doors opened early (7:10 P.M.)
Invocation	7:15 P.M.	7:17 P.M.	Minister delivers invocation	Stage manager	
Salad course	7:17 P.M.	7:30 P.M.	Salad served	Caterer	
Salad removed, entrée served	7:30 P.M.	7:50 P.M.	Entrée served	Caterer	

Figure 6.9 Typical Production Schedule

Task	Start Time	Stop Time	Details	Person(s) Responsible	Notes
Entrée removed, dessert served	7:50 P.M.	8:10 P.M.	Dessert served	Caterer	
Coffee and candies served	8:10 P.M.	8:20 P.M.	Coffee and candies passed	Caterer	
Welcome speech and introduction of entertainment	8:20 P.M.	8:30 P.M.	All waiters out of room; speeches	Stage manager	
Entertainment	8:30 P.M.	9:00 P.M.	Band	Stage manager	Entertainment started late (8:40 P.M.)
Dancing	9:00 P.M.	12 midnight	Dancing	Stage manager	
Close bars	11:45 P.M.	12 midnight	Stop serving	Caterer	
End of event	12 midnight	12 midnight	Lights up full	Event Leader	
Dismantle and load-out	12:30 A.M.	6 A.M.	All equipment dismantled and removed from venue	Event coordinator	
Reinspect venue	7 A.M.	8 A.M.	Venue checked for any damages or losses caused by event	Event Leader, event coordinator, venue official	

Figure 6.9   *(Continued)*

Anticipating and Resolving Operational Conflicts

During the coordination phase, numerous operational conflicts will develop. The key is for the Event Leader to anticipate and resolve these problems quickly by practicing what is often referred to as *damage control*. Some of the typical operational conflicts that arise and how you can resolve them quickly follow.

- ✦ *Late-arriving vendors.* Maintain cell-phone numbers and contact late-arriving vendors to determine their location.
- ✦ *Multiple vendors arriving simultaneously.* Sequence arrivals in logical order of installation.

Profile in Event Leadership:
Mary Jordan

GOODNESS MEETS GREATNESS AND CREATES SUSTENANCE

Whether pioneering in the world of business as one of the first successful female African American entrepreneurs or inspiring legions of young people through her professionalism, integrity, and hard work ethic, Mary Jordan exemplifies how successful event professionals create sustainable enterprises. Few have had the opportunity to not only sustain but also advance the profession for others in such a dramatic and important manner.

In the 1960s, when many U.S. communities still practiced segregation, Mary Jordan, a pioneering and prominent caterer in Atlanta, Georgia, outgrew her home kitchen, where she was catering meals for hundreds of persons each month. Due to her popularity in the white community, where she had served in their homes for many years, Mrs. Jordan leased a building on Howell Mill Road in a white section of Atlanta.

Almost before she could hang the "Open for Business" sign, a group of white ladies called on her to ask for her help in planning an upcoming society fundraiser. Mrs. Jordan thanked them for their visit and asked them to return the following week, when she would be better prepared to help them.

In the days between visits, Mrs. Jordan's staff created the most magnificent pastries and culinary delights to offer her future business prospects as a taste of the quality for which she was known. When the women arrived, she

Mary Jordan (1908–1996)
(As remembered by her
son, Windsor Jordan)
Mary Jordan Catering

served them tea from a silver service. The ladies asked if she would "donate" all of her services and food to help promote her new business.

Mary smiled and sweetly said, "I would be pleased to make a donation of my own choosing to your worthwhile cause, but please remember that I am in this business for the money, honey." She got the job, was well paid, and earned the respect of her customers as well as thousands of other clients in the six decades she would operate her firm.

In 1987, when the International Special Events Society (ISES) was founded, the first organizational meeting was held in Atlanta. Due to the newness of the organization, few hotels or even restaurants would agree to host the board for its first dinner together. However, Mary Jordan welcomed the leaders into her kitchen. She was also a visionary who understood that working together for the common good would help promote future business. Thanks in part to Mary Jordan, today there are over 5,000 members of ISES worldwide.

Indeed, she was a wise woman. According to her son Windsor, the current president of Mary Jordan Catering Service, Inc., these eight rules helped guide Mary and her children to future success.

1. Remember that image is everything and has to be consistently maintained and cul-

tivated. Mary always insisted that her children and staff were immaculately dressed and groomed.

2. An engaging smile exudes friendliness and encourages others to respond in kind. Even while negotiating complex contracts, Mary's smile helped her customers relax and grow confident in her abilities.

3. If you want to be successful, emulate the habits of successful people. She insisted that her children study successful people. Whenever possible, she invited prominent people to her home to entertain them and positively influence her children.

4. Befriending people in high places allows you access to influence. She encouraged her children to network long before the term became popular in the business world. As a result of networking, she was the preferred caterer for governors and presidents.

5. To enter the inner circle of the affluent, you often need a sponsor or someone already inside to grant you admission. Mary believed that everyone could benefit from having a mentor to open the doors to future success. As a black woman, this was especially important because so many doors had been closed to her.

6. Stay true to yourself, but learn the rules of the dominant culture. Mary practiced integrity; however, she also studied society in general and learned how to navigate the system of rules that would provide her with future access.

7. Try to never burn bridges, and remember the people who helped you. A burned bridge for Mary was a lost opportunity, and Mary Jordan was in the business of creating new opportunities. In doing so, she would continue to recognize those who had helped her.

8. Approach life systematically, methodically, and with steel determination to win. Mary

Jordan was both professional and determined. Her organizational skills and persistence provided a strong foundation for sustainable success.

The results of her labors over many years are perhaps best exemplified by her children. In addition to Windsor, her son Vernon served as special advisor to President Clinton. In his bestselling book *Vernon Can't Read* (Public Affairs, 2001), Vernon Jordan describes how his mother's fierce determination as "chief architect, contractor, and bricklayer of my life" helped promote his future success.

Due to all of the changes in business since the days when Mrs. Jordan started her company, Windsor Jordan states, "With all the forward thinking, you would think that the attendance at events in our city would now be 50 percent white and 50 percent black. However"—he smiles as he recalls his mother's wisdom—"Mother always said social integration wasn't really what it was about. She said it was about business."

One of Mary Jordan's grandsons, Windsor Junior, is a student at Swarthmore College in Pennsylvania, where he is president of the Black Students Organization on campus. When asked to describe his memories of his beloved grandmother, he quickly responded, "We loved and yet hesitated to visit her kitchen, because she always put us to work right away. She knew the value of work. Of course she would always feed us, but first we also had to finish our work."

Perhaps her strong work ethic was the result of her conviction that all of us have important unfinished work to do. And now, thanks to the early event leadership of Mary Jordan, all of us have new opportunities to further advance the special events industry that she helped establish over 60 years ago.

Windsor Jordan: www.maryjordancatering .com

✦ *Caterer running late in food delivery.* Monitor service carefully and use distractions such as dancing to cover long delays.

✦ *Speaker or entertainer cancels.* Use taped music or a pretaped video to cover.

✦ *Guests arrive too early.* Prepare for this and have appropriate staff greet and serve them.

✦ *Medical emergency.* Use standard operating procedures and work closely with venue to resolve.

As you can see, that wise Event Leader Murphy was prophetic when he wrote: "What can go wrong will go wrong." His cousin, O'Goldblatt, however, was perhaps even more prophetic when some years later he wrote: "Murphy is an optimist."

As a professional Event Leader, the coordination phase is the most exciting and often most grueling time during the event process. However, because you care deeply to achieve a high-quality outcome for the event, your ability to research, design, plan, and lead your team will smooth even the roughest edges during coordination of the event. The intersection of coordination can be crossed easily and safely because you are prepared, programmed, and ultimately polished in your ability to make the most difficult and intricate tasks appear easy and seamless.

Finally, during those maddening moments before guests arrive, you may wish to add one additional ritual to your arsenal of coordination tools. A colleague once told me that before she opens the doors to receive her guests, she closes her eyes for a few seconds and silently repeats three times: "This event is going to be easy, fun, and successful." Although events are rarely easy, and the fun comes after the guests leave, in fact your event may be more successful if you are relaxed in your approach to receiving the guests. Now relax and let's go on-site to begin coordinating the details that will produce your next successful event.

Career-Advancement Connections

 ### Global Connection

Moving events from city to city, state to state, or even country to country, is a complicated task with a number of challenges. One of the more important parts is transportation. Although many professionals are available to assist you in accommodating transportation needs, it is important for event professionals to have some basic knowledge of the issue. Transportation within one country involves mostly negotiations with a transport agency. A transportation agency usually provides services such as packing, loading, moving, unloading, and sometimes even unpacking as part of a contract. Event professionals should also remember about insurance. Usually transportation companies provide basic insurance on their services; however, it is important to confirm that the amount of insurance is sufficient to cover not only physical damage or/and loss of equipment but also potential losses that may occur due to event cancellation.

International transportation is more complicated than domestic. When conducting business internationally, event professionals should work with a much larger number of government and private institutions than for local events. Moving equipment to or from overseas venues often involves payment of import or export duties, various excise duties, various fees, and other payments. Before planning any international event activity, event professionals are strongly encouraged to consult international trade and tax professionals, who often will be affiliated with your international transport agency. An excellent reference for this task is *Global Meetings and Exhibitions* by Carol Krugman, CMP, and Rudy Wright, CMP (Wiley, 2006).

Technology Connection

Use a Microsoft Excel spreadsheet or other software to track all vendor agreements. Utilize event planning software such as Meeting Pro, Event Manager, Day to Day Event Manager, EVENTS, Special Event Management, and other products to efficiently organize and document your event planning operations.

For a more extensive list of event software, see Appendix 8. Software such as Microsoft Outlook will allow you to use the calendar function to set up appointments, reminders, and other date- and time-specific operations to ensure more accurate planning.

Resources Connection

Contact industry associations and local convention and visitors' bureaus for key contact information. Comprehensive listings may be found at the Convention Industry Council (*www.cic.org*), the Destination Marketing Association International (*www.iacvb.org*), the International Congress and Convention Association (*www.icca.nl*), or *www.ises.com*. These organizations will assist you in identifying qualified vendors to support your event. Interview prospective and current vendors and determine what systems they are using to manage events. This will help you ensure that your systems are congruent.

Learning Connection

Use the *Event Specification Guide* template to detail the arrangements for a association event for 1,000 persons with 100 exhibitors. The event's duration is three days and includes one opening reception, two luncheons, and one gala awards dinner.

Lighting truss demonstrates the color and complexity involved in on-site production for special events.

CHAPTER 7

On-Site Event Production

In This Chapter You Will Learn How To:

+ Understand the differences between the timeline, productions schedule, résumé, and Event Specification Guide (ESG)

+ Develop and implement event contingency plans

+ Monitor each element of an event during event operations

+ Establish and manage efficient registration operations

+ Coordinate industry and professional speakers

+ Identify and utilize appropriate amenities

+ Identify, create, and post informative signs

If policies and procedures provide a rationale and regulation for day-to-day event decision making, the timeline and production schedule serve as the road maps that ensure you will arrive safely at your destination. The policies, procedures, and practices comprise the rules of the road, but without the production schedule, you may never find the right road or navigate so poorly that your event is hopelessly lost before you even begin.

Timeline

The timeline is the sequential listing of all tasks and duties associated with the event project. It is divided by the five phases of the event process: research, design, planning, coordination, and evaluation. Within each of these tasks the Event Leader lists each task and duty that is required to develop and execute the event. These duties and tasks represent units of time or, as described by project managers, "work packages" that may be measured in hours or days. Therefore, the timeline is listed in calendar order by either dates, weeks, or months. The first task is reviewing previous data from preceding events, and the final task is to conduct a comprehensive evaluation and create and transmit a thorough final report to promote sustainability.

Production Schedule

The production schedule is one of the major series of tasks and duties within the timeline. In the *coordination* phase of the timeline the Event Leader coordinates the logistics of the event that has been planned. The first task in the production schedule is to inspect the venue prior to moving in any equipment. The final task in the timeline is to re-inspect the venue at the conclusion of the event after removing all equipment. This enables the Event Leader to observe and note any physical changes to the venue as a result of the event activity. The production schedule lists minute by minute (or, in the case of television production, second by second) each activity that is performed in sequential order. For example, the Event Leader would want to make certain the lighting company precedes the catering company when installing equipment. Lighting must be raised into place and requires a clear floor area. Therefore, tables may not be dropped and decorated until the major lighting has been hung and generally focused.

Résumé

Historically, meeting professionals have used the term *résumé* to describe all of the components for the meeting or function room. The résumé will not only list the time for each function but also the equipment and food and beverage that is required. This document

Date	Time	Function	Location	Setup	Attendance	Catering	A/V
Friday	10:00 A.M.– 12 P.M. (noon)	Board meeting	Room 102	Hollow square	20	Coffee, juice	Overhead

Figure 7.1 Typical Résumé

serves as a major communications tool for all stakeholders, including the hotel or convention center as well as individual vendors. A typical résumé is shown in Figure 7.1.

Event Specification Guide

Recently the Convention Industry Council (CIC) has adopted the term and format of an *Event Specification Guide* (*ESP*) through its successful APEX initiative. The *ESP* takes the production schedule and résumé to a higher level by providing a series of integrated components and, for the first time, encouraging universal adoption by all stakeholders in the meetings and events industry. The *ESP*, if widely adopted, has the potential for saving time and therefore saving money by promoting easier and better communication among event stakeholders. The *ESP* is available in a software package through the Convention Industry Council at *www.conventionindustry.org*.

Improving Event Performance

Hundreds or perhaps thousands of elements must be coordinated to produce a foolproof event. Just as a coach writes down plays and shares these plans with the team, the Event Leader must reduce his or her plans to writing and communicate these details with the event stakeholders. Using the timeline–production schedule will improve your event performance in many ways. A few of these are listed next to enable you to better understand the benefits of this planning tool:

+ A production schedule requires the Event Leader to schedule every element involved in an event systematically and logically.
+ It provides a unique comprehensive communications tool for the use of other team members.
+ It enables external stakeholders, such as police, fire, security, and medical personnel, to stay informed regarding event operations.
+ It is easily distributed to internal and external stakeholders via a computer modem for quick updates.
+ It provides an accurate historical accounting of the entire event.

Many of the competencies we have discussed in previous chapters, including history, communication, and logical and reasonable thinking, are incorporated in the production schedule process. However, the most important reason for implementing the time-line–production schedule into your planning process is that it absolutely improves event performance. This is accomplished through improved communications. Every member of your event team is able to refer to the timeline–production schedule and determine quickly and efficiently what is supposed to happen at what time. For this reason alone, it is a very valuable tool and should be used from the research period through the final evaluation.

Improving Financial Effectiveness

One area that governs all other areas of an event is financial management. The production schedule allows you to see, in spreadsheet fashion, how you are allocating your scarce event resources in the most efficient manner. Once you have assembled all the details in logical sequence, you can review them carefully to see if there are any duplications or ways in which resources may be reallocated for greater cost savings. For example, if you notice that the installation is scheduled for Sunday at 7:00 A.M. and that will result in paying time and a half to your crews, you can try to rearrange your Friday activities to schedule the setup within the straight-time rate.

Every element on the production schedule affects your event financially. Therefore, when using this schedule, you should look constantly for ways to best allocate your event resources in the most cost-effective manner.

Production Schedule

Creating the Schedule

The production schedule is the minute-by-minute (or in the case of television, second-by-second) running order for your event. It differs from the timeline in that it only reflects the time period from move in (referred to in Europe and Asia as "bump in") to move out (referred to in Europe and Asia as "bump out") for your event. It does not include the research, design, planning, or evaluation phases of the event. These phases, as well as the coordination phase, are included in the event timeline.

The first task in the production schedule is to *inspect the venue,* and the final task is *inspect the venue.* These inspections are critical as they allow the Event Leader to identify any physical or other challenges with the venue prior to the official move in and also to note any change in the condition of the venue prior to the conclusion of the move out.

There are three important resources to incorporate when creating your draft document. First, you must check with key informants to make certain that you have incorporated all critical information. Second, you will want to explain the production schedule at

Traditional dance in Bali, Indonesia. *Photo courtesy of Corbis Digital Stock.*

The National Constitution Center in Philadelphia, Pennsylvania hosted the Fiftieth Anniversary convention of the Professional Convention Management Association. Over 3000 persons effortlessly moved throughout the center and were astounded by aerial acrobatics by circus performers from over their heads.

This marching band in Austria is often used for ceremonial events such as opening ceremonies for international congresses. *Courtesy of Corbis Digital Stock.*

Bicycle race. *Photo courtesy of PhotoDisc, Inc.*

A living statue pours water to delight guests attending the Philadelphia ISES FRESH trade show. The living statue using a water effect is an effective way to take an older concept (living statue) to a new level (liquids).

Family celebrating Kwanzaa. *Photo courtesy of Purestock.*

The Philadelphia Flower Show attracts over 200,000 visitors and is regarded as one of the largest floral exhibitions in the world. This display demonstrates how floral products and lighting may produce multi-sensory impacts among guests.

Hot air balloons. *Photo courtesy of Corbis Digital Stock.*

The Batwa Pygmies of Uganda dance and conduct secret ceremonial rituals in their private place in the forest of the Mountains of the Moon. The pygmies have conducted and transmitted these rituals and ceremonies for thousands of year to cultivate pride, instill courage, transmit tradition, build kinship and pursue magic and mystery through their tribal events.

Wedding Cake with Sugar Flowers. *Photo courtesy of PhotoDisc/Getty Images.*

The Singapore Lantern Festival is held annually in Singapore to promote tourism and visitation. Hundreds of large scale illuminated cloth sculptures delight children and adults using a common theme such as Jungle Book™ or Disney™.

an upcoming group meeting to receive feedback from the entire group. Finally, you must recheck the timing, function, and assignment to check for gaps and make certain that your production schedule is logical.

■ Key Informants

Ask the senior members of your team to assist you with constructing the draft production schedule. Instruct each team member to create an individualized production schedule reflecting the operations of the individual departments. After you have received all the schedules, combine them into one integrated document. Then distribute the draft document to the same key informants and ask them to check your work for accuracy and see if there are additions, deletions, or changes. Typical key informants assisting you in preparing and reviewing the production schedule are:

- ✦ Admissions coordinator
- ✦ Advertising coordinator
- ✦ Assistant Event Leader
- ✦ Audiovisual coordinator
- ✦ Caterer
- ✦ Decorator
- ✦ Entertainment coordinator
- ✦ Exposition coordinator
- ✦ Facility management
- ✦ Fire department
- ✦ Food and beverage coordinator
- ✦ Legal advisor
- ✦ Lighting coordinator
- ✦ Medical coordinator
- ✦ Police
- ✦ Public relations
- ✦ Registration coordinator
- ✦ Rentals coordinator
- ✦ Risk management coordinator
- ✦ Safety coordinator
- ✦ Security coordinator
- ✦ Transportation coordinator
- ✦ Ushering coordinator

■ Group Meetings

Transfer the production schedule to a slide and use the next team meeting as an opportunity to explain this document. Walk through each step of the schedule slowly and carefully, pausing occasionally to ask if there are any questions. Solicit feedback from the group on how best to depict the schedule as well as ways to consolidate operations and improve efficiency.

■ Testing, Timing, Function, and Assignment

The production schedule is a table comprised of six columns. These columns allow you to enter the various key components or elements of the event in logical sequence. It is critical that you test your production schedule by seeking input from critical friends who have produced similar events of the same size and scope. Similar to a budget, the timeline–production schedule is a projection of how things should happen based on the knowledge available to you at this time. Figure 7.2 shows a typical event production schedule table. You may adapt this model for your own needs. Make certain the timeline–production schedule includes the five phases of Event Leadership: research, design, planning, coordination, and evaluation.

Task	Start Time	Stop Time	Details	Person(s) Responsible	Notes
Inspect venue	7 A.M.	7:45 A.M.	Check for preexisting damages, problems	Event Leader	
Lighting and sound company loads in	8 A.M.	9 A.M.	Arrivals and load-in	Event coordinator	
Lighting and sound company installs	9 A.M.	12 noon	Set up, hang, focus, test	Event coordinator	
Lunch break	12 noon	1 P.M.	Lunch for 10 stage hands	Caterer	
Florist loads in and installs	1 P.M.	3 P.M.	Decorate stage and prepare centerpieces	Florist	
Rental company loads in and sets tables, chairs, and cloths	1 P.M.	3 P.M.	Place tables and chairs and clothe the tables	Rental company	
Place centerpieces on table	3 P.M.	4 P.M.	Position centerpieces	Volunteers	
Caterer loads in and sets up preparation area	3 P.M.	4 P.M.	Set up staging area for food preparation	Caterer	
Caterer sets tables	4 P.M.	5 P.M.	Final setting of tables	Caterer	
Inspection of tables, décor, lighting, sound by Event Leader	5 P.M.	5:30 P.M.	Final review	Event Leader	

Figure 7.2 Typical Production Schedule

Task	Start Time	Stop Time	Details	Person(s) Responsible	Notes
Sound check and rehearsal with band	5:30 P.M.	6:30 P.M.	Final sound check	Event Leader, talent, technicians	
Waiters in position to open doors	6:45 P.M.	7 P.M.	Workers ready to open doors for guests	Event coordinator	
Open doors	7 P.M.	7:15 P.M.	Guests enter and are seated by waiters	Event coordinator	Doors opened early (7:10 P.M.)
Invocation	7:15 P.M.	7:17 P.M.	Minister delivers invocation	Stage manager	
Salad course	7:17 P.M.	7:30 P.M.	Salad served	Caterer	
Salad removed, entrée served	7:30 P.M.	7:50 P.M.	Entrée served	Caterer	
Entrée removed, dessert served	7:50 P.M.	8:10 P.M.	Dessert served	Caterer	
Coffee and candies served	8:10 P.M.	8:20 P.M.	Coffee and candies passed	Caterer	
Welcome speech and introduction of entertainment	8:20 P.M.	8:30 P.M.	All waiters out of room; speeches	Stage manager	
Entertainment	8:30 P.M.	9:00 P.M.	Band	Stage manager	Entertainment started late (8:40 P.M.)
Dancing	9:00 P.M.	12 midnight	Dancing	Stage manager	
Close bars	11:45 P.M.	12 midnight	Stop serving	Caterer	
End of event	12 midnight	12 midnight	Lights up full	Event Leader	
Dismantle and load-out	12:30 A.M.	6 A.M.	All equipment dismantled and removed from venue	Event coordinator	
Reinspect venue	7 A.M.	8 A.M.	Venue checked for any damages or losses caused by event	Event Leader, event coordinator, venue official	

Figure 7.2 *(Continued)*

Implementing the Schedule

After you have completed the production schedule, you must circulate a series of drafts to key constituents to ensure that approvals are received before issuing the final document. Always attach a cover memorandum instruction for each reader on how to analyze the production schedule and describe the kind of input you are seeking. For example, you may ask one reader to proof for typographical errors while another is to concentrate on validating the timing for the various activities. Each key constituent should have a specific role to play relevant to his or her level of expertise. However, each constituent should review the entire plan to check for overall gaps as well as his or her own particular area of expertise.

Monitoring the Schedule

Appoint several capable people to serve as monitors and oversee various stages of implementation of the production schedule. They should have a copy of the schedule and should, in the notes section, list any variances from the schedule published. If, for example, the event is late in starting, this should be noted with the actual start time. If the event runs overtime, this should also be noted with the actual stop time. This kind of information is extremely important when planning future events and budgeting adequate time to the various elements you will use.

The monitor should turn in his or her copy of the production schedule with the notes included immediately after completing his or her assignment. Figure 7.2 demonstrates typical notes that your monitor may insert.

Handling Changes

About the only thing you can count on today is that things will change and sometimes far too rapidly to update the production schedule. When a change must be made quickly, use a printed bulletin headlined "CHANGE NOTICE" to ensure that every member of your team is aware and able to adjust his or her schedule to accept this change. Figure 7.3 depicts a typical change notice.

■ Using the Timeline–Production Schedule to Manage Change

One of the most useful aspects of the production schedule is its ability to assist you in managing change. As literally hundreds of decisions must be made on a daily basis, the production schedule provides a solid framework for decision making.

Perhaps your celebrity has been delayed in another city and will be arriving late for your function. A quick glance at the production schedule allows you to make the necessary adjustments and see how these adjustments are affecting other elements of the event. In addition, by sharing a common document with your team members, you can solicit their input before making the adjustments, to ensure that you are in concert with one another.

Using integrated system design network (ISDN) technology, you will be able to send the most complex production schedule using fiber optics and involve as many people as

CHANGE NOTICE
Distribution: All event staff and volunteers.

Change: The opening ceremony previously scheduled to start at 10:00 A.M. on May 15, 2008, has been changed. **The new start time is 10:15 A.M.** The reason for this change is that the television feed has been moved and the new time is the actual start of the broadcast.

Summary: Note time changes for opening ceremony.

Previous time: May 15, 10:00 A.M.

New time: May 15, 10:15 A.M.

Figure 7.3 Typical Change Notice

necessary in your review and decision-making process. As each of you sits in front of a computer terminal sharing the same document, you will be able to make minute or major changes and immediately see and discuss the ramifications of your decisions. In a world fraught with accelerated change, this will be a major advancement in the Event Leadership process.

The deficiencies in the résumé shown in Figure 7.1 include the absence of a contact person or person responsible for this function and a cell for notes regarding the actual start and stop times for the event. Although the résumé is widely used in the meeting Event Leadership field, it has some gaps you must be aware of. When deciding which tool to use for your event, first share your template or model with the venue that will be responsible for handling most of the meeting event logistics. Confirm and verify that the tool you propose to use will be accepted and used by the venue's staff prior to implementation.

Evaluating the Schedule

The best way to evaluate the use of the production schedule is to ask the key stakeholders if the process was effective: "Did the schedule help you understand the big and little picture of the event? Was the production schedule useful in keeping track of start and stop times? Were there any deficiencies in the timeline–production schedule? How could the schedule be improved next time?"

A quantitative way to monitor the use of the schedule is to review the notes section and look for wide gaps between the scheduled start and stop times and the actual times. Carefully study those elements of the event where the gaps were inordinately wide, and seek solutions in planning your next event.

Remember that the production schedule is similar to a budget in that it is a broad project management tool with a history that may be used to improve the overall planning process. Make certain you are diligent about reviewing the final schedule and comparing your projected elements with the final event. From this process, improvements will be made and your production scheduling process will become more scientific in the future.

Audiovisual Effects Management

Audiovisual, lighting, sound, special effects, and video are growing in importance with emerging techniques, lower costs, and improved quality.

Standard Audiovisual Equipment

■ Liquid Crystal Display Projector

Technology
The liquid crystal display (LCD) projector is used in conjunction with a computer to project graphic text and video onto a screen. This technology, which allows a presenter to have maximum flexibility when preparing and showing slides, is rapidly replacing traditional overhead transparencies. It has largely replaced the 35-millimeter slide projection and overhead projector as the instrument of choice in the event industry.

Use
An LCD projector may be used to present complex charts and graphs, text, Internet Web sites, graphics, and video as well as other images in a lively format similar to that of television production incorporating wipes, crawls, rolls, and other moving images. Make certain that you have the proper cabling for the LCD panel, as the Macintosh and PC use different attachments. With additional technology, it is possible to incorporate video and audio into your presentations to create an attention-grabbing program and liven up even the most tedious lectures. Be careful not to allow your content to become buried under too much technological wizardry. Content must supersede presentation to maintain the integrity of your message.

■ Light Emitting Diode Screen

Technology
Light emitting diodes (LEDs) are essentially little colored light bulbs. They require a computer system, wires, and lots of power to operate.

Use
Use an LED screen in large outdoor and especially daylight situations where the brightest possible projection is required. LED screens are often used in large stadiums or in locations with high pedestrian and vehicle traffic, such as New York's Times Square area.

■ Flat-Panel Screen

Technology

The flat-panel screen uses liquid crystal display technology (LCD) (see earlier LED description).

Use

The most common use is computer screens in laptop computers. However, in recent years home entertainment systems have adopted the flat-panel screen, and it is often seen in private homes and offices. In the meetings and events industry, the flat-panel screen is often used in smaller events to magnify the speaker or live onstage activity. It may also be used as a alternative for the traditional teleprompter.

■ Microphone

Technology

The lectern microphone is perhaps the most common technology in use in conference events. Two primary types of microphones are available for use by Event Leaders. The *unidirectional microphone* is ideal for the individual speaker, and the *omnidirectional microphone* is designed for occasions when several people share the lectern. In addition to the lectern microphone, the *lavaliere* or *clip-on microphone* (sometimes the names are used interchangeably) allows a presenter to be mobile and move around the stage or room. Although more expensive, the wireless handheld or lavaliere microphone provides even greater freedom, as no cable is attached. Using an FM transmitter and receiver, the audio signal is patched directly into the audio system and produces high-quality sound.

Use

When using a clip-on microphone, placement of the microphone head is extremely important. The head should be as close to the mouth as possible. Therefore, it should be placed on the upper part of a man's necktie or coat lapel. Women should wear it high on the blouse or in the upper part of a jacket lapel. It is wise to provide redundant wired microphones for wireless systems. I usually place a wired microphone with 50 feet of cable in the lectern to provide security for the speaker and make the transition from wireless to wired as smooth as possible.

■ Projection Screens

Technology

Event Leaders use both rear and front projection screens for different reasons and different venues. A front projection screen generally provides brighter illumination; however, a rear projection screen makes it possible to hide the projection equipment from audience view. Typically, two types of screens are used. A *tripod screen* is supported by a metal tripod, and a *fastfold screen* is supported by a metal frame and may be either supported on legs or hung from above. Projection screens generally range in size from 6 feet high by 8 feet wide to 15 feet high by 20 feet wide. These screens accept slides produced in horizontal formats. In addition to the screen, most audiovisual suppliers will provide a dress kit for the fast-fold screen. This kit consists of a skirt, valance, and perhaps side drapes for masking. You may also wish to use other pipes and drapes to run off to the side of the room to further mask the backstage area. In addition to traditional screens, increasingly Event Leaders use a wider range of surfaces for front and rear projection. One such projection surface is a product known as Transformit™ (*www.transformitdesign.com*). See Figure 7.5 for an example of this product.

Use

Screens may be used for laser, slide, or video projection. Typically, screens are underutilized at conferences. Consider using the screen surface to project the names of your event's sponsor or other information in addition to the educational content of the conference. Avoid leaving screens blank by using a title slide to cover periods when no video or slides are required. In case of an emergency, to create an instant title slide without the expense of a slide projector, use the video camera to shoot the lectern sign that usually features the organization's logo or name. This shot will then be projected onto the screens as if it were a title slide.

■ Cost-Saving Measures

When renting audiovisual equipment, remember that this business, like many in the meetings and conference field, is somewhat seasonal. Therefore, the prices for the equipment may be negotiable. The price for labor is typically not negotiable. When bidding on audiovisual equipment, make certain that you list every possible application and amount of time required for labor so that the bidders may evaluate the total value of your event. Many (if not most) audiovisual rental firms will offer a 25 percent producer's discount. You may be able to receive greater discounts on equipment by adjusting the dates of your event to reflect periods when equipment is more readily available.

Still another way to save money is to find multiple uses for your audiovisual equipment during the same 24-hour period. Too often, Event Leaders use a video projector for one hour when, in actuality, the rental is factored on a 24-hour period. Preplan the use of this equipment to maximize the value. For example, can the projector be moved to a different room instead of renting a separate piece of equipment?

Finally, look for ways to share costs on audiovisual equipment with other groups. Perhaps there is another organization meeting in the same venue at the same time as your organization. Can you co-rent equipment with them to save costs?

Lighting

When, according to the old testament of the bible, the almighty proclaimed "Let there be light," it may have been the first time in recorded history that a lighting cue was called. Since that fateful day, lighting has come to symbolize safety, mood, atmosphere, and transition, as well as time of day and location. In almost every event environment, lighting improves the atmosphere. It may be used to focus attention on the speaker and to enhance the look of décor and food as well as to change the mood dramatically from one scene to another.

Miniaturization has affected the lighting field in major ways. Only a few years ago, a lighting control system would require enough space to fill a small bedroom. Today, the same system fits compactly on a card table. This major reduction in size has made lighting more flexible and available than ever before.

LEDs are the emerging lighting technology of choice by Event Leaders. LEDs provide lower cost and greater flexibility of lighting designers. Annually, the Lighting Dimensions International (LDI) (*www.ldishow.com*) exhibition showcases the latest new technologies in theatrical and event lighting.

Figure 7.4 demonstrates how lighting may be used in a variety of event situations. These applications are only the tip of the iceberg, because many Event Leaders combine different lighting effects, much as a visual artist combines color and texture to create the desired effect. Event Leaders commonly use the lighting technology that follows to achieve the desired effects.

■ Chase Lights or Rope Lights

Technology
Chase lights or *rope lights* are miniature lights that may be encased in clear or colored plastic flexible tubing or assembled on a string of electrical wire. They are a low-wattage way to create excitement and direct focus. The emerging standard for all chase or rope lights is the Light Emitting Diode (LED) format. This provides the designer with greater flexibility and significantly lower cost. The annual LDI trade show showcases this technology as well as many other new products that are quickly adopted for use by the live events industry.

Activity	Lighting Application
1960s or space age	Ultraviolet light
Atmosphere	Lighting projections (gobos)
Centerpieces	Pin spots
Change of mood	Backdrop colorization
Dance floor	Moving lights
Entertainer	Follow spotlights
High-tech focus	Laser light show
Product reveal	Chaser light
Space-age effect	Fiber-optic backdrop
Speaker at lectern	Key light for focus
Stage set	Set light and backlight

Figure 7.4 Applications for Lighting

Use

Chase lights may outline a new product or sign, edge a stage or arch, or be incorporated in ceilings to create a starlight effect.

■ Dimmer or Control Board

Technology

A dimmer or control board allows the lighting operator to fade, black out, and perform other lighting cues. Many, if not most, control boards are computer-driven, allowing the operator to store the cues in memory and then, at the press of one button, perform dozens of tasks.

Use

The control board sends the electronic signal to the individual lighting instrument, instructing it to perform on cue a specific effect. These cues may range from blackouts to slow fades to everything in between. Some control boards have a light organ built in that allows the lights to pulse to the beat of live or recorded music. The control board also can be used to cue the house lights, or make certain that the control board is placed near the house-light control so that you may coordinate these two functions.

■ Ellipsoidal Spotlight

Technology

The major difference between the ellipsoidal spotlight (also known as leko) and the par cam, which is discussed later, is the ability to focus light selectively and to use a template for projecting specific images.

Use

Using shutters, the ellipsoidal spotlight allows the Event Leader to focus light narrowly to highlight specific areas in a cylindrical, horizontal, or vertical format. Additionally, this instrument accepts a metal or glass template known as a gobo. The gobo uses a design that can be projected on a surface such as a curtain, wall, floor, or other area. These designs may be mixed and matched to create a variety of effects. Using a scrim curtain, you can project an image such as a window, and using a rear light source, an actor may actually appear to raise the window by adding a second gobo of an open window. Gobos may also be used to project text such as sponsor names. This is a quick and inexpensive way to add sponsor recognition to an event.

■ Fiber-Optic Drop or Curtain

Technology

Thousands of microthin fibers carry light from a central source and create changing colors or chase effects.

Use

This relatively new technology provides a dramatic backdrop for a stage set and may also be used in a theme event to create the illusion of a galaxy of stars.

■ Follow Spotlight

Technology
A manually operated, focusable spotlight with the ability to add color through gels, this spotlight can follow speakers, actors, or other persons as they perform.

Use
Follow spotlights focus attention on a principal performer or on a prop or other important symbol. This technology is also used to create excitement as the spotlight ballys (rapidly moves left and right) through the audience onto the stage.

■ Intelligent Lighting

Technology
Robotic lights are able to tilt, pan, turn, change color, change gobo patterns, change focus, and perform other maneuvers at the touch of a switch. One intelligent lighting unit may be able to replace a dozen other units, due to the flexibility it offers. Although significantly more expensive than traditional lighting instruments such as par cams (discussed next), these units are able to perform many more functions.

Use
Intelligent lighting is most appropriate for large-scale productions where high-tech lighting will support or enhance the production. I have used them for theme parties, inserting the client's gobo in the units and then ballying the image throughout the room. I have also used them when I required a flexible system that could change the look of the event environment several times over a short period of time.

■ Par Cam Lighting Instrument

Technology
If the LCD projector is the workhorse of the audiovisual field, the par cam performs that same function among the many instruments in the field of lighting. The par cam provides a broad floodlight and is used to fill a stage with light. This instrument is traditionally used to flood large areas and to provide color to create mood and atmosphere.

Use
From lighting the front area of a stage, to providing side fill light for a lectern, to creating dramatic mood lighting for a backdrop, the par cam has many uses. Gels may be inserted to provide color. To create an effect similar to *Star Trek*'s "Beam me up, Scotty" illusion, I used four par cams placed on the floor of each side of a platform. Adding fog, the lights projected up through the particulate matter and created a low-cost but highly effective impression.

■ Pin Spot

Technology
A pin spot is used to provide a narrow focused beam of light on a table centerpiece.

Use

This low-wattage instrument is extremely effective for lighting a specific area, such as a centerpiece.

■ Strobe Light

Technology

This rapidly flashing light creates the illusion of slow or fast motion when used with movement. It is available in a variety of sizes, including small egg-shape products that, when used in combination with other instruments, produce a starlight effect.

Use

In a theatrical production, strobe lights may be used to simulate slow motion. I have used strobe lights to create a space-age effect in an entrance tunnel and egg-shape strobes to decorate the exterior of a building.

Caution

Both chase lights and strobe lights may cause discomfort or even injury to guests with disabilities, such as hearing loss or epilepsy. When using these devices, post a sign at the entrance stating: *The following special effects are used during this event: strobe lights and chasing lights.*

■ Ultraviolet or Black Light

Technology

Popular during the 1960s, ultraviolet or black light technology has improved tremendously. Originally available only in tube format, its major drawback was the limited throw distance. In recent years, manufacturers have invented new technology that allows longer throw distance and focusable light to create fantastic new effects.

Use

This technology may be used to create a dark and haunting atmosphere or a space-age thrill. As the light excites the color in a sign, the graphic will suddenly pop out at the audience. I have effectively used this technology to reveal new products by outlining the new item in colors that are sensitive to black light and then, at the appointed time, illuminating the appropriate instrument.

■ Cost-Saving Measures

The easiest way to save money on lighting equipment and labor is to select a venue that has lighting equipment permanently installed in its facility. Sometimes the venue will include in the rental fee the use of some or all lighting equipment. You may also wish to share the costs of equipment rentals with other groups in the same venue.

When you must rent lighting equipment, make certain that you solicit bids. When possible, ask bidders to inspect the venue with you, as they may be able to offer additional ideas that you may not have thought of previously.

Finally, remember that costs escalate rapidly when work is performed outside normal business hours. Find the time frame for straight time and work within this window. Sometimes this will require renting the venue on a weekday to prepare for a weekend event. Compare the labor cost savings to the rental charges and determine which is better. Schedule labor carefully to avoid overtime charges.

Sound

The level of complexity and purpose of the event determines the level of audio support that is required. In most event environments, audio is used for simple, noncomplex productions. However, as the size of the audience increases or the complexity of the production rises, simple audio must be replaced by the services provided by a production sound company.

Sound is used for public address, entertainment, to project speakers, and to transmit sound from video or film as well as numerous other applications. Figure 7.5 describes some of these applications and the type of equipment that may be required.

Sound Equipment	Application
Audio console and rack	Full-sound production capability, including playback and recording.
Boom attachment	Television, film, recording, specific sound source, and large groups.
Cassette player/recorder	Recording live sound.
Compact disc player	Playback of instrumental music and other sound, including effects.
Delay speaker	Used to project sound to areas that are a greater distance from the original sound source. In a stage setting, the delay speakers may be mounted halfway over the audience. The signal received by these speakers is delayed to avoid an echolike quality.
Digital audiotape (DAT) machine	Synchronized music.
Fill speaker	A speaker used to send sound signals to dead spots such as the front center of an audience
Mixer	Used for blending sound sources through one central unit.
Omnidirectional microphone	Chorus.
Perimeter zone microphone (PZM)	Chorus, singers, and piano.
Reel to reel	Slide or audio synchronization.
Speaker	Used for projecting sound to either a specific area or a wide distribution.
Speaker cluster	A group of speakers clustered together to project a wide distribution of sound.
Speaker tripod	A speaker mounted on a tripod.
Stage or ear monitor	Playback from other instruments and vocalists.
Unidirectional microphone	Solo speaker.

Figure 7.5   Applications for Sound Equipment

■ Compact Disc Player

Technology

A compact disc (CD) player produces high-quality audio and video signals and provides enduring quality. Unlike its predecessor, the audiocassette player, the compact disc player allows for instant cueing and random access to specific audio or video segments. Data storage are also important uses of this technology.

Use

Instrumental music and/or video/slides may be retrieved instantaneously with this technology. CD players can be used for background or specific audio musical cues as well as to project photos or video images. They are ideal for instrumental music for background music, fanfares, or dancing.

■ Equalizer

Technology

The range between treble and bass is equalized using this valuable technology.

Use

A professional sound engineer is required to equalize the range between treble and bass. He or she will use either your prerecorded sound source or the live performance to equalize the sound to provide a full range of audio dynamics.

■ Mixer

Technology

A mixer is used to blend or mix different sound inputs or sources and transmit them into a central output. The number of inputs may vary from four to dozens.

Use

Instrumental musicians and multiple vocalists as well as event programs that feature both live and recorded sound sources will require the services of a mixing unit.

■ MP3 Player

According to the British Council, an organization represented by official charter and dedicated to promoting the creative arts among various nations, the MP3 player is associated with downloading music from the Internet. The device, smaller than a personal CD player, is very portable. You will need a computer to download songs, but you do not necessarily need the Internet. *MP3* is just the name of a type of computer file.

Event Leaders are increasingly using the MP3 player in place of the traditional compact disc (CD) due to its size and versatility. The audio quality of an MP3 player is comparable to a CD and enables the Event Leader to quickly download music from the Internet to satisfy the immediate need of a specific event.

When downloading music, it is critically important to ascertain who owns the rights to the material that is being downloaded. For example, some music may be downloaded for personal use only, such as iTunes music from Apple™ (*www.itunes.com*). If you wish to use the same material for commercial purposes or to synchronize the music with another media, such as video, you may need to negotiate additional rights with the music licensor.

■ Perimeter Zone Microphone

Technology
The perimeter zone microphone (PZM) is a flat microphone that picks up sounds in a 180-degree radius. It is used inside a piano, on the floor of a stage, to record choirs or large musical ensembles, and other applications where sound may originate from more than one point.

Use
Place the PZM inside the piano lid, on the center of a table for a group discussion, or on the floor of a stage to record or broadcast sound from multiple sources.

■ Sound Console or Rack

Technology
A sound console or rack is a multicomponent system that may feature a recorder, player (cassette and/or compact disc), equalizer, mixer, and other important technology.

Use
The term *rack* originates from the way the equipment is stacked on racks in a vertical system.

■ Stage or Ear Monitor

Technology
The stage monitor (sometimes referred to as a wedge due to its wedge-like shape) is used to monitor sounds from other instruments in a musical group, including vocals, as well as to monitor the sound level as the audience experiences it. Increasingly popular among entertainers is the ear monitor. This small hearing-aid type of device is custom-fitted to the ear and allows for monitoring of sound as well as cueing and synchronizing when singing or performing to a prerecorded track.

Use
Singers and musicians use stage monitors to communicate with one another and to review their sound as the audience hears it. Singers, television performers, and others use ear monitors to receive cues from the director and monitor their vocal performance.

■ Wireless Microphone

Technology
Both handheld and clip-on wireless microphones are regularly used for conferences, meetings, and live entertainment as well as video production. The speaker can move freely before and among the audience using this equipment.

Use

When conducting a presentation featuring audience questions and answers, the wireless microphone is ideal. It is also the instrument of choice for speakers who move randomly on the stage and among the audience. Remember to have redundant equipment in the form of a wired microphone in case the wireless microphone should fail.

■ Sound Opportunities

There are generally three periods when sound is utilized for most events.

1. Sound is utilized prior to the event to prepare certain audio products, such as sound tracks or fanfares, for the live performance.
2. Sound is used during the actual event for broadcasting both to the live audience attending the event and to those listening by radio and television.
3. Sound production may include a postproduction session when the live sound recorded during the event is further processed to documentary, marketing, or other use.

Preproduction

The preproduction period generally occurs during the design, planning, and coordination phases. Preproduction may include the design and production of specific audio elements for the event. These elements will vary depending on the complexity of the event. Your task could be as simple as selecting appropriate instrumental music tracks or as complex as mixing an entire symphony orchestra to provide recorded accompaniment for a major mega-event, such as the opening or closing ceremony of the Olympic Games. The preproduction period must be planned carefully, as others may need to review the finished product before use in the actual event. Therefore, allow sufficient time to identify the appropriate resources, produce the product, and receive feedback from your important event stakeholders. When budgeting this time, I usually allow 25 to 50 percent more time than estimated to handle last-minute changes and requests.

Production

During this period, the Event Leader *coordinates* the live, broadcast, or recording of sound from the actual event. Depending on the size and complexity of the event, the Event Leader may wish to assign a specific person from his or her staff to monitor the sound production. In most cases, a competent and capable sound technician will handle the myriad of details required for this function. However, in those circumstances when the event is new or highly specialized, it is wise to have one person supervise the sound department to ensure that this element of production is consistent with expectations. Too often, Event Leaders assign too low a budget for production sound. Do not fall victim to this error. Make certain that you have budgeted carefully for the level of quality required. One way to do this is to be certain that you have retained a sound console operator as well as a stage sound technician. Speakers, actors, singers, musicians, and others who are using sound equipment will benefit from the knowledge that a qualified sound technician is nearby to help prevent or correct problems. A simple mistake, such as failing to turn on the wireless microphone, can easily be prevented by investing in a professional sound technician to monitor these important details.

Postproduction

Once the event has ended, the sound responsibilities may continue. More and more events are being recorded for both documentary and marketing purposes. Therefore, during the design, planning, and coordination process of the event, careful attention must be paid as to how you may use the sound product after the live event has ended. Although the two most common uses are documentation and recording, it is also possible to use the sound portion of your event for communications as well as risk management purposes. For example, a well-edited sound version of your event may be an effective way to communicate with your volunteers. You may duplicate this program on cassette tapes and distribute them to volunteers to enjoy during their drive time to and from work. Should your organization become involved in a lawsuit resulting from a risk management incident, the sound recording may provide evidence that you practiced a standard of care acceptable in your area. For example, a recording of the evacuation announcement may provide you with evidence that you conducted this important activity with a reasonable degree of care to prevent injury. Throughout the research and design process, the Event Leader must carefully consider how he or she will later use the sound product created during the event.

■ Soundscaping

The Olympic Games and Super Bowl sound designer Bob Estrin of Creative Event Technology in Orange County, California, may have been the first person of his generation to soundscape a room. The soundscaper works very much like the landscape artist or architect in that he or she designs specific areas of the event venue to reflect the form and function of the event theme. Estrin has used miniature speakers to transform a themed environment into a symphony of sound effects that subtly transport the guest into a total experience.

■ Sound Ideas

There are no limits to the possibilities for exciting sound production for your event. However, implementing these ideas requires careful planning and well-executed coordination.

Famous Voices

To attract the attention of an audience in Houston, Texas, home of the U.S. space program, I quickly lowered the house lights and played an audiotape of President John F. Kennedy describing the United States aspirations for a space program that included (and succeeded in) landing a man on the moon. As President Kennedy spoke, we showed a video with sound effects of the launch of the space shuttle. Using surround sound, the entire room felt as if it were preparing to lift off. Carefully and selectively, we added one speaker at a time until the entire room thundered with sound. As the audio program concluded, a burst of fog appeared from stage left and the presiding officer entered the stage to greet the space-age delegates.

Invisible Actors

The president of a corporation wanted to reward his senior staff with a series of bonuses. To introduce this announcement dramatically, the president agreed to dress as Ebenezer Scrooge and meet the ghosts of Christmas past, present, and future. However, due to budget constraints, there were no funds to hire or wardrobe actors to play the ghosts. Once again, we solved the problem by prerecording the voice of one actor playing all three ghosts. When the ghosts appeared, we used fog and simple lighting effects to create the illusion of a ghost. The president impersonating Scrooge spoke to this area of the stage and the ghost answered him. At the end of the ghostly visit, the president agreed to distribute the bonuses to his senior staff.

Tracks

Only a few weeks before a major convention, the meeting planner changed the theme of the event to reflect an international program. To open the convention, we selected an international children's choir that featured children from over 50 different countries wearing native costumes. The children ranged in age from five to seven years. Concerned that their voices would not be strong enough to fill the event venue, I arranged for them to be prerecorded so that they could sing to tracks and be certain that they were in full voice on the day of the show. As it turned out, nearly half of the children had bad head colds; however, the audience heard only clear, beautiful tones prerecorded in a studio several days prior to the event.

The element of sound will be the technology that is noticed in most events. How many times have you attended an event and winced at the sound of screeching feedback pouring forth from the oversized speakers? I have often said that the only two things that most people have a strong opinion about at events are the temperature and the sound level. In most cases, the temperature will be either too hot or too cold and the sound too loud (usually) or too soft (sometimes).

The Event Leader must recognize that, today, many people have high-quality stereophonic sound systems in their homes and automobiles. Because of this new sophistication, your guests are extremely discriminating when it comes to the quality of sound used at your event. Make certain that you determine in advance the level of sophistication of your listeners and then allocate your resources effectively to satisfy their needs, wants, and desires.

■ Cost-Saving Measures

Wireless products are significantly more expensive than wired ones. Unless the production requires wireless products, avoid this costly equipment. In some cases, you will still pay for wired equipment, because you will want to have redundant equipment, as described earlier.

Labor can be a major cost in installing heavy-duty sound equipment. Consult with your sound rental expert and determine if small units can be used to avoid the rental of lifts and riggers required for the larger equipment. Bid sound equipment carefully to make certain that the experience of the operators and condition of the equipment will ensure that you meet the goals and objectives of your event. For example, in the Washington, DC, area, only three or four sound companies have the capabilities to handle the large-scale sound requirements for major demonstrations and marches. Using an inferior company can incur much greater costs than selecting the most qualified and perhaps higher bidder.

Special Effects

It is interesting that most special effects reflect variations in the weather of the planet. Effects such as fog, rain, thunder, lightning, and even pyrotechnics (fireworks) immediately conjure images of dramatic changes in the climatic conditions. Weather is perhaps the most talked-about subject in the world. As so much depends on it, including one's mood, it is natural that special effects have come to play an important role in the development of Event Leadership.

Event Leaders use special effects to attract attention, generate excitement, and sustain interest as well as startle, shock, and even amuse. The key to proper integration of special effects into an event scheme is to determine, during the design process, how special effects will support or enhance an event's goal and objectives. The most common error made by Event Leaders when using special effects is to add too many different components and thereby confuse the guests. Instead, special effects should be viewed as a natural and necessary part of the entire event strategy.

Figure 7.6 lists the most common special effects used in Event Leadership. However, it is important to remember that some event technicians also use the term *special effects* to describe a variety of specialty lighting devices, such as black or strobe lights.

Effect	Application
Air-propelled confetti cannons	Shower of paper flutters over and on guests as part of finale of entertainment
Balloon drop	Hundreds of balloons drop onto the heads of the audience from a net or bag suspended above
Dry ice	Low-level fog for ground cover
Flash pot/box	Explosion
Flying	Aerial effects such as outer space or illusions
Fog	Ghost, magic, laser-beam projection, explosion, and outer space
Hologram	Illusion, attraction, and communications
Laser	Communication, entertainment, focus attention, and reveal product
Pyrotechnics (indoor)	Reveal new product and finale of production
Pyrotechnics (outdoor)	Capture attention and finale of sport or other event
Wind machine	Blowing, billowing trees, flags, and other fabric

Figure 7.6 Applications for Special Effects

■ Balloon Drop

Technology

A bag or net suspended above the heads of the audience opens and releases hundreds of balloons.

Use

Traditionally used on New Year's Eve as well as at the conclusion of U.S. political party conventions, this technology is always appropriate as a capstone or finale element for a significant event. In some instances, prizes or slips of paper announcing gifts may be placed in the balloons.

■ Confetti Cannon

Technology

Air-propelled cannons range from small to huge and can propel large pieces of confetti 100 feet or more.

Use

A confetti cannon provides a fitting conclusion to an important meeting or conference or an effective way to attract attention through the introduction of a new product.

■ Dry Ice

Technology

A 50-gallon drum combined with dry ice, heat, and a blower will easily fog a large stage floor surface. Unlike chemical fog, this substance clings to the stage surface and creates the illusion of ground cover.

Use

A remote moat, graveyard, or lagoon at a theme party as well as a snowy winter wonderland can be established easily with this effect.

■ Flash Pot

Technology

A small amount of gunpowder and flash paper combined with an electric charge creates a flash followed by a small amount of smoke.

Use

The appearance of a genie, ghost, or other magical moment is appropriate for this startling effect.

■ Flying

Technology

Individuals, props, or both can appear to float effortlessly over the stage and sometimes over the heads of the audience.

Use

Flying is appropriate for a space-age illusion or theme incorporating magic. May be used to levitate individuals or new props being introduced to the audience. Two of the largest event flying specialists are Flying Inventerprises (*www.flybyfoy.com*) and Zfx (*www.zfxflying.com*), both of which are based in Las Vegas, Nevada.

■ Fog

Technology

Fog is usually dispensed from a small box using a chemical ingredient and heat. Chemical fog rises and may set off smoke sensors. It is available in a variety of scents or in an odorless form.

Use

From creating an eerie graveyard scene at a theme party to establishing a cone shape for a laser beam to highlight in producing a "Beam me up, Scotty" effect, fog has become an indispensable part of many events. When using this device, post a sign at the entrance stating: *The following special effects are used during this event: fog.*

■ Hologram

Technology

A hologram is the result of a film image and light combined to create a three-dimensional image.

Use

A hologram may be used to depict a product or spokesperson in a trade-show booth or onstage.

■ Indoor Pyrotechnics

Technology

Indoor pyrotechnics are small devices that emit little smoke and create sparks, flame, or other indoor effects.

Use

Over an ice rink at the conclusion of an opening ceremony a shower of sparks falls from the ceiling or on the front of a stage, or flames appear to leap from the footlights.

Note: Recent legislation in Rhode Island and other U.S. states has limited the usage of pyrotechnics to major venues, such as arenas, stadiums, and auditoriums. When pyrotechnics are utilized significantly, advance planning is required and, in most cases, a uniformed firefighter or a fire detail must be present during the rehearsal and presentation. Although there will be minimal smoke output, make certain the venue has an effective ventilation system to extract smoke.

■ Laser

Technology

A laser is a high-powered light source cooled by either water or air. The water-cooled laser projects beams many hundreds of feet.

Use

From creating a vertical laser cone to introducing the chief executive officer in a space-ship *Enterprise*™ "Beam me up, Scotty" effect, to creating a waving canopy over the heads of the audience, lasers can dynamically animate the activities of an event. Using graphics, the laser beams can create logos and animation to tell a story or set the tone for an event.

■ Outdoor Pyrotechnics

Technology

Outdoor pyrotechnics are large shells ranging in size from 3 to 12 inches that propel up into the night sky and burst, creating patterns and other colorful effects.

Use

Many professional sport events conclude with an aerial fireworks display, and some orga-nizations use fireworks as a way of celebrating the culmination of a historic meeting or holiday, such as Independence Day in the United States.

■ Pyrotechnic Set Piece

Technology

A pyrotechnic set piece is a large sign that is illuminated with pyrotechnics. Sometimes it includes movable pieces that spin, rotate, rise, and fall.

Use

A pyrotechnic set piece can be used to announce a new idea or product or celebrate a his-toric occasion or holiday. Sometimes it is used in combination with indoor or outdoor pyrotechnics.

■ Wind Machine

Technology

A wind machine is a large, high-powered fan mounted on a secure floor base.

Use

A wind machine can be used to blow curtains, flags, or other scenery or costumes to cre-ate the illusion of movement by wind.

■ Cost-Saving Measures

When using special effects, there are usually ancillary costs, such as site preparation and cleanup as well as additional security. Make certain that you factor in all costs before you blast the confetti cannon and later realize that a cleanup fee of several hundred dollars must be paid to the janitorial staff.

Some lighting and production companies will include special effects devices in the total bid for equipment. Consult with lighting and production vendors to determine what equipment they own and then include these items in your specifications.

Finally, use special effects only if they support the overall goals and objectives of the event. Special effects may be the first area of a budget that can be trimmed unless the added value is justified.

Video

Due to the growth of television and the rapid acquisition of digital video disc (DVD) players, video has become an integral part of many live events. Video is used to enhance the live image of the speaker or performer so that a person seated in the far reaches of a venue may see his or her facial reactions. Video is also used to document the entire event for future use, such as for historical or marketing purposes, or both.

The expansion of this field has placed the video camera in the hands of large numbers of the public, and as a result, guests are more sophisticated with regard to video production. Because of supply and demand, even editing equipment is now available to consumers, allowing them to perform simple editing functions for home-video features.

Figure 7.7 identifies the most common uses for video at an event and the types of equipment required for these purposes.

■ Character Generator

Technology
A character generator (CG) is an electronic device used to create titles and project text on the video image.

Use
It may be used to identify speakers, project messages to the audience, or create other communications through video production.

Use	Equipment
Audience interaction event	Multiple cameras and video switcher
Complex special-effects editing	Online editing equipment
Corporate communications	Animated character
Image magnification	VHS or four-chip camera and projector
Simple cuts-only editing	Off-line editing equipment
Video roll	Video player and projector

Figure 7.7 Video Uses and Typical Equipment

■ Off-line Editing

Technology

Off-line editing is designed primarily for simple edits, such as cuts only. During off-line editing the video product is refined further prior to the more expensive online editing session.

Use

Simple video products may be prepared during the off-line session or may be used to prepare the product for the online session.

■ Online Editing

Technology

Sophisticated, complex special effects may be achieved using online editing equipment.

Use

During online editing, complex digital effects are included to produce exciting transitions, sweeten the music, and add other technical elements to complete the production.

■ Switcher

Technology

A switcher enables the video operator to switch electronically between two or more cameras and also to cue prerecorded video products.

Use

Complex event production that requires two or more cameras and use of prerecorded video products must be programmed through a switching system.

■ Video Animation

Technology

An operator uses a mechanical device similar to a finger puppet and creates a dancing, talking electronic figure video-projected on a screen.

Use

Video animation can be used to establish a new image or character, interact with the main presenter at the meeting, improve corporate communications, or improve other communications. When Xerox introduced its new logo—the digitized X—I retained Interactive Personalities of Minneapolis, Minnesota, to create an animated character we named Chip. He immediately brought the new symbol to life for the guests and even endeared himself to them as they literally became friends during this conference.

■ Video Camera

Technology

Consumer as well as broadcast-quality cameras are available for rental from most audio-visual production firms. The broadcast camera is a four-chip model that may record on

Beta videotape, the highest quality available for editing. However, for simple events where editing will not be required, consumer equipment may be acceptable.

Use

Either live coverage for video magnification or live and recorded for future use, the video camera is the primary tool in video production. One drawback with regard to video production at live events is the presence of the video camera, tripod, and sometimes a platform to elevate the equipment. This complex setup may interfere with the audience's view of an event's live performance. Bob Johnson of Corporate Video Communications (*www.cvc.cc*) has overcome this challenge with the invention of robotic cameras designed for event production. In the Video Bob system™, each of the 12 broadcast-quality robotic cameras is placed on a thin metal rod and is operated electronically by one operator. This saves both labor and space. One experienced operator may be able to control up to eight different cameras simultaneously.

■ DVD Player

Technology

A digital video disc (DVD) stores video/audio media. A DVD shares the same overall dimensions of a CD, but has significantly higher capacity—holding from 4 to 28 times as much data. Single-sided DVDs can store 4.7GB for single-layer and 8.5GB for dual-layer disks.

Use

This player reads digital video files and may be precisely cued for a specific start/stop point.

■ Video Player/Recorder

Technology

Either 1/2-inch VHS or 3/4-inch Beta tape may be played or recorded on this machine. Beta 3/4-inch allows for sophisticated editing techniques.

Use

This equipment is used either to record the event activities or to play back prerecorded video products during the live event.

■ Video Wall System

Technology

A video wall system may include as few as 4 or up to 40 times video monitors that project a video image simultaneously. A separate processor allows the video signal to produce a variety of effects, including geometric images, to generate visual excitement.

Use

This is a high-tech solution for spreading a corporate message or introducing a new idea or product. It may also be used as a background for an event stage set.

■ Fragrance Systems and Other Trends

Bob Estrin, president of B.E. Creative, LLC in Orange, California has been creating technical innovations for special events for nearly three decades. Most recently, he saw the technical fulfillment of a prediction he made some 15 years ago. He explained, "When you first interviewed me for your book, I predicted that smell would become one of the most important and dominant of all the senses in event production. Now, through the new Envirodine Studios™ (*www.envirodine.com*) EnviroScents fragrance system, we are able to make this prediction a reality."

Estrin states that the fragrance system is a gel that creates powerful smells such as Grandma's kitchen, Christmas morning, and even a barbecue. These smells create moods and feelings among event attendees that revive memories and help develop their attitude during the event. He has used this new system to overcome negative smells in event facilities and also to stimulate the imagination of his guests through sense memory. According to Estrin, "You only have to fool a couple of the senses to develop the illusion of reality, and smell is one of the most powerful ways to do this effectively."

Estrin says that the biggest change in event technology is the development of virtual systems through computer projection. Once again, he predicted nearly a decade ago that this would be a simple and cost-effective way to create atmosphere. Now the technology finally exists to be able to do this reliably and cost-effectively.

New and/or aspiring Event Leaders must be extremely computer-literate, says Estrin. "Today, most events are programmed through computer show control systems where all technologies are controlled through a single powerful computer. Event Leaders must understand the significance of this change and be prepared to integrate all systems."

Bob Estrin also notes that, due to changing demographics and psychographics, sound will be louder and many, if not all, events will feature assisted-listening devices. "The most exciting change is that the cost is dropping for many of these technologies, which allow more widespread use. For example, an outdoor television screen that once would have cost $180,000 and required several days to set up is now only $4,000 and is usually working in a few hours."

Estrin cautions that safety for special events must become an everyday concern. Event Leaders must realize that safety is something that must be integrated throughout the entire event process if you are to reduce error and prevent harm. He points to the recent Rhode Island Station nightclub fire as one example of how a tragic event has affected the event industry throughout the world, with greater legislation and scrutiny concerning pyrotechnics.

■ Cost-Saving Measures

Contact a local university or college and determine if its radio, television, or film program can provide you with equipment for preproduction or postproduction. Significant savings may be available through use of these facilities.

When shooting, keep in mind that the better you plan your shots, the less time may be required in postproduction. Shoot with editing firmly in mind. Some video directors shoot in a style that requires very little postproduction by matching shots carefully and maintaining continuity.

Plan your postproduction schedule carefully. The majority of time should be devoted to off-line editing, as this costs less. The more you can accomplish in off-line editing, the greater the overall savings. Check with the postproduction editing facility to find out if you can use off-peak times to complete your project. Avoiding normal business hours may result in significant savings.

Retain an experienced crew that can handle multiple functions. For example, the shooter or cameraperson may also be able to coordinate the audio feed, and this will eliminate additional labor costs. Video crews can range from $750 to over $1,500 per day, depending on the type and quantity of equipment and labor required. Always solicit bids for these services and ask to see a demonstration reel of the crews' work.

Use robotic cameras for simple meeting and conference event production and include an option (with the permission of the speakers and entertainers) to sell tapes to the attendees. By selling the tapes, you may not only recover all video production costs but also generate additional net proceeds for your sponsoring organization.

Synergy of Audiovisual Effects

Carefully integrate audiovisual, lighting, sound, special effects, and video to ensure a smooth and seamless event. Avoid overproducing your event merely to demonstrate the latest high-tech wonders. Most production personnel will state that their work is designed to support and enhance, never to dominate. In fact, these technologies should be so well incorporated into event planning and coordination that they are invisible to guests. However, as a result of their combined power, a positive enduring effect should result.

The key elements of many events include musicians and other entertainers. Coordinating and presenting these artists is both an art and a science. The Event Leader must plan with precision and also incorporate sensitivity and thoughtfulness to achieve the desired outcome through their performances. Veteran entertainment producer Jack Morton once told me, "I always asked the performer to let me know how to help them succeed. After, all, every performer wants to be successful and my job is simply to help them."

Music and Entertainment Management

Mark Sonder, CSEP, author of *The Complete Guide to Event Entertainment and Production* (Wiley, 2004) observes, "A person who enjoys a certain event entertainment experience can be associated with a particular lifestyle, interest group, attitude, educational level, buying behavior, voting habits, and even a set of beliefs." Sonder notes throughout his book that event entertainment is a critical consideration when designing the mood, the atmosphere, and the outcome of many events.

Deciding whether to use music and entertainment at your event or not can mark the difference between captivating your audience and confusing them. Next we discuss the major issues that involve event entertainment.

Although most events benefit from music and entertainment, not every event needs to incur this expense. The Event Leader must assess the needs of his or her guests carefully and determine whether music and entertainment are appropriate for each event. For example, the groundbreaking of a historic battlefield site may require speeches, but it would be inappropriate to engage a Dixieland jazz band. Too often, music and entertainment are engaged based on the personal tastes and desires of the organizers with little regard for the appropriateness of the event or the interests of guests. To avoid making this mistake, use this checklist to conduct some preliminary research:

+ Research the history of the event to determine if music and/or entertainment were used in the past.
+ Interview the event stakeholders through a formal focus group or informally to ascertain their individual and collective tastes.
+ Determine how music and/or entertainment will be used to further the goals of the event.
+ Analyze the event budget to determine available resources for music and/or entertainment.
+ Review the time frame for planning and production to determine if sufficient time is available for incorporating these elements into the event.

Identifying the Resources

Once you have conducted the research to identify the need, the next step is to identify the most appropriate and cost-effective resources for your event. Fortunately, in the postmodern entertainment era, there are many more choices.

In most communities, literally dozens of resources are available for music and live entertainment. Many resources are available for both professional and amateur music and entertainment (see Figure 7.8).

Matching the best music and entertainment resource to the needs, wants, and desires of your guests, as well as the goals and objectives of your event, is a complex task. The first step is to comprehend the various musical and entertainment options that are available (see Figure 7.8). Although descriptions of music and entertainment are largely composed of industry jargon and may vary according to location, the terms are considered standard and customary in these fields. See Figure 7.9 for a list of music and entertainment terms. For further definitions, refer to *The International Dictionary of Event Management* (Wiley, 2000) or the APEX glossary of terms (*www.conventionindustry.org*).

Music for Mood, Atmosphere, Animation, and Transitions

According to veteran band leader Gene Donati of Washington, DC, music is used to create the proper mood, sustain the atmosphere, and, most important, to "animate" the room. According to Donati, "The music should begin before the doors open, to draw people into the room. Up-tempo songs should be used to energize this segment of the party." Donati and his colleagues not only conduct the musicians but in fact conduct the guests, using music to animate their actions.

1. *Academy Players Director,* a list of television and film stars (see Appendix 5)
2. Actor's Equity Association, the union of professional stage actors and actresses
3. Agents who represent a variety of acts
4. American Federation of Musicians
5. American Federation of Television and Radio Artists, the union of television and radio artists
6. American Guild of Variety Artists, the union of live-entertainment artists, such as circus performers
7. Amusement parks and permanent attractions, such as zoos
8. Arts advocacy societies and commissions
9. Bars, nightclubs, restaurants, and taverns
10. *Cavalcade of Acts and Attractions,* a directory of live entertainment (see Appendix 5)
11. Churches
12. *Circus Report,* a magazine for circus enthusiasts
13. Clubs, including fraternal organizations
14. Dance clubs, groups, and dance advocacy organizations
15. Educational institutions, including public, private, primary, middle, and secondary schools, as well as colleges and universities
16. *Event World,* the official magazine of the International Special Events Society (ISES)
17. Fraternal organizations, such as the Shriners
18. Historical reenactment organizations
19. Institutions, such as museums that may provide lecturers
20. Instrumental music organizations
21. Musical contractors
22. Native American organizations
23. Newspaper critics familiar with local arts organizations
24. Parks and recreation organizations that offer dance, music, and other arts programs
25. Producers of radio, television, or live-entertainment programs
26. Radio disc jockeys who are familiar with local bands and who may provide DJ services
27. Religious organizations other than churches and synagogues
28. Schools, colleges, and university music and theater departments
29. Screen Actors Guild, the union of film actors and actresses
30. Shopping centers that feature live music and entertainment
31. *Special Events* magazine (see Appendix 4)
32. Synagogues
33. Theatrical organizations from professional to community or amateur groups
34. Travel agents familiar with local entertainment resources
35. Very Special Arts, an organization representing disabled people who are artists
36. Zoological parks

Figure 7.8   Resources for Music and Entertainment

Act: a self-contained, rehearsed performance of one or more persons.

Agent: a person who represents various acts or artists and receives a commission from the buyer for coordinating a booking.

Amateur: a musician or entertainer who does not charge for his or her services, usually due to lack of professional experience.

Arrangements: musical compositions arranged for musicians.

Band: a group of musicians who perform contemporary music, such as rock 'n' roll, jazz, or big band.

Booking: a firm commitment by a buyer of entertainment to hire an act or artist for a specific engagement.

Combo: a musical ensemble featuring combined instruments (usually, piano, bass, and drums)

Commission: the percentage received by an agent when booking an act or artist.

Conductor: a person responsible for directing/conducting the rehearsal and performance by musicians.

Contractor: a person or organization that contracts musicians and other entertainers. Handles all the agreements, payroll, taxes, and other employment tasks.

Cover song: a tune popularized by another artist performed by a different artist or group.

Doubler: a musician who plays two or more instruments during a performance.

Downbeat: the cue given by a conductor to musicians to begin playing.

Drum riser: a small platform used to elevate a drummer above the other musicians.

Drum roll: a rolling percussive sound used for announcements and to create a suspenseful atmosphere.

Duo: an act with two persons. Also known as a *double*.

Fanfare: a musical interlude used to signal announcements of awards or introductions. Usually includes horns but not always.

Fife and drum corp: a small or larger musical ensemble featuring fifes and drums playing music from the eighteenth century.

Horn section: a group of musicians that specializes in wind instruments and is usually part of a larger ensemble.

Leader: a person who organizes and conducts a musical or entertainment group.

Manager: a person who provides management services to an artist, act, or several artists and acts. The manager normally handles all logistics, including travel, and negotiates on behalf of the artist or act. The manager is paid by the act or artist from fees that are earned through performing.

Marching band: a musical ensemble of persons who play and march simultaneously, usually comprised of percussion, horns, woodwinds, and other instruments.

Minimum: the minimum number of hours for which musicians must be paid.

Octet: a musical ensemble comprised of eight musicians.

Overture: the music performed before actors or entertainers enter the stage. Also known as preshow music.

Professional: a musician or entertainer paid for his or her services.

Quartet: a musical ensemble comprised of four persons.

Quintet: a musical ensemble comprised of five persons.

Road manager: a person who travels with an act or artist to handle all logistical arrangements.

Figure 7.9   Music and Entertainment Terms

Sextet: a musical ensemble comprised of six persons.

Sideman/men: musicians within a musical ensemble who accompany an artist.

Single: an act with one person.

Soloist: a single performer.

Stage manager: a person who coordinates the technical elements for the act or artist, cues the performer, and provides other services to support the performance.

Stand: the music stand used to hold sheet music.

Top Forty: the top 40 musical compositions/recordings selected by *Billboard* magazine. A Top Forty band is able to perform these selections.

Trio: a musical ensemble comprised of three persons.

Walk-in, walk-out music: live or recorded music played at the start and end of an event as guests enter or leave a venue.

Walk music: live or recorded music played as award presenters, speakers, and recipients enter or exit the stage area.

Windjammers: the slang name for circus musicians (mostly horn players).

Figure 7.9 *(Continued)*

Alice Conway, CSEP, director of the Event Management Program at Stratford University, recommends having her event clients close their eyes and describe what they see their guests doing as the music plays.

Music may be used as a transition to create punctuation marks in the order of a program. One of the best examples is the awards event. Using music associated with the presenters or award recipients helps the audience remain interested and focused on the program. Some typical tunes for awards programs are listed next.

✦ Person from California	"California Dreamin'"
✦ Person from New York City	"New York, New York"
✦ Sports-related award	Main theme from the film *Chariots of Fire*
✦ Championship award	Main theme from the film *Rocky*
✦ Chapter of the year	"We Will Rock You"
✦ Person of the year	"Hot, Hot, Hot"
✦ Volunteer of the year	"You've Got a Friend"
✦ Leadership award	*Masterpiece Theater* theme

Use awards music to introduce the presenters by sequencing the music in this manner. First, cue the drummer to perform a drum roll. Next, have your offstage announcer introduce the presenter using this text: "Ladies and gentlemen, please welcome the president of XYZ Corporation, from New Orleans, Louisiana, Ms. Jane Smith!" As the presenter's name is announced, the rest of the musicians should play a lively Dixieland jazz melody and conclude promptly when Ms. Smith reaches the microphone. This will help accelerate the action for the event and keep things running on time.

As Ms. Smith introduces the award recipient, the musicians should begin to play as soon as the name is called. Because musicians need a warning before they begin to play, I recommend that you give the cue to play as the first name is announced so that, as the surname is announced, the tune has begun. Here is an example: Ms. Smith: "And now welcome our award winner, from New York City, Mr. (cue conductor) John Doe (music begins)." The music should continue until Mr. Doe reaches Ms. Smith and then conclude with a brief fanfare as the award is presented. A generic walk-off melody may be played as Mr. Doe exits the stage.

Properly sequenced and timed, music can ensure that your event runs on time. Even Old Blue Eyes himself, Frank Sinatra, learned at the Grammy Awards that unless you sustain the interest of the audience, the music will abruptly change the mood, ending one segment and cueing another.

■ Musical Formulas for Success

Veteran and legendary society band leader Lester Lanin (1907–2004), who conducted orchestras for bar mitzvahs and weddings well into his nineties, recommended that Event Leaders carefully consider the number and type of guests who will be attending an event prior to the selection of musical performers. Lanin reports that, while at one time both opera and classical music were commonly used for social life-cycle events, today it is not uncommon to incorporate contemporary music.

Cantor and rabbinical student Arnold Saltzman of Washington, DC, cautions people involved in religious events to work closely with their clergy to select appropriate music that is in accordance with the traditions and customs of the religious denomination. As one example, a bride asked Saltzman for permission to use the theme from *Star Wars* as the processional music. Since the event was a secular occasion, no policies were set by the location. However, Saltzman correctly counseled the bride and groom that if this music was used for the processional, the guests might be distracted by this departure from tradition and the rest of the ceremony could suffer as a result.

Shown in Figure 7.10 are the staffing levels that Lanin recommends for musicians at specific events. Although a 30-member orchestra might have been standard fare a few years ago, in today's cost-conscious times, Lanin's formulas are more likely to be used.

Number of Guests	Minimum Number of Musicians
125	5–7
250	7
500	12
750	12 plus strings if budget allows
1,000	15–20

Figure 7.10   Attendance and Minimum Musicians Required as Recommended by Lester Lanin (1907–2004)

■ Electronic Music

Miniaturization in lighting and sound has also found its way into the orchestra. Many modern musicians use electronic instruments to perform the sounds of dozens of instruments. It is not unusual today to see four musicians performing music that once required a 100-member symphony orchestra. However, certain liabilities, such as losing the visual appeal of having live musicians, result from this economically driven change.

■ Managing Musicians

Musicians, as well as other personnel, require careful management to be able to deliver an optimum performance. Musical artists require the Event Leader to provide support systems that allow them to do what they do best: deliver a quality musical performance. The 15 most common considerations for effectively managing musicians include:

1. Provide clear, written instructions regarding date, time, and location.
2. Communicate a profile of the guests so that appropriate music may be selected.
3. Provide an event schedule, and supply the leader of the musical group with a summary of the musical activities.
4. Arrange for parking for the musicians and notify them of the locations authorized.
5. Identify and communicate to the musicians where equipment may be loaded into a venue.
6. Select and notify the musicians of a room where their cases may be stored during a performance.
7. Provide adequate dressing rooms for breaks.
8. Adhere carefully to required breaks.
9. Arrange for and provide food and beverage service if required by contract.
10. Assign a key contact person to serve as principal liaison to the leader of the musical group.
11. Locate adequate electric power.
12. Provide ample performance space as required by contract.
13. Adhere to schedule specified by contract.
14. Notify musicians if overtime is required.
15. Assist musicians with load-out/departure and offer thanks.

■ Union Requirements

Whether contracting union musicians or other entertainers affiliated with labor unions, it is important that the Event Leader study union contracts carefully and comply with the responsibilities that apply to the event sponsor. For example, union musicians must be compensated separately if their performance is audio- or videotaped. Failure to provide additional compensation can result in severe penalties for the event organizer. In addition, union members must be given a certain number of breaks during each performance or be paid additionally for performing continuously without the prescribed number of breaks. Therefore, it is important that the Event Leader work closely with his or her music contractor when engaging union musicians. Certain union locals have established trust funds that will provide some money for musicians to perform for worthwhile causes at no cost to the sponsor. Check with your local American Federation of Musicians to determine if your event may qualify for this outstanding opportunity.

■ Electronic Music

During the 1970s, as recording quality improved, disc jockeys became popular at many events. Indeed, in some situations electronic or recorded music is more appropriate than live music, for three reasons.

1. Electronic music may be easily controlled. Unlike live music, it may be faded, stopped, started, and refocused through different speakers.
2. It is usually less expensive than the engagement of live musicians.
3. Perhaps most important, for those events with space restrictions, electronic music solves important logistical problems.

Today, disc jockeys provide not only music but entire party production services, including lights, effects such as fog, and interactive games. In addition to providing music for dancing and background atmosphere, electronic music may serve other purposes as well.

In lieu of using a live orchestra, many professional entertainers and industrial productions use prerecorded tracks to supplement their live performances. When using these systems, it is critical that the Event Leader use redundant equipment in case of failure. In other situations, live musicians actually play along with the recorded tracks, creating a combination of live and recorded sound. In still other situations, the orchestra will perform some music live and pantomime to the prerecorded sound in other numbers.

When music is synchronized to video or film, separate rights must be negotiated and obtained. Usually these rights include a clause limiting use to certain mediums and time periods. Ultimately, someone will pay for the use of privately owned music each time it is used. Therefore, the Event Leader must budget for this expense.

■ Music Licensing

In the early 1990s, the two major music licensing firms in the United States decided to enforce their rights to collect fees from sponsors of meetings, conventions, and expositions as well as other events. Prior to this date, the American Society of Composers, Authors, and Publishers (ASCAP) and its competitor, Broadcast Music, Inc. (BMI), collected fees from restaurants, nightclubs, hotels, and even roller skating rinks. However, perhaps recognizing the enormous possibility for revenue from the meeting, convention, exposition, and event industry, these organizations made it clear that they planned to require sponsors of these events to pay for the use of live or recorded music they licensed.

The first organization to sign a separate agreement with ASCAP and BMI was the International Association for Exposition Management (IAEM), and soon the American Society of Association Executives (ASAE) convened a task force to study this issue. As a member of this task force, I asked both organizations to assign the responsibility for payment to either the musical contractors or the professional producers of these events. Both organizations rejected this request, and today there continues to be acrimony regarding who pays what to whom and why.

The official sponsor or organizer of an event, the entity that bears the financial responsibility for the event, is responsible for obtaining a license for the use of protected music from either or both ASCAP or BMI or other rights-licensing organizations. The only exception to paying these fees is for events that are small gatherings of people who are known to you. This usually means social life-cycle events, such as weddings, bar and bas mitzvahs, birthday parties, and other events attended by family and friends.

ASCAP and BMI each have separate licensing agreements that require careful consideration by Event Leaders. Both electronic and live music is covered in these agreements. According to ASCAP, the majority of popular music is licensed through its organization. However, most Event Leaders obtain, on behalf of their sponsors, agreements with both ASCAP and BMI for obvious reasons. Among these reasons is the problem associated with the live dance band and the guest who requests a tune from the band leader only to have the band leader decline because the rights are assigned to BMI and the license is with ASCAP.

For most events, the costs associated with music licensing are minimal, and the filing of the license agreement is merely another part of the long paper trail that is a natural part of Event Leadership. However, in the field of expositions, especially the larger ones that attract tens of thousands of persons, the costs can quickly mount. How are these fees assessed?

Both ASCAP and BMI assess fees based on the daily attendance at each event. The fees are, therefore, charged daily and are factored using separate formulas for recorded and live music. If both recorded (electronic) and live music are used, the costs are higher.

To enforce these licenses, both ASCAP and BMI use spotters who visit event venues randomly and investigate organizations that are using their licensed works unlawfully. The penalties for this illegal activity are substantial.

Recent court cases concerning expositions have somewhat weakened the position of ASCAP and BMI to require that sponsors of expositions assume responsibility for their individual exhibitors with regard to the use of music. However, ASAE continues to investigate the entire music licensing issue, with the major concerns relating to potential monopolies by ASCAP and BMI, which control the majority of all musical composition.

What music is covered? Literally any musical work licensed by ASCAP and BMI, and this includes "Happy Birthday." Even classical compositions may be covered if they have recently had a new, authored arrangement.

Alternatives to paying music licensing fees are limited. The Event Leader may, of course, elect to not use music at all. Or the Event Leader may commission an original work of music and purchase the song or selections for use at the event. Another option is for the Event Leader to purchase commercial music produced by a private firm. Commercial music may be obtained from recording studios or other private organizations and usually includes some sound-alike tunes that are appropriate for use at awards programs and events other than those where popular tunes may be requested. Still larger organizations may negotiate individually with ASCAP, BMI, or other rights-licensing organizations and seek to create a separate agreement. In some cases, licensing fees may be waived. However, this is a rare occurrence.

In order to play, you must pay. Failing to do so may adversely affect your event sponsor and your reputation. Therefore, it is the responsibility of the event organizer to fully comprehend the requirements for music licensing and allow sufficient planning and coordination time to attend to these important details.

Entertainment Options from A to Z

Figure 7.7 presents a variety of resources for music and entertainment. However, now it is time to consider entertainment as a separate resource. The most commonly used entertainers for live events include:

- Acrobats (Cirque-like performers as first introduced by Cirque De Soleil™)
- Animal acts
- Artists (working on large canvasses and accompanied by music)
- Balloon sculptors
- Ballroom dancers
- Bands
- Break dancers
- Cancan dancers
- Caricaturists
- Carnival games
- Carnival rides
- Chinese dragon dancers
- Circus performers
- Clowns
- Comedians
- Contortionists
- Dancers
- Disc jockeys
- Dixieland bands
- Escape artists
- Female impersonators
- Flamenco dancers
- Folk dancers
- Fortune tellers
- German oompah bands
- Giant heads and giant puppets
- Hat designers such as Party Hats™
- Horseshoes
- Hula hoop performers
- Humorists
- Hypnotists
- Ice skaters
- Illusionists

- Japanese koto musicians
- Jazz bands
- Jugglers
- Klezmer bands
- Limbo dancers
- Magicians
- Marching bands
- Marionettes
- Mentalists
- Mimes
- Modern dancers
- Opera singers
- Organ grinders
- Organists
- Palm readers
- Pep bands
- Photo booths
- Puppeteers
- Rap artists
- Reggae musicians
- Robots
- Roller skaters
- Sand dancers
- Sand painters (working on an opaque projector and accompanied by music)
- Singers/vocalists/gospel groups
- Spaceships
- Sport games
- Square dancers
- Stilt walkers
- Tap dancers
- Tattoo artists
- T-shirt designers
- Tight-wire walkers
- Trapeze artists
- Ventriloquists
- Wax hand artists
- World music

◼ Inexpensive Options for Live Entertainment

The term *amateur* implies one who has not yet begun to charge for his or her services. However, the term literally means "what one does for love." Every community is filled with hundreds and perhaps thousands of people whose vocational interests include performing. From barbershop and sweet Adeline singing groups to entire community orchestras, with a little detective work, you can identify a great deal of entertainment at low cost.

When using amateur performers, make certain that you supplement their performance with those elements that will achieve the level of sophistication required for your event. This may mean the addition of professional costuming, lighting, or other elements. In some cases, you will need to assign a professional producer to develop the amateur performers' act further to fit the needs of your event.

Amateur performers will require more time in advance, immediately preceding, and during the production. Therefore, although you will save significant dollars by using nonprofessional performers, you must allocate additional resources and allow more time for this opportunity.

Professional performers may be obtained directly by contacting the performer or his or her manager, through agents, or by holding auditions. When contracting professional performers, first identify all the tasks you wish the performers to handle during your event. List these tasks and then prioritize them so that if you find you cannot afford everything you want, you will be able to identify quickly the most important elements that must be preserved.

One way to save lots of money when using professional performers is to *block-book* the act or artists with other organizations. Block-booking entails contacting other organizations in your city or area that may also be able to use the services of the act or artists. By offering performers a series of engagements closely connected by time and location, you may be able to save as much as 50 percent of the cost.

Another way to save is to work with acts that are routed annually through your area. Major music and entertainment groups that tour frequently may be able to add your date to their tour at nominal expense. To identify the routing for these groups, track them through publications such as *Variety, Billboard, Amusements Business,* and *Performance* magazine.

Often performers will participate in additional events for the same basic fee. Therefore, determine well in advance what other activities, such as book signings, media conferences, and hospitality events, you want the performer to participate in and incorporate these into the agreement.

Travel expenses can often be a significant part of an act's cost, especially for those that require a large retinue of performers. To save money on travel, first determine if the act will travel coach versus first class. Next, contact the major airlines and seek sponsorships. Finally, although performers like to have flexibility, arrange the travel as far in advance as possible to take advantage of lower fares.

Whether contracting amateur or professional entertainers, the Event Leader is ultimately responsible for the final performance. To ensure the satisfaction of your client and guests, invite the client to attend the sound check or lighting rehearsal so that he or she can meet the performer in advance of the event. Furthermore, make certain that the performer mentions the name of the sponsoring organization during his or her act. To facilitate this, I write this information in large block letters on an index card and hand it to the performer during rehearsal. A second copy is given to the performer before he or she walks on stage for the final performance, in case the first copy was misplaced or lost.

Sourcing, contracting, and managing live entertainment carefully will further ensure the financial and artistic success of your event. When you make the decision to include live entertainment as an important element of your event, you have assumed a considerable and complex responsibility. Make certain that you devote the proper time and resources to fulfill this important responsibility effectively.

■ Celebrities and Speakers

The National Speakers Association in Tempe, Arizona, reports that its association represents over 3,000 people who earn some or all of their living by giving speeches, conducting seminars, or presenting workshops. Their topics may range from anthropology to zero population growth. However, as members of this association, they are committed to improving their performance on the public platform.

Previously, the professional speaker was an accomplished person whose credits from another field produced demand for public appearances and speeches. Consequently, people such as film and television stars, politicians, and leading religious figures delivered speeches to their devotees. According to most futurists, continuing education will be the major growth industry of the new millennium. As a result, there is greater demand than ever before for sales trainers, motivators, and other experts in both content and performance.

When contracting a professional speaker for an event, first identify the needs, wants, and desires of your audience. Next, identify how you will use the speaker from a marketing perspective. Will the speaker's name or subject matter help increase attendance? Finally, and perhaps most important, determine what you expect to happen as a result of the speaker's appearance. The outcome of the event is paramount to every other decision.

Matching the speaker type to the outcome is the most important task facing the Event Leader who has decided to use a professional speaker. Although speaking fees may range from a few hundred dollars to tens of thousands of dollars, the most important consideration is what value will be derived from this investment. For example, if the sales trainer's fee is $10,000 and there is the potential of generating $100,000 in sales as a result of his or her appearance, the outcome is well worth the investment.

Figure 7.11 lists the most popular types of speakers and the audience locations that may benefit from their content.

In addition to professional speakers, most organizations can provide you with outstanding lay speakers whose industry expertise qualifies them to speak to your audience. However, it is important to consider that the failure rate for lay speakers is extremely high. Therefore, plan to provide them with coaching or support equal to their stature on the program. For example, if the lay speaker is your plenary keynoter, you may wish to provide a speech coach to assist the speaker with his or her talk. However, if the speaker is presenting a workshop, it may be sufficient to work with him or her via telephone to fine-tune content and presentation techniques.

All speakers require an investment of time, and time is money. To maximize your investment, communicate clearly and often to the speakers what you want them to accomplish. Determine if they can perform other functions at your event (such as serving as emcee for the banquet) and perhaps author an article in advance for your newsletter or magazine.

Speaker	Plenary or General Session	Luncheon	Spouse or Partner Program	Evening Banquet
Author	X	X	X	X
Celebrity	X			
Futurist	X			X
News person	X	X		X
Humorist		X	X	X
Hypnotist				X
Magician		X		X
Motivational speaker	X	X	X	X
Psychologist	X	X	X	
Sales trainer	X	X		
Seminar leader		X	X	
Workshop leader		X	X	

Figure 7.11 Speakers and Their Audiences

Finally, ask if there is a discount for multiple engagements in one day or week. You may be able to save substantial dollars by block-booking your speaker as you would an entertainer.

Finding the appropriate speaker involves finding the right resources, auditioning the speaker either in person or using videotape, and then confirming your assumption by speaking directly with the speaker. Possible resources for locating the appropriate speaker for your event include:

+ Agents and bureaus that represent professional speakers
+ Churches
+ Colleges and universities
+ Corporate speakers bureaus
+ Industry speakers
+ National Speakers Association "Who's Who in Professional Speaking" (see Appendix 5)
+ Synagogues
+ Volunteer speakers bureaus

Negotiating with Celebrities and Speakers

Most personal appearances require some degree of negotiation prior to signing a contract. The success of the negotiation ultimately will depend on both parties' desire to complete the deal. The greater the desire from both parties, the more quickly the deal will come to fruition.

Remember that you are in search of a win-win-win outcome. In this scenario, the guest, the celebrity or speaker, and the Event Leader win because of hard work and persistence. Do your homework to determine the history of fees for celebrities or speakers. Also find out what other income they have generated from the sale of books, tapes, and other products. Next, explain to the celebrity or speaker, or his or her representative, your desire to book the person. Describe in detail the role the celebrity or speaker will play at your event. Explain the outcome you desire from his or her involvement. Then, and only then, ask him or her to quote a fee. Say that you would like to have a few days to consider this fee and then thank the person for his or her time. At this point, two things may happen: The celebrity or speaker or representative may call you back and offer a better deal, or the person may accept another engagement.

To prevent the latter, you can ask the person to put a tentative hold on this date for a specified period of time. A tentative hold implies that the person will contact you prior to accepting another engagement on the same date as your engagement. If another client calls the celebrity or speaker, he or she will tell the other client that he or she is tentatively holding the date for you and then will check with you first before accepting the other engagement.

After a few days, call the speaker, celebrity, or representative back, and ask him or her to reserve a time to discuss the engagement with you when he or she will not be interrupted. During the discussion/negotiation, offer other incentives in lieu of the full fee. For example, if you are projecting the speaker's image on a large screen to magnify his or her image, you could offer to provide the speaker with a professional video of his or her speech (estimated value of $3,000), or you could allow the speaker to sell books, tapes, and other products before, during, and after the engagement. Another valuable concession is to offer the speaker your mailing list or offer to promote his or her services to your guests. After determining the value of these concessions, ask the speaker to work with you on the fee so that you may complete the contract. Once you make your request, ask for his or her reaction. Tell the speaker to take his or her time to think about your offer, but set up a time frame to complete the agreement. When the person calls you back within the specified period of time, ask for his or her answer. Now you have the first news. It may not be the best news, but it is sufficient for you to provide a counteroffer. Make certain that you are prepared to make a counteroffer, such as shifting the date, shortening the responsibilities, or increasing the fee. When you use these techniques, step by step, you and your negotiating partners will move closer to closure.

If for any reason you fail to reach closure, always thank your negotiating partners for their time and interest and tell them you will recommend their services to others but are not able to work with them at this time. Do not be surprised if the other party calls you in a few days with a very attractive offer to use his or her services.

Contracting with Celebrities and Speakers

A letter of agreement, a contract, or a contract with rider must be prepared and/or executed by the Event Leader to engage a celebrity or speaker. In some cases, the celebrity or speaker will provide his or her own contract, and in others the Event Leader will be responsible for drafting the agreement.

The *rider* is the attachment on the contract that spells out the special conditions under which the celebrity or speaker will perform. The rider may specify lighting, sound, transportation, food, beverage, and other conditions. To make certain that you are providing only necessary items in the rider, contact previous clients and find out what they provided. In some instances, the rider may be used to incorporate everything, including the kitchen sink. You cannot allow the celebrity or entertainers to use the rider as a tool to abuse your limited resources.

■ Trends in Music and Entertainment

The music and entertainment field has undergone tremendous change during the past several decades since Howard Lanin and Jack Morton first organized their orchestras. However, changes in the last decade of the twentieth century have far surpassed all of the previous changes.

During the 1990s, many musicians were replaced by electronic instruments. The electronic synthesizer, the musical instrument digital interface (MIDI), and the development of additional computer software for composing have revolutionized the music field. Entertainment, too, has experienced great change. Perhaps the most significant change has been the incorporation of technology such as video and computers within the context of a live performance. This blend of live and electronic media is known as *interactive media.*

Interactive Media

The interactivity inherent in interactive media is supplied by online users, who provide both proactive and reactive techniques for event purposes. For example, a general session at an association meeting may require that a vote be taken by hundreds of delegates to settle an important issue. Instead of requiring a manual show of hands, a large screen flashes the command "Vote Now" and each delegate presses green for yes, red for no, or yellow for abstain. Their votes are recorded and tallied electronically, and in seconds the results are shown on the screen both numerically and graphically.

Another example of interactive media involves live performers interacting with electronic media. This engagement may be live action combined with pretape. In one such occasion, I produced a film of a car racing down a track, and suddenly the car came to a screeching halt. The film was shown using rear production on the back of a screen. The screen had a small door cut into the exact location where the driver would later emerge. When the car stopped, the door opened and the president of the corporation walked right through the screen. This is but one of many examples of live and electronic media interacting with one another.

It is in the education field that the potential for interactive media may be the greatest. Using technologies such as CD-ROMs, modems, and powerful personal computers, tomorrow's event may look something like this. First, the guest enters the venue and is greeted by a robotic registrar who requests that the guest insert his or her credit card in the "Welcome" station. Upon reading the card, the machine welcomes the guest to the meeting and issues a smart card, which contains all critical information about the guest, including medical data, to ensure a safe and productive visit. The same card may be used to gain access to his or her sleeping room.

Next, the guest reports to his or her first meeting and uses the smart card to receive a complimentary computer disc from the Communications Center, a multistation machine that provides workspaces for telecommuting with the home office. The computer disc will be used to record the lecture to be delivered by the keynote speaker.

Finally, the guest is seated in an ergonomically correct chair, fastens his or her seat belt, and "experiences" the opening ceremony. Such experience includes not only a visual and auditory presentation, but also sensory experiences, such as smell, taste, and touch. The visual images are delivered three-dimensionally as the guest wears glasses provided by a commercial sponsor. The chair moves hydraulically, controlled by dozens of levers and pumps as the visual images unfold on the 10-foot high-definition screen. The audio portion of the program is enhanced with over 100 miniature speakers positioned throughout the venue to create a total surround-sound effect. At the conclusion of the opening ceremony, the guest is invited to vote using his or her smart card to gain access to the ballot box. He or she will vote to select the topics the electronic speaker will address. Instead of merely receiving what the motivation speaker delivers, the guest will become an interactive learner, selecting those topics that are most useful at this time. Once the selection has been made, the prerecorded speaker will instantly process the choices and provide state-of-the-industry knowledge that the guest most requires. This is recorded directly onto a disc that is inserted in a DVD writer within the chair where the guest is sitting.

Have no fear. All of this new technology will not decrease the demand for in-person events. Instead, it will create even greater demand as people meet online and seek other opportunities and venues within which to interact in person. For example, asynchronous discussion groups such as one offered by the Temple University Event Leadership Executive Certificate Program (*www.temple.edu/sthm/EL*) encourage electronic discussants to meet in person for further inquiry. People who participate in list serves or other bulletin board–type communications technologies will discover new organizations and new groups where they want to affiliate in person to improve their skills or simply enhance their lives. These new technologies will serve as the catalyst for bigger and better events.

Virtual Reality

Perhaps one of the most startling and certainly most effective interactive media innovations is virtual reality. Since the early 1990s, it has been used for entertainment and education as well as sales. As an entertainment device, it can be used to engage the guest in navigating through a virtual game. Wearing a large helmet, the guest sees a virtual environment. Using movements from his or her hand, the guest can run, jump, and even fly through outer space. In education, virtual reality may be used to train pilots (for whom the technology was first developed) and other technicians, such as surgeons, to perform complicated maneuvers without risking human life. In sales, virtual expositions are fast becoming effective methods for introducing buyers to the concept of virtual shopping.

Teleconferencing: Up-Link, Down-Link, and Fiber Optic

Increasingly, meetings and conferences as well as other event fields are being linked using both satellite and fiber-optic technologies. In the case of video, the satellite technology is less expensive and more reliable. However, data transmission is more cost-effective via fiber-optic technology. This may change as economies of scale prevail in the telecommunications industry.

When assessing the need for a teleconferencing or data-transmission component for your event, first determine what resources currently exist and then review the added value of using these technologies. If the added value provides significant advantages, the added cost will be relative to the investment. However, some Event Leaders succumb to these technologies as the latest bells and whistles to use without careful thought regarding the need, the added value, and the return on the investment.

To select a firm to assist you with teleconferencing, first discuss your needs with the venue directors to find out what vendors they recommend. The venue is usually your best reference because the recommended vendors have probably transmitted or received communications successfully for a previous organization. In some instances, modern conference and congress centers have this technology in place and can purvey this service directly through their staff audiovisual or communications personnel.

Next, meet with those who will provide this service or those who will submit bids. Provide them with a list of transmission dates, times, content, purpose, locations, and other pertinent data. Seek their recommendations for reducing costs and improving quality.

Finally, put a contingency plan in place. Weather, power blackouts, and other unforeseen problems can affect your transmission or reception. Determine in advance how you will cover for an interruption in the signal. In some instances, it may be appropriate to ask the audience to adjourn and reconvene. In other cases, you may wish to have a local moderator lead a discussion and generate additional questions to be used when the teleconference continues. Regardless of what you decide, it is important to have an alternative plan or program firmly in place.

That's Edutainment!

The term *edutainment* may have been coined during the early 1970s, when a large number of corporations began to combine entertainment with education to motivate their human resources. Edutainment is simply the use of live or recorded entertainment to promote learning.

Edutainment productions may range from a group of actors who present short skits about sales, customer service, or negotiation, to an elaborate interactive multimedia program involving video, slides, teleconference, and live entertainment to motivate customers to invest in a new product. When designing edutainment programs for your event, start with behavioral objectives in mind. Focus carefully on what you want to happen as a result of your edutainment activities.

Perhaps the best example of edutainment is the murder mystery phenomenon, which became very popular during the mid-1980s. During this period, largely due to popular television programs such as *Murder She Wrote,* murder mystery companies began popping up all over the United States and other countries. In Harrogate, England, the Old Swan Hotel (where Agatha Christie was found mysteriously after having been missing for several days) stages a popular murder mystery weekend. During the opening reception, the guests witness a murder. The next morning a real coroner/medical examiner delivers the autopsy results as the "detectives" take exhaustive notes. By Sunday evening, the mystery is solved and everyone goes home satisfied that they participated in finding the murderer.

Andy Craven is a murder mystery producer at the Old Swan Hotel. Craven states that there are probably over 100 murder mystery companies actively performing in Great Britain. In fact, there are now 10 to 15 companies in the immediate area of Harrogate. When I interviewed the murder mystery director at the Old Swan for the first edition of the book, his troupe was the only one performing in Harrogate. Craven says that to differentiate his product now, he must carefully customize each performance. To remain competitive, he continually strives to offer greater value for the money that is expended rather than to lower his prices. Craven suggests that Event Leaders must at all times have a passion for their work and for trying new things. Prior to producing murder mysteries, Craven was a computer programmer; he sees the organization and creativity required for theatrical production as similar to the skills he needed for developing award-winning computer programs.

Corporations and associations in the United States as well as other organizations may use the murder mystery premise as a way of delivering important messages about sales, customer relations, membership development, ethics, and other principles. To use this medium as your message, first interview several murder mystery directors and select the one who will carefully customize his or her script to meet your goals and objectives. Next, make certain that you see his or her troupe in performance before you make engagement plans. While a videotape is a convenient audition device, it is far better to see them in person and determine how they handle the important audience participation segments of their production.

Whether you use a murder mystery, a musical production, or a tightly scripted three-act play, it is critical that the message be simple, repeated, and well produced. Too often, Event Leaders develop a complex message that requires too much explanation to make sense to the guests. In other instances, the message is used once and never repeated. This denies the guests the opportunity to review and have the message reinforced. Retention requires repetition. Finally, regardless of what budget is assigned to this production, make certain that it is produced with high-quality ingredients. The message will suffer if the packaging is not of sufficient quality.

Event Leader as Producer

The modern Event Leader is both consultant and producer. He or she not only must research, design, and plan, but also must coordinate all the event elements, as a producer does with a play, film, television show, or other theatrical presentation. While the music and entertainment will ultimately reflect the tastes of your clients and their guests, you must never allow your own taste to be compromised. Remember that your signature is part and parcel of every production. Your next opportunity to produce an event is tied directly to the one you produce today. Quality, and only quality, must prevail if you are to have the opportunity to produce future events. Therefore, see every Event Leadership opportunity as your personal and professional challenge to produce the very finest music and entertainment with the time and logistical and financial resources that may be allocated.

Profile in Event Leadership: George "Boom Boom" Zambelli

Zambelli Fireworks International, founded in 1893 and based in what is known as the fireworks capital of the world, New Castle, Pennsylvania, is one of the world's largest and most prominent pyrotechnics firms. Connie Zambelli is now the chairman of the board, and her beloved husband, George "Boom Boom" Zambelli, served as the longtime leader of this internationally acclaimed company in the special events industry. Equally important, he served as the head of a large and loving family that enjoyed numerous celebrations, most of which featured elaborate fireworks displays.

George "Boom Boom" Zambelli (1924–2003) (As remembered by his family, Connie, Danabeth, and Marcy Zambelli)

Danabeth Zambelli, president of the firm, recalls, "Daddy would bring me to the International Festivals and Events Association (IFEA) annual convention when I was eight or nine years old. He always made sure I had lots of ice cream to eat. So, even today, as an adult, I remember the ice cream and the many friends Daddy made, so the IFEA is like a family reunion for me where we celebrate his life."

When Danabeth was born, her father was at the White House in Washington, DC, producing a pyrotechnic display for President John F. Kennedy. Immediately after the display concluded, with the cheers of the crowd still ringing loudly in his ears, he hurried home to greet his new daughter.

George and Connie celebrated their fiftieth wedding anniversary, and the entire Zambelli tribe went on a Caribbean cruise. However, unlike other more staid anniversary parties, their unique golden anniversary celebration included both a gigantic "Happy Anniversary" banner *and* spectacular aerial fireworks display directly over the ship.

Zambelli's daughters remember that their father always talked about the value of hard work. All of the children grew up traveling the world with their famous parents. Marcy Zambelli says, "They never gave us anything that was extravagant. When we earned money, we would go to the store and buy a big flower for Mom."

However, what their parents did give them was priceless. Danabeth says, "We all had to go to college. Our parents promoted the value of education. They wanted us to have a great future." Of the five Zambelli children, one is a physician and another a dentist.

George Zambelli has been described by his family and professional colleagues as a perfectionist. Although his faith was tested numerous times with the usual ups and downs of business and the tragic loss of his beloved sister, he never lost faith.

According to his daughters, he lived his faith by quietly helping others throughout his long life. His daughters say, "He often would buy breakfast for a hungry person and performed many other acts of loving-kindness for his employees, customers, and strangers."

"He loved people. One day, the legendary Radio City Music Hall productions, Super Bowl Half Time Show spectacular, and Walt Disney Company special event producer, Bob Jani, came to our home in New Castle. Our mother greeted him so warmly and entertained him so beautifully that he often described that first meeting as the beginning of a lifelong relationship with Zambelli International," says Danabeth, as her mother smiles with pride at this memory.

A protective father, George would sometimes create discomfort for his daughters at their school dances when he would ominously stand in a corner of the gymnasium in his hat and rain coat watching their every move. Furthermore, he would sometimes embarrass their dates by wearing mismatched pajamas when the boys came to call on his daughters.

Today, the pyrotechnics empire developed by George Zambelli Sr. every year produces over 1,500 displays, which have increased from only about 200 per year 50 years ago. The number, size, and types of displays have dramatically changed during the past several years, and firework displays are now a year-round business. Marcy says that today "weddings are huge, and also New Year's Eve is growing fast,"

which now creates a year-round desire for spectacular fireworks displays.

Connie Zambelli cherishes her late husband's memory and recalls, "When we were first married, his sister had a restaurant, and he ran the hotel. He was a student at Duquesne University and would take the train to Pittsburgh. He always worked hard and put other people first."

In 2003 a new book chronicling Zambelli's achievements was written by Dr. Gianni DeVincent Hayes and published by Paul S. Eriksson. Entitled *Zambelli: the First Family of Fireworks: A Story of Global Success* (Paul S. Eriksson, 2003). Dr. Hayes has successfully revealed much of the mystery and majesty of the Zambellis' numerous pyrotechnic achievements.

Today, the Zambelli family continues to cultivate the many traditions and values that were produced by Boom Boom. According to his daughters and wife, he believed that a good life consisted of three important values. "First, be proud of what you do. Second, do it with love. And finally, work hard to make others happy."

The first family of fireworks has worked hard to sustain and honor their father's memory by continuing to paint the skies with new innovations. By annually amazing and delighting millions of people, the unique and eternal legacy of George "Boom Boom" Zambelli rises to new heights each year. His is indeed a colorful and beautiful legacy for the family and industry that he loved.

Zambelli Fireworks: zambelli@zambelli-fireworks.com

Career-Advancement Connections

 ## Global Connection

Do your homework to be certain that you are aware of the subtle but important language and cultural differences when conducting on-site management. For example, in the United States, if you request shag, the vendor will deliver carpeting. However, in Great Britain, the vendor may give you a curious look because the term *shag* refers to sexual favors. Furthermore, body language has significant cultural implications. In North America, the index finger curled to join the thumb signifies that everything at your event is "OK." However, in Brazil, this gesture is an insult that could erupt into a fistfight. Therefore, it is important that you review books such as *Gestures: The Do's and Taboos of Body Language Around the World*, by Roger E. Axtell (Wiley, 1990).

Technology Connection

Invest in radios (walkie-talkies), cell phones, pagers, clear-com headsets, and other forms of communication to ensure that you are connected to all critical stakeholders during an event. Assign appropriate codes for emergencies, such as first aid, evacuation, criminal activity, and other issues, that may develop during the event. Test all communications equipment carefully prior to the start of the event to ensure stability. If you are using simultaneous interpretation systems, rehearse with speakers and interpreters to ensure that the rate, language ability, and other critical factors are synchronized to provide consistently excellent communications for your participants.

Resource Connection

Read *Professional Event Coordination* by Julia Rutherford Silvers. See also the *CIC Manual and Glossary of Terms* (Connection Industry Council, 2000) for additional techniques to improve on-site operations.

Learning Connection

✦ Create a sample *Event Specification Guide* (*www.conventionindustry.org*) for your event. Once you have completed the *Event Specification Guide*, adjust the times by 15 minutes to allow for last-minute changes.
✦ How will this change affect the financial, operational, and other outcomes of your event?
✦ Now you must also teleconference or videoconference this event to another country. How will the production schedule be affected by the different time zones?

PART FOUR

Event Marketing

The Singapore Lantern Festival advertises its event using a colorful three-dimensional outdoor billboard.

CHAPTER 8

Advertising, Public Relations, Promotions, and Sponsorship

In This Chapter You Will Learn How To:

◆ Conduct event marketing research

◆ Develop an integrated marketing program

◆ Use the five P's of event marketing

◆ Incorporate both internal and external marketing programs

◆ Develop retail marketing events

◆ Promote fairs and festivals

◆ Launch new products

◆ Develop, design, and execute print, electronic, and other advertising programs

◆ Develop comprehensive public relations programs

◆ Organize street promotions and creative stunts

◆ Develop and manage effective sponsorship programs

◆ Create and conduct successful cause/event-related marketing programs

◆ Integrate the Internet into the event marketing strategy

◆ Comprehensively evaluate event marketing programs and measure return on event

The international television program *Who Wants to Be a Millionaire*™ was described in the media as *event television,* and the Broadway musical version of *Saturday Night Fever* was labeled *event theater* by the *Wall Street Journal* because the audience is encouraged to dance in the aisles at the conclusion of each show. It seems that, everywhere you look, someone is marketing events or events are being used to market products and services.

The first step in the Event Leadership process, research, is mirrored in the marketing process. Without valid and reliable research, you may waste scarce time and resources. Therefore, the first step in the event marketing process must be careful, thoughtful, and comprehensive research. The outcome of this research must result in the identification of measurable goals and objectives for your event marketing campaign or program.

A campaign is usually an extended series of marketing activities designed to market an event, cause, product, or service, whereas a program may include many campaigns targeted at a wide variety of different market segments. For example, regional shopping centers design and implement annual marketing programs that may include a separate campaign for each of the four seasons or for specific events, such as the expansion of the center or introduction of a new major anchor store.

Regardless of whether you are designing a campaign or an entire program of marketing activities, the resources and channels available to you are expanding rapidly. However, with this expansion, there is also greater competition than ever before. This growth and competition is well documented.

In 2000, *Advertising Age,* the weekly tabloid that many in advertising consider the bible of their profession, added a feature to its editorial section in addition to the traditional mix of advertising, public relations, and promotions. The new section is titled "Events and Promotions." According to an editorial in *Advertising Age,* the editors have determined that events are a critical component of marketing.

Traditionally, marketing students have recognized that product, promotion, price, public relations, and location, or place, are critical components in the marketing process. Each of these five *P*'s of marketing is a catalyst for sales. Although marketing has become more sophisticated in the twenty-first century, savvy event marketers recognize that, ultimately, *marketing* is only a three-syllable word for *sales.*

The founder of *Parade* magazine, Red Motley, once wrote: "Nothing really happens until someone sells something." According to some marketing experts, the most efficient and cost-effective way to make sales is through events. Whether you are selling a product, service, idea, or cause, an event allows you to use all of the senses to persuade the prospect to make an investment. The components of product, promotion, price, public relations, and place directly influence the desire and decision to make this investment. However, it is important to remember that a festival, fair, wedding, meeting, exposition, or other event is a legitimate product that also must be developed and sold.

Product

Successful salespeople have both expert product knowledge and effective sales skills. Expert product knowledge is essential in today's competitive environment. The expertise the salesperson demonstrates regarding the sponsorship package or other event component will differentiate this person from the competition. More important than sales skills, demonstrated product expertise shows the client that he or she is making a purchase that has added value and helps to develop confidence as well as long-term loyalty.

Every event product combines history, quality, and value to produce a unique program. Even new events may draw from the experience or history of the organizers. This demonstration of consistent capability to produce similar events will influence prospective clients to recognize the overall quality of the event organization. Finally, every event product must convey not only perceived value, such as dollar-for-dollar worth, but also added value. The concept of added value is perhaps best described with the Cajun word *lagniappe*. This term literally means "everything one deserves and a little bit more." The little bit more may mean providing the client with the home telephone number of the key contact person, developing a unique approach to achieving the event objectives, or perhaps simply spending additional time with the client to better understand his or her needs.

Promotion

You may have the best-quality event product, but unless you have a strategic plan for promoting this product, it will remain the best-kept secret in the world. Even large, well-known mega-events such as the Super Bowl, Rose Parade, and Olympic Games require well-developed promotion strategies to achieve the success they require.

Following is a five-step list to assist you with identifying and budgeting for your event promotion:

1. Identify all event elements that require promotion from the proposal through the final evaluation.
2. Develop strategies for allocating scarce event promotion resources with efficient methods.
3. Identify promotion partners to share costs.
4. Target your promotion carefully to those market segments that will support your event.
5. Measure and analyze your promotion efforts throughout the campaign to make corrections as required.

The promotion strategy you identify for your event requires a careful study of past or comparable efforts, expert guidance from people who have specific expertise in this field, and, most important, benchmarks for specific measurement of your individual promotion activities.

There are a variety of ways to measure promotion efforts. First, you may measure awareness by your target market. Anticipation of the event may be tantamount to ultimate participation. Next, you may measure actual attendance and the resulting investment. Finally, you may measure the post-event attitudes of the event promotional activity. Did the promotions you designed persuade the participants or guests to attend the event?

Promotion is the engine that drives the awareness of your event. Throughout event history, legendary promoters such as Bill Veck, Joe Engel, and, perhaps most important, P. T. Barnum realized that you must shamelessly promote your event product to attract the attention of the public.

Veck did this in Major League Baseball by hiring midgets as players. At the time of this stunt, there was no height requirement, and Veck took advantage of this oversight to promote his Chicago team. Engel, a Minor League Baseball promoter in Chattanooga, Tennessee, staged a fake elephant hunt on the baseball diamond to generate capacity attendance for his losing team. And, of course, P. T. Barnum continually amused the public with his legendary promotions, such as the smallest man (Tom Thumb) and the biggest mammal (Jumbo).

Most event marketers use a variety of media to promote their products. However, it is essential that Event Leaders carefully select those media outlets that will precisely target the market segments that are appropriate for their events. Targeting promotion strategies is essential to ensure the alignment of the event's attributes with the needs, wants, and desires of potential attendees.

Price

Market research will help you determine price. Part of this market research will include conducting a competitive analysis study of other organizations offering similar event products. You may initially believe that your product is uniquely different from every other event. However, when you interview potential ticket buyers or guests, you may be surprised to learn that they consider your event similar to many others. Therefore, you must carefully list all competing events and the prices being charged to help you determine the appropriate price for your event.

Typically, two factors determine price. First, the Event Leader must determine the financial philosophy of the event. If the event is a not-for-profit venture, the organization may not be concerned with a large commercial yield from the event. Instead, the philosophical purpose of the event may be to generate overall awareness and support. However, if the event is a commercial venture, the goal is probably to generate the greatest potential net profit. Once the philosophy is clear, the Event Leader will be able to determine price. The price must reflect the cost of all goods and services required to produce the event, plus a margin of profit or retained earnings.

The second factor is the perceived competition from similar events. If your event ticket costs $100 and does not offer the same *perceived value* as a similar event selling for $50, your prospective guests are more likely to select the latter event. Therefore, you must be price-competitive. Becoming price-competitive does not mean lowering your ticket price. Rather, it may require raising the perception of value (as discussed earlier) to justify the slightly higher price.

These two factors—the cost of doing business and the marketplace competition—certainly influence price. A third area that may also influence price is the general economic conditions, not only in your area but also in the region, your country, and, increasingly, the world. During times of recession, some events with lower ticket prices will flourish, while other upscale event products may not be as successful. Keep a close eye on market economic indicators to make certain that your price matches the purchasing power of your target market.

Public Relations

Advertising is what *you* say about your event whereas public relations is what *others* (their perceptions) are saying about your event. Since many events require a second-party endorsement or even review to encourage people to attend, public relations is significantly more valuable and effective than traditional advertising.

In the 1930s and 1940s, public relations consisted primarily of press agents who worked diligently to convince the print media to devote editorial space to their clients. With the influence of leaders such as Edward Bernays (1891–1995), the public relations effort soon became more complex and respected. Bernays, credited as being the father of public relations, was both a blood nephew and nephew-in-law to the father of psychoanalysis, Sigmund Freud. Bernays recognized the psychological factors that govern a person's decision-making ability. Therefore, he advocated that public relations professionals first engage in research, including focus groups, to determine the values, attitudes, and lifestyles of their target markets and carefully match their messages to these important factors.

Today, in many event marketing campaigns, public relations is at least equal to and, in many cases, even more important than traditional advertising. However, public relations involves much more than merely grinding out a short press release.

The effective event public relations campaign will involve research with event consumers as well as the media; the development of collateral materials such as media kits, fact sheets, and other tangibles; the organization and implementation of media conferences; the development of a speaker's bureau; and on-site media relations assistance at the event.

Event public relations help create the overall impression that others will develop about your event. In that regard, it is significantly more valuable than advertising because it implies greater credibility. For that reason, the Public Relations Society of America, an organization whose members include professionals in the public relations profession, states that public relations exposure is more valuable financially than advertising. For example:

✦ Half-page newspaper advertisement

cost = $5,000

✦ Editorial about your event in the same space as the advertisement

value = $15,000 to $35,000 (3 to 7 times more) depending on placement

Use the power of public relations to beat the drum loudly for your event. Carefully select those public relations tools that will most effectively and cost-efficiently help you inform and persuade others to support your event.

Place

In real estate, location is everything. In event marketing, distribution of your product may be everything as well. The location of your event often determines the channels of distribution.

If your event is located in a rural area, it may be difficult to promote the event due to limited media resources and for your target market to make the purchase due to logistical constraints. However, in the post–September 11, 2001, world, rural events are growing in number and size in the United States. This may be due to the perception of safety and security and convenience of local guests. Therefore, despite these limitations, demand due to lack of competition and need for tourism dollars has overcome these obstacles.

The place where you locate your event ultimately will determine the marketing efforts you must exert to drive sales. For example, it has been shown that those events that are close to inexpensive, safe public transportation or those events that feature closed-in reasonably priced parking will attract more guests than those that do not offer these amenities. Furthermore, those events that are connected to other nearby attractions or infrastructures (such as shopping malls) may also draw more attendees due to the time efficiency of the destination. For upscale events, the addition of valet parking may improve the chances of attracting guests to a new or nontraditional location.

The Event Leader must seriously consider place when designing the marketing program for the event. *Place* does not only imply the taste or style of the event; it also, in large part, defines the type of person that will be persuaded to invest in the event. In this regard, the event marketer must determine the place in the early stages through research and design. This is the perfect time to convene a focus group or conduct a survey to determine who is likely to attend your event when they are given a variety of location choices. Making certain you have thoughtfully analyzed this important issue will save you time and money throughout the entire event marketing process.

According to Leonard H. Hoyle Jr., in his book *Event Marketing* (Wiley, 2002), there is an additional *P* that is critical to the marketing mix. Hoyle describes *positioning* as the proper positioning of the product. Hoyle maintains, "Positioning is the strategy of determining through intuition, research, and evaluation those areas of consumer need that your event can fulfill." He further states that the five key considerations when positioning an event include location, attention span, competitive costs, the program, and the simplicity of the marketing plan. Hoyle states:

> Issues of location must be continuously evaluated, because interests of the markets change constantly. Maintaining the attention of the prospective event attendee is very important because people have so many images and messages competing for their attention. Competitive costs include the critical factor of cost of admission, which further defines the market. The program must be something that no one else can offer. Finally, the most important variable of all may be the plan itself. Keep it short and sweet and easy to track. The plan should spell, as briefly as feasible, the strengths and weaknesses of your organization and event, the objectives, the needs of your potential market niche, economic considerations, and elements that make the enterprise unique from others.

Internal versus External Event Marketing

Event Leaders may use an event or a series of events as one of the marketing methods to promote external events, products, or services, such as shopping malls, tourist destinations, or attractions (e.g., amusement parks or zoos), or any entity that is appropriately promoted through events.

However, in most cases, Event Leaders use marketing forces such as advertising, public relations, promotion, advertising specialties, stunts, and other techniques to promote individual events. These traditional marketing techniques should be used to inform, attract, persuade, sustain, and retain potential customers for your event.

Increasingly, a blend of internal and external event marketing is being utilized to promote events. In some cases, Event Leaders use miniature events as a means of promoting major events. The Sydney Organizing Committee for the Olympic Games (SOCO) staged a major fireworks display to celebrate the decision by the International Olympic Committee to stage the games in Sydney, Australia. The fireworks spectacular began the marketing process of identifying Sydney as the city of the next Olympic Games. Smaller events, such as a torch run, are used throughout the days preceding the opening ceremonies to promote this event.

On a smaller scale, fundraising organizations such as the National Symphony Orchestra use smaller focus-type events (e.g., receptions) to promote larger events (e.g., the Symphony Ball or the annual Designer's Show House). These ancillary events serve to promote the larger event to different market segments and maintain excitement about the overall event product.

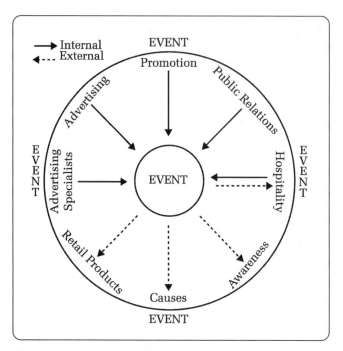

Figure 8.1 Internal and External Event Marketing Model

Therefore, both internal and external event marketing are important strategies for your event. Figure 8.1 depicts how this process is used to market your event product. Since resources for marketing are always limited, it is important to select those internal or external elements that will reach and influence your target market most effectively.

External Event Marketing

Using events to market products and services is increasing. As mentioned earlier, *Advertising Age* has declared that events are now critical in the total marketing effort. Therefore, although using an event marketing strategy may be more costly due to the additional labor required, it must be considered seriously when promoting products and services.

Retail Events

Our firm began by producing fashion shows, petting zoos, Santa Claus appearances, and other retail events. During the mid- to late 1970s, regional mega–shopping centers opened throughout the United States, and mall developers such as the Rouse Company and Homart recognized that they were the new Main Streets of America. To attract the appropriate target market, a series of events was developed and implemented to position the shopping mall as an attraction.

Using the fashion show as one example, shopping mall management could satisfy the needs of both its internal and external customers. First, the store owners and managers could showcase their goods and services to a highly targeted audience in a cost-effective manner. Second, the external customer—the shopper himself or herself—would be held captive during the 20- to 30-minute production and then directed to visit each store for special discounts immediately following the show. According to the International Council of Shopping Centers, the trade association that educates and promotes the shopping center industry, many marketing directors are earning the Certified Marketing Director (CMD) designation to develop specialized knowledge of this increasingly complex and competitive profession.

Figure 8.2 lists several retail events that have proven successful and the market to which they are best targeted. You will note that most of these events target women, as historically women have comprised the largest customer bases for retail businesses. However, these demographics are shifting as two-income families have emerged in the United States, and now both men and women increasingly share the responsibilities and pleasures of shopping. Therefore, successful Event Leaders will look for events that they may use to develop other markets with disposable income, such as men, teenage boys, and even senior citizens.

Timing is everything when developing and producing the retail event. To allow the consumer to devote as much time as possible to spending money, the live event should be brief in duration (under 20 minutes) and offered frequently throughout the day to allow a

Event	Target Market
Arts and crafts shows	Women and senior citizens
Children's entertainer	Young children
Circus and petting zoo	Young families
Computer show	Men
Cooking demonstration/ tasting	Women
Fashion show	Women and teenage girls
Fine art show	Women and men
Health fair	Senior citizens
Magician	Young boys
Model railroad show	Young boys and men
Puppeteer	Young children
Soap-opera-star appearance	Women and teenage girls
Sport-celebrity appearance	Men and boys
Sport-memorabilia festival	Men and teenage boys

Figure 8.2 Retail Events and Their Target Markets

variety of customers to experience the event activity. Obviously, due to the increase in working adults, the middle-of-the-week day should be avoided so that the most consumers can witness the event. Finally, many retail events are tied directly to paydays. Find out what the pay period is from large organizations such as factories, government, or other sources of large numbers of consumers, and then time your event to coincide with this window of time when there will be a large amount of expendable income available.

Fairs and Festivals

Fairs, festivals, and other public events may also serve as temporary retail locations (TRLs). These events often contract space to vendors, craftspeople, and others to demonstrate and sell their products and services. However, like their permanent retail counterparts, to be successful such events must be marketed aggressively through both internal and external event marketing efforts.

A media preview event is an excellent way to inform the media about the size, scope, and excitement being offered at your fair or festival. Designing a ribbon-cutting event featuring prominent local citizens along with celebrities is an important way to announce "open for business." Finally, a series of ongoing ancillary events held at other public venues, such as sporting event halftime shows, is an important form of external marketing to introduce and remind other market segments of your event's importance.

Launching New Products

Perhaps one of the more important activities within the event marketing area is that of launching new products developed by corporations. Each year in the United States and other countries, billions of dollars are invested in advertising to promote new products. Before these products are introduced to the general public, they are usually showcased to retailers or dealers. An event such as the launch of a new automobile serves several constituent groups. The trade media may be invited to promote the product to others. Then the general media (newspapers, radio, and television) may be invited to help make the general public aware of the new product benefits and features. Finally, and perhaps most important, the product launch must target those people who will either sell the item to others or purchase it themselves.

The organization and presentation of the product launch event may be one of the most important steps in the overall marketing effort. Whether introducing the latest software or an attraction such as a new hotel resort, great thought must be given to the goals, objectives, and desired outcomes to create a successful event.

Following is a 10-step list for developing and producing consistently successful product-launch events.

1. Determine the goals and objectives of the product-launch event.
2. Identify the target market(s).
3. Coordinate planning with sales promotion, public relations, human resource development, and other critical departments.

4. Conduct research to refine your general production plans.
5. Use creativity to introduce your product in a nontraditional yet attractive manner.
6. Use creativity to unveil a new product.
7. Identify who will speak, for what length of time, and why.
8. Identify ways to reach those who could not attend the event (such as through a video program or satellite presentation).
9. Measure and analyze your results by how sales are affected.
10. Develop opportunities for added value the next time you produce a similar event.

Lavish plans for product-launch events sometimes are foiled by circumstances beyond the control of the Event Leader. However, most circumstances can be controlled easily through close communication with other parties. Make certain that you contact the corporate communications or public relations department early in the process to identify their goals and incorporate them into your plans. Next, and equally important, make certain that the vice president or director of sales is closely involved in your planning, as your activities will directly affect his or her efforts. Finally, ensure that senior management, including the chief executive and operating officers, understands, supports, and is committed to your success. However, despite all this careful interaction with other stakeholders, sometimes old Murphy raises his devilish head.

Event Promotion Techniques

Five typical or traditional techniques are used to promote events: advertising, public relations, cross promotions, street promotions, and stunts. Some events use only one of these techniques; others may use all of them to ensure that their message is received and acted on by their target market.

Advertising

Advertising includes print and electronic media, transportation media (such as bus and rail), advertising specialties (calendars, key rings, coffee mugs, and other products), and outdoor media (billboards). Larger events may use many of these media resources, while smaller events may carefully target their message to one or two media.

Print advertising is not limited to magazines and newspapers. It may also include membership directories, inserts in local newspapers, flyers (sometimes called *one sheets*), posters, church and synagogue newsletters, brochures, and virtually any printed media. When analyzing your print advertising needs, make certain that you test your advertising product in advance with a small distribution to test its effectiveness. Specialists in direct mail recommend that you use a *split-test* approach. This requires that you mail one type of advertising printed matter to one group and a different type to another to test the best response from both types. Varying items such as the color of the ink, copy, type, and weight of the paper, or other decisions may produce different results. Test your print advertising using focus groups to make certain that your event product is well positioned for success.

Classic advertising terms such as *free, discount, now, sale,* and *new* may help you influence the consumer to invest in your event. Clever graphics, endorsements, testimonials, and other credibility-building devices will help differentiate your event product from others.

Electronic media include radio, television, the Internet, and any form of advertising that involves electronic delivery. Radio advertising is typically used to remind the listener about the event, whereas television is used to build excitement. The Internet is an excellent means with which to reach upscale consumers and those who are interested in science, technology, and travel. Before you select electronic media as a means to advertise your event, examine all potential media outlets.

Within television media, you may elect to cast your event broadly through major networks or narrowly cast by selecting a finely targeted cable station. For example, if you are promoting an arts-related event, you may select a cable station with arts programming. Selecting the appropriate media outlet may require the assistance of experts in media buying or from an advertising agency specializing in radio or television media.

Transportation media require that you place your message on buses, subways, and other forms of transportation. Usually these media are aimed at a very wide market and have proven effective for circuses, fairs, festivals, and other events that require large attendance from diverse groups.

Advertising specialties are those items that are usually given away or offered as a premium, as an incentive to purchase a product or service. Advertising specialties include thousands of products; however, the most typical are calendars, refrigerator magnets, coffee mugs, writing instruments, and key chains. In recent years, clothing has become popular as an advertising specialty, and some event organizers give away clothing to the media and other key constituent groups and sell the rest at souvenir stands. Once again, research this purchase carefully to ensure that the recipient values the item and will use it. Prolonged use will serve as reminders of your event.

Outdoor advertising was, at one time, one of the major forms of advertising in the United States. However, during the late 1960s, many billboards were banned in a "beautify America" campaign. Still, the outdoor billboard is an excellent way to reach large numbers of potential event participants for an extended period of time.

Regardless of the type of advertising media you select, first conduct market research and follow up with tests to determine actual response. Once you have found a medium that effectively reaches your target market, use repetition to build reinforcement and retention. Finally, measure all responses to develop history and determine where your advertising dollar will pull best for each event.

Public Relations

Public relations involves informing the media and your target market about your event and persuading them to support your programs. Public relations activities for your event may include designing, printing, and distributing media kits, producing public service announcements for radio and television, producing and distributing audio and video news releases, or even producing events. In fact, according to many public relations professionals, events are the fastest-growing segment of the public relations strategy.

The media kit is typically a presentation-type folder that contains a fact sheet, request for coverage notice, media releases, and even a public service announcement (either written or recorded). This kit is distributed well in advance of the event to the print and electronic media to inform them of opportunities for coverage. In smaller markets, some media outlets may print your media releases word for word; in larger, more sophisticated markets, members of the media may use the kit for background information alone.

Leonard H. Hoyle Jr., suggests that press kits should include these materials:

+ Press or media releases
+ Photos
+ Media alerts
+ Requests for coverage
+ Press conference announcements and invitations
+ Speeches
+ Background news stories
+ Videotapes of the event
+ CDs and DVDs of the event
+ Organizational information
+ Biographies of the key individuals leading the event or appearing at the event (speakers, entertainers)
+ Folders, brochures, postcards
+ Advertising specialty items

A *public service announcement* (PSA) is a written or prerecorded audio or video announcement about your event. Broadcasters in the United States are required by federal law to allot a certain amount of time for public service announcements. In some cases, the broadcaster may provide help, as a further public service, in producing these announcements. Often a local celebrity or nationally prominent person will participate at no charge, to add credibility to your announcement.

The audio or video news release, while a relatively new phenomenon, is one of the most effective ways to distribute your event message. Audio news releases (ANRs) and video news releases (VNRs) require that you pretape a news story about your event and then, by overnight mail or use of satellite transmission, send the story to local stations that you would like to have air the story as part of their news programming. Since news programs are often the most watched segments of television programming, this type of public relations has the potential of reaching a large, well-targeted audience in a credible and cost-effective manner.

Finally, events themselves often become major public relations vehicles. To promote the opening of a new shopping center, movie actress Teri Garr starred in a public service announcement to benefit the National Center for Missing and Exploited Children. Garr filmed the announcement in the mall. Later she appeared on *The Tonight Show* with Johnny Carson and described in detail her activities on behalf of the national center, including the filming of the public service announcement in the mall. This *event-within-an-event* serves to further position you firmly in the minds of those in the target audience.

Remember that the two chief goals of public relations are to inform and persuade. Therefore, using collateral materials, public service announcements, and audio and video news releases as well as smaller events are excellent ways to accomplish these two important goals of an overall marketing campaign.

Cross Promotions

To allocate market resources in the most efficient manner, you must identify and incorporate marketing partners into your campaign. These organizations may actually contribute marketing dollars or may provide in-kind services, such as providing celebrities, tagging their ads with your event date and time, or contributing other valuable components to your campaign.

When seeking marketing partners to develop a cross-promotional strategy, study the advertising and marketing activities of compatible businesses in your area. Determine which of these activities will benefit your event. Next, develop a proposal that clearly describes the resources that you can bring to the event. Finally, present the proposal to your prospective marketing partners and answer any questions they may pose.

Tagging advertising involves your marketing partner adding a line of copy to his or her regular advertising placements that promote your event. It may read "Official supporter of XYZ event" or "Meet us at XYZ event, date and time." Tag lines may appear in both print and electronic advertising.

Make certain that you chronicle all marketing activities so that you can report to your partners after the event and describe in specific detail those placements that were successful. Cross promotions and tie-in activities are sensational ways to reach a much larger market in a cost-effective manner.

Street Promotions

This marketing activity requires that you literally take your message to the street. Street promotions may include the handing out of flyers by a clown in a high-traffic area, the appearance of a celebrity at a local mall, contests, or other promotional activities designed to draw high visibility to your event. Before *leafleting* (handing out flyers), make certain that this is allowed by local code. You certainly do not want to generate negative publicity by having the clown arrested for causing a disturbance. A celebrity appearance can help generate significant publicity if it is handled properly. Schedule the celebrity to include radio and television interviews, appearances at a local children's hospital or other public facility, and ceremonial events with local, state, provincial, or federal leaders. At each appearance, make certain that the celebrity is well informed about the event and articulates your event message in a consistent manner. Contests and other promotional events also require analysis to ensure that they are within the bounds of the local code and that they are appropriate for your event. For instance, selling raffle tickets at a nonprofit event may require that you file legal forms.

Stunts

During the early 1950s in the United States, advertising agencies used stunts as an important method of breaking through the clutter of traditional print and electronic advertising. Today, stunts continue to be effective but must be crafted carefully to ensure that the integrity of the event is preserved.

A stunt involves an activity designed to generate media coverage and attendance by spectators to promote a specific event or series of events. Radio stations continue to rely heavily on stunts and will often provide remote broadcasts to cover stunts involving their on-air personalities. Stunts can be tied to charitable endeavors, such as locking up prominent officials until enough donations are raised to cover their release. Other stunts may involve creating the world's largest pizza, cake, sandwich, or other product. Before you incorporate a stunt in an event marketing program, it is important to analyze how the stunt will further your marketing objectives and to determine all associated costs. Finally, make certain that you chronicle all media coverage that results from the stunt, distribute bounce-back coupons to attendees, and track all responses resulting from the stunt.

Invitation

Whether your invitation is a print or electronic advertisement, a flyer, or a formal engraved document, the copy that is composed, art that is created or selected, and paper that is chosen will greatly influence the response. The five central components of all effective invitations are:

1. Name of host or event organizer
2. Date, time, and location
3. Dress requirements
4. Transportation and parking
5. RSVP

Six additional components may include:

1. Purpose of the event
2. Names of honorary board or committee members
3. Names of prominent speakers
4. Frequency or historic nature of the event (second annual, 100th anniversary celebration, or biannual event)
5. Limited supply of tickets
6. VIP status

Remember that an invitation is an official offer to the consumer or guest to participate in your event. Therefore, from a legal perspective, it is important that you choose your words carefully to reflect the actual event you are promoting.

Each of these components is designed to generate a specific response from the recipient. The most important response is to build anticipation toward acceptance followed by actual attendance.

Marketing Thrust

The late Ira Westreich, noted corporate marketing expert and eloquent professional speaker, described the word *event* as an acronym that represents *"Extract Value with Every New Thrust."* The purpose of your event marketing campaign is to ensure that every decision you make provides greater value for the overall event outcome. To do this, you must carefully match the objectives to the strategies, test all ideas using feedback from actual event consumers, and, perhaps most important, use creativity and innovation to differentiate your event product as a unique and valuable investment. By integrating marketing activities such as advertising, public relations, cross promotions, street promotions, and stunts, you will be able to build a strong campaign that will effectively promote your event to your target audience.

Event Sponsorship

According to the International Events Group (IEG) of Chicago, sponsorship worldwide is a $25 billion industry (IEG, 2004). IEG is a recognized leader in the field of sponsorship research and education. Although the vast majority of sponsorship dollars is invested in sports-related events, there is a trend to diversify funding into festivals, fairs, and cultural events. The primary reason for this diversification of investment is due to the need of advertisers to reach more targeted demographics. Sports have generally attracted broad demographics, whereas cultural events are able to target high-income and well-educated consumers.

Sponsorship becomes more valuable if the event organization is able to offer precise targeting that matches the marketing objectives of the prospective sponsor. The growth in sponsorship is due primarily to the need of advertisers to find alternative marketing channels to inform, persuade, promote, and sell their products and services. However, the number of events that require sponsorship has also grown in recent years.

Without sponsorship, many events would not be financially feasible. Other events would not be able to provide the quality expected by event participants. Still other events would not be able to achieve their specified goals and objectives. Suffice it to say that, more often than not, sponsorship provides the grease that allows the event wheel to function smoothly.

Historically, sponsorship has its earliest modern origin in professional sporting events. These events have always appealed to the widest demographics and were, therefore, perfect event products for sponsorship. Sponsorship is a uniquely American invention brought forth from the need of advertisers to reach certain markets and the need of event organizers to identify additional funding to offset costs not covered by normal revenue streams, such as ticket sales.

In recent times, there has been a noticeable shift in sponsor dollars away from sporting events and toward arts events. The reason for this shift is that sponsors are seeking more highly targeted upscale demographics and the arts' audience delivers that market segment. Therefore, those events that deliver the higher-income demographics are predicted to benefit most from sponsorship dollars in the future.

Perhaps the best example of sport sponsorship is the 1984 Summer Olympic Games in Los Angeles, California. For the first time in the history of the modern Olympic Games movement, sponsors were aggressively solicited as marketing partners for this unprecedented event. Offers were made, deals were cut, and the Los Angeles Olympic Organizing Committee received net earnings of over $200 million.

From fairs to festivals to hallmark events such as a world's fair, the role of the sponsor has earned a permanent place in the marketing lexicon of events. Following are typical types of sponsors for a variety of events.

+ *Fair:* bottler, grocer, automotive, and bank
+ *Festival:* department store and record store
+ *Sport:* athletic wear manufacturer, bottler, brewery, and hospital or health-care facility
+ *School program:* children's toy stores, children's clothing stores, and amusement park
+ *Meeting/conference:* printer, bank, insurance broker, and associate member firms

Use this list as a guide to begin to identify sponsors for your event.

Sponsorship Needs Assessment

Although most events may benefit from sponsorship, not every event is appropriate for this component. Sponsorship is a commercial endeavor and is extremely time-consuming. Therefore, unless you are prepared to enter into a commercial relationship with other parties and have the time resources to devote to this activity, you may instead wish to solicit donations.

Many Event Leaders confuse sponsorship with benevolence. A fundraising event where donors contribute without any expectation of commercial benefit is a benevolent activity. Sponsorship, however, is a commercial transaction in which two parties agree by way of an offer and acceptance. The offer generally involves marketing services provided by the event organizer in exchange for the sponsor's cash or in-kind contribution to the event. The marketing services may range from advertising, to banner displays, to hospitality, to a full-blown marketing plan involving public relations, advertising, and promotion.

As you can see, these marketing services place new demands on the event organizer. Therefore, event resources may need to be reallocated to handle this new demand. Not every event is able to do this.

Before you give the green light to soliciting sponsorships, use the next checklist to determine if your event is appropriate for this activity:

1. Does the event require an infusion of sponsor dollars to achieve the quality required?
2. Are there sufficient internal and external resources to support this activity?
3. Is commercial sponsorship appropriate for the nature of the event?
4. Are there sufficient prospects for sponsorship sales, and is the timing appropriate to approach them?
5. Is this activity legal, ethical, and appropriate for the spirit of the event organization?

These questions can save many event organizations much wasted time, energy, and heartache. Examining the internal and external resources may be one of the most important aspects of this process.

Although sponsors may provide much needed funding for your event, to help you achieve the quality that is required, sponsors also require that your own financial resources meet their objectives. They may, for example, require that you commit a certain amount of marketing dollars. They also may require minimal or substantial hospitality services that may amount to hundreds or thousands of dollars per day. If you are going to retain these sponsors, assign one or more people to monitor the activities, service these accounts, and develop long-term relationships. Yes, sponsors can provide needed funding; however, as in any commercial transaction, they must also receive a fair return on their investment. You are responsible for orchestrating this return.

Your event may benefit from additional exposure through sponsorships. Earlier, we discussed using tag lines in advertising as one way to increase your exposure inexpensively. Sponsors may also provide you with shelf space in their retail stores to promote your event through coupons. Your sponsors can also help you with the development of a public relations campaign or can supplement their own public relations efforts with your message. Some sponsors have celebrity athletes, television stars, and movie personalities on contract whom they may wish to involve with your event.

Perhaps one of the more important reasons event organizers align themselves with commercial sponsors is the opportunity to achieve greater credibility for the event. Securing the sponsorship of AT&T, IBM, Coca-Cola, or other Fortune 500 firms immediately positions your event as a major player and may help your event organization secure additional funding from other sources.

Developing Sponsors

The competition by event organizers for sponsors is keen at every level. Whether your event is a local event or a national one, you must first conduct a competitive analysis to identify all competing events and study their sponsorship history and current activities. Several suggestions on how to identify appropriate sponsors for your event follow.

1. Determine the financial level of sponsorship you require. Not every sponsor can make a five- or six-figure decision.
2. Review trade journals such as *Advertising Age* and *Sponsorship Report* to track sponsor activities.
3. Review the local business tabloid in your area to search for prospective sponsors.
4. Network with advertising and public relations agency officials to find out if their clients have an interest in your event.
5. Conduct a focus group with prospective sponsors to solicit and later analyze their opinions and attitudes toward your event.

Once you have developed a list of prospective sponsors, the next step is to qualify them for solicitation. Do not waste your valuable resources by making endless presentations to sponsors who do not have the interest or resources to support your event financially. Instead, qualify your sponsors by contacting local organizations, such as the chamber of commerce, board of trade, banks, and other centers of commerce, to inquire about the financial viability of the prospective sponsor. Next, thoroughly review the sponsor's past marketing efforts to determine if its overall marketing plans are conducive to sponsoring your event. Finally, talk to advertising and public relations executives and attempt to forecast where your prospective sponsor may put his or her marketing dollars in the future. Perhaps the logical place for investment is your event.

Selling Sponsorships

Always do your homework regarding the sponsor's needs, wants, and desires prior to attempting to sell a sponsorship. To make the sale, the sponsorship offer must be an exact fit with the needs, expectations, goals, and objectives of the commercial sponsor. Customize the offer to achieve these goals and objectives prior to your presentation.

Constructing a successful proposal is equal parts of art and science. As an artist, you must design an attractive, enticing, and aesthetically pleasing product that the sponsor will want to purchase. Therefore, describe the capability of your organization and past sponsors (if any), incorporate testimonials and references from leading individuals, and package the proposal in a professional design. Avoid being clever. Remember that the sponsor will be making an important business decision and will prefer a serious business plan rather than one that demonstrates cleverness. The science part involves carefully identifying your target market and linking all sponsorship activities to sales or recognition that will benefit the sponsor. List the benefits and activities the sponsor will enjoy as a sponsor of your event. For example, the sponsor may be able to provide free samples of his or her product or service and conduct marketing research. He or she may be able to offer his or her product or service for sale and measure the results. Or the sponsor may benefit from public relations exposure. Regardless of the benefit or feature, detail each potential activity that may result from the sponsorship.

Include in the proposal sponsorship terms for payment and any requirements the sponsor may have in addition to these payments. In some events, the sponsor is allowed to provide an exhibit at his or her own cost. In others, the exhibit is provided as part of the sponsorship costs. Describe any additional costs or services the sponsor is required to contribute to avoid any future surprises. This list summarizes the key elements in a winning sponsorship proposal:

1. Describe the history of the event.
2. Include a capability statement about your organization's resources.
3. Incorporate testimonials and references from other sponsors.
4. Describe the benefits and features that the sponsor will receive.
5. List all financial responsibilities that the sponsor must accept.
6. Describe any additional responsibilities that the sponsor must accept.
7. Describe how you will chronicle the sponsorship activity.
8. Include a time and a date for acceptance of the offer.
9. Include a provision for renewal of the sponsorship.
10. Include an arbitration clause in case you and the sponsor disagree regarding the sponsorship activities.

One of the more effective ways to persuade sponsors to participate in an event is to organize a prospective sponsor preview program. During this program, you and your staff describe the benefits and features of your sponsorship activities to a large number of prospective sponsors. You may wish to invite a couple of previous sponsors to provide in-person testimonials about the benefits of the sponsorship. You may also wish to presell one or two sponsors so that when you ask for a reaction from those in attendance, at least two from the group will respond favorably. Their favorable response may, and usually does, influence others. Avoid trying to hard-sell during this program. Use this program to plant seeds that will be further cultivated during meetings with individual sponsors.

Overcoming Sponsor Objections

Most sponsors will want their sponsorship activities customized to achieve their specific goals and objectives. Therefore, they may have some preliminary objections after receiving your initial offer. Once you have presented the offer, ask them for their reaction on each benefit and feature. Listen carefully and list these comments. Make two lists. One list is for approvals, those items that they see the value in sponsoring. The second list is for objections, those items that they cannot see the value of at this time. Your goal is to move all the items from list 2 to list 1. To do this, ask sponsors what their organization requires to overcome their objections on each point. In some cases it may be additional exposure. In other cases it may be the price of the sponsorship. To overcome these objections, be prepared to provide sponsors with the tools they need to make a positive decision. For example, if their objection is cost, you may be able to combine their sponsorship with others and lower their contribution. If their objection is limited exposure, you may be able to reposition their involvement inexpensively to provide them with greater and more sustained visibility. Handling objections is an integral part of the sponsorship sales process. Rehearse these discussions with your internal stakeholders to identify other common objections, and be prepared to provide the solution your sponsors need to remove these barriers.

Negotiating Your Sponsorship

Almost every sponsorship will require intense negotiations to move it to fruition. Whenever possible, conduct these negotiations in person with the decision maker. Assign a specific date and time for these negotiations and confirm that the sponsor is a feasible prospect before entering into a serious negotiation. In most negotiations, both parties desire a win-win-win outcome. In this type of negotiation, you win as the event organizer, the sponsor wins as the event funding agent, and the stakeholders of your event win from your mutual efforts to secure these dollars.

Carefully analyze what your sponsor expects from the sponsorship prior to your negotiating session. Determine in advance what additional components you may be able to offer if required. Also, list those concessions that you cannot make. Finally, list these items that may require further approval from your board or others before you agree to them. Begin the negotiation by asking the prospective sponsor to list all items that are acceptable, bundle them, and have the sponsor approve them. Now you are prepared to focus on those items that require further resolution. Ask the sponsor to describe his or her concerns about each negotiation point and take careful notes. Look at your list of concessions and decide if any item you have listed will help resolve these concerns. If it is appropriate to offer a concession, do so and ask the sponsor for his or her approval. Once the sponsor has approved, ask him or her to provide you with an additional service, usually at modest additional cost to the sponsor, to balance his or her end of the negotiation. If the sponsor is unable to provide you with an additional service or product, determine if you are able to proceed to the next point.

Do not be afraid to walk away. In some cases, the concession that the sponsor will ask for may sacrifice the credibility or reputation of an event. In other cases, the sponsor will want a concession that may undermine the financial wealth of your event. Do not concede your reputation or the financial success of the event. Instead, thank the sponsor for his or her time, offer to work with him or her in the future under different circumstances, and leave the room as quickly as possible. In some instances, event organizers have reported that this approach has forced the prospective sponsor to reexamine his or her position. It is not unusual to have the sponsor call the event organizer the next day and offer a greater concession to save the sponsorship.

Closing the Sponsorship Sale

You must always *ask for the order* when presenting your sponsorship proposal. State at least three times that you want to develop a positive relationship with the sponsor. Start your discussions by stating that your desired outcome is to ensure that the sponsor understands all the benefits and features of your event and will desire to become a sponsor.

Throughout your presentation, ask for feedback from the sponsor and build on the sponsor's positive reactions by saying that you are pleased that he or she recognizes the value of your event product. Finally, at the conclusion of your presentation, ask the sponsor for his or her overall impression and state, once again, that you would like his or her business.

Unfortunately, these techniques may not be enough to get a clear answer. In some cases, you may have to say something like "So, can we count on you to sponsor our event?" Sometimes you need to secure the answer to this question in order to plan your next step in sponsorship negotiations or to decide to move forward with the next sponsor. The word *ask* is the most powerful three-letter word in sponsorship sales. Unless you ask, you will never know. Remember to ask early, often, and before leaving to confirm the sponsorship sale.

Servicing Sponsorship Sales

Once the sponsor has accepted your offer, the next task is to service the sale in order to retain his or her support in the future. One of the more common reasons that sponsors fail to renew their sponsorship is due to poor communications. In Part One of this book, we discussed in great detail the importance of open and continuous communications. Make certain that you develop methods for implementing positive communications with your sponsors. Some event organizers use newsletters to update their sponsors, others provide regular briefings, and still others offer their sponsors marketing seminars to help them design a booth or target their product or service to event guests. It is wise to assign one or more persons on your staff to service all sponsorships and communicate regularly with sponsors to make certain they remain informed, excited, and committed to the event activities.

Another reason that some sponsorships go sour is the inability of the event organizers to deliver what they promise. If you promise that the sponsor's banner will be suspended on the main stage above the head of the performing artist, you must first confirm with the artist that this is acceptable. It is unacceptable to renege later on your commitment to the sponsor. It is always best to underpromise and overdeliver when stating the benefits of sponsorship. Exceeding the sponsor's expectations is how you turn a one-year sponsorship into a five-year plan with options to renew forever.

Every sponsor has a hidden agenda. It can be as simple as the chair of the board wanting to meet his or her favorite celebrity or as complex as the sales manager's bonus and promotion decision resting on this particular sponsorship activity. Ask the sponsor's representative what else you need to know about the needs of his or her organization as you design the sponsorship measurement system. For example, if the sponsor's representative is in the public relations department, his or her interest may be in seeing lots of ink and television time devoted to the name of the sponsor. Therefore, you will want to measure these outcomes carefully to assist your sponsor. Remember that you may sign a sponsorship agreement with a large corporation or organization, but the day-to-day management of this agreement is between people. Find out what these people desire and try to provide them with these outcomes.

Although communications between you and your sponsors is critical to your success, perhaps even more important are the internal communications between the Event Leader and his or her operations personnel. You must first confirm that your personnel will be able to support sponsorship activities at the level required by the individual sponsors. Determine if you have sufficient internal resources to satisfy the requirements both in contract as well as implied to ensure the well-being of your sponsor's investment. For example, if your sponsor wants a hospitality setup arranged at the last minute, do you have a catering operation that can handle this request? One way to ensure that the sponsors' needs are handled expeditiously is to create a written system of orders, changes, and other instructions that clearly communicates those activities required by your sponsors. Prior to distribution of these forms, have the sponsor's representative sign one copy. Then have the event's representative initial approval before forwarding it to the appropriate department or team leader.

Evaluating Sponsorships

To secure multiple-year sponsorships, it is important that you develop and implement a system for measuring the sponsor's activities. First, decide what needs to be evaluated and why. The answers to these questions typically may be found in the goals and objectives of the sponsorship agreement.

To collect these data, conduct sponsorship evaluations that are comprehensive in scope. You may wish to interview the sponsors, your own staff, the sponsor's target market, and others to solicit a wide range of opinions regarding the effectiveness of the sponsorship. Furthermore, you may wish to include in the event survey-specific questions about the sponsor's participation. Finally, ask the sponsor for tracking information regarding sales that have resulted from the sponsor's participation in your event.

You may measure the sponsor's public relations benefits by measuring the number of minutes of television and/or radio time, as well as the number of inches and columns of print media, that was devoted to the sponsor's products or name. List the comparable value using the 3:1 ratio provided by the Public Relations Society of America.

Ask the sponsor how he or she would like to see the data you have measured presented. Some may prefer an elaborate in-person presentation using video clips and slides; others will prefer a simple summary of the goals, objectives, and outcomes that were achieved. Make certain that you present this information in a manner that is useful to the sponsor and that you take the time to prepare this presentation professionally to address the sponsor's needs. All future sponsorship activities will come from this important activity.

Timing Is Everything

The process for identifying, soliciting, negotiating, securing, servicing, and evaluating sponsorships is a complex one. However, as is true with most things, timing is everything. Allow a minimum of 12 to 18 months to formulate and consummate a successful sponsorship program. A typical timeline for the various stages just described follows.

18 months in advance	Conduct needs assessment and research.
16 months in advance	Identify prospective sponsors.
14 months in advance	Develop and present proposals.
12 months in advance	Negotiate proposals and sign agreements.
9 months in advance	Implement sponsorship operations plan.
6 months in advance	Audit sponsor's changes and additions.
4 months in advance	Review changes and additions with staff.
2 months in advance	Meet with sponsor to provide update on event progress.
1 month in advance	Begin sponsor public relations campaign.
1 month after event	Meet with sponsor to provide analysis of results.

Some event organizers have come to see sponsorship as the goose with the golden egg. However, while specific benefits come from individual sponsorships, prior to engaging in this time-consuming and expense-laden activity, an Event Leader must audit for each event the needs, resources available, and benefits offered. When developing sponsorship activities, always start small and build a base of sponsors year by year or event by event from your ability to deliver high-quality and successful events consistently. This is the best way to make sure that your goose lays a golden egg, not a rotten one, for your event organization.

Internet Event Marketing

Not since the invention of the printing press has advertising been changed as dramatically as with the introduction of the Internet. For example, the number of Internet users in the events industry grew from 50 percent to over 80 percent between 1996 and 1998. Today, virtually every event industry worker uses the Internet to search for resources, reserve or contact vendors, and promote continuous communication. Event marketing has now fully embraced the electronic marketplace. Reggie Aggarwal, CEO of Cvent.com, a leading Internet event marketing firm, told the Convention Industry Council Forum attendees that "the fastest, most precise, easiest, and most cost affordable way to reach prospective event attendees is through e-mail." According to Aggarwal, the penetration of the Internet will soon be 100 percent and will soon be equal to or even replace traditional television and radio in some segments as an electronic source for daily information and communications.

Cvent.com is one example of how the technological revolution is driving the Event Leadership industry. Aggarwal started the firm after he used e-mail invitations and reminders to promote registration for a local association that he directed. He soon discovered that he could increase the response rate significantly and better target his prospects using e-mail communications. For example, Cvent.com technology enables meeting planners and Event Leaders not only to send e-mail messages but also to note whether they have been read or not. Direct-mail marketers cannot monitor whether their communications are read; they can only note when a purchase or inquiry has been received. This innovation gives Cvent a competitive edge in the event market because the firm can determine quickly whether the e-mail event invitation has been opened and read. If it has been opened, the event marketer can assume that there is interest and build on that interest with follow-up communications. This customized marketing approach is one of the many benefits of the new technologies that are being developed to assist event marketers.

When developing event marketing, Internet marketing must be considered as a central part of any strategy. For example, regardless of size, all events should have a Web presence through a dedicated Web home page, a banner on an existing Web home page, or a link to a separate page. Following are points to consider when developing a comprehensive e-marketing event strategy.

- Identify your event market segments and targets.
- Design your Web strategy to reach your target market quickly, efficiently, and precisely.
- Use a focus panel of prospective event attendees to review your plans and suggest modifications to your overall design.
- Audit and evaluate the competition to determine how your Web presence can be more effective.
- Match the color scheme and design components to your printed matter.
- Determine whether you require a separate home page for your event or a link from an existing home page to a unique page.
- Identify and establish links with all marketing partners.
- Determine whether you will need a transaction page and ensure security for your ticket buyers.
- Determine whether you, your staff, or others can build the pages and/or make changes should they be needed.
- If consultants are contracted to build your site or pages, determine how they will be maintained (frequency, speed, and reliability).
- Use viral marketing (e-mails copied to prospective attendees) to promote your event.
- Use search engines to promote your event, with careful selection and registration of your URL.
- Use e-mail reminders to increase attendance during the last two weeks of an event.
- Use online registration systems.
- Use online evaluation systems to collect survey information before, during, and after an event.
- Use online chat rooms to create discussion areas for preregistered attendees and to generate follow-up discussion post-event.
- Carefully monitor all online activity for potential data mining to determine future needs, wants, and desires of your target audience.

The Internet will continue to drive the development of the global Event Leadership industry. You must use this dynamic technology quickly and accurately to ensure that your event remains competitive throughout the twenty-first century.

Event Marketing Evaluation

Reggie Aggarwal, founder and CEO of Cvent.com, and I coined the term *return on event* (ROE) in 2000 to identify the percentage of earnings returned to an event organization sponsoring the event based on marketing efforts. The ROE is an important concept for all event marketers, regardless of event size. For example, if you are marketing a small event for 100 persons and you increase attendance by 25 percent due to your new e-marketing strategies, you may, in fact, not only have saved a significant amount of money but also have generated a sizable net profit that may be directly attributable to this marketing activity. Figure 8.3 outlines how this formula may be used to identify the ROE.

The income statement shows a significant increase in total revenues in Year 2 as well as a slight increase in net income. Now we measure the increase in return on marketing and see how the marketing function performed as part of the overall financial analysis (Figure 8.4). By careful monitoring, tracking, and measuring of each marketing activity, you are able to identify that, in Year 2, your event generated a 160 percent return on marketing investment as compared to Year 1, with only 39 percent. To monitor, track, and measure each of these separate marketing functions, you need to use a variety of simple but effective systems.

	Year 1	Year 2
Expenses		
Advertising		
Newspaper	$25,000	$35,000
Radio	15,000	20,000
Television	50,000	60,000
Direct mail		
Design and printing	10,000	10,000
Postage	5,000	5,000
Internet	10,000	15,000
Promotions	5,000	5,000
Public relations	5,000	10,000
Subtotal	$120,000	$160,000
Income		
Ticket sales	$100,000	$125,000
Sponsorships	25,000	45,000
Subtotal	$125,000	$170,000

Figure 8.3   Measuring the Return on an Event: Income Statement for Family Festival of Fun

Expenses	Year 1	Year 2	Penetration (%)	Response (%)
Advertising				
Newspaper	$25,000	$35,000	25–40	5–10
Radio	15,000	20,000	10–15	1–5
Television	50,000	60,000	5–7	20–25
Direct mail				
Design and printing	10,000	10,000		
Postage	5,000	5,000	75–85	5–10
Internet		15,000	0–55	1–90
Promotions	5,000	5,000	1–2	3–10
Public relations	5,000	10,000	5–7	5–10
Subtotal	$120,000	$160,000		39–160

Figure 8.4 Evaluating the Return on an Event

Coding

Make certain that you assign a unique code to each marketing response item. For example, if you allow your attendees to register by mail, phone, newspaper, radio, and Internet, each marketing channel should have a separate code. Figure 8.5 demonstrates how to code and track each response. By identifying the response ratios from each marketing channel, you are better able to adjust your marketing efforts during the promotional period prior to the event and evaluate where to place your marketing dollars in the future.

Determining the return on your event accomplishes three fundamental purposes that are critical to your future marketing success.

Response Method	Code	Total		Response (%)
		Year 1	Year 2	
Direct mail	DM99	100	200	<100
Internet	IN99	1000	3000	<200
Newspaper				
Daily Courier	DC99	1000	1200	<20
Weekly Standard	WS99	500	750	<25
Radio				
WLAC	R-WLAC	15	25	<10
WPIR	R-WPIR	10	15	<5
Television	WNEW	150	300	<100

Figure 8.5 Coding and Tracking Event Marketing Responses

1. You are able to track where your responses are being generated.
2. You are able to compare investment versus actual marketing performance by each channel.
3. You are able to compare return on marketing with other economic performance indicators, such as risk management, labor, and utilities, on an annual basis and determine whether you need to increase or reduce the budget accordingly to achieve your revenue targets in future years.

Other Marketing Evaluation Tools

The ROE is a quantitative system for evaluating marketing response. However, in addition to quantifying your responses, you must also qualify them. Using a focus panel to review marketing promotional campaigns, including ink colors, logo design, and copy, will help you fine-tune your visual impressions to match the tastes of your prospective event attendees.

You may also wish to use personal interviews to determine why nonattendees refuse to accept your invitation to participate in your event offer. These telephonic interviews can reveal important information that will help you in marketing your event in the future. For example, a nonattendee may reveal that he has trouble finding a babysitter. If this comment is replicated with a large enough sample, you may wish to consider offering on-site child care to increase attendance by families with young children or add more children's activities to your event programming.

The overall benefits associated with marketing should not be focused solely on the economic performance of an event. Remember, even if someone did not attend your event, he or she may have recommended it to others. Furthermore, he or she may be positively influenced to attend in the future. Following are some of the qualitative areas you may wish to measure in your marketing analysis and measuring techniques for each.

- *Image improvement:* survey, interviews, focus panel
- *Recall of event name:* interviews, focus panel
- *Recall of event slogan:* interviews, focus panel
- *Increase in number of volunteers:* survey, focus panel
- *Increase in sponsorship:* focus panel, survey
- *Increase in gifts (philanthropy):* interviews, survey
- *Improved political relations:* interviews
- *Improved media relations:* interviews, clipping, and clip monitoring
- *Improved community relations:* interviews, focus panel

The overall purpose of marketing analysis and evaluation is to provide you with the essential information you need to make better decisions in the future. Whether your event is one that recurs year after year or is a one-time affair, the data you collect from your marketing analysis will help you in the development of many different types of future events. Make certain that you assign a line item in the event budget for marketing evaluation.

Some of the typical costs include: survey development and printing; focus panel facilitation; interviewer fees; data collection, tabulation, and analysis; and report writing. In addition, you may wish to contract with third parties, such as a clipping services firm, to track the media generated about your event. Your ability to measure the return on marketing for your event comprehensively will provide you with dividends for many years to come. Do not miss this opportunity to improve your competitiveness, your event's image, and your profitability now and in the years to come.

Leonard (Buck) Hoyle suggests that at least 10 trends will influence event marketing in the near future.

1. The aging demographics throughout the world will require that marketers use larger print to aid failing eyesight.
2. It is projected that there will be more disposable income for consumers to invest in your event, so you may wish to add pre- and post-events to your main event and combine your promotion for these packages.
3. Through improved technological delivery, such as wireless application protocol (WAP), you will be able to better promote your event in real time through cell phones and other wireless systems.
4. Through faster technology (broadband), you will be able to send much more information to potential attendees at faster and faster speeds.
5. A wide range of new media outlets (including schools, colleges, clubs, amusement parks, and other locations) will develop where your potential target market can receive your message.
6. Your copywriters will need to develop a new vocabulary to communicate effectively with new event consumers including generations X and Y.
7. Event marketers will be able to achieve greater success if they emphasize the health benefits associated with attending their events as the baby boomers age and generations X and Y have greater interest in health and wellness.
8. A seamless registration system, wherein the consumer can arrange transportation, registration, accommodation, tours, restaurant reservations, and much more with a visit to one Internet site, will be essential for event marketers to remain competitive.
9. As the multicultural trend continues to escalate, it is essential that event marketers use multiple languages to communicate with their constituencies.
10. Due to heightened concerns about terrorism, event marketers must focus their messages on safety and security and also emphasize the need to be there to benefit fully from the event.

Profile in Event Leadership: David Rich

ILLUSIONS + PHYSICS = CREATING THE ULTIMATE EXPERIENCE

From the time David Rich was a youngster, he was a fan of magicians, especially those who worked with large-scale illusions. In magic, he saw in action the irrefutable laws of physics and how they could be used to create significant impressions. He also may have been witnessing a future career path beginning to open for him.

David grew up in a suburb of Boston, Massachusetts, and by the time he was a teenager, he was performing magic at corporate trade shows. For example, he contracted with the largest chain of grocery stores in his area and served as the magical emcee of Club Party. At these community performances representing the chain, he would use magic to dramatize how customers could stretch their dollars by shopping at this store.

In 1978, a major event took place in David's career when he met the New England television star Rex Trailer and became a performer on his TV show. As one example of Trailer's fame, *Tonight Show* host Jay Leno once said that as a boy he dreamed of one day becoming not Johnny Carson, but Rex Trailer. Finally, after 20 years of local stardom, Rex left the airwaves and started an agency with David Rich booking entertainment for corporate and college events.

A few years later, Rex decided that his real passion was video production, so he left the

David Rich
Vice President, Program
Strategy/Worldwide
George P. Johnson
Company

agency. In 1987, David sold his roster of clients to the venerable lecture and entertainment bureau Lordly and Dame and went to work for them placing speakers and entertainers. At Lordly and Dame, David and his supervisors soon discovered that he had a unique way of thinking. He recognized early that events and meetings were strategic business opportunities. Clients would request a specific speaker or entertainer, who at that time charged between $3,000 and $40,000, but David encouraged them to first think strategically about what they wanted to accomplish before deciding on the specific choice of personality.

During this same period, he brought full-scale event production to the agency based on his prior experience in TV, coupled with his understanding of the strategic opportunity events provide. For example, for one of his clients he created a *Wizard of Oz* themed event, which invited the audience to "go over the rainbow" and see their future in a bold new way. David says that his mission is to help the client decide in advance what action the audience is to perform as a result of the experience and through events help to achieve that same action.

While at Lordly and Dame, EMC Corporation, the world's largest data storage technology firm, asked David to help them design a trade show presentation to inform customers about their products. With only six weeks and $60,000, David created a *Star Trek* themed presentation using a professional impersonator who portrayed all of the major characters in the popular television series: Captain Kirk for the live, in-booth performance, who interacted with himself as he played the other characters pretaped and projected on screen. The skit dramatized the story of a chief technology officer and the challenges that he faced, which were solved by business solutions provided only by EMC. This presentation could be performed up to 25 times per day for crowds of 60 people or more at each performance.

When asked to describe his thinking process for this event, David says, "First, my job is to arrest their attention, often with entertainment, next, to emphasize the key personal and professional benefits of the product or service, and finally to communicate a call to action in a compelling way."

EMC achieved 435 percent of its lead generation result due to this thinking process. Ultimately EMC offered David the chance to join the company as its first-ever manager of event strategy and marketing.

Shortly after being hired by EMC, a friend working for George P. Johnson Company (GPJ) called David stating that one of their executives had a similar, strategic point of view of events and thought they might enjoy meeting. David was intrigued by this synergy because for many years he felt as if he was often alone in terms of developing a strategic vision for events.

Originally founded as a flag and decoration company in 1914, today GPJ has 17 offices in 10 countries. The company provides strategic experience marketing and management services for Fortune 500 corporations throughout the world. In 2006, *Advertising Age* ranked GPJ

nineteenth on the list of largest marketing agencies in the world, and in 2005, *Special Events Magazine* listed GPJ as the largest event marketing company globally, in terms of annual billings.

David Rich found a natural home at GPJ. As the vice president of Program Strategy/Worldwide, he has led the creation of the company's strategic marketing practice and has been instrumental in helping GPJ advance into the twenty-first century. He states that these challenges and opportunities face event and experience marketers today:

"First, we have to be better understood in the eyes of our clients and consumers. Second, we have to push this concept of legitimacy from the concept of need. Historically, event marketing was focused on creativity for creativity sake. There has been a significant topographic shift toward creativity that relies less on popular culture for themes for events and is now driven by the need to bring the brand value alive in creative and meaningful ways. Third and finally, we need to determine the best measures for confirming our legitimacy."

David believes that the future is boundless for event management and marketing professionals. When asked what he looks for in recruiting new staff, he mentions four critical factors:

First, successful event marketing and management professionals must have an unquenchable thirst for knowing how things work. This is an intellectual habit that must be cultivated and developed.

Second, it is important to think in terms of principles. It is all about understanding how and why things work from the standpoint of principles, and then applying those principles to new work. According to David, "You will always bring value if you think in terms of principles. For example, the iPod succeeded not

(continues)

(continued)

because it provides music in a way that is portable. We had that before through other devices. Rather, it is in the volume of music made portable, and moreover, the principle that it allows individuals to customize their music experience.

Third, it is critical that one takes responsibility for his or her own success. He or she must be self-accountable and focus not on what appears to be limiting about their current career, but acknowledge that they own everything about themselves and can change in order to surmount whatever obstacles they face. David says that one of the hiring considerations at the George P. Johnson Company is that the individual must score high on the "plays well with others" and the "takes responsibility for outcomes" meter.

Finally, David believes that flexibility and adaptability are paramount in this rapidly changing business environment. He says that, more and more, "flexibility is key to long-term success, as our 90-plus year-old company has proven over time."

David Rich began his career by studying magicians and later became one himself. He has grown from practicing magic to producing strategic business outcomes, and today, he has used his own unquenchable curiosity to help his clients travel over the rainbow and even to galaxies of greater fortune in the future.

David Rich: marketing@gpj.com

Career-Advancement Connections

Global Connection

When marketing to two or more cultures, make certain that you use focus group research to review all marketing communications. Simply translating a marketing slogan into a language other than English will not always achieve the meaning or intent you require. Furthermore, some cultures are sensitive to certain colors and may not respond favorably to your design. Convene a focus panel comprised of people from various cultures to review your marketing plan and designs prior to implementation.

Technology Connection

Use desktop publishing software to create simple advertisements, flyers, brochures, and other print matter. Use the Internet to distribute your media releases to targeted media. Use audio and video news releases (ANRs and VNRs) to broadcast your event news item to television and radio stations worldwide.

Resource Connection

The Public Relations Society of America (*www.prsa.org*) publishes the informative *PR Journal,* which documents the latest trends in public relations research and methodology. The American Advertising Federation (*www.aaf.org*) offers extensive research information at the World Advertising Research Center. The International Events Group (*www.sponsorship.com*) offers an annual sponsorship seminar that includes informative seminars concerning how to find, recruit, and keep sponsors. The American Marketing Association (*www.ama.org*) *Journal of Marketing* offers an online journal that includes marketing research and many other resources. The most comprehensive book on the subject of event marketing, *Event Marketing* by Leonard Hoyle (Wiley, 2002), is part of the John Wiley & Sons Event Management series.

Learning Connection

Develop a marketing plan for your event that identifies the competitive advantages, target market(s), strategies, tactics, budgets, schedule, and evaluation methodologies. Describe how you will increase your marketing performance through creative and innovative tactics despite a significant reduction in the marketing budget.

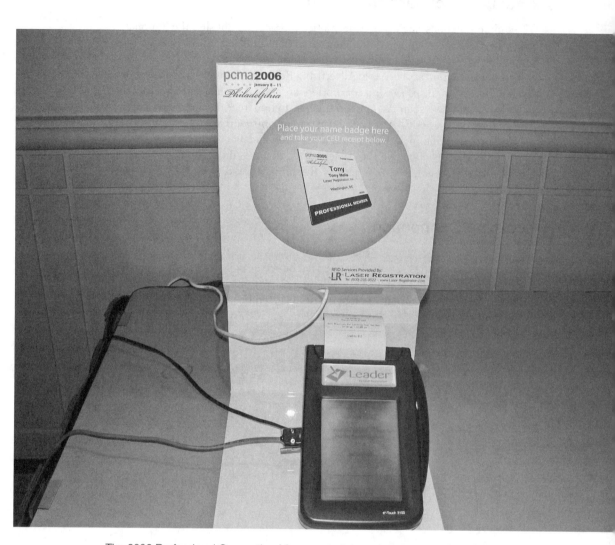

The 2006 Professional Convention Management Association convention in Philadelphia, Pennsylvania, utilized Laser Registration™ to record participant attendance at meetings. Guest name badges contained microchips with their information. As guests passed by the small receiver shown, a printer automatically provided them with official evidence of their attendance. This data could be used to track continuing education credits.

CHAPTER 9

Online Marketing and Computer-Generated Media

In This Chapter You Will Learn How To:

+ Understand the role and scope of the emerging Internet marketplace

+ Differentiate the major advantages in online marketing

+ Maximize your Web marketing opportunities

+ Determine the major types of Web sites and their characteristics

+ Identify, prevent, and correct common mistakes in Web site management

+ Include security and confidentiality for your Web site

+ Incorporate special features for your Web site

+ Develop and effectively utilize blogs and podcasts

+ Measure and evaluate the data collected through your online marketing activities

There is no question that the development of the Internet has become the most important communication and marketing media breakthrough since the printing press in the mid-fifteenth century. It has fundamentally reshaped understating of sales and marketing. However, because so few years have passed since the Internet has become available for widespread public use, the marketing tools used in cyberspace are still works in progress. You can take an active role in developing Internet marketing rules and standards for Event Leadership.

Internet Marketing for Events

The Internet can be a highly efficient tool in the marketing programs of Event Leadership organizations. At the same time, it can be a major financial burden if an Event Leadership organization does not formulate specific goals for its Internet marketing policy. The objectives for each event management organization may vary depending on company size, dynamics of operations, financial and staff resources, location, overall development strategy, and client base. The Web site for a small Event Leadership startup will differ from that of a large multinational Event Leadership conglomerate. Major marketing concepts enhanced by online tools include brand building, direct marketing, online sales and online commerce, customer support, market research, and product or service development and testing.

Leonard H. Hoyle Jr., in *Event Marketing* (Wiley, 2002), states that there are six advantages of Web marketing for your event.

1. Web marketing can help build and extend your brand.
2. Web marketing eliminates many of the costs customarily associated with direct mail.
3. You can immediately begin making online sales in an interactive and secure environment.
4. By posting frequently asked questions (FAQs), you can provide easy access to common questions.
5. Through conducting online surveys and analyzing the data from Web visits and transactions, you may acquire valuable marketing research.
6. You can use the Web to publish information that has resulted from your event (abstracts, papers, and reports).

Brand Building

Online marketing combined with television, media, and print is a major brand-building tool. The biggest advantage the Internet has over television and old-fashioned media is the favorable cost/benefit ratio. Event Leadership organizations can achieve a much higher return on their marketing investments in Internet promotions than in a traditional campaign. The research conducted by Millward Brown Interactive, a 20-year-old international advertising research group, found that an organization can achieve significant progress in brand recognition simply by placing its logo on banners of search engines or online databases. It is important for an Event Leadership organization to secure the presence of its logo on the Web. You can start simply by trading space on the banner section of your Web site with a partner organization. You place your logo on your partner's Web site and create a hyperlink from his or her Web site to yours, in exchange for placing your partner's information on your Web site. It is very important to submit your company's profile to all major search engines. A few years ago, when students were conducting a search on Yahoo using the key words *event management,* they obtained only a few matches, whereas now there are thousands. Submitting your company's profile to most search engines is free, so there is no reason not to do it.

Use these four steps to register your Web site with a search engine:

1. Enter a search engine (Google™, AltaVista™, DogPile™, Yahoo!™, etc.).
2. Go to "register your site."
3. Carefully describe your site's profile.
4. Try it, after submission.

Direct Marketing

According to Bruce Ryan, vice president and general manager of Media Metrix, a research firm that studies Web users' characteristics and profiles, more than 80 percent of personal computer (PC) owners have at least one college degree. Their average household income is about $50,000 per year, well above the $35,000 U.S. household average. These consumers could be a prime market niche for Event Leadership organizations. Customers with household income of less than $40,000 per year often cannot afford to contract a professional Event Leader. By placing well-designed information and ads about your Event Leadership services on the Internet, you gain immediate direct contact with your target market group. In addition, on the Internet, larger competitors have no significant advantage over smaller organizations.

Online Sales

An online sales concept is more applicable to companies that sell consumer goods, not services. However, Event Leadership organizations can still benefit greatly from Internet electronic commerce features. Event Leadership organizations conduct registration, ticket sales, and distribution of materials over the Internet. All of these are segments of event sales. By putting them online, Event Leadership companies achieve financial savings and preserve resources that can now be reallocated.

Among the most important problems of online commerce is the problem of security. If an Event Leadership organization conducts financial transactions over the Internet, security of clients' personal financial information is the top priority. Data that contain such information as credit card and Social Security numbers are very sensitive. It is important to ensure that these data are protected. Since this is a critical point, it is highly recommended that you involve security professionals in this aspect of your Web site development.

Customer Support

Event customer support is one of the areas where the Internet can prove truly indispensable. To date, few Event Leadership companies have realized the full potential of this opportunity. Industry analysts predict that, in coming years, many Event Leadership companies will shift their telephone customer support services to the Web. This does not mean that telephone-based services will disappear, but they will become a secondary source that customers will use if they need to get a more detailed response or resolve a problem. The primary source will be the Internet.

The first step in shifting at least part of their customer support services online is to start a FAQ Web section. Simply by adding this section to an Event Leadership organization Web site, an organization can achieve better customer service and improve efficiency. The Event Management Certificate Program at George Washington University started an FAQ Web section in 1998. Before that happened, a large portion of all questions that the program received from students were about the same issues: location of classes, directions, and registration process. By posting answers to these frequently asked questions on the Web at *www.gwu.edu/emp,* the program was able to direct a majority of telephone questions to online answers. This move contributed greatly to customer satisfaction and enhanced the positive image of the program.

The next step after posting an FAQ page is to personalize online customer service. This can be accomplished by adding an interactive feature to a customer-support site. A customer is asked to type his or her question and submit an e-mail address. Then the customer receives an answer within a certain time frame via either e-mail or telephone. By adding this feature, an event organization can achieve much more personalized customer service and can also collect very valuable data about its clients.

Market Research

Increasingly, Event Leadership organizations are recognizing the Internet potential for market research. Burke, Inc., a leading international market research firm with a history of over 65 years, conducts online focus-group meetings for its clients in addition to face-to-face interviews and telephone surveys. Using Internet technology, the company was able to bring together participants from different parts of the world for small, real-time chat sessions. Clients can observe these chat sessions from anywhere in the world. Software such as Aptex, Autonomy, Adforce, and Accrue can monitor users' behavior constantly. This information can then be used to improve the site or services or to personalize content for users.

Web sites can be used to conduct market research by surveying visitors. This information can be effective if the process is well planned. Unfortunately, many Web sites require users to complete online registration forms without providing incentives. As a result, users often submit incorrect information or simply ignore the forms. This behavior can be explained by the desire of users to guard their privacy online and fear that their e-mail addresses will be sold to third parties. The best way to overcome this constraint is to build a sense of trust between the event organization and clients or to compensate users for submitting their data.

Product or Service Development and Testing

The Internet is an ideal place for event companies to test new products/services before they are launched. An event organization can post information about a conference that it is planning to organize online and monitor the interest that users express toward the conference. By doing this, the organization can see a market's reaction to the conference before it invests large amounts in actual planning. This testing refers to the first stage of successful Event Leadership, event research. One of the biggest advantages that the Internet has over other marketing tools is real-time contact. Marketing professionals use a number of special technical features to leverage this point. Chat rooms, live broadcasting, and time-sensitive promotions are only a small part. The Internet allows marketing professionals to change and update content in almost no time, ensuring that customers have the most recent information.

Web Design and Management

Today, after experiencing five consistent years of cyber growth, event marketing specialists are speaking about second and third generations of Web sites. The best definition I have heard of all three stages of online marketing development comes from Jupiter Communication, a leading Internet research firm based in New York. The company's analysts describe three types of Web sites, from least to most effective from the Internet marketing point of view:

1. *Brochureware* is the name for the first and least developed type of Web site. This type of Internet event marketing material has long been recognized as the most primitive and boring type of marketing material. Web sites of this type are static and contain basic information about an organization, including its address and services. The site reflects a paper brochure placed on the Web. These kinds of sites miss the entire idea of marketing on the Web, and their effectiveness today is not very high.
2. *Show-biz* is the name for the second group of Web sites. These sites try to amuse visitors through interactive features, flashing pictures, news reports, or press reviews. Although these features can serve the purpose of making an Event Leadership organization's Web site more attractive, often they are not appropriate for the content and only distract the viewer's attention.
3. *Utilitarian* is the last and most developed type of Web sites. These sites offer viewers a unique and balanced interactive service that is both highly informative

and helpful in building brand recognition and loyalty. A classic example mentioned by Rick E. Bruner in *Net Results: Web Marketing That Works* (Hayden Books, 1998) is FedEx online services. The company's Web site does not contain a lot of flashy effects, is easy to navigate, and contains useful features, such as shipment tracking and customer address books. The result of such a well-performed online marketing strategy is that, today, about two-thirds of all FedEx customer contacts are conducted electronically. In addition to offering great customer service via the Internet, the company's Web site saves millions of dollars a year in regular customer support costs and marketing expenses.

Blogs and Podcasts

The relatively new phenomena of *blogs* and *podcasts* are dramatically changing the online marketing environment for special events. These new tools are offspring of consumer-generated media (CGM) where online content is created and managed entirely by consumers. As a result of CGM, E-pinions or online consumer opinions are formed. The forums for these E-pinions are often blogs. A blog is a web log of comments and opinions created, controlled, and driven directly by consumers. Obviously, in the democratic world of the Internet, these opinions can both help and harm your ability to market your event. A site for developing a blog is www.blogger.com. You may list your blog on search engines such as *www.newsgator.com* or *www.bloglines.com*. One of the best examples of using a blog to promote travel and tourism events is the Visit Pennsylvania Web site at *www.visitpa.com.*

Additional tools that are the result of CGM include podcasts and wikis. A podcast may be audio or video or both and provides brief, high-content information for consumers through streaming on the Internet. It can be used to promote entertainers or speakers who will appear at your event as well as to provide instructions, information, and education for your participants or volunteers. The millennial generation loves podcasts because they can download them and listen to them at a later time. For a directory of podcasts, visit *www.itunes.com* or *www.podcastalley.com.* According to experts in this field, there are about 10 million listeners to podcasts, and this number is growing quickly. For example, there are nearly 350 National Public Radio broadcasts. You should also endeavor to have your podcast available through iTunes (www.itunes.com), which has become the most popular Internet download site.

The wiki is perhaps best evidenced by Wikipedia™ (*www.wikipedia.org*) which is the world's largest online consumer-generated encyclopedia. You may wish to list your event on a wiki site or create a wiki of your own to direct consumers to your event.

The rapidly growing online environment for promoting events will increasingly include blogs, podcasts, RSS technology [which means Really Simple Syndication (RSS 2.0)], Rich Site Summary (RSS 0.91, RSS 1.0), or RDF Site Summary (RSS 0.9 and 1.0). This is a family of Web feed formats used to transmit frequently updated digital content such as podcasts or other published materials through the Internet, as well as other advancements. You should continue to review consumer publications such as *Advertising Age*™ to keep abreast of these developments. Specific information about consumer-generated media in the travel industry may be obtained from *www.holtz.com*/travel.

Mobile Phone Marketing

The online environment has rapidly extended to and converging with mobile phone technology. Advertisers are regularly using mobile phone technology to market directly to consumers. Text messaging is rapidly evolving into full-motion video. Very soon you will be able to send streaming video of your event directly to mobile phones. This technology has enormous potential for reaching the millennial generation. However, with every advancement in communications, there is also the increasing concern about privacy issues. Make certain you thoroughly research the laws and regulations regarding sending unsolicited advertisements through telecommunications systems prior to implementing your plan.

RFID Technology and Target Marketing

At the 2006 fiftieth anniversary of their first convention, the Professional Convention Management Association (PCMA) launched a new service using Laser Registration (*www.laser-registration.com*) technology. This technology involves using Radio Frequency Identification (RFID) to track the attendance of participants. A small microchip is attached to the name badge of the event participant. This microchip contains all of their critical information. In the future, this technology may be used to further target to whom you will market your event by determining levels of interest through tracking people's engagement with activities at your event.

In addition to tracking attendance and participation (or lack of attendance and participation), this technology may be also used to segment your market to provide you with better return on marketing (ROM) investment. The ability to achieve higher return on event (ROE) will be a critical measurement tool for event organizers and marketers in the future.

The examples and models just described are applicable to many different professional services, including Event Leadership. You can visit Web sites of various Event Leadership organizations and observe how lack of proper planning or understanding of online marketing concepts results in boring Web sites, useless online questionnaires, and annoying e-mail listservs. At the same time, those event organizations that carefully plan their online activities and balance design and content succeed in achieving their Internet marketing goals.

Profile in Event Leadership:
Dessislava Boshnakova, Ph.D.

LEADING THE EXPANSION OF SPECIAL EVENTS IN EASTERN EUROPE

Prior to the fall of the communist government system in Bulgaria, special events were still celebrated, albeit quietly, and somewhat differently—the main theme of all events was the bright future. As communism fell, a new industry arose, greatly influenced by the considerable efforts of Dr. Dessislava Boshnakova, a graduate of and a senior assistant professor at New Bulgarian University in Sofia, Bulgaria. She is the managing director of ROI Communication, a public relations firm also located in Sofia.

Dessislava Boshnakova
Chief Executive Officer
ROI Communication

According to Dessislava, or Dessi as she is known to friends and colleagues, "Before the end of communism, we conducted our events; however, we did not celebrate Christmas on Christmas day. Rather, we celebrated on New Year's Day instead because it was not considered appropriate to celebrate on a religious holiday."

Dessi served as a flight attendant for Balkan Bulgarian Airlines from 1990 to 1995 and through her travels discovered various festivals and other types of events. One day she would turn these discoveries into a thriving business in the new Bulgarian free marketplace.

In the mid-1990s, Dessi discovered the very textbook you are holding in your hands. With the many changes occurring in Bulgaria, she quickly surmised that new opportunities would emerge to train professionals to produce events. Therefore, she began teaching a course at New Bulgarian University that incorporated event planning, and simultaneously she translated this textbook into Bulgarian. In 2006, it became the first events management textbook to be published in the long history of Bulgaria.

Bulgaria was founded in 681, and the first kingdom existed until 1018. In 1018, Emperor Basil II Bulgaroctunos conquered Bulgaria and made it a province of the Byzantine Empire. The Second Bulgarian Kingdom (1185–1396) was created after a successful uprising of the Bulgarian aristocracy. It remained an Ottoman province for five centuries.

The Third Bulgarian Kingdom was established in 1878, and territorial boundaries were established. During this period, a constitutional monarchy was created and capitalism flourished. During World War II, although an ally of Germany, Bulgaria did not allow any of the Jewish people within its borders to be killed.

After World War II and the agreements of Churchill, Roosevelt, and Stalin, Bulgaria fell under the influence of the Soviet Union. All political opposition was silenced, the Bulgarian private sector was privatized, and communism became the dominant economic system.

In 1989, Bulgaria's longtime leader was forced to resign, initiating a period of great hope as the country once again embarked on the road to democracy. Bulgaria is currently a fully functioning market economy, a member of both NATO and the World Trade Organization, and is expected to join the European Union in 2007.

Today, in the new Bulgarian economy, Dessi produces events for companies. For the magazine *Bacchus,* she helped with the organization of a gala dinner that recognizes the "Restaurant of the Year—Bacchus—Chivas Regal." Many restaurants are included, and 200 guests attend. In 2004, her firm was selected by seven jurors to receive the top award from the Bulgarian Public Relations Society for special events entitled "Keep Exchanging Business Cards." The goal of the event was to instigate networking for business purposes. While the concept of business card exchanges is well established in most capitalistic systems, this is a new custom for Bulgarians in the postcommunist era. As yet another indicator of the country's emerging economy, the number of guests at the second networking event increased by 50 percent since Dessi developed this innovative concept in Bulgaria.

For the second year, her firm is producing the Public Relations Christmas Raffle, where the public relations community of Bulgaria raffles all of their leftover marketing and promotional items. Each of these unique business-related special events demonstrates how influential Dessi has been in helping develop the burgeoning Bulgarian economy.

When Dessi was asked if her personal familial celebrations influence her corporate events, she shook her head and said, "Just the opposite. The more I learn from my business about events, the more I am able to improve my family celebrations. For example, it was once traditional to celebrate a child's birthday at home. Now it must include McDonald's Restaurant and all of the various animations from this popular business enterprise."

Since the end of communism, events that were once discouraged, such as Easter celebrations, are now commonplace and in fact growing every year.

Dessi smiles with satisfaction as she says, "Now for the first time in the history of Bulgaria, there is an opportunity to rediscover classical events in a different and more dynamic way. Every day we are creating new rituals from our history."

When asked to describe her aspirations for the future of her country, she states, "I want Bulgaria to become *the* event capital of Eastern Europe. We have already seen over 100 percent growth with many new wedding planners, congress organizers, and others operating successful event enterprises. Bulgarians recognize they need help in planning and producing these events, and they will pay for professional consultation."

She also firmly believes in the importance of education as a means of growing the events industry in Bulgaria. "If we want to compete with the greater European market, we must earn certifications and diplomas [degrees] to maintain a competitive advantage."

Her goal in producing events, she states, "is to create positive memories for her guests to cherish forever." While creating these memories, she is simultaneously transforming one of the world's oldest countries into a modern-day special events capital.

Dessislava Boshnakova: dboshnakova@roibg .com

Career-Advancement Connections

Global Connection

Carefully evaluate the type of coding and bandwidth required for your data transmission. Remember that your ability to reach prospective event customers through the Internet depends largely on their communication infrastructure. Therefore, you must first determine if your target market can download your event e-marketing message easily and quickly. Also be very careful to ensure that the design, color, and language are appropriate and effective for the market you are trying to influence.

Technology Connection

Familiarize yourself with these software applications: Microsoft FrontPage and Netscape Composer.

Resource Connection

Read these books about Internet marketing: *Net Results: Web Marketing That Works,* by USWeb and Rick E. Bruner (Hayden Books, 1998); *Creating Killer Web Sites,* by David Siegel (Hayden Books, 1998).

Learning Connection

✦ Locate 15 event organizations randomly on the Internet using any search engine. Visit their Web sites and try to divide the sites into the three major categories described in this chapter.
✦ Develop a blog for your event.
✦ Create a podcast to inform and educate your volunteers about the policies and procedures of your event organization.

PART FIVE

Legal, Ethical, and Risk Management

Smirnoff Ice Dry promotion in Tokyo, Japan, achieves a reasonable standard of care by posting these notices throughout the area where alcohol is being served.

CHAPTER 10

Risk Management: Legal and Financial Safeguards

In This Chapter You Will Learn How To:

- ✦ Recognize and comply with standard and customary event regulations and procedures

- ✦ Read, understand, and evaluate legal event documents

- ✦ Understand and comply with the general requirements of U.S. regulations related to the Sarbanes-Oxley Act

- ✦ Access, plan, manage, and control potential event liabilities

- ✦ Obtain necessary permits and licenses to operate events

- ✦ Develop and manage risk management procedures

Whether you are the Event Leader for a wedding or the Olympic Games, according to risk management and safety expert Dr. Peter Tarlow, author of *Event Risk Management and Safety* (Wiley, 2002), "All events carry two risks, (1) the risk of a negative occurrence both on site and off site, and (2) the negative publicity that comes from this negative occurrence." Tarlow, a sociologist and rabbi who has studied tourism and other types of events throughout the world, realizes that whenever we bring people together, there is an element of risk.

Most modern events have a potential for negligent activity that can lead to long and costly litigation. As the number of professionally managed events has increased, so has the concern for risk management and other legal and ethical issues. During the mid-1970s in the United States, many events were held to celebrate the 200th anniversary of American independence. During this period most events were organized by amateurs. As a result of a lack of understanding or training in risk management, there was a corresponding interest by the legal profession in bringing litigation against negligent event managers. This relationship continues today with one notable difference. Event Leaders are becoming smarter with regard to legal, ethical, and risk management issues.

Attorney James Goldberg, J.D., the author of *The Meeting Planners Legal Handbook* (*http://assnlaw.com/publications.htm*), addresses in this book critical issues for association meeting and event specialists such as taxation, antitrust issues, tort liability, and intellectual property challenges. In addition, Goldberg offers seminars and workshops. Courses are also being offered throughout the United States covering recent developments in the areas of legal, ethical, and risk management and Sarbanes-Oxley issues relating to Event Leadership. Perhaps the best evidence of this change has been the development of alternative dispute resolution (ADR) programs to avoid lengthy and expensive litigation. Indeed, the paradigm has shifted dramatically from an environment governed by ignorance to one where education and proactive measures may reduce the level of risk and the resulting cost to event organizers.

Sarbanes-Oxley Act

In 2002 the United States Congress approved and the President signed into law the Sarbanes-Oxley Act. According to the American Institute of Certified Professional Accountants (*www.aicpa.org*), the act, which generally applies only to publicly held companies and their auditing firms, dramatically affected these companies and the entire accounting profession. The legislation was created as a reaction to the court actions against U.S. companies such as Enron, MCI WorldCom, and others.

As a direct result of this new legislation, there is much greater transparency in the accounting industry and within the companies they represent. For example, an auditor working for an accounting company must now report to a company's audit committee rather than only one or two executives within the firm. Furthermore, the chief executive officer of public companies must certify the auditing report; if there are errors, he or she may also face criminal prosecution.

Therefore, when you are producing events on behalf of a public company, it is important that you carefully review the Sarbanes-Oxley legislation (*www.aicpa.org/info/Sarbanes-Oxley2002.asp*) and seek counsel from your accountant as well as your client's accounting department regarding any specific compliance issues that may involve you as you comply with this new law.

Contracts, Permits, and Licenses

Most public events in the United States and other countries require some type of official permission to be held. The larger the event in terms of attendance or technical complexity, the more official oversight is usually required. Official review may come from local (town, city, county), state or province, or federal agencies. There are numerous reasons why an event must comply with existing laws and regulations. The four primary reasons are to protect your legal interests, to abide by ethical practices, to ensure the safety and security of your event stakeholders, and to protect your financial investment.

Protecting Your Legal Interests

Preparing proper contracts, researching the permits and licenses that are required, and complying with other legal requirements helps ensure that your event may proceed without undue interruption. Contracts or agreements may range from a simple letter or memorandum of understanding to complex multipage documents with lengthy *riders* (attachments). The Event Leader should utilize the services of competent legal counsel to review all standard agreements, such as hotel contracts, to ensure validity prior to execution. Furthermore, when writing new agreements, local legal counsel must make certain that the contract conforms to the code of the jurisdiction where it is written and executed (usually where the event takes place). Lawyers are admitted to the state bar in the United States and must be experts on the state *code* (laws). Therefore, it is important to use an attorney who is admitted to the state bar where your event is being held or where, in the case of litigation, the case may be tried.

The majority of permits and licenses will be issued by local agencies. However, some state, provincial, or federal authorities may also issue licenses for your event. Therefore, it is wise for the Event Leader to audit past and similar events carefully to identify the customary permits and licenses that are required for an event.

The permitting and licensing process may require weeks or even months to accomplish, so the Event Leader must carefully research each jurisdiction where he or she will produce an event and meet these time requirements. The cost for permits and licenses is typically nominal. However, some larger events or events that pose high risk (such as Grand Prix auto racing) may require the posting of expensive bonds.

The major reasons why you must convince your event stakeholders of the importance of legal compliance and the need to obtain all necessary permits and licenses follow.

✦ Event Leaders are legally required to obtain certain permits and licenses to conduct many events. Failure to do so may result in fines, penalties, interest, or cancellation of an event.

✦ You have a fiduciary responsibility to event stakeholders to plan, prepare, and provide evidence of compliance. Avoiding compliance can have dire economic consequences.

✦ You have an ethical responsibility (as stated by various industry codes of ethics) to comply with all official regulations and to provide written agreements.

✦ Although an oral agreement may be binding, the written agreement usually takes precedence. Written agreements provide all parties with a clear understanding of the terms, conditions, and other important factors governing the event.

✦ One of the primary ultimate responsibilities of an Event Leader is to provide a safe environment in which to conduct an event.

Although developed countries have many more regulations and compliance requirements, developing countries are rapidly instituting controls to ensure the safe and legal operating of events.

Honoring Ethical Practices

One of the primary definitions of a profession is adherence to a code of ethical conduct. As Event Leadership has emerged as a modern profession, a code of ethics has been developed by the International Special Events Society (ISES) (see Appendix 2). Many related industry organizations, such as Meeting Professionals International, have separate but similar codes. The code of ethics is different from biblical moral laws and from legal codes voted by governing bodies.

A code of ethics reflects what is standard and customary in both a profession and a geographic area. In that sense, it is somewhat elastic in that it is applied in various degrees as needed for different circumstances. For example, when a hotelier offers an Event Leader a complimentary lunch at the first meeting, should this be construed as a bribe by the Event Leader and, therefore, refused? Attorney Jeffrey King, an expert in the field of event legal procedures, states that he advises his Event Leader clients always to pay for their lunch when meeting with a hotelier for the first time. "This immediately lets the hotelier know that the relationship is equal and represents a business transaction," according to King. It also sets an ethical standard for future discussions and the building of a relationship.

Although many professional societies, including ISES, enforce their code of ethics with a grievance procedure, in most cases it is up to the Event Leader to determine what is and is not appropriate ethical behavior using the code of ethics as a guide. Robert Sivek of The Meeting House Companies, Inc., suggests that Event Leaders use the front-page-of-the-newspaper rule. "Ask yourself if you would like to wake up and see your decision or action plastered across the front page of the newspaper," says Sivek. This may quickly determine whether your proposed action is one that is acceptable not only to you but to others in your events community. Ethics are covered in detail in Chapter 13.

Ensuring the Safety and Security of Event Stakeholders

A *safe event environment* implies that it is free from hazards. A *secure environment* is one that is protected from future harm. The Event Leader is responsible for constructing a safe, secure environment and sustaining it during the course of an event. Do not transfer this responsibility to others. The Event Leader either extends the invitation or coordinates the event at the invitation of others. You have both a legal and an ethical responsibility to event stakeholders to design and maintain a safe and secure event environment.

Protecting Your Financial Investment

The legal, ethical, and safety-security aspects of an event can affect the bottom line dramatically. Therefore, every decision you make that is proactive may reduce your risk of unforeseen financial impacts. Practicing thorough legal, ethical, and risk management proactive measures may actually help your event produce greater revenues.

Although not every contingency can be anticipated, the more adept you are at strategically planning preemptive measures to prevent contingencies, the better your balance sheet may look at the end of the event. Lapses in legal, ethical, and risk management judgment may cause not only loss of property, life, and money, but loss of your event's good name as well.

Key Components of an Event Management Agreement or Contract

The Event Leadership contract reflects the understanding and agreement between two or more parties regarding their mutual interests as specified in the agreement. A binding contract must contain the key components described in this section.

Parties

The names of the parties must be clearly identified. The agreement must be described as being between these parties, and the names that are used in the agreement must be defined. Typical Event Leadership agreements are between the Event Leader and his or her client or the Event Leader and his or her vendor. Other contracts may be between an event professional and an insurance company, an entertainment company, or a bank or other lending institution.

Offer

The *offer* is the service or product tendered by one party to another. The Event Leader may offer consulting services to a client, or a vendor may offer products to an Event

Leader. The offer should list all services that an event professional offers to provide. Any miscommunications here may lead to costly litigation in the future.

Consideration

The *consideration clause* defines what one party will provide the other upon acceptance of an offer.

Acceptance

When both parties accept an offer, they *execute* (sign) the agreement confirming that they understand and agree to comply with the terms and conditions of the agreement.

Other Components

Although the key components are the parties, the offer, consideration, and acceptance, Event Leadership agreements usually include many other clauses or components. The most typical clauses are listed next.

▪ Terms

The *terms clause* defines how and when the funds will be paid to the person extending the offer. If the Event Leader offers consulting services, he or she may request a deposit in the amount of the first and last month's retainer and then require that the client submit monthly payments of a certain amount on a certain date each month. These terms define the financial conditions under which the agreement is valid.

For some large events, payments are made during a specified period. In this case, or in case of another complicated payment arrangement, a separate *payment schedule* should be attached to a contract. This schedule should be treated as an essential part of the contract and signed and dated by both parties. In case an advance payment is mentioned in the payment term section, special attention should be paid to the provisions of how the deposit is returned in the case of event cancellation. For example, is the deposit credited toward future transactions within a specific time period, or is a cash refund offered?

Within the Event Leadership industry, event professionals are increasingly concerned with reducing internal or operational risk in order to improve profitability of their enterprise. Internal risk issues include theft, slippage, and intellectual property safeguarding. Event professionals must work closely with colleagues to put in place procedures aimed to reduce internal risks.

▪ Cancellation

Events are always subject to cancellation. Therefore, it is important to provide for this contingency legally with a detailed cancellation clause. Usually the cancellation clause defines under what circumstances either party may cancel, how notification must be provided (usually in writing), and what penalties may be required in the event of cancellation.

■ *Force Majeure* (Act of God)

In the *force majeure clause,* both parties agree on which circumstances, deemed to be beyond their control, will permit an event to be canceled without penalty to either party. The force majeure clause must always be specified to reflect the most common or predictable occurrences. These may include hurricanes, earthquakes, floods, volcanic eruptions, tornadoes, famines, wars, or other catastrophic disasters such as terrorism.

■ Arbitration

It is common practice to include in Event Leadership agreements a clause that allows both parties to use arbitration in place of a legal judgment when they fail to agree. The use of arbitration may save the parties substantial costs over traditional litigation.

■ Billing

Because many events involve entertainers or are theatrical events in and of themselves, the agreement must define how entertainers will be listed in advertising and in the program. Generally, a percentage, such as 100 percent, is used to describe the size of their name in relation to other text.

■ Time Is of the Essence

The *time-is-of-the-essence clause* instructs both parties that the agreement is valid only if it is signed within a prescribed period of time. This clause is usually inserted in order to protect the offerer from loss of income due to late execution by the purchaser.

■ Assignment

As employees have shorter and shorter tenures with organizations, it is more important than ever that agreements contain clauses indicating that the contract may not be assigned to other parties. For example, if Mary Smith leaves XYZ Company, the agreement is between XYZ Company and the offerer and may not be transferred to Smith's successor, who may or may not honor the agreement as an individual. Therefore, Mary Smith has executed the agreement on behalf of XYZ Company.

■ Insurance

Often agreements detail the type and limits of insurance that must be in force by both parties, as well as a requirement that each party coinsure the other. Some agreements require copies of certificates of insurance that name the other party as additional insured in advance of the event date.

■ Hold Harmless and Indemnification

In the event of negligence by either party, the negligent party agrees to hold the other party harmless and to defend them (indemnify) against harm.

■ Reputation

The production of an event is a reflection of the personal tastes of the event organization and sponsors. Therefore, some Event Leaders include a specific clause that recognizes the importance of the purchaser's reputation and states that the Event Leader will use his or her best efforts to protect and preserve the reputation during management of the event.

■ Complete Agreement

Typically, the *complete agreement* is the final clause and states that the agreement constitutes the full understanding of both parties. Figure 10.1 demonstrates how a complete agreement is used in a typical Event Leadership consulting agreement.

Rider

A *rider* is an attachment to a main agreement and usually lists the important ingredients that support the main contract. These may include sound equipment and labor, lighting equipment and labor, food and beverages, transportation, housing for artists/entertainers, or other important financial considerations other than the artist's fee (e.g., a payment schedule). The rider should be attached to the main agreement, and it should be initialed or signed separately to signify acceptance by both parties.

Changes to the Agreement

Most agreements will require negotiation prior to execution, and the result of these executions will be changes. If only two or three nonsubstantial changes are made, you may choose to initial and date each change prior to returning the agreement for execution by the other party. Your initial and date signify your acceptance of the change but do not obligate you to fulfill the entire agreement until you have affixed your signature. If there are substantial changes (such as in the date, time, venue, or fees) or more than three changes, it is best to draw up a new agreement.

Terms and Sequence of Execution

First and foremost, always require that the purchaser sign the agreement prior to affixing your signature. Once both signatures are affixed, the agreement becomes official. If you sign the agreement and forward it to the other party, and the purchaser makes changes and signs it, you may be somewhat obligated for those changes. It is always wise to request the purchaser's signature before affixing your own.

Second, never use facsimiles. Should you be forced to litigate the agreement, the court will seek the "best copy," and that is usually an original. You may use a facsimile for an interim memorandum of understanding, but binding, official agreements must be originals.

Third, take the time to sign the agreement in person. Explain to the purchaser that the terms implied in the agreement are only as valid as the integrity of the persons signing the document. Offer your hand in friendship as you jointly execute this agreement.

Agreement

This agreement is between Jane Smith Productions (otherwise known as Event Leader) and ABC Corporation (otherwise known as Purchaser).

Event Leader agrees to provide the following services:

1. 50 hours of research regarding XYZ festival.

2. 40 hours of design regarding XYZ festival.

3. 30 hours of planning regarding XYZ festival.

4. 20 hours of coordination regarding XYZ festival.

5. 10 hours of evaluation regarding XYZ festival.

A total of 150 hours of consulting time will be provided by Event Leader.

Purchaser agrees to provide:

1. A total fee in the amount of $7,500.

Terms:
The Purchaser agrees to provide a nonrefundable deposit in the amount of seven hundred and fifty dollars (U.S.) ($750.00) to officially retain the services of Event Leader. The Purchaser furthermore agrees to provide monthly payments in the amount of seven hundred and fifty dollars (U.S.) ($750.00) on or before the fifteenth day of each month commencing August 15, 2005, until the balance has been paid in full.

Cancellation:
In the event of cancellation, notice must be received in writing. Should Purchaser cancel 90 days or more prior to event, Event Leader shall be entitled to retain all funds paid as of this date. Should Purchaser cancel less than 90 days prior to event, Event Leader shall receive full payment as specified in the agreement above.

Force Majeure:
This agreement is automatically null and void if event is canceled due to an act of God, including hurricane, earthquake, flood, volcanic eruption, tornado, famine, or war. In the event of cancellation due to an act of God, neither party shall be liable for any further payments.

Insurance:
Both parties shall maintain in full force one million dollars ($1 million) per occurrence comprehensive general liability insurance. Each party shall name the other as additional insured for the duration of the event. Both parties shall provide a certificate of insurance demonstrating evidence of additional insured status prior to the start of the event.

Hold Harmless and Indemnification:
Both parties agree that if either party is negligent, they will defend the nonnegligent party and hold them harmless against future action.

Figure 10.1   Event Leadership Sample Consulting Agreement   *(Continued)*

Arbitration:

Both parties agree that if a dispute arises concerning this agreement, a professional arbitrator certified by the American Arbitration Association or the alternative dispute resolution process through the Conventional Liaison Council will be used in place of normal litigation.

Reputation:

Both parties agree to use their best efforts to preserve and protect each other's reputation during the conduct of this event. The Event Leader recognizes that the Purchaser has, over time, developed good standing in the business and general community and will use the best efforts available to protect and preserve his reputation from harm.

Billing:

The Event Leader shall be listed in the official program of the event with the following text in type the same size and style as the body copy:

This event managed by Jane Smith Production.

The Event Leader shall be listed in the official program with other staff in the following manner with text in type of the same size and style as the body copy:

Jane Smith, Event Leader

Time Is of the Essence:

This agreement must be executed by July 15, 2005. After this date this agreement must be considered null and void and a new agreement must be created:

Assignment:

This agreement may not be assigned to others. The persons executing this agreement have the full authority to sign this agreement on behalf of the organizations they represent.

The Full Agreement:

The agreement and any riders attached represent the full understanding between both parties. Any amendments to this agreement must be approved in writing and separately attached to this agreement.

Execution:

The signatures below confirm complete understanding and compliance with the terms and conditions described in this agreement.

_____   _____
ABC Corporation, Purchaser   Date

_____   _____
Jane Smith, Event Leader   Date

Figure 10.1   *(Continued)*

Other Agreements

In addition to the main event consulting agreement, the Event Leader may be required to prepare and execute other types of agreements. Samples of these agreements may be found in Appendixes 9 and 10. Typical Event Leadership agreements include :

+ *Consulting agreement:* an agreement whereby one party (usually the Event Leader) agrees to provide consulting services for another party
+ *Employment agreement:* an agreement whereby an employee agrees to specific terms for employment
+ *Exhibitor contract:* an agreement between an individual exhibitor and the sponsor of an exposition to lease space for a specific booth at the exposition
+ *Hotel contract:* an agreement between a hotel and the organization holding an event to provide rooms and function space as well as other services (food and beverages) for a specific event or series of events
+ *Noncompete agreement:* an agreement whereby an employee agrees not to compete within a specific jurisdiction or marketplace for a specified period of time following termination of employment
+ *Purchase order:* an order to a vendor to provide services or products
+ *Sponsorship agreement:* a contract between a sponsor and an event organizer in which the organizer agrees to provide specific marketing services to the sponsor for a prescribed fee and/or other consideration
+ *Vendor agreement:* an agreement between a vendor and an Event Leader or client to provide specific services or products for an event

These agreements, along with many others, may be required to ensure the professional operation of an event. To identify all the agreements that may be required, check with other event organizers and local officials as well as your vendors to determine the critical documents that must be executed prior to the start of the event.

Permits

Permits are issued by local, state, provincial, or federal governmental agencies and allow you to conduct certain activities at your event. Figure 10.2 details the typical permits that may be required. Allow sufficient time to obtain the permits. A permit may be issued only after you have submitted the appropriate documentation and have paid a fee. Determine well in advance what type of documentation is required by the issuing agency and how funds are accepted.

Remember that permits are not issued automatically. A permit reflects that an agency is permitting your event organization to conduct certain activities provided that you conform to the regulations established. Make certain that you are able to comply with these regulations prior to applying for the permit. If you are denied a permit, you may consider

Permit	Source
Bingo	Lottery or gaming department
Food handling	Health department
Lottery	Lottery or gaming department
Occupancy	Fire department
Parking	Transportation and parking department
Park use	Park department
Public assembly	Public safety and police department
Pyrotechnics	Fire department
Sales tax	Revenue or tax collector's office
Signs and banners	Zoning department
Street closing	Transportation and parking department

Figure 10.2 *Typical Event Leadership Permits and Where to Obtain Them*

appealing your case. In some cases, Event Leaders have sued an agency to obtain permission to conduct an event. However, since most Event Leaders rely on the goodwill of local agencies to conduct an event successfully, litigation should be the absolutely final resort.

Licensing

A license is granted by a governmental institution, a private organization (as in music licensing), or a public entity to allow you to conduct a specific activity. The difference between a permit and a license may be slight in some jurisdictions. Usually the requirements for obtaining a license are much more stringent and require due diligence (evidence of worthiness) prior to issuance.

Figure 10.3 lists the more common licenses required for events and their sources. Additional licenses may be required for your event. To determine what licenses are required, make certain that you examine the event's history, check with organizers of similar events, and confirm and verify with the appropriate agencies that issue these licenses.

Permit	Source
Alcohol	Alcohol beverage control boards
Business	Economic development agency; recorder
Food	Health department
Music	American Society of Composers, Authors, and Publishers or Broadcast Music, Inc.
Pyrotechnics	Bureau of Alcohol, Tobacco, and Firearms; fire department

Figure 10.3 *Typical Event Leadership Licenses and Where to Obtain Them*

One of the best sources of information will be your vendors. Audit your vendors, especially in the technology field, and determine if licenses are required (as in the case of laser projection) or if the Event Leader must obtain a license.

For many events, both permits and licenses must be secured. The larger the event, the more likely the number of permits and licenses will increase. Remember that licenses and permits are the government's way of establishing a barrier to entry to protect its interests. Work closely with government agencies to understand their procedures, time frames, and inspection policies. A close working relationship with the agencies that issue licenses and permits will help ensure the success of your overall event operation.

Contracts, Permits, and Licenses: A Synergistic Relationship

Professional Event Leaders understand, and use to their advantage, the synergy between a well-written and executed contract and the acquisition of proper permits and licenses. All three instruments are essential for the professional operation of modern events. When developing an agreement, determine in advance who is responsible for obtaining and paying for specific permits and licenses and incorporate this language into the agreement. Failure to specify who is responsible for obtaining and paying for permits and licenses can lead to an interruption of your event and conflicts among the various stakeholders.

Therefore, conduct research carefully during the planning stage to identify all necessary permits and licenses and determine who will be responsible for coordinating this process. Include this information in your master event consulting agreement as well as your vendor agreements. Since permits and licenses are unavoidable in most event situations, it behooves the Event Leader to practice the maxim that an ounce of prevention (or risk management) is worth a pound of cure. Use the planning phase to examine potential permit processes, and then use the coordination stage to link these two important steps within the event management process.

Contracts, permits, and licenses have legal, ethical, and risk management ramifications. To ensure that these impacts are positive, Event Leaders must understand their importance and work diligently to communicate with the required agencies as well as to prepare and execute valid agreements.

Risk Management Procedures

"Hundreds of people burned to death in tent during graduation ceremony in India," shouted the headlines. Whenever human beings assemble for the purposes of celebration, education, marketing, or reunion, there is an increased risk of loss of life or property. This has been proven many times, as similar newspaper headlines have reported accidents that have occurred at events.

With increased injuries, thefts, and other misfortunes come, of course, increased expense. This may stem from two sources: the loss of revenue resulting directly from the occurrence and increased insurance premiums when underwriters are forced to pay large settlements as a result of negligence. Perhaps the most profound loss is the loss of business opportunity that results from the bad publicity attached to such tragedies. After all, who wants to visit an event where a tent might collapse and injure people or where there is a risk of food poisoning?

Alexander Berlonghi, an expert in the field of risk assessment and risk management, has devised a method for attempting to identify and contain the many risks associated with events. Berlonghi describes the first step in the risk assessment process as that of holding a risk assessment meeting. A step-by-step guide to holding such a meeting follows. I suggest that you use it for each of your events—it could be a lifesaver.

Organizing a Risk Assessment Meeting

The first question to ask when organizing a risk assessment meeting is: Who should attend? Ideally, all key event stakeholders should be involved in this meeting, and you may wish to use a written survey to audit their opinions regarding risks associated with an event. However, for practical purposes, you must first identify those event team leaders who can bring you the best information from which to manage present and future risks associated with your events. These event team leaders should be included in the risk assessment meeting:

- ✦ Admissions manager
- ✦ Advertising manager
- ✦ Animal handler
- ✦ Box-office manager
- ✦ Broadcast manager
- ✦ Catering manager
- ✦ Comptroller
- ✦ Computer or data processing manager
- ✦ Convention center safety director
- ✦ Department of Homeland Security
- ✦ Electrician
- ✦ Entertainment specialist
- ✦ Environment safety specialist
- ✦ Federal Bureau of Investigation (FBI)
- ✦ Fire department liaison
- ✦ Food and beverage manager
- ✦ Hotel security director
- ✦ Insurance broker
- ✦ Laser specialist
- ✦ Lighting specialist
- ✦ Office manager
- ✦ Parking specialist
- ✦ Police liaison for event

+ Public relations manager
+ Pyrotechnic specialist
+ Security director for event
+ Sound specialist
+ Special-effects specialist
+ Transportation specialist
+ Venue safety director
+ Weather and meteorological experts

Before the Meeting

Once you have identified the participants for a risk assessment meeting, it is time to put them to work. Assigning prework helps meeting participants focus on the seriousness of the meeting and will probably improve the efficiency of the meeting. Figure 10.4 demonstrates a typical risk assessment meeting announcement that you may customize for your own use.

Make sure that you follow up with meeting participants to ensure that all lists have been returned and that you understand the risks they have identified as important to their area. Once you have received responses, it is time to compile a master list of all risks that have been identified. You may list these risks in alphabetical order or subdivide them by event area.

The final step in preparing for a risk assessment meeting is to prepare a detailed agenda that may be used to conduct the meeting. Prior to the meeting, circulate the agenda and seek feedback from the participants. Figure 10.5 provides a sample agenda and pre-meeting announcement that you may customize for a risk assessment meeting.

TO:	Event Risk Assessment Team
FROM:	Event Leader
SUBJECT:	Meeting Announcement and Instructions
DATE:	August 15, 2008
ACTION REQUIRED:	Return your list of potential risks by July 15, 2008.

A risk assessment meeting will be held on July 20, 2008 at 1 P.M. for the purpose of identifying and managing the major risks associated with this event. Prior to this meeting you should audit your area and prepare a comprehensive list of risks associated with your event responsibilities.

Interview the team members in your area and ask them to assist you in this important task. Risks may involve potential injuries, loss of life or property, or other risks.

Submit this list to me by the close of business on July 15, 2008. Thank you for your contribution to this important process.

Figure 10.4 Risk Assessment Meeting Announcement

TO: Event Team Leaders
FROM: Event Leader
SUBJECT: Event Risk Assessment Meeting Agenda
DATE: July 15, 2008
ACTION REQUIRED: Return the enclosed agenda to me with your com-
                                   ments by July 18, 2008.

Tentative Agenda

    I. Welcome and introduction
   II. Explanation of purposes, Event Leader
  III. Comprehensive risk review, all participants
  IV. Additional risks not covered in listing, all participants
   V. Recommendations for risk management, all participants
  VI. Economic impacts of risk management, all participants, comptroller
 VII. Post-meeting work assignment, Event Leader
VIII. Adjournment

Figure 10.5   Risk Assessment Meeting Sample Agenda/Announcement

Conducting the Meeting

After the agenda has been distributed, corrected, and approved, it is time to convene the risk assessment meeting. Use a hollow square seating design and prepare tent cards for each participant, listing his or her name and event area of responsibility. A flip chart displayed on an easel stand should list the agenda for the meeting, and subsequent pages should list the risks previously identified by meeting participants. In addition, participants should receive a typed copy of the agenda and the comprehensive list of risks, along with any other collateral material that will help them make the important decisions that will be required during the meeting.

As the Event Leader, you are also the meeting facilitator. To facilitate the participation of all, first welcome the participants and explain that the meeting will be successful only if they participate actively by offering their expert opinions and engaging in a lively discussion concerning recommendations for reducing or alleviating the risks that have been identified.

After you have set the tone for the meeting, review the list of risks and ask the meeting participants to study them for a few moments and identify any gaps. What risks have been overlooked?

The next stage of the meeting is to begin discussions on how to reduce, control, transfer, or eliminate the risks that have been identified. This is a good time to ask the participants to form small groups that represent cross-disciplinary task forces. For example, you may ask the admissions, box office, and comptroller team members to work on reducing the risk of theft from the box office or eliminating the risk of gate crashing. Allow 15 to 30 minutes for this activity.

When you reconvene the group, ask participants to communicate their recommendations to the entire group and try to seek consensus from group members. Do not rush this process. During these discussions, important concerns may be expressed. You must make sure that you address and attempt to satisfy these concerns before moving on to the next stage.

Every risk decision will have corresponding financial impacts. This is a good time to use a Likert scale to rate the importance of each risk in terms of the overall event. For example, to identify risks that should receive the greatest consideration when considering the financial impact on your event, ask each participant to assign a number to each risk, with 1 representing least concern and 5 representing most concern. Theft from the box office might rate a 5, while rain might receive a 1. Once you have reached consensus on the level of importance of each risk, you may concentrate the discussion on risks that the group deems most important.

■ Documenting the Meeting's Recommendations

The final stage of a risk assessment meeting is to document your recommendations and assign post-meeting work groups to continue to address the important issues covered in the meeting. Assign one person as a scribe during the meeting and ask him or her to prepare review notes to be circulated within three business days. The notes should reflect the substance and content of the discussion and list the recommendations the group has agreed to pursue.

The work groups are responsible for conducting additional research to identify ways in which to better manage the risks that were discussed and perhaps lower the cost of the event. Their work may include interviewing external experts or brainstorming with their fellow event stakeholders to seek better solutions.

The review notes also serve the important purpose of preserving the history of the meeting. Should there be an incident at your event that requires evidence that you conducted risk assessment and management procedures to attempt to prevent this occurrence, the review notes may serve as valuable proof documenting your proactive stance.

Safety Meeting and Other Considerations

Before you allow vendors to install the various event elements, you must conduct a brief safety meeting to alert all event stakeholders to the standards your organization has established with regard to safety. Notify the event stakeholders in writing and explain that this meeting is required for participation in the event. Usually the meeting is held prior to installation and is conducted by the Event Leader. Survey the event stakeholders to determine if they have particular expertise in event safety. You may wish to call upon this expertise during the safety meeting.

Use a checklist or written agenda distributed to each participant at the meeting to remain focused on the goals and objectives of the meeting. Detail your expectations of minimum safety requirements for the event. These may include taping or ramping of exposed cables, grounding of all electric power, keeping the work areas cleared of debris, nonsmoking policies, and other important issues.

Ask those assembled if they have been trained in the Heimlich maneuver or CPR (cardiopulmonary resuscitation) during the past three years. Ask those who have been trained to serve as first responders for the event if someone requires this level of response. The Event Leader should be trained in both the Heimlich maneuver and CPR and be prepared to use these techniques to sustain or save lives, if required. Make certain that you ask each person to sign in when he or she attends the meeting. This will provide you with a record of those who participated and may be helpful if there is a later claim against the event. Conclude the meeting by reminding all participants that the overall goal of this event is zero percent tolerance of unsafe working conditions.

Inspections

Prior to opening the doors to admit guests to your event, conduct a final inspection. Walk the entire event site and note any last-minute corrections that must be made to ensure the safety of guests. Walk-throughs are best conducted by a team that includes your client, key vendors, key event team leaders, and, when possible, police, fire, and other officials.

During the walk-through, use a digital camera and/or video camera to record corrections you have made, and post caution signs where appropriate to notify guests of possible risks.

These areas must be reviewed when conducting a walk-through prior to admitting guests to your event:

- ✦ Accreditation/credentialing systems are in working order.
- ✦ Admissions personnel are in place.
- ✦ Air walls are in working order in case of evacuation.
- ✦ Bar personnel have received alcohol management training.
- ✦ Doors are unlocked from inside the venue in case of evacuation.
- ✦ Edge of stage is marked with safety tape.
- ✦ Electric boxes are labeled with caution signs.
- ✦ Electric cables are grounded.
- ✦ Electric cables traversing public areas are taped or ramped.
- ✦ Elevators are working.
- ✦ Light level is sufficient for safe ingress and egress.
- ✦ Lighting has been properly secured with safety chains.
- ✦ Metal detectors are in place and operational for VIP appearances.
- ✦ Ramps are in place for the disabled.
- ✦ Security personnel are posted.
- ✦ Signs are visible and well secured.
- ✦ Staging has chair and handrails.
- ✦ Stairs have handrails, and individual steps are marked with safety tape to highlight the edges.
- ✦ Ushering personnel are in place.
- ✦ Final visual inspection of all areas and verbal confirmations with support staff and volunteers prior to opening doors/admitting guests.

These are but a few of the areas that must be inspected prior to admitting guests. You may wish to prepare a checklist to inspect each area systematically or simply use a small pad of paper and note areas that must be corrected prior to the event. The walk-through should be conducted one to two hours prior to the official start time of an event. This will give you time to make any minor corrections that are required.

Documentation and Due Diligence

Each of the steps included in the walk-through demonstrates to officials, and perhaps one day to a jury, that you have attempted to do what a reasonable person would be expected to do under these circumstances to ensure the safety of guests. Documenting your risk assessment, management, and prevention steps may assist you in demonstrating that you have practiced due diligence for your event. The goal is to achieve or exceed the standard of care normally associated with an event of this size and type. The steps just listed will help you move rapidly toward this goal.

Obtaining Insurance

Insurance is used by Event Leaders to transfer the risk to a third party: the insurance underwriter. Many venues require that the Event Leader or event organization maintain in full force a minimum of $1 million per occurrence of comprehensive general liability insurance. Some municipalities require similar limits of insurance for events to be held in their jurisdiction. Events that are more complex and pose greater risks may be required to have higher limits of insurance.

Identifying a properly qualified insurance broker is an important first step in receiving expert advice regarding the types of insurance that may be required for your event. After checking with the venue and municipality to determine the level of insurance required, you will need a well-trained specialty insurance broker to advise you further on coverage available.

A specialty insurance broker has insurance products and services specifically relevant for the Event Leadership profession. For example, large firms such as Arthur J. Gallagher & Co. or K & K insurance provide products for clients ranging from the Super Bowl to local parades and festivals. They are experienced experts in providing advice and counsel for the unique risks associated with events.

■ Identifying the Appropriate Premium

After you have contacted two or more specialty insurance brokers and determined the type of insurance products that may be required for your event, you will request quotes from each broker. The brokers will ask you to complete a detailed form listing the history of the event, specific hazards that may be involved (e.g., pyrotechnics), and other critical information. The broker will submit this information to several underwriters and present you with a quote for coverage.

The most cost-effective premium is an annual policy known as comprehensive general liability insurance. Some Event Leaders pay as little as $2,000 annually for coverage for a variety of risks for which they may be liable. Other Event Leaders pay their premiums on a per-event basis. Your insurance broker will help you decide what the best system is for you.

For example, the Summer Olympic Games in Athens, Greece reportedly paid, according to Bloomberg News Service, over thirty million dollars for insurance coverage for the first Summer Olympic Games following the tragedy of September 11, 2001. Therefore, it is critically important for you to carefully assess your potential risks and work closely with your insurance professionals to purchase sufficient insurance coverage.

These insurance products are typically associated with events:

+ Automotive liability
+ Board of directors' liability
+ Business interruption
+ Cancellation
+ Comprehensive general liability
+ Disability
+ Earthquake
+ Errors and omissions
+ Fire
+ Flood
+ Health
+ Hurricane
+ Key person
+ Life
+ Nonappearance
+ Office contents
+ Officers
+ Rain
+ Terrorism
+ Workers' compensation

Your client or others involved with your event may ask that they be named as an additional insured on your policy. The term *additional insured* means that, if for any reason there is an incident, your insurance policy will cover claims against those listed as additionally insured. Before agreeing to name the other party or parties as additional insured, check with your insurance broker to find out if there is an additional charge or if this is appropriate. You may also want to ask the other parties to name you as additional insured on their policies.

■ Exclusions

Every insurance policy will list certain hazards that are excluded from coverage. Make certain that you check with your broker and review your policy carefully to make sure that there are no gaps in coverage for your event. For example, if your event is using pyrotechnics and they are excluded specifically from your current coverage, you may wish to purchase additional coverage to protect your event. Oftentimes, especially during the Y2K period of 2000, a typical insurance included computer systems. Today, some policies may exclude terrorist acts. Make certain you carefully review all exclusions to eliminate any gaps in coverage.

■ Preexisting Coverage

Before purchasing any coverage, audit your existing coverage to check for gaps regarding your event. Your event organization may already have in force specific coverage related to the risks associated with your event. Once you have conducted this audit, your specialty insurance broker can advise you with regard to additional coverage for your event.

Risk Control

■ Theft Prevention

The best strategy for theft prevention is segregation of duties. All transactions that involve cash handling, returns, and deposits should have at least two employees performing that transaction.

■ Cash

Cash must be handled accurately. I encourage you to establish a special cash log where all cash transactions should be recorded. Even small petty cash numbers add up to a substantial amount, so if you think that $20 cash expense is not worth recording, you are wrong; $20 per week turns into $1,080 per year. Anyone who handles cash should be given occasional unscheduled vacation days to check his or her cash-handling practice. While an employee is away, a replacement is in a very good position to catch all illegal activities set up by the employee.

■ Inventory

One of the more important tools in preventing theft of inventory is incorporation of special procedures for inventory management. Storage facilities should be monitored; two people should be involved in storage operations. All records of inventory disbursement should be stored and checked on a random basis. In a real-time computer system, inventory should have bar codes that have to be entered into the system as soon as inventory is disbursed.

As an Event Leader and supervisor, you should approve all equipment breakdowns and/or replacements. Management of Event Leadership organizations should analyze the level of breakage that is typical for their operations. Any constant abnormalities should be investigated in more depth. Physical inventory counts should be taken regularly. Shortages should be reviewed, comparing them to acceptable loss levels.

Profile in Leadership:
April Harris

PLANNING FOR SUCCESS, SHE CREATED A MODERN PROFESSION

In the late 1980s, very few books focused solely on the emerging field of professional event management. Prior to this period, most events were implemented and organized by a secretary or administrative support person. That changed significantly in 1988 when April Harris, a longtime leader in the events community within higher education, published her first book, *Special Events: Planning for Success* (CASE, 1988).

This book was the first to describe in comprehensive detail the public relations rationale behind campus events for alumni and development, as well as the myriad of steps required to consistently produce professional results. Nearly 20 years later, the book is in its third edition and is still one of the most popular books offered by the Council for the Advancement and Support of Education (CASE). In addition to this revolutionary book, Harris is also the author of *Etiquette and Protocol: A Guide for Campus Events* and *Academic Ceremonies: A Handbook of Traditions and Protocol*, both published by CASE (*www.case.org/Publications*).

April Harris
Director of Alumni Relations
University of Alabama at
Huntsville

Harris, who has a degree in journalism, began her career in alumni relations at Bowling Green State University in Ohio. She was eventually named director of special services, which included event management. "My boss was quite visionary," Harris recalls. "He could see why events were valuable to the campus community and the overall advancement function."

In 1985, she left Bowling Green and tried to find a similar position. Because special events was such a new concept and did not exist at many universities at that time, her job search proved fruitless. Frustrated at what she perceived as a lack of understanding, while unemployed, she wrote *Special Events: Planning for Success*. Despite its cautious reception, the book sold briskly among the 3,000 colleges and universities in the United States.

In 1989, Harris suggested that the special events community of higher education should gather for the first time and allow for an exchange of best practices. CASE cautiously assigned her a small room at their annual meeting. Nearly 150 people attended, and when seating was no longer available in the room, people stood in the hallways to participate. Today, the CASE annual conference for events planners is one of the organization's largest.

Looking back on these early experiences, Harris finds it puzzling that it took so long to develop the field when, after all, "colleges and universities were from the beginning well grounded in the roots of event design, etiquette and protocol."

During her career within higher education, she has seen the position of events professional evolve from "pink collar" to "white collar" with most salaries currently ranging the high thirties to low fifties. However, some may earn as little as $23,000 while others may earn $60,000 or more, depending on the size of their institution and the portfolio of events they supervise.

"I believe the role of the event planner within higher education is not as respected as it could be, but we're certainly gaining ground. Event planners have a complex skill set that deserves greater recognition and respect," Harris suggests. "Today it's uncommon to find a college or university that doesn't have special events planners, but we're still working to join the highest ranks of the advancement team."

Events within higher education are often the first (recruiting and development events), final (commencement), and continuing (alumni events) impression that stakeholders receive from their institution. These events are more complex and high risk than ever before due to various regulations, especially in the field of athletics, and the wide range of stakeholders. In addition, media scrutiny of higher education has made these events more visible than ever before to larger audiences.

April Harris believes that event planners in higher education must think of themselves as strategists and must plan and manage events so that they consistently reflect, support, and advance the overall mission of the institution.

Harris's interest in events first began as a young girl while she was involved in Girl Scouting. She enjoyed the requirements, traditions, and regulations associated with scouting. Many of these traditions included the organization of ceremonies and conducting specific rituals. "Our academic heritage is rich with tradition. By keeping our traditions alive, event planners become the next link in a chain that extends back to the Middle Ages," she says.

Harris believes in having standards for quality and demonstrating care and thoughtfulness to the details of each event. She believes that in the future, society will return to more structure, and that is why it is important for event planners to understand the rules of etiquette.

Harris is confident that society will always value the high standards required for leading quality ceremonies and rituals. "Standards and etiquette are indeed comforting because they give us a common set of expectations that help facilitate a good outcome from our actions."

For nearly two decades, April Harris has been a groundbreaking, seminal, and positive influence on thousands of event planners worldwide. As a result of her commitment to "higher standards," the events industry within higher education, and in many other fields as well, has risen to greater heights.

■ Copyright

Some Event Leadership organizations have their brand names listed separately in their assets. This is an important part of their goodwill. Any Event Leadership organization should protect its brand. Event professionals should consult copyright and intellectual property specialists to evaluate copyright areas where an organization can have potential problems. All brand names and logos of event organizations should contain clear copyright marks and warning statements.

■ Terrorism and Biochemical Risk

Dr. Peter Tarlow, the author of *Event Risk Management and Safety* (Wiley, 2002), advises soberly, "It takes only small amounts of a biochemical substance to murder hundreds of people, including those in charge." He advises that personnel should know when to enter and when to avoid possibly contaminated areas, types of equipment to use, and what the signs of a biochemical attack might be.

Events are often considered soft targets for terrorists. A soft target is one that is easily penetrated due to many different vulnerabilities. Tarlow has identified eight reasons for the interaction between terrorism and events and why terrorists see them as soft targets:

1. Events are often close to major transportation centers.
2. Events are big business.
3. Events impact other industries, such as restaurants, hotels, and entertainment.
4. Events draw media coverage.
5. Events require tranquility or places where business can be conducted in a peaceful manner.
6. Events must deal with people who have no history; thus, risk managers often do not have databases on delegates or attendees.
7. Events are based on a constant flow of guests; thus, it is hard to know who is and who is not a terrorist.
8. Events are the point where business and relaxation converge, and, therefore, guests often let down their guard.

Managing Risk: Everyone's Responsibility

The field of event risk management has grown so rapidly that there is emerging a specialization within the profession for risk experts such as Alexander Berlonghi and others. Larger events, such as the Pope's visit to Colorado, may require a risk manager to manage them from a risk perspective. However, for most events, the event manager is also the risk manager.

To improve your event operations, as the risk manager, you must assemble a risk management team that will assist you in identifying and managing risks. You must communicate to all event stakeholders that event risk management is everyone's responsibility.

Career-Advancement Connections

Global Connection

Create a list of written risk management policies, procedures, and practices, and ask a colleague in another country to examine these statements to determine if they are standard and customary in their country.

Technology Connection

Use a Computer Assisted Drawing and Design (CADD) system to prepare the final diagram for review by public officials.

Resource Connection

The American Society for Individual Security (*www.asisonline.org*) provides a wide range of books, articles, and videos to help you understand the many issues regarding safety, security, and risk management. The most comprehensive book in this field is entitled *Event Risk Management* by Peter Tarlow (Wiley, 2002).

The American Institute of Certified Public Accountants (*www.aicpa.org*) is the best source of information concerning how accounting firms must comply with Sarbanes-Oxley legislation.

Learning Connection

Design a risk management plan for an event for a publicly traded corporation. Describe how the plan will change based on various weather conditions. Explain how you will conduct, if necessary, a mass evacuation due to a catastrophic condition, such as fire or violence. List the types of insurance you must purchase to reduce your financial exposure. Describe how Sarbanes-Oxley legislation may or may not affect your event.

This technician is wearing protective clothing as he fabricates props for one of the themed events decorated by Party Design Ltd. in Johannesburg, South Africa. When creating and producing special events, your staff, vendors, and volunteers must carefully observe safety precautions.

CHAPTER 11

Inclusivity, Morality, Law, and Ethics in Event Leadership

In This Chapter You Will Learn How To:

✦ Develop special events within events to satisfy the needs of all guests and perhaps increase attendance

✦ Organize and conduct appropriate accompanying-persons programs

✦ Promote principles of inclusiveness throughout your event plan and production

✦ Comply with the U.S. Americans with Disabilities Act

✦ Understand the difference among morals, laws, and ethics

✦ Identify common ethical problems in the special events industry

✦ Avoid some ethical problems

✦ Establish policies and procedures for ethical issues

✦ Identify and use industry ethical guidelines

✦ Appoint an "ethical brain trust" to guide your ethical decision making

Two decades ago, this chapter probably would have not appeared in this book or any business book, for that matter. However, as businesses have grown and the Event Leadership industry in particular has expanded rapidly, more and more ethical issues have appeared.

Headlines screaming about Enron, Arthur Andersen, and other major ethical failures in business have made all of us more aware of the potential for loss of reputation through ethical missteps. Therefore, it is essential that issues of inclusiveness, morality, ethics, and law be discussed in this book.

Only a few years ago, when I introduced a required unit on ethics in my master's degree courses, several students told me that the other business professors found this to be ironic in a business school curriculum. I have persevered and continue to include this unit, and slowly but surely more and more business schools are now requiring not only units but also entire courses in business ethics. Largely prompted by the corporate supporters that ultimately employ their graduates, business schools have come to realize that their discussion of business ethics may be the first and last time students are exposed to this important issue. Indeed, the majority of the population may never earn an advanced degree, so providing this discussion at the baccalaureate or graduate level could fill in a gap left by parents and teachers. I often tell my colleagues that we must teach ethical decision making because ultimately it may affect and influence students' actions at the university and beyond. As faculty and mentors, we have a responsibility to help students make the personal and professional decisions that ethical behavior requires. I suggest that Event Leaders also have a responsibility to themselves and those they mentor to understand the requirements for making sound ethical decisions.

Differences among Morals, Laws, and Ethics

Etymologically, the term *moral* is derived from the Latin term *moralis,* that is, related to the word *custom* or *right or wrong in terms of behavior.* When Moses received the original 613 commandments, he may have also realized that if he or his followers disobeyed, there would be penalties. Morals are personal decisions that have personal consequences for right or wrong behavior. The legal system is a series of laws (many based on the Mosaic code) that are linked to specific punishments. Laws are enacted by groups, and punishment is imposed by peers (juries) or judges. Unlike morals, laws use third parties to enforce them and issue the punishment based on the degree of the violation. Professional ethics are, however, neither morals nor laws. Some argue that professional ethics incorporate both law and morals, but in actuality, ethics are the principles of conduct governing individuals or groups. These principles are based on the business culture that is accepted at the time of the action. Although ethics are personal decisions, they are guided by group behavior and group acceptance.

To better understand the interrelatedness of morals, laws, and ethics, ask yourself a series of questions. Let us start with a moral question: "Would you kill another person?" A moral person would immediately answer, "No, never." However, what if your children were being attacked by a violent person and the only way to stop the attack would be to kill the assailant? "Would you steal?" Once again most people would answer, "No." However, let us suppose that your children are starving and their very lives are threatened unless they receive some food to nourish them. Now what would you do?

"Would you attack someone?" Most of us would answer negatively. However, if your country was attacked, and you were part of the army that must defend your nation, you would answer in the affirmative or face serious punishment.

As you can see, many moral questions also have legal and ethical repercussions. Most of us will not be confronted on a daily basis with serious moral or legal decisions; however, many members of this profession regularly face serious ethical dilemmas.

Common Ethical Problems in the Special Events Industry

Ethical problems often vary according to type of industry and geographic location. In the special events industry, some ethical problems faced by hoteliers may or may not affect those in the party rental industry. The same may be said about the Event Leader in the country of Brazil versus the Event Leader in the United States. For example, in Chapter 10 you examined some risk management and legal issues associated with the consumption of alcohol. In the United States, the person who pours the alcohol may be legally responsible if a person being served overindulges and causes injury to others. In Brazil, just the opposite is true. The legal system of Brazil places the responsibility on the drinker rather than on the server. This has important ethical ramifications. If you are serving alcohol in Brazil, is it ethical to allow your guests to drink until they are inebriated and capable of causing injury to others? As you can see, the type of industry (or industry segment) and the geographic location often dictate the customs, practices, and values that are practiced by members of that community. These customs, practices, and values of the industry and local culture often drive the ethical decision making within the event organization.

Numerous typical ethical issues are addressed on a regular basis by members of the Event Leadership industry. Figure 11.1 lists some of the ethical issues that you will encounter most often.

Avoiding or Addressing Ethical Problems

The proactive methods described in Figure 11.1 illustrate some of the simple and practical steps that you can take to avoid the pitfalls of unethical behavior. Realistically, you cannot predict every ethical dilemma that may arise. You can, however, be prepared to resolve these problems with a proven three-step process: admission, remorse, and correction.

Despite your best efforts to avoid ethical misconduct, you can always recognize the mistake and notify the person or persons who may have been affected and tell them, "I made a mistake. I'm sorry. I will try not to let it happen again." Too often, individuals and organizations attempt to avoid confronting the problem of ethical misconduct, and the

Issue	Those Affected	Proactive Measures
Breach of confidentiality	Staff members	Include a confidentiality clause in employment agreements and policies and procedures.
Gifts versus bribes	Buyer and seller	Define gifts, set limits for receipt of gifts, and establish policies and procedures.
Sexual harassment	Staff members, supervisors, clients, guests	Establish written policies and procedures in accordance with federal laws, conduct training for new staff, and notify clients of policies and procedures.
Staff members soliciting clients from previous employment at new place of employment	Staff members	Establish employment agreements that limit this exposure.
Taking credit for others' work	Staff member and organization	Clearly identify who is responsible for work produced.
Theft of ideas by clients and competitors	Clients, competitors	Insert a copyright statement on proposals, and notify others of infringement.
Vendors accepting work directly from clients	Vendors and clients	Establish written policies.

Figure 11.1   Typical Event Industry Ethical Issues

misdeed festers like a wound that never heals. From the highest office in the land to local places of worship, most of us know far too many examples of ethical violations that are swept under the rug with the supposition that they will go unnoticed. Despite the rug, these ethical infractions continue to smell, and the small lump under the rug may grow and trip others in the future unless you address the problem promptly.

There are numerous successful examples of the three-step process for handling the problem of ethical violations. This is why it is important that you and your organization develop policies, procedures, and practices to address ethical issues when they arise. One of the best examples of professional handling of a major ethical situation is the 1982 Tylenol tampering incident. Johnson & Johnson, the maker of Tylenol, immediately withdrew the product from all shelves worldwide and issued a statement describing its plans for researching the problem and improving the safety measures for its products. As a result of its response, Johnson & Johnson received plaudits from the media and customers, and sales remain strong today.

How did Johnson & Johnson know how to respond to this ethical issue? The Johnson & Johnson credo states in the first paragraph that its company exists for the purpose of providing safe products and services: "We believe that our first responsibility is to the doctors, nurses, and patients, to mothers and fathers and all others who use our products and services." You can create your own credo to guide you as you face the many ethical decisions you will encounter in your career. One of the important facets of the Johnson & Johnson credo is the statement: "We must constantly strive to reduce our costs. . . . We must be good citizens. . . ." These statements not only reflect the credo of the organization but also address the operational aspects to enable managers and other employees to make decisions on a daily basis that are congruent with the values of Johnson & Johnson. When you draft your credo, make certain that it is more than cold type on a page; instead, it should burn like a branding iron into the hearts and minds of all persons who are responsible for serving as the stewards of your organization's good name. One of the many ways that Johnson & Johnson communicated its strong ethical message was through a series of internal events produced by one of the leading firms in the industry: Jack Morton Worldwide (*www.jackmorton.com*).

According to Bill Morton, chairman of Jack Morton Worldwide, "We were given a very small window to develop and produce these events. However, Johnson & Johnson entrusted us with their brand because of our long relationship with them. And ultimately, we were successful, despite the short time frame for development and production." Jack Morton Worldwide also has a strong credo that is based on *integrity*. It is a credo first solidified by the founder Jack Morton in 1939. And this is one of many reasons why the Athens, Greece, Olympic Games Organizing Committee (ATHOC) selected Jack Morton Worldwide to produce the opening and closing ceremonies of the 2004 summer Olympic Games.

Nearly 50 years ago, my father opened his small hardware store in Dallas, Texas. Instead of hanging a grand opening banner or blowing up balloons, he sat down and composed a simple but profound message to his customers. The message was then transformed into elegant calligraphy and displayed just inside the front door of his store, where it greeted customers for almost 50 years. As I write these lines, that message faces me, and it reads:

Once upon a time, I met a stranger . . . not so many years ago . . . in a distant city. When he learned that he knew my grandfather, the stranger looked at me and said, "You have a good name." He went on to explain that my grandfather held the respect and esteem of his fellow businessmen, his customers bestowed their confidence upon him, and his compassion and service for others was an inspiration to all. It is the hope of this business that we will so conduct our affairs that someday, somewhere one of our descendants will meet a stranger who will say, "You have a good name."
                                                                    —Max B. Goldblatt (1911–1995)

Establishing Policies and Procedures for Ethical Issues

In Appendix 17, you will find the Code of Ethics of the International Special Events Society (ISES). This is one example of how an industry establishes standards for ethical behavior. Some ways to avoid or resolve many of the issues within the code of ethics are:

+ *Do not accept expensive gifts.* Ban or set a financial limit on gifts.
+ *Avoid confusion regarding a change in an agreement.* Put all agreements (and changes) in writing and have both parties initial acceptance.

♦ *Avoid improper promotion of your services.* Seek written authority while working for another Event Leader.

♦ *Avoid claiming credit for an event you produced while working for another firm.* Clearly disclose the circumstances concerning the production of the event.

♦ *Avoid submitting photos of an event as an example of your work.* Clearly disclose that you helped produce your specific contributions to this event.

Inclusiveness Is an Ethical Responsibility

Perhaps one day the ISES Code of Ethics will be further amended to reflect the growing importance of promoting and achieving diversity and inclusiveness within event organizations. The statistics in the event industry reflect that females continue to outnumber males. What is not evident unless you attend industry conventions is that the percentage of minorities is relatively small as compared to the general population. While many industry organizations have made significant strides in promoting minority participation at the top level of their organizations, many minorities still prefer to form their own independent organizations that may more closely address their own needs and issues.

In the late 1990s, the Washington, DC, chapter of ISES held its annual awards event at the television studios of Black Entertainment Television. As a result of this decision, the percentage of African Americans attending this event was much greater than in previous years.

This is one example of how traditional members of this profession must rethink their locations, programming choices, and other considerations to promote and achieve diversity and inclusiveness. Without diversity and inclusiveness within our events, they and the entire profession will not be as successful and may, in fact, fail to be sustainable. Every living system requires diversity to ensure sustainability. The event industry is no different. Through active and effective programs promoting diversity and inclusiveness, you can expand your event market rapidly. To do this effectively, you must regularly look beyond your own sphere of knowledge to find out what you are missing.

For example, although in 1999 nearly 25 percent of the students in The George Washington University Event Management Program were African American females, no photographs of African American females appeared in the catalog used to promote the program. When a staff member brought this to my attention, I wondered what other groups might be underrepresented.

As Gene Columbus, manager of entertainment casting for Walt Disney World, stated, it is time for Event Leaders to ensure "places for everyone" and make certain that every possible opportunity is developed within the events industry to create a future that is both inclusive and representative of the diversity within the new world of Event Leadership.

Identifying and Using Industry Ethical Guidelines

In addition to the ISES, many related industry organizations use guidelines for professional practice or ethical beliefs to guide decision making. One criterion that you may wish to use for joining a professional organization is whether it has established a strong code of ethics along with appropriate enforcement procedures. Although these guidelines are at best guideposts rather than firm edicts, they will be useful not only to you but also to your clients as they raise the image of your profession.

Appointing an Ethical Brain Trust to Guide Your Ethical Decision Making

I have always relied on wise counselors and advisors to help me when faced with making a difficult ethical decision. Instead of assembling this brain trust at the last minute or on a case-by-case basis, I recommend that you identify people who know you well enough to provide you with critical input during times of ethical decision making.

A colleague of mine was faced with a tough ethical decision when he discovered some papers that contained highly personal information in a file left by a recently deceased relative. The papers included letters describing the circumstances of a death that took place 60 years earlier. After consulting with his immediate family members, he decided to contact his minister, who had been a friend of the family for nearly 60 years. The minister listened to the dilemma and asked a few questions relating to the medical consequences of the case. Finally, the minister offered simple but important advice that would spare much future pain to the survivors of the person who had died. "There is a reason the letters were hidden for 60 years. Burn the letters and do not discuss this with anyone." Obviously, the minister had faced this dilemma many times before and knew the framework for reaching this critical decision.

In another instance, someone's will granted lifetime use of a house for a longtime friend of the family. When told of the gift, the friend declined to live in the house and authorized sale of the property. The heirs wanted to share with the friend some of the proceeds from the sale, but a question arose as to how much would be appropriate. Once again, a brain trust was contacted. This time three wise and experienced persons were consulted: a minister (and longtime family friend), an attorney, and a peer of the same chronological age who had recently had a similar experience. The consensus of the advisors was to use the rule of tithing and provide a gift of 10 percent of the net proceeds to the friend but to forward the funds in the form of a specific gift for past services rather than an arbitrary amount.

These are the types of complex and difficult decisions that require the collective wisdom of the community to reach an appropriate ethical conclusion. Once you reach this conclusion, you can feel confident that your judgment has not only been tested but also strengthened by the counsel of others, who in many instances are more experienced than you yourself. Therefore, once you make the decision, do not look back. Instead, look forward to the next ethical decision you will face, because you will use the experience of all your past decisions to make future ones.

According to the *Washington Post,* the Washington, DC, Millennium-Bicentennial Celebration resulted in $290,500 in unpaid bills. The *Post* also reported that there were questions of ethics violations. The District of Columbia established a not-for-profit organization for the purpose of raising funds to plan and coordinate the millennium and bicentennial celebrations for the District. However, there were questions about whether the organization used DC government employees to raise money for the event.

Polly A. Rich, the ethics counselor in the District of Columbia corporation counsel's office, wrote in a memo that city employees should not raise money for nonprofits or solicit contributions from companies and individuals who do business in the District. Anthony W. Williams, mayor of the District of Columbia, responded to the criticism by stating: "Clearly, the lesson from the millennium-bicentennial events and the loss of a substantial amount of money from a lot of this nonprofit fund-raising is: 'What is the proper mechanism to do it?'" The question of appropriateness is not solely moral or legal but also an ethical dilemma that every Event Leader must address.

Furthermore, the Event Leader must realize that his or her event is only as good as its ability to include everyone in the process. Therefore, it is critically important that Event Leaders carefully analyze their board, planning committee, volunteers, and staff to insure that they have attempted to include as many diverse opinions and groups as possible.

Including Everyone: Arranging and Organizing Activities

Many events use tours and other off-site visits to expand the educational value of the program. Other events regularly incorporate tours of the destination and its attractions to provide guests with added value. Finally, some event organizers incorporate tours to offer diversions for accompanying persons, such as spouses, partners, friends, or young people attending with their parents. Regardless of the reason, increasingly, the arrangement and organization of tours is a critical component of most conferences, conventions, reunions, and even weddings.

There are three steps to consider when planning and coordinating tours for your event:

1. You must conduct an audit of the destination to determine if there are attractions or activities that are of interest to your guests. You can obtain this information from the local convention and visitors' association or from the chamber of commerce. Make certain that you ask the providers of this information what programs are most appropriate for specific market segments (females, males, children, mature guests, etc.).

2. Use this research to begin to assess the interest levels of your prospective guests with a brief survey of their interests. If you can match their strong interests with the best attractions and activities in the destination, you are well on your way to finding a winning combination guaranteed to increase attendance and produce excellent-quality reviews.

3. Find a price point that will be acceptable to your guests and perhaps provide excess revenues for your organization. To do this, you will need to obtain bids from local providers. In many destinations, a for-profit organization known as a *destination management company* (DMC) provides tour services. These services

are generally priced on a per-person basis and require a minimum number of participants to operate the program successfully.

In addition to tours, the DMC can provide services such as planning and coordinating local transportation, receptions, parties, and other events within your large event, as well as a wide range of other services. Outside the United States, the term *professional congress organizer* (PCO) is often used to refer to DMCs. The PCO generally provides an even greater range of services than the DMC. In addition to tours and events, the PCO may provide travel bookings, marketing of the event, and registration services, among many other services.

Two organizations represent the top DMC and PCO organizations. In the United States, the Association of Destination Management Executives (ADME) represents the leading destination management companies, and in Europe, the International Association of Professional Congress Organizers (IAPCO) represents the most respected PCO firms. Both organizations are listed in Appendix 2.

Developing Special Events within Events

The Event Leadership professional is often required to organize numerous individual events with a larger special event. In fact, this is so prevalent that the certified special events professional programs require that candidates understand and be able to coordinate accompanying-person events, tours, and other auxiliary programs related to special event management. Typical activities that often help form the context of a larger special event include:

- ✦ Accompanying person programs
- ✦ Arts and crafts displays and/or sales
- ✦ Auctions (live and silent)
- ✦ Book signings
- ✦ Carnivals
- ✦ Children's activities
- ✦ Coffeehouses
- ✦ Cyber Internet café(s) areas
- ✦ Dance lessons or parties
- ✦ Educational programs
- ✦ Etiquette seminars
- ✦ Exercise classes
- ✦ Exhibitions
- ✦ Fashion shows
- ✦ Festivals
- ✦ Films

◆ Formal dinners
◆ Golf tournaments
◆ Health lectures
◆ Hospitality rooms
◆ Hot-air ballooning
◆ Lifestyle lectures
◆ Museum tours
◆ Personal finance programs
◆ Pilates
◆ Races, runs, and marathons
◆ Sports activities or programs
◆ Tea ceremonies
◆ Team-building activities
◆ Tennis tournaments
◆ Tours (city, scenic, historic, cultural, walking)
◆ Yoga
◆ Youth programs featuring motivational speakers
◆ Zoological programs and tours

The Event Leader must assess, through research, how the internal or external events will support the overall goals and objectives of the total event. These events should be seen as the frame of a large umbrella. Each spoke or event must carefully support the individual objectives of the overall event. If any one event is poorly planned or weakly coordinated, the entire structure may weaken. Therefore, the Event Leader should conduct an audit of typical event guests, as well as those who are atypical and nonattendees, to determine their interests, needs, wants, and desires. These data can be very helpful in determining which events to offer and during which times they will be most popular.

Once the audit is completed, the Event Leader will usually contact a third party, such as an entertainment, production, or other professional, to obtain proposals to present the type of event or attraction that is required. Make certain that you encourage the proposers to use their creativity to develop your event ideas further. For example, a game show requested by a major corporation became an "event" when the game company supplier suggested a hostess who was a Vanna White look-alike and a set that reflected the popular game show *Wheel of Fortune*. The creativity of others can quickly embellish your event design and bring added value without additional cost.

The final consideration when selecting the events that will comprise your larger event is to confirm the reliability of the vendors. Too often, event organizations driven by committees will develop extraordinary ideas with ordinary budgets and resources. It is much better to select those event elements that will bring high quality and consistent excellence to your event than to stretch the event to the breaking point. To confirm the reliability of individual vendors, it is best to inspect the event during operation before a similar group of guests or to seek references from organizers of events that are similar to the one you are producing.

Organizing and Conducting Spouse and Partner Programs

One of the key competencies in the coordination knowledge domain of the certified special events professional program is the organization and coordination of spouse and partner programs. The term *spouse* is actually somewhat antiquated and has been replaced with the term *accompanying person* to reflect the broader spectrum of persons who are attending an event with the invited guest. The actual taxonomy of the guest list is:

1. Delegate or principal invitee or guest
2. Guest of principal invitee or accompanying person
3. Observer

The accompanying person may have a wide range of interests that must be satisfied during the overall event experience. Typically, the accompanying person will be invited to all social events with the principal invitee, delegate, or guest. In addition, special programming as discussed earlier may be organized to provide diversions while the delegate, principal invitee, or guest is involved in official functions, such as education, governance (debate, discussion, elections), or other similar activities that generally are not of interest to the accompanying person.

The Event Leader must strike a balance between diverting the accompanying person and totally disengaging him or her from the basic goals and objectives of the overall event. To ensure that the accompanying person is fully engaged and recognized, the person should be identified through credentials as a guest, accompanying person, or observer. In addition, an orientation program should be organized at the beginning of a conference or other multiday event to help accompanying persons to understand the opportunities available during the larger event, as well as to make them feel welcome and answer any pertinent questions.

The accompanying person very often influences the principal guest or delegate to return to an event year after year, so it is critically important that the person has an excellent experience that is equal although different from that of the person he or she is accompanying. To monitor the experience, it is important that accompanying persons be surveyed or surveyed through a focus group to thoroughly analyze their event experience, to allow you to improve your practice continually in the future.

Complying with the Americans with Disabilities Act

It is projected that the number of persons in North America with disabilities will grow exponentially in the next several years as the baby boomers show the natural signs of the aging process. As a result, the large number of persons with visual, auditory, and physical disabilities will significantly affect the research, planning, design, and coordination phases of twenty-first century Event Leadership.

During the research phase, the Event Leader must assess the types of disabilities that are most likely to be reflected by event participants. These important data may be obtained through historical information or through a survey of potential guests. Research will include learning about individual disabilities in order to best prepare and serve the population that will be attending your event.

The design phase enables the Event Leader to work closely with the disabled community to determine the services and accommodations that must be implemented to ensure the comfort and satisfaction of all guests. During the design phase, many creative solutions may be suggested by members of the disabled population to help the event organizer satisfy his or her needs with little or no additional investment.

During the planning and coordination phases, the Event Leader fine-tunes the recommendations proposed by the disabled community and works with event vendors and staff to implement the best ideas to achieve the best outcomes for the overall event. These two phases should include the identification of contingency plans for serving disabled individuals who were not identified previously but must be accommodated once they arrive at the event.

Event Sensitivity

At one time the term *handicapped* was used to describe individuals with limited abilities. In recent years, the disabled community has asked that this term be replaced with the term *disabled*. When conducting staff and volunteer training, I prefer to use the term *different abilities* because in my experience, every human being has different abilities with which to enjoy your event. Your job is to find these abilities and through the event plan and practice, satisfy the needs, wants, and desires of all guests regardless of their individual abilities.

There is a fine line between attending to the needs of guests with special needs and interfering with their personal space. According to the International Association of Amusement Parks and Attractions video resource titled *Disability Etiquette*, here are some key methods for helping rather than intruding.

■ Visually Challenged Guests

When approaching guests who have visual challenges, first speak and offer to assist them. Do not touch them first as this may startle them; rather, use a soft voice and offer your help by saying, "May I help you?" Consider providing additional services including Braille programs, Braille signs, and infrared technology that will verbally alert guests when there is a step up or step down or turn.

■ Physically Challenged Guests

When speaking to persons in wheelchairs, bend down to their level so you are making face-to-face contact. The chair is a physical extension of the individual; therefore, ask before touching it. According to the U.S. Department of Justice, parking is a critical issue for persons who are physically challenged. Event leaders, therefore, are required to make certain that they provide sufficient accessible parking for their physically disabled guests. Furthermore, the Americans with Disabilities Act (ADA) requires that van parking spaces provide three additional features: a wider access aisle (96 inches) to accommodate a wheelchair lift; vertical clearance to accommodate van height at the van parking space, the adjacent access aisle, and on the vehicular route to and from the van-accessible space; and an additional sign that identifies the parking spaces as "van accessible." Figure 11.2 lists the minimum requirements for accessible parking spaces according to the U.S. Department of Justice.

■ Auditorily Challenged Guests

Make eye contact with your guest so he or she may be able to read your lips as you speak. Do not raise your voice; rather speak slowly and carefully enunciate. Keep a pad of paper nearby and write down your communications, if necessary. If possible, seek help from a American Sign Language (ASL) interpreter to help with communications. The U.S. Department of Justice provides an excellence business connection web page to help individual

Total Number of Parking Spaces Provided (per lot)	(Column A) Total Minimum Number of Accessible Parking Spaces (60" & 96" aisles)	Van-Accessible Parking Spaces with min. 96" wide access aisle	Accessible Parking Spaces with min. 60" wide access aisle
1 to 25	1	1	0
26 to 50	2	1	1
51 to 75	3	1	2
76 to 100	4	1	3
101 to 150	5	1	4
151 to 200	6	1	5
201 to 300	7	1	6
301 to 400	8	1	7
401 to 500	9	2	7
501 to 1000	2% of total parking provided in each lot	1/8 of Column A*	7/8 of Column A[†]
1001 and over	20 plus 1 for each 100 over 1000	1/8 of Column A*	7/8 of Column A[†]

*One out of every eight accessible spaces.
[†]Seven out of every eight accessible parking spaces.

Figure 11.2 ADA Standards for Accessible Design of Parking Lots 4.1.2(5)

Source: U.S. Department of Justice, ADA Business Brief, "Re-striping Parking Lots," *www.usdoj.gov*

Profile in Event Leadership: Zeren Earls

SHE WROTE THE BEST-SELLING BOOK ENTITLED *FIRST NIGHT*

Thirty years ago, artists Clara and Bill Wainwright invited nine creative co-conspirators including Zeren and the late Paul Earls to their Boston home to conceive a plot to transform New Year's Eve. Paul Earls, a talented composer, and Zeren, a creative artist, wondered each year how they could best celebrate New Year's Eve with their young child. Their co-conspirators also faced the same challenge with their families. Together this small band of New Englanders reinvented New Year's Eve through First Night Boston (*www.firstnight.org*).

Zeren Earls
Founder of First Night

According to Zeren Earls, "The goal of First Night is to mark the turning of year by engaging the public's imagination. New Year's Eve is loaded with memories and expectations, and we seek to connect, engage, and tap into the audience just as a great writer reaches his or her readers." Earls believes the event planner is similar to a great novelist and, therefore, must create images that engage the audience. Furthermore, events, like great novels, must be page-turners, arresting and holding the audience member's attention as the story dramatically unfolds.

The spectacular First Night celebration achieves this through the Grand Procession, the opening event that is ritualistic, symbolic, and participatory. It features hundreds of costumed people and musicians. "In the early years of First Night, we invited

businesses better comply with the standards and guidelines of the ADA act. Visit *www.usdoj .gov/crt/ada/business.htm* for additional ideas on how to better serve this population.

Providing for Special Needs of Your Guests

Once you have gathered all the quantitative data from the site inspection, it is time to analyze your findings and determine what implications emerge for your event environment design. Most important considerations include the legal, regulatory, and risk management issues that are uncovered during site inspection.

Peter Schumann of Bread & Puppet Theater in Vermont to bring his giant puppets to be carried in the procession. The scale of these giant figures captured the audience's imagination."

First Night celebrations are a kaleidoscope of live performers, visual artists, and audience members. "We soon became a victim of our own success," says Earls as she describes the evolution of First Night Boston. "We ran out of venues to showcase our performers and, therefore, had to shorten the performances to allow more audience members to interact with as many different types of live performance and visual art as possible in one evening." When First Night Boston was first launched, early requests for proposals to dozens of artists attracted only six responses. The initial event attracted 60,000 persons and today, 30 years later, over 1 million people participate in First Night Boston each year.

The event grew in both quality and size because the founders agreed from the beginning that they would emphasize artistic excellence and that they would focus on thinking big. One example of thinking big during the nation's 1976 bicentennial year was Paul Earls's assembling 1,000 high school band musicians to perform under the direction of the legendary conductor of the Boston Pops Orchestra, the late maestro Arthur Fiedler.

The first year the Boston event was offered free to the public; however, today's numerous First Night celebrations feature colorful buttons that are sold in advance and on site and admit audience members to all performances. Today, over 150 First Night celebrations are conducted throughout the world. There is also First Night International (*www.firstnight.com*), an organization that promotes and encourages the development of First Night celebrations.

Zeren Earls believes that New Year's Eve is demarcation on our calendar, and we can either live in fear or in hope. "We have to work at cultivating community, to develop cultural habits, to help us be in 'dignity' with others," she says, "and the procession is the 'emblem' of the event. It is the tapestry that weaves all of the cultures together."

Thanks to Zeren Earls, millions of people throughout the world are helping write the next chapter in the developing story of First Night.

Zeren Earls: zearls@verizon.net

If the venue is not in full compliance with the Americans with Disabilities Act (signed into law in 1992), you may need to make certain modifications in your design. For example, a large quasi-government corporation asked me to create a tropical theme, including a small bridge at the entrance where guests would stroll over a pond containing live goldfish. In creating this design, we factored in the need to provide full and equal access for disabled guests and ramped both ends of the bridge to satisfy this need.

The statute states:

Title III-Sec. 302 a) General rule. No individual shall be discriminated against on the basis of disability in the full and equal enjoyment of the goods, services, facilities, privileges, advantages, or accommodations of any place of public accommodation.

Profile in Event Leadership: Gene Columbus

A PLACE FOR EVERYONE

In 2005, Gene Columbus was the first person from the Walt Disney Company to be inducted into the Event Solutions Event Industry Hall of Fame. From serving as an assistant stage manager for the touring production *Disney on Parade* to managing entertainment staffing for Walt Disney Entertainment, Columbus has served as an Event Leader for the world's largest live entertainment company for over 30 years. Columbus believes that the difference between managers and leaders is best defined with these comparisons: "A

Gene Columbus
Manager of Entertainment Staffing
Walt Disney World

manager administrates and a leader innovates. A manager maintains the status quo and a leader develops the future. A manager relies on systems and a leader relies on people. A manager counts on control and a leader counts on trust."

Columbus advises new Event Leaders to occasionally look behind and see if they are being followed. This is one of the many important tests for successful Event Leaders. One way to insure that the Event Leader has followers is to actively promote diversity and inclusiveness. He recalls that,

As a result of this historic legislation, wheelchair ramps, Braille menus and signs, sign-language interpreters, and other elements have become commonplace at events. Event Leaders are responsible for complying with this law, which affects nearly 50 million Americans.

A comprehensive checklist for incorporating the Americans with Disabilities Act into an event environmental design follows.

+ Survey your guests in advance of the event to determine what accommodations will be required.
+ Include the following language on all brochures or other offerings: "If you require special accommodations, please describe below."
+ Survey the venue to determine what gaps must be closed prior to your event.
+ Establish wheelchair seating positions.
+ Maintain a clear line of sight for guests who will be using sign-language interpreters.

30 years ago, as a young stage manager, he would announce to his company a few minutes before the curtain went up, "Places, please." Today, he recommends changing the announcement to "Places for *everyone*" to reflect the diverse and inclusive culture that is the hallmark of successful event organizations.

Columbus, who is hearing impaired, greatly understands the importance of a place for everyone. "When I attend meetings in my organization, the other attendees make certain that I have a seat at the table that allows me to comfortably hear all of the discussion. They ask me if I am comfortable. During the meeting, they will check with me to make certain I understand what is being discussed and if I have any questions or input. This type of sensitivity to individuals with special needs is a natural part of our culture."

As a champion of diversity and underrepresented groups, Columbus was instrumental in establishing a scholarship program at a local university to promote greater opportunities for minorities in technical theater. "On stage, it is obvious that we are making great strides with diversity; however, offstage we still struggle. This scholarship program is designed to seed the field with role models from underrepresented groups that others can follow."

Columbus believes that we must start even before college by reaching out to youth at the high school level. "Whether it is giving a speech or volunteering in other ways, it is important that we reach young people when they are moldable and introduce everyone to our profession," he says. Columbus believes that accommodating special needs for events is really about serving the audience. "Our challenge is every time to bring to the audience a unique experience, with quality values that are inspiring and motivating. Courage and integrity are paramount in achieving this goal."

Gene Columbus exemplifies the courage and integrity that is needed to guide others toward a more inclusive, diverse, and caring event industry for the new world.

Gene Columbus: gene.columbus@disney .com

+ Work with speakers with disabilities to provide access to the podium.
+ Provide audio-transcription services of the stage action for the visually disabled.
+ Select venues with, or provide, handrails for guests with physical infirmities.
+ Provide tables with appropriate height for wheelchair users.
+ Contact the U.S. Department of Justice if you have additional questions about designing an event environment that meets compliance regulations. Telephone the ADA information line at (800) 514–0301.
+ Train your staff to better meet the needs of people with disabilities.

After seeking written feedback from your prospective guests regarding their special needs, it is important to take one additional step to meet their expectations fully. You may wish to invite people with special needs to conduct their own site inspection of your proposed venue and become part of the planning team. People in wheelchairs, older guests with limited mobility, and sight- and hearing-impaired persons can provide you with important information to improve the total event environment. Local organizations, such as Easter Seals or the Muscular Dystrophy Association, can refer you to people who will volunteer to offer their advice and counsel during the planning stage. Listen carefully to their suggestions and incorporate them where feasible. Your goal is to produce an event environment that is accessible and effective for everyone.

Every guest has special needs. Abraham Maslow recognized these needs with his hierarchy of needs, which ranged from basic needs to ephemeral requirements, including the need to be loved. The professional Event Leader may not be able to forecast or satisfy every need his or her guests bring to an event. However, guests must sense that the Event Leader or host is genuinely concerned with their welfare and will work diligently to attempt to anticipate, identify, and satisfy their needs to provide them with a total high-quality event experience. When this occurs, the guest experience rises to a heightened level, as defined by Maslow. When guests begin to feel appreciated or even loved, this ultimately defines in an intangible but powerful way their enduring memories or experiences from your event.

Career-Advancement Connections

Global Connection

Working with multicultural organizations can be challenging unless the Event Leadership professional does his or her homework. For example, many events held outside the United States suggest that guests wear formal attire or national dress or costume to a formal dinner. It is appropriate to further define national costume as "that which reflects the culture, ethnicity, or national pride of the country where the guest has sworn national allegiance."

Once you have created a list of written ethical policies, procedures, and practices, ask a colleague in another country to examine these statements to determine if they are acceptable in that culture. To avoid committing an offense, use advisors in other countries to guide you in your ethical practices.

Technology Connection

The Internet has numerous sites that provide valuable information concerning disabilities as well as the Americans with Disabilities Act. The U.S. Department of Justice administers the act and may be contacted at *www.usdoj.gov.*

Use appropriate etiquette when using the Internet. Avoid spamming (marketing without permission), flaming (using all capital letters, exclamation points, and harsh language), or inappropriate language that may offend the reader. Visit the ISES Web site (*www.ises.com*) and other industry sites to review their codes of ethics.

Resource Connection

+ The Ethics Resource Center (*www.ethics.org*) in Washington, DC, provides a wide range of books, articles, and videos to help you understand the many issues affecting ethical decision making.
+ The International Association of Amusement Parks and Attractions has an excellent video training tool entitled *Disability Etiquette* (*www.iaapa.org*).
+ For comprehensive information on the Americans with Disabilities Act visit *www.usdoj.gov/crt/ada/business.htm*.

Learning Connection

+ You have been offered an expensive gift from a vendor in exchange for your business. Is there any situation or circumstance in which it would be acceptable to accept this gift? How do you know this? Where will you get the information? How will you make the decision? How could the decision be different if this occurred in another culture, where the giving and receiving of expensive gifts is accepted, usual, and customary?
+ One of your event guests complains to you about inappropriate behavior from one of your vendors. Although the vendor is not your employee, do you have an ethical responsibility to intervene on behalf of your event guest? How do you know what to do? Where will you get the information? What steps will you take to make the decision?
+ You have been asked to bid on a future event. You are asked by your prospective client to show examples of your past work. Some of the work you have completed was when you were in the employ of others. Do you explain to your prospective client that some of this work was completed while you worked for another firm, or do you simply ignore this fact and present the work to the client as if you were responsible as an individual? How do you know what to do? Where will you get the information to make the proper ethical judgment? How do you know that this judgment is correct?
+ To improve your professional Event Leadership skills, practice completing this exercise: Describe how you will provide relevant and appropriate programming for each of the following groups who will be accompanying your guests to a three-day medical conference: youth, young children, heterosexuals, and homosexuals. Twenty-five percent or more of your delegates have visual, auditory, or physical-mobility disabilities. Describe how you will accommodate these delegates. Finally, describe how you will evaluate your performance for serving each of these populations to ensure continual quality improvement at your event.

PART SIX

Technology and Professional Development

A robot promotes a trade show exhibit at the Western Fairs Association annual convention in Reno, Nevada.

CHAPTER 12

Technology for Modern Event Leadership

In This Chapter You Will Learn How To:

- ✦ Understand the role and scope of emerging technology within the event industry
- ✦ Find resources for efficient technological solutions
- ✦ Differentiate data processing systems
- ✦ Apply technological solutions to solve problems

The major task of the technology and information system in modern Event Leadership is to collect, store, and provide data to the different levels of users. The comparative advantages of technology over manual systems are:

+ Opportunities to use data in a more efficient and timely manner
+ Greater reliability; less possibility of human error
+ Consistency of operations
+ Better data security
+ Real-time analysis and review

The current trend of most Event Leadership organizations is to move toward a paperless office, where a company relies fully on software collection, storage, and retrieval of data. Many types of computer technology systems are currently in use. These systems are distinguished by the method they use to process information, by the type of filing systems used for data storage and retrieving, and by hardware configuration.

Data Processing Systems

There are three major types of event data processing systems: (1) batch processing, (2) online real-time processing, and (3) time sharing and service bureaus.

Batch Data Processing

In batch-processing systems, event transactions are accumulated and processed in groups. All revenues and invoices for a day are viewed as batch transactions, to be processed as a group. For example, sales divisions of an Event Leadership company see all sales for a single day as one "day sale" and are entered into a computer system as one batch. Simplicity and reliability distinguish this system. The general rule in technology is that the more complicated the system, the greater the potential for mistakes. The biggest advantage of batch processing systems is their cost. Since the systems do not require networks, instant backup, and training of the entire staff, they are relatively cheap. However, a batch-processing system does not allow the quick processing of transactions. Therefore, Event Leaders do not always have the ability to retrieve current information. Because of their characteristics, batch processing systems are rarely used in large Event Leadership companies. They are more common for small and mid-size Event Leadership companies.

Real-Time Data Processing

In a real-time processing system, transactions are entered as they occur. Given the continuous updating of the database as transactions are entered, the status of all major accounts—such as admission revenue, sales revenue, and inventory—can be determined at any moment. Data processing systems of several Event Leadership subsidiaries can be connected to the main office's processing unit. The main office can process the data either in real time or using the batch processing principle. Event Leaders may have different levels of access to the central data processing unit. Middle-level managers can be authorized to retrieve all the data from all units or may be limited in their ability to browse through the data.

The system tracks all activities through an Event Leadership company. It allows Event Leaders to set their activities schedule in the most beneficial manner. The system provides Event Leaders with a great tool for inventory control and for control over collection of revenue and of comparison data. Since this system requires real-time transactions and networking, it is more expensive than batch processing. Real-time systems are common for mid-size Event Leadership companies with diverse operations and/or for large Event Leadership companies.

Time Sharing and Service Bureaus

Time sharing occurs when a system services more than one branch of an Event Leadership company at the same time. A service bureau is a company that processes transactions for other entities. Many small and mid-size Event Leadership companies hire bureau companies to handle small operations (e.g., payroll and collection of receivables). In this case, the event company's internal data processing system can be either linked or not linked to the bureau company's data processing system.

Hardware Configuration

Three basic types of hardware configuration are common in the Event Leadership industry: (1) online systems, (2) personal computer (PC) systems, and (3) distributed data processing.

Online Systems

Online systems are unique in that each transaction is entered via a communication device connected to a computer. Magnetic cards are a good example for such systems. Online systems may or may not be real-time systems, depending on whether transactions are processed and updated immediately as they happened.

Electronic data interchange (EDI) is currently being adopted by an increasing number of large Event Leadership companies. EDI is a computer-to-computer exchange of intercompany information and data in a *public standard form*. In an EDI system, documents such as purchase orders, invoices, attendance projections, and checks are converted into standard form, permitting other companies to read and accept them. There are two methods available for implementing EDI: direct and indirect. The direct method links the computer system of an Event Leadership company with a major client or a supplier, such

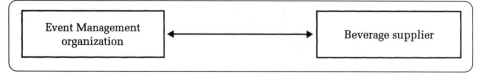

Figure 12.1 Direct Method for Implementing EDI

as a major beverage supplier (see Figure 12.1). When an Event Leadership company makes adjustments to its attendance numbers, the system informs the supplier, which helps to eliminate inventory shortages.

The indirect method utilizes a network of various companies' computers and companies, and provides a "mailbox" for use by all (see Figure 12.2). The network transforms senders' messages into the format preferred by receivers. The advantage of this method is that the sender can transmit documents to several receivers without changing the format each time. For example, an Event Leadership company submits all information about a forthcoming event (e.g., attendance menu, list of beverages, setup requirements) to the mailbox. Then suppliers visit the mailbox and submit offers matching the requirements.

PC Systems

PC systems may consist of stand-alone computers used by a single Event Leader, or they may be connected to one another and/or to mainframe computers through a form of networking.

Distributed Data Processing

Many large Event Leadership companies use PCs extensively for both data processing and analysis. Event Leadership companies with branches in various locations frequently

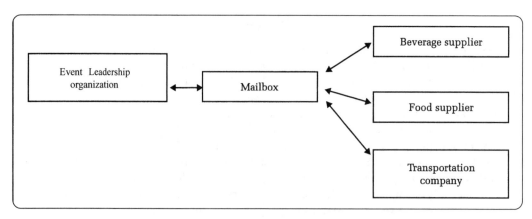

Figure 12.2 Indirect Method for Implementing EDI

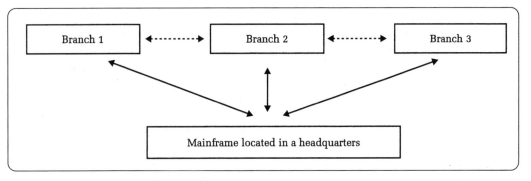

Figure 12.3   Distributed Data Processing System

use networks to process each branch's transactions and transmit them to the major office via communications links. At the same time, local Event Leaders can use a PC for various kinds of analyses. Distributed data processing systems are usually connected to a mainframe computer located at the headquarters office of an Event Leadership company (see Figure 12.3). Additionally, they can be linked to one another through a networking system, such as a local area network (LAN) or a wide area network (WAN). Networks are used to enable PCs to communicate with one another and share workloads.

Access Control

To prevent unauthorized use and alteration of files and data, access must be limited to authorized individuals. In an online, integrated file system and EDI, access limitation is archived through control over *passwords,* codes used to access various parts of a database. Some passwords allow only examination and retrieval of data; others allow data alteration. Database control includes voiding and changing passwords. However, it is important to ensure that at least two people have master access to a database so that if a person with master access is unavailable, the company's operations will not suffer.

Interactive Web

Development of the Internet was one of the most significant events of the last decade. At first it was available only to academia and the military, but very soon it became an integrated part of the business environment. As the technology becomes more affordable, more companies are entering cyberspace. As a starting point, companies set up Web sites. At the beginning sites may be viewed as simply an informative tool. Small event management companies usually start Web sites to post basic information about their services, employees, history, and information on how to contact them. However, the effect of posting the information is similar to listing your company in the yellow pages. The moment an Event Leadership company develops a Web site, it starts to create ways to attract potential customers to the site. All the information becomes immediately available to the general public and, if presented correctly, can serve as a great marketing tool.

Companies attract potential customers in several ways using their Web sites. As a starting point, new sites should create general visitor traffic. This can be accomplished by registering the site with various search programs, such as Google, AltaVista, Yahoo!, and HotBot. Once you register a Web site with all major search engines, you can be reasonably sure that it will be available to a potential client who is conducting a search. Usually a search is conducted using *keywords,* such as "event leadership," "event leadership New York," or just "event." The more general the keywords, the more potential matches a search program generates.

A Web site is an excellent marketing tool that can be either used or misused. A site can provide these advantages to an Event Leadership company:

✦ Wide market reach
✦ Ability to update information quickly and easily
✦ Ability to track and collect data about potential clients
✦ Ability to cut marketing expenses

The Internet is a great equalizer. Small and mid-size Event Leadership companies have the same opportunities as industry giants to reach potential customers. Although larger companies have more technical resources to invest in the development of Web sites, the difference usually comes down to having more cookies or action. Web sites that are too complicated and contain much flashier but unnecessary effects may be annoying and make the information difficult to read. In my experience, user-friendly, well-developed, well-designed Web sites are often those of smaller and mid-size Event Leadership companies or even individual event professionals. At the end of the day, all companies have the same opportunity to reach clients.

If you think that you must be a programmer to operate a Web site, you are wrong. In the early days, you had to know one or even several programming languages (e.g., HTML, Java) to make simple changes in a Web site. Today, many computer applications, including Microsoft FrontPage and Netscape Composer, allow users to change sites without learning the coding. Working with your site using these software applications is similar to writing a letter using Microsoft Word. The program automatically transforms the changes you want to make into HTML format. The most difficult part is posting the contents you have created to the World Wide Web, but you can learn to do this in a one-time professional consultation. After your site is designed and launched (which usually requires professional assistance), you can maintain it yourself.

A Web site can be an excellent tool for collecting information about existing and potential clients. Often Event Leadership companies ask their site visitors to register. Usually visitors are asked to provide their e-mail address, area of interest, basic geographic data, and other material. This information turns into a customized database of clients that you can use later. If a person visited your site and registered, it means that this person is interested, or at least potentially interested, in your services. By collecting and analyzing these data, you can optimize your marketing expenses. You can use your Web site as a tool for customizing services. Major site-development software applications provide site owners with an opportunity to monitor not only traffic in general but also to obtain more detailed information about what parts of the site generate the most clicks and who is doing the clicking. If, for example, your site contains information about two major services that your company offers—private banquet services and corporate events—and the corporate event service generates much more traffic, this should send you a strong signal about current and future market needs.

Event Leadership Databases

The Event Leadership industry is growing rapidly. Although there are several large Event Leadership companies in the market, new players enter every day. A major challenge that companies face in every fast-growing industry is the problem of keeping a database up to date. How often do you dial a number that you found in a catalog only to find that the number has been changed? It happens to me all the time. Almost every catalog is outdated the moment it leaves the print shop. The accuracy of documents decreases dramatically over time. Getting online is one way of ameliorating this problem. Internet databases are the most reliable in the event industry. One event association executive told me that within a few days of allowing members to update their online records, over 200 persons made changes to the electronic directory.

Two major criteria distinguish a database. The first is its resources. The more resources that a database has, the more valuable it is. Because resources are collected over time, young databases usually contain less data than older ones. The second criterion relates to search features. You can search a database in a number of ways: alphabetically, by region, by service offered, by price, and by age. The more criteria a database has, the more valuable it is. Search criteria should be user-friendly and easy to customize. Even users with moderate database-search experience should be able to find necessary data quickly. Some databases make their search engines overly complicated and the search process becomes very confusing.

Development of the Internet has provided new opportunities for Event Leadership, such as real-time information databases, interactive databases, and commercial databases. Content can be updated online, and users have access at any time. You can receive catering quotes immediately after answering required questions and can book event facilities all over the world. Search criteria can be customized and changed much easier than in a paper version. The search itself can be customized to an unbelievable extent. In electronic databases, users can enter keywords and the database will conduct a global search based on these words. I encourage you to visit DOME, one of the best available Event Leadership industry databases, to familiarize yourself with the vast online Event Leadership resources. You can find this database by visiting *www.domeresearch.org*.

Profile in Event Leadership:
Steven Wood Schmader, CFE

HEADING FOR THE FUTURE

Steven Wood Schmader, CFEE
President and CEO
International Festivals and Events Association

In the 1980s, singer-songwriter Neil Diamond's hit song "Heading for the Future" could easily have served as a battle cry for Steven Wood Schmader, president of the International Festival and Events Association. Schmader has helped lead us into the future of the festival and special events industry for the past quarter of a century.

As a member of the cast of the international touring company "Up With People" in the mid-1970s, Schmader realized the power and influence of live events. He transitioned from cast member to promotion manager in the late 1970s, and then was promoted to director of special events. As director he was responsible for major projects, such as the involvement of the company in Macy's Thanksgiving Day Parade, the NFL Super Bowl Halftime Spectacular, and the inauguration of President George H. W. Bush.

As a leader in the events industry, Schmader, along with Robert Jackson, wrote one of the first books in the field, *Special Events Inside & Out* (Sagamore Press, 1990).

This early work continues to profoundly influence the events industry today.

Jackson was asked to conduct a feasibility study for the city of Boise, Idaho, to determine how to develop a festival or major event for the city. After Jackson issued his recommendations, the city conducted a national search and chose Steven Wood Schmader to serve as the first leader and founder of the Boise River Festival. This event, which began with a modest budget of $310,000, grew to require a budget of over $1.6 million with a staff of five employees and 4,000 volunteers, lasting four days, and featuring 400 events. The aggregate attendance at this event was over 1 million people, and it was named one of the top 100 events in North America by the American Bus Association.

When asked what the motivating force that propels his leadership abilities is, Schmader quickly answers, "You must love the unknown." According to Schmader, to advance in this profession, you must use your leadership skills effectively at every level. By using his leadership skills throughout his career, he was able to become the leading spokesperson for the festival and special events industry as president of the International Festival and Events Association (IFEA).

"I saw IFEA as an event," says Schmader, "exciting, fresh, an opportunity to learn, to get better, and, yes, to dream about the future of our industry." When asked to describe a defining moment during his leadership of IFEA, he carefully considered the question and then thoughtfully responded, "I suppose it was at the very beginning. I proposed to move the offices from Port Angeles, Washington, to Boise, Idaho, and demonstrated how this would not only create greater efficiencies but also provide new resources for the organization. Immediately following our move, September 11, 2001, occurred and we were forced to postpone and relocate our annual convention." Schmader emphasizes that he recommended they "go on with the show" rather than cancel the convention because the industry, his members, needed to get together to continue to move the industry into the future.

Since assuming the presidency of IFEA, Schmader has faced numerous challenges. However, he has also been able to advance many important new ideas, including redeveloping the Certified Festival Executive (CFE) program, reformatting and renaming the association publication from *Festivals Magazine* to *International Events,* and using technology to improve and accelerate communications with members. "We must continually look for better and faster ways to communicate with our members and other constituencies, and IFEA plans to be at the forefront of this important area," says Schmader.

According to Schmader, there are three important propellants of leadership that he continues to use to head for the future:

1. Relationships are critical to a leader's success because they enable leaders to build a network, to nourish friendships, and to treat all people with the highest respect and esteem.
2. A leader must be committed to do whatever it takes to accomplish his or her goals. There should be no limits to a leader's ability to achieve successful outcomes.
3. It is critically important never to forget what business you are in.

He believes we are first and foremost in the *people* business. Events change people's lives. Through events we can impact millions of lives in a positive way every day. Schmader says we must embrace this responsibility and use our leadership abilities to continually advance toward future success.

From performer, to producer, to president of one of the industry's leading associations, Steven Wood Schmader's illustrious career demonstrates how relationships, commitment, and respect for people can be carefully woven together to create a strong and beautiful tapestry that, similar to a magic carpet, will carry the special events industry into a future of which we may all be extremely proud.

Steven Wood Schmader: steve@ifea.com

Technology Trends

Twenty years ago, technology was a luxury for small and mid-size companies. The situation is different now. It is hard to imagine any Event Leadership office without a computer, Internet access, and e-mail. Although it is hard to predict what will happen with technology in 10 years, there are recognizable trends. The technology will become more customized. Several years ago, small and mid-size Event Leadership companies did not have a lot of options when choosing software applications, as the number of major software packages was limited. Software programming services were not very affordable. But the situation has changed. There is much more technology and many more software development companies today than existed even a few years ago. Development of the Internet has allowed software development start-ups to sell their products directly to customers. As a result, the software development market has become more competitive, services more user-friendly, and prices more affordable. People who a short time ago did not know how to create a document are now getting more and more comfortable with computers. With this in mind, we can talk about the growth of virtual offices and the amount of online business and overall globalization of event management services.

One of the most important innovations in the global high-technology revolution is the development of the wireless application protocol (WAP). WAP was developed within the wireless industry, from companies such as Phone.com, Nokia, and Ericsson. The WAP standard is to provide Internet contents and services to wireless clients using WAP devices such as mobile phones and terminals. The opportunities for use of WAP-driven products in the Event Leadership field is significant. According to *The Profile of Event Management* (International Special Events Society, 1999), over 90 percent of event professionals regularly use cellular technology. Due to the mobility of the Event Leadership field, the cell phone is an indispensable tool. However, what about the potential use for event guests?

In Japan, firms are testing the use of WAP technologies to improve networking among guests attending events. By having the event organizer or guests themselves preprogram the guests's cell phones with vital demographic information, WAP technology enables event guests to quickly identify others with similar interests within a few feet of the venue space. Imagine walking into a reception, and as you approach a guest, your cell phone vibrates. You glance quickly at the cell phone screen and see the message "buyer" and can connect instantaneously as seller and buyer. Furthermore, all critical buying information is downloaded via the Internet to the expanded computer memory within your cell phone.

Indeed, WAP technology is going to make connecting with others locally and globally easier, faster, more cost-efficient, and ultimately more profitable. One excellent source for WAP information is *www.openmobilealliance.org.*

Career-Advancement Connections

Global Connection

Developments in technology are rapidly erasing geographical borders in the global event industry. Event Leadership companies conduct registration, planning, control, and supervision of the events over the Internet. An Event Leadership company located in the United States can produce an event in Germany, and vice versa, without physically relocating its staff and/or setting up an office. As the Event Leadership industry becomes more competitive, the development of technology will further amplify and accelerate competitive factors.

Technology Connection

In using technology, especially the Internet and other networks, it is important to remember that all processes should be available for all participants. If one of your partners has a very slow Internet connection, the entire network should be designed around this limitation to ensure that the user with the slow connection can receive the same services as others can.

Resource Connection

Cvent.com provides online event marketing, regulations, and data analysis services (*www.cvent.com*). An excellent reference book is *Internet World: Essential Business Tactic for the Net,* by Larry Chase and Eileen Shulock (Wiley, 1998).

Learning Connection

Your Event Leadership organization is about to acquire a small Event Leadership company with inadequate technology resources. You are assigned to manage the technology transition. Prepare a checklist describing possible high-risk areas in technological integration that your organization may face during and after the acquisition.

Temple University event students at the PCMA Annual Convention "Student Day" event represent the future of the industry.

CHAPTER 13

Career Development, Advancement, and Sustainable Success

In This Chapter You Will Learn How To:

✦ Advance your Event Leadership career through formal and informal education

✦ Gain more professional experience to build your résumé

✦ Become a Certified Special Event Professional (CSEP)

✦ Earn the credentials you need for employment, promotion, and long-term success

✦ Build both a life and a career

Following 12 years of sustained economic growth in North America, the economy began to slow in the third quarter of 2001 and finally ground to a halt immediately after the tragedy of September 11. Although there were early signs of life as world leaders encouraged people to travel and support the economy, consumer confidence continued to decline in the first quarter of 2002. Finally, following a series of macroeconomic shocks (including anthrax attacks; the nervousness of going to war in Iraq; the fear surrounding the Washington, DC, snipers; the actual declaration of war with Iraq; and finally the development of SARS in Asia and then later in North America), some realities began to come into focus. One of these realities is rising unemployment.

Most of the economists and business leaders in the hospitality and tourism industry predict that the slow economy will continue for the short term. Therefore, you may be asking: What does this mean in terms of my career future? Will I be able to find employment? Will I be able to find job security? Will I be able to find career-advancement opportunities? The answer to each of these questions is resoundingly affirmative.

Despite the uncertainty of the current economy, several factors are, in fact, very certain. First, the world population is aging. In the United States, nearly 70 million people will turn 50 by 2010. As individuals age, so do their institutions and organizations. Therefore, the need to hold more life-cycle celebrations (birthdays, anniversaries, bar and bat mitzvahs) grows accordingly. Second, experiential marketing has become the marketing channel of choice for many if not most sellers of services and markets. As one example, *Sports Illustrated* magazine invested several million dollars in 2003 to promote its publication with a series of events produced by Jack Morton Worldwide. Third and finally, the rapid expansion of technology has actually resulted in the development of more live events as individuals of common interest meet on the Internet and then seek to meet in person to conduct business. As a result of these and many other positive signs, job growth in the hospitality, tourism, and event sectors is expected to increase rapidly. In fact, many economists believe that this field will be one of most demanded in the future.

In order to benefit from this future growth, Event Leaders must continually develop their skill sets and gain as much related experience as possible. Fortunately, there are innumerable opportunities to do this.

Education

Only a few years ago, education was considered to be a minor requirement for employment as an Event Leadership professional. I remember participating in the first meeting designed to develop questions for the Certified Special Events Professional (CSEP) examination. I argued that the questions should be more rigorous. The professional educators attending this meeting reminded me that, because there was so little formal education in the field at that time, it might be difficult for even experienced Event Leaders to pass the test.

A few months later, a brave group of industry veterans sat for the first CSEP examination. They literally trembled as they walked into the examination room. Although combined they represented hundreds of years of professional experience, none had the benefit of formal education in the special events field. Today, the landscape is dramatically different. According to studies conducted by Temple University, 172 colleges and universities throughout the world offer curriculum, certificates, and/or degrees in the Event Leadership–related studies field (see Appendix 2). These courses include:

- Advertising
- Anthropology
- Art
- Beverage management
- Business administration
- Catering
- Communications
- Culinary
- Design
- Education
- Floral
- Folklore
- Hospitality
- Hotel
- Information systems and information technology
- Law
- Museum studies
- Music
- Political science
- Public relations
- Recreation
- Sport management
- Television
- Theater
- Tourism
- Travel
- Web design and management

In addition to these related fields of studies, many colleges and universities offer specific programs in the field of Event Leadership. Temple University, The George Washington University, the University of Nevada at Las Vegas, and other universities offer concentrations in special events, entertainment, and meetings and expositions. Northeastern State University in Tahlequah, Oklahoma, may have been the first college in the United States to offer specialization in the field of meeting planning and destination management. In addition, several colleges and universities throughout the world have adopted The George Washington University Certificate Program, so it is now possible to receive standardized training in this field in many different parts of the world as well as the United States. In 2005, Temple University, School of Tourism launched a comprehensive industry certificate program leading to six interrelated event fields.

This growth in formal education for Event Leaders may be compared to the related field of information technology. In both areas of expertise, specific skills are required to ensure that high-quality performance is achieved consistently over time. However, unlike information technology, Event Leaders must also master the critical human resource skills essential for working effectively in teams. This dimension adds challenge and opportunity for educators as they work to develop a standardized field of study similar to that of medicine, law, accounting, or public relations.

Since over 60 percent of event professionals have earned a bachelor's degree and nearly 10 percent have a postgraduate degree, it may be assumed that professionals in this field are highly educated compared to the general working population in the United States. This means that those entering this competitive profession should expect to have a formal education plus experience in order to succeed. Increasingly, a major part of this formal education is specialized in the area of Event Leadership studies.

A Body of Knowledge

Organizations such as the Convention Industry Council, the International Association for Exhibition Management, and the International Special Events Industry have identified specific bodies of knowledge within their industry sector. This knowledge is encapsulated in the certification programs that each organization has developed. While the body of knowledge varies according to the organization, generally each of these fields includes knowledge in these domains:

- ✦ Administration
  - ✦ Communications
  - ✦ Financial planning, management, and analysis
  - ✦ Information technology
  - ✦ Organizational development
  - ✦ Scheduling
  - ✦ Tax liabilities and regulations
  - ✦ Time management
    - ✦ Strategic planning
- ✦ Coordination
  - ✦ Amenities
  - ✦ Advertising
  - ✦ Awards
  - ✦ Catering
  - ✦ Décor
  - ✦ Entertainment
  - ✦ Etiquette
  - ✦ Human resource management
    - ✦ Conflict resolution
    - ✦ Staff recruiting, training, supervision, and reward
    - ✦ Volunteer recruiting, training, supervision, and reward
  - ✦ International customs
  - ✦ Lighting
  - ✦ Parking
  - ✦ Prizes
  - ✦ Protocol
  - ✦ Sound
  - ✦ Speakers
- ✦ Strategic management
- ✦ Transportation
- ✦ Venues
- ✦ Marketing
  - ✦ Advertising
  - ✦ Analysis
  - ✦ Assessment
  - ✦ Conflict resolution
  - ✦ Evaluation
  - ✦ Negotiation
  - ✦ Planning
  - ✦ Promotion
  - ✦ Proposal development and writing
  - ✦ Public relations
  - ✦ Sales
  - ✦ Sponsorship
  - ✦ Strategic marketing
  - ✦ Stunts
- ✦ Risk management
  - ✦ Assessment
  - ✦ Compliance
  - ✦ Contracts
  - ✦ Financial impacts
  - ✦ Insurance
  - ✦ Licensing
  - ✦ Management
  - ✦ Permits
  - ✦ Planning
  - ✦ Safety
  - ✦ Security

In addition to these broad categories, each specialized field emphasizes additional requirements, such as exhibit planning and management, hotel and convention center negotiation, and catering. However, through consolidation, perhaps there will soon be an era of unprecedented collaboration among the various industry subfields. Event Leadership should, in my opinion, adopt the model generated by medicine many years ago. Event Leaders should be trained as general practitioners (such as the CSEP program), then earn additional certifications as specialists in individual fields. With this model, clients and employers worldwide will be able to use a global standard for Event Leadership training and identify specialists who have advanced training in certain areas.

Education and Your Event Leadership Career

Obviously, it is important for you to obtain a strong general studies education at the undergraduate and perhaps graduate levels. In addition to general studies, you may wish to focus your education in areas where the majority of Event Leaders have earned degrees (business administration, education, and tourism, in that order).

Increasingly, Event Leadership professionals are earning advanced credentials, such as professional certificates in events, meetings, expositions, and related fields. The professional certificate is often more valued by industry employers because it represents a specialized body of knowledge that is immediately useful to organizations that employ event professionals. Therefore, to be successful, it is important for Event Leaders to understand both the theory and practice of Event Leadership. To sustain your career, you should carefully design an educational blueprint from which to construct your future career. This blueprint should include a thorough understanding of the history and theory of the profession, skill training, and practical observation and application. A model blueprint for developing your Event Leadership education follows.

- ✦ *General studies education:* arts and sciences, business administration (observation/ internship)
- ✦ *Postgraduate education:* business administration, tourism, Event Leadership (practical training/externship)
- ✦ *Executive development:* certificate in Event Leadership, meetings, expositions, or related field (observation/externship)
- ✦ *Certification:* CSEP, Certified Meeting Professional, or other respected industry certification program (practical training)
- ✦ *Continuing industry education:* through professional associations, such as the International Special Events Society (ISES), Meeting Professionals International, and others (observation/practice)

In addition to this formal education, successful Event Leaders combine classroom experience with extensive practical training. Our students at Temple University have benefited from internships and externships ranging from small Event Leadership consulting organizations to the Olympic Games. They have coordinated expositions for up to 40,000 people and have observed small social events. Every opportunity has provided a rich learning experience for these professionals. I strongly suggest that you invest a minimum of 15 to 30 hours per year observing or practicing under the aegis of another event organization. By observing the best (and sometimes worst) practices of others, you will find that the educational theory and skills you studied earlier will synthesize into a new foundation for future success.

Professional Experience

Finding a worthwhile internship or externship can be a daunting task, especially for a newcomer to the industry. First, it is important to understand the difference between internship and externship. Generally, *internship* is used to describe a supervised experience that an undergraduate or graduate student affiliated with a college or university receives while earning academic credit. *Externship* refers to the practical experience that a senior professional employed in the Event Leadership industry receives in an organization other than his or her own.

Internships and externships should both include a blend of observation and practice. One of the earliest descriptions of formal education is that provided by the philosopher Socrates, who described the educational process as including observation and questioning. Using the Socratic method, you should find outstanding organizations or individuals or both, observe them, ask lots of questions, and then draw your own conclusions from this experience. In the best scenario, your industry teachers or mentors will simultaneously question and challenge you (just as Socrates did with his protégés in ancient Greece).

Finding an Internship or Externship

One of the easier ways to identify a high-quality practical training opportunity is through a formal institution of learning, such as a college or university. Another way is through professional networking in an industry organization. Using the auspices of a college or university may provide you with additional credibility for obtaining a high-quality practicum experience. In fact, a professor of Event Leadership studies can help you open doors that were closed to you heretofore. Many Event Leadership employers may even be suspicious of persons who wish to engage in a practicum for fear that this is merely a ploy to steal ideas for use in their own companies. Therefore, the intervention of a college professor or mentor can provide an employer with reassurance that the practicum experience is required for graduation and that students will be supervised to ensure proper ethical behavior.

Once you have identified an appropriate practical experience, you should send the potential supervisor a one-page brief description of the observations, experiences, and outcomes you desire from this experience. Figure 13.1 is an example of such a document.

Some internships are paid, others include a small stipend, a few provide living expenses, and still others provide no compensation or expenses. You must determine the best setting for your needs and whether compensation is required. If you are an Event Leader who is providing a practical training opportunity, it is important to remember that U.S. labor laws prohibit displacing a paid employee with an unpaid intern. Therefore, Event Leadership and other employers may use interns to support staff but should not utilize them as a means of displacing current employees to reduce expenses.

During the internship or externship, you should exhibit good work habits (e.g., attendance, punctuality, dress) and conduct yourself in a highly ethical manner. For example, it is important to ask your supervisor about proprietary information and then to abide

Date

Dear Employer, Supervisor, etc.:

Your organization is one of the most respected in the special events industry and, therefore, I am requesting the opportunity to receive a practical training experience under your auspices. The training will require the following commitment from your organization:

1. Five to ten hours per week on-site at your place of business, observing your operations

2. Participation in practical experiences you design for me to enhance my learning experience

3. Your supervision of my practical training

4. Completion of a brief form evaluating my performance at the end of my practical training

5. Submission by your firm of a letter of recommendation for me (if appropriate) to assist me in career development

I will be contacting you in a few days to discuss this opportunity, and I thank you in advance for your consideration of this request.

Sincerely,

Jane Event Manager

cc: Dr. Joe Goldblatt, CSEP, Senior Lecturer, Executive Director for Professional Development and Strategic Partnerships, Temple University School of Tourism and Hospitality Management, Philadelphia, Pennsylvania.

Figure 13.1 Proposal for Practical Experience Opportunity

absolutely by his or her requests for confidentiality. Finally, remember that you are there primarily to learn from these people, who are more experienced than you. Therefore, refrain from offering unsolicited advice. Instead, carefully write down instructions, observations, and other notes in a journal to help you document what you are learning. At the same time, note any questions and then ask for time with your supervisor to probe him or her with questions concerning any areas of the practicum where you need further clarification.

At the end of the practicum experience, both you and your supervisor should have a debriefing session to evaluate the practicum. The supervisor should complete forms describing your attendance, punctuality, performance, and learning capacity, as well as write a letter of recommendation for use with future employers. You should promptly write a thank-you letter to the supervisor expressing your appreciation for this unique opportunity.

A good practicum experience requires the commitment of both a generous supervisor and a curious and loyal student. When you plan this experience carefully, you will find that you have not only established a rich learning opportunity but built a lifelong connection with mentors who will encourage your success.

Certification

Professional certification is the sign of professions that have matured and seek a uniform standard to ensure consistent levels of excellence. Most professional certification programs, such as Certified Public Accountant, were developed early in the twentieth century. One of the reasons for the development of industry standards and certification was to limit the role of government in licensing emerging professions. The Event Leadership industry has followed this historic pattern.

The International Special Events Society established the Certified Special Events Professional (CSEP) certification program based on the empirical studies conducted by the Canadian government. ISES elected to consolidate the Event Manager and Event Coordinator into one comprehensive vocation titled Event Manager or Special Event Professional.

According to the Canadian government and the ISES certification committee, the vocation of Event Leadership requires competence in four knowledge domains. These represent the body of knowledge in the field of Event Leadership and, therefore, require a high degree of competence in administration, coordination, marketing, and risk management. ISES further ratified the findings of the Canadians by stating that the critical path for the production of a professional event required administration, followed by coordination, succeeded by marketing, and then finally reduction of exposure through well-developed risk management.

Today, over 100 persons worldwide hold the title of Certified Special Events Professional (CSEP). To obtain this difficult and challenging designation, they must exhibit a high degree of professional experience, formal education, and service to the industry and pass a three-part examination process. The CSEP is the most rigorous examination in the Event Leadership industry, and those who earn this designation are considered to be the preeminent practitioners in the industry. You should aspire to join their growing ranks. I often point to the example of doctors as one reason why it is so important to ensure that professional Event Leaders function at a consistently high level. Doctors have the ability to save lives but also lose lives one person at a time. Event Leaders, by contrast, can save or lose hundreds or thousands of lives at one event, depending on their level of training, experience, and that illusive quality called judgment. Therefore, the Event Leader, in my opinion, has an even higher degree of responsibility than doctors. In addition, Event Leaders often organize seminars or educational programs that train current and future doctors, so our responsibility extends into their profession as well.

How to Become a CSEP

The CSEP affirms that you have achieved the highest level of training, experience, and recognition by your peers in the Event Leadership industry. This recognition is achieved in three steps:

1. Enroll in the CSEP program through ISES ([800] 688-ISES or *www.ises.com*).
2. Obtain a minimum of 35 points through service to the industry, education, and experience.
3. Pass the CSEP exam.

ISES provides a form to assist you in documenting your points to submit to ISES staff for review and approval. ISES also provides study materials (including this textbook) to help you prepare for the CSEP examination. The CSEP exam consists of three parts. Part 1 comprises 100 multiple-choice questions drawn directly from the *International Dictionary of Event Management,* Second Edition (Wiley, 2000). These terms represent the vocabulary of the profession. Two hours is allowed for this exam. Part 2 is an essay-style exam in which you are given a choice of two case studies and are required to use the CSEP blueprint of administration, coordination, marketing, and risk management to develop a theoretical event. The exam may be completed by hand or using a personal computer. The time allowed for part 2 is four hours. Part 3 of the examination process is the submission of a professional portfolio documenting that you have produced a professional event during the previous two years. Extensive guidelines are provided to aid in the development and preparation of the portfolio.

The exams are reviewed by academics in the field of Event Leadership studies as well as other Certified Special Event Professionals. Using a blind review process, each exam is marked by a panel of three industry professionals and/or academics, and the results are forwarded to the certification committee for validation. Successful certification candidates are notified by ISES by certified mail that they have now joined the ranks of the preeminent leaders in the special events industry. Many new CSEPs remark that, when they receive the envelope with their name listed "Jane Event Leader, CSEP," it is one of the proudest moments of their professional lives.

Recertification

Many certification programs require that certified leaders be recertified every few years to ensure that they are currently engaged in the industry and that they remain knowledgeable about developments in the field. The process for recertification typically requires documentation of education, experience, and service to the industry. The CSEP program requires recertification every five years after the initial certification has been granted.

Credentials

I am often asked by prospective students to quantify the value of a master's degree versus a certificate. Typically, the questioner asks: "What do I need to be successful in Event Leadership—a certificate or a master's degree?" The question automatically assumes that credentials or third-party validation is important to success in the special events industry. This is a correct assumption. Although it has not always been the case, the facts clearly indicate that, in the U.S. economy, those who have credentials earn more, are promoted more often, and enjoy more economic and career opportunities than those who do not have appropriate credentials.

The type of credential you earn depends largely on which sector of the events industry you decide to enter. For example, in the government and education sectors, it is generally known that the education you attain affects the promotion or appointment by salary grade, whereas in the association sector, although education is important, it is also acceptable to obtain certification to demonstrate your training, competence, and experience level. However, in the corporate sector, increasingly, it is not unusual to find MBAs who are responsible for coordinating major events.

Bill Morton, chairman and chief executive officer of Jack Morton Worldwide, the world's largest Event Leadership firm, once told me that his firm actively recruited MBA students from leading business schools for senior management positions. He explained that the blend of strategic thinking skills, marketing analysis and execution, and financial management training and experience helped his firm ensure that strong management leaders would sustain and advance the mission of the 60-year-old firm.

It is interesting that Morton did not mention the need for experience in Event Leadership as a prerequisite for appointment as a leader in his firm. In fact, Event Leadership experience, although important, is not essential to succeed in many organizations today. What is essential is proof or evidence that you are competent to advance the goals and objectives of your employer. Increasingly, employers are turning to third-party organizations, such as colleges, universities, and certification organizations, to vouch for this competence.

When I give references for student Event Leadership programs, potential employers ask the typical questions about persistence, punctuality, and intellectual capacity. However, ever more frequently, they ask questions about the ability of the candidate to work in a team, to communicate, and to lead an organization to accomplish specific goals and objectives. Although it is difficult to quantify, much less rate, these abilities, employers count on them to determine if the person they will hire will succeed quickly after he or she is appointed. This is another reason why it is important to obtain a credential. Behind every credential are people who tested, assessed, and can vouch for the integrity, persistence, communications, and leadership abilities of the person holding the credential. Whether they are former professors, industry certifiers, or even internship supervisors, each one has had a prolonged, intimate, and objective opportunity to evaluate the candidate. For this reason alone, it is important to earn a credential, for with it comes references and contacts that will help you gain employment and promotion.

So you may ask what credential is most valuable. The simple answer is: all of them. I recommend that you determine what your industry sector demands in terms of a credential and, as soon as you earn it, begin exploring how you can earn the next credential. In today's competitive global business environment, you must demonstrate your competence continually. Whether you are in Asia, the Americas, Europe, Africa, or other parts of the world, governments as well as nongovernmental organizations are developing higher standards for Event Leaders. For example, the governments of Great Britain, South Africa, and Australia have joined Canada in developing standards for Event Leadership professionals. These standards require high levels of professional education as well as experience. Therefore, to compete in the global Event Leadership industry, you must continually seek the credentials that future employers demand to ensure your long-term success in this growing field.

Power Tools

Once you have mapped your journey, you need transportation tools to ensure that you arrive speedily at your destination. Historically, the most powerful tools have been the résumé and cover letter. I recommend that you follow these 10 steps to best apply these tools:

1. Create a preliminary list of employers who have (or are likely to have) open positions in your field.
2. From this short list of 25 to 50 people, create a computer database using Access, Filemaker Pro, or a similar contact program.
3. Send a cover letter to each contact as shown in Figure 13.2. Customize the letter for each organization based on the homework you have completed to learn about the person and the organization's strengths.
4. Wait two weeks after the letter has been mailed, and then call each contact between 7 and 9 A.M. or between 5 and 7 P.M. These are the best times to reach your contact directly without interception by an administrative assistant.
5. When you reach the contact, reintroduce yourself and assume that the person has received your letter. ("I am calling about the letter I sent you requesting a personal interview.")
6. Ask for an interview at one or two specific times. ("Could we meet in person or by telephone on Tuesday at 10 A.M. or Thursday at 4 P.M.?")
7. If the contact agrees to meet with you in person or by telephone, thank the person immediately and reconfirm in writing via e-mail or other correspondence.
8. If the person refuses to see you, ask if there are others whom you should see or other organizations that could benefit from your skills to which the person can refer you. Get at least three to five referrals. Add these names to your database.
9. If you confirmed the meeting in person or by telephone, conduct further research about the organization so that you are prepared to ask pertinent questions.
10. During the personal interview session, do not offer your résumé unless requested. Instead, show your portfolio of an event or events that you have produced. Conclude the session by asking directly: "What would be necessary for me to earn the opportunity to work for your outstanding organization?" Do not speak again until the contact tells you specifically what is necessary to earn the job.

Finding a great job in this field is a combination of timing, persistence, and talent. Timing is the most illusive part of the equation because rarely is a job created specifically for you. Instead, you have to wait until a position needs to be filled. This is why persistence is important. You may wish to create a postcard that has your photograph and a few lines about your experience, skills, and credentials, and mail this to your contact list on the same date each month as a reminder of your interest in working for them. Personalize

Date

Name

Title

Organization name

Address

City, state, postal code

Dear (Ms., Mr., Dr.),

Dr. Joe Goldblatt, CSEP (or other person whose name will be immediately recognized by the employer), referred me to you to request a personal interview about your outstanding organization. Your organization is one of the leading organizations in this field and I would like to learn more about your unique attributes in this rapidly growing field. (Use research to customize this paragraph with a concluding sentence such as "For over _____ years, your organization has provided _____ to clients and I am impressed with your excellent reputation in the industry.)

    I am currently completing my (degree, certificate, or other credential) in the Event Leadership field (or I have been employed as a professional Event Leader for over _____ years) and am confident that my training, experience, and contacts can be of great benefit to your organization. Therefore, I am requesting a personal interview to explore future opportunities in this profession.

    This interview may be conducted in person at your office or by telephone at a time that is convenient to you. In that regard, I will telephone you in the next week to determine the best date and time for you to conduct this interview. Thank you for your interest, and I look forward to speaking with you soon.

Sincerely,

Jane Event Manager

P.S. Dr. Joe Goldblatt, CSEP (or other referral) sends his best regards. I look forward to speaking with you soon and sincerely appreciate your time and interest.

Figure 13.2 Model Cover Letter

the card with a handwritten note that says: "I am writing further to indicate my interest in working for your outstanding organization. Please let me know if there is an opportunity to work with you in the near future."

    The postcard technique has been highly effective with my students for the last decade, as the tenure of employees in an organization has shrunk from two and one-half years to less than one year. During a period of full employment, employers are constantly on the lookout for capable people able to start work immediately. Your postcard may arrive at just the right moment and, instead of conducting a formal search for candidates, the

Résumé
Jane Event Manager, CSEP
1234 Main Street
Celebration, Florida
Telephone: (304) 544-1234
E-mail: jem@eventsrus.net

Career Objective

To assist a leading event organization to achieve high quality and rapid growth through my contributions as an Event Leadership professional.

Professional Experience

- Managed a 2000-person health-care exposition with a budget of $150,000 in March 2000
- Coordinated a 500-person legal conference with a budget of $50,000 in September 1999
- Developed and managed a 50-person executive education retreat with a budget of $19,000 in July 1999

Related Experience

- Conceived and coordinated a 1000-person community festival with a budget (including in-kind contributions) of $50,000 in Spring 1999
- Led a 25-person event planning workshop/retreat with a budget of $1,000 for the purpose of organizing an annual conference for a community-services organization

Volunteer Experience

- Founded a 500-person bazaar with 50 exhibitors and a budget of $500 for Holy Name Church
- Created and managed a 250-person banquet for Cub Scout Awards with a budget of $1,200
- Organized and managed a 100-person fundraising walking event for AIDS prevention with a budget of $3,000

Education and Training

- Candidate to receive the George Washington University Professional Certificate in Event Management (May 2001)
- Recipient of the George Washington University Master of Tourism Administration, Concentration in Event Management, degree (May 2000)
- Certified Special Event Professional (1995, recertified 2000)

Awards and Recognition

- International Special Events Society Volunteer of the Year, 2000
- Dean's List, Johnson Wales University, 2001
- Employee of the Month, Regent Hotel, May 1997

Technology Skills

Access, computer-assisted drawing, Excel, Word, World Wide Web, Web design (HTML)

Languages

Spanish (high verbal and written)
Portuguese (moderate verbal and written)
French (low to moderate verbal)

References

Available upon request

Figure 13.3 Model Résumé
Note: Résumé should not exceed one page.

employer may telephone you to interview for the job. You have already shown interest, enthusiasm, organization, and persistence, and these are qualities that employers value. You have also made the company's job easier by helping it find you quickly.

The two critical tools, the résumé and the cover letter, must be consistent with the standards used traditionally in the Event Leadership field. Figures 13.2 and 13.3 provide models for you to use in the future.

The purpose of the résumé and the cover letter is to reduce to writing the impression you will make in person. These important tools rarely help you obtain a job unless they are supported by a good reference, your homework about the organization, and, most important, the impression you make in person. I strongly suggest that you work with a career coach through a local university or college or someone in private practice to help you optimize your abilities when you are ready to make that all-important first impression.

Life and Career

Too often, Event Leadership professionals build a successful career and at the same time risk ruining their personal lives. Although mental and physical stress are not unique to the events industry, the constant demand for creativity, innovation, and the increasing speed of delivery can cause Event Leadership professionals to literally burn the candle at both ends until exhaustion and illness require professional intervention.

Recently, a leader in the festival industry grew irritated with me when I explained that many of the generation described by demographers as cuspers or busters do not want to work a traditional workweek of five eight-hour days. Instead, according to research, many prefer to work a shorter workweek with longer workdays. The reason for this major paradigm shift is the recognition that the seven-day workweek of preceding generations ultimately led to rapid burnout. In protest, the cuspers and busters choose to work a shorter number of days and a longer number of hours per day. This schedule permits them to separate work and leisure activity and grants them longer weekends (three days as opposed to one). Furthermore, they prefer to separate work from leisure in order to fully enjoy recreation, culture, and other activities.

Perhaps there is a lesson to be learned here—or several lessons. In an age defined by technology, it is often difficult to escape from the world of work. Therefore, to find a life in addition to a career, one must be ever vigilant about understanding the difference between these two values. Experts in leisure study define work as the absence of leisure. However, for work to be enjoyable, it must be rewarding and fulfilling. Therefore, to sustain life and career, it is important to understand the nuances that define the difference between each of these two similar but different states of being.

Because the special events industry is perceived by guests as "a fun business," practitioners often forget that, in fact, this is the business of fun. As a business it requires hard work, persistence, and talent. Each of these tasks is bound to deplete your energy. You must replenish this expenditure of energy with a healthy lifestyle that includes proper exercise, nutrition, and spiritual nourishment. This replenishment is essential if you are going to experience both the joy of work and the joie de vivre (joy of life).

From Invention to Reinvention

To achieve long-term career success, it is important to develop a historical perspective of careers in this field. Compared to other more established professions, such as medicine and law, the relatively new profession of Event Leadership is better positioned as a career for long-term sustainability and growth. At the turn of the twentieth century, Event Leaders were unknown despite the fact that many events, including world's fairs and expositions, were produced in abundance. Like many modern professions, Event Leadership began as a craft that was learned through an informal apprentice system. However, in the 1930s, pioneers such as Jack Morton and Howard Lanin used their organizational skills in music and personnel management to conduct successful social and later corporate events. As events grew in size in the 1960s (Woodstock, Hemisphere in San Antonio), there developed a need for specialists to plan and manage these large-scale events. Specialists with experience in film, television, writing, music, and public relations/communications, such as the late Robert Jani, Tommy Walker, and David Wolper, used their skills to produce many of the marquee events of the twentieth century. These events included the opening and closing ceremonies of the Los Angeles Olympic Games in 1984, the Knoxville and New Orleans world's fairs, the 100th Anniversary of the Statue of Liberty, the inauguration of President Ronald Reagan, and the ubiquitous Super Bowl Halftime Spectaculars throughout the 1980s.

This telling story from David Wolper's autobiography, *Producer* (Scribner, 2003), summarizes the newness of this field. Peter Ueborroth, president of the Los Angeles Olympic Games Organizing Committee, invited Wolper to lunch and asked him to produce the opening and closing ceremonies of the 1984 Olympic Games. Wolper discussed it with his wife and she asked, "Do you know how to do something like that?" Although he had attended three previous Olympics and had received numerous awards for television and film production, he had not produced events of the magnitude of the Olympic Games opening and closing ceremonies. He spent the night convincing himself and the next day accepted the job.

As the twentieth century came to a close, the demand for trained, experienced Event Leaders grew largely due to the need for professionals who could fill the positions that were being created in this new field. For example, in the early 1990s, there were few classified ads listed under the heading of Event Manager, Event Coordinator, or Director of Special Events. However, by the end of the century, several ads appeared under these headings on a daily basis.

Through the development of formal education programs such as Temple University's School of Tourism Event Leadership Executive Certificate Program, The George Washington University Event Management Certificate and Master's Degree Program (and their licensees throughout the world), Leeds Metropolitan University Diploma in Events Management and Great Britain Center for Events Management, Northeastern Oklahoma University's Destination and Meeting Management Program, the University of Nevada at Las Vegas Tourism and Convention Administration Program, The University of Technology, Sydney, Australian Center for Event Management, and, most recently, Johnson &

Wale University's Master of Business Administration (MBA) degree concentration in Event Leadership, thousands of students throughout the world are learning prescribed systems for leading events toward success.

As a result of the rapid development of this field, many of the early pioneers may shake their heads in amazement at how far the profession has come. While the first generation of Event Leaders (Bacon, Jani, Morton, Walker, Wolper, and others) may be amazed at the progress the field has made in such a short time, the current generation of educators is hopeful that, through formal education, the profession will become better respected by the general public and will encourage sustainable careers.

I characterize three periods of economic growth of this profession: First was the age of the practitioners (those who learned by doing), which was roughly from 1930 to 1980. Next came the age of the educators (those who have learned through a combination of formal education coupled with guided experience in the field), which covers the period of 1980 to the present day. However, now as we are on the cusp of the second 50 years of this young profession, we are entering the age that will be dominated by Event Leaders.

In the first edition of *Special Events,* I interviewed David L. Wolper and asked him how he was able to motivate 100,000 people during the closing ceremonies of the Los Angeles Olympic Games in 1984 to spontaneously join hands and sing "Reach Out and Touch (Somebody's Hand)" (Ashford & Simpson with vocals by Diana Ross), and he told me that a producer must "know how to use special events to produce specific emotions in people. As a producer, I know how to invoke laughter, tears, joy, and, of course, love."

Nearly 15 years after that interview, Wolper wrote his biography, which charts his successful career as one of the preeminent producers of the twentieth century. According to Wolper, "The producer is the man or woman with the dream." Wolper examines his many successes as a producer from television's *Roots,* to the 100th anniversary of the Statue of Liberty, through *Liberty Weekend,* to hundreds of other television spectaculars and special events. In fact, Wolper's work created the term *special event television.* In his own words:

> I have been successful as a producer primarily because I had the natural ability to recognize a good idea, whether it came from my mind, or someone else's. I could sell the idea: I worked as hard as I asked anyone working for me to work to bring it to fruition. I was not afraid to take risks to achieve quality, and maybe just as important, I hired good people and gave them all the responsibility they could handle. I was always there in the background. I was never afraid to dive in and get dirty, but I had the good fortune to find great people and recognize their talent. And with my banking experience, I knew finance, so I could build a company. I was the orchestra conductor who picked the music. I was the cook who mixed the ingredients. And I was the judge who made the decisions. I picked the people who worked from my documentary company. I picked the right people when I created the ceremonies for the Olympics (1984 Los Angeles Olympic Games). I picked the right people to make Roots. I suspect that not one of the hundreds of people who worked for a Wolper company would state that I was an easy person to work for; I wasn't. I demanded quality.

Event Leaders must now embrace the traditions and educational opportunities of the past 50 years while simultaneously using their strategic planning skills to chart a course for the future of the profession. This merger of practice, theory, and the ability to balance life and career will be essential as Event Leaders address the many new and unknown challenges in the new world.

As Event Leaders, it is important that we lead, but also record, remember, and celebrate the triumphs, joys, and even sorrows of our lives. You are responsible for leading this effort. You are a modern pioneer destined to explore, expand, and improve the global event management industry in the twenty-first century. The global technological revolution we have created can hollow us, or hallow us, depending on how we embrace it. I prefer to use the metaphor that the twentieth-century scientist Albert Einstein envisioned when describing his theory of relativity. Einstein wrote that "science without religion is lame and religion without science is blind." He envisioned that, one day, he would be able to ride a laser beam of light into the twenty-first century; indeed, his theories and ideas continue to challenge and illuminate us today. Einstein continues to ride into the future taking us along with him, as our dreams become realities, just as his theories became scientific fact.

Sometimes a lamplighter must turn his or her light toward dark places to provide greater illumination or all. Mandla Mentoor is one example of this practice with the work he is doing in Soweto, South Africa. Mentoor, a community activist, has taken one of the most impoverished areas in South Africa and helped transform it into a tourism destination by using events featuring local artisans and performers to attract economic development. Describing himself as the founder, member, and director of the Soweto Mountain of Hope, Mentoor has proven that lives and places may be transformed through events. However, numerous other lamplighters in many of the dark corners of our world are also bringing illumination through events.

On the morning of August 29, 2006, Hurricane Katrina entered the American lexicon as this category 3 storm roared into the Mississippi Gulf Coast of the United States. The communities affected by Hurricane Katrina were devastated. New Orleans, Louisiana, once the crown tourism jewels in world tourism and hospitality, lost one-half of its population as people were left homeless, fled, or, worse, died as a result of this catastrophe.

In the third edition of *Special Events* I invited my cousin, Eva Barkoff, who is a columnist for the *New Orleans Times Picayune* daily newspaper, to write the foreword. Eva listed all of the many celebrations that are held in New Orleans and throughout the Gulf Coast region, not the least of which is Mardi Gras. She reminded us that events are often about families and communities coming together through food, music, and celebration. She also stated that our roots are often formed and strengthened through these milestone celebrations.

Eva and my other cousins in the New Orleans area were driven from their homes as a result of Hurricane Katrina. Many of them have now rebuilt their homes and have returned to some form of normalcy. Due to Hurricane Katrina and Hurricane Wilma, which soon followed, significant time and resources will be required before there ever is true normalcy in the region.

However, one family demonstrated celebrations that must continue regardless of the challenges associated with daily life. The Shea family's daughter, Rhyan Shea, had planned her dream wedding in New Orleans one year before Hurricane Katrina destroyed much of the city.

According to the knot (*www.theknot.com*), perhaps the most popular U.S. wedding planning Internet site, 2.5 million weddings in the country annually generate $72 billion. The average budget for a U.S. wedding is $20,000; however, in the Northeast, average budgets can climb to $50,000 and higher.

Like most brides, Rhyan, who lives in Atlanta, Georgia, dreamed of a once-in-a-lifetime event that would provide many years of happy memories for herself and her groom. However, those dreams would take several twists and turns before being fulfilled.

She had flown into New Orleans the weekend Katrina struck to attend a baptism. As the hurricane approached, she did not have any grave concerns because storms and hurricanes are so common in this area. However, when she tried to return to Atlanta through the New Orleans airport, her father said, "I do not think anyone is going into New Orleans." The magnitude of this disaster finally was apparent, and Rhyan spent the next several weeks trying to find lost friends and deal with the additional challenges of the two hurricanes. During this troubling time she did not think very much about her upcoming nuptials.

Rhyan and her mother, Virginia, decided they needed to allow the people of New Orleans, including their vendors, to recover as much as possible before contacting them to determine the viability of going through with their original wedding plans. At the same time, Rhyan said, "We knew we needed to set a deadline to make a decision on our final plans. We chose October 1 (four months prior to the wedding date) as the date by which we must make our final decisions."

According to Rhyan, during post–Hurricane Katrina recovery period, three things helped her maintain patience, calm, and even confidence in the planning process. "First, my mother reassured me that I would be married! Second, we decided to give our vendors in New Orleans time to try and restore some normalcy before we made any final decisions. And finally, as is often our philosophy in southern Louisiana, we decided to 'go with the flow' and be flexible and deal with any new situation that arose." During this same time she also regularly visited the knot Web site to find out what other brides did when weather incidents disrupted their wedding plans.

On February 11, 2006, only five months after the tragedy of Hurricane Katrina, nearly 350 people, including the governor of Louisiana, were dancing on the twenty-third floor of the famed Windsor Court Hotel in New Orleans, Louisiana, as they celebrated Rhyan and Kerby Wheeler's nuptials.

The obstacles that had to be overcome, according to Rhyan, were actually minor ones. They included finding a new limousine company, waiting a little longer to receive the bridesmaids' dresses that had been ordered, and relocating the official wedding family photographs to a new room at the hotel because the original one had been damaged by the hurricane.

After Hurricane Katrina, Hurricanes Rita and Wilma arrived, bringing their own disruption to Rhyan's family and wedding plans. "Hurricane Rita flooded our family business and Hurricane Wilma came through Mexico and forced us to move our honeymoon location from Mexico to St. Martin in the U.S. Virgin Islands." (According to the knot, Americans spend $8 billion per year on honeymoons.) The challenges of a flooded business and relocated honeymoon were minor, says Rhyan, compared to the serious personal and business challenges others in the Gulf Coast region of the United States were experiencing at the same time.

Many of the people involved in the wedding suffered very serious personal losses, including two of her bridesmaids and the wedding coordinator. "I was impressed and very grateful with their fortitude in dealing every day with their own losses, while at the same time helping me move ahead with the plans for our wedding," remembers Rhyan.

However, never once did Virginia or Rhyan seriously consider relocating the wedding. "New Orleans is the city I envisioned for my wedding because I love the energy and culture of the place. Also, it was convenient for Kerby's family who are from Tennessee and my family from Louisiana."

And, perhaps it is worth noting that the Sheas do not actually live in New Orleans. Rather, they make their home in New Iberia, a two-hour drive from the Crescent City.

During the same time as the Shea wedding, the first post–Katrina Mardi Gras parade rolled into the historic French Quarter. During the months following Katrina, there was enormous debate about whether to hold a Mardi Gras celebration that year. The debate grew quite heated with the opposition stating that the costs of the celebration would further injure the city's rebuilding. However, a majority of the residents, including the political leaders, supported the idea of restoring some semblance of normalcy through the Mardi Gras celebration and also the potential for economic injection through new tourism dollars.

Ultimately, city leaders approved a somewhat smaller-than-usual Mardi Gras celebration, and plans soon commenced for the first parade. I stood on Decatur Street in the French Quarter, and despite the unusually cold temperatures, I felt enormous warmth (despite the unseasonably cold temperatures) surrounded by thousands of Mardi Gras revelers who cheered loudly as the floats appeared in the distance, their roars of appreciation representing a true example of joie de vivre. For these survivors, the parade sounded the first trumpets of triumph over the storm for them. Life would go on. This milestone marked the beginning of a new era of celebrations in New Orleans. They had rediscovered their roots.

Whether in Kazakhstan, the Mountains of the Moon in Uganda, or Ayres Rock (Uluru) in Australia, there is a common reason and purpose for perpetuating and growing these celebrations. In my studies with the Batwa Pygmies of Uganda, the aboriginal tribes of Uluru, and other indigenous people throughout the world, I have identified five common motivations for celebration. According to my research findings, human beings celebrate to remember their ancestors, promote kinship within their tribe, demonstrate pride in their culture, and transmit rituals to future generations. However, according to the aboriginal elders I interviewed and whose commentary I researched at the Strehlow Research Center in Ayres Rock, Australia, there is a fifth motivation that may surpass all of the others in terms of power. The aboriginal elders told me that I would perhaps never really understand why these rituals, traditions, and celebrations were so important because, indeed, they were motivated and invested with *magic and mystery*. As one of the elders looked penetratingly into my eyes and revealed this belief to me, I reacted in a suspicious and typically skeptical manner. Although my reaction was motivated by the requirements of scientific inquiry, for the first time in my research, I realized something more important was being revealed to me than mere opinion.

For literally thousands of years traditional people throughout the world have preserved and transmitted their celebrations for a common purpose. There is obviously a reason for this cultivation and transmission of the cultural symbols of celebration. And the reason, I have concluded, is that these celebrations imbue their very lives with meaning. In fact, without these celebrations, people lack reasons for life itself. Anthropologists and sociologists who study linguistics have learned that when a common language is removed from a tribe, the roots of civilization are also destroyed. Celebrations are a common language that is perpetuated and expanded by all people to illuminate their lives.

Perhaps our greatest challenge as Event Leaders is not merely to light the lamps for those who will follow us in this growing industry, but also to shine our lamps into the darker corners of the world and on those who will most benefit from our talents. As you find new places to shine your light in the future, I raise my glass in a celebratory toast to you as you begin or continue your journey in the field of eventology. The celebratory toasts that follow indicate the many global opportunities ahead of you as an Event Leader. May your celebratory roots grow stronger and your wings beat faster as they take you and others further to rapidly advance the global celebrations industry!

- ✦ Afya!/Vifijo! (Swahili)
- ✦ Apki Lambi Umar Ke Liye (Hindi)
- ✦ À votre santé!/Santé! (French)
- ✦ Ba'sal'a'ma'ti! (Farsi)
- ✦ Cheers! (Great Britain)
- ✦ Chook-die!/Sawasdi! (Thai)
- ✦ Egészségedre! (Hungarian)
- ✦ Fee sihetak! (Egyptian)
- ✦ Fi sahik! (Arabic)
- ✦ Gan bei! (Mandarin)
- ✦ Gesondheid! (Afrikaans)
- ✦ Gia'sou (Greek)
- ✦ Hipahipa! (Hawaiian)
- ✦ Kampai! (Japanese)
- ✦ Kippis! (Finnish)
- ✦ Konbe! (Korean)
- ✦ Kong chien! (Chinese)
- ✦ Le'chaim! (Hebrew)
- ✦ Mabuhay! (Tagalog)
- ✦ Minum! (Malaysian)
- ✦ Na zdorov'ya! (Ukranian)

- ✦ Na zdrowie! (Polish)
- ✦ Nazdrave! (Bulgarian)
- ✦ Noroc! (Romanian)
- ✦ Nqa! (Sesotho)
- ✦ Oogy wawa! (Zulu)
- ✦ Prieka! (Latvian)
- ✦ Prost! (German)
- ✦ Prost!/Zum Wohl! (Austrian)
- ✦ Proost! (Dutch)
- ✦ Saha wa'afiab (Moroccan)
- ✦ Salud! (Creole, Spanish)
- ✦ Sanda bashi (Pakistani)
- ✦ Saúde! (Brazilian, Portuguese)
- ✦ Salute!/Cin cin! (Italian)
- ✦ Serefe! (Turkish)
- ✦ Skål! (Danish, Norwegian, Swedish)
- ✦ Sláinte! (Irish Gaelic)
- ✦ Vashe zdorovie! (Russian)
- ✦ Zivjeli! (Bosnian)
- ✦ Zivjeli!/U zdravlje! (Croatian, Serbian)

Note: For more toasts, visit *www.awa.dk/glosary/slainte.htm*.

Epilogue

In the dark days following September 11, 2001, I received a somber call from a family friend. Shelia Campbell, my mentor and friend of 30 years, had died following a long illness. Despite the challenges of flying, I returned to Texas, the state of my birth, to serve as a pallbearer for my longtime friend.

As friends and family gathered from near and far, we told stories about this remarkable woman who had positively influenced so many lives. In my own case, Shelia was directly responsible for me returning to college and completing my undergraduate degree. As a result of her help, today I am able to share my scholarship with others throughout the world.

The morning after the funeral I departed early for the airport. I stopped at a gas station to refuel and when I returned to the car noticed a small brown bird sitting on the passenger seat. Despite my shouts of "shoo, shoo" to encourage the bird to fly away, the bird remained firm. It appeared to look me directly in the eye and with silent language say, "I will never leave you."

A few years later Shelia's grandson Christopher announced his engagement to Courtney, a beautiful young woman (and event planner) from California. During this same period, Christopher's grandfather announced that he had lung cancer. Therefore, this wedding, to be performed in part by Christopher's grandfather, Jeff, a Methodist minister and professor of English for nearly half a century, was very special. Although very ill, Jeff's presence that weekend and his words that day were an inspiration to all. The love returned to their grandfather by Christopher and Courtney spoke volumes about the power of family and ritual.

As my wife and I sat quietly in the chapel awaiting the beginning of the ceremonies, my eye turned to the clear glass panels on the left side of the room. There, high above us, were three small brown birds. One flapped its wings incessantly while the others remained calm. I turned to my wife, pointed at this sight, and reminded her of my experience with the small brown bird immediately following Shelia's funeral. She smiled and nodded her head at me as if to say "She's back."

As this manuscript was in the final stages of preparation, Jeff Campbell succumbed to cancer and other ailments. When I called his family from Tokyo, where I was teaching and conducting research, to offer condolences, they reported that on the morning of his death, Christopher, now working in Minneapolis, saw two birds that suddenly appeared as if to once again affirm "We are here."

And so it goes with the global celebrations industry. Despite unending catastrophes seeking to destroy the very spirit of human beings, we go on. Perhaps the Aboriginal elders and Pygmy leaders understand this better than most as they have overcome so much during their life on earth. And they also know that it is the *magic and mystery* of these celebrations, such as I witnessed in the chapel that day, that give us the courage, stamina, and hope to further advance our lives and indeed all civilization through special events.

Profile in Event Leadership:
Lucky Morimoto and Jin Kawamura

OLD SOULS PRODUCE NEW PROFESSION

The thirteenth through the sixteenth of August is one of the most important times for the people of Japan. It is during this time that the Obon Festival is held, and the Japanese people believe that their ancestors' spirits will return to their homes to be reunited with their loved ones. Two leaders of the modern events industry in Japan are indeed old souls who are separated in age and experience by over 30 years. One is looking toward retirement while the other is looking forward to the role he will play in further advancing his profession. However, they are both united in their passionate desire to listen to their clients and help them have fun and find happiness through well-produced events.

Lucky Morimoto, founder, owner, and president of Event Services Inc., one of the largest event firms in Asia, and his colleague, professional event planner Jin Kawamura, appear to be old souls who have returned to give birth to a new industry in the Land of the Rising Sun and throughout the world. Their colorful Web site (*www.eventservices.co.jp*) proclaims: "We listen. We are serious about fun," and for 26

Lucky Morimoto
Owner, President
Event Services
Tokyo, Japan

Jin Kawamura,
Event Planner
Event Services
Tokyo, Japan

years they have been advancing the modern events industry in Asia and throughout the world.

Morimoto, 68, was a political science major at Waseda University in the 1960s. Upon graduation, he worked for a trading company and then found his true passion in the travel industry. For 16 years he served as tour guide, inbound tour coordinator, and ultimately vice president and outbound tour promoter and conductor for a mid-size travel agency in Tokyo.

During this period, Morimoto guided numerous incentive travel groups from Japan to destinations throughout the world. (Incentive travel is vacation travel arranged by an employer as a motivational bonus for qualifying employees or salespeople.) It was during this period that Morimoto learned that his true calling was using his experience and talent to make others happy.

In 1981 he decided to start his own business to focus exclusively on incentive events. However, he had no clients and, therefore, the business struggled for the first three of four years. "Finally, a major client, the American Family Life Insurance Company (better known as AFLAC) commissioned me to create a series of incentive events in Banff, Canada. The events took place at the Banff Springs Hotel and included about 550 AFLAC employees."

For entertainment he turned to performers from the famed Calgary Stampede (*www.calgarystampede.com*). However, to insure further lively interaction, he conceived the idea of inviting 55 Canadian students who were studying Japanese and inviting them to sit at each table and converse with the Japanese guests in their native language. Lucky offered each student a gift of a Japanese/English dictionary plus dinner for their participation. He did not, however, anticipate that some students might not show up. Much to the frustration of the guests and Lucky, some tables did not have students. Nevertheless, the overall incentive program was a major success, and the guests especially liked Lucky's idea of involving the students. This kind of customization of incentive travel events remains an important element today as does the AFLAC, which has been Lucky's client for 26 years.

According to Jin Kawamura, it is important to ask entertainers to do something new and different that will satisfy the needs of the individual group for which they are performing. For example, in Japan, Cirque de Soleil™ (*www.cirquedesoleil.com*) performers are very popular. Although Japanese people are generally shy and reserved, Jin believes that younger generations want to be amazed and engaged by entertainers at events. This engagement and amazement, according to Jin, may require clients to spend $300 per person or more.

Event Services Inc. bills their clients for the direct services they provide, such as lighting, sound, décor, and entertainment as well as arrangements (planning) and coordination (on site production) fees. Generally in Japan, clients will not pay for a proposal; however,

Lucky states that one client paid four firms $2,000 each to create a comprehensive proposal for a series of events. Although his firm was not selected to produce the events, he was pleased that the client was willing to make the investment to receive a truly comprehensive plan. "In fact, I further invested another $2,000 U.S. dollars to compete for this business."

Jin Kawamura, 38, has a professional background that is quite different from his employer. Raised in Tokyo and later Nagano (home of the 1998 Winter Olympic Games), Kawamura became interested in events as a student. "I was always involved with producing events in my school," he says. His family also organized Olympic Games–style competitions for the family members, and Jin liked to participate. Later, as a young adult, he was selected to be a member of the cast of the internationally acclaimed *Up With People*™ (*www. upwithpeople.org*) performing group. He quickly transitioned from performer to show coordinator, and he, like Lucky, also discovered that his passion was to make people happy through producing live events.

In 2001, Lucky Morimoto ran an advertisement seeking someone who "likes to make people happy," and Jin applied. However, Jin was not selected for the position because Lucky felt that his extensive résumé made him overqualified for what was essentially a position that involved only coordinating rental equipment. Six months later, Lucky once again decided that he really needed a talented professional like Jin and asked him if he was still available. The job position was redefined as an event planner, and Jin accepted the position. According to Jin, "I accepted the position because of the experience and respect Event Services Inc. and especially Lucky himself had established. In addition, Lucky's aspirations and philosophy were similar to my own, and that included producing events all over the world."

(continues)

(continued)

As one example of these opportunities, Jin recently produced an event in Cairns, Australia, in a hotel ballroom. The event theme reinforced the location attributes that included the famed Great Barrier Reef. At this event, guests entered the ballroom and were greeted by dancing sea creatures (actually professional ballet dancers), dramatic underwater lighting effects, aquatic theme music, and even beautiful mermaids.

When asked what this event might look like 10 years into the future, these two old souls provide different responses. Morimoto says, "I never imagined when I began this company 25 years ago that we would be producing events as technologically advanced as we are today. I suppose technology that has yet to be invented will play a larger role in the future of events."

However, Jin's eyes brighten as he peers into the future and says, "We will actually produce these events *under the real sea.* We will find new ways to transport our guests to even greater experiences in the future."

Both Lucky and Jin acknowledge that the modern event industry is first and foremost a team effort. Thanks in large part to the Internet, they are now able to assemble international teams all over the world to produce events. Jin says, "Therefore, it is more important than ever to communicate effectively with the team members using email, facsimile, and most important, face-to-face meetings whenever possible."

Three years ago *Special Events Magazine* selected Event Services Inc. as one of the top 50 event companies in the world. According to Lucky, "This recognition meant a great deal to me as I had such humble beginnings with this business." As the future continues to unfold for Event Services Inc., despite their age and generational differences, both Lucky and Jin share a common passion and commitment to the growing events industry in Asia and throughout the world.

These two old souls are working together and with their event team members throughout the world to give birth to a new profession. Rather than waiting for the annual Obon festival to commemorate their ancestors, Lucky and Jin are celebrating their rich event legacy in Japan and Asia every day. By using their talents and creativity, they are establishing a legacy that both honors their ancestors and insures that their successors are even prouder of their achievements that ultimately result "in making people happy."

Lucky Morimoto: lucky-m@eventservices .co.jp

Jin Kawamura: jin-k@eventservices.co.jp

Career-Advancement Connections

Global Connection

There are infinite opportunities for global event careers. From multinational corporations to international associations, the opportunities are rich for travel, transnational experiences, and multicultural stimulation. To identify international career opportunities, you need to network through international organizations such as MPI Europe or the International Congress and Convention Association (ICCA). ICCA represents professionals in the meetings and events industry in over 100 countries around the world. The ICCA membership list is available at *www.icca.nl*. Click on "Membership" and then search in the category "Professional congress organizers."

Technology Connection

The breadth and depth of online education has grown dramatically in the past decade. This growth reflects the overall growth of the Internet itself. Leading providers of distance-learning programs in Event Leadership–related studies include The George Washington University Event Management Program (*www.gwu.edu/emp*), the University of Nevada at Las Vegas (*www.unlv.edu*), the American Society of Association Executives (*www.asaenet.org*), and Meeting Professionals International (*www.mpinet.org*).

Resource Connection

The American Society of Association Executives publishes a newsletter listing hundreds of jobs in the not-for-profit sector. The newsletter is available by subscription. Contact ASAE at *www.asaecenter.org*. The International Special Events Society also lists jobs on its Web page at *www.ises.org*. George Washington University (GWU) also lists dozens of global career opportunities on its password-protected Web page. To obtain access to this page, you must register for one of the certificate courses at GWU. You may also wish to visit *www.monster.com* and use keywords such as *special events, event management, meeting planning*, and *exposition management*. When I checked this listing, there were over 1,000 part- and full-time positions being advertised in the event-related categories just listed.

Learning Connection

Develop and write a new résumé that includes the skills and abilities you have mastered as a result of studying this book. Include in this résumé related lifetime experiences that are relevant to the Event Leadership profession. Invite an experienced Event Leadership professional to review your résumé and provide you with honest feedback. Just as the growth in online programs has been dramatic in the past decade, the same growth has been experienced in the classroom. Over 140 universities and colleges throughout the world offer courses, curriculum, degrees, or certificates in event-related studies. Today, you can obtain a bachelor's degree with a major in meeting planning from Northeastern Oklahoma University, a master's degree with a concentration in Event Management from George Washington University, and certificates in Event Leadership–related studies from dozens of universities and colleges throughout the world. Each year institutions of higher education expand their event studies–related course offerings. To identify an educational provider for your continuing education needs, contact the International Congress and Convention Association (*www.icca.nl*) and click on "Education" or go to *www.unlv.edu* and click on "William Harrah School of Hotel Management." Both sites provide comprehensive listings of Event Leadership–related courses in numerous universities and colleges throughout the world. Finally, contact Temple University, School of Tourism, at *www.temple.edu/sthm*, for information about the new Event Leadership System.

CHAPTER 14

Best Practices in Event Leadership

The term *best practice* is defined by different industries and different organizations in numerous ways. Fletcher Petroleum defines a best practice as "management practices and work processes that lead to world-class superior performance." Industries ranging from information technology to project management utilize different definitions to achieve the same purpose. The overarching purpose of a best practice in the field of Event Leadership is to establish a benchmark or leading example that may positively influence your ability to lead future events.

I define a best practice in the field of Event Leadership as an event organization that demonstrates one or more of five key attributes:

1. Best practice event organizations continually, over time, advance their mission through consistent performance improvement.
2. They continually innovate to improve and enlarge their body of knowledge.
3. They create new opportunities for the expansion of the profession.
4. They seek to promote positive global impacts through their individual contributions.
5. They promote sustainability through each event.

In this edition of *Special Events* I have subjectively selected five event organizations that, in my opinion, best emulate this definition. There are perhaps thousands of best practice event case studies to choose from each year; however, these selections represent, in my own personal and professional judgment, those that deserve recognition and meet the criteria just identified.

The choices are eclectic and include a professional association, a leading experiential marketing agency, a publisher, a community college foundation, and a university school of business. Despite their vastly different fields, all of them share a common outcome as they are advancing, innovating, and promoting the future of the special events industry through their events.

In future editions I will continue to search the world for best practice Event Leadership organizations, and I welcome your recommendations. Only through careful scrutiny and evaluation of these and future best practices will all Event Leaders be able to continually improve this profession.

Best Practice in Event Advancement

The Temple University Fox School of Business Musser Awards for Excellence in Leadership

For 10 years, Temple University's Fox School of Business has produced the Musser Award for Excellence in Leadership, which promotes the ethic, personified by the first recipient, that exceptional achievement by those seeking business success and exceptional effort on behalf of the community are compatible, mutually supportive goals. The first recipient of the award was business leader Warren V. "Pete" Musser.

Recipients during the next 10 years have included internationally recognized business leaders such as Sidney Kimmel, founder and chairman of Jones Apparel Group and Ralph Roberts, the founder of Comcast Corporation, among others. The event includes a dinner program especially designed to complement the philosophy and values of the honoree.

For example, in 2005 the honoree was James Nevels, chairman of The Philadelphia School Reform Commission and The Swarthmore Group. Because of Nevels' commitment to the public schools, the event featured schoolchildren singing and dancing during the program. However, more important, the 6,000 students of Temple University's Fox School of Business collected over 22,000 books to be used by the School District of Philadelphia.

In addition to recognizing outstanding business leaders, the annual Musser Awards also recognizes faculty, researchers, student, and staff leaders. In just 10 years, this event has become one of the hottest tickets in the greater Philadelphia region.

As a direct result of the excellence and popularity of this event, hundreds of thousands of dollars have been raised to support student scholarships. Furthermore, through events such as the Musser Awards, the Temple University Fox School of Business has advanced its external reputation and was ranked by *Financial Times* as the number-one Master of Business Administration (MBA) program in urban universities in the world in terms of value for money and one of the top 50 MBA programs in the United States.

Sponsor: Temple University Fox School of Business
M. Moshe Porat, Ph.D., Dean
www.sbm.temple.edu
Producer: The Creative Group
Fred Stein, President
www.cre8ivegrp.com

Best Practice in Event Creativity

Event Solutions Idea Factory™

In 2006, *Event Solutions* magazine celebrated the tenth anniversary of its annual conference and trade show titled "The *Event Solutions* Idea Factory." This annual event features a series of educational seminars, a trade show, and an awards competition called the "Spotlight Awards." Among the many creative ideas that publisher and president John Baragona and his staff have developed is the industry's first and only international Event Industry Hall of Fame. First introduced in 2002, the Event Industry Hall of Fame includes international luminaries such as the late Jack Morton, lifestyle expert Martha Stewart, and David Wolper, Academy–and Emmy–award-winning producer of the 1984 Olympic Games Opening and Closing Ceremonies, among others.

Members of the hall of fame are annually inducted in a lavish ceremony that also includes awards in 18 other categories, including Convention Center of the Year, Hotel Event Site of the Year, Event Planner of the Year, and Samaritan Service. Voting for the award's finalists is democratic, another *Event Solutions* creative contribution, using a unique Internet-based ballot box.

The 2006 educational program included a case study of the Recording Academy's annual Grammy awards™ to enlist the most creative event minds to help refresh this live televised event. In addition, the educational program was integrated within the exhibit floor displays to merge, for the first time in the industry, keynote presenters and exhibitors.

In addition to these creative ideas, *Event Solutions* was the first publisher to conduct in-depth industry research to produce their *Black Book* of event industry statistics. This publication has become a critical annual reference guide for new and established event professionals who seek to better understand the rather impressive statistics behind this industry.

Baragona and his team continually seek ways to not only showcase the creativity within the global special events industry but also to engage this creativity to help others. At each *Event Solutions* Idea Factory a special fundraising event benefiting the industry's SEARCH foundation is conducted and raises thousands of dollars to help those in need.

When asked how he continually delivers one of the most creative programs in the events industry, Baragona modestly says, "An Event Leader is only as good as his team. The Event Leader must select the best people, the right people. The Event Leader must continually shape the team to produce the desired excellence within the organization."

As the *Event Solutions* Idea Factory™ enters their second decade of helping manufacture the creative solutions event professionals require for long-term success, their efforts can be seen in the thousands of live events resulting from the stimuli often first experienced within this unique laboratory.

Sponsor: Event Publishing LLC
John Baragona, President
www.event-solutions.com

Education Director: Corinne Dudine
corrine@event-solutions.com

Best Practice in Event Innovation

The Fiftieth Anniversary Professional Convention Management Association Annual Meeting in Philadelphia, Pennsylvania

For half a century the Chicago, Illinois-based Professional Convention Management Association (PCMA) has raised the level of performance in the global meetings and events industry primarily through education. As PCMA prepared to return to the site of its first annual meeting, Philadelphia, Pennsylvania, it also sought ways to innovate through the design of this event.

By incorporating a variety of new, sometimes untested educational formats, PCMA proved to the thousands of participants that this was no longer their grandparents' industry. Through *Meetings Xperiments* PCMA sought new, innovative ideas from members to better deliver cutting-edge education. As a result of this process, several innovative features were offered for the first time.

Partnering with the prestigious Wharton School of Business at the University of Pennsylvania, PCMA offered senior professionals a in-depth and highly relevant Executive Edge Program.

General session programs were hosted by Ralph Archbold, portraying Dr. Benjamin Franklin, whose 300th birthday was celebrated the same year as PCMA turned 50. Dr. Franklin introduced panels of experts who deconstructed the industry's response to international terrorism and natural disasters such as Hurricane Katrina. Among the panel participants was General Richard Myers (Retired), former chairman of the U.S. Joint Chiefs of Staff.

In addition, PCMA offered other added value innovations such as *Open Space Technology,* which promoted a free flow of ideas; the content was entirely driven by the participants. Furthermore, many technological innovations were utilized, including a radio frequency identification (RFID) system to track delegates' continuing education units (see Chapter 11).

Another example of PCMA's many innovations is the annual event called *Party with a Purpose.* This event has been produced for over a dozen years, and the funds raised benefit both the local community where the meeting is held as well as other charitable organizations.

The official host organization for the 2006 fiftieth anniversary annual meeting was the Philadelphia Convention and Visitor's Bureau. According to Jack Ferguson, executive vice president of the convention division of this organization, "Hundreds of local volunteers worked tirelessly for many years to help produce the many innovations that occurred at this meeting."

As one example of innovative destination promotion, the opening reception for over 3,000 persons was held at the National Constitution Center (see menu in the appendices), and Ferguson and his team recruited local and state elected officials to serve as hosts at the event. PCMA annual meeting delegates were impressed to meet the local and state leaders and saw this as further evidence of their support of the growing convention industry in Philadelphia. Not only did the event feature elected officials, but acrobatic performers danced overhead as the guests dined at dozens of food stations below.

The closing event was hosted by the Pennsylvania Convention Center Authority and featured five decades of music culminating with a performance by The Village People. Décor and food and beverage representing each decade of music further enhanced the positive final impression that each guest received. The primary producer of this event was Global Event Partners of Philadelphia (*www.gepphilly.com*).

In addition to the education and best practiced events developed for the PCMA professional members, over 200 college and university students participated in special programming at the annual meeting. PCMA was the first and is currently the most extensive provider of education for college and university students studying hospitality, tourism, meeting, and event management. Through PCMA student chapters and the in-depth programming provided for them at the annual meeting, students receive real-world opportunities to learn about and eventually enter the profession of meeting and event management.

For over 50 years PCMA has pioneered in meeting and events education. The 2006 annual meeting in Philadelphia further demonstrated that PCMA will have even more to celebrate in the years to come.

Sponsor: Professional Convention Management Association
Deborah Sexton, President and CEO
www.pcma.org
Host partner: Philadelphia Convention and Visitors Bureau
Tom Muldoon, President
Jack Ferguson, Vice President for Convention Division
www.pcvb.org

Best Practice in Event Global Impacts

Opening and Closing Ceremonies of the 2004 Summer Olympic Games in Athens, Greece, produced by Jack Morton Worldwide

According to Bill Morton, son of founder Jack Morton and current chairman of Jack Morton Worldwide (*www.jackmorton.com*), "Leadership is hope." Morton believes that true leaders provide hope for their followers no matter how unsteady the journey may appear at the time. Morton, who was a 2005 inductee into the Event Industry Hall of Fame, led Jack Morton Worldwide for 40 years.

This philosophy certainly was tested during the production of the XXVIII Summer Olympic Games in Athens, Greece, in 2006. Jack Morton Worldwide was selected by the Athens Organizing Committee (ATHOC) to produce the event first conceived by the Greek avant-garde choreographer Dimitris Papaioannou.

Under the leadership of the international president, Lois Jacobs, the Jack Morton Worldwide team developed and successfully produced what the global media described as "the most beautiful ceremonies ever."

Jacobs, who formerly was a leader with the international major events firm Caribener, replied in this way when asked why she joined the Jack Morton Worldwide organization: "I believed in Bill Morton. I had known him for many years and he consistently demonstrated the business acumen and creative passion to lead the business." Jacobs further stated that, in her opinion, leadership is not only about hope, it is also about performance. "Bill and his team performed day after day, year after year in a stable and yet forward-moving manner, and I suppose that cultivates a sense of hope within those who choose to follow him."

And Jack Morton Worldwide certainly performed in Athens. Technologically, the opening ceremony was perhaps the most complex event in special event history. The Olympic Stadium floor was covered in water, and the ceremonies began with a white paper boat sailing across the water carrying a small Greek boy waving the flag of Greece. Soon the boy was greeted by a mythological centaur, then a huge Cycladic head rose from the center of the stadium floor. Within seconds, the giant head separated into several individual sections that were first suspended high above and then descended to the stadium floor. A laser helix depicted the DNA of the Games, and a dramatic pageant featuring figures from Greece's storied past paraded into the stadium.

The opening ceremonies also included a tribute from the American and Russian astronauts aboard the International Space Station. The ceremonies traditionally culminate with the lighting of the Olympic cauldron (which is actually a replica of the Athens Olympic torch). A massive pyrotechnic display framed the finale, and tens of thousands of spectators and over 10,000 athletes cheered as the Games officially returned to Greece.

According to International Olympic Committee president Jacque Rogge, an estimated 3.9 million people had television access to the Athens Olympic Games, which is the largest television audience in the history of the Games. Rogge further stated, "Athens has set a new benchmark with the highest audience, images of spectacular quality, expanded coverage of sport, new technologies and, I am delighted to say, a high level of satisfaction amongst our rights-holding broadcast partners" (Rogge, 2004).

Another symbol of the success of the 2004 Olympic Games ceremonies was seen in the overwhelmingly positive reaction of the live audience. Despite the numerous global political rivalries and controversies, as each country's athletes entered the Olympic Stadium, the cheers were long and loud.

Therefore, in terms of global impacts, the spectacular and splendid images created by Jack Morton Worldwide for the 2004 Summer Olympic Games in Athens, Greece, once again advanced the special events industry. Since 1939, the Jack Morton Worldwide team has been a pioneer, first in the global convention industry and now in the Olympic Games. When Bill Morton was asked at the conclusion of the 2004 Summer Olympic Games what the next advancement might be, he smiled proudly and said, "The technology has not even been invented to fulfill the dreams we have for the future." Thanks to Jack Morton Worldwide's contribution to the special events industry, these technological advances must rapidly accelerate to keep pace with the ambitions of Morton's dream makers.

Sponsor: Athens Organizing Committee for the Olympic Games (ATHOC)
Producer: Jack Morton Worldwide
Josh McCall, Chief Executive Officer
www.jackmorton.com

Best Practice in Sustainability

The Dallas County Community College District Max & Rosa Goldblatt Endowment Scholarship Awards

Twenty years ago, two children decided to honor their parents' 50 years of marriage by establishing a scholarship fund at a local community college that the parents had been instrumental in establishing. Unbeknownst to their parents, the children had contacted the newly formed Dallas (Texas) County Community District Foundation executive director, Carol Shlipak, and asked for her help in arranging this surprise.

Shlipak immediately recognized the potential for this award and offered her guidance. She had long admired Max and Rosa Goldblatt and welcomed the opportunity to develop a scholarship program in their honor.

Max Goldblatt was a member of the original steering committee that helped create the Dallas County Community College District. Now recognized as one of the leading community college programs in the world, the Dallas project had become stalled due to a lack of signatures on petitions needed to call an election to fund the colleges.

The first step in funding the college system was to call for an election for voters to approve the initial bond issue. The chairman of the board of the college, R. L. Thornton, asked Goldblatt to help collect signatures for a petition that was required to call an election. Goldblatt enlisted the help of hundreds of young people by offering the student who collected the most signatures the use of a red Mustang convertible for a week. Within a few weeks Max Goldblatt and his team had not only collected enough signatures, but had in fact exceeded the number by several thousand.

In planning the fiftieth wedding anniversary celebration, the Goldblatt children and their spouses contacted friends and family and invited them to secretly contribute to the Max and Rosa Goldblatt Endowment Award for Community Service. A few thousand dollars were raised; however, on the day of the event a long-term friend of the Goldblatt family contributed an additional $40,000 to fully fund the endowment.

Today, 20 years later, every other year seven students who have high academic performance and also are leaders in their community receive Max and Rosa Goldblatt Scholarships. These students are generally older and have families and full-time jobs; however, to exemplify the Goldblatt ideals of leadership, they are active community volunteers. Whether delivering Meals on Wheels™, rebuilding a local playground, caring for AIDS patients, or counseling at-risk youth, the Goldblatt scholars are changing their community one life at a time.

Every other year an awards luncheon is held in Dallas to honor the recipients. Tears flow freely as these adult students describe what it means to them to give back to their community. They also speak with pride about the honor they have received, which, for many, is their first public recognition. This remarkable program was documented in a video program narrated by a longtime friend and admirer of Max and Rosa Goldblatt, Jim Lehrer, host of the U.S. National Public Broadcasting television program *The News Hour with Jim Lehrer*. In the video, Lehrer quotes Dr. Margaret Mead, who said, "Never doubt that a small group of thoughtful, committed citizens can change the world. Indeed, is the only thing that ever has." The recipients of the Goldblatt awards exemplify this spirit.

During the past 20 years, over 100 students have received the Goldblatt scholarship award, and countless lives have been positively affected as a result of this sustainable event that was inaugurated in 1986. This event demonstrates that every event, regardless of size, has the potential of being sustained long after the original creators have completed their work.

Author, motivational speaker, and business leader Stedman Graham delivered remarks at one of the Goldblatt Awards ceremonies and stated, "This unique program is a perfect reflection of the college and the Goldblatt family whose commitment to servant leadership is an inspiration to all."

Sustainable events may be seen and experienced in many different sizes and forms. However, the Dallas County Community College District Foundation and its first executive director, Carol Shlipak, exemplify the ideal that sometimes the potential long-term positive outcome of live events far surpasses the impact of the original celebration.

Sponsor: Dallas County Community College District Foundation
Betheny L. Reid, Executive Director
www.dcccd.edu
Producer: Kathryn J. Hammontree
Director of Administration
khammontree@dcccd.edu

CHAPTER 15

Case Studies in Twenty-First-Century Event Leadership

A case study of an event problem is an excellent device to compare, contrast, explore, and perhaps expand discussion regarding critical issues in the field of Event Leadership. The case studies that follow examine many of the types of problems you have or probably will encounter in the Event Leadership field. Through these case studies, you may be able to develop an efficient early-warning system as well as identify new strategies for managing events efficiently now and in the future.

Taking a Gamble

Corporate Product Launch

A major casino developer organized a televised launch for his billion-dollar resort and contracted with an independent Event Leader to research, design, plan, coordinate, and evaluate this important project. The independent Event Leader also took a huge gamble with his client as he planned and executed this corporate product launch. First, the client did not arrange for the proper permits for a pyrotechnic display, and this required that the Event Leader had to hold innumerable meetings with the fire department as well as the pyrotechnics operators. In addition, the last pyrotechnics display had caused injuries and left debris all over the event area. Therefore, the Event Leader needed to work closely with the fire department to provide the necessary assurances that this would not recur.

Next, on the day of the major event, a man who identified himself as the chief steward of the drapery motion addressed the Event Leader. According to the steward, the Event Leader had not used union labor to hang a large red grand-opening bow, and now he would have to pay exorbitant penalties and fines. After further negotiation, the Event Leader agreed to hire members of the union to observe the bow, and they were paid even though they did not perform any work.

Finally, the independent Event Leader received a telephone call from a firm that had also bid to produce this corporate product launch. The other firm claimed that the Event Leader stole their original ideas and demanded compensation or threatened a lawsuit. According to the other firm, the Event Leader used an Aladdin's lamp as a prop, and this was in the proposal they submitted during the bidding process.

Most of the problems listed in this case study could easily have been avoided. In his contract with the client, the Event Leader should have required that all usual and customary permits be provided by the client no later than three weeks before the event dates. In addition, the Event Leader should have investigated the union requirements thoroughly and transferred any oversights to the client. Finally, the Event Leader should have required the client to state in writing that all ideas that were provided for the event (including the Aladdin's lamp) by the client were the sole creation and property of the sponsoring organization (the client's organizations).

Case Questions

✦ How does the Event Leader protect the image and corporate brand when producing a corporate product launch?

✦ What legal and ethical issues typically are present in corporate product launch events that may not be as critical in other types of events, such as social life-cycle events?

✦ How does the Event Leader know to whom in the corporation to report and to whom to turn when he or she has a question or needs a decision made?

Festival Challenge

Festival

As a festival approach, the Event Leader had only five crafts vendors committed to take part in the marketplace. She and her assistant were frantic. They had been pounding the streets, attending festivals all over the city trying to recruit artists and vendors to sell artwork, crafts, authentic items, and concessions at the event. With only nine days before the event and only a few vendors confirmed, they were afraid that the event would be a failure.

At the end of April, the Event Leader had been asked to plan the festival; she had only two months to put everything together. In addition, the budget was minimal and was heavily dependent on vendor participation. The festival was supposed to be a positive community event promoting a neighboring shopping center where the event would take place. The opening was promoted in local newspapers as an event that would bring the community together.

Charlottesville, Virginia celebrates First Night (the non-alcoholic new years eve celebration) using giant puppets for their grand procession that annually commences the evening activities.

The Philadelphia Flower Show created a sumptuous display of various floral and other natural products to create this setting. Once again demonstrating that creativity and innovation are unlimited as décor an lighting combine to arouse the senses.

The stage set for the 2005 Event Solutions Idea Factory in Atlanta, Georgia uses lighting, projections, gobos and video to create a dramatic and eye appealing setting for speakers and performers.

The annual Senso-Ji festival in Tokyo, Japan attractions nearly 1 million participants and spectators. Safety and security, risk management, crowd control and other critical factors are carefully planned and controlled by local officials to insure a successful outcome for everyone.

Fireworks Over the Arc de Triomphe. *Photo courtesy of Digital Vision.*

As the sound of drums was heard from the Krewe's marching in the French Quarter of New Orleans, thousands of local citizens and tourists began to cheer. Despite all of the fears and challenges, the Mardi Gras returned to New Orleans only a few months after Hurricane Katrina tried to dash the hopes of local residents. This photo depicts volunteer members of one of the first Krewe's to march in the 2006 Mardi Gras parade in New Orleans.

The Philadelphia Museum of Art's block buster Dali exhibition was advertised using a unique visual communications system employing design on the steps that faced hundreds of thousands of cars each day. Finding unusual locations in high visibility areas to promote your event, such as the steps in this picture, promote creative approaches to marketing your event.

Serving traditional fare, such as oysters, in a new style can often enliven the senses of your guests. This oyster shooter bar was extremely popular at the 2006 Conference for special Events Professionals produced by the Council for the Advancement and Support of Higher Education.

Indian Male Dancer in Mexico City, Mexico. *Courtesy of Flat Earth.*

Man running through finish line. *Photo courtesy of Corbis Digital Stock.*

A food presentation Tokyo, Japan illustrates how food and beverage must first appeal to the eye, then the olfactory before finally satisfying the taste buds.

The Mummers Parade in Philadelphia, Pennsylvania delights hundreds of thousands of tourists and residents in the City of Brotherly Love each New Years day. This photo shows the bold and bright colors used to costume and design the floats that appear in the parade.

The problem was that, despite the fact that the shopping mall was located in an unpopular neighborhood, the main stakeholders wanted to have a first-class celebration with upscale vendors and the best entertainers. However, the shopping mall where the event was taking place mainly featured stores that targeted middle- and low-middle-income shoppers. Therefore, the vendors selected could not benefit from people living in the area, because they did not have the income to purchase upscale merchandise or simply were not interested. However, all the entertainers and contractors were confirmed, and the local shop owners were determined to have a neighborhood festival and marketplace. The Event Leader and her assistant made the decision to reduce the vendor participation fee from $25 to $15. Due to the short time frame, they went to comparable festivals and distributed flyers to prospective vendors. Fortunately, 25 vendors were recruited, close to their goal of 30. However, both the Event Leader and her assistant felt that they should have talked with the owners about raising donations and sponsorship money to offset the cost instead of recruiting more vendors for the marketplace.

Case Questions

✦ What could the Event Leader and her assistant have done to market their event effectively to vendors?

✦ What integrative marketing techniques would be most effective for this type of event, given the low budget?

✦ Do you think the situation would have been the same if the Event Leader had more time?

✦ How could the Event Leader incorporate cause marketing in this event? Would it have been appropriate?

✦ What types of sponsors would have been appropriate for this event?

✦ What negotiation strategy would you use to negotiate sponsorship for this event?

Shower Surprises

Wedding/Bridal

It was late December, and Jen was becoming more and more excited about the prospect of marrying David in June of the following year. They had been engaged for almost six months now, and planning was in full swing. Just as she was daydreaming about the wedding, the phone rang and brought her back to reality. It was her sister Marcy. She wanted to throw Jen a bridal shower but was worried about not having enough time or money to make all the arrangements. After a couple of minutes chatting about some options, Jen suggested involving other people. Perhaps David's sister, Alyson, would be interested in helping with the planning. Jen wanted a bridal shower so badly that she knew she had to overcome Marcy's objection about paying for the event. Marcy had just graduated from medical school and gotten married herself; she was overburdened with debt. Then it hit them: Their aunt, Carol, was a single, successful businesswoman with plenty of financial resources at her disposal. Marcy quickly got off the phone and called her aunt. Carol welcomed the idea but warned that she was too busy to do any of the grunt work. She would pay for the event—that was it. Excitedly, Marcy called Alyson to enlist her help. Alyson accepted readily, despite the fact that she realized that she would be doing much of the research, design, planning, and coordinating. Alyson knew that the first stage in planning an event is to do research about previous events similar in size and scope. She was eager to begin discussing possible dates and general locations (i.e., Philadelphia or Wilmington, Delaware) so that she could start gathering data. By early February, Alyson and Marcy had engaged in some initial brainstorming about the design of the event. Together, the three hostesses selected a date: Saturday, May 13, 2006. Both Marcy and Carol gave Alyson permission to proceed in researching specific venues in the Wilmington area. They selected this location because nearly all the guests were located between New York and Washington, DC. There were three essential benefits of having the event in Delaware:

1. The groom's parents lived in Wilmington and could accommodate a number of overnight guests in their home.
2. Everything tended to be less expensive in Delaware than in Philadelphia.
3. Alyson was from Wilmington and was very familiar with a number of venues and vendors, whereas none of the three hostesses was from Philadelphia, nor do they have any contacts there.

Alyson spent much of the first two weeks in February collecting costs and specifications about various venues in the Wilmington area. Alyson told Carol that she would fax all the information she had collected by the end of the business day on Friday, February 11. When 5 P.M. rolled around, however, Alyson was still awaiting the response of one very nice hotel, the Hotel duPont. Instead of faxing the incomplete information, she decided to wait until Monday, when she hoped the information would be complete. To Alyson's surprise, Jen called on Sunday to express her excitement at having the bridal shower in Philadelphia. Confused, Alyson asked Jen who had told her that the shower would be held in Philadelphia. Jen explained that Carol had changed her mind and decided to book a hotel in Philadelphia instead of Wilmington, as the three hostesses had decided previously. Alyson was enraged and hurt. She faxed Carol a letter expressing her disappointment, accompanied by all the information she had collected on possible venues up until that point. In the letter, she "graciously decline[d] the honor of being a hostess," as she felt that she had little value to add to the planning function should it be located in Philadelphia.

The next day, Jen called Alyson and begged her to rethink her decision. Alyson refused until she received an apology directly from Carol. Just over a week later, Carol e-mailed Alyson an apology and expressed how impressed she had been with the information that Alyson had collected and faxed to her. She had been so impressed, in fact, that she had selected the Hotel duPont in Wilmington as a venue for the event. She asked Alyson to rethink her decision and to rejoin the effort to plan Jen's shower. Alyson knew how much it meant to Jen and agreed. Throughout the remainder of the planning, Alyson and Carol remained very distant and communicated only when it was critical to the success of the event. The event, however, turned out to be an overwhelming success.

Case Questions

+ Who was the Event Leader in this scenario?
+ What type of leadership style did Carol use? Was it successful? Why or why not?
+ What policies, procedures, or practices could have eliminated this conflict?
+ What would have been some effective ways to motivate Alyson to cooperate more fully with Carol?

Unhappy Tournament

Sports

The Shoot for the Cure: 3-on-3 Basketball Tournament, organized by the American Cancer Society (ACS) and coordinated by Mark, the Event Leader, was going smoothly. The games were running on schedule and everyone seemed to be enjoying the entertainment. Overall, the event seemed to be a success. Suddenly, the atmosphere of the event changed drastically. Sally, a participant in the next game, reported to the basketball court for the beginning of the last 3-on-3 game. The game began, then all of a sudden there was a loud cry from the courts. Sally had been struck by a falling basket. The entire apparatus had fallen on Sally. The volunteer first-aid squad assigned to monitor the event was on the scene immediately. The injury was severe. Sally lay on the court with the apparatus lying across her body. She was not breathing and was losing blood. Her arms were severely torn. Sally was airlifted to the closest trauma center, where she received a high level of treatment.

Sally survived the incident. After an extended stay at the hospital, she was released; however, almost a year after the incident, Sally still did not have full function in her right arm and hand. The prognosis was poor. As full function had not returned by this point, there was little hope that it would ever return. Sally would invest much time and energy in occupational therapy to relearn life skills that she had previously taken for granted.

During Sally's recovery time, the ACS and the Event Leader were busy gathering all of the paperwork that they would need in the event that, after recovery, Sally would press charges and demand payment for her injuries. While gathering the paperwork, they noticed that Sally's parents had not signed a release form for her to be cared for or transported by event medical personnel. They also realized that their registration package did not include a form for participants to sign that indicated that they understood that there were risks involved in participation and that they assumed these risks. Because a precedent had already been set in the courts of New Jersey, the location of the event, these missing documents would be extremely detrimental to the society and the Event Leader. The ACS knew that it would be targeted as the deepest pockets and that the Event Leader would be accused of negligence.

Sally's parents did bring a lawsuit against Mark and the ACS. They claimed that their daughter did not receive proper medical attention and that they did not consent to having their daughter airlifted to a hospital outside the local community. They claimed that the time spent waiting for the helicopter should have been spent transporting their daughter to the local hospital, where she would have received treatment sooner. They also claimed that they were not informed that such a serious injury could result from their daughter's participation in the event. The complaint ended with the assertion that the ACS and the Event Leader were negligent in using equipment that could fall on and injure participants.

The ACS and the Event Leader had no defense in this matter and eventually had to settle, even though the incident was an accident and the equipment had been inspected prior to use. The ACS agreed to assume a large portion of the financial burden, and the Event Leader agreed to forfeit all profits and pay an additional sum out of his own pocket.

Case Questions

✦ What should the Event Leader have done to ensure that both she and the ACS were protected against lawsuits brought by an injured participant?

✦ What forms should the Event Leader have included in the registration package?

✦ What specific details should be included in a medical release form?

✦ How could the Event Leader prove that she had inspected the equipment, and was it an issue in this case?

We Are Sold Out!

Association Convention

A professional trade association holds an annual meeting every October for the purpose of education and networking for its 12,000 members. Traditionally, the meeting is held in convention hotels, and the site is reserved three years in advance. These plans are made based on past growth of the meeting and the projected increase in membership of the association. In budgeting for the meeting each year, the association carefully considers the break-even point as well as the goal for increased attendance and membership in each progressive year. Since this is a not-for-profit organization, the primary goal is to attract enough attendance from its membership base to cover the costs of the meeting and allow the meeting to continue each year.

During the preconference meeting held two days before the annual meeting, the Event Leader constantly heard herself telling the convention manager to max out every meeting room in theater-style seating. Over the last few weeks of registration, the meeting staff began to worry about the ramifications of allowing too many members to register for the meeting based on the space available in the hotel. Trying to find this balance between earning increased revenues based on more registrations and providing a high-quality event for a smaller number of attendees given the space parameters is an issue facing many Event Leaders. It is critical to plan ahead for these circumstances to ensure a high-quality event that will also fulfill financial expectations.

Three weeks before the meeting was to be held, the director of meetings realized that registration income had more than exceeded the projected level of income for the year, based on the number of registrations in each of three price categories. Since previous meetings had never been sold out, and members had always been able to register on-site, the meetings department decided to keep registration open to all members waiting to register until the last minute. The association did not want to disappoint members who counted on being able to register at the late date.

In the last three weeks of registration, a disproportionately large number of people registered for the meeting. The meeting manager did not cut off registration until 5:00 P.M. on the last day of business before the meeting. For convenience, the association had three different ways that members could register. The most traditional way was to send the registration form through the mail with the registration check. The second was to fax the registration form and include a credit-card number for payment. Third, the attendee could register online and provide credit-card information. Regardless of the method, registrations were tracked and accounted for through an online registration database.

When attendees preregistered, they could choose from all the sessions, and it was not necessary to provide both first and second choices. The database was not equipped for this type of selection. Therefore, the registrants were essentially guaranteed that they would be able to attend their first choice of sessions. In reality, preregistration was only for the purpose of reserving meeting room space, and attendees could go to any session in a time slot regardless of which they preregistered for. The association did not have the staff to monitor each session room to be sure that everyone preregistered for a specific session.

About one month before the meeting, the director of meetings needed to assign session rooms at the hotel so that room assignments could be published in the program guide and so that speakers would know ahead of time where they were going to present. When this scheduling of rooms occurred, the director of meetings knew that several sessions were completely full but figured that some people would attend different sessions in the end and that some of the registrations would be canceled. Since registration was much greater in the last month than was expected, many session rooms were overbooked. The registration database was not equipped to close out certain sessions or to alert registrants that a session was full.

Also, after the final room assignments were made, there was no way to change them to make certain rooms larger and others smaller. The managers knew that there would be some unhappy attendees, especially those who preregistered months in advance; however, they felt that there was no flexibility for the location, and they wanted to try to satisfy the greatest number of members.

After evaluating the results of the 2000 annual meeting, the association directors began to seriously contemplate the goals of the annual meeting. The directors knew that, for the meeting in three years, they would be able either to find a hotel with even larger meeting facilities or to use a small convention center. However, the problem lies in the location of the meetings for the next two years, for which the hotel has already been reserved based on smaller attendance numbers.

Case Questions

+ Ethically, should the association allow unlimited registration in order to earn more revenue from increased demand, or should it limit registration and focus on the quality of the event?
+ If the association limits registration, how should members be notified about the change in procedure?
+ When booking a location for the meeting in three years, how can the meetings department predict how large demand for registration will be?
+ What could the association do to allow members to access information from the meeting if they get cut off from registration?

Trials of the Trade Show

Exhibition

The trade show Event Leader stood on the loading dock with sweat dripping down her brow as she watched dozens of trucks and other vehicles line up for what seemed like miles in the distance. As the sun continued to beat down on the loading-dock area, two union workers began to exchange heated words about who had the jurisdiction of work. Finally, the Event Leader glanced at her watch and realized that the load-in for the event was running two hours behind schedule, thus incurring thousands of dollars in overtime charges. And this was only the beginning of trials for the trade show Event Leader.

Once the doors to the exhibition opened, hundreds of buyers streamed in and promptly clogged the aisles on one side of the exhibit floor. For nearly four hours, buyers virtually ignored exhibitors on the other side of the exhibit floor. A few minutes after the exhibition began, several exhibitors complained to the Event Leader that other exhibitors were playing loud music and stepping into the aisles to bring people into their booths. Legal counsel also reminded the exhibit manager that it was illegal for the exhibitors to play recorded music without permission from the American Society of Composers, Authors, and Publishers or Broadcast Music, Inc.

These problems could easily have been prevented if the Event Leader had conducted proper research, design, and planning. For example, the load-in should have been smooth and seamless because of proper advance scheduling and a nearby marshaling facility for the vehicles. The issue of labor jurisdiction should have been clarified immediately and resolved by the union steward or union business manager. The problems with crowding and crowd flow could have been anticipated and rectified in advance by establishing attractions (such as food and beverage), entertainment, or perhaps human traffic directors to route the arriving buyers. Finally, the issue with activities being conducted in the booths should have been prevented by a policy statement in the exhibitors' regulations, policies, and procedures. Each exhibitor should have been required to initial or sign the regulations documents to confirm compliance with these policies. This would have eliminated the issue of music in the booths and given the Event Leader the necessary tools to enforce these policies.

Case Questions

+ What should be included in the exhibitors' policies, procedures, and practices, and regulations?
+ How do you design the exhibit floor to avoid crowding, gridlock, and other crowd-control issues?
+ What do you do if an exhibitor violates regulations?
+ How do you communicate effectively with union workers?
+ What are some creative solutions to ensure that buyers visit underutilized areas of an exhibit area?

Cutting the Ribbon and Healing the Community

Civic Celebration

For several weeks, the Event Leader has been inquiring how to get a permit to hold a major municipal parade to celebrate the grand opening of a convention center in a mid-size Southern city. The night before the parade, he was introduced to the mayor. "Mr. Mayor," the Event Leader asked, "how do I get a permit to hold the parade? None of your staff can tell me where to request permission." The mayor smiled, held out his hand, and said, "You have my permission." Most Event Leaders know that receiving a parade permit is neither that simple nor that secure. The Event Leader was lucky to meet the mayor and receive permission, but it would have been much safer to get it in writing or at least to document the conversation.

This municipal celebration offered many other challenges for the novice Event Leader. First, the convention center was a controversial municipal project and required a great deal of public relations effort to convince the local citizens that this was not just another civic boondoggle. Second, the board of the convention center wanted to be sure that multiple stakeholders were involved and that the programming attracted a wide variety of audience members. Third, the staff of the convention center wanted to showcase their human resources along with the new building. To be successful, the Event Leader would have to satisfy all these needs.

To combat a potential negative public relations reaction, the Event Leader designed a media luncheon as the first event to introduce the new convention center. At the luncheon, the media were captivated by a troupe of singers and dancers who performed an original musical called *Something for Everyone: A Convention Center Now*. In the musical, a villain named Mr. Sleeze represented downtown before the center was built. The actors encourage the media to boo and hiss Mr. Sleeze and, by the end of the show, the entire audience was standing and singing along to the closing lyrics of "Something for Everyone: A Convention Center for Us."

To ensure that multiple stakeholders were involved in the program, the Event Leader met with dozens of local professional and amateur performing artist organizations. The cast included church choirs, ethnic folk dance troupes, and professional musicians, dancers, and singers. As a result, many audience members were family and friends of the cast and represented the entire rainbow of this Southern city.

Finally, the Event Leader included in the production schedule for the event two days of customer-service training. The entire staff of the convention center was trained to become members of the cast and was costumed and scripted for the three-day celebration. Many of the media reports commented favorably on the new era of customer service that had arrived at the new convention center.

Case Questions

✦ How can you determine the public relations challenges for a municipal event and work with your client to mitigate potential problems?

✦ What type of programming can you incorporate in a municipal event to ensure that you represent every facet of the community as well as to maintain a level of quality and professionalism throughout the program?

✦ Why is the permanent full- and part-time staff an important consideration at the venue where the event will be held? How can you raise the level of their performance without circumventing their existing training programs?

Good Luck, Grads!

University

Sometimes an event has many planners and organizers. This was true in the case of this year's graduation luncheon for a graduate program. Each year for the past three years, a graduate school of a small regional university held an event for its winter graduates. There is a luncheon on campus to recognize the graduates, give them a chance to assemble, and present them with a small gift as they continue their lives beyond the university. The stakeholders in this graduate luncheon include the new graduates, the university, and the community. In the beginning of November, Chris was given the job of printing the programs. This did not appear to be a difficult task, as he had a sample from the previous year; therefore, he did not begin to work on the job seriously until the beginning of December. As he set to work finalizing the content for this year, Chris quickly began to realize that not only were several people in the department working on different aspects of the luncheon, but also the actual luncheon programming was not being taken care of. Specifically, the previous year's luncheon had involved a student speaker and a faculty member who presented the graduation gift. This year, however, Chris learned that a student speaker still needed to be nominated. Quickly compiling and mounting an e-mail campaign, less than two weeks before the luncheon, he was still receiving nominations. Issues of which faculty members would be involved in the event also arose, and the Event Leader's job grew to include the task of deciding and scheduling this element of the program.

In the end, a student speaker was selected and included in the program. The luncheon was a total success, and the graduates were unaware of the last-minute scrambling. However, an unclear organizational chart can lead to miscommunications and dropped balls. When the structure of the planning group is unclear or unknown, as it was in this case, important details such as nomination of a graduation speaker can be missed.

Case Questions

✦ How can the university clearly identify who is in charge of planning the luncheon when it arranges for next year's event?

✦ What type of efficient organizational chart would you recommend for such events in an academic environment?

✦ What other techniques would be helpful to save, track, and retrieve in the event history?

✦ How would you create a checklist for the various elements of the event?

Show Me the Money

Financial

ASEM is a major professional organization dedicated to the science and art of engineering management. The goal of the ASEM 2000 conference was to bring together the nation's leading engineering managers, with a special emphasis on evaluation of technical leadership in the vibrant information systems technology sector in the Washington, DC, metropolitan area. This annual conference is highly respected among technical professionals in the United States. ASEM 2000 was held from October 4 to October 7 in Washington's Marriott Hotel. The main stakeholders included ASEM, the conference management service at one large metropolitan university, engineering managers from high-tech organizations, and other organizations interested in the electronic communication's development.

The annual budget for the conference is close to $100,000, and the organization committee traditionally raised these funds by soliciting contributions from sponsors and by charging participants an attendance fee. The conference organizers had several contracts in place with major vendors: a conference facility, caterers, and a transportation company. These vendor contracts, signed five years ago and not revised since, were fixed-fee contracts.

Approximately 10 months before holding the event, the conference committee faced a serious problem. There was a serious deficit of funds to complete the conference organization. Due to a sales decline, one of the conference's sponsors was not able to contribute a pledge this year, and others made clear that they would not be able to cover the gap. During a special meeting held by the organizers, two possible solutions were identified:

1. Generate more revenues by attracting additional sponsorship funds.
2. Reduce the costs of the event by better expense management.

One of the possible solutions was to renegotiate the vendors' contracts. However, the organizers were not sure how to start the negotiations. It was very unlikely that the vendors would agree simply to cut their prices without strong reasons from the conference organizers' side. You were asked to prepare your recommendations to the organization committee on how to turn around the finances of the conference.

Case Questions

✦ How would you prepare for the meeting with your vendors?
✦ What kind of research should be done before any financial contract negotiations?
✦ What incentive can organizers provide to sponsors and participants earlier to generate cash?
✦ What other solutions could organizers use to attract funds?

Homeland Security Alert: From Yellow to Orange

Change in Federal Security Threat Level

At 10:00 A.M. on the first day of a large convention/exposition held in a major U.S. city, the Event Leader received a telephone call from the manager of the venue where the event was being held. "I just received an e-mail from the Department of Homeland Security announcing that they are changing the threat level from yellow to orange effective immediately," said the venue manager. "What would you like to do with regard to the start of your convention?" The Event Leader drew a deep breath; this was the first time her organization had heard the ominous phrase "change of threat level" since this process had been established by the U.S. Department of Homeland Security.

"What is the standard operating procedure when there is a change of threat level in the venue?" the Event Leader inquired. "We increase our security operations, inspect all bags coming into the venue, and use wands to search for weapons," replied the venue manager.

"How will this affect the event operations for our programs?" asked the Event Leader.

"These additional procedures could delay your guests as they enter the building and it could raise some concerns as well regarding the perception of safety for your event. With some events, the change in threat level has resulted in lower attendance than what was projected," the venue manager cautioned.

The Event Leader paused for a few moments to digest this information and then said, "I am going to ask my staff to send an e-mail to the preregistered attendees informing them that, for their benefit, we are increasing our normal security procedures and, therefore, they should allow more time to arrive at and enter the venue. Furthermore, I would like to order large signs for the entrance doors informing our attendees of these procedures and thanking them for their cooperation. Can you help me do this?"

"These are excellent ideas," said the venue manager. "We will work closely with you and also keep you apprised of any changes as our director of security works closely with local public safety officials who, in turn, are connected to the Department of Homeland Security."

A few hours later, guests began arriving for the opening reception and, as predicted, long lines began to form at security as the new procedures were implemented. Some guests appeared frustrated and irritated, and others were genuinely concerned for their safety. However, eventually all guests were admitted to the venue in time to attend the opening reception. The final conference evaluations confirmed that the plans implemented by both the Event Leader and the venue manager were satisfactory, as guests gave high marks for the venue operations and the safety and security procedures for the event.

Case Questions

+ Should the Event Leader have checked with other officials (and if so, whom) in addition to the venue manager prior to formulating the final code-orange plan?
+ What other questions should the Event Leader have asked in addition to those listed in the case study?
+ What could the Event Leader have done in advance to anticipate a change in the threat level so that the event would have been prepared for this new development?
+ During the ingress for the event, what else could the Event Leader have done to satisfy his or her guests and increase their feeling of security and comfort?

APPENDICES

APPENDIX 1

References

Professional speaker Charles "Tremendous" Jones has been widely quoted as having originated the simple philosophy that, many years from now, most of us will be exactly the same person we are today except for two things: the books we read and the people we meet along the way.

I encourage you to develop the rigor of reading one new book per week and surveying other written resources daily, such as magazines and newsletters. This will help ensure that you stay current in your profession and will provide you with many new ideas to accelerate the growth of your career.

I am often asked, "Where do you get all your ideas?" The questioner assumes that I reach into Pandora's fabled box and divine new wonders of creation. Usually I reply to this question by stating: "Plato, Aristotle, Shakespeare, Keats, Browning, Hemingway, Dickinson, Stein, Eyre, Barrett, Seurat, Beethoven, Bach, Brahms, Picasso, Vermeer, and other renowned writers, painters, and composers."

The resources I describe next have guided my career and will further ensure your professional success.

Books Specifically for Event Leaders

Adcock, E., D. Buono, and B. McGee (1995). *Premium, Incentive, and Travel Buyers.* New Providence, NJ: Salesman's Guide.

Allen, J. (2000). *Event Planning: The Ultimate Guide to Successful Meetings, Corporate Events, Fundraising Galas, Conferences, Conventions, Incentives, and Other Special Events.* Toronto, Ontario: John Wiley& Sons.

American Society of Association Executives (1999). *The Law of Meetings, Conventions, and Trade Shows: Meetings and Liability.* Washington, DC: ASAE.

Anderson, N. *Ferris Wheels: An Illustrated History.* Bowling Green, OH: Bowling Green State University Popular Press.

Association of National Advertisers Event Marketing Committee (1995). *Event Marketing: A Management Guide.* New York: ANA.

Astroff, M.T., and J.R. Abbey (1998). *Convention Sales and Services,* 5th ed. Cranbury, NJ: Waterbury Press.

Badger, R. (1979). *The Great American Fair: The World's Columbian Exposition and American Culture.* Chicago, IL: Nelson-Hall.

Baghot, R., and G. Nuttall (1990). *Sponsorship, Endorsements and Merchandising: A Practical Guide.* London: Waterlow.

Bagley, N.F. (1994). *Reunions for Fun-Loving Families.* St. Paul, MN: Brighton Publications.

Bailey, D. (1999). *American Nightmares: The Haunted House Formula in American Popular Fiction.* Bowling Green, OH: Bowling Green State University Popular Press.

Baines, P., J. Egan, and F. Jefkins (2003). *Public Relations: Contemporary Issues and Techniques.* London: Butterworth-Heinemann.

Baldridge, L. (1993). *Letitia Baldridge's New Complete Guide to Executive Manners.* New York: Rawson Associates, Maxwell Macmillan International.

Batterberry, A.R. (1976). *Bloomingdale's Book of Entertaining.* New York: Random House.

Bergin, R., and E. Hempel (1990). *Sponsorship and the Arts: A Practical Guide to Corporate Sponsorship of the Performing and Visual Arts.* Evanston, IL: Entertainment Resource Group.

Berlonghi, A.E. (1990). *The Special Event Risk Management Manual.* Dana Point, CA: Author.

Berrige, G. (2006). *Events Design and Experience.* London: Butterworth-Heinemann.

Bodde, D. (1975). *Festivals in Classical China.* Princeton, NJ: Princeton University Press.

Boehme, A.J. (1999). *Planning Successful Meetings and Events: A Take-Charge Assistant Book.* New York: AMACOM.

Boothman, N. (2000). *How to Make People Like You in 90 Seconds or Less.* New York: Workman Publishing.

Bowdin, G., J. Allen, W. O'Toole, R. Harris, and I. McDonnell (2006). *Events Management,* 2nd ed. London: Butterworth-Heinemann.

Bowman, J. (1992). *Family Reunions: A Guide to Planning, Organizing and Holding Exciting Family Reunions.* Carson, CA: Akila Publishers.

Brashich, C. (1990). *World Manual for Group and Incentive Travel.* Livingston, NJ: Networld.

Brody, M., and B. Pachter (1994). *Business Etiquette.* Burr Ridge, IL: Irwin Professional Publishing.

Brown, R., and M. Marsden (1994). *The Cultures of Celebrations.* Bowling Green, OH: Bowling Green State University Popular Press.

Browne, R.B. (1981). *Rituals and Ceremonies in Popular Culture.* Bowling Green, OH: Bowling Green State University Popular Press.

Breuilly, E., J. O'Brien, M. Palmer, and M. Marty. (2002). *Festivals of the World: The Illustrated Guide to Celebrations, Customs, Events, and Holidays.* New York: Checkmark Books.

Calabria, F.M. (1993). *Dance of the Sleep-Walkers: The Dance Marathon Fad.* Bowling Green, OH: Bowling Green State University Popular Press.

Carey, T. (ed.) (1999). *Professional Meeting Management: A European Handbook.* Dallas, TX: Meeting Professionals International.

Cartmell, R. (1987). *The Incredible Scream Machine: A History of the Roller Coaster.* Bowling Green, OH: Bowling Green State University Popular Press.

Catherwood, D.W., and R.L. Van Kirk (1992). *The Complete Guide to Special Event Management: Business Insights, Financial Advice, and Successful Strategies from Ernst & Young, Advisors to the Olympics, the Emmy Awards and the PGA Tour.* New York: John Wiley & Sons.

Charsley, S.R. (1992). *Wedding Cakes and Cultural History.* New York: Routledge.

Church, B.R., and B.E. Bultman (2000). *The Joys of Entertaining.* New York: Abbeville Press.

Church, B.R., and L.R. Harrison (1993). *Weddings Southern Style.* New York: Abbeville Press.

Clynes, Tom (1995). *Wild Planet: 1,001 Extraordinary Events for the Inspired Traveler.* Detroit, MI: Visible Ink Press.

Cole, H. (1995). *Jumping the Broom: The African-American Wedding Planner.* New York: Henry Holt.

Convention Industry Council (2003). *The Convention Industry Council,* 5th ed. Washington, DC: CIC.

Dance, J. (1994). *How to Get the Most Out of Sales Meetings.* Lincolnwood, IL: NTC Business Books.

Deal, T.E., and A.A. Kennedy (1984). *Corporate Cultures: The Rites and Ritual of Corporate Life.* Reading, MA: Perseus Publishing.

Delacorte, T., J. Kimsey, and S. Halas (1984). *How to Get Free Press: A Do-It-Yourself Guide to Promote Your Interests, Organizations or Business.* San Francisco: Avon.

De Lys, C. (1989). *What's So Lucky about a Four-Leaf Clover and 8414 Other Strange and Fascinating Superstitions from All Over the World.* East Brunswick, NJ: Bell Publishing.

Devney, D.C. (2001). *Organizing Special Events and Conferences: A Practical Guide for Busy Volunteers and Staff.* Sarasota, FL: Pineapple Press.

Dittrich, K. (ed.) and A. Geppert. (2004). *Component Database Systems.* San Francisco, CA: Morgan Kaufman

Dlugosch, S.E. (1980). *Folding Table Napkins: A New Look at a Traditional Craft,* 9th ed. St. Paul, MN: Brighton Publications.

Dlugosch, S.E. (1990). *Table Setting Guide.* St. Paul, MN: Brighton Publications.

Dlugosch, S.E. (1991). *Tabletop Vignettes.* St. Paul, MN: Brighton Publications.

Dlugosch, S.E. (1989). *Wedding Hints and Reminders.* St. Paul, MN: Brighton Publications.

Dlugosch, S.E. (1993). *Wedding Plans: 50 Unique Themes for the Wedding of Your Dreams,* 3rd ed. St. Paul, MN: Brighton Publications.

Dunkins, M., and J. Gray-Miott (1994). *The Perfect Choice: Wedding and Reception Sites.* Silver Spring, MD: Gray, McPherson and Associates.

Ehrenreich, Barbara (2007). *Dancing in the Streets: A Collective History of Joy.*

Fenich, G. (2004). *Meetings, Expositions, Events and Conventions: An Introduction to the Industry.* New York: Prentice Hall.

Fields, D., and A. Fields. (2002). *Bridal Bargains: Secrets to Throwing a Fantastic Wedding on a Realistic Budget,* 6th ed. Boulder, CO: Windsor Peak Press.

Finkel, C.L. (1991). *Powerhouse Conferences: Eliminating Audience Boredom.* East Lansing, MI: Educational Institute of American Hotel and Motel Association.

Flanagan, J. (1999). *Successful Fund Raising: A Complete Handbook for Volunteers and Professionals.* New York: McGraw-Hill Trade.

Foster, J.S. (1991). *Business Insurance for Independent Planners.* Atlanta, GA: John S. Foster, Esq., Law Offices.

Foster, J.S. (1991). *Choosing a Business Form: What's Best for You?* Atlanta, GA: John S. Foster, Esq., Law Offices.

Foster, J.S. (1995). *Hotel Law: What Hoteliers Need to Know about Legal Affairs Management.* Atlanta, GA: John S. Foster, Esq., Law Offices.

Foster, J.S. (1995). *Independent Meeting Planners and the Law.* Atlanta, GA: John S. Foster, Esq., Law Offices.

Foster, J.S. (1991). *Independent Planner Checklists*. Atlanta, GA: John S. Foster, Esq., Law Offices.

Foster, J.S. (1995). *Meeting and Facility Contracts*. Atlanta, GA: John S. Foster, Esq., Law Offices.

Foster, J.S. (1995). *Meetings and Liability*. Atlanta, GA: John S. Foster, Esq., Law Offices.

Foster, J.S. (1992). *Sample Contract Clauses for Independent Planners*. Atlanta, GA: John S. Foster, Esq., Law Offices.

Freedman, H.A., and K.F. Smith (1994). *Black Tie Optional: The Ultimate Guide to Planning and Producing Successful Special Events*. Farmington Hills, MI: Taft Group/Thomson Gale.

Fulmer, D., and N. Eddy (1991). *A Gentleman's Guide to Toasting*. Lynchburg, TN: Oxmoor House.

Gartell, R.B. (1994). *Destination Marketing for Convention and Visitor Bureaus*, 2nd ed. Dubuque, IA: Kendall/Hunt.

Getz, D. (1991). *Festivals, Special Events, and Tourism*. New York: John Wiley & Sons.

Getz, D. (2007). *Event Studies: A Multi-Disciplinary Approach*. London: Butterworth-Heinemann.

Giblin, J.C. (2001). *Fireworks, Picnics and Flags: The Story of the Fourth of July Symbols*. Boston, MA: Clarion Books/Houghton-Mifflin.

Gilbert, E. (1990). *The Complete Wedding Planner: Helpful Choices for the Bride and Groom*, rev. ed. Lake Wales, FL: Lifetime Books.

Global Media Commission Staff (1988). *Sponsorship: Its Role and Effect*. New York: International Advertising Association.

Goldblatt, J., and K.S. Nelson (1996). *The International Dictionary of Event Management*. New York: Van Nostrand Reinhold.

Goldblatt, J.J. (1995). *The Ultimate Party Handbook*. Philadelphia, PA: Goldblatt Company.

Graham, S., J.J. Goldblatt, and L. Delpy (2001). *The Ultimate Guide to Sport Event Management and Marketing*. New York: McGraw-Hill Trade.

Greier, T. (1986). *Make Your Events Special: How to Produce Successful Special Events for Nonprofit Organizations*. New York: Folkworks.

Grimes, R. (2002). *Deeply Into the Bone*. Berkley, CA: University of California Press.

Gumley, L. (2001). *Practical IDL Programming*. San Francisco, CA: Morgan Kaufmann.

Hall, C.M. (1992). *Hallmark Tourist Events: Impacts, Management and Planning*. New York: Belhaven Press.

Hall, S.J. (1992). *Ethics in Hospitality Management: A Book of Readings*. East Lansing, MI: Educational Institute of the American Hotel and Motel Association.

Hansen, B. (1995). *Off-Premise Catering Management*. New York: John Wiley & Sons.

Harris, A.L. (2005). *Academic Ceremonies: A Handbook or Ceremonies and Protocol*. Washington, DC.: Council for Advancement and Support of Education.

Harris, A.L. (1999). *Etiquette and Protocol: A Guide for Campus Events*. Washington, DC: Council for Advancement and Support of Education.

Harris, A.L. (1988). *Special Events: Planning for Success*. Washington, DC: Council for Advancement and Support of Education.

Heath, A. (2001). *Windows on the World: Multicultural Festivals for Schools and Libraries*. Metuchen, NJ: Scarecrow Press.

Hayes, G.D. (2003). *Zambelli: The First Family of Fireworks*. Middlebury, VT: Paul S. Eriksson.

Hildreth, R.A. (1990). *The Essentials of Meeting Management.* Englewood Cliffs, NJ: Prentice Hall.

Hoffman, L.J. (1999). *The Reunion Planner: The Step-by-Step Guide Designed to Make Your Reunion a Social and Financial Success.* Los Angeles, CA: Goodman Lauren Publishing.

Holbrook, M.B. (1993). *Daytime Television Game Shows and the Celebration of Merchandise: The Price Is Right.* Bowling Green, OH: Bowling Green State University Popular Press.

Howe, J.T. (1993). *The International Travel Resource for International Meeting and Congress Professionals.* Dallas, TX: Meeting Professionals International.

Howe, J.T., and H.M. Schaffer (1992). *Keeping in Step with Music Licensing.* Dallas, TX: Meeting Professionals International.

Howe, T. H. (1996). *U.S. Meetings and Taxes,* 3rd ed. Dallas, TX: Meeting Professionals International.

Howell, M. D. (1997). *From Moonshine to Madison Avenue: A Cultural History of the NASCAR Winston Cup Series.* Bowling Green, OH: Bowling Green State University Popular Press.

Hoyle, L. (2002). *Event Marketing.* Hoboken, NJ: John Wiley & Sons.

Hoyle, L.H., D.C. Dorf, and T.J.A. Jones (1989). *Managing Conventions and Group Business.* East Lansing, MI: Educational Institute of the American Hotel and Motel Association.

International Association of Business Communicators (1990). *Special Events Marketing* (IABC Communication Bank Series). San Francisco, CA: IABC.

International Association of Professional Congress Planners (2000). *Meeting Industry Terminology,* 4th ed. Brussels, Belgium: IAPCP.

International Events Group (1995). *Evaluation: How to Help Sponsors Measure Return on Investment.* Chicago, IL: IEG.

International Events Group (1995). *Media Sponsorship: Structuring Deals with Newspaper, Magazine, Radio and TV Sponsors.* Chicago, IL: IEG.

International Special Events Society (1993). *ISES Gold.* Indianapolis, IN: ISES.

Jackson, I. (ed.) (2002). *Great Festivals of the World.* London: Pilot Guides.

Jarrow, J., and C. Park. (1992). *Accessible Meetings and Conventions.* Columbus, OH: Association on Higher Education and Disability.

Jewell, D. (1992). *Public Assembly Facilities: Planning and Management,* 2nd ed. Melbourne, FL: Krieger Publishing.

Jolles, R.L. (2000). *How to Run Seminars and Workshops: Presentation Skills for Consultants, Trainers and Teachers,* 2nd ed. Hoboken, NJ: John Wiley & Sons.

Jones, J. (1984). *Meeting Management: A Professional Approach.* Stamford, CT: Bayard Publications.

Jones, J.E., and C. Phypers (1985). *Incentive Travel: The Professional Way.* Stamford, CT: Bayard Publications.

Jones, P., and A. Pizman (1993). *The International Hospitality Industry: Organizational and Operational Issues.* London: Pitman Publishing.

Kahan, N.W. (1992). *Entertaining for Business: A Complete Guide to Creating Special Events with Style and a Personal Touch.* New York: C. N. Potter.

Kaiser, T.A. (1995). *Mining Group Gold: How to Cash in on the Collaborative Brain Power of a Group.* New York: McGraw-Hill Trade.

Karasik, P. (1995). *How to Make It Big in the Seminar Business.* New York: McGraw-Hill.

Keegan, P.B. (1990). *Fundraising for Non-profits.* New York: Harper Perennial.

Kerzner, H. (2003). *Project Management: A Systems Approach to Planning, Scheduling, and Controlling.* Hoboken, NJ: John Wiley & Sons.

Klausner, S.Z. (1968). *Why Man Takes Chances: Studies in Stress-Seeking.* New York: Doubleday.

Kring, R. (1994). *Party Creations: A Book to Theme Event Design.* Denver, CO: Clear Creek Publishing.

Krueger, C. (1993). *Dream Weddings Do Come True: How to Plan a Stress-Free Wedding.* St. Paul, MN: Brighton Publications.

Krugman, Carol, Wright, Rudy (2006). *Global Meetings and Expositions.* Hoboken, NJ: John Wiley & Sons.

Kurdle, A.E., and M. Sandler (1995). *Public Relations for Hospitality Managers.* New York: John Wiley & Sons.

Levi-Strauss, C. (1990). *The Origin of Table Manners, Vol. 3: Mythologies.* Chicago, IL: University of Chicago Press.

Levitan, J. (2000). *Proven Ways to Generate Thousands of Hidden Dollars from Your Trade Show, Conference and Convention.* Vernon Hill, IL: Conference and Exhibition Publisher.

Levy, O., and A. Davidson (1991). *Party Planner.* New York: Langson Press.

Lewis, C.L. (1992). *How to Plan, Produce, and Stage Special Events.* Chicago, IL: Evergreen Press.

Liebold, L.C. (1986). *Fireworks, Brass Bands, and Elephants: Promotional Events with Flair for Libraries and Other Nonprofit Organizations.* Phoenix, AZ: Oryx Press.

Lindsay, D.J. (1994). *Bravo Meeting Planner's Organizer: A Step-by-Step Road Map to Planning a Successful Meeting or Event.* Portland, OR: Bravo Publications.

Lippincott, C. (1999). *Meetings: Do's, Don'ts and Donuts: The Complete Handbook for Successful Meetings.* Pittsburgh, PA: Lighthouse Point Press.

MacCannell, D. (1999). *The Tourist: A New Theory of the Leisure Class.* Berkeley, CA: University of California Press.

Mack, W.P., and W. Connell (1981). *Naval Ceremonies, Customs and Traditions,* 5th ed. Annapolis, MD: Naval Institute Press.

Mackenzie, J.K. (1990). *It's Show Time! How to Plan and Hold Successful Sales Meetings.* Homewood, IL: Dow Jones-Irwin.

Malouf, D. (1993). *How to Create and Deliver a Dynamic Presentation.* Alexandria, VA: American Society for Training and Development.

Malouf, L. (1999). *Behind the Scenes at Special Events: Flowers, Props and Design.* New York: John Wiley & Sons.

Mangels, W.F. (1952). *The Outdoor Amusement Industry, From Earliest Times to the Present.* New York: Vantage Press.

Manning, F.E. (1983). *The Celebration of Society: Perspectives on Contemporary Cultural Performance.* Bowling Green, OH: Bowling Green State University Popular Press.

Marsh, V. (1994). *Paper-Cutting Stories for Holidays and Special Events.* Atkinson, WI: Highsmith Press.

Martin, E.L. (1992). *Festival Sponsorship Legal Issues.* Port Angeles, WA: International Festivals Association.

Masciangelio, W.R., and T. Ninkovich (1991). *Military Reunion Handbook: A Guide for Reunion Planners.* San Francisco, CA: Reunion Research.

Masterman, G. (2004). *Strategic Sports Event Management: An International Approach.* London: Butterworth-Heinemann.

McDonnell, I., J. Allen, and W. O'Toole (2002). *Festival and Special Event Management.* Hoboken, NJ: John Wiley & Sons.

McGinnis, C. (1994). *202 Tips Even the Best Business Travelers May Not Know.* New York: McGraw-Hill Trade.

McKinzie, H. (1992). *Reunions: How to Plan Yours.* Los Angeles: McKinzie Publishing Company.

McMahon, T. (1996). *Big Meetings, Big Results.* Lincolnwood, IL: NTC Publishing Group.

Meeting Professionals International and Canadian Council and the Government of Canada, The Department of Human Resources Development (1994). *Meeting Coordinator Standards.* Dallas, TX: MPI.

Meeting Professionals International and Canadian Council and the Government of Canada, The Department of Human Resources Development (1994). *Meeting Manager Standards.* Dallas, TX: MPI.

Mikolaitis, P., and W. O'Toole (2002). *Corporate Event Project Management.* Hoboken, NJ: John Wiley & Sons.

Miller Brewing Company (1999). *Good Times: A Guide to Responsible Event Planning.* Milwaukee, WI: MBC.

Miller, S. (2000). *How to Get the Most Out of Trade Shows.* New York: McGraw-Hill Trade.

Montgomery, R.J., and S.K. Strick (1995). *Meetings, Conventions, and Exposition: An Introduction to the Industry.* New York: Van Nostrand Reinhold.

Monroe, James (2006). *The Art of the Event,* Hoboken, NJ: John Wiley & Sons.

Morrisey, G.C. (1996). *Morrisey on Planning, Vols. I-III.* San Francisco, CA: Jossey-Bass.

Morrow, S.L. (1997). *The Art of Show.* Dallas, TX: IAEM Foundation.

Morton, A., A. Prosser, and S. Spangler (1991). *Great Special Events and Activities.* State College, PA: Venture Publishing.

Morton, J. (1985). *Jack Morton (Who's He?) Story.* New York: Vantage Press.

Morton, J. (1993). *The Poor Man's Philosopher.* Washington, DC: Jack Morton Worldwide NY.

Mothershead, A.B. (1982). *Dining Customs around the World: With Occasional Recipes.* Garrett Park, MD: Garrett Park Press.

Museum of Fine Arts (1992). *Wedding Planner.* New York: Rizzoli International Publications.

National Association of Broadcasters (1991). *A Broadcaster's Guide to Special Events and Sponsorship Risk Management.* Washington, DC: NAB.

Neel, S.M., and R. Wray (1995). *Saying "I Do": The Wedding Ceremony. The Complete Guide to a Perfect Wedding.* Colorado Springs, CO: Meriwether Publishing.

Neuhoff, V. (1987). *Scientists in Conference: The Congress Organizer's Handbook: The Congress Visitor's Companion.* Weinheim, Germany: VCH.

Newman, P.J., and A.F. Lynch (1983). *Behind Closed Doors: A Guide to Successful Meetings.* New York: Prentice Hall.

Nichols, B. (1999). *Professional Meeting Management,* 2nd ed. Birmingham, AL: Professional Convention Management Association.

Ninkovich, T. (1991). *Reunion Handbook: A Guide for School and Military Reunions,* 2nd ed. San Francisco: Reunion Research.

Norris, D.M., J.F. Loften, & Associates (1995). *Winning with Diversity: A Practical Handbook for Creating Inclusive Meetings, Events, and Organizations.* Washington, DC: Foundations of Meeting Planners International, Professional Convention Management Association, Association of Association Executives, International Association of Convention and Visitors Bureaus, and International Association of Exposition Management.

Oldenwald, S.B. (1993). *Global Training: How to Design a Program for the Multinational Corporation.* Chicago, IL: Irwin Professional Publishing.

Packham, J. (1993). *Wedding Parties and Showers: Planning Memorable Celebrations.* New York: Sterling Publishing Company.

Petersen, K. (1992). *Historical Celebrations: A Handbook for Organizers of Diamond Jubilees, Centennials, and Other Community Anniversaries,* 3rd ed. Boise, ID: Idaho State Historical Society.

Pinto, J., and J. Trailer. (eds.) (1998). *Leadership Skills for Project Managers.* Newtown Square, PA: Project Management Institute.

Pizam, A. (2005). *International Encyclopedia of Hospitality Management.* London: Butterworth Heinemann.

Plenert, G. (2003). *Reinventing Lean: Introducing Lean into the Supply Chain.* London: Butterworth-Heinemann.

Plessner, G.M. (1986). *The Encyclopedia of Fund Raising: Charity Auction Management Manual.* Arcadia, CA: Fund Raisers.

Plessner, G.M. (1980). *The Encyclopedia of Fund Raising: Golf Tournament Management Manual.* Arcadia, CA: Fund Raisers.

Plessner, G.M. (1980). *The Encyclopedia of Fund Raising: Testimonial Dinner and Luncheon Management Manual.* Arcadia, CA: Fund Raisers.

Polivka, E. (ed.) (1996). *Professional Meeting Management,* 3rd ed. Birmingham, AL: Professional Convention Management Association.

Post, E. (1991). *Emily Post's Complete Book of Wedding Etiquette,* rev. ed. New York: Harper-Collins.

Powers, T., and J.M. Powers (1991). *Food Service Operations: Planning and Control.* Melbourne, Australia: R.E. Krieger.

Price, C.H. (1989). *The AMA Guide for Meeting and Event Planners.* Arlington, VA: Educational Services Institute.

Professional Convention Management Association (1985). *Professional Meeting Management.* Birmingham, AL: PCMA.

Quain, B. (1993). *Selling Your Services to the Meetings Market.* Dallas, TX: Meeting Professionals International.

Ramsborg, G.C. (1993). *Objectives to Outcomes: Your Contract with the Learner.* Birmingham, AL: Professional Convention Management Association.

Ray, C. (2001). *Highland Heritage: Scottish Americans in the American South.* Chapel Hill, NC: University of North Carolina Press.

Reed, M.H. (1989). *IEG Legal Guide to Sponsorship.* Chicago, IL: International Events Group.

The Reunion Network (1992). *Class Reunions: Lesson 1, A Planner's Guide.* Hollywood, FL: Reunion Network.

The Reunion Network (1992). *Survival Guide for Military Reunion Planners.* Hollywood, FL: Reunion Network.

Reyburn, S. (1997). *Meeting Planner's Guide to Historic Places.* New York: John Wiley & Sons.

Reynolds, R., E. Louie, and E. Addeo (1992). *The Art of the Party: Design Ideas for Successful Entertaining.* New York: Penguin Studio.

Richards, G. (2007). *Eventful Cities: Cultural Management and Urban Revitalisation.* London: Butterworth-Heinemann

Ritchie, J.R.B. and C.R. Goeldener (2002). *Tourism Principles, Practices and Philosophies,* 6th ed. Hoboken, NJ: John Wiley & Sons.

Riverol, A.R. (1992). *Live from Atlantic City: A History of the Miss America Pageant.* Bowling Green, OH: Bowling Green State University Popular Press.

Rogers, T. (2003). *Conferences and Conventions: A Global Industry.* London: Butterworth-Heinemann.

Rooney, C. (1998). *The Knot Ultimate Wedding Planner: Worksheets, Checklists, Etiquette, Calendars, and Answers to Frequently Asked Questions.* New York: Broadway Books.

Roysner, M. (2000). *Hotel Contracts: A Road Map to Successful Hotel Negotiations.* Dallas, TX: IAEM Foundation.

Rutherford, D.G. (1990). *Introduction to the Conventions, Expositions, and Meetings Industry.* New York: Van Nostrand Reinhold.

Rutherford Silvers, J. (forthcoming[DM1]). *Risk Management for Meetings and Events.* London: Butterworth-Heinemann.

Rutherford Silvers, Julia (2003). *Professional Event Coordination.* Hoboken, NJ: John Wiley & Sons.

Scannell, E.E., and J.W. Newstrom (1994). *Even More Games Trainers Play.* New York: McGraw-Hill.

Scannell, E.E., and J.W. Newstrom (1991). *Still More Games Trainers Play.* New York: McGraw-Hill.

Schaumann, Pat (2004). *The Complete Guide to Destination Management.* Hoboken, NJ: John Wiley & Sons.

Schindler-Rainman, E., and J. Cole (1988). *Taking Your Meetings Out of the Doldrums,* rev. ed. San Diego, CA: University Associates.

Schmader, S.W. (1997). *Event Operations.* Boise, ID: IFEA.

Schmader, S.W., and R. Jackson (1997). *Special Events: Inside and Out: A "How-to" Approach to Event Production, Marketing, and Sponsorship.* Champaign, IL: Sagamore Publishing.

Schreibner, A.L., and B. Lenson (1994). *Lifestyle and Event Marketing: Building the New Customer Partnership.* New York: McGraw-Hill.

Shaw, M. (1990). *Convention Sales: A Book of Readings.* East Lansing, MI: Educational Institute of the American Hotel and Motel Association.

Sheerin, M. (1984). *How to Raise Top Dollars from Special Events.* Hartsdale, NY: Public Service Materials Center.

Shenson, H.L. (1990). *How to Develop and Promote Successful Seminars and Workshops: A Definite Guide to Creating and Marketing Seminars, Classes and Conferences.* New York: John Wiley & Sons.

Shock, P.J., and J.M. Stefanelli (1992). *Hotel Catering: A Handbook for Sales and Operations.* New York: John Wiley & Sons.

Simerly, R. (1990). *Planning and Marketing Conferences and Workshops: Tips, Tools, and Techniques.* San Francisco, CA: Jossey-Bass.

Simerly, R.G. (1993). *Strategic Financial Management for Conferences, Workshops, and Meetings.* San Francisco, CA: Jossey-Bass.

Sinclair, M.T., and M.J. Stabler (1997). *The Tourism Industry: An International Analysis.* Wallingford, Oxon, England: C.A.B. International.

Skinner, Bruce (2002). *Event Sponsorship.* Hoboken, NJ: John Wiley & Sons.

Slocum, S.K. (1992). *Popular Arthurian Traditions.* Bowling Green, OH: Bowling Green State University Popular Press.

Soares, E.J. (1991). *Promotional Feats: The Role of Planned Events in the Marketing Communications Mix.* Westport, CT: Greenwood Publishing Group.

Society of Incentive Travel Executives (1990). *The Incentive Travel Case Study Book.* New York: SITE.

Sokolosky, V. (1990). *Corporate Protocol: A Brief Case for Business Etiquette.* Dallas, TX: Valerie and Company.

Sokolosky, V. (1994). *The Fine Art of Business Entertaining.* Dallas, TX: Valerie and Company.

Sonder, Mark (2004). *Event Entertainment Production.* Hoboken, NJ: John Wiley & Sons.

South Australia Department of Tourism (1982). *Planning Festivals and Special Events.* Adelaide, Australia: SADT.

Sowden, C.L. (1992). *An Anniversary to Remember: Years One to Seventy-Five.* St. Paul, MN: Brighton Publications.

Sowden, C.L. (1990). *Wedding Occasions: 101 New Party Themes for Wedding Showers, Rehearsal Dinners, Engagement Parties, and More.* St. Paul, MN: Brighton Publications.

Starsmore, I. (1975). *English Fairs.* London: Thames and Hudson.

Stern, L. (2001). *Stage Management,* 7th ed. Boston: Allyn & Bacon.

Stewart, M. (1988). *The Wedding Planner.* New York: C.N. Potter.

Stewart, M. (1987). *The Weddings.* New York: C.N. Potter.

Storey, B.T. (1997). *One Hundred and One Event Ideas I Wish I'd Thought Of.* Port Angeles, WA: International Festivals and Events Association.

Strick, S. (1995). *Meetings and Conventions.* New York: Van Nostrand Reinhold.

Supovitz, Frank (2004). *The Sports Event Play Book.* Hoboken, NJ: John Wiley & Sons.

Surbeck, L. (1991). *Creating Special Events: The Ultimate Guide to Producing Successful Events.* Louisville, KY: Master Publications.

Swarbrooke, J. (2002). *Development and Management of Visitor Attractions.* London: Butterworth-Heinemann.

Swartz, O.D. (1988). *Service Etiquette,* 4th ed. Annapolis, MD: Naval Institute Press.

Swiderski, R.M. (1987). *Voices: An Anthropologist's Dialogue with an Italian-American Festival.* Bowling Green, OH: Popular Press.

Talbot, R. (1990). *Meeting Management: Practical Advice for Both New and Experimental Managers Based on an Expert's Twenty Years in the "Wonderful Wacky World" of Meeting Planning.* McLean, VA: EPM Publications.

Tarlow, Peter (2003). *Event Risk Management & Safety.* Hoboken, NJ: John Wiley & Sons.

Tassiopoulos, D. (ed.) (2000). *Event Management: A Professional and Development Approach.* Johannesburg, South Africa: Juta Education.

Tepper, B. (1993). *Incentive Travel: The Complete Guide.* San Francisco, CA: Dendrobium Books.

Thomsett, M.C. (1991). *The Little Black Book of Business Etiquette.* New York: American Management Association.

The 3M Meeting and Management Team with Jeannine Drew (1994). *Mastering Meetings: Discovering the Hidden Potential of Effective Business Meetings.* New York: McGraw-Hill.

Torrence, S.R. (1991). *How to Run Scientific and Technical Meetings.* New York: Van Nostrand Reinhold.

Turner, V. (1982). *Celebration: Studies in Festivity and Ritual*. Washington, DC: Smithsonian Institution Press.

Van Der Wagen, L., and B. Carlos (2004). *Event Management*. New York: Prentice Hall.

Veeck, B. (1972). *Thirty Tons a Day: The Rough-Riding Education of a Neophyte Racetrack Operator*. New York: Viking Press.

Verbruiggen, H. (2002). *New Technologies for Computer Control 2001*. London: Pergamon.

Von Bornstedt, M., and U. Prytz (1987). *Folding Table Napkins*. New York: Sterling Publishing Company.

Walford, C. (1968). *Fairs, Past and Present: A Chapter in the History of Commerce*. New York: A.M. Kelly.

Washington, G., and Applewood Books Staff (1994). *George Washington's Rules of Civility and Decent Behavior in Company and Conversation*. Mount Vernon, VA: Applewood Books.

Watt, D.C. (1998). *Event Management in Leisure and Tourism*. London, UK: Pearson Education UK. .

Weirich, M.L. (1992). *Meetings and Conventions Management*. Albany, NY: Delmar Publishers.

Weissinger, S.S. (1992). *A Guide to Successful Meeting Planning*. New York: John Wiley & Sons.

Wiersma, E.A. (1991). *Creative Event Development: A Guide to Strategic Success in the World of Special Events*. Indianapolis, IN: Author.

Wigger, E.G. (1997). *Themes, Dreams, and Schemes: Banquet Menu Ideas, Concepts, and Thematic Experiences*. New York: John Wiley & Sons.

Williams, W. (1994). *User Friendly Fundraising: A Step-by-Step Guide to Profitable Special Events*. Alexander, NC: World Comm., Associated Publishers.

Wilson, J., and L. Undall (1982). *Folk Festivals: A Handbook for Organization and Management*. Knoxville, TN: University of Tennessee Press.

Wisdom, E.J. (1992). *Family Reunion Organizer*. Nashville, TN: Post Oak Publications.

Witkowski, D. (1994). *How to Haunt a House*. New York: Random House.

Wolf, T. (1983). *Presenting Performances: A Handbook for Sponsors*. New York: American Council of the Arts.

Wolfson, S.M. (1995). *The Meeting Planner's Complete Guide to Negotiating: You Can Get What You Want*. Kansas City: Institute for Meeting and Conference Management.

Wolfson, S.M. (1986). *The Meeting Planner's Guide to Logistics and Arrangements*. Kansas City, Missouri: Institute for Meeting and Conference Management.

Wolfson, S.M. (1991). *Meeting Planner's Workbook: Write Your Own Hotel Contract*. Kansas City, Missouri: Institute for Meeting and Conference Management.

Wright, R.R. (1988). *The Meeting Spectrum: An Advanced Guide for Meeting Professionals*. San Diego, CA: Rockwood Enterprises.

Yeoman, I., M. Robertson, J. Ali-Knight, S. Drummond, and U. McMahon-Beattie (eds). (2003). *Festivals and Events Management: An International Arts and Culture Perspective*. London: Butterworth-Heinemann.

Zuckerman, M. (1979). *Sensation Seeking: Beyond the Optimal Level of Arousal*. Hillsdale, NJ: Lawrence Erlbaum Associates.

General Interest Business Books for Event Leaders

American Society of Association Executives (1985). *Achieving Goals.* Washington, DC: ASAE.

Axtell, R.E. (1993). *Do's and Taboos around the World,* 3rd ed. New York: John Wiley & Sons.

Axtell, R.E. (1994). *The Do's and Taboos of International Trade: A Small Business.* New York: John Wiley & Sons.

Axtell, R.E. (1997). *Gestures: The Do's and Taboos of Body Language around the World.* New York: John Wiley & Sons.

Baker, D.B. (1992). *Power Quotes: 4,000 Trenchant Soundbites on Leadership & Liberty, Treason & Triumph, Sacrifice & Scandal, Risk & Rebellion, Weakness & War and Other Affairs Politiques.* Detroit, MI: Visible Ink Press.

Bartlett, J. (2002). *Familiar Quotations: A Collection of Passages, Phrases, and Proverbs Traced to Their Sources in Ancient and Modern Literature,* 14th ed. Boston, MA: Little Brown & Co.

Collins, Jim (2001). *From Good to Great.* New York: HarperCollins.

Davidson, J.P., and G.A. Fay (1991). *Selling to the Giants: A Key to Become a Key Supplier to Large Corporations.* New York: McGraw-Hill.

Goldblatt, J.J. and F. Supovitz. (1999). *Dollars & Events: How to Succeed in the Special Events Business.* New York: John Wiley & Sons.

Goldsmith, C.S., and A.H. Waigand (1990). *Building Profits with Group Travel.* San Francisco, CA: Dendrobium Books.

Harris, T.L. (1993). *The Marketer's Guide to Public Relations: How Today's Top Companies Are Using the New PR to Gain a Competitive Edge.* New York: John Wiley & Sons.

Humes, J.C. (1993). *More Podium Humor: Using Wit and Humor in Every Speech You Make.* New York: HarperCollins.

Kawasaki, G. (1991). *Selling the Dream: How to Promote Your Product, Company or Ideas—and Make a Difference—Using Everyday Evangelism.* New York: HarperCollins.

Piltzeker, T., B. Barber, M. Cross, and R. Dittner. (2006). *How to Cheat at Managing Microsoft Operations Manager 2005.* Sebastopol, CA: Syngress Publishing.

Wolfram, S. (2002). *A New Kind of Science.* Champaign, IL: Wolfram Media.

Anthropological and Folklore Resources of Interest to Event Leaders

Baron, R., and N.R. Spitzer (1992). *Public Folklore.* Washington, DC: Smithsonian Institution Press.

Browne, R.B. (1981). *Rituals and Ceremonies in Popular Culture.* Bowling Green, OH: Bowling Green State University Popular Press.

Browne, R.B., and A. Neal (2001). *Ordinary Reactions to Extraordinary Events.* Bowling Green, OH: Bowling Green State University Popular Press.

Cannadine, D., and S. Price (1993). *Rituals of Royalty: Power and Ceremonial in Traditional Societies.* New York: Cambridge University Press.

Farmer, S. (2002). *Sacred Ceremony: How to Create Ceremonies for Healing, Transitions, and Celebration.* Carlsbad, CA: Hay House.

Grimes, R. (2002). *Deeply into the Bone: Re-Inventing Rites of Passage*. Berkeley, CA: University of California Press.

Grimes, R. (1995). *Readings in Ritual Studies*. Upper Saddle River, NJ: Pearson, Allyn & Bacon.

Jensen, V. (1993). *Where People Gather: Carving a Totem Pole*. Vancouver, British Columbia: Douglas & McIntyre.

Johnston, W.M. (1991). *Celebrations: The Cult of Anniversaries in Europe and the United States Today*. New Brunswick, NJ: Transaction Publishers.

Mason, A. (2002). *People Around the World*. Boston: Houghton-Mifflin.

St. Aubyn, L. (1999). *Everyday Rituals and Ceremonies: Special Ways to Mark Important Events in Your Life*. London: Piatkus Books.

Turner, V.W. (1982). *Celebration Studies in Festivity & Ritual*. Washington, DC: Smithsonian Institution Press.

Visser, M. (1999). *Much Depends on Dinner: The Extraordinary History and Mythology, Allure and Obsessions, Peril and Taboos, of an Ordinary Meal*. New York: Grove Press.

Visser, M. (1992). *The Rituals of Dinner: The Origins, Evolution, Eccentricities and Meaning of Table Manners*. New York: Penguin USA.

York, S. (1992). *Developing Roots & Wings: A Trainer's Guide to Affirming Culture in Early Childhood*. St. Paul, MN: Redleaf Press.

APPENDIX 2

Organizations and Resources

The Event Leadership–related organizations and resources listed in this appendix can help propel your career success.

1. Do your homework and contact listed associations via e-mail and request information about their educational and networking programs and resources.

2. Join a primary organization based on your field of interest. For example, if you are interested in the broad category of Event Leadership, the International Special Events Society should be your first choice. However, if your selection is narrowly confined to expositions, you will want to join the International Association for Exposition Management. The primary organization will be where you devote the majority of your time and energy, while the secondary organization is one whose resources and programs can further assist you in developing your career.

   Most organizations have local, state, or provincial chapters where you can easily meet people who could serve as future mentors.

   Many national and international leaderships begin their leadership progression at the local, state, or provincial level.

3. Set a three- to five-year goal that includes committee involvement and board leadership and, ultimately, serving as one of the officers of the organization's local chapter or national organization. In many industries, the most successful people are those who are also the leaders within their industry's professional organizations.

4. Once you have set your goal, annually keep track of how you are doing. Continually remind those who are more established in the organization of your career goals and seek their help in making sure that you are advancing properly within the leadership of the organization.

In summary, do not merely join and expect success. Success comes naturally from your investment of time and talent.

Definitions

+ *Professional trade association:* a national or international organization whose purpose is to actively promote the industry within which its members are active
+ *Professional society:* a national or international organization that provides research and educational services for its members and the general public
+ *Regional association:* an organization whose members are located in one regional location
+ *Local chapter:* A local (city, state, province based) affiliate organization of a national association.

Event Management–Related Organizations

American Rental Association
1900 Nineteenth Street
Moline, IL 61265
(800) 334–2177
www.ararental.org
A professional trade association whose members own and operate rental stores, including party rental stores. It offers the Certified Rental Professional (CRP) certification program.

American Society of Association Executives (ASAE)
1575 I Street, N.W.
Washington, DC 20005–1103
(202) 626-ASAE
www.asaecenter.org
A professional trade association whose members are executives in professional, trade, and civic associations, as well as those who provide services and products for this industry. The Meetings and Exposition Section is composed specifically of Event Leaders. Allied associations exist throughout the United States and Europe.

Association for Convention Operations Management
191 Clarksville Road
Princeton Junction, NJ 08550
(609)-799–3712
Fax: (609)-799–7032
www.acomonline.org

A professional trade association whose members are employed as convention service managers and in other conference positions.

Association for Events Management Education (AEME)
Glenn Bowdin, Chair
c/o UK Centre for Events Management
Leeds Metropolitan University
Civic Quarter, Leeds, LS1 3HE, UK
+44 (0)113 283 3484
Fax: +44 (0)113 283 3111
E-mail: g.a.j.bowdin@leedsmet.ac.uk
www.aeme.org
AEME is a professional association for educators in the field of events management. It is based in the United Kingdom, but membership is open to educational institutions worldwide. It provides conferences for faculty and students as well as publications through its Web site.

Association for Fundraising Professionals
1101 King Street, Suite 700
Alexandria, VA 22314
(703) 684–0410
Fax: (703) 684–0540
www.nsfre.org
This organization provides training and information related to fundraising and development for not-for-profit organizations. They have a national convention and active local chapters, as well as provide a wide variety of helpful written materials.

Association of Bridal Consultants (ABC)
56 Danbury Road, Suite 11
New Milford, CT 06776
(860) 355–0464
Fax: (860) 354–1404
E-mail: office@bridalassn.com
www.bridalassn.com
A professional trade association that offers
educational programs and certification for its
members.

Association of Destination Management
Executives (ADME)
P.O. Box 2307
Dayton, OH 45401–2307
(937) 586–3727
Fax: (937) 586–3699
E-mail: info@adme.org
www.adme.org
This is the leading organization in North
America of professional destination management specialists. A destination management
executive is an expert in the assets within
their local destination and provides among
many other services airport and local shuttle
transportation, tours, event planning, registration, and other critical local needs. ADME
offers a certification entitled Certified Destination Management Executive (CDME)
which is considered the highest level of professional qualification in this field.

Association of International Meeting
Planners (AIMP)
2547 Monroe Street
Dearborn, MI 48124
(313) 563–0360
Fax: (313)-563–1448
A professional trade association whose mem-
bers organize international meetings.

Connected International Meeting
Professionals Association
9200 Bayard Place
Fairfax, VA 22032
(512) 684–0889
Fax: (267) 390–5193

www.cimpa.org
An association of meeting professionals who
utilize the Internet as a major tool in their
work.

Convention Industry Council (CIC)
1620 I Street, NW, 6th Floor
Washington, DC 20006
Toll Free: 1–877–429–8634
Phone: (202) 429–8634
Fax: (202) 463–8498
www.conventionindustry.org

Council of Engineering and Scientific
Society Executives (CESSE)
P.O. Box 130656
St. Paul, MN 55113
(952) 838–3285
Fax: (651) 765–2890
www.cesse.org
A professional society whose members
organize meetings in the engineering and
scientific industries.

Council of Protocol Executives (COPE)
101 West Twelfth Street, Suite PH-H
New York, NY 10011
(212) 633–6934
E-mail: copeorg@aol.com
www.councilofprotocolexecutives.org
A professional society whose members are
engaged primarily as experts in protocol.

Destination Marketing Association
International (DMAI) (formerly known as
the International Association of Convention
and Visitors Bureaus)
2025 M Street, N.W., Suite 500
Washington, DC 20036
(202) 296–7888
Fax: (202) 296–7889
www.iacvb.org
A professional trade association whose
members manage and market convention
and visitors' bureaus for individual destinations and supply goods and services for
these bureaus.

First Night International, Inc.
67 Broad Street, Suite 210
Johnson City, NY 13790
(607) 772–3597
Fax: (607) 772–6305
www.firstnight.com
A community celebration of the New Year through the arts. It is an alcohol-free, public festival that marks the passage from the old year to the new with art, ritual, and festivity. All First Night Celebrations are licensed by First Night International and adhere to a set of standards.

Foundation for International Meetings (FIM)
1110 N. Glebe Road, Suite 580
Arlington, VA 22201
(703) 908–0707
Fax: (703) 908–0709
www.imnsolutions.com
A professional association whose members specialize in organizing international meetings.

Healthcare Convention and Exhibitors Association
1100 Johnson Ferry Road, Suite 300
Atlanta, GA 30342
(404) 252–3663
Fax: (404) 252–0774
www.hcea.org
A professional trade association whose members are exhibitors and others in the healthcare industry.

Hospitality Sales and Marketing Association International (HSMAI)
8201 Greensboro Drive, Suite 300
McLean, VA 22102
(703) 610–9024
Fax: (703) 610–9005
www.hsmai.org
A professional trade association whose members are professional salespeople in the hotel, convention center, and hospitality industry and those who provide services and products for this industry. HSMAI sponsors a confer-

ence called "Affordable Meetings." This conference provides low-cost resources for Event Leaders in the convention industry.

Insurance Conference Planners Association
401 N. Michigan Avenue, 22nd Floor
Chicago, IL 60611
(312) 245–1023
Fax: (312) 321–5150
www.icpanet.com
A professional association whose members are planners of conferences in the insurance industry.

International Association for Exhibition Management
8111 LBJ Freeway, Suite 750
Dallas, TX 75251–1313
(972) 458–8002
Fax: (972) 458–8119
www.iaem.org
A professional trade association whose members manage trade and public expositions and provide services and products for this industry.

International Association of Amusement Parks and Attractions (IAAPA)
1448 Duke Street
Alexandria, VA 22314
(703) 836–4800
www.iaapa.org
A professional trade association whose members own, manage, market, and consult in the amusement park and attraction industry and provide services and products for this industry.

International Association of Assembly Managers
635 Fritz Drive, Suite 100
Coppell, TX 75019–4442
(972) 906–7441
Fax: (972) 906–7418
www.iaam.org
A professional trade association whose members own, manage, operate, market, consult, or supply services and products for arenas, auditoriums, stadiums, and other venues.

International Association of Conference
Centers
243 North Lindbergh Boulevard
St. Louis, MO 63141
(314) 993–8575
www.iacconline.org
A professional trade association whose members own, operate, manage, market, consult, and supply goods and services for conference centers.

International Association of Fairs &
Expositions (IAFE)
P.O. Box 985
Springfield, MO 65801
(800) 516–0313
Fax: (417) 862–0156
www.fairsandexpos.com
A professional trade association whose members organize and manage fairs and expositions.

International Association of Professional
Congress Organizers (IAPCO)
42 Canham Road
London W37SR, UK
+44–20–8749–6171
Fax: +44–20–8740–0241
E-mail: info@iapco.org
www.iapco.org
A professional trade association whose members are professional congress organizers.

International Balloon Association
1600 Lynnhurst
Wichita, KS 67212
(866) 413–7358
(316) 943–7223
Fax: (316) 941–4097
E-mail: Marty@IBAonline.net
www.ibaonline.net
Individuals and suppliers in the balloon
industry. They conduct an annual convention each year that provides numerous ideas
for balloon designers.

International Caterers Association
1200 17th Street, N.W.
Washington, DC 20036
(888) 604–5844
Fax: (202)-973–5371
www.icacater.org
Founded in 1981, to provide education and
networking for caterers.

International Congress & Convention
Association
The International Meetings Association
Entrada 121
1096 EB Amsterdam, The Netherlands
+31–20–398–1919
www.icca.nl
A professional trade association whose members are travel agents, congress centers, professional congress organizers, and others
involved in the organization and servicing of
international meetings.

International Council of Shopping Centers
(ICSC)
1221 Avenue of the Americas, 41st Floor
New York, NY 10020–1099
(646) 728–3800
Fax: (732) 694–1755
E-mail: icsc@icsc.org
www.icsc.org
A professional trade association whose members own, operate, manage, market, and supply goods and services for shopping centers.
ICSC administers the Certified Marketing
Director (CMD) exam and designation. This
program includes competencies relating to
shopping center promotion, including special
event leadership.

International Festivals & Events Association
(IFEA)
2601 Eastover Terrace
Boise, ID 83706
(208) 433–0950
Fax: (208) 433–9812
www.ifea.com

A professional trade association whose members own, operate, manage, market, and supply goods and services for festivals and events. IFEA in conjunction with Purdue University administers the Certified Festival Executive (CFE) designation/certification.

International Institute of Convention Management
9200 Bayard Place
Fairfax, VA 22032
(703) 978–6287
A professional trade association whose members are active in managing conventions.

International Special Events Society (ISES)
401 North Michigan Avenue
Chicago, IL 60611–4267
(800) 688-ISES
Fax: (312) 673–6953
www.ises.com
The only umbrella organization representing all aspects of the special events industry.

Japanese Association for the Promotion of Creative Events (JACE)
Japanese Institute for Eventology
3 F Ichibancho-Hohgenzaka Building
13 Ichibancho, Choiyoda-Ku Tokyo
102–0082
Japan
81–3-3238–7821
Fax: 81–3-3238–7834
E-mail: watanabe@jace.or.jp
www.jace.or.jp
The leading association in Japan for event professionals. It is connected to a wide range of event organizations, including Japan's Ministry of Economy, Trade and Industry. JACE provides workshops, training, seminars, and offers certifications for professional event managers in Japan. JACE is also the home of Japan's Institute for Eventology, which studies and evaluates the impacts of events in Japan.

Meeting Professionals International (MPI)
3030 LBJ Freeway, Suite 1700
Dallas, TX 75234–2759
(972) 702–3000
Fax: (972) 702–3070
www.mpiweb.org
A professional trade association whose members include corporate, association, and other meeting planners, as well as those who provide goods and services for meeting planners.

National Association of Casino and Theme Party Operators
7815 S. 108th
Kent, WA 98032
(800) 35-LUCKY
www.casinoparties.com
Founded to provide education and professional networking for individuals in the casino and theme party field.

National Association of Catering Executives (NACE)
9881 Broken Land Parkway
Columbia, MD 21046
(410) 290–5410
Fax: (410) 290–5460
www.nace.net
A professional trade association whose members provide on- and off-premises catering services as well as goods and services for the catering industry.

National Association of Reunion Managers
P.O. Box 50713
Renton, WA 98058–2713
(800) 654–2776
www.reunions.com
A professional trade association for persons who professionally organize reunions.

National Ballroom & Entertainment Association (NBEA)
2799 Locust Road
Decorah, IA 52101–7600

(563) 382–3871
www.nbea.com
A professional trade association whose members provide or organize entertainment.

National Bridal Service (NBS)
1004 West Thompson Street, Suite 205
Richmond, VA 23230
(804) 342–0055
Fax: (804) 342–6062
www.nationalbridal.com
A professional trade association whose members consult in the bridal industry.

National Coalition of Black Meeting Planners (NCBMP)
8630 Fenton Street, Suite 126
Silver Spring, MD 20910
(202) 628–3952
www.ncbmp.com
A professional trade association whose members are black meeting planners or those who provide goods and services for meeting planners.

National Restaurant Association (NRA)
1200 Seventeenth Street, N.W.
Washington, DC 20036–3097
(202) 331–5900
Fax: (202) 331–2429
www.restaurant.org
A professional trade association whose members own, operate, manage, market, consult, or supply goods and services to the restaurant industry.

National Association of Fundraising Executives
1101 King Street, Suite 700
Alexandria, VA 22314
(703) 684–0410
www.nsfre.org
A professional trade association whose members are employed in development, fundraising, or consulting in the philanthropic field and provide goods and services for this profession.

North American Association of Commencement Officers
Kellie A. Southards, President
Special Events/Travel Manager
University of Wyoming
1000 E. University Avenue
Laramie, WY 82071
(307) 766–4122
E-mail: KSouth@uwyo.edu
www.naaco.info
An association whose members are responsible for planning and producing college and university comment exercises and related programs.

Professional Convention Management Association (PCMA)
2301 South Lake Shore Drive, Suite 1001
Chicago, IL 60616–1419
(312) 423–7262
A professional trade association whose members plan and manage meetings and supply goods and services for meeting planners.

Public Relations Society of America (PRSA)
33 Maiden Lane, 11th Floor
New York, NY 10038–5150
(212) 460–1400
Fax: (212) 995–0757
www.prsa.org
A professional trade association whose members are involved in public relations activities or supply goods and services for this profession.

Religious Conference Management Association (RCMA)
One RCA Dome, Suite 120
Indianapolis, IN 46255
(317) 632–1888
www.rcmaweb.org
A professional trade association whose members are professional meeting planners for religious organizations and those who provide goods and services for this industry.

Resort and Commercial Recreation
Association
P.O. Box 1564
Dubuque, IA 52004
www.r-c-r-a.org
An association of commercial recreation
directors, their suppliers, and other professionals as well as students and faculty in
commercial recreation programs in higher
education. They provide annual networking
and education programs through conventions and workshops as well as career fairs.

Society of Corporate Meeting Professionals
(SCMP)
217 Ridgemont Avenue
San Antonio, TX 78209
(210) 822–6522
Fax: (210) 822–9838
A professional trade association whose members are involved in corporate meeting planning and supply goods and services for this
industry.

Society of Government Meeting
Professionals (SGMP)
908 King Street, Lower Level
Alexandria, VA 22314
(703) 549–0892
Fax: (703) 549–0708
www.sgmp.org
A professional trade association whose members are involved in planning government
meetings and those who supply goods and
services for this industry.

Society of Government Travel Professionals
(SGTP)
6935 Wisconsin Avenue, Suite 200
Bethesda, MD 20815
(301) 654–8595
Fax: (301) 654–6663
www.government-travel.org
A professional trade association for travel

professionals involved in government and
those who supply goods or services for this
industry.

Society of Incentive & Travel Executives
(SITE)
401 North Michigan Avenue
Chicago, IL 60611
(312) 321–5148
www.site-intl.org
A professional trade association whose members organize incentive activities and supply
goods and services for this industry.

Stage Managers' Association
P.O. Box 275, Times Square Station
New York, NY 10180–2020
(212) 543–9567
E-mail: info@stagemanagers.org
www.stagemanagers.org
A professional trade association whose mem-
bers are theatrical stage members. Many
professional stage managers work in the
Event Leadership profession.

Trade Show Exhibitors Association (TSEA)
McCormick Place
2301 South Lake Shore Drive, Suite 1005
Chicago, IL 60616
(312) 842-TSEA
Fax: (312) 842–8744
www.tsea.org
A professional trade association whose members exhibit at international meetings.

Western Fairs Association
1776 Tribute Road, Suite 210
Sacramento, CA 95815–4410
(916) 927–3100
www.fairsnet.org
A regional association whose members
organize and manage fairs.

Miscellaneous Organizations and Resources

Actors' Equity Association (AEA)
165 West 46th Street
New York, NY 10036
(212) 869–8530
www.actorsequity.org
A professional union representing professional actors, actresses, and stage managers working in live theater.

Air Transport Association of America
1301 Pennsylvania Avenue, N.W., Suite 1100
Washington, DC 20004–1707
(202) 626–4218
www.airlines.org
A professional trade association whose members are active in the air-transport industry.

American Federation of Musicians
(AF of M)
1501 Broadway, Suite 600
New York, NY 10036
(212) 869–1330
Fax: (212) 764–6134
www.afm.org
A professional union representing musicians.

American Federation of Television & Radio Artists (AFTRA)
260 Madison Avenue
New York, NY 10016–2402
(212) 532–0800
www.aftra.com
A professional union representing television and radio performers.

American Floral Marketing Council
1601 Duke Street
Alexandria, VA 22314–3406
(703) 836–8700
www.aboutflowers.com
A trade association that promotes the floral industry.

American Guild of Variety Artists (AGVA)
184 Fifth Avenue, Sixth Floor
New York, NY 10010
(212) 675–1003
No web site available for this organization.
A professional union representing performers in nightclubs, cabarets, circuses, and other variety venues.

American Hotel & Lodging Association (AH&LA)
1201 New York Avenue, N.W., Suite 600
Washington, DC 20005–3931
(202) 289–3100
Fax: (202) 289–3199
www.ahla.com
A professional trade association representing owners, managers, and marketers of hotels and motels and those who provide services and products for these industry-allied organizations.

American Institute of Floral Designers
720 Light Street
Baltimore, MD 21230
(410) 752–3318
www.aifd.org
A professional trade association whose members represent floral designers and those who provide products and services for this industry.

American Pyrotechnics Association (APA)
P.O. Box 30438
Bethesda, MD 20824
(301) 907–8181
Fax: (301) 907–9148
www.americanpyro.com
A professional trade association representing manufacturers, designers, and producers of professional pyrotechnics.

American Society for Training &
Development (ASTD)
1640 King Street, Box 1443
Alexandria, VA 22313–2043
(703) 683–8100
www.astd.org
A professional trade association whose members are trainers and those who provide services and products for this industry.

American Society of Composers, Authors
and Publishers (ASCAP)
One Lincoln Plaza
New York, NY 10023
(212) 621–6000
www.ascap.com
A music licensing organization representing composers, authors, and publishers for live and electronic music for events.

Broadcast Music, Inc. (BMI)
10 Music Square East
Nashville, TN 37203
(615) 401–2000
www.bmi.com
A music licensing organization representing composers, authors, and publishers for live and electronic music for events.

Exhibit Designers & Producers Association
(EDPA)
5775 Peachtree-Dunwoody Road
Atlanta, GA 30342
(404) 303–7310
www.edpa.com
A professional trade association whose members design and produce exhibits for expositions.

Exhibition Services & Contractors
Association
2260 Corporate Circle, Suite 400
Henderson, NV 89074
(702) 319–9561
Fax: (702) 450–7732
www.esca.org
A professional trade association whose members provide services for expositions.

International Association of Speakers
Bureaus (IASB)
7150 Winton Drive
Indianapolis, IN 46268
(317) 328–7790
Fax: (317) 280–8527
www.igab.org
A professional trade association whose members own, operate, and manage professional speakers' bureaus.

International Communications Industries
Association (ICIA)
11242 Waples Mill Road, Suite 200
Fairfax, VA 22030
(800) 659–7469
Fax: (703) 278–8082
www.infocomm.org
A professional trade association whose members provide communications services.

LED Lighting Products
STA Enterprises International Ltd.
33–59 Farrington Street
Flushing, NY 11354
or
P.O. Box 462
Flushing, New York 11352
(888) 353–0805
(718) 353–0805
Fax: (718) 353–6350
E-mail: sales@stawwholesale.com
www.stawholesale.com
Provides dozens of different LED-powered products ranging from plastic ice cubes to champagne, wine, and beer glasses.

The Balloon Association
Katepwa House
Ashfield Park Avenue
Ross-on-Wye, Herefordshire
England HR9 5AX
01989–762–204
Fax: 01989–567–676
E-mail: admin@nabas.co.uk
www.nabas.co.uk
A professional trade association whose members provide balloon products and services.

National Limousine Association
49 South Maple Avenue
Marlton, NJ 08053
(856) 596–3344 ext. 15
www.limo.org
A professional trade association for persons
who own, manage, market, and supply goods
and services to the limousine industry.

National Speakers Association (NSA)
1500 South Priest Drive
Tempe, AZ 85281
(480) 968–2552
www.nsaspeaker.org
A professional trade association whose members are professional speakers and those who
provide services and products for the professional speaking industry.

North American Association of
Ventriloquists (NAAV)
P.O. Box 420
Littleton, CO 80160
(800) 250–5125
www.maherstudios.com
A professional trade association for people
involved in ventriloquism.

Pyrotechnics Guild International (PGI)
3944 Carthage Road
Randallstown, MD 21133–4517
(410) 655–8594
www.pgi.org
An organization comprised of people
engaged in fireworks (pyrotechnics).

Screen Actors Guild (SAG)
5757 Wilshire Boulevard
Los Angeles, CA 90036–3600
(323) 954–1600
www.sag.com
A professional trade union for actors,
actresses, and others in the film and television industry.

Society of American Florists (SAF)
1601 Duke Street
Alexandria, VA 22314
(703) 836–8700
Fax: (703) 836–8700
www.safnow.org
A professional trade association for florists
and those who provide goods and services
for the floral industry.

Special Events Office of the Military
District of Washington
Fort Lesley J. McNair
Fourth and P Streets, S.W.
Washington, DC 20319–5058
(202) 475–1399
www.usdod.gov
An organization responsible for providing
military units such as bands, color guards,
and others for special events in the Washington, DC, metropolitan area.

Travel Industry Association
1100 New York Avenue, N.W., Suite 450
Washington, DC 20005
(202) 408–8422
Fax: (202) 408–1255
www.tia.org
A professional trade association whose members promote, market, research, and provide
information about the travel industry.

United States Department of Homeland
Security
Washington, DC 20528
(202) 282–8000
www.dhs.gov/dhspublic
The U.S. federal agency responsible for
homeland security issues.

Internet Sites

Cities and Convention and Visitors' Bureaus

50states.com
Find businesses in a particular area of the United States.
www.50states.com

Big Book
Directory of addresses of any business in the United States, as well as maps and restaurant reviews.
www.bigbook.com

City Net
A comprehensive guide to communities all over the world.
www.citynet.org

ClickCity.com
Provides news and resources for travel and entertainment of various cities.
www.clickcity.com

ConventionBureaus.com
Directory of official convention bureau and national tourist office Web sites around the globe.
www.conventionbureaus.com

Destination Marketing Association International
This organization administers CINET, one of the larger databases of information about group histories (conventions, meetings), and provides education programs, including certifications in destination management.
www.iacvb.org

Google Earth
Learn more about a specific location by using this three-dimensional interface to the planet
http://earth.google.com

LA, Inc.: The Convention and Visitors Bureau
This comprehensive guide includes accommodations, event calendars, and travel information for the city of Los Angeles.
www.lacvb.com

NYC & Company
Use this Web site to organize professional events and meetings in New York City. From the homepage, click on "Meeting and Event Professionals."
www.nycvisit.com

Tourism Offices Worldwide Directory
Searchable database of offices throughout the world.
www.towd.com

USA CityLink Project
A directory of U.S. city sites on the Web listed by state. Focuses on two types of sites: tourism sites and sites whose mission is to support their local community.
www.usacitylink.com

Weather.com
Plan appropriate clothing based on the weather forecast.
www.weather.com

Windows Live Local
Combines online mapping with local searches.
http://local.live.com

General

American Society for Training and Development
The world's largest society dedicated to workplace learning and professional training.
www.astd.org

Eagle's Talent Connection, Inc.
An all-inclusive speaker bureau specializing in helping corporate meeting planners select and stage motivational speakers, sports stars, celebrities, and corporate entertainment.
www.eaglestalent.com

FabJob: Event Planner
How to get an event leadership job and create a business.
www.fabjob.com/eventplanner1.asp

International Association of Professional Congress Organizers
A nonprofit organization that represents professional organizers and managers of international and national congresses, conventions, and special events.
www.iapco.org

International Association of Speakers Bureau
The worldwide trade association of speaker agencies and bureaus, with members in Canada, England, Australia, The Netherlands, South Africa, Spain, Singapore, Brazil, France and New Zealand as well as the United States. IASB member bureaus subscribe to a code of ethics, take part in ongoing professional development and adhere to a high level of professional standards.
www.iasbweb.org

International Congress and Convention Association
Represents the main specialists in handling, transporting, and accommodating international events and comprises over in almost 80 countries worldwide.
www.icca.nl

International Institute for Peace through Tourism
A not-for-profit organization dedicated to fostering and facilitating tourism initiatives that contribute to international understanding and cooperation, an improved quality of environment, and the preservation of heritage, and, through these initiatives, helps to bring about a peaceful and sustainable world.
www.iipt.org

National Speaker's Association
A national nonprofit association that educates and creates networks among professional speakers. It is affiliated with international speaker's organizations throughout the world.
www.nsaspeakers.org

Pacific Asia Travel Association
Representing the travel and tourism industry in Asia and the Pacific Islands.
www.pata.org

Toastmasters International
An organization aimed at helping you improve your communication and leadership skills.
www.toastmasters.org

Union of International Associations
Uses programs oriented toward the community of international associations whose actions are designed to facilitate through both special studies and new uses of information.
www.uia.org

Washington Speaker's Bureau
Washington, D.C.'s leading lecture agency.
www.washingtonspeakers.com

World Tourism Organization

A specialized agency of the United Nations, which is the leading international organization in the field of tourism.
www.world-tourism.org

World Travel and Tourism Council

The forum for global business leaders comprising the presidents, chairs, and chief executives of 100 of the world's foremost companies. It is the only body representing the private sector in all parts of the Travel and Tourism industry worldwide.
www.wttc.org

Hotels and Alternative Venues

These sites provide online booking capability for leisure and group business.

Accor Hotels

www.accorhotels.com

All the Hotels on the Web

www.all-hotels.com

Choice Hotels Europe

www.choicehotelseurope.com

Choice Hotels International

www.choicehotels.com

Directory of Hotels Online

www.hotels.com

Guide to Campus, Nonprofit, and Retreat Meeting Facilities

A site that lets planners search by geographic location for a selection of less customary venues. Free. Over 500 sites listed.
www.USAHotelGuide.com

HotelFormule1

www.hotelformule1.com

HotelBook

www.utell.com
The following Web sites provide online booking capability for travel accommodations for younger travelers all over the world.
Hostelworld.com
Kasbah.com

Online Publications

Bizbash.com
Resources, discoveries, and news for special event planning, branding, and business entertaining.
www.bizbash.com

BizTravel
Online magazine for the business traveler from e-publishers.
www.biztravel.com

Meetings and Conventions Online
Helps meeting and event planners in corporations, associations, incentive houses, and independent planning companies effectively manage their careers.
www.meetings-conventions.com

Newspage
A clipping service creating news pages for the travel, hospitality, and gaming industry.
www.individual.com

Nightclub and Bar Magazine
Provides information on nightclubs and bars.
www.nightclub.com

Successful Meetings
An electronic version of the magazine.
www.successmtgs.com

Valuation Resources
A free resource guide to business valuation publications, industry information, economic data, market transaction data, valuation multiples, legal and tax resources, and more.
www.valuationresources.com

Professional Associations/Listservs

American Society of Association Executives
A membership organization for the association management profession.
www.asaenet.org

American Travel Association
Carriers that are members of the American Travel Association.
www.airlines.org (click on "Current ATA Members")

Hospitality Net
Internet home page for the global hospitality industry. Provides a global communication platform for professionals and students, as well as vendors.
www.hospitalitynet.org

Infotec-Travel
A moderated Internet work mailing list dedicated to the exchange of information about information technology in travel and tourism.
www.infotec-travel.com

International Association of Exhibition Management
Represents the interests of trade show and exposition managers. The IAEM is the leading association for the global exhibition industry and represents over 3,500 individuals who conduct and support exhibitions around the world.
www.iaem.org

International Special Events Society
The home page for the ISES, the only international association serving the events industry.
www.ises.com

MPINet
Available through Meeting Professionals International on CompuServe. An excellent method for planners and suppliers to network, get education online via the message sections and library, conduct real-time conversations, and have meetings.
www.mpiweb.org

National Association of Catering Executives
The oldest and largest professional association that addresses all aspects of the catering industry through the collective efforts of members, local chapters, committees and the Foundation of NACE.
www.nace.net

Professional Convention Management Association
An association dedicated to delivering breakthrough education and promoting the value of professional convention management.
www.pcma.org

TEAM Net
An exclusive membership of special events companies in separate major North American cities that network together to support the traveling needs of their clients.
www.go2teamnet.com

Trade Show Listserver
The Tourism and Convention Department at the University of Nevada–Las Vegas operates the Convention Educator's Listserver.
groups/yahoo.com/group/conventioneducators

Airlines of the United States of America

Airtran Airways
www.airtran.com

Alaska Airlines
www.alaskaair.com

American Airlines
www.aa.com

American Trans Air
www.ata.com

Continental Airlines
www.continental.com

Delta Airlines
www.delta.com

Frontier Airlines
www.frontierairlines.com

Hawaiian Airlines
www.hawaiianair.com

Jet Blue
www.jetblue.com

Midwest Airlines
www.midwestairlines.com

Northwest Airlines
www.nwa.com

SkyWest Airlines
www.skywest.com

Southwest Airlines
Discount airfares within the United States
www.southwest.com

Spirit Airlines
www.spiritair.com

Sun Country Airlines
www.suncountry.com

United Airlines
www.united.com

US Airways/America West Airlines
www.usairways.com

Examples of Major International Airlines

Argentina
Aerolineas Argentinas
www.aerolineasargentinas.com

Australia
Qantas
www.qantas.com.au

Austria
Austrian Airlines
www.aua.com

Brazil
Varig
www.varig.com

Canada
AirCanada
www.aircanada.com

China
China Airlines
www.china-airlines.com

France
AirFrance
www.airfrance.us

Germany
Lufthansa
www.lufthansa.com

Great Britain
British Airways
www.britishairways.com

Greece
Aegean Airlines
www.aegeanair.com

Italy
Alitalia
www.alitalia.com

Japan
Japan Airlines
www.jal.co.jp.en/

Mexico
Mexicana Airlines
www.mexicana.com

Russia
Aeroflot
www.aeroflot.com

Singapore
Singapore Airlines
www.singaporeair.com

South Africa
South African Airways
www.flysaa.com

Spain
Iberia
www.iberia.com

Thailand
Thai Airways
www.thaiair.com

Zimbabwe
Air Zimbabwe
www.airzimbabwe.aero

Transportation

Amtrak
Information about Amtrak's rail service.
www.amtrak.com

Easyjet.com
Provides discount airfares within Europe. Available in 15 different languages.
www.easyjet.com

Greyhound Lines
Provides information for bus travel for the United States, Canada, and Mexico.
www.greyhound.com

Peter Pan
Provides information for bus travel within the United States.
www.peterpanbus.com

Ryanair.com
Provides discount flights within Europe. Available in 20 different languages.
www.ryanair.com

Discount Travel Sites

Each of these Web sites provides discounted travel and hotel fares.

www.airgorilla.com
www.bargain-airfares.org
www.expedia.com
www.flyaow.com
www.hotwire.com
www.lowestfare.com
www.orbitz.com
www.priceline.com
www.travel.yahoo.com
www.travelocity.com
www.travelzoo.com

United States Government

United States Department of Commerce
The U.S. federal agency designed to foster, promote, and develop the foreign and domestic commerce of the United States
www.commerce.gov

United States Department of Health and Human Services: Center for Disease Control
This Web site provides information about vaccinations and health for travelers.
www.cdc.gov.travel

United States Department of Homeland Security
The U.S. federal agency responsible for homeland security.
www.usdhs.gov/dhspublic

United States Department of Housing and Urban Development
This U.S. federal agency is responsible for economic development and strengthening communities.
www.hud.gov

United States Department of the Interior
Use this Web site to acquire information on acquiring passes to national parks and how to promote education about conservation.
www.doi.gov

United States Department of Justice
Primary federal criminal investigation and enforcement agency.
www.usdoj.gov

United States Department of Labor
Provides information on the Americans with Disabilities Act.
www.dol/odep
www.disabilityinfo.gov

United States Department of State
Use this Web site to learn about travel warnings, travel tips, visa information, and U.S. passport information
www.state.gov/travelandbusiness

The White House
The official Web site for the White House.
www.whitehouse.gov

APPENDIX 4

Periodicals

To remain current with the overwhelming amount of Event Leadership literature that crosses my desk each month, I prioritize publications into three stacks. The first stack represents information I am currently in need of, and I set aside a specific time each day to review this material. The second stack goes in my travel bag and is read when I have time during travel or other downtime. The third stack is filed under the topic of the article so that when I need the information, I am able to retrieve it quickly.

Advertising Age. Weekly. Bill Publications, Chicago, IL; *www.advertisingage.com;* E-mail: subs@crain.com.

Agenda New York. Annually. Agenda USA, Inc., 686 Third Avenue, New York, NY 10017; (800) 523–1233.

Amusement Business. Weekly. Box 24970, Nashville, TN 37202; (615) 321–4250.

Association Management. Monthly. American Society of Association Executives, 1575 I Street, N.W., Washington, DC 20005; (202) 626–2740; *http://am.meetingsnet.com.*

Association Meetings. Monthly. Primedia, 43 L Nason Street, Maynard, MA 01754; (978) 897–5552.

Association Trends. Weekly. 7910 Woodmont Avenue, No. 1150, Bethesda, MD 20814; (301) 652–8666.

Backstage. Weekly. BPI Communications, 770 Broadway, New York, NY 10003; (212) 764–7300.

Billboard. Weekly. Billboard Publications, 770 Broadway, New York, NY 10003; *www .billboard.com.*

Business Events. Quarterly. Sullivan Group Corporate Meeting and Event Production, 510 Bering Drive, Suite 455, Houston, TX 77057.

Conference and Incentive Management. Bimonthly. CIM Verlag für Conference, Incentive and Travel Management GmBH, Nordkanalstrasse 36, D-20097 Hamburg, Germany; 40 237 1405.

Convene. 10 times a year. Professional Convention Management Association, 2301 South Lake Shore Drive, Suite 1001, Chicago, IL 60616–1419; (312) 423–7262.

Convention Industry: The International Magazine for Meeting and Incentive Professionals. Monthly. Association Internationale des Palais de Congres, European Association of Event Centers, and European Federation of Conference Towns, Mainzer Landstrasse 251, 60326 Frankfurt am Main, Postfach 200128, 60605.

Conventions and Expositions. Bimonthly. Conventions and Expositions Section of the American Society of Association Executives, 1575 Eye Street, N.W., Washington, DC 20005; (202) 626–2769.

Corporate and Incentive Travel. Monthly. Coastal Communications Corporation, 488 Madison Avenue, New York, NY 10022; (212) 888–1500.

Corporate Meetings and Incentives. Bimonthly. Laux Company, 63 Great Road, Maynard, MA 01754; (508) 897–5552.

Entertainment Marketing Letter. Monthly. EPM Communications, 488 East Eighteenth Street, Brooklyn, NY 11226–6702; (718) 469–9330.

Event Management. Quarterly. Cognizant Communication Corporation, 3 Hartsdale Road, Elmsford, NY 10523–3701; (914) 592–7720; *www.cognizantcommunication.com.*

Event Solutions. Monthly. Event Publishing LLC, 5400 South Lakeshore Drive, suite 101, Tempe, AZ 85283; (480) 831–5100; *www.event-solutions.com.*

Hollywood Reporter. Weekly. 5055 Wilshire Boulevard, Los Angeles, CA 90036–4396; (213) 525–2000.

Hospitality Research Journal. Quarterly. Council on Hotel Restaurant and Institutional Education, 2613 North Parham Road, 2nd Floor, Richmond, VA 23294; (804) 346–4800.

IAAM News. Bimonthly. International Association of Assembly Managers, 635 Fritz Drive, Coppell, TX 75019.

IEG Sponsorship Report. Bimonthly. International Events Group, 640 North LaSalle, Suite 600, Chicago, IL 60610; (312) 944–1727.

Incentive. Monthly. (847) 647–7487; *incentivemag.com.*

Insurance Conference Planner. Bimonthly. 132 Great Road, Suite 200, Stow, MA 01775; (603) 679–4320.

In-Tents. Biannually. Industrial Fabrics Association, 1801 County Road, B-West, Roseville, MN 55113; (651) 222–2508.

International Events. Quarterly; International Festival and Events Association (IFEA), 2603 West Eastover Terrace, Boise, ID 83706; (208) 433–0950.

International Journal of Hospitality Information Technology. HITA/HFTP.NAU, Box 5638, Flagstaff, AZ 86011–5638.

International Meetings News. Monthly. International Congress and Convention Association, Ashdown Court, Lewes Road, Forest Row, East Sussex RH18 5EZ, United Kingdom; 144 (0) 1342 824044; *www.icca.nl.*

Journal of Convention and Exhibition Management. Quarterly. Haworth Hospitality Press, 10 Alice Street, Binghamton, NY 13904–1580; (607) 722–5857.

Journal of Travel Research. Quarterly. Travel and Tourism Research Association and the Business Research Division, University of Colorado at Boulder, Boulder, CO 80309–0420.

Leisure Management. Monthly. Leisure Media Company, Portmill House, Portmill Lane, Hitchin, Hertfordshire SG5 1DJ, England; 144 (0) 1462 431385.

Lighting Dimensions International. 9 times a year. Entertainment Technology Communications Corporation, 32 West Eighteenth Street, New York, NY 10011–4612.

Medical Meetings. 8 times a year. Adams/Laux Company, 63 Great Road, Maynard, MA 01754; (978) 466–6358.

Meeting News. VNU Business Publications USA; (847) 763–9050; *www.meetingnews.com.*

Meeting Planners Alert. P.O. Box 404, Derry, NH 03038.

The Meeting Professional. Monthly. Meeting Professionals International, 4455 LBJ Freeway, Suite 1200, Dallas, TX 75244–5903; *www. mpiweb.org.*

Meetings and Conventions. Monthly. Reed Travel Group, 500 Plaza Drive, Secaucus, NJ 07096; (201) 902–1700; subscription service: P.O. Box 5870, Cherry Hill, NJ 08034.

Performance Magazine. 2 times a year. 1203 Lake Street, Suite 200, Fort Worth, TX 76102–4504; (817) 338–9444.

Public Relations Journal. 845 Third Avenue, New York, NY 10022.

Religious Conference Manager. 5 times a year. Primedia, 43 L Nason Street, Maynard, MA 01754; (507) 455–2136.

Rental Management. American Rental Association, 1900 Nineteenth Street, Moline, IL 61265; (800) 334–2177; (309) 764–2475.

The Reunion Network News. Reunion Network, 2450 Hollywood Boulevard, Suite 504, Hollywood, FL 33020; (954) 922–0004.

Sales and Marketing Management. 15 times a year. Bill Communications, 355 Park Avenue South, 5th Floor, New York, NY 10010–1706; (212) 592–6200.

Show Business News. Weekly. 102 W. 38th Street, 6th Floor, New York, NY 10018; (800) 562–2706.

Special Events Forum. 6 times a year. Dave Nelson, 1973 Schrader Drive, San Jose, CA 95124; (408) 879–9392.

Special Events Magazine. Monthly. 23805 Stuart Ranch Road, Suite 235, Malibu, CA 90265; (310) 317–4522.

Successful Meetings. 13 times a year. Bill Communications, 770 Broadway, New York, NY 10003; (646) 654–5049.

Tent Rental Report. Tent Rental Division of the Industrial Fabrics Association International, 345 Cedar Street, No. 800, St. Paul, MN 55101; (612) 222–2508.

TLL The Licensing Letter. Monthly. EPM Communications, 160 Mercer Street, 3rd Floor, New York, NY 10012–3212; (212) 941–0099.

Tradeshow Week. Weekly. 5700 Wilshire Boulevard, Suite 120, Los Angeles, CA 90036; (323) 965–2437.

Training. Monthly. VNU Business Publications, P.O. Box 2104, Skokie, IL 60076; (800) 255–2824.

Training and Development Journal. Monthly. American Society for Training and Development, 1640 King Street, Alexandria, VA 22313; (703) 683–8100.

U.S. Association Executive (USAE). Weekly. Custom News, 4341 Montgomery Avenue, Bethesda, MD 20814; (301) 951–1881.

Variety. Weekly. 5700 Wilshire Boulevard, Suite 120, Los Angeles, CA 90036; (323) 857–6600.

World's Fair. Weekly. International (0161) 683–8000.

Youth Markets Alert. Monthly. 160 Mercer Street, 3rd Floor, New York, NY 10012–3212; (212) 941–0099.

APPENDIX 5

APEX Resources

The Convention Industry Council (*www.conventionindustry.org*) has developed an initiative that is designed to bring together all stakeholders in the development and implementation of industry-wide accepted practices to create and enhance efficiencies in the meetings, conventions, and exhibitions industry. This initiative is the result of many years of hard work by panels of volunteers who are experts in various fields within the meetings, conventions, and exhibitions industry.

The overarching goal of Accepted Practices Exchange (APEX) APEX is to reduce time, reduce costs, and improve efficiency by creating accepted practices that may be exchanged throughout the industry.

APEX has several deliverables that help meeting, convention, and exhibition professionals save time and effort while simultaneously improving quality. All of these products, which can be accessed at *www.conventionindustry.org,* include:

+ *APEX Industry Glossary:* A key source of terms and definitions for the meetings, conventions, and exhibitions industry.
+ *APEX Post-Event Report:* According to APEX, a report of the details and activities of an event is called a "Post-Event Report" (PER). A collection of PERs over time will provide the complete history for an event. This template is the industry's accepted format.
+ *APEX Event Specifications Guide:* This template is the *official* format for the meeting, convention, and exhibition industry for delivering information clearly and accurately to appropriate venue(s) and/or suppliers regarding all requirements for an event.
+ *APEX Housing & Registration Accepted Practices:* These accepted practices are for the collecting, reporting, and retrieving complete housing and registration data for meetings, conventions, and other events; and for housing issues such as housing providers, Internet issues, international housing, and disclosure.
+ *Request for Proposal (RFPs) Forms:* These forms are used to create consistent and thorough requests for proposals that address core information and unique needs for meetings, conventions and exhibitions.

APEX has also produced a software product that contains a collection of more than 200 event management and business templates, including those developed through APEX as the industry standard. It is designed to interface with the Microsoft Office suite of software programs, specifically Word, Excel, and PowerPoint.

For more information about APEX or to purchase their products, visit *www.conventionindustry.org.*

APPENDIX 6

Directories

Directories are an invaluable resource for Event Leaders. Many libraries stock directories in the reference section. However, for day-to-day use, you will want to own your own copy for quick reference.

Academy Players Directory. Academy of Motion Picture Arts and Sciences, 60 E. Magnolia Boulevard, Burbank, CA 91502. List of hundreds of television and film stars and their contact telephone numbers.

ACCED-I Membership Directory. Association of Collegiate Conference and Events Directors International, Colorado State University, 8037 Campus Delivery, Fort Collins, CO 80523–8037; (970) 491–515; *ACCED-I.com.*

The Almanac of Anniversaries (1992). By Kim Long. ABC-CLIO, 130 Cremona Drive, Santa Barbara, CA 93117; (805) 368–6868.

America's Meeting Places (1984). Facts On File, 11 Pennsylvania Plaza, New York, NY 10001; (212) 967–8800. List of event venues.

ASAE Convention Themes. American Society of Association Executives, 1575 Eye Street, N.W., Washington, DC 20005. List and description of successful convention themes.

The ASAE Meetings and Expositions Section Networking Directory. Annually. American Society of Association Executives, 1575 Eye Street, N.W., Washington, DC 20005–1168. List of meeting and exposition managers.

Auditorium/Arena/Stadium Guide. Amusement Business/Single Copy Department, Box 24970, Nashville, TN 37202. List of venues for events.

Banquet Guide (1995). Banquet Guide, 8948 Southwest Barbour Boulevard, Suite 132, Portland, OR 97219.

The Beverly Hills International Party Planner. Jan Roberts Publications, 139 South Beverly Drive, Suite 312, Beverly Hills, CA 90212. List of resources for events in various cities.

Cavalcade of Acts and Attractions. Amusement Business/Single Copy Department, Box 24970, Nashville, TN 37202. List of live acts for events ranging from musical performers to circus attractions.

Chase's Annual Events: Special Days, Weeks, and Months. Annually. Contemporary Books, 180 North Michigan Avenue, Chicago, IL 60601. List of thousands of annual events.

456

CHRIE Member Directory and Resource Guide. Council on Hotel, Restaurant and Institutional Education, 2613 North Parham Road, 2nd Floor, Richmond, VA 23294; (804) 346–4800; Fax: (804) 346–5009; E-mail: info@chrie.org. List of scholars and others involved in the hotel and restaurant education field.

Circus and Carnival Booking Guide. Amusement Business/Single Copy Department, Box 24970, Nashville, TN 37202. List of circuses and carnivals.

Culinary and Hospitality Industry Publications Services. C.H.I.P.S., 1077 Mazoch Road, Weimar, TX 78962; (979) 263–5685; *www.chipsbook.com.* List of books selected specifically for the hospitality industry.

DC Tech Membership Directory. Washington, DC Technology Council, 1401 New York Avenue, N.W., Suite 600, Washington, DC 20005; (202) 637–9333.

Destination: Washington, DC. Washington, DC Convention and Visitors Association, 1212 New York Avenue, N.W., Suite 600, Washington, DC 20005–3992; (202) 789–7036.

Directory of City Policy Officials. National League of Cities, 1301 Pennsylvania Avenue, N.W., Washington, DC 20004; (202) 626–3150. List of people, including event managers, who work for municipal governments.

The Garden Tourist: A Guide to Garden Tours, Garden Days, Shows and Special Events (1995). Garden Tourist Press. *www.gardentourist.com.* List of events specifically related to garden tours.

The Government Contracts Reference Book (1992). George Washington University, National Law Center, Government Contracts Program, Suite 250, 2100 Pennsylvania Avenue, N.W., Washington, DC 20037–3202. Guide to obtaining government events contracts.

The Guide to Campus and Non-profit Meeting Facilities. acced-i.colostate.edu. ACCED-I List of venues on campus for event managers.

A Guide to College Programs in Hospitality, Tourism, & Culinary Arts. International Council on Hotel Restaurant and Institutional Education, John Wiley & Sons, New York.

The Guide to Unique Meeting and Event Facilities. AMARC, P.O. Box 279, 164 Railroad, Suite 250, Minturn, CO 81645; (970) 827–5500.

Here Comes the Guide: Hawaii (1994–1995). Hopscotch Press, Inc., 930 Carlton Street, Berkeley, CA 94710–9727; (510) 548–0400. List of venues for events and weddings in Hawaii.

Here Comes the Guide: Northern California (1993–1994). Hopscotch Press, 1563 Solano Avenue, Suite 135, Berkeley, CA 94707; (510) 548–0400. List of venues for events and weddings in Northern California.

ICCA Membership Directory. International Meetings Association, Entrada 121, NL-1096, EB Amsterdam, The Netherlands; 131–20–398–1919.

IEG Directory of Sponsorship Marketing. International Events Group, 640 North Lasalle, Suite 600, Chicago, IL 60610; (312) 944–1727. List of individuals and organizations involved in sponsorship marketing.

IEG Guide to Sponsorship. International Events Group, 640 North LaSalle, Suite 600, Chicago, IL 60610; (312) 944–1727. List of sponsorship agencies.

Insurance and Financial Services Directory (2001). American Society of Association Executives, 1575 Eye Street, N.W., Washington, DC 20005.

International Association of Amusement Parks and Attractions Directory and Buyers Guide. IAAP, 1448 Duke Street, Alexandria, VA 22314.

International Association of Assembly Managers, Inc. Members and Services Directory. IAAM, 635 Fritz Drive, Suite 100, Coppell, TX 75019–4442; (972) 906–7441.

Locations, etc.: The Directory of Locations and Services for Special Events (1992). Innovative Productions; *www.locationsetc.com*. List of event locations.

The Management Sourcebook. American Rental Association, Rental Management, 1900 Nineteenth Street, Moline, IL 61265–4198; (800) 334–2177. List of rental resources.

Morris Costumes. Morris Costumes, 6900 Morris Estate Drive, Charlotte, NC 28262; (704) 332–4443. Annual catalog of inexpensive costumes for events.

MPI Membership Directory, Annual. Meeting Professionals International, 3030 LBJ Freeway, Suite 1700, Dallas, TX 75234–2759; (972) 702–3000. List of over 10,000 people involved in meeting planning and related services.

Oriental Trading Company Inc. (800) 875–8480. Extensive catalog listing over 10,000 novelty items for use at events.

The Original British Theatre Directory (1990). Richmond House Publishing Company, 70–76 Bell Street, Marylebone, London NW1 6SP, England; (020) 7224–9666; *www.britishtheaterdirectory.co.uk*. List of equipment rental for events in Great Britain.

Perfect Places: Northern California, 2nd ed. Hopscotch Press, Inc. 930 Carlton Street, Berkeley, CA 94710–9727; (510) 548–0400. List of event venues in California.

Publications and Electronic Products. World Tourism Organization, Calle Capitan Haya, 42, 28020 Madrid, Spain; (+34) 91–5678100.

RCRA Membership Directory. Resort and Commercial Recreation Association, P.O. Box 1564, Dubuque, IA 52004–1564. List of members and resources for resorts and commercial recreation.

Sites and Insights: The Special Event Location and Resource Directory. Site Network, 550 Orange Avenue, Suite 132, Long Beach, CA 90802; *www.sitesandinsightstours.com*.

Sourcebook, Annual. Bill Communications, Successful Meetings, P.O. Box 888, Vineland, NJ 08362; (800) 266–4712. List of resources for meeting planners.

Tent Rental Directory (1993–1994). Tent Rental Division of the Industrial Fabrics Association International, 1801 County Road B-West, Roseville, MN 55113. List of resources for tent firms.

Tradeshow and Convention Guide. Amusement Business/Single Copy Department, Box 24970, Nashville, TN 37202. List of venues and resources for events.

Travel and Tourism Research Association Membership and Supplier Directory. Association of Travel Research and Marketing Professionals, P.O. Box 2133, Boise, ID 83701; (208) 429–9511; *www.ttra.com*.

UFI Directory of International Fairs and Expositions. 35 bis, rue Jouffroy d'Abbans F-75017, Paris, France; 33(0) 1–43–67–99–12.

Unique Meeting, Wedding, and Party Places in Washington, A directory of unusual and unique venues for meetings, weddings, and parties in the Washington, DC area. DCon (1997). By Elise Ford. Charlottesville, VA: Howell Press. List of unusual venues for events in Washington, DC.

Washington Speakers Bureau Guide. WSB, 1663 Prince Street, Alexandria, VA 22314; *www.washingtonspeakers.com*.

Who's Who in Association Management, ASAE Membership Directory. American Society of Association Executives, 1575 Eye Street, N.W., Washington, DC 20005; (888) 950–2723. List of association executives (including meeting planners) and their suppliers.

Who's Who in Professional Speaking (2007–2008). National Speakers Association, 4747 North Seventh Street, Phoenix, AZ 85014. List of over 3000 professional speakers.

Who's Who in Religious Conference Management (1994–1995). Religious Conference Management Association, One RCA Dome, Suite 120, Indianapolis, IN 46225; (317) 632–1888. List of professional meeting planners employed by religious organizations and their suppliers.

Worldwide Convention Centres Directory. Conference and Travel Publications, Ashdown Court, Lewes Road, Forest Row, East Sussex RH185EZ, England; 144(0) 1342–824044.

Your Special Event Planning Guide. Patty Sachs, 250 Seagrape Circle, Coconut Creek, FL 33066; (954) 974–7907; *PartyPlansPlus.com*; E-mail: PartyPlansPlus@aol.com.

APPENDIX 7

Audio and Video Resources

Many of the major Event Leadership organizations, such as the International Special Events Society (ISES), maintain extensive audio recordings of seminars held at their annual conferences. These audiotapes may be purchased directly from the organization.

The Gelman Library of George Washington University maintains a complete set of all audio recordings from ISES conferences. These recordings may be used within the confines of the library media resources division.

Additionally, the Gelman Library maintains an extensive video collection containing footage of corporate, association, civic, retail, and other types of events, including large-scale programs such as Super Bowl halftime shows and the opening and closing ceremonies of the Olympic Games, the Goodwill Games, and the Olympic Festival. These videotapes may also be viewed within the confines of the library and, with permission of the copyright holder, may be duplicated for scholarly or professional use. To receive a complete list of these resources, contact the Gelman Library Media Resources Division at (202) 994–6378.

Although the resources of the Gelman Library and the Event Leadership and Marketing Archives are too numerous to list (in fact, each collection has its own finding aid listing dozens of resources), I have a few personal favorites.

First, review the 1988 Super Bowl half-time spectacular produced by Radio City Music Hall Productions. This event is a masterful depiction of logistics, both mechanical and human.

Next, view the Goodwill Games opening ceremonies in Russia. The use of cards by thousands of spectators was so impressive that the television newscaster reporting the games stated that "this was the most memorable moment."

Finally, review the opening ceremonies for the 1984 Olympic Games in Los Angeles, California. This video depicts the transformation of the opening ceremonies from a one-dimensional live event into a multidimensional production staged for a live audience as well as hundreds of millions of television viewers. As a result of this production, the format of the Olympic Games' opening and closing ceremonies shifted to include effects that are more spectacular.

In addition to these resources, I recommend these sources for scholarly and professional use:

The 5 Essential People Skills: How to Assert Yourself, Listen to Others, and Resolve Conflicts (2005). Nightingale-Conant. Audio CD.

American Rental Association, Certified Event Rental Professional (C.E.R.P.) video education program. 1900 19th Street, Moline, IL 61265; (800) 334–2177; Fax: (309) 764–1533.

The Articulate Executive: How to Look, Act, and Sound Like a Leader (2003). American Media International. A detailed description of how to develop yourself as a successful leader and manager. Audio CD.

Communication Skills for Project and Team Management: The Soft-Skills Video (2006). Paul G. Ranky, Ph.D. A comprehensive overview of communication, team building, team management, interviewing, and listening.

Ethics Resource Center. 1747 Pennsylvania Avenue, Suite 400, Washington, DC 20006. (202) 737–2258; E-mail: ethics@ethics.org.

The Event Marketing Process (1988). Produced by Petit Communications, Don Mills, Ontario, Canada. A description of the various competencies involved in event marketing.

Globe Trekker: Great Festivals (2002). Pilot Productions. An outline and glimpse at various festivals around the world.

Holtz consulting for information on consumer-generated media including blog and podcast development: *www.holtz.com/travel.*

How to Be a Great Communicator: In Person, On Paper, and At the Podium (2005). Coach Series. Audio CD.

How to Get Your Point Across in 30 Seconds or Less (1999). Simon & Schuster. A detailed guide to effectively communicating with others. Audio CD.

How to Start Your Own Business (2004). Ryan Video Productions, David Felder. A brief description of beginning a personal business.

IAAPA Training Videotape Series. International Association of Amusement Parks and Attractions, Alexandria, VA; (703) 836–4800; *www.iaampa.org.*

Labor Relations: A Partnership for the Future. IAEM Foundation, 2000. (972) 458–8002; *www.iaem.org.*

A Matter of Judgment, Conflicts of Interest in the Workplace. A brief vignette entitled "Special Events Director" dealing with the subject of Event Leaders who receive gifts from hotels and other vendors and the consequences that may follow. This is an excellent way to begin an in-depth discussion of ethics in Event Leadership. Ethics Resource Center, Barr Media Group, Irwindale, CA.

Making Work Work: New Strategies for Surviving and Thriving at the Office (2004). Harper Audio. Provides assistance for being successful in the work environment. Audio CD.

Political Money for Senate Candidates (1989). Produced by Purdue University Public Affairs Video Archives, West Lafayette, IN. Subject matter deals with raising funds for U.S. Senate candidates.

Successful Special Events with Virgil Ecton, CFRE. A lecture by Virgil Ecton, CFRE of the United Negro College Fund, dealing with brainstorming, budgeting, operations, and other factors that help to ensure the success of special events for fundraising purposes. National Society of Fundraising Executives, Alexandria, VA.

Ten Commandments of Networking (1994). Victoria Multimedia. An outline of how to build a network of relationships in your career.

Time Management from the Inside Out (2006). PBS Paramount. Audio tracks available with the DVD.

Women in Business (1987). Warner Home Video. An outline of the benefits that women add to the workplace.

APPENDIX 8

Software

Using the following software listed may save you time and money. However, remember that part of your investment is the learning curve that must be mastered, and this may require a considerable investment of time. Compare software carefully prior to purchasing to ensure that you are maximizing your scarce resources with the most efficient software solutions available for your Event Leadership practice.

Software is typically divided into four categories:

1. Word processing
2. Financial and data analysis
3. Publishing, such as the development of diagrams and site plans
4. Compiling extensive databases

Whenever possible, try to obtain a software product that combines as many of these functions as possible. In some instances you may wish to purchase a standard product and customize the functions to solve your individual Event Leadership business challenges.

a2zShow. A Web-based application that helps associations and independent show organizers to market and manage their live trade shows and conferences online. NeoTech Center, 9250 Bendix Road, North, Columbia, MD 21045; (410) 480–7220; *www.a2zshow.com.*

ALERT Computer Systems. Rental management package. Colorado Springs, CO; (800) 530–8050; (719) 634–7755.

Campagne Associates: Fundraising Software Solutions. 195 McGregor Street, Suite 410, Manchester, NH 03102; *www.campagne.com.*

Culinary Software Services. Catering package. Boulder, CO; (800) 447–1466; (303) 447–3334.

Dean Evans and Associates Event Management Software. 5775 DTC Boulevard, Suite 210, Englewood, CO 80111; *www.dea.com.*

Devron Integrated Systems Ltd. Nova Building, Herschel Street, Slough, Berks SL1 1XS, England; 144(0) 1753 701 014; *www.devron.net.*

EKEBA International. P.O. Box 15131, Columbus, OH 43215–0131; (614) 459–7178.

Event Automation Services, Inc. 3230 Anton Drive, Aurora, IL 60504; (800) 535–1253; *www.wineasi.com.*

Event Business Management System. 87 Hubble, St. Charles, MO 63304; (800) 400–4052; *www.ungerboeck.com.*

EventMaker Pro. Special events management software. Campagne Associates, Nashua, NH; (800) 582–3489.

Event Planner Plus. Certain Software, One Daniel Burnham Court, Suite 330C, San Francisco, CA 94109–5460.

Event Software. 540 West Iron Avenue, Mesa, AZ 85210; (480) 517–9990.

InScribe, Inc. Calligraphy/printing package. Cambridge, MA; (800) 346–3461; (617) 868–5743.

International Hospitality and Tourism Database CD-ROM: The Guide to Industry and Academic Resources. The consortium of Hospitality Research Information Systems. Available through MPI, Dallas, TX; (214) 712–7742.

Microchips, Inc. Function Space Management. St. Louis, MO; (800) 373–0693; (314) 645–2800.

Mom 'N' Pops Software. A shareware company offering party and event planning programs. Springhill, FL; (352) 688–9108.

MPI Net. The first global communications network for the meeting industry. Dallas, TX; (214) 712–7742.

Parsons Technology. A large company with software for both PCs and Macs. Hiawatha, IA; (800) 243–6169.

Peopleware, Inc. Registration package. Bellevue, WA; (800) 869–7166; (206) 454–6444.

RE: Event (a component of The Raiser's Edge for Windows). Manufactured by Blackbaud, Inc. Helps planners organize and manage their events. Charleston, SC; (800) 443–9441.

Synergy Software International. Catering package. Arlington, VA; (800) 522–6210; (703) 522–6200.

Terrapin Systems. Special event planning/management package. Silver Spring, MD; (301) 933–5599.

Unique Business Systems. Rental management package. Santa Monica, CA; (800) 669–4827.

Venue Technology. Summitlink, North American Headquarters, Washington, DC. (888) 852–9614.

The Wedding Planner. Ninga Software, Calgary, Alberta, Canada; (800) 656–4642; (403) 383–2772.

Note: Many new software versions and applications emerge every week. Conduct a search of the Internet using the key words *event management software* to identify the latest technologies available to assist you.

APPENDIX 9

Sample Client Agreement

The client agreement must be reviewed by a local attorney, as each state requires individual language to conform with the code. However, this template provides Event Leaders with the conceptual framework for a basic client agreement.

Client Agreement

Account number: XYZ-1

This agreement is between ABC Event Leadership Company (hereafter referred to as EVENT LEADER) and XYZ Firm (hereafter referred to as CLIENT).

I. *EVENT LEADER agrees to provide:*
   1. Research, design, planning, coordination, and evaluation of the event entitled "The Night of a Thousand Stars."
   2. Research that will commence with the joint execution of this agreement.
   3. A professional event that will begin on July 15, 2007 at 8 P.M. central time in the city of Kansas City, Kansas, and conclude on the same date at 11:00 P.M. central time.
   4. A comprehensive evaluation including financial and attitudes and opinions will be submitted to CLIENT by August 15, 2007 at 5:00 P.M. central time.
   5. Comprehensive general liability insurance with a $1 million limit per occurrence, naming CLIENT as additional insured for the period of the event.

II. *CLIENT agrees to provide:*
   1. One person as principal contact and decision maker for the EVENT LEADER.
   2. General liability insurance with a $1 million limit per occurrence, naming EVENT LEADER as additional insured for the period of the event.

3. Decisions in a timely manner as required by the final approved production schedule.

4. Ten (10) volunteers to coordinate registration and guest relations during the event from 7:00 P.M. central time to 11:00 P.M. central time.

III. *INVESTMENT*

The EVENT LEADER will receive a fee for professional services in the amount of $10,000 exactly. The EVENT LEADER will receive fees for all direct expenses approved by CLIENT.

IV. *TERMS*

The CLIENT agrees to provide the following payments to the EVENT LEADER as compensation for the services described above.

June 30, 2007: 25% of fee ($2,500) plus 50% of direct expenses.

July 15, 2007: 65% of fee ($6,500) plus balance of pre-approved direct expenses.

August 15, 2007: 10% of fee plus any additional charges approved by client plus the balance of all approved direct expenses.

V. *CANCELLATION*

Should the EVENT LEADER cancel his or her services for any reason other than acts of God, the CLIENT shall receive a refund of all prepaid fees less any costs expended on behalf of the event. Should the CLIENT cancel his or her event, the following payments shall be due:

Cancellation more than 120 days prior to event date: 25% of professional fee and 50% deposit of all direct expenses.

Cancellation less than 120 days prior to event date: 50% of professional fee and 50% deposit of all direct expenses.

Cancellation less than 60 days prior to event date: 75% of professional fee and 100% of all direct expenses.

Cancellation less than 30 days prior to event date: 100% of professional fee and 100% of all direct expenses.

VI. *FORCE MAJEURE*

This agreement is canceled automatically if the event is interrupted due to acts of God, including, but not limited to, hurricanes, tornadoes, strikes, war, volcanic eruption, earthquakes, or pestilence.

VII. *ARBITRATION*

The American Arbitration Association is designated as the official body for arbitrating any disputes resulting from this agreement.

VIII. *HOLD HARMLESS and INDEMNIFICATION*

The EVENT LEADER and CLIENT agree to hold one another harmless from negligence caused by either party and mutually indemnify one another.

IX. *TIME IS OF THE ESSENCE*

The services and related costs described in this agreement are guaranteed through 5:00 P.M. central time March 15, 2007. After this date, these services and related costs must be renegotiated.

X. *THE FULL AGREEMENT*

This agreement and any attachments constitutes the full agreement. Any changes, additions, or deletions to this agreement must be approved in writing by both parties.

XI. *ACCEPTANCE*

The parties whose signatures are affixed below agree to accept the terms and conditions stated within this agreement.

_____   _____
CLIENT   DATE

_____   _____
EVENT LEADER   DATE

Note: Sign both copies and return one signed original to the EVENT LEADER.

Sample Vendor Agreement

Account Number: DEF-1

This agreement is between ABC Event Leadership Company (hereafter referred to as EVENT LEADER) and DEF firm (hereafter referred to as VENDOR).

I. *EVENT DATE: July 15, 2008.*
II. *EVENT ARRIVAL TIME: 7:30 P.M. central time.*
III. *EVENT START TIME: 8:00 P.M. central time.*
IV. *EVENT STOP TIME: 11:00 P.M. central time.*
V. *VENDOR shall provide:*
   1. Three (3) magicians performing walk-around magic suitable for young children ages 5 to 12 years. Magicians shall wear black tuxedoes.
   2. Eight- (8-) member Top-40 band entitled "Starlight," wearing matching black tuxedoes.
   3. Balloon drop of 500 nine-inch silver Mylar balloons. Rigging to be completed by 2:00 P.M. central time and drop to occur between 10:00 P.M. and 11:00 P.M. central time.
   4. Comprehensive general liability insurance with a $1 million limit per occurrence, naming EVENT LEADER as additional insured for period of event.
   5. Refrain from distributing promotional literature at event and direct any and all inquiries for future business resulting from event to EVENT LEADER.
VI. *EVENT LEADER shall provide:*
   1. Complimentary parking for VENDOR and his or her personnel.
   2. Two dressing rooms.
   3. One lift for rigging balloon drop. Lift to be available from 12:00 P.M. to 2:00 P.M. central time.
   4. On-site event coordinator to liaison with VENDOR.

VII. *FEES*

EVENT LEADER shall pay the following fees to VENDOR:

1. Magicians $1,000
2. Band $3,000
3. Balloon drop $1,500
   Total: $5,500

VIII. *TERMS*

EVENT LEADER shall pay VENDOR 50% deposit ($2,750) upon execution of agreement, and the balance net 30 days of event date.

IX. *CANCELLATION*

If the VENDOR cancels for any reason, he or she forfeits all funds received or due and shall promptly repay EVENT LEADER any funds advanced for this event. If the EVENT LEADER cancels for any reason, he or she must provide the following payments to VENDOR:

Cancellation before 120 days of event date:	No fees due.
Cancellation of up to 90 days of event date:	15% of total fee.
Cancellation of up to 60 days of event date:	25% of total fee.
Cancellation of up to 30 days of event date:	50% of total fee.
Cancellation less than 30 days prior to event date:	75% of total fee.

X. *FORCE MAJEURE*

This agreement is canceled automatically if the event is interrupted due to acts of God, including, but not limited to, hurricanes, tornadoes, strikes, war, volcanic eruption, earthquakes, or pestilence.

XI. *ARBITRATION*

In the event of disagreement pertaining to this agreement, the parties agree to submit to mandatory nonbinding arbitration. The American Arbitration Association is designated as the official body for arbitrating any disputes resulting from this agreement.

XII. *HOLD HARMLESS AND INDEMNIFICATION*

The EVENT LEADER and VENDOR agree to hold one another harmless from negligence caused by that party and to mutually indemnify one another.

XIII. *TIME IS OF THE ESSENCE*

The services and related costs described in this agreement are guaranteed through 5:00 P.M. central time March 15, 2007. After this date these services and related costs must be renegotiated.

XIV. *THE FULL AGREEMENT*

This agreement and attachments contain the final and entire agreement between the parties, and neither they nor their agents shall be bound by any terms, statements, or representations, oral or written, not contained herein.

XV. *ACCEPTANCE*

The parties whose signatures are affixed below agree to accept the terms and conditions stated within this agreement.

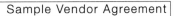

_____   _____
CLIENT   DATE

_____   _____
EVENT LEADER   DATE

Note: Sign both copies and return to EVENT LEADER. A fully executed original will be provided once signed by the EVENT LEADER.

Sample Insurance Certificate

ACORD™ CERTIFICATE OF LIABILITY INSURANCE

DATE (MM/DD/YYYY)
03/29/2006

PRODUCER (212)994-7086 FAX (212)994-7021	
Arthur J Gallagher Risk Management Services Att: Alice Prine 444 Madison Ave, 20th Fl New York, NY 10022	THIS CERTIFICATE IS ISSUED AS A MATTER OF INFORMATION ONLY AND CONFERS NO RIGHTS UPON THE CERTIFICATE HOLDER. THIS CERTIFICATE DOES NOT AMEND, EXTEND OR ALTER THE COVERAGE AFFORDED BY THE POLICIES BELOW.

	INSURERS AFFORDING COVERAGE	NAIC #
INSURED "Special Event" Promoter 155-157 Franklin Street New York, NY 10013	INSURER A: Insurance Company providing coverage	
	INSURER B:	
	INSURER C:	
	INSURER D:	
	INSURER E:	

COVERAGES

THE POLICIES OF INSURANCE LISTED BELOW HAVE BEEN ISSUED TO THE INSURED NAMED ABOVE FOR THE POLICY PERIOD INDICATED. NOTWITHSTANDING ANY REQUIREMENT, TERM OR CONDITION OF ANY CONTRACT OR OTHER DOCUMENT WITH RESPECT TO WHICH THIS CERTIFICATE MAY BE ISSUED OR MAY PERTAIN, THE INSURANCE AFFORDED BY THE POLICIES DESCRIBED HEREIN IS SUBJECT TO ALL THE TERMS, EXCLUSIONS AND CONDITIONS OF SUCH POLICIES. AGGREGATE LIMITS SHOWN MAY HAVE BEEN REDUCED BY PAID CLAIMS.

INSR LTR	ADD'L INSRD	TYPE OF INSURANCE	POLICY NUMBER	POLICY EFFECTIVE DATE (MM/DD/YY)	POLICY EXPIRATION DATE (MM/DD/YY)	LIMITS	
A		**GENERAL LIABILITY** [X] COMMERCIAL GENERAL LIABILITY [ ] CLAIMS MADE [X] OCCUR	12345	MM/DD/YY	MM/DD/YY/	EACH OCCURRENCE	$ 1,000,000
						DAMAGE TO RENTED PREMISES (Ea occurance)	$ 100,000
						MED EXP (Any one person)	$ 0
						PERSONAL & ADV INJURY	$ 1,000,000
		GEN'L AGGREGATE LIMIT APPLIES PER: [ ] POLICY [ ] PRO-JECT [ ] LOC				GENERAL AGGREGATE	$ 2,000,000
						PRODUCTS - COMP/OP AGG	$ 1,000,000
		AUTOMOBILE LIABILITY [ ] ANY AUTO [ ] ALL OWNED AUTOS [ ] SCHEDULED AUTOS [ ] HIRED AUTOS [ ] NON-OWNED AUTOS				COMBINED SINGLE LIMIT (Ea accident)	$
						BODILY INJURY (Per person)	$
						BODILY INJURY (Per accident)	$
						PROPERTY DAMAGE (Per accident)	$
		GARAGE LIABILITY [ ] ANY AUTO				AUTO ONLY - EA ACCIDENT	$
						OTHER THAN EA ACC AUTO ONLY: AGG	$ $
		EXCESS/UMBRELLA LIABILITY [ ] OCCUR [ ] CLAIMS MADE [ ] DEDUCTIBLE [ ] RETENTION $				EACH OCCURRENCE	$
						AGGREGATE	$
							$
							$
							$
A		**WORKERS COMPENSATION AND EMPLOYERS' LIABILITY** ANY PROPRIETOR/PARTNER/EXECUTIVE OFFICER/MEMBER EXCLUDED? If yes, describe under SPECIAL PROVISIONS below	12345	MM/DD/YY	MM/DD/YY	[X] WC STATU-TORY LIMITS [ ] OTH-ER	
						E.L. EACH ACCIDENT	$
						E.L. DISEASE - EA EMPLOYEE	$
						E.L. DISEASE - POLICY LIMIT	$
		OTHER					

DESCRIPTION OF OPERATIONS / LOCATIONS / VEHICLES / EXCLUSIONS ADDED BY ENDORSEMENT / SPECIAL PROVISIONS
Venue Owner is included as an additional insured but only as respects negligence arising out of the named insured's operations.

CERTIFICATE HOLDER	CANCELLATION
Name of Venue Owner Att: Person Requesting Certificate Address City	SHOULD ANY OF THE ABOVE DESCRIBED POLICIES BE CANCELLED BEFORE THE EXPIRATION DATE THEREOF, THE ISSUING INSURER WILL ENDEAVOR TO MAIL __30__ DAYS WRITTEN NOTICE TO THE CERTIFICATE HOLDER NAMED TO THE LEFT, BUT FAILURE TO MAIL SUCH NOTICE SHALL IMPOSE NO OBLIGATION OR LIABILITY OF ANY KIND UPON THE INSURER, ITS AGENTS OR REPRESENTATIVES. AUTHORIZED REPRESENTATIVE

ACORD 25 (2001/08)   ©ACORD CORPORATION 1988

Courtesy of Arthur J. Gallagher & Co., Alice Prine, Area Senior Vice President, Alice_Prine@AJG.com, www.ajg.com.

APPENDIX 12

Sample Catering Menu*

Max & Me Catering Proposal for
The Professional Convention Management Association (PCMA)
*50th Anniversary Convention Opening Reception at the
National Constitution Center
Philadelphia, Pennsylvania*

Client: Philadelphia Convention & Visitors Bureau
Sunday January 8th 2006
Event Timing: 6:00pm–8:00pm
3,000 Guests

Passed Hors D'Oeuvres (Passed for the first 30 Minutes)
Chicken and Shrimp Wontons with a Rice Wine and Red Pepper Sauce
Wild Mushroom Tartlet with White Truffle Oil and Chervil
Filet on Croutons with Piperade and a Roasted Garlic Aioli
Smoked Salmon Napoleons with a Chive Cream

Potato Station
Short Rib Chili with Baked Russet Potatoes, Sour Cream and Scallions
Slow-Cooked Pork with Red Bliss Potatoes, Fresh Thyme and Garlic
Potato Gnocchi Gratin with Porcini Mushrooms and Pepato

Mushroom Station
Veal Stew with Cremini Mushrooms, Fresh Rosemary and Pearl Onions
Fettucine with Oyster Mushrooms and a Light Cream Sauce, Prosciutto
and Reggiano Parmesan
Shrimp Stir-Fry with Shiitake Mushrooms, Sugar Snap Peas,
Baby Corn and Fresh Ginger
Baguettes and Mini French Rolls

*Menu courtesy of Max & Me Catering (*www.maxandmecatering.com*)

Beef Station
Pan-Seared Filet Mignon with Roasted Shallot Sauce
Multi-Peppercorn Rubbed and Roasted Sirloin
(We will keep this hot using a heat lamp) sliced to order and served with a Spicy Cinnamon
and Cumin Tomato Jam and
a Dijon Mustard–Horseradish Sauce
Slow-Roasted Beef Brisket with Red Wine and Caramelized Onions
Stirato and Soft Onion Rolls

Winter Squash Station
Roasted Butternut Squash with Duck Confit, Fresh Thyme and White Truffle Oil
Baked Acorn Squash with a Vegetarian Rice Pilaf with Garlic Bread Crumbs
Puree of Calabash Soup with Smoked Bacon and Crème Fraîche

Shore/Seafood Station
Pan-Seared Nova Scotia Salmon with Cucumbers, Medjool Dates,
Lemon Zest, Dill and Extra Virgin Olive Oil
New Orleans–Style Barbecued Shrimp with Rosemary and Black Pepper
Grilled Tuna Tacos with Jalapeño Cabbage Slaw and Charred Tomato Salsa

Chicken Station
Free-Range Chicken with Ratatouille and a Fresh Thyme Jus
Grilled Chicken Breasts with a Tomato Olive and Caper Sauce
Pad Thai with Chicken, Rice Noodles, Light Peanut Dressing,
Shredded Cucumber, Scallions and Toasted Peanuts

Dessert Stations

Termini's South Philly Italian Delicacies
Pignoli Cookies, Variety of Mini Cannolis, Mini Chocolate and Hazelnut Mousse Tarts,
Macadamia Dark Chocolate Clusters, Lemon Curd Tartlets with Fresh Raspberries, Mini
Strawberry Tartlets with a Vanilla Pastry Cream, Mini Éclairs and Mini
Cappuccino Cheesecakes

Philadelphia's *Tasty Cakes*®
Peanut Tandy Cakes, Butterscotch Krimpets and
Chocolate Ice Cream–Filled Cupcakes
Etc.
A Variety of Salt Water Taffy
Macaroons

APPENDIX 13

Sample Incident Report

Note: The incident report should be completed as soon as possible after an incident has occurred. Copies of this form should be easily accessible to all event personnel.

1. Name of event: _____

2. Name of venue: _____

3. Report of incident: (check one) ____ Injury ____ Theft ____ Lost person
   ____ Lost property ____ Violent activity ____ Other ____
   Describe _____

4. Location of incident: _____

5. Date and time of incident: _____

6. Date and time of report: _____

7. Exact location of incident: _____
   _____

8. Complainant: _____
   _____

9. Gender/race of complainant: _____

10. Complainant address: _____
    _____

11. Complainant city, state, zip code: _____

12. Complainant telephone contact: (Home) _____
    (Office) _____ (Fax) _____

13. Additional means to contact complainants/reporting persons:

    _____

    _____

14. Illness/injury received: _____

    _____

15. Description of illness/injury: _____

    _____

16. _____ Admitted for treatment

17. _____ Released
    Property code: V, vehicle from which theft occurred; S, stolen; R, recovered;
    L, lost; I, impounded; E, evidence; F, found; O, other.

18. _____

Code	Items	Value Estimated by ID#	Purchase by Complainant	Value Estimated by Date	Reporter
Example:					
S	Purse	12/31/04	$100	12/15/04	$75
___	___	___	___	___	___
___	___	___	___	___	___
___	___	___	___	___	___

19. Description of automobile:
    Year: _____ Make: _____ Model: _____
    Color: _____ Body: _____ Tag/state/year: _____
    Vehicle identification number: _____

20. Suspect description:
    Race: _____
    Gender: _____
    Age: _____
    Height: _____
    Weight: _____
    Eye color: _____
    Hair color: _____
    Complexion: _____

Scars: _____

Hat: _____

Coat: _____

Jacket: _____

Pants: _____

Shirt: _____

21. Narrative. Describe and state the action taken by the Event Leader.

_____

_____

_____

_____

22. Reporting person: _____

23. Status:

_____ Open

_____ Closed (List date and if closed by arrest list arrest

number): _____

24. Internal review: (Describe supervisor's findings below): _____

_____

_____

_____

Sample Purchase Order

Note: To control payments, the purchase order must be issued to vendors prior to authorization of purchase. The purchase order is not an invoice; rather, it is an official order to the vendor to provide your event organization with specific goods and services. The vendor's invoice will serve as the agreement and, therefore, must be inspected carefully to ensure that it meets the specifications of the purchase order.

Purchase Order

Tracking number: XYZ-1

    I. Event date: _____

   II. Vendor name: _____

  III. Vendor address: _____

  IV. City, state, zip: _____

  IV. Vendor telephone: _____

  VI. Vendor facsimile: _____

VII. Quantity Example:

Quantity	Item Description	Cost per Unit	Total Cost
32	Black derbies	$1.00	$ 32.00
10	Red garters	0.50	5.00
100	Red bandanas	3.00	300.00
Subtotal:			$337.00

   VIII. Applicable taxes (if tax exempt, attach appropriate documentation): Tax exempt

    IX. Total amount authorized for this purchase: _____ $337.00

     X. Terms: Net 30 days upon receipt of invoice.

    XI. Delivery date and time: _____

   XII. Delivery address: _____

  XIII. Delivery contact person (receiving agent): _____

  XIV. Telephone number at delivery site: _____

   XV. Note to vendor: No substitutions or changes may be made to this order without the written consent of the purchaser.

  XVI. Name of Event Leadership organization _____
            Address _____
            Telephone _____

XVII. _____
            Authorized signature

Sample Event Evaluations

Quantitative Survey

Event Leadership Survey on Educational Programs

1. *Please select only ONE discipline that best describes your company's products and/ or service.*
   - ☐ Event planning and coordination
   - ☐ Design, décor, and graphics
   - ☐ Technical services and products
   - ☐ Entertainment
   - ☐ Food service and products
   - ☐ Travel and transportation services
   - ☐ Event public relations and marketing
   - ☐ Other (specify) _____

2. *How many years have you been in the special event industry?*
   - ☐ Less than 1 year   ☐ 1–4 years   ☐ 5–10 years   ☐ 10 or more years

3. *What is your highest level of education? (Check only ONE.)*
   - ☐ Some high school   ☐ Some college   ☐ Graduate degree
   - ☐ High school diploma   ☐ Undergraduate degree

4. *Have you previously attended chapter educational seminar(s)?*
   - ☐ Yes
   - ☐ No

   If yes, when and on what topic(s)? _____

   If no, please indicate a reason for nonattendance and **skip to question 6.**

   _____

5. *How satisfied are you with the overall quality of the seminar(s)?*
   ☐ Very satisfied   ☐ Not too satisfied
   ☐ Fairly satisfied   ☐ Not satisfied at all

6. *Please mark ALL the seminar topics that you would like to attend in the future.*
   ☐ Strategic planning   ☐ Fundraising
   ☐ Building your own business   ☐ Corporate sponsorship
   ☐ Legal, ethical, and risk management   ☐ Budgeting and financial planning
   ☐ Creating effective proposals   ☐ Recruitment, motivation, and
                                                  coordination of volunteers

   ☐ Technology   ☐ Cross-cultural Event Leadership
   ☐ Marketing through Internet   ☐ Strategic entertainment
   ☐ Marketing through print promotion   ☐ Other (specify) _____
   ☐ Design and creative concept generating

7. *What ONE time is the most convenient for you to attend such educational seminars?*
   ☐ Morning   ☐ Afternoon   ☐ Evening

8. *Who would you like to hear as a guest speaker at a monthly meeting?*

   _____

9. *What location(s) would you suggest for future meetings? (Identify a specific location.)*

   _____

   If you can, please list the contact person at the location (name and telephone number)

   _____

10. *Would you volunteer to be a speaker in your area of expertise at an upcoming meeting?*
    ☐ Yes
    ☐ No
    On what topic?

    _____

    If you answered **yes,** we would be happy to know your name and contact telephone number.

    _____

11. *Are you currently a member?*
    ☐ Yes
    ☐ No

Thank you very much for your cooperation! Someone will collect your completed questionnaire.

Quantitative Survey

Road Financing and Road Fund Management Workshop Evaluation Survey

Kiev, Ukraine

Please fill out the questionnaire below and drop it at the registration desk on your way out. In appreciation for your feedback, we have a small souvenir for you that you can exchange for a completed questionnaire.

1. *Do you believe that you have learned something new during this workshop?*
   ☐ Yes
   ☐ No

2. *Do you believe that the workshop was applicable to the current road situation in Ukraine?*
   ☐ Yes
   ☐ No

3. *On a scale of 1 to 10, how strongly did the workshop influence your vision of road financing and road fund management?* (1, did not influence at all; 10, greatly influenced)

   1   2   3   4   5   6   7   8   9   10

4. *Which, if any, message(s), were in your opinion, communicated throughout the workshop? (Please check all that apply.)*
   ☐ Importance of having an autonomous road agency
   ☐ Managing the road agency along commercial lines
   ☐ Involving road users to win public support for increased road financing
   ☐ The need to manage the road fund more actively

5. *Which presentation did you find most useful for your future work? (Please check ONE box only.)*
   ☐ EBRD Consultant Study   ☐ South African Road Experience
   ☐ EU Accession Criteria   ☐ Latvian State Road Fund Experience
   ☐ Commercially Managed Road Funds

6. *Which presentation did you find least useful for your future work? (Please check ONE box only.)*
   ☐ EBRD Consultant Study   ☐ South African Road Experience
   ☐ EU Accession Criteria   ☐ Latvian State Road Fund Experience
   ☐ Commercially Managed Road Funds

7. *On a scale of 1 to 10, how would you evaluate the quality of translation?*
(1, poor; 10, excellent)

    1   2   3   4   5   6   7   8   9   10

8. *On a scale of 1 to 10, how would you evaluate facilitation of the discussions?*
(1, poor; 10, excellent)

    1   2   3   4   5   6   7   8   9   10

9. *Would you be interested in attending similar workshops in the future?*

☐ Yes

☐ No

10. *You can identify the organization that you are representing at this workshop as (please check ONE box only):*

☐ Governmental   ☐ Engineering   ☐ Other (please specify)

☐ Association   ☐ Research _____

☐ Commercial   ☐ Regional governmental

We encourage you to use the back of this questionnaire for any comments or suggestions that you might have regarding the workshop.

Thank you very much for your cooperation!

Qualitative Event Evaluation Methods

Focus Groups

Utilize these steps to conduct an effective focus group or panel:

1. Qualify 9 to 12 persons who have one or two homogeneous characteristics. For example, they may be both men and women but all have a college degree. Or they may all be midlevel managers or between the ages of 35 and 50.
2. Use a survey instrument or interviews to qualify participation.
3. Distribute a confirmation letter to the qualified participants listing the date, time, location, and topics for the focus panel.
4. Offer a reward or gift for their participation, such as a book.
5. Make certain that you recruit 15 to 25 percent more participants than you will actually need to allow for attrition.
6. Appoint a trained focus group facilitator. A good facilitator will be skilled at remaining neutral during the focus group session and probing to elicit the most valid responses from the participants.
7. Call the participants the day before the focus group session to remind them and reconfirm their participation.
8. At the beginning of the focus panel, you should announce the agenda and format. Encourage the participants to express themselves fully even if they wish to speak to one another.
9. Record the focus panel using an audio recorder or video recorder.

10. Transcribe the recording and notes from the focus panel.
11. Analyze the focus panel transcription and note areas of agreement as well as areas of dissonance among the participants.
12. Submit your final report, including your recommendations based on the focus group comments:

Key Informant Interviews

The following steps will assist you in targeting key informants to provide high-quality information about your event.

1. Identify those persons with the highest level of expertise.
2. Request an interview that will last no more than 15 minutes.
3. Prepare up to 10 questions to ask the key informants.
4. Use a quantitative approach for some of the questions, such as "How would you rate the potential location for this event on a 1 to 5 scale, 1 being unacceptable and 5 very acceptable?"
5. Use open-ended questions, such as "How would you describe the overall quality of the event?"
6. Probe to extract more information for the key information using questions such as "Tell me more about this" or "Why do you feel this way?"
7. Reduce your field notes from the interview questions to a short written report using initials for the key informants' responses and the letter Q for your questions.
8. Summarize and analyze the report, listing the key points that were identified by the key informants and how you will use these recommendations to resolve the issues associated with the event or improve overall performance.

Ethnographic Studies

The ethnographic study is an excellent research tool to employ when seeking in-depth knowledge of the event environment. The ethnographic researcher participates and observes the stakeholders who are associated with the event to report on subtle nuances and unspoken issues. The purpose of ethnographic research is to identify meanings associated with event behaviors. Use the following steps to conduct effective ethnographic studies for your event.

1. Establish an outline and timeline for the study.
2. Request permission from event stakeholders to conduct the study.
3. Utilize a trained field researcher.
4. Develop interview questions for the various stakeholder groups.
5. List the events, programs, and meetings that the field researcher should attend to participate and observe the critical activities of the stakeholders.
6. Record in the field notes not only the verbal responses but also the physical behavior of the stakeholders.
7. Analyze the field notes to identify trends, patterns, and ultimately meanings of stakeholder responses and behaviors.
8. Reduce your findings to a short written report that describes your findings and offers recommendations for using this information to develop the event strategically.

APPENDIX 16

Sample Event Survey

EDINBURGH MILITARY TATTOO 2005

Win Tattoo CDs & DVDs

Please complete this questionnaire, by ticking the boxes or writing in the answer as required. Once completed simply fold over and seal the flap on the inside cover and post to The Tattoo Office (no stamp is required in the UK). If you return your questionnaire by 30th September you will be entered into our prize draw with 50 Tattoo CDs and DVDs to be won. Thank you.

Veuillery remplir cette questionnaire en cochant les cases correpondantes ou en répondant aux questions. Si vous renvoyez la questionnnaire avant le 30 Septembre, vous aurez la chance de gagner 50 DVDs du "Tattoo" ou des CDs. Merci beaucoup.

1. What gave you the idea of coming to the Tattoo this year?

Recommendation from a friend or relative	☐
Advertising by the Tattoo	☐
Programme organised by a coach or tour operator	☐
I visit the Tattoo regularly	☐
TV or radio programme	☐
I've always wanted to	☐
Enjoyed previous visits and wanted to come again	☐
Show content	☐
Other reason:	

2. How long ago did you decide to attend this year's Tattoo?

Within the last week	☐
1 – 8 weeks ago	☐
2 – 6 months ago	☐
7 – 12 months ago	☐
More than 1 year ago	☐

3. How many times have you visited the Tattoo before?

Never - this is the first time (Go to Q5)	☐
1 – 4 times (Go to Q4)	☐
5 times or more (Go to Q4)	☐

4. When did you first attend the Tattoo?

Less than 5 years ago	☐
5 years ago	☐
10 years ago	☐
20 years ago	☐
More than 20 years ago	☐

5. Have you ever seen or heard any advertising for the Tattoo?

Yes	☐	No	☐

6. If yes, where did you see or hear the Tattoo advertised?

Television news	☐
Television advertisement	☐
Television programme	☐
Radio	☐
Local newspaper	☐
National newspaper	☐
Internet	☐
Poster	☐
Leaflet	☐
Magazine	☐
Bus side	☐
Other: (Please specify)	☐

7. What is the name of the main sponsor of the Tattoo?
(Please write your answer below)

8. What is your opinion of the Tattoo performance overall?

Excellent	☐	Okay	☐
Good	☐	Poor	☐

9. How much did you enjoy each of the items in the Tattoo performance?
Please rate each of the following items on a scale of 1 (did not enjoy at all) to 10 (enjoyed greatly). Please write in your score out of 10 in the spaces below.

Fanfare	__
The Massed Pipes & Drums	__
The Imps Motorcycle Team	__
The Band and Bugles of the Light Division	__
Massed Highland Dancers	__

9. (Continued)

The Royal Marines Display	__
Trinidad and Tobago Defence Force Steel Orchestra	__
Russian Cossack State Dance Company	__
The Guard of His Majesty The King of Norway	__
The Massed Military Bands / Celebration of Trafalgar	__
The Massed Military Bands and Massed Pipes & Drums	__
The Finale	__

10. How did you obtain your ticket for the Tattoo?

By post from the Tattoo Ticket Office	☐
By visiting the Tattoo Ticket Office	☐
By telephone from the Tattoo Ticket Office	☐
From a ticket booking agency	☐
From a coach or tour operator	☐
At the Castle Esplanade	☐
By email from the Tattoo web site	☐
From a tourist information centre	☐
Other: (Please specify)	

If you live in Edinburgh, please go to Q18

11. If you do not live in Edinburgh, are you staying overnight in Edinburgh as part of your visit to the Tattoo?

Yes (Go to Q11a)	☐
No (Go to Q15)	☐

11a. If yes, why are you staying overnight in Edinburgh?

On holiday / short break / just to see the Tattoo	☐
On business	☐
On an educational course	☐
Other reason: (please specify)	☐

12. How many nights are you staying in Edinburgh in total? _____

13. How many of these nights are you staying in paid for accommodation, e.g. in a hotel or guesthouse? _____

14. If staying in paid for accommodation, which of the following statements best describes how you booked your accommodation for staying in Edinburgh?

I booked my accommodation as part of a tour / coach operator's package	☐
I booked my accommodation arrangements through a travel agent	☐
I booked my own accommodation arrangements directly myself	☐
Other: (please specify)	☐

15. Was this visit to the Tattoo your:

Main reason for coming to Edinburgh	☐
One of a number of reasons for coming to Edinburgh	☐
Was not one of the reasons for coming to Edinburgh	☐

15a. Which of the following visitor attractions have you visited during this trip to Edinburgh?

Edinburgh Castle (paid to enter)	☐	Royal Museum of Scotland	☐
Edinburgh Zoo	☐	Royal Botanic Gardens	☐
Our Dynamic Earth	☐	The Royal Yacht Britannia	☐
		None of these	☐

16. Are you staying elsewhere in Scotland on this trip?

Yes	☐	No	☐

17. If yes, how many nights are you staying in other parts of Scotland?
_____ nights

18. Where is your home (i.e. your normal place of residence)?

Edinburgh	☐	USA	☐
The Lothians	☐	Canada	☐
Rest of Scotland	☐	Europe	☐
England (Please specify)	☐	Asia	☐
		Australasia	☐
Wales	☐	Other: (please specify)	☐
Northern Ireland	☐		

19. What types of transport did you use to get to Edinburgh and the Tattoo itself?

Air	☐	Rail	☐
Bus service	☐	Coach tour or excursion	☐
Own car	☐	Other: (please specify)	☐
Hire car	☐		

20. If you looked at our Tattoo show programme, how would you rate, firstly, its quality, and secondly, its value for money?

	Quality			Value
Very good	☐	Very good		☐
Good	☐	Good		☐
Okay	☐	Okay		☐
Poor	☐	Poor		☐
Very poor	☐	Very poor		☐
Did not see the Tattoo show programme				☐

21. Which of the following events at the Edinburgh Festival have you visited or do you intend to visit this year?

Fringe	☐	International Festival	☐
Film Festival	☐	Book Festival	☐
Jazz Festival	☐	Fireworks Concert	☐
Fringe Sunday	☐	Edinburgh Cavalcade	☐
		None	☐

21a. Are you aware of the new 'Spirit of the Tattoo' visitor centre located at the top of the Royal Mile?

Yes	☐	No	☐

21b. If yes, have you visited the new 'Spirit of the Tattoo' visitor centre?

Yes	☐	No	☐

22. Are you likely to come back to see the Tattoo again in the future?

Yes	☐	No	☐
Unsure	☐		

22a. If yes, when do you intend to return to the Tattoo?

Next year	☐	More than 5 years from now	☐
Within 5 years	☐		

22b. If no, why will you not come back to see the Tattoo again? (Please write your answer below)

_____

23. Do you have access to the Internet?

Yes, at home	☐	Both at home and at work	☐
Yes, at work	☐	No	☐

24. If you have internet access, did you see the Tattoo web site at www.edintattoo.co.uk?

Yes	☐	No	☐

25. About you…

Male	☐	Female	☐

26. Which age group are you in?

18 – 24	☐	45 – 54	☐
25 – 34	☐	55 – 64	☐
35 – 44	☐	65+	☐

27. How many people are in your party tonight including yourself? (i.e. the number of people for whom payment was made as part of one booking)

Men _____ Women _____ Children (under 16 yrs) _____

28. What is the occupation of the chief wage earner within your household. If he/she is retired, please state the occupation before retiring. (Please write your answer below)

If you would like to be entered into our prize draw competition, please complete your name, address, postcode and telephone number below.

Name: _____

Address: _____

_____

Postcode: _____

Telephone: _____

Email: _____

Thank you for taking the time to complete this questionnaire. The Edinburgh Military Tattoo would like to contact you again in the future to keep you up to date with news of its activities. If, however, you would rather not be contacted please tick this box ☐. Please note that we will not pass your details onto any other companies for marketing purposes.

BUSINESS REPLY SERVICE
Licence No. EH 2791

ROYAL MAIL

POSTAGE PAID GB
EDINBURGH 50

The Edinburgh Military Tattoo

32 Market Street

Edinburgh

EH1 0AB

International Special Events Society Principles of Professional Conduct and Ethics*

Each member of ISES shall agree to adhere to the following:

1. Promote and encourage the highest level of ethics within the profession of the special events industry while maintaining the highest standards of professional conduct
2. Strive for excellence in all aspects of our profession by performing consistently at or above acceptable industry standards.
3. Use only legal and ethical means in all industry negotiations and activities.
4. Protect the public against fraud and unfair practices, and promote all practices which bring respect and credit to the profession.
5. Provide truthful and accurate information with respect to the performance of duties. Use a written contract clearly stating all charges, services, products, performance expectations, and other essential information.
6. Maintain industry accepted standards of safety and sanitation.
7. Maintain adequate and appropriate insurance coverage for all business activities.
8. Commit to increase professional growth and knowledge, to attend educational programs, and to personally contribute expertise to meetings and journals.
9. Strive to cooperate with colleagues, suppliers, employees, employers, and all persons supervised in order to provide the highest quality service at every level.
10. Subscribe to the ISES Principles of Professional Conduct and Ethics, and abide by the ISES Bylaws and policies.

*Courtesy of International Special Events Society (*www.ises.com*)

INDEX

Accepted Practices Exchange (APEX). *See* APEX (Accepted Practices Exchange)

Accountants, selecting, 149

Accounting. *See* Finance and accounting

Accounts payable, 153–157

Accounts receivable, 153, 154

Advertising, 6, 9, 271, 272, 274, 301. *See also* Event marketing

Affinity marketing, 27

Airlines, 447, 448

Alternative dispute resolution (ADR), 308

Amenities, 76, 77, 88

Americans with Disabilities Act (ADA), 77, 135, 343–350

Anniversaries, 13. *See also* Social life-cycle events

APEX (Accepted Practices Exchange):
    APEX Meeting and Event Toolbox by Office Ready, 115
    Event Specification Guide, 199, 209
    initiative, 174, 209
    resources, 454, 455
    standard RFP form, 174

Approval process, 51

Arbitration clause, 313

Attendance, tracking, 301

Audio news releases (ANRs), 272, 273, 292

Audiovisual effects, 194
    lighting, 218–223, 229
    management, 216–237

    resources, 460, 461
    sound, 73–75, 217, 223–229, 460, 461
    special effects, 229–233
    standard equipment, 216–218
    synergy, 237
    video and audiotapes, 62, 233–237

Balloons, 96, 97, 230

Bar and bas mitzvahs, 13. *See also* Social life-cycle events

Benchmarks, 26, 30

Best practices, 393–400

Boshnakova, Dessislava, 302, 303

Bowling Green State University Center for Popular Culture, 140

Brands, 296, 297, 330

Break-even point, 151, 152

Budgets, 144–148. *See also* Costs
    case study, 411, 412
    importance of, 144, 160
    marketing evaluation, 288, 289
    samples, 161–166
    theme events, 104

Business development, 26, 27

Career development:
    certifications. *See* Certifications
    cover letters, 377–380
    credentials, 375–377
    economic factors, 368

Career development *(Continued)*:
 education, 18, 28–31, 34, 35, 39, 368–371, 375, 376, 391
 Event Leadership profession, 19–26
 international opportunities, 391
 internships and externships, 372, 373
 overview, 381–387
 and personal considerations, 380
 résumés, 377–380
Cash flow, 153, 154, 157
Catering, 177–192, 472, 473
Celebration, 5–8, 10, 11, 13, 128, 129, 387
Celebrities, 12, 227, 250, 251, 273, 274
Cell phones. *See* Mobile phones
Centerpieces, 88, 91, 97
Ceremony and ritual, 5, 6
Certifications, 18, 34
 Certified Marketing Director (CMD), 269
 Certified Special Events Professional (CSEP), 19, 368–371, 374, 375
 recertification, 375
Changes, notice of, 214, 215
Checklists:
 music and entertainment, 238
 site inspection, 196–198
 use of, 56
Civic events, 10, 51, 409, 410
Client agreement, sample, 464–466
Collaboration, 121, 122, 127
Colleges and universities:
 Bowling Green State University, 140
 Dallas County Community College District, 399, 400
 education, 34
 George Washington University, 115, 298, 369, 381, 391
 Johnson & Wales University, 185, 381, 382
 Leeds Metropolitan University, 381
 Northeastern State University, 369, 381
 Temple University, 34, 68, 118, 369, 371, 381, 394
 University of Nevada (Las Vegas), 369, 381, 391
 University of Technology, 381
Columbus, Gene, 338, 348, 349
Communication:
 barriers to, 62
 devices, 258

forms of, 62
 importance of, 52, 61, 282
 Internet, use of, 114, 140, 296. *See also* Internet
 leadership skills, 123, 124
 mobile phones, 301
 online discussions, 65
 policies, procedures, and practices, 134, 135
 research findings, 43
 schedule, 210, 211, 214
 and servicing sponsorship sales, 282, 283
 teamwork challenges, 125
 written, 62
Compensation (salaries and benefits), 7, 156, 157
Competitive advantage, 26, 27
Computer Assisted Drawing and Design (CADD), 198, 199, 331
Conferences, 10, 12
Confidence, 120, 121
Conflicts, resolving, 201, 204
Conservation, 105, 106
Consumer-generated media (CGM), 300
Contracts:
 celebrities and speakers, 251, 252
 clauses and terms, 312–314
 client agreement, sample, 464–466
 consulting agreement, sample, 315, 316
 described, 309
 elements of, 311, 312
 negotiation, 314
 permits and licenses, 319
 purchase orders. *See* Purchase orders (POs)
 riders, 314
 signing, 314
 types of agreements, 317
 vendor agreement, sample, 467–469
 written and oral, 310
Contributional margin, 151, 152
Convention Industry Council (CIC), 115, 174, 199, 205, 209, 370, 432, 454
 APEX initiative. *See* APEX (Accepted Practices Exchange)
Coordination phase of Event Leadership, 38, 58, 59, 63, 65, 111, 172. *See also* Vendors
Copyright, 330

Costs:
   audiovisual equipment, 218
   catering, 190, 191
   decorating, 99
   entertainment, 247–249
   expenses, 146–148, 150, 151
   factors, 41, 51
   funerals, 100, 104
   lighting, 222, 223
   reducing, 152, 153, 190, 191
   sound equipment, 228, 229
   special effects, 232, 233
   theme events, 104
   video production, 236, 237
Cover letters, 377–380
Creativity, best practices, 395
Cross promotions, 274
Crowd control, 79
Currency and foreign exchange rates, 158–160
Customer service, 127, 128, 298

Dallas County Community College District,
   399, 400
Damage control, 201, 204
Databases, 34, 356–359, 361
Deadlines, 131, 132
Decision-making, 58, 59, 65, 121, 122
Decorating, 91–94, 99
Demographics, 7, 16, 17
Design phase of Event Leadership, 38,
   46–51, 72
Destination management companies (DMCs),
   340, 341
Diagrams, 198, 199
Directories, 456–459
Disabled guests, provisions for. *See* Americans
   with Disabilities Act (ADA)
Disorganization, 53, 54
Diversity, 129, 338
DOME, 361
Down-links, 253, 254
Downie, Jay, 112, 113

Earls, Zeren, 346, 347
Education, 368–371
   and achieving goals, 35
   colleges and universities, 34. *See also*
      Colleges and universities

continuing education (lifelong learning),
   28–31
distance learning programs, 18, 391
edutainment, 9, 254, 255
event-related studies, 18
events, generally, 9
meetings and conferences, 12
postgraduate, 375, 376
and public assembly, 8, 9
Edutainment, 9, 254, 255
Egress, 56
Electronic data interchange (EDI), 357, 358
Electronic music, 243, 244, 252
Employees, 129, 131. *See also* Human
   resources
Employment agreements, 157, 158
Entertainment, 237–255, 438–440
Entrances and reception areas, 81–84
Ethics, 310, 334–340, 350, 351, 487
Evaluation phase of Event Leadership, 4, 38,
   59–61, 68, 111, 479–483, 485, 486
Event Leader, 6, 255
Event Leadership process, 38–61
Event Leadership profession, 8, 14–18, 26–28.
   See also Career development;
   Certifications; Education; Ethics
Event Management Body of Knowledge
   (EMBOK), 63–65
Event Manager, 19
Event marketing, 9, 27, 63, 65, 262–289,
   296–299. *See also* Advertising
Event philosophy, 47, 48
Event plan:
   amenities, 76, 77
   conservation, 105, 106
   distribution of, 108, 109
   environment considerations, 72–80
   environment design, 81–99
   guests, identifying needs of, 77–80
   importance of, 72
   innovative sites, 87, 88
   parades and float design, 95–99
   preplanning, 107, 108
   reliability, 108
   security concerns, 79, 108, 109
   sensory stimulation, 73–77
   size, weight, and volume considerations,
      77–79

Event plan (*Continued*):
  strategic planning, 106, 107
  stretching limits of the event, 72
  themed events, 99–104
  timeline, 109–111
  transportation and parking. *See*
    Transportation and parking
  validating, 108, 109
Event production, 199, 208–237
Event Specification Guide (ESP), 199, 209
Event sponsorship. *See* Sponsorship
Event strategic plan (ESP), 106, 107
Eventologist, 18
Eventology, 15
Expenses, 146–148, 150–153
Expositions and exhibitions, 10–12, 408, 409
Externships, 371–373

Fairs and festivals, 10, 11, 14, 270, 402, 403
FAQs, customer support, 298
Fees, 49, 153, 154
Festivals. *See* Fairs and festivals
Fiber-optics:
  lighting, 220
  teleconferencing, 253, 254
Finance and accounting:
  account codes, 148
  accountant, selecting, 149
  accounts payable, 153–156
  accounts receivable, 153, 154
  budgets. *See* Budgets
  cash flow, 153–154
  challenges and solutions, 156–158
  costs, controlling, 152, 153
  expenses, 146–148, 150–153
  and failure of Event Leadership concerns, 24
  financial management, 210
  foreign exchange rates, 158–160
  importance of understanding, 22, 23, 144
  income, 146
  profit, 149–152
  purchase orders, 156
  software, 149
Fire regulations, 94, 109
Fireworks. *See* Pyrotechnics
"Five w's," 43, 44, 48, 178
Focus groups, use of, 73, 135, 288, 292, 482, 483

Foreign exchange rates, 158–160, 167
Function area design, 85–87
Funerals, 13, 100, 104

GANTT charts, 53, 115
Gap analysis, 58
Gender opportunities, 18
George Washington University, 115, 298, 369, 381, 391
Globalization:
  cultural differences, 258
  diversity issues, 140
  and Event Leadership, 4
  international events, 114
  international transportation, 205
  online communication, 65
  World of Events, 34
Goals:
  and educational resources, 35
  financial, 23
  personal and professional, 19, 20
  self-improvement, 30
  and time management, 20–22
Goldblatt, Max B., 337, 399, 400
Goldblatt, Rosa, 399, 400
Government departments, 449, 450
Graduations, 410, 411
Graham, Sheila, 138, 139
Greeters, 81, 83, 84
Gross profit, 151
Guests:
  changes over past decade, 4
  disabled. *See* Americans with Disabilities
    Act (ADA)
  identifying needs of, 77–80
  transportation and parking issues. *See*
    Transportation and parking
  uninvited, 81

Hallmark events, 10–12
Hargrove, Earl Jr., 93–96
Hargrove, Earl Sr., 93, 94, 96
Harris, April, 328, 329
Historical background, 5–7
Hospitality, 10, 12
Hotels, 444, 449
Hoyle, Leonard H., Jr. (Buck), 267, 273, 289, 296

Human resources:
  diversity, 129
  and feasibility of event, 51
  management, 24, 25, 127–131
  temporary employees, 131

Incident report, sample, 474–476
Industry associations, 65, 430–440
Ingress, 56, 77, 80
Innovation, 87–90, 396, 397
Insurance:
  certificate, sample, 471
  contract provisions, 313
  and risk management, 325–327
  transportation companies, 204, 205
Integrated system design network (ISDN),
    214, 215
Integrity, 120, 121
Interactive events, 104
Interactive media, 252, 253
Internal events, 128, 129
International Special Events Society (ISES),
    19, 65, 141, 205, 350, 371, 375, 391,
    435, 446
  code of ethics, 310, 337, 487
  Esprit prizes, 172
  and Event Leadership positions, 17, 29
  resource directory, 88
Internet:
  communications, 140
  customer support, 298
  as developing medium, 296
  etiquette, 350
  event marketing, 284, 285, 296–299
  impact of, 25
  interactive data management, 34
  listservs, 445, 446
  market research, 298, 299
  media releases, 292
  music downloads, 224, 225
  online chat rooms, 62, 299
  online publications, 445
  online sales, 297, 298
  product/service development and testing, 299
  research, 114
  and resource development, 27, 28
  search engines, registering with, 297
  Web design and management, 299–301

Internships, 371–373
Invitations, 275, 276
iTunes, 225, 300

Jack Morton Worldwide, 65, 136, 137, 337,
    376, 397–399
Johnson & Wales University, 185, 381, 382
Jordan, Mary, 202, 203

Kagwa, Peter, 32, 33
Kawamura, Jin, 388–390

Laser Registration, 301
Leadership:
  characteristics of effective leaders, 119–125
  human resource management. See Human
    resources
  importance of, 118
  policies, procedures, and practices,
    developing, 134–135
  roles, 118
  styles, 118, 119
  teamwork challenges, 125–127
  volunteers, 131
Leeds Metropolitan University, 381
Legal compliance:
  Americans with Disabilities Act, 77, 135,
    343–350
  permits, 309, 310
  policies, procedures, and practices, 135
  Sarbanes-Oxley Act, 308, 309
Liability issues. See also Legal compliance;
    Risk management
  fog special effects, 231
  incident report, sample, 474–476
  negligence, 308
  and proposals, 173
  strobe lights, 222
Licensing, 244–246, 309, 310, 318, 319
Lighting, 218–223, 229
Listservs, 445, 446
Live production, 192, 193. See also Technology
Local area network (LAN), 359
Location of event. See Venues
Logos, 75, 96

Management theory, 121, 122
Marketing. See Event marketing

Mass customization, 7
Max and Rosa Goldblatt Endowment
    Scholarship Awards, 399, 400
McCall, Josh, 136, 137, 399
McFaddin, Jean, 66–68
Media kits, 273
Meeting Professionals International (MPI),
    141, 371, 391, 435, 446
Meetings:
    with caterer, 189, 190
    and communications, 62
    and conferences, 10, 12
    planning meeting, 107, 108
    production schedule, 210, 211
Mega events, 11. See also Hallmark events
Microphones, 217, 225, 226
Milestones, 53
Mixers, 224
Mobile phones, 301, 364
Morimoto, Lucky, 388–390
Morton, Bill, 337, 376, 397, 398
Morton, Jack, 73, 381, 397
Muyonjo, Patrick, 32, 33
Murder mystery productions, 254, 255
Music:
    downloading, 224, 225
    licensing, 244–246
    management, 237–255
    resources, 238–241
Musicians, 242–244

Needs assessment and analysis, 48, 50, 51
Negotiation:
    accounts payable, 155, 156
    caterers, 189
    celebrities and speakers, 250, 251
    contracts, 314
    salaries and benefits, 156
    sponsorships, 281
Net profit, 149–151
New product launches, 270, 271
Northeastern State University, 369, 381

Occupancy. See Size, weight, and volume
    considerations
Off-line editing, 234
Online chat rooms, 62
Online editing, 234

Online marketing. See Internet
Organizational structure, 52, 53, 132–134, 140
O'Toole, William, 52, 53, 63, 174
Outsourcing, 166, 167
Overhead, 150

Pandemics and epidemics, 79
Parades and float design, 95–99
Parking. See Transportation and parking
Parkinson rule, 132
Passwords, 359
Performance measurement, 26
Periodicals, 451–453
Permits, 51, 98, 309, 310, 317–319
Persistence as leadership characteristic, 120,
    121
Personal computers (PCs), 358, 359
PERT charts, 115
Planning phase of Event Leadership:
    and disorganization, 53, 54
    event plan. See Event plan
    event strategic planning (ESP), 106, 107
    gap analysis, 58
    as part of process, 38
    pre-planning, 107, 108
    project management systems, 52, 53
    space, 56
    tempo, 57, 58
    timing, 54, 55
Policies, procedures, and practices, 134, 135,
    157
Problem solving, 122, 123
Product development and testing, 299
Product launch case study, 401, 402
Professional congress organizer (PCO), 114,
    341
Professional Convention Management
    Association (PCMA), 141, 301, 396–397,
    436, 446
Profiles in Event Leadership:
    Boshnakova, Dessislava, 302, 303
    Columbus, Gene, 348, 349
    Downie, Jay, 112, 113
    Earls, Zeren, 346, 347
    Graham, Sheila, 138, 139
    Harris, April, 328, 329
    Jordan, Mary, 202, 203
    Kagwa, Peter, 32, 33

Kawamura, Jin, 388–390
McCall, Josh, 136, 137
McFaddin, Jean, 66–68
Morimoto, Lucky, 388–390
Muyonjo, Patrick, 32, 33
Rich, David, 290–292
Schmader, Steven Wood, 362, 363
Supovitz, Frank, 168
Zambelli, George ("Boom Boom"), 256, 257
Profit, 149–152
Project breakdown structure (PBS), 52
Project management systems, 52, 53
Projection screens, 217, 218
Promotions:
    cross promotion, 274
    event marketing, 263, 264
Proposals:
    request for (RFP), 173–175, 188, 189
    reviewing, 174
    tracking system, 176
Psychographic change, 7, 16
Public relations, 6, 9, 265, 266, 272–274, 283
Public service announcement (PSA), 273, 274
Purchase orders (POs), 156, 357, 477, 478
Pyrotechnics, 42, 231–232, 257, 401, 440

Radio Frequency Identification (RFID), 301
RDF Site Summary (RSS 0.9, RSS 1.0), 300
Reading log, use of, 30
Really Simple Syndication (RSS 2.0), 300
Reason for event (why), 43
Receivables, 153, 154
Recycling, 105, 106
Relationship marketing, 27
Reliability:
    of event plan, 108
    of information in proposal, 173
    of research, 42
    vendors, 342
Religious events, 242
Request for proposal (RFP), 173–175, 188, 189
Research phase of Event Leadership:
    communication, 43
    cost factors, 41
    deductive, 72
    and event plan, 72
    "five w's," 43, 44

importance of, 38, 39, 46, 262
inductive, 72
Internet, use of, 114
interpretation of data, 42, 43
market research, 39, 298, 299
as part of process, 38
quantitative and qualitative research, 39–42
reliability, 42
and risk reduction, 38
and SWOT analysis, 44–46
timeline, 109
types of, 39
validity, 42
Resources:
    American Society for Training and
        Development (ASTD), 140, 439, 442
    APEX. See APEX (Accepted Practices
        Exchange)
    audio, 460, 461
    books, 417–429
    career advancement, 391
    colleges and universities. See Colleges and
        universities
    development of, 27, 28
    directories, 456–459
    entertainment, 246, 247
    financial management, 167
    industry associations, 65, 430–440
    innovative sites, 88
    locating, 172–174
    marketing, 293
    music and entertainment, 238–241
    online publications, 445
    organizational charts, 140
    organizations, 65, 430–440
    periodicals, 451–453
    planning phase, 115
    public relations, 293
    risk management, 331
    software. See Software
    vendors, 205
    Web sites, 431–440, 442–444
Résumés, 377–380
Retail events, 10, 12, 268–270
Retained earnings, 149
Return on event (ROE), 286–289, 301
Return on marketing (ROM), 301
Rich, David, 290–292

Rich Site Summary (RSS 0.91, RSS 1.0), 300
Risk management:
  background, 308
  and certification programs, 19
  documentation, 325
  due diligence, 325
  hold harmless waivers, 104
  importance of, 319, 320
  inspections, 324, 325
  insurance, 325–327
  proactive measures, 311
  research, importance of, 38
  responsibilities, 330
  risk assessment meeting, 320–323
  risk control, 327, 330
  safety meeting, 323, 324
  and security concerns, 79
  and synergy, 63, 65
RSS technology, 300

Safety. *See also* Risk management
  incident report, sample, 474–476
  meeting, 323, 324
  as primary concern, 310
  safe event environment, 311
  secure environment, 311
Salaries. *See* Compensation (salaries and
  benefits)
Sales:
  closing the sale, 281, 282
  compensation for salespersons, 156, 157
  customer support, 298
  and event marketing, 262, 263
  online, 297, 298
  servicing sales, 282, 283
Sarbanes-Oxley Act, 308, 309
Scheduling, 53, 199–201, 208, 210–216
Schmader, Steven Wood, 362, 363
Search engines, 297, 300, 360
Seating arrangements, 85–87
Security concerns:
  case study, 412, 413
  and event plan, 108, 109
  risk management, 79
  Web sites, 297, 298
Sensitivity analysis, 53
Sensory stimulation, 73–77

Service bureaus, 357
Show-biz Web sites, 299
Silvers, Julia Rutherford, 63, 78, 118, 124,
  129, 160
Size, weight, and volume considerations,
  77, 78
Skype, 140
Smell, sense of, 73, 75, 236
Social life-cycle events, 10, 13, 242, 368
Software:
  Computer Assisted Design and Drawing
    (CADD), 198, 199, 331
  desktop publishing, 292
  event planning, 205
  Event Specification Guide, 209
  and market research, 298, 299
  Microsoft FrontPage, 304
  Microsoft Outlook, 205
  Netscape Composer, 304
  planning matrix, 115
  resources, 462, 463
  templates for event planning, 115
  trends, 364
  Web site design, 360
Sound, 73–75, 194, 217, 223–229, 460, 461
Space planning, 56, 81–85, 87
Speakers, 249–252
Special effects, 229–233
Special events:
  defined, 5, 6
  within events, 341, 342
  television, 382
Sponsorship, 276–284
Sports events, 10, 11, 13, 14, 405, 406
Spotlights, 220, 221
Spouse and partner programs, 340, 341, 343
Stage monitor, 225
Stakeholders:
  defined, 14
  determining, 43
  and event timeline, 109, 110
Standard of care, 111
Street promotions, 274
Strengths, weaknesses, opportunities, and
  threats (SWOTs), 44–46, 58
Stunts, 275
Subfields of Event Leadership, 9–14, 29

Supovitz, Frank, 168
Suppliers. *See* Vendors
Sustainability, 399, 400
SWOT analysis, 44–46, 58
Synergy, 63, 65, 237, 319
Tactile elements, 73, 75

Tasks, 53
Taste, sense of, 76
Teamwork, 125–127, 172
Technology:
    access to data, control of, 359
    audiovisual effects. *See* Audiovisual effects
    capabilities of venue, 114
    changes over past decade, 4
    communication devices, 258
    data processing, 34, 356–359, 361
    desktop publishing, 292
    and financial management, 167
    hardware configurations, 357–359
    importance of mastering, 23, 24
    integrated system design network, 214, 215
    interactive media, 252, 253
    interactive Web sites, 359–361
    Internet, use of, 25. *See also* Internet
    mobile phones, 301
    and need for continuing education, 17, 18
    production schedule, 199–201
    and purpose of event, 193, 194
    Radio Frequency Identification (RFID), 301
    resources, 365
    site inspection and analysis, 195–199
    software. *See* Software
    spreadsheets, 205
    teleconferencing, 62, 140, 253, 254
    telephone systems, 114
    time band, creation of, 115
    trends, 364
    videoconferencing, 140
    virtual reality, 253
    Web-based applications, 34, 65
Teleconferencing, 62, 140, 253, 254
Temple University, 371
    certificate programs, 118, 369, 381
    Fox School of Business, 394
    Musser Awards for Excellence in
        Leadership, 394

    National Laboratory for Tourism and
        eCommerce, 68
    School of Tourism and Hospitality
        Management, 34
Tents, 97–99
Terrorism, 79, 330
Theft, 79, 327
Themed events, 99–104
Time management, 20–22, 131, 132
Time sharing, 357
Time/space/tempo laws, 54–58
Timeline, 109–111, 208, 283, 284. *See also*
    Scheduling
Timing, 44, 54, 55
Toasts, translations of, 386
Tours and activities, 340, 341
Training, 52, 130
Transportation and parking:
    and event marketing, 266
    event plan considerations, 79, 80
    importance of, 80
    insurance, 204, 205
    international, 205
    parking lot concerns, 79, 80
    physically disabled guests, 345
    site inspection, 195
    and venue selection, 56
    Web sites, 448, 449
Travel industry:
    consumer-generated media, 300
    tourism, 10–12, 14, 16
    Web sites, 444, 447–449
Trends in Event Leadership:
    catering trends, 182, 191, 192
    event marketing, 289
    event production, 236
    music and entertainment, 252–255
"Tribing," 7
Triple Bottom Line theory, 61

Unions, musicians and entertainers, 243, 244
Universities. *See* Colleges and universities
University of Nevada (Las Vegas), 369, 381,
    391
University of Technology, 381
Up-links, 253, 254
Utilitarian Web sites, 299, 300

Validity:
of event plan, 108
of research, 42
Vendors:
accounts payable, 154–156
agreement, sample, 467–469
caterers. See Catering
conflicts, resolving, 201, 204
and licensing requirements, 319
policies and procedures, 157
purchase orders. See Purchase
orders (POs)
reliability, 342
resources, 205
technology. See Technology
types of, 174, 176
Venues:
calculating and sizing event environment,
78, 79
diagrams of, 198, 199
and event marketing, 266, 267
examples of event sites, 89, 90
hotels, 444
ingress and egress, 56, 77, 80
innovative sites, 87, 88
inspection, 195–199, 210, 324, 325, 346,
349, 350
location of event, 44
and off-premises catering, 178
resources for innovative sites, 88
size, weight, and volume considerations,
77, 78
and soundscaping, 74, 75
venue selection, 56
Web sites, 444
Video, 62, 233–237
Video news releases (VNRs), 272, 273,
292
Virtual reality, 76, 77, 104, 253
Vision as leadership characteristic, 124
Visual elements, 73, 75, 460, 461
Volunteers, 129–131

Web sites:
airlines, 447, 448
Americans with Disabilities Act guidelines,
346, 351
APEX initiative, standard RFP form, 174
blogs, 300
cities, 441, 442
convention and visitors' bureaus, 441, 442
creating, 359, 360
design and management, 299–301
designing, 140
discount travel and hotels, 449
event management organizations, 431–437
FAQs, 298
financial management and markets, 167
hotels, 444
listservs, 445, 446
as marketing tool, 360, 361
online publications, 445
organizations, 431–440
PERT charts, 115
podcasts, 300
privacy policies, 298, 299
registering, 360
resources, 438–440, 442–444
search engines, registering with, 297
security, 297, 298
transportation, 448, 449
travel industry consumer-generated media,
300
types of, 299, 300
U.S. government, 449, 450
visitors to, registering, 360, 361
Weddings, 13, 384, 403–405. See also Social
life-cycle events
"Welcome" translations, 4
Wide area network (WAN), 359
Wireless application protocol (WAP), 364
Work breakdown structure (WBS), 53
Work package, 53

Zambelli, George ("Boom Boom"), 256, 257